MICROWAVE GOURMET
HEALTHSTYLE
COOKBOOK

Also by Barbara Kafka

MICROWAVE GOURMET
FOOD FOR FRIENDS
AMERICAN FOOD AND CALIFORNIA WINES

MICROWAVE GOURMET HEALTHSTYLE COOKBOOK

Barbara Kafka

WILLIAM MORROW AND COMPANY, INC., NEW YORK

Library of Congress Cataloging-in-Publication Data

Kafka, Barbara.
    Microwave Gourmet Healthstyle Cookbook/Barbara Kafka.
        p.   cm.
    ISBN 0-688-07572-X
    1. Low-calorie diet—Recipes.   2. Microwave cookery.   3. Nutrition.   I. Title.
RM222.2.K19   1989
    641.5′635–dc20   89-15380
                                                                                       CIP

Printed in the United States of America

First Edition

1 2 3 4 5 6 7 8 9 10

BOOK DESIGN BY JOEL AVIROM

For Ernest, Nicole and Michael

Who are the pleasure
and have shared the food,
the good times and the bad

ACKNOWLEDGMENTS

Finally, a writer works alone; but readers and critics, good and bad, make it less lonely and I would like to thank them for the kind words and the corrections, the appreciation and the friendship.

Even though I write alone and am alone responsible for this book, I have been helped by many people who merit more gratitude than I can convey.

The past helps, so even though he cannot hear me, I thank James Beard.

Joy Horstmann has been my alter ego on this book. I relied on her organization, trusted her taste and we laughed a lot.

Ann Bramson, my editor, has once again—our fourth book together—been a support and a goad. The people around her at Morrow, Al Marchioni, Lisa Queen and others unfortunately too numerous to mention, have been loyal and professional; things that make it possible for a writer to work.

Lynn Hill of Hill Nutrition is for me, as for so many others, a source of expert nutritional advice going far beyond her assigned work of analyzing recipes and menus, often in a hurry.

Corby Kummer has helped with conversation, enthusiasm, shared eating and cooking and manuscript reading without stinting.

Sherry Arden provided the title and first brought me to Morrow.

Leo Lerman made me a food writer and keeps me thinking.

Chris Styler once again loaned me some time when the testing got heavy. Anna Brandenburger tested with zeal and flair. Jean Marcus had the heavy job of keeping track of the manuscript and the nutritional information. Jan Newberry has recently gotten into the testing swing.

Greg Campora cannot be defined; but he does everything else.

I have been fortunate to have good editors at magazines and newspapers, people who supported me, encouraged me and taught me. Some of them I can even call friend: Jean Hewitt, Margot Slade, Angela Dotson, Jane Montand, Julia Read, Amy Gross, Warren Picower, Malachy Duffy and Ruth Gardner.

There are more and more wonderful chefs, food writers, food journalists and food historians. If I were to thank all the ones who are important to me, it might sound like showing off.

The debts of friendship can never be paid; but without my friends, or as Helen says, "the buddies," life would be poorer indeed.

I would also like to thank a book, *The California Nutrition Book,* or rather those who wrote it. It is the best general guide that I have seen and I have used it often.

CONTENTS

INTRODUCTION

When I was a child, I hated being described as healthy, robust or sturdy. I realized that they were euphemisms for the word no one was cruel enough to use, "chubby." I got all the way to my preteen years without despairing confrontation. When I reached eleven, I went shopping for a dress for a party. After several awkward attempts to get into dresses that I longed for, dresses with waists and even sashes, I had to retreat to a department ignominiously labeled "chubette," with not a waist in sight. From that time onward my life has been one long struggle with roundness.

In the early days, caught in the vicious cycle—I'm overweight; no one loves me; so I'll eat to make myself feel better—I committed most of the dieter's cardinal sins. I starved. I went on eccentric diets. There was the brief period of all the hard-boiled eggs you can eat. Nobody can eat enough hard-boiled eggs to gain weight. At that time, I hadn't heard of cholesterol—pouring into my body from all those eggs—and if I felt groggy, I thought it was hunger; I didn't know about ketosis, the body being poisoned by excess ketones produced when there is only protein in the diet, which the liver cannot detoxify without glucose that must come from foods other than protein.

I bought clothes a size too small, thinking I would diet my way into them, and had them stare out of my closet as a constant reproach. I bought clothes that were too large or shapeless, thinking no one would notice me. I bought shoes; they almost always fit. I avoided exercise; I thought I looked silly and it was so much work. I didn't become anorexic and I didn't take pills.

I had friends who could eat anything. A childhood friend was constantly being coaxed to eat by one and all, tempted with mid-morning milkshakes for which I would have killed. One beauty, a friend at college, would eat breakfast, meet a boyfriend for coffee and a donut, have lunch, have a mid-afternoon milkshake, eat dinner at the dorm and then go out on a dinner date. Just thinking about what she ate made me fat. In those days, they said it wasn't glands; no one had heard of fat cells and they blamed it all on my diet. My diet was to blame all right. After all, if I ate nothing I wouldn't gain weight. However, it turns out I was right; they could eat more than I could or can.

Eventually, I got the whole thing pretty much under control, except, of course, for the times when I was pregnant and felt released from bondage. It was a constant battle. I didn't know how to respond when people would meet me and say: "How come you're thin if you write about food?" The answer was constant dieting; but it seemed rude. By now the evidence was coming in that it wasn't just vanity and self-respect that were at stake; it was my general health—not so much the length of my life, but the quality of that life. What started as a simple search for slim and what I thought went with it—self-esteem, beautiful clothes and boyfriends—matured into a search for health.

It wasn't enough to fit into my clothes. I had to eat healthfully. It took a while to figure out what that was, especially since the doctors and the researchers seem to keep changing their minds.

An odd thing happened a few years ago as I began to cook a great deal in the microwave oven. It was less hard to lose weight when it started to go up, and it was easier to keep it off. Partly, my way of eating had already begun to change, and the change was becoming an automatic part of my approach to food. Partly, it was indeed the microwave oven. After a while, I figured it out. The microwave oven doesn't need fat to cook. Food doesn't stick to the pan without it. The microwave oven cooks fish, poultry and vegetables brilliantly, so I was eating fewer steaks. The flavors of fruits cooked in the microwave oven were so intense they didn't need sweetening. I discovered that risotto and other high-carbohydrate dishes I loved cooked effortlessly. Rapidly made breakfast cereals replaced eggs and bacon and I was on my way.

Perhaps, the microwave wouldn't have helped so much if I didn't love to eat. The sad fact is I do and always have. Just about any food will do; but I prefer something that is mouth-filling and wonderful. In the past, I spent too much time in the kitchen, or to avoid it ate anything, and anything turned out to be unsatisfying so I kept on eating. The microwave oven let me cook quickly at the same time the food was inside a closed box; I couldn't reach in and "taste," shoveling in uncounted calories. Suddenly, I could cook good food with a minimum of fuss, and my mouth was happy.

Even the microwave oven wouldn't have helped if I hadn't learned some hard lessons on the way. I had to learn to eat less. It wasn't as hard as I thought. Often I wasn't eating from hunger. I had to stop being a member of the clean-plate club, constantly being told about the starving children in Armenia, China, the current disaster spot. One day at a great French restaurant my closest friend said to me: "You don't have to finish it." That simple but radical notion had never occurred to me. I put down my fork and stopped finishing up right then and there.

I tasted all sorts of things; but I ate less. I found that more different flavors made me happier than a humongous quantity of one.

I realized that as a privileged American child, privileged because brought up with plenty, I didn't know what hunger was. Not eating for the better part of a day let me experience the physical sensation so that I never again would confuse "I want to eat" with "I'm hungry."

I spent a day with one of my lean friends and watched her put away a Gargantuan breakfast while I had my usual cup of coffee. I thought it was another example of the unfairness of life, that she could eat more. As the day went on and I picked, I realized that she wasn't eating. I learned that the maternal instruction to have a good breakfast wasn't foolish. If I have some breakfast—not Gargantuan—I eat less. I don't really want anything until lunch.

I learned that starving and fads didn't work. Most of all, I learned that I had to give myself frequent doses of pleasure, that food was one of my great pleasures and that without it I became cranky and didn't stay on a diet. Pleasure is good for us.

The lessons multiplied, and as they did I tried to find out why. This book is about the whys, how to comply with them and how to make it easy for you and for me. If you don't know how to use a microwave oven, now is the time to learn, so skip right to the last chapter, Learning Microwave (page 597). It's easy. All you really need to know is the wattage of your oven and how to set the timer and turn it on. The recipes will do the rest.

BEING HEALTHY AND SLIM

We all want to get in the healthful-food habit and to be slim. This book has diets, recipes and nutritional information to help you do just that. It contains weight-loss diet plans, diet plans for those who do not need to lose weight but want to be healthy, and many menus to make balancing your general and weight-loss diet easier (pages 48–56).

There is a common misconception that being on a diet means trying to lose weight, and that may be so for many of us. In truth, a diet is whatever we eat. This book is about two things that come together to make a whole. It is about weight-loss diets and about diets for people who do not need or want to lose weight, but who want to eat in a healthful fashion. Fortunately, the two overlap. A good weight-loss diet can easily be adjusted for those who wish to be healthy but not lose weight, by increasing the amounts of certain foods eaten in a day or a week.

Many of us don't need to lose weight, or we need to watch it only from time to time. We may still have trouble understanding all the new information about what we should and should not be eating, let alone creating menus and recipes that fit these new guidelines. The nutritional information in this chapter and the menu plans should be a help. I still suggest that everybody get on the scale every morning so that if weight starts to slide up, a weight-loss diet can be started before things get out of control.

I have tried to make the food taste wonderful. If this is to be the beginning of a new way of eating, a new life-style, it needs to be rewarding so that you will stay with it. Those of you who are already convinced that this is the way to eat will find a wide variety of recipes. There are simple everyday recipes, done without taking too much time, fussing or money, and more complicated recipes for days when you are in the mood or want to give a party.

Eating healthfully, getting exercise and achieving a good weight won't make anybody live forever; but I intend to give my best shot at living out my biologically determined span to its full and to do it in the best shape that I can.

Quick Tips to Get You Started

Here are a few quick tips for weight loss and health the microwave way:

1. Start the day on the scale, then have a hot whole-grain cereal or muffin quickly made in the microwave oven.

2. Weigh your food. It will cook better. Measure your servings. You will look better.

3. Don't start your cooking with fat. The food won't stick; the pounds will. Use fat only for flavor—olive oil when possible.

4. Keep fish, shellfish, chicken and meat portions to about four ounces (113.5 g). The cholesterol isn't only in the fat; it's in the cell walls of the meat.

5. Skin that poultry to halve the calories. Trim the meat.

6. Make lots of salads with diet dressings (pages 486–499). Stay away from most bottled dressings—even diet—if you're reducing salt.

7. Cook vegetables. They fill you up and give you vitamins. Purée them in a blender for light soup and sauce bases.

8. Make basics (see list of staples on page 45) to reduce salt, improve nutrition and save money.

9. Eat more carbohydrates. See Good Grains and Other Starches (pages 148–225).

10. Spices and herbs don't cost calories. They have vitamins. Full-flavored food tastes better; you eat less. If the chili burns your mouth, the fork stops sooner.

11. Vary your diet: avoid boredom; balance nutrition.

12. Eat more than one course. It slows you down and keeps you happy.

13. Get at least twenty minutes of mild exercise twice a day—walks will do.

14. Don't clean your plate unless it's filled with a proper portion of food from this book, or you are sure exactly what and how much is on it. No one will tell your mother.

15. Avoid impulse. Wait ten minutes and find something to do. It may go away.

16. See pages 514–529 for good snacks and have them ready so that bad ones don't take their place.

17. Shop less often; shop with a list; spend less time in the kitchen . . . easy, the microwave way.

18. See your doctor.

If you don't want to read all the nutritional information now, skip to The Diet-Ready Kitchen (page 25) or to Microslim Gourmet Diets and Menus (page 46).

The foods on this diet are prepared almost entirely in a microwave oven. What are its advantages? It's quick. The less time you or I spend in the kitchen, the less we are exposed to temptation. Since it is quick, we are more likely to cook for ourselves, our friends and our families with fresh foods, whereby we will get more variety, more control, and avoid the often excessive salt or unwelcome saturated fat or excessive cholesterol in prepared foods such as pasta sauces and frozen dinners—let alone the unpronounceable chemicals. You need almost no fat to cook with.

There are some recipes in this book for foods to be cooked conventionally, foods that don't cook as well in a microwave oven. There are breads and some desserts, as well as general indications for grilling (page 346). Almost every culinary technique has a place in a balanced diet.

See Your Doctor

Your doctor is the only person who can say what your individual needs are and what your weight should be, based on your body type, your metabolism and, sad possibility, your diseases. In this book, there is no attempt to treat diseases. Instead, it outlines ways of eating: eating to lose weight, ways of losing weight while staying healthy, ways to maintain your weight and increase your chance of being healthy. I have taken into account the current information about healthful eating, weight loss and exercise. I have had the recipes and weight-loss diet plans checked by a registered dietician.

If you use the recipes but don't follow the diet and menu plans in the chapter on diets and menus, which are balanced to give you good overall nutrition, talk to your doctor about taking a pill with a balance of minerals and vitamins. They work better together.

My advice is for adolescents and adults, not for infants or small children. However, if you are on a healthful diet and keep in shape, your children are more likely to follow that pattern.

The Balancing Act

Weight-losers and non–weight-losers alike still need that old-fashioned thing, a balanced diet. It's just that the balance is different than it used to be. Eating less fat is important not only for your weight but also for your heart, blood vessels and for cancer avoidance. It's virtually impossible to remove all fat from your diet and it shouldn't be tried. There are essential fatty acids. We should eat less animal protein, more carbohydrate, less sodium and still get a balance of vitamins and minerals. As you read the book, you will find more nutritional information in each chapter.

FATS

Fats should be less than 25 to 30 percent of your diet, because in excess they are fattening and bad for our health. My recipes will give you even less, to help with weight loss. There are many different kinds of fats. Fats can be defined by where they come from, either animal or plant sources, or by their structure. The various kinds of fat are saturated, polyunsaturated, monounsaturated and Omega-3 fatty acids, which are all triglycerides, and then there is cholesterol. I will have to discuss cholesterol separately because, while related to the others, it is so different. The fat we eat should be—as much as possible—not the saturated kind that comes along with butter, fatty cheeses, chocolate, meat and poultry and some odd things like coconuts. These saturated fats should make up less than 10 percent of your diet. That doesn't mean the polyunsaturated fats such as corn oil are the best. New information shows that they may cause problems. At best, they don't help clear them up. Omega-3 fatty acids, the kind found in cold-water fish (see page 226), and monounsaturated fats like olive oil actually help clear up your arteries. Be careful with the Omega-3 if you are on anticoagulants; they work in a similar fashion. Check with your doctor.

While cholesterol is technically a fat, it is so special that it is not included in the fat counts that accompany each recipe. It has a number all its own. It is found only in animal foods. It is found not only in the fat of those foods but also in the cell walls of animal proteins.

The cholesterol that your doctor measures with tests is not a direct reflection of what you eat. Your body manufactures cholesterol and does so from a wide variety of foods. The body uses saturated fats to make cholesterol, but it also uses some proteins. Turkey protein and wheat gluten, for instance, provoke twice as much cholesterol production as pork does.

Cholesterol in your body occurs in two kinds of lipoproteins, HDL and LDL. HDLs are good and LDLs are bad. While all together they should probably stay under two hundred, the higher the ratio of HDLs to LDLs the better. Diet can only partially control your system's cholesterol. It is highly dependent on your heredity and your level of tension. Nevertheless, general wisdom tells us to limit our saturated fat and cholesterol intake.

To summarize, when you look at the nutritional profile of a food, it can be very fatty—bad—and low in cholesterol, or low in fat and high in cholesterol—bad. Some foods are high in both fat and cholesterol—very bad. The goal is to get the maximum of general nutrition with the least saturated fat and cholesterol. To compare different kinds of meat, fish, shellfish and chicken for fats, cholesterol and nutrients, see pages 341–345.

PROTEIN

We all grew up believing that proteins were good for us, that eggs were the perfect protein along with whole milk. Watch it. Much of the protein from animal sources carries cholesterol along with it. Egg yolks have a high proportion of cholesterol. Eggs from organically raised chickens have less. Whole milk has fat. If you're watching your cholesterol, use nonfat milk products. While some health-concerned organizations have recommended keeping protein down to 30 percent of the diet, the instruction is confusing. Many grains and legumes, which are desirable parts of the diet, and nonfat milk products—yogurt, cottage cheese, ricotta, etc.—are high in protein. As fats go down in your diet, protein may go up; but most of it shouldn't be from meats of any kind.

CARBOHYDRATES

The big news is carbohydrates. I remember when superior-sounding friends would say: "Oh, I have no trouble with my weight. If it starts to go up, I just cut out bread and potatoes for a while." Turns out they weren't doing themselves much good. Today's best advice is to try to get about 40 percent of your calories from carbohydrates. If you are on an 1,100-calorie weight-loss diet, you should be eating at least sixty grams of carbohydrate. Where possible, use whole grains and potatoes, apples and the like with their skins on.

FIBER

Don't worry too much about fiber. If you start the day with a whole-grain cereal or Majic Whole Grain Bread (page 152) and have as many vegetables, salads and fruits as I suggest, you won't have any problem. However, too much fiber isn't good. It can eliminate good nutrients from your body. Fiber is both soluble and insoluble. Soluble fiber, like that in brown rice and oat bran, helps reduce clotting in veins and arteries. Insoluble fiber, like that in celery and wheat germ, aids digestion and, in moderation, reduces the likelihood of bowel cancer.

Is That All There Is?

No, there are lots of other things we need from our foods. We need minerals like zinc, iron, calcium and potassium. We need a wide assortment of vitamins. With each passing year, research reveals more things that are essential to our well-being. There are even discoveries of things that may not be essential but are beneficial, like elements in garlic and onions that act as blood thinners and work against infection.

There is also sodium. Our bodies have and need it. Most of the sodium we get in our foods comes from salt or salty condiments and prepared foods. Soy sauce, hot sauces, ketchup, canned tomatoes, canned broth, pickles and the like may add a lot of sodium of which we are not aware. Making our own sauces, beans, broths and other basic foods (see Index for recipes) avoids the problem. Almost nobody gets too little sodium. Most of us do not have problems with sodium as long as we drink enough water or other fluids. Even so, cutting down on salt cannot hurt us and is now generally recommended by health organizations. We quickly become adjusted to a less salty taste and can compensate for its reduction by increasing other seasonings. Even if we add no salt to our foods, we will get sodium since almost all foods naturally contain it.

Some athletes who exercise in the sun and have tried to sharply limit the sodium in their diet may be salt-deprived after a workout. They should not take salt tablets. They should drink lots of water and some juice.

If there is a medical recommendation for you to be on a low-sodium diet, eliminate even the small amount of salt in these recipes and beware commercially prepared foods suggested as alternatives in their preparation.

FLUIDS

Which brings up water, something most of us may not consider a food. Our bodies are mostly water and we need a lot of it in order to function well. We get water in liquids like soups, sodas, vegetables and fruits; but we should still drink water. Try to drink about five glasses a day, some of them before meals. They help you to register full. As long as it's clean, it's the only thing we ingest that carries no concealed problems.

That isn't necessarily true of bottled waters, mineral waters and sodas. Look at their labels; many of them, including the low-calorie sodas, have lots of sodium. Many sodas, coffee and tea contain caffeine, which acts as a diuretic, so that you may actually not be retaining much of the water you are getting in them.

Other than water, what should we drink? Some people have a problem with alcohol and shouldn't drink it. Nobody should have too much. Don't worry about foods cooked in a microwave oven that have wine or liquor in the recipe. Alcohol evaporates quickly. If having the stuff is a problem, choose other recipes.

Some studies show that a moderate amount of alcohol can be good for adult males, relaxing them and reducing their cholesterol. There are more questions where women are concerned. I drink wine because I like the taste and the way it goes with food; but it is never necessary. A four-ounce (120 ml) glass of wine or an eight-ounce (240 ml) glass of light beer has about one hundred calories. Light beer has one-third fewer calories than regular beer has. You can stretch your wine by mixing it half-and-half with seltzer to make a spritzer. If a day or a menu (pages 46–56) calls for some wine, you can have an extra snack or portion of fruit if you don't have the wine.

Fruit and vegetable juices are full of vitamins, especially fresh. Canned may have substantial sodium contents. They vary widely in calories (page 73). Check even sodas and bottled water for sodium levels.

Consider freshly made and unsweetened lemonade or iced tea, or use a sugar substitute if you are losing weight. Mint and herb teas are drunk in many parts of the world and go well with food. Some of the herb teas, like chamomile, are soothing, which is a plus at night.

If you must have diet sodas, do; but studies have shown that they don't help people diet and some indicate that they may actually create a desire for real sugar.

SUGAR

Sugar is not a mortal sin. A teaspoonful has only sixteen calories. The problems come when sugar replaces other elements in a diet or when its consumption becomes excessive. Sugar is like a version of the old Chinese restaurant joke: It may pick you up, but it also is quick to let you down. I flirted with someone like that once. You don't need it. You may want it. I don't use much sugar in the recipes in this book, but there are some desserts and preserves that call for it.

Reading All Those Numbers

Every recipe in this book and many basic ingredients have nutritional information attached to them that is given numerically. Here is what the numbers mean.

All the numbers given are rounded off to the nearest whole number. All numbers given for a recipe are for the first ingredient in a list of possibilities. Optional ingredients will change things to a greater or lesser degree. Herbs and spices will generally change only vitamin and mineral counts. Substituting canned products for fresh will usually add sodium and sometimes fat.

PORTIONS

The first nutritional information given about any recipe is the size of the portion. Portions of fish, poultry and meat will be smaller than those to which you are accustomed; but it is important to get used to them if you want to follow the Surgeon General's, the American Heart Association's and the Cancer Prevention Association's guidelines.

If you are on a weight-loss diet, it's even more important not to cheat on the size of portions. If the recipe is for a soup or a stew, use a ladle whose capacity you know, or use a measuring cup of the right size as a ladle. Get a scale and use it for major solid ingredients. It's hard to eyeball a portion of fish or meat.

CALORIES

The number of calories is given per serving. Weight-loss diets are based on roughly 1,100 calories per day. See Diets and Menus (pages 46–73) for more information. If you are large and/or active, up your intake to about 1,400 calories per day, even on a weight-loss diet, by adding more carbohydrates.

Those of us who do not need to lose weight may need as few as 1,500 calories a day to maintain our weight if we are small, have a slow metabolic rate and are inactive. Athletes training for the triathlon who are of large frames may need as many as 6,000 calories per day.

If you don't need to lose weight, you can eat more. Start with about 1,700 calories. Every few days, increase the calories by 200 until you reach a point where you find yourself gaining weight. Drop back to the previous number of calories. Keep doing that until you reach a point where your weight varies little from day to day.

You can average out calories and other nutrition over a period of days; but it gets harder the farther you get from the basic diet. Vegetarians who are organizing their nutrition around complementary vegetable proteins will have to eat them at the same meal.

CHOLESTEROL

The amount of cholesterol in a portion of a recipe reflects what you are eating, not what is in your body. You don't need to eat cholesterol. Your body manufactures what you need. Some people cannot control their cholesterol by diet. They have a medical problem and need medical help. The rest of us can help ourselves.

The dietary recommendation of most government groups and health associations concerned with protecting our health is that we eat no more than 100 milligrams of cholesterol per 1,000 calories. Since the weight-loss diet in Diets and Menus has about that number of calories, that's about the most cholesterol you should eat in a day if you are on it.

OTHER FATS

All the kinds of fat other than cholesterol are given in grams. Since a gram of fat has more calories than a gram of protein or carbohydrate, it makes sense to keep the fat down; but you do need some. Monounsaturated fats, like those in olive oil, are better for you than the saturated ones. If you are taking in about 1,000 calories a day on a weight-loss diet, then you should eat only about 250 milligrams of fat, of which less than 100 should be saturated.

SODIUM

Between 1,100 and 3,300 milligrams per day is considered the safe range. It sounds like a lot; but one teaspoon of table salt has 2,200 milligrams of sodium. The kosher salt that I use is coarsely ground and contains only 1,475 milligrams of sodium per teaspoon. If you use table salt, use only—for taste reasons as well as to control sodium intake—one-third as much as the quantity given in the recipe. Tamari soy sauce, which is frequently used in the recipes, has 336 milligrams of sodium per teaspoon. I rarely suggest light soy because I don't like the flavor.

Watch out for onion salt and other seasoning mixtures; they are mainly sodium. Sodium exists naturally in all kinds of foods. I have reduced overall sodium by keeping the salt added to recipes low, since a major part of salt is sodium. If you need to reduce sodium further, eliminate salt and soy and make the basic products listed on page 45. Commercially prepared products tend to be high in sodium, even weight-loss products. Fresh is best.

Table salt is fortified with iodine in order to protect us from goiters, unless specifically marked. This practice started many years ago. Today, Americans are not iodine-deficient. We eat many prepared foods and food in restaurants, almost all of which are made with iodized salt. We eat seafood as well as vegetables grown in soil near the seashore, both of which are rich in iodine. When we cook at home, we can avoid the bitter taste of iodine and the chemicals that make salt pour out of shakers in humid weather by using kosher salt. Pickling salt also contains no iodine; but it is not as pure and is more finely ground.

RDA

Most of the remaining nutritional information given with each recipe or with individual foods is given in terms of a percentage of RDA. RDA means recommended dietary allowance. These figures are determined by the National Academy of Sciences. They are not provided for everything we need to eat.

PROTEIN

If a recipe is listed as having four grams of protein, which is 10 percent of the RDA, the total RDA would be forty grams. As I say on page 16, don't worry too much about the percentage of protein; consider instead where it comes from. Protein from flesh should be kept down due to the associated cholesterol. Sometimes, when recipes are extremely low in protein, I don't give the number.

OTHER NUTRIENTS

Every recipe also has a separate list of nutrients, each of which is given with a number that tells us what percentage of the RDA for that nutrient is supplied by a portion of that recipe. Calcium, phosphorus, iron, vitamins A and C, riboflavin, thiamin and niacin are all listed in this way as percentages. Potassium is also listed, even though there is no RDA. It is listed in milligrams, and 1,900 to 5,600 seems to be the best daily range. All of this information is not listed for every recipe. What is given are the strengths of each recipe. Although there is no RDA for carbohydrate, the gram amount is usually given because most of us need to increase our intake of carbohydrate. To find out about zinc, look at pages 341–342.

Since it is clear that not everything that needs to be known about nutrition is known today, your best shot is to eat a wide variety of foods. That way you will get something of everything. You'll also have more fun.

The only time you need to worry is if you aren't following the diet plans on pages 46–73.

Exercise

I know some of us practically didn't graduate from high school because we didn't complete the gym requirement. Exercise can sound punishing and painful. Maybe if we called it activity instead it would sound more attractive. Whatever we call it, we all need it. Lying in bed all day isn't good for us and only burns the minimum number of calories used to keep us alive. I once got out of the hospital after eating—for medical reasons—what I was convinced was nothing. To my shock I found I had only lost a pound. I also felt weak as a sick kitten. All my muscles had turned to jelly.

There are all sorts of health reasons why we need to keep our bodies and muscles active and get our breathing and pulse rates up. It's good for hearts. Muscles waste away if unused. Fat, especially above the waist, is less good for our bodies than the same weight in muscle. From the point of view of the weight-loss dieter, it may be less a question of extra calories actually burned—you need to do a lot of exercise to burn off a donut—than of getting our motors, metabolisms, to run at an efficient rate.

While a vigorous hour of exercise three times a week may be good for developing or maintaining muscles, twenty minutes twice a day is better for keeping up the metabolic rate. Fast walking, swimming, a vigorous rather than languorous bicycle ride, chugging up and down a flight of stairs, or calisthenics if you prefer, will all fill the bill. Make the exercise periods convenient; but space them out. Walking briskly to and from work may do the job—but not if you live in the suburbs and work in the city.

Getting to the Proper Weight

Unfortunately, at some point we cannot consider health and food without considering weight. Many of us are overweight and placing a strain on our bodies—our hearts, our joints. Some—never me—are underweight and constantly short-changing their bodies. The important thing is to find out what you should weigh and to get there and stay there. One person's slim is not another's, and what you or I will have to do to achieve and maintain our own best shape may be different even as it respects balanced nutrition.

On our way to the proper weight, it is important that we don't do silly things that will damage our bodies as we slide down the scale.

Understanding good, balanced nutrition, simply outlined above, will help; but there are bad things done to lose weight that need to be avoided. Starving, although effective in the short term, is very bad for us and bad for our long-term chances of keeping our weight off. It is tempting because many of us who love food find it is easier not to eat at all than to control the amount that we eat.

Unfortunately, if we starve, our bodies decide: "Whoops, something bad is happening; it's time to conserve energy." The body then begins to metabolize— burn up—food more slowly to help us out. Little does it know that we are not living in the Australian Outback, but are simply trying to lose some weight. If the body uses calories more slowly, we lose weight more slowly. When we stop dieting it doesn't rev up again, so we still have to eat less to stay in the same place. One result is that once we have painfully lost the weight, we regain it easily and have to start all over. That's discouraging. What is more important is that this up-and-down pattern, called yo-yo dieting, may actually be as bad or worse for us than never losing the weight at all.

Starvation metabolism goes into effect when our bodies are fed less than about 1,000 calories for any length of time. If we are very large or exercise regularly, we probably need to go up to about 1,400 calories per day even when losing weight. An athlete may require many more calories a day. Most of us don't do that much exercise. Therefore, we have to reduce our calories consistently without hitting the trigger point for lowering our metabolisms.

Any diet at a lower range of calories should be supervised by a doctor, and you need to be careful when you come off of an extreme diet or your starving body will fight to regain calories and weight.

Suppose you are in my shoes and starved before you knew it was bad for you. The best you can do now is to go on an exercise program to try to boost your metabolism and to make sure that if you are planning to lose weight you do it sensibly so that you don't immediately gain it back.

The Diet-Ready Life

For many of us the simple everyday things of life seem to be what get in the way of eating healthfully or getting slim. Children need to be fed; we go out to dinner; we have to entertain; there's a business lunch; we're on a once-in-a-lifetime trip. We are tired and frazzled, and thinking too much about our food seems overwhelming if not impossible. There isn't any food in the house; I live alone; it's not worth bothering. What we need is a strategy to see us through until the new style becomes automatic. It will.

One of the simplest things to do is to get your kitchen stripped for a new way of eating and filled with the basics for a healthful and/or slimming meal. See The Diet-Ready Kitchen (page 25).

Even if you are making food only for yourself, a diet-ready kitchen will work. If the salad's washed, the dressing's made or bought and pasta sits on your shelf just waiting for you to cook it and add the sauce you will defrost from the freezer, and if there's a piece of fruit for dessert, dinner need not be an effort. Consider cooking what you really want. The microwave oven will make it short work. You can make just as much as you need or enough so that leftovers will be ready for another meal.

Don't tell the world that you're changing the way you eat or that you plan to lose weight. You do have to tell the people you live with. Children will gradually accommodate to a healthful home diet.

If the people you live with don't need to lose weight and you do, serve them more bread, grains, pasta and other carbohydrates or a little more of the main course. Look at individual recipes to see where the quantities can be increased without unbalancing nutritional goals.

Always eat breakfast before you leave the house. You may be pleasantly surprised to find that others will join you.

If you go out to work, consider taking your food with you. It can be leftovers, cold food or even something that is quickly cooked in the office if there is a microwave oven. Many offices have one. The soup or stew can be quickly heated. A washed salad brought in a plastic bag can be shaken in the bag with dressing brought along in a small container or from a bottle kept in the office. There are microwavable plastic plates that come with snap-on lids. You can put the raw ingredients for lunch on the plate. Refrigerate it until just before you want to eat. Then pop it in the microwave oven for the short time it will take to cook.

At home or at work, keep a selection of diet snacks (page 529) on hand to avoid the cart that rolls through the office or the temptations lurking in your refrigerator.

If you work someplace that has a cafeteria or other food service, get active in requesting that they provide healthful alternatives such as nonfat yogurt and cottage cheese, salads with diet dressings on the side, fresh fruits and even well-made, small, healthy main courses. You will delight more of your co-workers than you suspect.

If you're tired when you get home and dinner won't be ready for a while, try that twenty minutes of brisk exercise. I know it sounds silly; but you will probably find yourself much less tired and hungry after the exercise than before. If you still need a pick-me-up, have a piece of fruit or Spicy Chicken Broth (page 59).

EATING OUT

If the outside meal is lunch in a restaurant and you are trying to lose weight, you may want to make it the equivalent of dinner so as to feel less conspicuous. Eating the larger meal in the middle of the day is actually better for you. For lunch or dinner, almost any restaurant will offer simply grilled fish, chicken or a paillard (a thin slice) of veal or beef. Many will offer a vegetarian main course or vegetable plate. If you order meat, remove the skin or trim it and try not to eat the entire portion if it seems hefty. If a first course seems in order, you are probably better off with a clear soup or a small order of pasta with a noncreamy vegetable sauce, such as tomato. Refuse the cheese and don't eat bread. Skip dessert or have some melon or berries without cream.

If lunch is a matter of just leaving work, try to avoid fast-food restaurants. At cafeterias and lunch counters, the Alternate Weight-Loss Meals (page 52) should be easy to accommodate.

When you are invited to a party, it is all right to say when accepting: "I prefer not to eat red meat"; or, "My doctor has put me on a low-fat diet." It happens to me all the time these days and I cope. You don't have to finish what's on your plate; but try not to refuse a dish unless you are allergic. Taste the gooey dessert if you want to. Pay for it tomorrow.

It often pays off to play Scarlett O'Hara by eating a little something before going to a party. It will help cut your appetite and you will eat less, particularly of the seductive and often pernicious hors d'oeuvres. Either a portion of fruit (pages

531–533) or Spicy Chicken Broth (page 59) is good. Drink several large glasses of water and go off fortified.

Watch out for cocktail parties and hosts who have long cocktail hours before dinner. It's easy to overeat when it just seems like bits and pieces. If I know that there is to be a long cocktail hour before dinner, I often arrive a little late.

Don't accept too many invitations in a row unless they are to homes where you feel comfortable telling the host or hostess you are on a diet—of whatever kind.

The worst part of traveling may be airline food. You can bring your own, or order ahead a fruit plate or a vegetarian meal. Other strategies for any kind of dieting and business travel are like those for eating in restaurants. Breakfast is the great exception, especially when it's included in the price of the room. Avoid breakfast buffets like the plague. You always eat too much. You can get cereal, fruit and something to drink delivered to your room. Other room-service meals are easy to arrange to your satisfaction.

ENTERTAINING

Giving a party is no problem. There are dinner-party menus on pages 67–68 that will not make a guest feel short-changed. Make somewhat larger quantities than you make for yourself and your family. Your guests may want to eat a lot; who are you to stop them? Just watch your own portions.

I find one odd benefit from giving a dinner party and doing the extra work and cooking. By the time the guests arrive, I'm often not very interested in eating anymore. I eat lightly.

PLANNING A MEAL

Microslim Gourmet Diets and Menus (pages 46–73) has menus that are simple and fancy, for one or two or a family, for parties, for weight loss and for healthy eating. There are even vegetarian menus. When you look in the chapters about main courses—The Fish and Shellfish Advantage (pages 226–288), Perfectly Poultry (pages 289–339) and For the Carnivore (pages 340–387)—you will find menu suggestions in the introductions to many of the recipes.

If your larder is stocked, you will probably only need to buy some vegetables and fish, chicken or meat. Make a list of what you need and get out of the store fast if you are trying to lose weight, or begin by going to the store and seeing what is fresh and interesting. Look in the Index and make a recipe that uses what you have found.

Don't omit first courses, soups, salads and even desserts or fruit. The fancy spas serve a sequence of six or seven small courses. I don't expect you to go that far; but having more than one course give you a wider variety of foods, slows down your eating and provides lots of different taste and texture sensations. You'll eat less and better. You won't feel deprived.

PLANNING THE WEEK

If you can make the time, it pays to plan the week ahead. Check The Diet-Ready Kitchen, beginning on the opposite page, and make a time to replenish staples that you buy and make. Make a shopping list for the meals that you know are going to be eaten at home. Stay flexible.

THE DIET-READY KITCHEN

Before you set out to lose weight or to change your ways for healthier eating, it's a good idea to strip for action . . . not you, the kitchen. You can also strip yourself and get a base weight—not a bad idea; but this chapter is about changing your kitchen. First remove temptation. You may have to be ruthless with yourself. It may be useful to enlist a friend to hold the garbage bag and to help you avoid wolfing down the quart of ice cream you are about to throw out. If there is a lot of food and it's in good condition, call a charitable organization that will come and pick it up and make good use of it. You'll be inclined to get rid of more and feel better about it.

Then you can go out and splurge on new supplies and any equipment that might be useful.

Some minutes may be sad. Tossing out the half-eaten package of filled chocolate cookies or sugar-coated donuts may only hurt a little. The worst to me was scraping the mayonnaise out of the bottle and into the trash; that was before I discovered how to make Egg White Mayonnaise (see page 482). Disposing of old, crusty marshmallows and sugar-drenched breakfast cereals really isn't bothersome. If you have a lot of expensive jams and jellies you can't bear to part with, put them on a high shelf that's out of sight. Save them until the weight comes off, when a little sugar won't hurt. Frozen desserts including ice cream, chocolate syrups, sugary sodas, cans of coconut cream (piña colada mix), cake mixes and packages of lard must all go. You really in your heart of hearts know what shouldn't be there; get rid of it. Discard temptation so you don't have to fight it constantly. Freeze the butter.

Now make a list of what you have that seems reasonable. Check it against The Shopping List (page 28–44) and make a second list of things to buy. If you have a store nearby that will take a telephone order and deliver, do that. Avoid the temptation of shopping. Second best is to order the food over the telephone and pick it up. If you must pick out food, go with your list and buy nothing that isn't on it. You can add to the list the foods needed for a few days or a week of menus. Look in Diets and Menus (pages 46–73). Just carrying all that food is exercise.

Now look at your equipment. If you don't have a scale, you need one in addition to the one on which you weigh yourself every morning. I find it convenient to have two kitchen scales. One is for weighing larger amounts and the other is for weighing a few grams or ounces and is reliable down to a fraction of an ounce. Not only will you work more efficiently with your microwave oven if you know the weights of the foods you are using; but you are also less liable to cheat on your diet.

Buy a small instant-read thermometer so that you can quickly tell if your food is fully cooked. See page 230 for fish temperatures and page 290 for chicken.

A scale that has the capacity to
weigh up to 2½ pounds (1.13 g) or
up to 5 pounds (2.27 g) of food is an
important tool for microwave and
healthy cooking.

A food mill comes with three discs
with different-sized holes to
purée cooked vegetables and fruits
while removing skins, seeds
and membrane.

Most of what you need you may already have on hand. In addition to your microwave oven—if you don't have one, look at pages 597–604 for features before buying—you will find life easier with a food processor, a blender, a food mill, a small electric coffee grinder reserved for spices, a cheese grater, a four-sided grater, a ricer and a citrus juicer.

Why so many ways to grind and cut things up? It's mainly to speed things along and make less work. Why cook rapidly in a microwave oven and spend an endless time on preparation? These tools also make a wide variety of soups, sauces and drinks as well as helping with your basic preparation.

While a blender and a food processor can often be used interchangeably, they give different results. A blender will make finer, more liquid purées, cream soups, shakes and other drinks that tend to ooze out of a food processor. A food processor can chop vegetables and fruits without turning them to mush and without the addition of liquid. The food processor can also grind meat; but the blender will make a more finely textured fish mousse or pâté.

A food mill has the delightful property of removing skins and seeds from foods put through it to purée. You can regulate the fineness of the purée by buying a food mill with three discs that fit into its bottom; changing the disc will change the fineness of a purée. A food mill cannot chop and can purée only cooked fruits and vegetables or those that are very soft, such as tomatoes.

Spices quickly lose their flavor when ground and stored. If you have a small electric coffee mill, you can grind them as you need them for more perfume and flavor. While it is worthwhile to grind pepper that way when you are making a large meal, you still need a pepper mill for small quantities and the table. Cheese that has been grated—at home or in the store—also dries out and loses flavor. It is best to have a little rotary grater and grate what you need as you need it.

While you can use the grating discs that come with your food processor, I often find it convenient to resort to an old-fashioned four-sided grater. There is less waste and less cleanup. I use it to grate fresh gingerroot, which eliminates a lot of the stringy fiber. It can be used for cheese, particularly soft cheeses like part-skim mozzarella, which does not do well in the rotary cheese grater. Nutmeg, a little onion and countless other things can be handled quickly.

A potato ricer, looking like a giant garlic press, is useful only for mashed potatoes; but if you like them as much as I do, there is no better tool—no lumps, no gluteny texture.

A citrus juicer is essential if only for breakfast. I use lots of lemon juice in everyday cooking.

Every cook needs sharp knives in a variety of sizes. You also need a potato peeler and an apple corer. In addition to peeling, the peeler is used to remove long, widish strips of lemon zest without pith.

While metal pots generally do not go in a microwave oven, there are many other possibilities. Glass measuring cups in many sizes, up to an eight-cup size that may take some looking for, are very useful for cooking as well as measuring. The best have some space over the last of the measured numbers. You may already have glass pie plates or ceramic quiche dishes, two-and-a-half-quart (2.5-1) soufflé dishes, five-quart (5-1) and two-and-a-half-quart (2.5-1) glass or ceramic casseroles with tightly fitting lids. Glass and ceramic loaf pans and baking pans are also useful, along with custard cups, small soufflés and even individual ceramic or glass tart pans. Some of the glass pans such as the loaf pans now come with a transparent nonstick interior surface—very nice for avoiding sticking (particularly of breads cooked in a conventional oven) and fat. The largest-sized flattish dish that will fit in all ovens is an oval pan, about $13 \times 9 \times 2$ inches ($33 \times 23 \times 5$ cm) or $13 \times 10 \times 2$ inches ($33 \times 25.5 \times 5$ cm). It comes in glass and in ceramic—often as a French gratin pan. You may find that you already have many of these things in your kitchen.

I have one favorite cooking dish that does not fit in all ovens; but it is wonderful if you have a full-size full-wattage oven. It is a $14 \times 11 \times 2$-inch ($35.5 \times 28 \times 5$-cm) rectangle made of vitrified china. The corners are rounded so that the dish can fit on a carrousel.

If your microwave oven doesn't have a carrousel, you may want to buy an inexpensive wind-up plastic carrousel for more even cooking. If you often cook

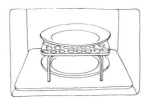

Use a rack for cooking two plates of food; switch plates halfway through cooking time. If recipe calls for cooking portions for two in one dish, add 30 seconds to the cooking time.

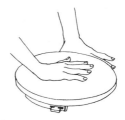

A wind-up carrousel is useful if the oven does not have a carrousel.

for two, buy an equally inexpensive plastic rack with folding legs (useful for storage). It will permit you to cook food for both of you at the same time on two plates, saving some washing up.

Every cook needs spoons, slotted spoons, measuring spoons and cups (dry and liquid measure), whisks, ladles, sieves and colanders. A salad spinner can hasten the drying of greens.

While many of your conventional cooking pots will get less use, you still need large pots to boil pasta, smaller pots to boil rice and some baking tins for things that just don't do well in the microwave oven. If you don't have one, invest in a small—for one or two portions—sauté pan with a nonstick coating for days when you want a browned piece of meat.

You will need an ample supply of microwave plastic wrap, some paper toweling that is marked microwavable and a little parchment paper. Buy freezing containers, if you don't have them—one-half cup, one cup and one pint—that are usable in a microwave oven. They can be used for freezing individual portions of soup and leftovers and to take lunch to the office. You may also want to buy a couple of plastic blue-plate divided dishes with snap-on lids, also for taking to the office. Do not use any of their lids in the microwave oven.

Part of setting up your kitchen is to gradually make a store of basic preparations from this book that freeze well and permit your cooking to be more spontaneous, more rapid. There is a list on page 45.

The Shopping List

THE PANTRY

"Pantry" is an old-fashioned word. It used to be a place or even a group of places. The pantry itself was where the dry staples of a household were kept along with hanging bunches of dried herbs. Sometimes it also held the jams, jellies, pickles, preserves, vinegars, syrups, jars of tomatoes and preserved meats—pickled or smoked. If there was a large, cool, dry cellar, the put-up foods would be kept there. There might be a root cellar for cold storage of root vegetables and hard fruit. A very fancy house would have a butler's pantry for the good dishes, crystal and silver.

The kitchen itself would have the pots and pans and bowls and the food for the day's meal, much of it perishable. Today, we have some cabinets, a refrigerator and freezer; but we need the same groups of foods even if we store them differently.

GRAIN PRODUCTS

Good Grains and Other Starches (pages 148–225) will tell you why this list is so large and give you the basic nutritional analysis for food in this category. Rather than keeping a lot of half-used boxes that spill around and because I have a house in the country where white mice are frequent winter visitors, I empty all grain products as well as sugar and cornstarch into clean plastic containers with tightly fitting lids. I mark the plastic with a china marker, or cut out the label from the original boxes and bags for identification and nutritional information and tape it on, or put on a piece of masking tape and write on that. Anything that is easily removed is good. It is a good idea to store things in categories. Grains and everything for baking do well together.

Grains, flours and other dry ingredients should be measured by dipping a dry measure—that is, one that holds just the amount to be measured—into the ingredient and leveling the top with the blade of a knife or any other straight edge.

Many of the somewhat unusual grains may be more easily found in health-food stores or from mail-order sources. As long as grains are kept cool and dry, they will last virtually indefinitely. Flours should be used more quickly.

BARLEY gets points just for longevity as one of the world's oldest cultivated grains. It is usually used as pearl barley, which has had the husk removed. It may be less nutritious; but it's a lot more enjoyable (page 196).

BREAD particularly if you are not making Majic Whole Grain Bread (page 152). See page 69 for nutritional comparisons of breads.
> *French or Italian bread,* preferably whole wheat, made without milk or eggs
> *Pita breads,* small (whole wheat or white)
> *Whole-grain crackers or flat breads,* about 22 calories each, unless making Oat Bran Wafers (page 161)
> *Whole wheat or a low-calorie bread*

BUCKWHEAT is a whole grain that is often ground into flour and made into pancakes or added to bread. It has a dark color and strong smell. Whole, it is cooked in the husk. Husked, it is called **kasha** (page 199).

BULGUR WHEAT, also called burghul and cracked wheat, is whole grains of wheat that have been boiled until they cracked and then dried and ground. When finely ground it is called **tabbouleh** and can be prepared by simply soaking in hot liquid (page 195).

CORNMEAL, white or yellow, fine or coarse. The coarse yellow kind is **polenta** in Italy. It can be cooked on its own (pages 215–217) or used in breads.

CORNSTARCH is a fine white powder that is particularly useful as a thickening agent in microwave cooking. When using cornstarch, it is always best to mix it first with a very small amount of liquid to make a lumpless paste. Then stir in the remaining liquid slowly, again avoiding lumps. This is called a **slurry**. If the slurry sits, the cornstarch will tend to separate. Stir it well before adding it to sauces and stews as a thickening agent. It needs to boil for 2–3 minutes in order to thicken. Boiling for a very long time may cause the mixture to thin. When cornstarch has been used as a thickener, always stir the cooked mixture well while scraping the bottom of the dish, in order to make sure that all of it has been incorporated.

FARINA can be any type of flour, but is most often a cereal to be served hot and made from coarsely ground hulled wheat (page 160).

GRITS in this book are intended to be the American dried corn whose grains are treated to make **hominy**. Then they are dried again and coarsely ground. The best are white grits with specks of black, which are the germ (page 218).

KASHA see Buckwheat.

MILLET is a grain held in rather low esteem, and yet I like it as a change from the more ordinary starches (page 199).

OAT BRAN is just the outer husk of oats; but it is rich in soluble fiber. It is sold as oat bran cereal for hot preparation. I don't like it that way; but I use it in baking.

OATMEAL (old-fashioned type, not quick-cooking) is used for cereals (pages 158–159) and in breads and cookies.

PASTAS (pages 162–179). Italy alone has countless kinds of pasta, fresh and dry. If you add to that the Oriental pastas, you have an almost unending variety. Since dry pasta keeps well, it is easy to vary your meals by having several kinds in the cupboard. Pasta shapes are generally chosen by the way they hold sauces, glide through clear soups (vermicelli and capellini), and stand up to chunky soups (small shells and tubetti). Many pasta shapes are available as whole wheat, semolina, spinach or tomato. Nutritional information is unavailable on Oriental pastas.

> *Artichoke noodles* are made without wheat and are a gray-green in color. They are good for people who are allergic to wheat.
>
> *Capellini and capelli d'angelo* are fine and finest round pastas often used in soups. They cook extremely quickly and should be used only with very light sauces. The capelli d'angelo often come rolled into nests.
>
> *Couscous,* plain or quick cooking, is a tiny pasta often mistaken for a grain that is found in Morocco, Sicily and southern Spain. Traditionally steamed, it may also be cooked like a risotto, or, if quick-cooking, swelled with hot water like tabbouleh (page 195).
>
> *Egg noodles,* dry or fresh, are the traditional soup noodles and come thin, thick and medium. While it is nice to make fresh pasta *al uovo* (with eggs) from time to time, on a day-to-day basis I count on dry. The Chinese also have egg noodles, which are somewhat chewier in texture than the Western variety. If cholesterol is a problem, avoid egg noodles.
>
> *Fettuccine* is a long, flat pasta the size of spaghetti, sometimes made with eggs. It is best for unctuous sauces.
>
> *Macaroni* was for many years the compendium name for pasta in America. Today, it is the name for tubular pasta, most of which is curved like an unformed "c" and called **elbow macaroni**. Short little macaroni, about one-quarter inch, are called **tubetti** and are good in minestrone.

Mung bean noodles become transparent when cooked and are good in soups and side dishes.

Orzo is not an Italian noodle. In Italy, "orzo" is the word for barley. In this book it is a small, rice-shaped pasta that is very popular in Greece. I particularly like it in soups. It also gives a creamy texture when stirred into stews.

Pastina is the smallest of the noodles and usually used as baby food. There are days when I want to be soothed like a baby, and pastina it is. Pastina also cooks quickly and can be used in stuffings in place of rice or bread crumbs.

Rice noodles are whitish, almost transparent sticks that soften in hot water and can be used in salads without cooking. They seem to disappear into soups and stews, ending up as a mystery texture.

Shells are unsurprisingly shaped like shells and are striated on the outside. They come in three sizes: small (usually used in soups), medium (used with thickish sauces) and large (cooked and stuffed).

Soba is a Japanese buckwheat noodle that is pale brown in color. It is eaten cold in the summer with a dipping sauce and hot in the winter as part of made dishes.

Spaghetti was the name for pasta when I was growing up in a more innocent America. It was usually served with a thick red sauce—with or without meatballs. In truth it is a group of long, rod-shaped pastas of lesser or greater width. Most typically we call rods that are about ⅛-inch (.3-cm) thick spaghetti. The thinnest spaghettis, such as capellini and vermicelli, are sometimes sold with the strands twisted into 1-ounce (28-g) nests.

Spaghettini is a thin spaghetti and is better with the thinner tomato sauces and light seafood sauces.

Udon is a white Japanese wheat noodle usually served in a broth as a meal with cut-up vegetables, a poached egg or with tempura on top.

RICE (page 181)

Ambra is an Italian rice used in seafood risottos that is golden in color and a little less starchy than arborio.

Arborio rice is a short oval grain with an opaque white spot in the middle and comes from the Po Valley in Italy. It is perfect for risotto.

Basmati rice is a long-grain Indian rice perfect for pilafs. It can be bought brown as a whole grain.

Brown rice is an unhusked whole-grain rice that can be of any variety. It takes about three times as long to cook as white rice, but is more nutritious and has a pleasantly nutty taste. On pages 181–182 are instructions for precooking, refrigerating and reheating in the microwave oven. If you are Oriental or cook for one, the odds of brown rice being accepted are slim. Don't push it or the carbohydrate may go uneaten.

Converted rice takes longer to cook than other kinds of rice. It is treated in such a way that more minerals and vitamins are retained than in other types of white rice.

Instant rice has been parboiled and takes relatively little time to cook. I don't use it. I don't find the time saving worth the difference in quality.

Long-grain rice (Carolina) is what Americans call their all-purpose long-grain rice.

RICE GERM AND BRAN are the most nutritious parts of the rice and are combined in pellets that are soluble in hot water. Using that liquid in bread-baking recipes will increase the nutritional component of the bread.

WHEAT FLOUR

White flour made without the husk or germ is whitish. It is whiter when bleached. It will vary in gluten in different parts of the world and in different parts of the United States. If your normal flour is rather soft, as it is in England, France and the South, mix one part of your standard flour with one part of bread flour to approximate the all-purpose flour used in this book.

All-purpose enriched is a relatively hard wheat flour that is the American standard.

Bread flour or high-gluten flour is useful for bread baking, although I don't use it, as it is hard to find and the studies on gluten are in a state of flux.

Cake flour, unleavened, is a weak low-gluten flour usually made from summer wheat, and is close to standard British and French flours.

Whole wheat flour is made from the whole wheat berry and has more nutrients but less gluten than white flours.

WHEAT GERM, toasted and unsweetened, can be used in baked foods or sprinkled on fruits or breakfast cereals for extra nutrition and fiber.

YEAST, DRY, often comes in packets with ¼ ounce (7 g) yeast (about 2 teaspoons).

LEGUMES

Dry legumes are the major source of protein and other nutrients for vegetarians and are good for all of us. Dried legumes that have been around for a long time are liable to take slightly more water and cooking time than those that are new.

BEANS There is a plethora of varieties. The more you make, the more kinds you will be tempted to try, as they have different flavors. They can be cooked ahead and then refrigerated covered with water. See page 202.

CHICK-PEAS have the most protein of all the legumes and are much used in Italy (*ceci*) and the Middle East. Dry ones need soaking—par cooking—and then must be popped out of their skins. It's a lot of work, and unless you are on a strict salt-reduced diet, use canned.

LENTILS come in different colors. Red, orange and yellow are commonly used in Indian cooking and cook more quickly than the green and brown lentils more typical in the West.

CANNED OR BOTTLED FOODS

Canned or bottled foods should all be refrigerated after opening.

BEANS AND LEGUMES OF MANY KINDS, if you don't regularly make them from scratch. They will be high in sodium (page 19).

CHICKEN BROTH, unsalted, if possible, if not making Basic Chicken Broth (page 460). Avoid bouillon or stock cubes if at all possible because of their high sodium content (page 115). You may want to keep canned chicken broth in the refrigerator so that when you open the can it will be easy to remove the blob of fat that floats on the surface. (A good tip from a reader.)

JAMS AND JELLIES, diet, if not making. Vegetarians can look for those made with agar agar.

MAYONNAISE, low-calorie, if not making Egg White Mayonnaise (page 482).

PINEAPPLE packed in juice, no extra sugar

SALAD DRESSINGS, diet, if not making (pages 486–492). Read labels for sodium and cholesterol contents.

TOMATO PRODUCTS commercially prepared are high in sodium. (See page 19). If you have the time, make fresh and freeze to keep on hand. Do it in season when tomatoes are plentiful, good and cheap. All processed tomato products will taste fresher if a little lemon juice is added to them when using.

American tomatoes in cans are round, peeled and look like most of the tomatoes in produce departments. They have a fresher, brighter flavor than the fleshier Italian plum tomatoes. I like them in stews and soups when good fresh tomatoes are unavailable. Avoid tomatoes packed in purée or paste, which have more salt, more calories and a less fleshy flavor.

Plum (Italian) tomatoes are canned in Italy and America with or without basil (no problem) and with or without purée or paste added (avoid). San Marzano and Roma are the plum tomato varieties for which to look. These are the tomatoes used to make paste; they have more flesh than juice.

Tomato juice has half the calories of orange juice. Health-food stores may carry less-salty brands.

Tomato paste is better in tubes than in cans and there is less waste.

Tomato purée and crushed tomatoes are helpful if not making Fresh Tomato Purée (page 468). Purée has a thick, smooth texture. The best packaged comes from Italy sterile-packed in cartons and has less salt and is less sickly sweet than canned products. If you cannot find it you may prefer to put American canned or crushed tomatoes through a coarse sieve or food mill. There are some salt-free products on the market.

Tomato sauce, tomato-pasta sauce and marinara sauce can be used pretty much interchangeably if not making Tomato Sauce Casalinga (page 167). Tomato sauce is my last choice of these emergency rations, as it is sweeter and less fresh in flavor than homemade.

TUNAFISH, water-packed, in small (3½ ounces, 99 grams) cans will produce less waste.

DRY STORES

AGAR AGAR is a vegetarian gelatin made from seaweed.

COCOA, Dutch process, unsweetened, contains none of the fat that is in chocolate.

NORI, a Japanese seaweed, is sold in packages of thin, brittle, dark green sheets and is used to wrap sushi. It can be toasted and thinly sliced as an iron-rich garnish.

NUTS may be something you want to refrigerate or put in the freezer if you buy them in bulk or the container in which you bought them has been opened. They will keep much better. Broken nuts, pieces or sliced nuts are often cheaper than whole nuts.
   Almonds that are blanched are easier to use.
   Hazelnuts
   Peanuts, dry-roasted and unsalted
   Pecans

OILS, aside from coconut and palm, are unsaturated or monounsaturated. In microwave cooking, they are used mainly as flavorings. Always buy the best. Mono-unsaturated oils such as canola, olive and avocado are the best for you.
   Nut oils, optional, hazelnut and walnut, are expensive and go rancid easily. Store in a cool, dark place.
   Olive Which is best is a question of opinion. I always have two or three different olive oils on hand. One is fruity and elegant, golden in color, but not too heavy. I save it for salads. I usually have one that is less expensive and less definite in flavor to use in mayonnaise—sometimes cut with canola oil, which is neutral tasting. I may also have a coarser, greener, more robust oil to use sparingly in cooked vegetable dishes and with pastas. Olive oils can vary in acidity, color, strength of flavor and perfume. They will taste and look different made from different varieties and ripeness of olives and in different countries. Cold-pressed extra-virgin is generally considered to be premium; but you should suit yourself and your budget. Buy the smallest sizes available and taste until you find oils that you like. You may be able to share the tasting cost and fun with friends. Do not buy so-called light olive oils. They have no fewer calories, but much less flavor.
   Peanut oil should be bought in cans and kept in a cool place; otherwise it rapidly goes rancid. It is often used in Chinese recipes.

Sesame, toasted (Oriental), is dark brown and very perfumed. Small amounts add a great deal of flavor to a dish. Do not mistake for plain sesame oil, which is white and virtually flavorless.

Vegetable oils can be of many different kinds. You will have to read labels to see what a brand is actually made from. Do not buy any that include coconut or palm oil. Canola oil has the best ratio of polyunsaturated and monounsaturated fats to saturated fat. Unfortunately, it is also rather tasteless. Use it when you are moistening spices for precooking in the microwave oven, or when you think that olive oil will be too strong a flavor. I often blend it with olive oil when I don't want the olive taste to be too strong.

Vegetable oil in a spray can is useful to add a minimal amount of oil to grills, sauté pans and molds so food will not stick.

RAISINS

SWEETENERS should be bought in small quantities; you will be using less.

Artificial sweeteners, see Sugar substitute.

Granulated sugar

Honey is not for babies; but it is sweeter by volume than sugar, so you may use less of it than you would sugar and many like the taste.

Light or dark brown sugar can harden once its package is opened. Soften by removing from package and placing in a bowl covered with plastic wrap and heating at 100% for 1–2 minutes.

Molasses, not black strap, in the smallest possible container, or omit altogether; rarely used.

Sugar substitute, artificial sweeteners. Only aspartame can be used in cooking. Add others to foods after cooking.

FLAVORINGS

Flavorings are the palate pleasers that keep our food from getting too salty, too bland and boring. Properly kept they retain their savoriness for a long time, awaiting inspiration. All flavorings called salts, such as celery, garlic and onion salt, should be avoided. They are mainly salt.

DRIED HERBS should be used in smaller quantities in microwave cooking than in conventional cooking. Microwave cooking brings out every iota of their energy. Try to buy herbs in small quantities and keep in tightly closed opaque containers or in a dark cupboard. Do not store near heat.

Basil is increasingly available fresh, which is infinitely preferable; but you might want some dried on hand for desperate moments.

Bay leaf comes from either the European bay laurel or the American bay tree. Both are usable; but they have different flavors. Unlike the other dried herbs, slightly more bay may be used in microwave cooking than otherwise since bitterness will not develop in the short cooking time. Overwhelming amounts are called for in many recipes. We seem to forget that a bay leaf can be broken in half. A bay leaf is a nice addition to pasta-cooking water. Remove bay leaves before serving food; they can make people choke.

Chamomile looks like a tiny daisy and makes a relaxing nighttime tea. It is also nice in fruit-poaching liquids.

Dillweed can often be found fresh, which is infinitely preferable.

Lemon grass, dried, fresh or powdered, is a nice addition to soups, often used in Thai and Vietnamese cooking.

Mint is used in Indian and Middle Eastern dishes and also makes a delightful, refreshing tea.

Oregano is one of the world's most widely used herbs—no doubt because it dries so well. Oddly, due to the many plant varieties, we rarely know what we are getting. I prefer Greek hand-picked oregano. It is more costly; but one uses so little, the price difference barely matters.

Rosemary dries shortly after picking; but the fresh sprigs make beautiful garnishes. Go slowly with rosemary; it is very pungent and needs to be used sparingly, as in polenta, or more aggressively with a strongly flavored meat such as lamb. Buy leaves; they are better than crushed or powdered. Dried rosemary can be ground or pulverized in a mortar and pestle, like a spice.

Sage is a common ingredient in stuffings, sausages and other pork dishes.

Savory makes a nice addition to the stew herbs and goes well with green beans.

Summer savory dries relatively poorly.

Tarragon is much better fresh than dried; but dried can be used in hot preparations. Use one third as much of the dried as the fresh.

Thyme that comes dried is mostly English or common thyme. There are many other fresh kinds worth experimenting with. They are very decorative in the herb garden, as pathways and as edgings.

KOSHER SALT see Sodium (page 19).

SPICES that are bought whole will keep their flavor better than those that are ground. Buy a small electric coffee grinder and keep it just for spices, or use a mortar and pestle. Peppers that are not seeds but are pods will, when dried, need to be heated in a little oil or other fat to bring out their flavors (see procedure with paprika in Goulash Soup, page 134). Treat composite seasonings containing peppers—chile and curry—the same way.

Allspice is used mainly by bakers.

Anise seed tastes slightly like licorice and can be used in baking; it can also be used instead of fennel seed in fish stews and pork dishes.

Black peppercorns for grinding are essential. There are many varieties. Keep trying until you find those you like the best. I don't use white pepper. It is used mainly by chefs who don't like the black flecks in white sauces.

Caraway seeds are the flavoring for rye bread, sauerkraut and other cabbage dishes.

Cardamom comes in papery pods with tiny seeds inside. Hit the pod to break it and use the seeds or grind them.

Cayenne pepper usually comes ground and is very spicy. A very little bit can pick up a bland sauce.

Celery seed goes well in salad dressings and coleslaw or to intensify the celery flavor in soups and stews.

Chili powder, pure, is just ground hot peppers; it is red in color and is preferable. Most chile powders are brownish and have cumin, oregano and even cloves, coriander, allspice and salt added. Read labels.

Chinese salted (fermented) black beans can be found in Oriental markets and specialty food stores. Normally, they are soaked before cooking. This is unnecessary in microwave cooking. They add a smoky flavor, but also add salt. Do not increase quantities.

Cinnamon can be used in sticks—curled bark strips—or ground. It is used primarily in baking, but is also found in Moroccan and other savory foods.

Cloves are often found studding a baked ham or ground in baked goods. Sometimes they are stuck in an onion when stock is being made. The flavor is very dominant, so use with care, but experiment combining cloves and fruits such as pears and oranges.

Coriander seeds taste nothing like the fresh leaves; but they are used in some Indian and Middle Eastern dishes.

Cumin is underused in most European and American cooking except for chili; but it pairs well with carrots, mushrooms and many other warmly flavored foods.

Curry powder is a mixture of many seasonings. I prefer the more aromatic imported Indian curry powders, or you can make your own. They may be designated as hot or mild. Milder curries are used mainly in French-style cream curries.

Dill seed is not interchangeable with fresh or dried dillweed. The seeds are used mainly in pickles, salads and vegetable dishes.

Fennel seed is another of the many seasonings with a licorice-like flavor. It is used in many sweet and savory dishes, from fish soups to Moroccan breads to fruit dishes.

Ginger is used fresh in most recipes in this book, but is used dried and ground for baking.

Hot pepper sauce is usually red but sometimes green, depending on the kind of pod peppers it is made from. It comes from all the countries where people like their food spicy. The bottle is often kept on the table as we might keep salt and pepper. It is meant to be added at the end of cooking, whereas dried or fresh hot peppers are used in the actual cooking. Be careful. These sauces are loaded with salt.

Juniper berries are the flavor of Dutch gin and are good with cabbage dishes and pork.

Mace is the poor man's nutmeg.

Mustard seeds, whole black (for Indian cooking) or brown. Yellow, dried and ground into a powder, is usually used to make English and Chinese prepared mustard and is used in salad dressings and chutneys, Italian *mostarda* and sauces. Mustard sauces can vary from the sharp English variety to the standard smooth, yellow French style to grainy, dark ones made with a proportion of whole seeds and often wine. Prepared mustards are salty and some—I'm not too fond of them and don't use them in cooking—add sugar or honey.

Paprika, both the sweet and hot kinds, if possible. It is dried red pod peppers ground to a powder. Imported Hungarian paprikas are excellent. Also look for paprika paste in tubes. See also Cayenne and Chile powder.

Red pepper flakes are the same hot, red pod peppers, dried and crushed into flakes with their seeds rather than being powdered. You may be accustomed to seeing them in pizza places.

Red pepper sauce, see Hot pepper sauce.

Saffron is a very expensive spice; but there is no true replacement, although turmeric is sometimes used to mimic its color. Saffron comes in threads and in powder. I prefer the threads, which are a little cheaper, and I know they have had no cheap filler added. It is used in curries, rice dishes and some baked goods, and adds a fabulous perfume and flavor to Mediterranean fish soups.

Salted black beans (see Chinese salted black beans)

Sesame seeds are the seeds that are toasted and pressed to make sesame oil. On their own, naturally white or toasted to a light brown, they can add flavor and nutrition to savory foods and to baked goods.

Star anise is usually used in Chinese cooking. It is good, but not often used by most Westerners.

Turmeric is bright orange-gold in color and most often used in curries. It is mildly hot, like its cousin ginger, and is used in cakes, cookies and relishes as well.

LIQUID FLAVORINGS

MIRIN is a mildly alcoholic and gently sweet Japanese flavoring used in dipping sauces and in some of my recipes.

TAMARI SOY SAUCE is made exclusively from soy rather than being a mixture of soy and wheat by a process of fermentation. It is salty. See Sodium, page 19. It has a round rich flavor that is a nice addition to many dishes other than the Oriental ones with which we commonly associate it.

VANILLA EXTRACT AND/OR BEANS can come from many parts of the world and will vary in flavor. Good beans are plump and dark brown. They are often cooked in a liquid and then removed or cut open, and the pulpy insides are scraped back into the dish. Vanilla beans should be tightly wrapped and kept in the refrigerator or freezer. An unused bean or one that has been steeped once and then dried can be stored with sugar to flavor it. Many recipes call for only a piece of bean. Vanilla extract is made with alcohol and is used mainly for baking. Do not use artificial vanilla, vanillin.

VINEGARS can have very different flavors and acid levels. Balsamic vinegar and rice wine vinegar taste less sharp than white or malt vinegar, which actually have less acid.

> *Balsamic vinegar* is a dark red-brown and aged in a succession of woods; it is aromatic with a round flavor that can enhance fruits as well as salads, chicken and fish dishes. Its price will usually depend on its age. While high in acetic acid, it is gentle in flavor and proportionately more of it can be used in salad dressing than other vinegars, reducing the oil and calories.

> *Cider vinegar* is made from apples and is a gentler all-purpose vinegar than white vinegar. Do not use in pickles.

> *Fruit vinegars* are made in three ways. The best are made by simply fermenting the fruit. Others are made by macerating the fruit in vinegar. The least good and the ones to watch out for are made by adding a fruit concentrate or syrup to vinegar. The last kind is often slightly sweet. Read labels. Fruit vinegars, such as raspberry, can give a nice taste to bland foods like chicken and fish and can even be used on fruits and in fruit salads.

> *Malt vinegar* is brown and popular in England. It can often be substituted for cider vinegar.

> *Red wine vinegar* is often used in salad dressings. Good ones are made in America, Spain, Italy and France. It is also used in stews and red cabbage dishes.

> *Rice wine vinegar* is a Japanese ingredient that is absolutely clear and rather light in flavor. You can use more of it in cooking than American white vinegar without getting a harsh taste or unpleasant smell. By using more in proportion to the oil, you can bring down the calories in salad dressings.

> *Sherry (Xerex) vinegar* has a nice nutty taste and can be used on subtle salads and in cooking. It is brown.

> *Tarragon vinegar* is the most common and successful of the white wine vinegars in which herbs are steeped to add flavor. I prefer the French imports.

> *White vinegar* is the American standard, good for making pickles.

WINES AND LIQUORS

These are for drinking with meals and for flavoring foods.

BRANDY, preferably Cognac

FRUIT BRANDIES that are clear and unsweetened are nice flavorings for fruits and desserts. Orange-flavored ones are most often used.

PERNOD is an anise-flavored liquor. Do not use anisette, which is sweetened. This makes a big difference in fish soups. There are many less-expensive liquors of a similar flavor, such as raki, arak and ouzo, which can be substituted. Typically they are clear in the bottle and turn milky when water is added.

RED WINE for cooking should be robust but not heavy or musty-tasting. It need not be expensive.

WHITE WINE, dry and crisp, not too acidic or fruity when used for cooking. For drinking there is an infinite variety. The fruitier wines as well as the somewhat acidic ones make good spritzers—drinks mixed with bubbly water to dilute them and make them go further.

REFRIGERATOR

All foods stored in the refrigerator should be left out until they reach room temperature before using in cooking, except for butter, which is rarely used. If they have not reached room temperature, the cooking time will be longer.

FRESH FRUITS, VEGETABLES AND HERBS

Keep these on hand as seasonally good and available at a reasonable price. If they're there, you'll use them. See pages 532–533 for nutritional values of fruits. See Index for location of nutritional information on the vegetable that interests you. Organic fruits and vegetables are better, more expensive and harder to find.

APPLES Try to find unsprayed ones.

BANANAS—not in refrigerator

BROCCOLI

CARROTS. Some to cook with, some to peel, cut in strips and put in cold water in the refrigerator for snacks.

CELERY. Some to cook with, some to peel, cut in strips and put in cold water in the refrigerator for snacks. Celery is high in sodium.

FRESH HERBS, when available. I grow a wide variety in summer and a more limited group in the house in winter. Experiment with any you can find in the store; but keep the following on hand as you find them. All will keep well washed, the stems set in a glass of cold water and refrigerated, except for dill, which is best kept refrigerated unwashed with the stems wrapped in wet paper and washed just before using.

> *Basil* comes in many kinds: bush, Italian and opal are the most common. A plant will grow well indoors. Basil should be washed as little as possible and cooked as little as possible for maximum intensity. Dried basil is almost never a good substitute.
> *Coriander* (Chinese parsley, cilantro) is a green herb that looks something like parsley and should always be used fresh. Some people hate the flavor. Substitute flat-leaf parsley.
> *Dillweed* is feathery and should not be too finely chopped or it will taste gritty. Add at the end of the cooking time or it will lose its color and fresh taste.
> *Mint* should be grown away from other herbs as it is very invasive. There are many varieties. While dried mint is good for tea and some dishes, fresh mint

will add sprightliness to vegetables such as peas and carrots and to cut-up fruits.

Parsley, flat leaf (Italian) or curly, is a standard, but is usually used more for garnish than flavor. Think of it as an ingredient that can give you flavor, vitamins and minerals.

GARLIC is bought in fresh bulbs composed of many cloves. Do not substitute oil-packed, dried or garlic salt. Garlic is a bulb and can be planted. Try to buy garlic that has no green shoots beginning to grow. Different kinds of garlic will vary in flavor. Be careful with elephant garlic; it goes bad quickly.

To separate the cloves, put a cloth over the head so that cloves don't fly all over the kitchen. Hit the covered garlic with a heavy pan or knife. Remove the cloth and any papery skins that are loose. Select the number of cloves you need and hit again with the pot or with the flat of the knife. I call this smashing. The skins will now be loose and easy to remove. If when you look at the garlic there is a shoot in the middle, pull it out; it has a bitter taste.

For most microwave cooking, the garlic does not need to be cut or mashed. It will cook quickly to a creamy state, which means that you may need to use more in microwave cooking than you are accustomed to. If you are using it raw or barely cooking it, mince or slice it. Garlic is very good for you—not against the evil eye, but to deal with blood clots and infections. See page 601 for getting the smell out of your oven. To keep garlic, see Garlic to Go (page 470).

GINGER is a rhizome that grows under the ground and is one of the wonderfully fresh, spicy and acidic flavors in Chinese and Japanese food. A whole piece is called a hand of ginger because of its protuberances. Ginger is better when young, when the skin is pale in color and thin. If you are just using slices to flavor a liquid and will remove them, you do not need to peel the ginger. Otherwise, peel and proceed as the recipe directs. I often like to grate ginger; this removes the fibrous part, which can be unpleasant.

GRAPEFRUIT doesn't need to be painstakingly sectioned. Simply cut it in wedges, remove the seeds, eat.

GRAPEFRUIT JUICE. Home-squeezed will taste better, not bitter.

LETTUCE see Salad greens

LEMONS are an essential part of my cooking. I always have them on hand. Ripe lemons will give slightly when squeezed. The dimples in the skin will be flattish.

MELON. There are many good ones. They are sweet and filling, and make a good dessert, snack or part of breakfast as a caloric bargain.

ONIONS—red, white and yellow. Size indications and weights are given in recipes. Pearl onions can be briefly blanched in a half-cup (120 ml) of water, tightly covered, in the microwave oven so that they can be peeled. Frozen pearl onions are very satisfactory.

ORANGES often have dye on their skins. If you are using the zest—the outer skin without any of the white pith—use juice oranges that are not dyed. Juice oranges give the most juice. Navel oranges are easier to peel for eating. To eat juice oranges, proceed as with grapefruit. To remove zest, use a potato peeler, not a zester. In this book a piece of zest will be what comes off with the potato peeler, about 2 inches (5 cm) long. If you want thinner strips, slice with a knife.

ORANGE JUICE, fresh or refrigerated, but not from concentrate, if possible

PEARS

POTATOES used to be regularly sold in fifty or more varieties. A few of the old varieties, like purple and yellow Finns, are coming back. Try them for their attractive colors and unusual flavors. Cook them like new potatoes. All basic cooking instructions for potatoes are on pages 219–220. Potatoes are done when a knife slips in easily.

> *Baking or Idaho* potatoes will be mealy and are good for eating cooked whole, or making mashed potatoes.
> *California* potatoes have the same shape as baking potatoes and yellow to pale-beige skins. They do not bake well, as they are firm rather than mealy. Use as white potatoes.
> *New* potatoes can be red-skinned or brown-skinned, the smaller the sweeter and better. Scrub clean; don't peel. Skins are good and nourishing. In the microwave oven, they will cook by weight, not by number. They will not shrivel if cooked with a little water (page 220).
> *White* potatoes are often round and have dark-brown skins and come from Maine or Long Island. Wash well before peeling or they can have a dirty taste.

SALAD GREENS, a selection. If you can make time, wash, trim and tear up when you bring them home. Put them loosely in a plastic bag with a few ice cubes. That way they will always be at the ready. Also see pages 391–392.

> *Bibb lettuce*
> *Boston lettuce*
> *Endive*
> *Mâche,* field salad, corn salad
> *Radicchio*
> *Romaine*
> *Spinach*
> *Watercress*

SCALLIONS are good raw with dips or cut up in salads. They are also good to use in cooking.

SPINACH. Treat as salad greens, but be sure to remove the stems so it will be ready for use.

STRAWBERRIES of all kinds and sizes are good in season and low in calories.

TOMATOES in season, of all colors and kinds, for eating, salads and cooking.

DAIRY

DAIRY PRODUCT NUTRITION

The following data are based on an 8-ounce (240-ml) serving, unless otherwise noted. The abbreviations "Cal.," "Prot.," "Carb.," "Calc.," "Sod.," "Pot.," "Chol," "tr" and "N/A" stand for calories, protein, carbohydrate, calcium, sodium, potassium, cholesterol, trace and not available, respectively. Eight hundred milligrams of calcium is the RDA. See also page 520.

PRODUCT	CAL.	PROT. (g)	FAT (g)	CARB. (g)	CALC. (mg)	IRON (mg)	SOD. (mg)	POT. (mg)	CHOL. (mg)
Butter, unsalted (1 tbsp.):	100	0	11	0	tr	tr	2	4	30
Margarine, unsalted (1 tbsp.):	100	0	11	0	tr	tr	95	5	0
Cheeses (used in this book):									
Cottage (low-fat, 2%) (1 cup; 240 ml)	203	31	4	8	155	0.36	918	217	19
Ricotta (part-skim) (1 cup; 240 ml)	340	28	19	13	669	1.08	307	308	76
Parmesan (1 oz.; 28 g)	129	12	9	1	390	0.27	528	30	22
Romano (1 oz.; 28 g)	110	9	8	1	302	—	340	—	29
Fromage Blanc (2 oz.; 56 g)	40	6	tr	4	approx. .5	N/A	70	N/A	5
MILK AND MILK SUBSTITUTES:									
Buttermilk, unsalted	99	8	2	12	285	0.12	123	371	9
Low-fat milk (1%)	102	8	3	12	300	0.12	123	381	10
Low-fat milk (2%)	121	8	5	12	297	0.12	122	377	18
Skim milk	86	8	tr	12	302	0.10	126	406	4
Whole milk	150	8	8	11	291	0.12	120	370	33
Sour cream (1 tbsp.)	26	tr	3	tr	14	0.01	6	17	5
Yogurt, low-fat (8 oz.; 120 ml)	144	12	4	16	415	0.18	159	531	14

Some adults have a problem digesting milk products. They may have less with yogurt and cheese. Acidophilus milk or tablets may solve the problem. If not, talk to your doctor about calcium tablets.

BUTTER AND MARGARINE are rarely used for cooking in this book. They have been included in the analysis list above so that you can see what you are doing if you add or substitute them for other fats. Some of the menus call for butter as a spread for bread. Use the best unsalted butter and keep it in the freezer. It can be cut frozen and softens quickly.

BUTTERMILK has no fat and has a pleasant acidity. It's good for baking and sauces.

EGGS. Buy only six, Grade A large; make Egg White Mayonnaise (page 482) and a dessert that uses egg whites. Ruthlessly throw the yolks away, or give them to a neighbor who loves to bake. Organic eggs are lower in cholesterol, have more flavor and are less likely to be diseased.

FROMAGE BLANC. See page 518 to make it, or buy it if you can find it. Now, made in America, it's a totally nonfat, low-salt cheese usually thought of as French, or make Yogurt Cheese (page 514). Fromage Blanc gives a wonderful smooth texture to sauces without any cream. Both cheeses can be served with crushed berries as a dessert.

LOW-FAT, LOW-SALT CHEESE for eating. There are good ones—some imports—on the market. Look around. Cut cheese into one-ounce portions and wrap individually.

LOW-FAT COTTAGE CHEESE is a good lunch or snack.

LOW-FAT OR, BETTER STILL, NONFAT RICOTTA CHEESE has a creamy and slightly sweet taste.

LOW-FAT MOZZARELLA can be eaten as a snack or used in salads or cooking.

NONFAT YOGURT that is unflavored is a good snack; you can add your own fruit and a sugar substitute if you want. It is also good in cold sauces and to stir into hot foods when they are cooked. Think of it as a substitute for fatty sour cream.

SKIM MILK for coffee and tea and cooking. Skim-milk products or nonfat products have no fat; part-skim products have the amount listed on the label. Watch it.

FREEZER

Frozen vegetables should be defrosted, after unwrapping, in a sieve under warm-to-hot running water until they are at room temperature.

APPLE JUICE CONCENTRATE See page 73

ARTICHOKE HEARTS

DIET SORBETS

PEARL ONIONS

SPINACH

TINY GREEN PEAS

TINY LIMA BEANS

Staples to Consider Making

You can make your cooking life much easier if you spend some time making staples to freeze or refrigerate. They will also help your diet by keeping you from substituting a more caloric, saltier or more cholesterol-laden alternative because you are in a hurry. These lists are divided into a group of most desirable staples, frozen and refrigerated, and pleasant but not essential staples. See Basics, Sauces and Snacks (pages 458–529).

ESSENTIAL STAPLES

Frozen

Basic Broths (pages 460–466)
    Chicken
    Meat
    Vegetarian
Fresh Tomato Purée (page 468)
Tomato Sauce Casalinga (page 167)

Refrigerated

Diet salad dressings
    (pages 486–492)
Egg White Mayonnaise (page 482)
Majic Whole Grain Bread
    (page 152)

PLEASANT BUT NOT ESSENTIAL

Frozen

Diet Pesto Sauce (page 476)
Diet Duxelles (page 477)

Refrigerated

A dessert that you like
    (pages 530–596)
Brown rice, cooked
    (pages 181–182)
Diet jams
    (pages 587–594)
Diet pickles (pages 526–529)

Parcooked dried beans (page 202)
Peanut Butter (page 478)
Pickled Jalapeño Peppers
    (page 473)
Red Pepper Purée (page 500)
Silky Pepper Strips (page 472)

MICROSLIM GOURMET
DIETS AND MENUS

Planning Your Diet

Making one healthful dish or weight-loss dish is never a problem—just follow a recipe. Changing your ways to have a healthful diet requires revamping your kitchen so that it doesn't tempt you with things you shouldn't eat and provides you with the makings of healthy meals. See pages 46–73 for suggestions. You also need to develop an approach to eating outside the home. See pages 23–24. It is important to know your own body (page 13) to judge how many calories and other nutrients you need in a day. Take into account your own eating pleasures and patterns. You will not keep eating in a healthful way for the rest of your life unless your food gives you pleasure. Eating is one of the easiest ways to make ourselves feel good, to treat ourselves (that doesn't mean spoil). If we don't have pleasure, it's just no good.

I love to eat, and if my food doesn't taste good, if it doesn't please me, I cannot stay well or virtuous about my diet. Part of health is happiness. Healthy eating requires very little self-deprivation. As you change your eating and cooking styles, the new way will become largely automatic. An occasional fall from grace—a Thanksgiving indulgence, a butter sauce in a restaurant, a dish of ice cream—is not the end of the world. Simply be a little better than usual for a day or so before or after. You may find that an odd thing happens with a changed eating pattern; you may crave the rich foods less often.

In addition to healthful diets, we need diets to lose weight. Losing weight is hard. I have tried to make it as easy as possible with as many ways to vary your food and as many good recipes as possible. Until you get used to eating less—particularly meat—you may feel punished; but you shouldn't feel hungry.

About the Menus

In this chapter, there is a week of very simple weight-loss menus for one, and another, more complicated set requiring cooking for weight-loss menus for two. You will also find a day's liquid menu that is not meant to be followed regularly or often; but it may be a good way to start your diet. Use that day to prepare some staples for future cooking. There are also alternate breakfast menus and a whole section of menus for yourself, your family and entertaining. As you get used to using this book, feel free to substitute recipes from any part of it. Also note the week of healthful menus for those who do not need to lose weight.

A good way to plan your own menus is often to decide what you want as a main course—a kind of meat, poultry, fish or a vegetarian meal. Turn to the proper section of recipes or look in the Index to find a dish that pleases you and is appropriate to the number of people, the time you have and the seasonally available foods. Often, you will find menu suggestions in the head note before the recipe. You can replace the suggested recipes with others that have a similar nutritional profile: amount of calories, vitamins and cholesterol. There will also be hints as to how to enlarge the meal and/or portion size for those who are not losing weight or are large and/or active.

Don't eliminate the starch: the rice, pasta, noodles, beans, potatoes and bread. Getting more of our calories from carbohydrates is good for us. In fact, when increasing the calories in the meal from weight-loss standards for a small person to those for a large or active person or to lifetime levels, it is better to increase the carbohydrates, salads, vegetables and even desserts than to increase the meat component.

The weight-loss plans can be used until you reach your desired weight. They are carefully balanced to give decent nutrition and variety during the course of a week. Your body doesn't know if it had its vitamin C every day, or had two days with a lot and a day with less, or even if it had too much cholesterol on a day with a big party as long as the rest of the week had been virtuous. The exception is needing to have a vitamin C–rich vegetable with a meat meal (page 340 for explanation). Once again, I am not your doctor. Check with your doctor before beginning a prolonged diet, and should she or he recommend, take a vitamin-mineral supplement. Also, follow medical advice for dealing with diseases with specific dietary needs or restrictions.

While you may be tempted just to plunge ahead with the diet, it is a good idea to read Being Healthy and Slim (pages 13–45) so that you know what you are doing and how to adjust the diet for yourself.

The weight-loss menus are based on about 1,100 calories per day for an average-sized woman. An average man can go up to about 1,400 calories a day and still lose weight unless he never gets out of bed. A very active or large person may be able to increase these amounts somewhat and still lose weight.

Add calories and food by increasing amounts of carbohydrates—say, two slices of toast instead of one—or snacks, soups, vegetables, fruit and nonfat dairy products. Do not add large amounts of meat, as that will increase your fat and cholesterol intake.

THE MEALS

You can always substitute for an item on a weight-loss menu a dish from the book that you particularly like as long as it has a similar calorie count and about the same nutritional levels.

Breakfast is a matter of personal taste. You can have the same breakfast every day or vary. If you do not care for any of the alternatives given below, look in the Index for ideas and recipes. Keep breakfast at around 200 calories. Do not skip it.

Lunch is fairly specific, but again, keeping yourself within the calorie limits, you may eat something different. If you are at home for lunch, you can make something more involved than the choices given below. Look at the menus at the end of the chapter for suggestions, or pick an item from any chapter that pleases you. You can use leftovers from dinner for lunch. Try to keep to 300 calories. Pages 69–73 have some simple sandwich suggestions.

For dinner I often specify lean meat, chicken or fish, grilled or broiled (pages 346–347). If you want to cook your food simply in the microwave oven, place on a dinner plate with a deep rim or in a quiche dish or pie plate and follow microwave instructions in Fish and Shellfish (pages 226–228), Perfectly Poultry (pages 289–339) and For the Carnivore (pages 340–387). Add herbs and healthy vegetables such as broccoli or carrots. Cover with plastic wrap and cook. On any night you can substitute a frozen diet main course—homemade or store-bought. A small pita, a small baked potato or a half-cup (120 ml) of cooked pasta with a low-calorie sauce such as Tomato Sauce Casalinga (page 167) would be good accompaniments. For dessert each night, you can have a portion of fresh fruit from the list on pages 532–533, or make a dessert (pages 530–596) ahead to have for several nights. Peach Sorbet, Mango Mousse and Tricky Chocolate Pudding are all good choices. You can also buy diet sorbets or diet canned or frozen fruits. Diet gelatins can be used as well. They do have artificial sweeteners.

Remember that frozen and prepared foods—even those specially created for weight loss—will often have more salt and cholesterol than the recipes in this book. It is a good idea to get in the habit of doing at least some simple food preparation. If salt is not a problem for you, add a little more salt at the table.

See page 529 for snacks that can be added at hungry times. You can always save a portion of fruit or your salad to eat as a snack, or have a warming cup of Spicy Chicken Broth (page 59). Don't have too many snacks or you will be in trouble. You can have carrots or celery between meals if you need some extra nourishment. Another good idea is to save your fruit from lunch and have it as a mid-afternoon snack.

Stick to water, seltzer (club soda without salt), diet sodas, or unsweetened or artificially sweetened iced tea or coffee with your meals. Also see pages 17–18.

You should have plenty to eat and the flavors will keep you happy. These weight-loss diets can be followed for as long as need be; it's healthy.

Weight-Loss Menus

The menu given below is easy to follow and effective for moderate weight loss—one to three pounds a week, depending on the individual body frame and activity level. Each day involves some planning but not much cooking. For those who like the structure of eating the same thing every day, there is a standard breakfast, lunch and dinner. You may eat these meals every day or follow the varied daily menus as given, substituting the standard meal if and when desired. Commercial diet foods such as preserves and sorbets can be used instead of homemade. Use artificial sweeteners as desired. From time to time, a Liquid Meal may be substituted for breakfast or lunch. This is for convenience, not as a regular habit. When a piece of fruit is indicated on the menus, the calories range from 80 to 100. If you are on a strict weight-loss diet, stick to 80-calorie portions. Look at the fruit chart on pages 532–533 for more ideas. Where a green salad with 1 tablespoon of diet dressing is indicated, look at page 391 for salad-ingredient ideas and page 392 for dressing ideas.

THE STANDARD DAY

Breakfast each day: 150–200 calories
1 slice whole wheat toast, or 1 slice Majic Whole Grain Bread
1 tablespoon Cinnamon Spread
1 tablespoon Strawberry Jam
1 portion fruit

Black coffee or tea, with ¼ cup (60 ml) skim milk, 21 calories

or

½ cup (120 ml) nonfat yogurt
1 tablespoon raisins, 1 tablespoon walnuts or 1 piece fruit
Black coffee or tea, with ¼ cup (60 ml) skim milk, 21 calories

or

1 Steamed Banana Muffin
1 portion fruit
Black coffee or tea, with ¼ cup (60 ml) skim milk, 21 calories

or

½ cup (120 ml) dry cereal (choose unsweetened whole-grain cereals or sweetened with fruit juice)
1 cup (240 ml) skim milk
1 portion fruit
Black coffee or tea

Lunch each day: 300–400 calories
3 ounces (85 g) lean meat or fish, or 1 cup (240 ml) low-fat yogurt *with*
1 slice Majic Whole Grain Bread (page 152) or 1 small pita

Snack:
1 portion fruit *or*
small tomato with lunch

Dinner each day: 500–600 calories
4 ounces (113.5 g) lean meat or fish*, steamed, broiled or grilled *with*
½ cup (120 ml) cooked white or brown rice *or*
1 small potato (8 ounces; 227 g), baked or steamed *or*
½ cup (120 ml) cooked pasta with ¼ cup (60 ml) Tomato Sauce Casalinga or bottled tomato sauce *and*
1 cup (240 ml) basic microwave-cooked green vegetable (see Index)
1 portion fruit

*Try to have at least three portions of cold-water fish a week, such as swordfish or salmon or water-packed tuna.

A WEEK OF WEIGHT-LOSS MENUS FOR ONE
Total daily calories equal those of the Standard Day

MONDAY

Lunch:
Tuna Salad, 175 cal.
1 slice Majic Whole Grain Bread, whole wheat bread, rye bread, small pita, or 2 slices protein bread, 80 cal.
1 portion fruit, 80 cal.

Dinner:
Veal Savarin, 256 cal., *with*
½ cup (120 ml) boiled rice, 90 cal.
Mixed Green salad with 1 tablespoon diet dressing, 35 cal.
Peach Sorbet or store-bought diet sorbet, 87 cal., *or*
1 portion fruit, 80 cal.

TUESDAY

Lunch:
8 ounces (240 ml) low-fat yogurt, 110 cal.
1 cup (240 ml) unsweetened, sliced fresh strawberries or fruit salad, 50 cal. You can use an artificial sweetener.
2 Wasa crackers, 45 cal.

Snack:
1 small pita with ¼ cup (60 ml) Cottage Cheese Dip, 136 cal.

Dinner:
Swordfish with Pesto, 199 cal.
Salad with 1 tablespoon diet dressing, 35 cal.
Tricky Chocolate Pudding, 75 cal., *or*
1 portion fruit, 80 cal.

WEDNESDAY

Lunch:
Turkey Sandwich, 350 cal.
½ portion fruit, 40 cal.

Snack:
If having spaghetti for dinner: 1 cup (240 ml) clear soup, 70 cal., *or*
1 portion fruit, 80 cal.

Dinner:
1 cup (240 ml) cooked spaghetti with ½ cup (120 ml) Lean Bolognese, 275 cal., *or*
Frozen diet entrée, under 300 cal.
Mixed green salad with 1 tablespoon diet dressing, 34 cal.
Tricky Chocolate Pudding, 75 cal., *or*
1 portion fruit, 80 cal.

THURSDAY

Lunch:
1 cup (240 ml) Semi-Irish Stew, 362 cal., *or*
Curried Chicken Salad, 335 cal.
1 slice Majic Whole Grain Bread, whole wheat bread, rye bread, small pita, or 2 slices protein bread, 80 calories
1 portion fruit, 80 cal.

Dinner:
1 cup (240 ml) Spicy Chicken Broth, 70 cal.
Large salad with vegetables of choice, 100 cal. (approx.)
2 tablespoons diet dressing, 70 cal.
1 small pita or 2 Wasa crackers, 80 cal.
Peach Sorbet, 86 cal., *or*
½ cantaloupe melon, 94 cal.

FRIDAY

Lunch:

½ cup (120 ml) Cinnamon Spread, *or* low-fat cottage cheese, 90 cal.

Fruit salad made with ¼ orange, ¼ apple, 1 cup (240 ml) sliced strawberries, ¼ melon, and ½ banana, 170 cal.

1 tablespoon chopped walnuts, 48 cal.

1 tablespoon raisins, 32 cal.

Snack:

1 cup (240 ml) clear soup or Spicy Chicken Broth, 70 cal.

Dinner:

1 small potato (8 ounces; 227 g), baked or steamed, 220 cal., *with*

4 ounces (113.5 g) broiled or grilled lean steak, 200 cal.

1 portion fruit, 80 cal.

SATURDAY

Lunch:

Pita Pizza, 194 cal.

1 portion fruit, 80 cal.

Dinner:

Standard dinner *or*

Raw vegetables with ½ cup (120 ml) Eggplant Purée with Tomato and Green Pepper, 48 cal.

1 cup (240 ml) Skinny Chili, 186 cal.

1 small potato (8 ounces; 227 g), baked or steamed, 220 cal.

Gingered Oranges, 79 cal., *or*

2 cups (470 ml) fresh strawberries (sweetened with artificial sweetener, if desired), 45 cal., *with*

1 Meringue Cloud, 8 cal.

SUNDAY

Brunch:

Standard breakfast and lunch *or*

Salmon Scrambled Eggs, made with 1 whole egg, 1 egg white, 2 ounces (56 g) smoked salmon, chives and 1 teaspoon butter per person, 230 cal.

½ bagel, 75 cal.

1 tablespoon whipped cream cheese, 50 cal.

1 portion fruit, 80 cal., *or*

1 Bloody Mary cocktail, 110 cal.

Dinner:

Skinny Chili, left over from the night before, 186 cal.

½ cup (120 ml) rice, 110 cal., *or*

Skinny Burger, 170 cal.

Mixed green salad with 1 tablespoon diet dressing, 34 cal.

1 portion fruit, 80 cal.

Alternate Weight-Loss Meals

Lunch:
Sandwiches (pages 70–73)

1 cup (240 ml) of any of the soups
1 small pita (80 g)

8 ounces (240 ml) low-fat yogurt
1 tablespoon raisins
1 tablespoon walnuts *or with*
1 cup (240 ml) unsweetened fruit salad

Salad bar (lettuce and assorted vegetables,
    bought or brought)
2 tablespoons diet dressing

8 ounces (240 ml) low-fat cottage cheese
1 small apple or a navel orange or a ba-
    nana

Liquid Meal (pages 57–63)

Dinner:
Frozen diet entrée, purchased
Spinach, Mushroom and Celery Salad
    with Buttermilk Dressing
1 small hard roll
1 teaspoon butter
1 portion fruit

1 slice take-out pizza
Take-out salad with your own diet
    dressing
1 portion fruit or frozen-fruit bar

2 Pita Pizzas
½ cantaloupe melon

3 ounces (85 g) dry pasta, cooked
½ cup (120 ml) Tomato Sauce Casalinga,
    or bottled plain tomato or pasta sauce
1 tablespoon grated Parmesan cheese
Green salad with diet dressing, or store-
    bought
1 portion fruit

4 ounces (113.5 g) loin or rump steak,
    broiled
Salad with 2 tablespoons diet dressing
1 piece of bread
1 portion fruit

1 cup (240 ml) diet soup (pages
    114–147)
5 ounces (142 g) fish with vegetables
½ cup (120 ml) cooked rice
1 portion fruit

Chicken breast
Baked potato *with*
1 tablespoon nonfat yogurt
Green salad with 1 tablespoon diet
    dressing

First course (pages 74–113) of your
    choice, or pasta (pages 162–166), or
    risotto (pages 187–191)
1 small steamed lobster
6-ounce (170-ml) vegetable plate
1 slice bread
1 portion fruit

Vegetarian Dinner:
Dried Shiitake with Parsley, 51 cal.
Summer Vegetable Stew, 100 cal.
Black Bean Salad, 170 cal.
Coleslaw, 110 cal. *or* Fennel Salad, 81 cal.
½ cup (120 mi) Chocolate Sorbet, 134
    cal.

Chilied Red Bean Soup, 224 cal.
Stuffed Eggplant, 195 cal.
Sesame Broccoli Sauté, 57 cal.
Honey Baked Apple, 117 cal. *with*
    Whipped Ricotta Topping, 19 cal., op-
    tional

A WEEK OF WEIGHT-LOSS MENUS FOR TWO

These menus are designed for those who like to eat well and don't mind cooking. If you are not up to preparing things this involved, you can substitute less-complicated dishes, or even a diet frozen entrée if you are particularly tired.

It is a good idea to pick a weekend day before you start this week of menus to do some do-ahead cooking. If you want that to be a diet day, try one of the easy Liquid Days (pages 57–63) to give you a head start. On the cooking day, make some diet jam, a large batch of Basic Chicken Broth (page 460) and a few diet dressings to keep in the refrigerator and get a head start on the week.

Diet fruit ices can be bought along with diet fruit preserves. Melon or grapefruit can be dessert. Later in this chapter, after the week's menus, you will find simple substitute menus. Some may call for something as easy as grilling—trim the fat and weigh the meat, please—a piece of steak or a chop. Another possibility is a frozen diet main course. Look in your freezer and see if you have a single serving of another recipe from the book waiting to be defrosted.

One of the best places to look for substitutes is in other sections of this book or in the Index. If you want lamb instead of chicken, look in the Index.

When making substitutions, try to choose foods with roughly the same calorie count and nutritional profile. This will ensure that you get your vitamins and won't get too much cholesterol or fat. Eggs, for instance, are often an attractively quick and easy low-calorie meal; but you don't want many of them in any given week—they are very rich in cholesterol.

I have included a modest portion of wine. If omitted, have extra fruit.

If you don't like whole-grain diet flat breads—look on the package; a piece should have about twenty-two calories—you can substitute a slice of commercial diet bread (forty-five calories per slice), toasted or plain, or an Oat Bran Wafer (page 161) or a slice of Majic Whole Grain Bread (page 152), which has more calories but is better for you. One advantage of the flat breads and Oat Bran Wafers is that they keep virtually indefinitely—no spoilage—and make healthy low-calorie snacks; just don't eat too many. If you live alone or will be tempted by an open loaf of bread sitting around, wrap the individual slices in plastic wrap and freeze. Toast them as you want them, which will also defrost them. Delaying the eating is a good idea. Think before you pop something into your mouth.

Most of the luncheon menus are designed for people who work or are alone at lunch. If you prefer a larger lunch and a lighter dinner—actually better for you—take one dish, such as a soup, from the nighttime menu and add it to your lunch.

You will notice that some of the recipes for stews and soups can be made in larger-than-needed quantities. You can freeze the extra in individual serving portions in microwavable freezing containers. Use as main courses for dinner when you don't have time to cook. They may also be substituted for lunch; but you cannot then have the other things listed for lunch on that day. To defrost, remove container cover; cover tightly with microwave plastic wrap; microwave cook on high for six minutes; stir. If not thoroughly heated, cook for two minutes longer.

Breakfast:
Oatmeal, 102 cal. *topped with*
1 tablespoon Strawberry Jam, 13 cal., or
  store-bought diet preserves
Café au lait (½ skim milk and ½ coffee),
  40 cal., or black coffee (and add ¼ cup
  [60 ml] skim milk to your oatmeal)

Lunch:
Spinach, Mushroom and Celery Salad, 58
  cal.
Pita bread, 80 cal. (see heating instructions)
1 ounce (28 g) part-skim mozzarella, 114
  cal.
1 small apple or a navel orange, 81 cal.

Dinner:
Steamed artichokes, 53 cal.
Balsamic vinegar for dipping, 5 cal. each
  tablespoon (approx.)
Semi-Irish Stew, 362 cal.
Raspberry Poached Pears, 76 cal.
Either 4 ounces (120 ml) dry wine, alone
  or as a spritzer with salt-free soda, or a
  pita bread

If wine or pita bread is not eaten at dinner, a small serving of fruit may be
  eaten as a before-bed snack.

Breakfast:
1 slice Majic Whole Grain toast (page
  152), or store-bought whole wheat
  bread, 80 cal.
1 tablespoon Strawberry Jam, 13 cal., or
  store-bought diet jam
6 ounces (180 ml) tomato juice with
  lemon, 35 cal.

Snack:
1 banana, 105 cal.

Lunch:
Cold artichoke, left over from the day
  before, 53 cal.
2 tablespoons Orange-Yogurt Dressing,
  18 cal., or commercial diet dressing
⅓ cup (80 ml) Curried Ricotta Spread, or
  ½ cup (120 ml) low-fat cottage cheese,
  90 cal.
2 Wasa or flat-bread crackers, 44 cal.
Navel orange, 65 cal.

Dinner:
Fat-free Risotto, 200 cal.
Chicken in Red Wine, 230 cal.
Mixed green salad with 1 tablespoon diet
  dressing, 35 cal.
Rummy Baked Pineapple, 115 cal. (eat
  the refrigerated leftovers as snacks, or
  have a portion of diet sorbet)
Optional: 4 ounces (120 ml) dry wine,
  alone or as a spritzer with salt-free
  soda

WEDNESDAY

TOTAL CALORIES 1,098

Breakfast:
Steamed Banana Muffin, 136 cal.
½ pink or red grapefruit, 38 cal.
Coffee or tea with skim milk

Lunch:
Turkey Sandwich, brought or bought, 350 cal.
Diet soda, or coffee or tea with skim milk
Small apple, 81 cal.

Dinner:
Hearty Vegetable Soup with Pesto, 70 cal.
Paupiettes with Parsley Stuffing, 195 cal.
Watercress Sauce, 5 cal. per tablespoon
½ cup (120 ml) steamed rice, 100 cal.
Tapioca Pudding, 98 cal.
4 ounces (120 ml) dry wine

8 ounces (240 ml) skim milk, 85 cal., for snack if wine is not had at dinner

THURSDAY

TOTAL CALORIES: 1,081

Breakfast:
1 banana, 105 cal.
1 slice Majic Whole Grain toast (page 000), 80 calories
¼ cup (60 ml) Cinnamon Spread—to eat with the banana or on your toast with a sprinkling of wheat germ, 55 cal.
Coffee or tea with skim milk

Snack:
1 orange, 65 cal.

Lunch:
Hearty Vegetable Soup with Pesto, left over from previous dinner (¾–1 cup; 180–240 ml), 70 cal.; you can have 2 cups (470 ml) and omit the sandwich
3 ounces (85 g) water-packed tuna, drained, with lemon juice, dill seed and 1 tablespoon diet mayonnaise (optional), 162 cal.
1 slice whole wheat bread, 61 cal.
Lettuce, if desired

Dinner:
Stuffed Peppers, 284 cal.
Chicken with Celery, 145 cal.
Salad with Skinny Tomato Dressing, 34 cal.
Apple Snow, 85 cal., or 4 ounces (120 ml) dry wine, 100 cal.

FRIDAY

TOTAL CALORIES: 1,110

Breakfast:
Farina, 81 cal.
1 cup (240 ml) sliced strawberries, 45 cal.
Coffee or tea with skim milk, if desired

Lunch:
Cold Stuffed Pepper, 284 calories
1¼ ounces (35 g) goat cheese or ½ cup
  (120 ml) low-fat cottage cheese, 90 cal.
2 Wasa crackers, 44 cal.

Dinner:
Watercress, Fennel and Romaine Salad
  with Pernod Dressing, 123 cal.
Risotto with Lamb and Dill, 335 cal.
Steamed zucchini—½ cup (120 ml)
  sliced, 14 cal.; 4 ounces (113.5 g) raw
  per person
½ cantaloupe melon, 94 cal.

SATURDAY

TOTAL CALORIES: 1,031

Breakfast:
½ cup (120 ml) low-fat yogurt, 55 cal.
1 banana, sliced, 105 cal.
Coffee or tea with skim milk

Lunch:
1 cup (240 ml) Winter Vegetable Salad,
  100 cal., or 2 cups (470 ml) Summer
  Vegetable Salad, 88 cal.
1 pita bread, 80 cal.
1 portion fruit, 80 cal.

Dinner:
Jade Soup, 110 cal.
Salmon with Cucumbers and Dill, 194
  cal.
1 piece sourdough bread, 70 cal.
Honey Baked Apple, 117 cal.
Optional: 4 ounces (120 ml) dry wine,
  alone or as a spritzer with nonsalt
  soda, 100 cal.

SUNDAY

TOTAL CALORIES: 1,174

Breakfast:
1 slice sourdough toast, 70 cal., with
  Strawberry Jam, 13 cal.
Coffee or tea with skim milk

Lunch:
1 cup (240 ml) low-fat yogurt, 144 cal.,
  with 1 tablespoon raisins (27 cal.), 1
  tablespoon chopped walnuts (47 cal.),
  and sugar substitute
Rye crackers, 44 cal.
Honey Baked Apple (left over from night
  before), 47 cal., or a piece of fresh
  fruit, 80 cal.

Dinner:
Asparagus—8 spears, with 1 tablespoon
  Orange-Yogurt Dressing, 37 cal.
Skinny Chili, 186 calories, with ½ ounce
  (14 g) grated Cheddar cheese, 57 cal.
  (optional)
1 small baked potato with skin, 220 cal.
Light Poached Pear, with Tart Apricot
  Sauce, 129 cal.
4 ounces (120 ml) dry wine, alone or as a
  spritzer with salt-free soda, 100 cal.

Liquid Meals and Days

I must open this section with a precaution: Do not use these liquid days or meals as a total diet for more than a day at a time, widely separated. While I have tried to make them as nutritionally balanced as possible, they are not intended to replace food for an extended period. Some of the recipes, which will be pointed out, can be used instead of a single meal such as breakfast; but try not to rely on them too much. The main purpose of these menus and recipes is to get you started on your diet, or to compensate for a few holiday days of overeating. They do not have as many calories as I recommend for a normal weight-loss day. Prolonged use will put your body on fasting rations, which is not good for you or your diet. See pages 21–22.

This is not an attempt to go into the liquid-diet business. Liquid diets are designed for the seriously overweight. They must be supervised by a doctor. Since they do put you on fasting rations, they have long-term implications that make it imperative that your doctor decide whether it is worth it for you. If you have been on a liquid diet, it is important that you recognize that you cannot go back to so-called normal eating when you finish the diet or you will immediately gain back the lost weight. Up-and-down weight may be harder on your system than overweight. Of course, neither is recommended. Instead, try my weight-loss diet for one.

LIQUID DAY NUMBER ONE

Liquid Day Number One is cathartic and diuretic. Use it on a day when you plan to be at home. Do not assume when you get on the scale the morning after that you have actually lost as much weight as the scale says. Much of the apparent weight loss will be water. You cannot and should not keep yourself permanently water-deprived. Water—it can come in any liquid and many solids—is necessary for your body to function properly. Nevertheless, if I am bloated from too much salt in my food or my weight seems out of hand, a day like this can get me back on the track. Make the entire recipe for Strawberry Shake. Have one glass for breakfast and space the rest out through the day as you get hungry. Have the Carrot Shake for lunch or divide it in half and have the other part at dinner. Have the Spicy Chicken Broth as snacks or as a meal. The total calories are 591. The protein, iron, calcium, carbohydrates, fiber and vitamins are complete as well.

Other recipes can be used on other days, or as substitutes on this day, or instead of specific meals.

STRAWBERRY SHAKE

MAKES 3½ CUPS (825 ML), 3 SERVINGS

For each generous 1-cup (240-ml) serving: 116 calories; 2 milligrams cholesterol; 0 milligrams fat; 82 milligrams sodium; 8 grams protein (18% RDA); 21 milligrams carbohydrate

RDA: calcium 22%; phosphorus 24%; iron 7%; thiamin 11%; riboflavin 32%; niacin 10%; vitamin C 98%

2 cups (470 ml) strawberries, washed and hulled
½ cup (120 ml) skim milk
8 ounces (240 ml) nonfat yogurt
2 packages dry yeast (¼ ounce; 7 g)

1 tablespoon sugar, or artificial sweetener to taste
1 cup (240 ml) smallish ice cubes (1½ cups [355 ml] if very large)

1. Put strawberries, milk, yogurt, yeast and sugar or sweetener in blender. Blend until thoroughly puréed.
2. With the blender running and the lid on but the center cup removed, drop in a few ice cubes at a time and continue to blend until the ice is in tiny crystals.

CARROT SHAKE

You may not think of shakes as things to cook; but the microwave oven makes this so rapidly and the carrots give you so much nutritional value that it's well worth doing. It tastes good too. *SERVES 1*

Per 1½-cup (355-ml) serving: 129 calories; 7 milligrams cholesterol; 2 grams fat; 145 milligrams sodium; 8 grams protein (18% RDA); 19 grams carbohydrate

RDA: calcium 22%; iron 20%; vitamin A 56%; thiamin 9%; riboflavin 16%; niacin 9%; vitamin C 30%

¼ pound (113.5 g) carrots, peeled and cut across into ½-inch (1-cm) slices
½ cup (120 ml) Basic Chicken Broth (page 460), or unsalted or regular canned chicken broth

½ cup (120 ml) skim milk
1 tablespoon part-skim ricotta cheese
½ clove garlic, smashed and peeled
Pinch cumin
1 tablespoon fresh lemon juice

1. Place carrots in a 10-inch (25.5-cm) quiche dish. Cover tightly with microwave plastic wrap. Cook at 100% for 4 minutes in a 650- to 700-watt oven. Prick plastic to release steam.

2. Remove from oven and uncover. Scrape carrots into a blender or food processor. Add remaining ingredients except lemon juice and purée until smooth. Transfer to a glass or a soup bowl and chill for one hour if eating chilled. If eating as soup, heat, uncovered, for 2 minutes. Stir in lemon juice just before serving.

FOR 400- TO 500-WATT OVENS

To serve 1 Cook for 7 minutes. Reheat, if desired, for 5 minutes.

SPICY CHICKEN BROTH

*U*se this as an opportunity to make Basic Chicken Broth (page 460) for the week. Make at least four cups (1 l); but consider making eight cups (2 l). Skim it well. Refrigerate or freeze what you do not need. If you cannot bear the thought of cooking at all, make this the day you buy lots of cans of low-sodium chicken broth. Try to make yourself eat the garlic; it will be creamy and well cooked; it's good for you. Once again, you can have one cup (240 ml) right away and another cup mid-afternoon. If you plan to save a cup to reheat, add half the lemon juice to the first cup. Add the rest of the juice to the second cup after reheating for one and a half minutes.   *MAKES 2 CUPS (470 ML), 2 FIRST-COURSE PORTIONS*

Per 1-cup (240-ml) portion: 52 calories; 0 milligrams cholesterol; 2 grams fat; 56 grams sodium; 3 grams protein (7% RDA); 7 grams carbohydrate

RDA: vitamin C 18%

2 cups (470 ml) Basic Chicken Broth (page 460), or unsalted canned chicken broth	1 pinch red pepper flakes 2 tablespoons fresh lemon juice
8 cloves garlic, smashed, peeled and sliced	

1. Combine chicken broth, garlic and red pepper flakes in an 8-cup (2-l) glass measure or in a 2-quart (2-l) soufflé dish. Cover tightly with microwave plastic wrap and cook at 100% for 10 minutes in a 650- to 700-watt oven. Prick plastic to release steam.

2. Remove from oven and uncover. Stir in lemon juice and drink from a mug.

BANANA SHAKE

*T*his makes a sufficiently large amount that you can have half at breakfast and save the other half, in the refrigerator, to eat mid-morning. On a normal day, substitute it for lunch with a portion of fruit or a small salad.
MAKES 1¾ CUPS (410 ML)

Per whole shake: 259 calories; 5 milligrams cholesterol; 2 grams fat; 151 milligrams sodium; 13 grams protein (29% RDA); 51 grams carbohydrate

RDA: calcium 39%; phosphorus 37%; 1,086 milligrams potassium; thiamin 15%; riboflavin 35%; vitamin C 25%

1 medium peeled banana (5 ounces;
   142 g)
½ cup (120 ml) nonfat yogurt

½ cup (120 ml) skim milk
1 tablespoon oat bran
⅛ teaspoon pure vanilla extract

1. Cut banana in chunks. Combine all ingredients in a blender and blend until there are no pieces of banana. Drink or refrigerate or freeze.

PINEAPPLE-PROTEIN SHAKE

Each one-half recipe serving can substitute for a lunch or a breakfast. The whole thing can be a dinner with calories left for a snack.
MAKES 2½ CUPS, 2 1¼-CUP (300-ML) SERVINGS

Per 1¼-cup (300-ml) serving: 205 calories; 1 milligram cholesterol; 2 milligrams fat; 45 milligrams sodium; 5 grams protein (12% RDA), 45 grams carbohydrate

RDA: calcium 15%; phosphorus 22%; iron 8%; thiamin 26%; vitamin C 44%

2 tablespoons (½ ounce; 14 g) rice fiber (germ and bran)
½ cup (120 ml) hot tap water
1 ripe 8-ounce (227-g) pear, peeled, halved, cored and diced (about 1½ cups; 355 ml)
Large pinch ground ginger
Large pinch ground cumin
Large pinch ground nutmeg
½ cup (120 ml) nonfat yogurt
Scant ¼ cup (60 ml) orange juice
¾ cup (4 slices; 180 ml) canned pineapple packed in juice (no added sugar)
¼ cup (60 ml) juice from canned pineapple

1. Stir rice fiber into hot water. It will dissolve in about 2 minutes.
2. Place all ingredients in blender. Blend until smooth. Refrigerate.
3. Serve a portion poured over ice cubes.

CURRIED YOGURT DRINK

Not all yogurt drinks need to be sweet or fruity. This variation of an Armenian drink is served in nonalcohol homes without the curry. I like it and find it filling and satisfying. It can also be the base for an easy cold soup. Just add some chicken broth or vegetarian broth.   *MAKES 2 CUPS, 2 SERVINGS*

Per 1-cup (240-ml) serving: 69 calories; 2 milligrams cholesterol; 0 milligrams fat; 7 grams protein (15% RDA); 10 grams carbohydrate

RDA: calcium 23%; phosphorus 18%; riboflavin 15%

2 cloves garlic, smashed and peeled
¼ teaspoon curry powder
1 cup (240 ml) nonfat yogurt

1 cup (240 ml) smallish ice cubes (1½ cups [355 ml] if very large)
1 tablespoon fresh mint or coriander leaves, optional

1. Place garlic, curry powder and ½ cup (120 ml) of the yogurt in a blender. Blend until puréed. Add remaining yogurt and blend briefly.
2. With the blender running and the lid on but the center cup removed, drop in a few ice cubes at a time and continue to blend until the ice is in tiny crystals. If using fresh herbs, add with ice cubes.
3. Drink immediately or refrigerate. May be served over ice.

HOT COCOA

*S*urprise! There is no reason not to enjoy this hot, soothing drink on a lazy Sunday morning, or before being lulled to sleep at night. Hot milk helps you to relax, just as mother said. If you substitute an artificial sweetener for the sugar, put it in after the cocoa cooks. You save 32 calories.   *SERVES 1*

Per 1-cup (240-ml) serving: 123 calories (91 if using artificial sweetener); 5 milligrams cholesterol; 0 grams fat; 128 milligrams sodium; 9 grams protein (19% RDA); 21 grams carbohydrate

RDA: calcium 30%; phosphorus 26%; vitamin A 10%; riboflavin 20%

1 teaspoon unsweetened Dutch-process
   cocoa
2 teaspoons granulated sugar

2 drops vanilla extract
1 cup (240 ml) skim milk

   1. Put cocoa, sugar and vanilla in a 4-cup (1-l) glass measure. Stir in just enough milk to make a smooth paste. Stir in remaining milk. Cover tightly with microwave plastic wrap and cook at 100% for 1 minute 30 seconds in a 650- to 700-watt oven. Prick plastic to release steam.
   2. Remove from oven; uncover; serve in a mug.

Healthful Diets Without Weight Loss for Small People

or

WEIGHT-LOSS DIETS FOR LARGE AND/OR ACTIVE PEOPLE

Leave breakfast the same as for the Standard Day (page 49) and have a piece of fruit in the middle of the morning if you get hungry. If you can eat more calories without gaining weight, add more carbohydrates, fruits and vegetables, or add snacks from pages 514–529. Breakfast can also be increased.

BASIC CALORIE COUNTS FOR A DAY ARE ABOUT 1,400–1,500 CALORIES. CALORIES ARE DISTRIBUTED IN MEALS AS FOLLOWS:

Breakfast:	*Lunch:*	*Dinner:*
200–300 calories	500 calories	600–800 calories

MONDAY
TOTAL CALORIES: 1,459

Lunch:
Chopped Salad (page 417), 285 cal.
1 small whole wheat pita, 87 cal.
1 portion fruit, 100 cal. (approx.)

Dinner:
Stuffed Peppers (page 98), 284 cal.
Anna's Fish with Black Bean Sauce (page 255), 173 cal.
Mixed green salad with 1 tablespoon diet dressing, 34 cal.
2 slices whole wheat bread, 170 cal.
Pumpkin Pudding (page 571), 126 cal.

TUESDAY
TOTAL CALORIES: 1,421

Lunch:
Stuffed Pepper, left over from the night before, 284 cal.
Double portion Oriental Spinach Salad (page 79), 108 cal., *or*
Double portion Spicy Chicken Broth (page 59), 104 cal.
2 cookies (pages 574–576), 100 cal. (approx.)

Dinner:
Herb-Stuffed Mussels (page 97), 170 cal.
Winter Pork Stew (page 370), 224 cal.
2 slices bread with 1 teaspoon butter, 155 cal.
Mixed green salad with 1–2 tablespoons diet dressing, 80 cal. (approx.)
1 portion fruit, 100 cal. (approx.)

WEDNESDAY
TOTAL CALORIES: 1,456

Lunch:
Double portion Hearty Vegetable Soup with Pesto (page 130), 196 cal.
Small pita, 87 cal.
2 ounces (56 g) part-skim mozzarella cheese, 144 cal.
1 portion fruit, 100 cal. (approx.)

Dinner for company:
Cauliflower Timbale (page 106) with Rich Watercress Sauce (page 506), 92 cal.
Fish Couscous (page 262), 288 cal.
Light White Ice Cream (page 558), 168 cal.
Chocolate Sauce (page 580), 47 cal.
2 Meringue Clouds (page 585), 16 cal.
¼ cup (60 ml) wine, or 1 slice bread

THURSDAY
TOTAL CALORIES: 1,490

Lunch:
Double portion Warm Chicken Salad Oriental (page 311), 220 cal.
½ cup (120 ml) white rice, 100 cal., *or*
1 slice bread, 70 cal.
1 portion fruit, 100 cal.

Dinner:
Gala Meat Loaf (page 352), 353 cal.
Double portion Olive Oil Mashed Potatoes (page 221), 254 cal.
Carrots and Mushrooms with Cumin (page 82), 44 cal.
Mixed green salad with 1 tablespoon diet dressing, 34 cal.
Strawberry Bavarian (page 560), 115 cal.

FRIDAY
TOTAL CALORIES: 1,508

Lunch:
Turkey Sandwich (page 71), 350 cal.
Coleslaw (page 394), 110 cal.
1 portion fruit, 100 cal. (approx.)

Dinner:
Jade Soup (page 124), 110 cal.
Jambalaya (page 323), 383 cal.
1 piece French bread, 100 cal.
Bibb and Tarragon Salad (page 393), 81 cal.
Plum Timbales (page 562), 74 cal.

SATURDAY

Lunch:
Quick Tomato Soup (page 126), 48 cal.
Lentil Salad (page 209), 136 cal.
2 ounces low-fat cheese, such as goat cheese, 150 cal.
3 Wasa crackers or 3 Oat Bran Wafers (page 161), 75 cal.

Dinner:
Optional entertaining meal or dinner out
Spicy Southwestern Soup (page 132), 110 cal.
José Lampreia's Poached Beef (page 360), 480 cal.
Steamed potatoes (page 220), 119 cal.
Mixed green salad with Buttermilk Dressing (page 491), 33 cal.
Tangerine Pudding (page 563), 147 cal.
¼ cup (60 ml) wine, or 1 slice bread

SUNDAY
TOTAL CALORIES:1,518 (brunch and dinner); 1,551 (breakfast, lunch and dinner)

Brunch:
Omelette made with 2 eggs, 1 egg white, 2 ounces part-skim mozzarella cheese, mixed fresh herbs, 318 cal.
1 bagel with 1 tablespoon butter, 330 cal.
2 tablespoons Lemon Marmalade (page 592), 104 cal.
1 portion fruit, 100 cal. (approx.)

Snack:
(pages 514–529), 100 cal. (approx.)

See Dinner opposite

OR
Breakfast

Lunch:
Hearty Chick-pea Soup (page 135), 197 cal.
1 large or 2 small whole wheat pitas, 174 cal.
Salade Niçoise (page 91), 214 cal.
1 portion fruit, 100 cal. (approx.)

Dinner:
Skinny Chili (page 357), 186 cal.
1 small potato (8 ounces; 227 g) baked or steamed (page 220), 220 cal.
1 tablespoon butter, 100 cal.
Mixed green salad with 1 tablespoon diet dressing, 34 cal.
Pumpkin Pudding (page 571), 126 cal.

Entertaining Menus the Weight-Loss Way

Calories below are approximate, especially for meals like cocktail parties; but they should be fairly exact if you don't let the portions get out of control. Feel free to have two small glasses of wine at any of these parties. I usually allow a few extra portions of the main course for the more robust eaters among my guests.

The Cocktail Party

400 calories
Crisp raw vegetables with Eggplant Purée with Lemon and Chives (page 89)
Sweet potato, cooked (page 221), cubed and served on a skewer with Aïoli as a dip
(page 483)
Gravlax with Dill Buttermilk Sauce (page 90)
Herb-Stuffed Mussels (page 97)
Spinach Roulade with Cheese Filling (page 109)

A Spring Dinner for 8

499 calories
Asparagus with Summer Green Dip (page 519)
Salmon in Red Wine (page 259)
New Potato Salad (page 224)
Watercress, Fennel and Romaine Salad with Pernod Dressing (page 405)
Peppered Strawberries (page 535)
Meringue Clouds (page 585)

Celebration Dinner for 2

738 calories
Fat-free Risotto (page 187)
Steamed Whole Fish (page 258)
Bibb and Tarragon Salad (page 393)
1 ounce goat cheese with 1 slice bread
Armagnac-Prune Soufflé (page 583)

An American Feast for 8

697 calories
Spicy Southwestern Soup (page 132)
Gala Meat Loaf (page 352)
Fennel and Potato Purée (page 222)
Mixed green salad with 1 tablespoon Spicy Buttermilk Dressing (page 495)
Summer Fruit Compote (pages 540–541)

Vegetarian Dinner

583 calories
Spinach Roulade with Duxelles (page 107)
or
Oriental Spinach Salad (page 79)
Vegetable Couscous (page 452)
Orange and Red Onion Salad (page 402)
Peaches with Cherry Sauce (page 547)
Ginger Crisps (page 586), optional

Ladies' Lunch

577 calories
24 Karat Soup (page 144)
Chopped Salad (page 417)
2 Oat Bran Wafers (page 161)
Peaches with Cherry Sauce (page 547)

Sunday Dinner

693 calories
Winter Vegetable Soup (page 128)
Chicken Paprikás (page 318)
Cooked orzo
Angel Food Cake (page 582)

Making Lunch Sandwiches and Such

SANDWICHES

All these sandwiches can be taken to the office. If you plan on doing so, place a piece of lettuce on each slice of bread to keep it from getting soggy. If you want some tomato on your sandwich, take the slices in a plastic bag and put them on the sandwich at the last minute so the sandwich doesn't get soggy. You can take a pita pocket with you and heat it in the microwave at lunchtime. Fill it with a cup of Chunky Tomato Basil Salad (page 407) and enjoy a midday feast. If you are running low on calcium, have half a cup of Cottage Cheese Dip (page 518) on 1 slice of Majic Whole Grain Bread (page 152).

All of these sandwiches are in the 350-calorie range. If you don't need to lose weight, add a bowl of soup and some fruit or a dessert to your lunch.

COMPARISON OF DIFFERENT TYPES OF COMMERCIAL SANDWICH BREADS

It makes no difference to their nutritional profile whether breads are plain, heated or toasted. Heat pita bread so that it puffs up and is easy to split in half or to fill as a pita pocket. Place it on paper toweling if desired, and heat as specified below.

1 small (3-inch) pita
650- to 700-watt oven: 30 sec.
400- to 500-watt oven: 45 sec.

2 small (3-inch) pitas
650- to 700-watt oven: 45 sec.
400- to 500-watt oven: 1 minute 30 sec.

TYPE	CAL.	PROT. (g)	CARB. (g)	SOD. (mg)
Cracked-wheat bread 1 slice (.9 oz.; 25 g)	66	2	13	108
French bread 5 × 2½ × 1-in. slice				
(1.2 oz.; 35 g)	102	3	19	203
Hamburger/Hot-dog roll 1 bun (1.4 oz.; 40 g)	119	3	21	202
Hard roll 3¾-in. (9.5-cm) diam. slice (1.8 oz.; 50 g)	156	5	30	313
Italian bread 4½ × 3¼ × ¾-in. (11 × 8 × 2-cm) slice				
(1.1 oz.; 30 g)	83	3	17	176
Majic Whole Grain Bread (page 152) 1 slice (1 oz.; 28 g)	88	4	17	139
Mixed grain bread 1 slice (1 oz.; 28 g)	73	3	13	117
Multi Grain Bread (page 153) 1 slice (1 oz.; 28 g)	46	1	9	44

Pita-pocket bread
This book calls for small 3-inch (7.5 cm) pitas. The others are here for the purpose of comparison, or if you are not on a weight-loss diet.

TYPE	CAL.	PROT. (g)	CARB. (g)	SOD. (mg)
White, 3-in. (7.5-cm) diam. (1 oz.; 28 g)	87	3	19	182
Whole wheat, 3-in. (7.5 cm) diam. (1 oz.; 28 g)	84	3	18	182
Onion, 3-in. (7.5-cm) diam. (1 oz.; 28 g)	89	3	19	182
White, 6-in. (15-cm) diam. (2 oz.; 56 g)	174	5	37	363
Whole wheat, 6-in. (15-cm) diam. (2 oz.; 56 g)	167	6	35	364
Onion, 6-in. (15-cm) diam. (2 oz.; 56 g)	178	6	37	364
Pumpernickel bread 1 slice (1.1 oz.; 32 g)	82	3	15	173
Raisin bread 1 slice (.88 oz.; 25 g)	70	2	13	94
Rye bread 1 slice (.88 oz.; 25 g)	66	2	12	174
White bread 1 slice (1 oz.; 28 g)	76	2	14	146
Whole wheat bread 1 slice (.88 oz.; 25 g)	61	2	11	159

COMPARISON OF VARIOUS COMMERCIALLY AVAILABLE CONDIMENTS

See Basics, Sauces and Snacks (pages 458–529) for more healthful homemade products.

TYPE	CAL.	SOD. (mg)	FAT (g)	CHOL. (mg)
Horseradish (1 tsp.)	2	5	1	—
Tomato ketchup (1 tbsp.)	18	180	1	—
Mayonnaise, regular (1 tbsp.)	99	78	11	8
Mayonnaise, diet (1 tbsp.)	50	115	5	5
Mustard, brown (1 tsp.)	5	65	1	—
Mustard, yellow (1 tsp.)	4	63	1	—
Butter, sweet (1 tbsp.)	100	2	11	30
Margarine, unsalted (1 tbsp.)	102	2	12	—

SANDWICH FILLINGS

The portions and calories given are for one sandwich with two slices of bread—not for the filling alone.

TUNA SALAD

*T*his is made with leftover cooked tunafish; but you can substitute water-packed tuna for about the same nutrition.   *MAKES 1½ CUPS*

Per generous ⅓-cup (80-ml) serving: 271 calories; 27 milligrams cholesterol; 22 grams fat; 118 milligrams sodium; 17 grams protein (38% RDA)

8 ounces (227 g) cooked tuna, flaked
   with a fork, or canned and water-
   packed tuna
1 rib celery, peeled and chopped (about
   ⅓ cup; 80 ml)
¼ cup (60 ml) chopped onion—about
   1 small onion (2 ounces; 56 g)

½ cup (120 ml) Egg White Mayonnaise
   (page 482), or bottled diet
   mayonnaise
Pinch kosher salt
Freshly ground black pepper, to taste
1 tablespoon fresh lemon juice

   1. Combine all ingredients in a small mixing bowl and toss to mix.

WHITE FISH SALAD

While you can cook fish especially for this spread (page 229), it is a good way to use up leftovers. You can make it with any firm-fleshed white fish.   *MAKES 3 CUPS*

Per ⅓-cup (80-ml) serving: 210 calories; 34 milligrams cholesterol; 17 grams fat; 107 milligrams sodium; 13 grams protein (28% RDA)

1 pound (450 g) cooked white-fleshed fish in small flakes
1 cup (240 ml) Egg White Mayonnaise (page 482), or bottled diet mayonnaise
¼ cup (60 ml) chopped mint leaves

2 scallions, cut into 1-inch (2.5-cm) pieces
1 tablespoon lemon juice
1 red bell pepper (about 6 ounces; 170 g), cut into small dice (about 1 cup; 240 ml)

1. Combine all ingredients in a small mixing bowl and toss to mix.

TURKEY SANDWICH

Per sandwich: 312 calories

4 ounces (113.5 g) thinly sliced turkey, store-bought or leftover (page 330)
2 slices rye bread

1 tablespoon mustard
Lettuce
2 ounces (56 g) tomato, sliced—about 2 medium slices

BEEF SANDWICH

Per sandwich: 362 calories

3 ounces (85 g) thinly sliced leftover beef (page 359), or lean store-bought roast beef
1 teaspoon Rouïlle (page 484), or commercial diet mayonnaise

2 slices rye bread
2 ounces tomato

MEAT LOAF SANDWICH

Per sandwich: 327 calories

½-inch (1-cm) slice Gala Meat Loaf
   (page 352)

2 slices rye bread
2 teaspoons Dijon mustard

CURRIED CHICKEN SALAD SANDWICH

Per sandwich: 344 calories

½ cup (120 ml) Curried Chicken Salad
   (page 418)
Lettuce, if desired

2 slices whole grain bread, or 1 small
   pita

PITA PIZZA

*T*his makes a quick, nutritious lunch; but half a pita topped with half the ingredients makes a good snack for a child or an adult who isn't trying to lose weight.

Per 2 open sandwiches: 298 calories

1 small whole wheat pita
1 ounce (28 g) part-skim mozzarella
   cheese, grated (about ¼ cup; 60 ml)
2 tablespoons freshly grated Parmesan
   cheese

2 ounces (56 g) tomato, sliced—about
   2 medium slices
2 leaves fresh basil

    1. Warm pita (page 69) and split in half. Place halves on a dinner plate or 10-inch (25.5-cm) quiche dish. Place a slice of tomato and a basil leaf on each half. Sprinkle on both cheeses. Cook at 100% for 1 minute 30 seconds in a 650- to 700-watt oven.

                FOR 400- TO 500-WATT OVENS

To make 2 open sandwiches. Cook for 3 minutes.

PEANUT BUTTER AND JELLY SANDWICH

Per sandwich: 370 calories (approx.) If you use commercial peanut butter, this will have more calories, sodium and fat

2 tablespoons Peanut Butter (page 478), or commercial peanut butter
1 tablespoon Strawberry Jam (page 590)

2 slices Majic Whole Grain Bread (page 152)

COMMON FRUIT JUICES

The following data are based on 8-ounce (240-ml) glasses of juice, unless otherwise noted. The United States Department of Agriculture uses the term "canned juice" to indicate juice packed in cans, bottles or jars. Some juices do not naturally have much vitamin C—apple juice, for example—but a fair amount is added by commercial packers. If you get a fall treat of fresh sweet cider, it will have only 1.4 percent of the RDA of vitamin C, versus 60 percent in processed juice.

TYPE	CAL.	CARB. (g)	IRON. (mg)	POT. (mg)	VIT. C (%RDA)
Apple juice					
reconstituted frozen	111	28	0.61	301	61.4
frozen concentrate (1 tbsp.)	29	7	0.16	79	16.4
Cranberry juice cocktail					
canned, with vitamin C	144	36	0.38	46	89
Grapefruit juice					
fresh	96	23	0.49	400	94
canned sweetened	116	28	0.89	405	67
canned unsweetened	93	22	0.50	378	72
Grape juice					
canned	155	38	0.60	334	.20
reconstituted sweetened					
frozen concentrate	128	32	0.26	53	60
Orange juice					
fresh	111	26	0.50	496	124
canned	104	25	1.10	436	86
reconstituted frozen					
concentrated	112	27	0.24	474	97
Pineapple juice					
canned	139	34	0.65	334	26
frozen concentrate	129	32	0.75	340	30
Prune juice					
canned	181	45	3.03	706	10.6

FIRST COURSES

What First Course?

I like a first course. I have been known to eat two or three in a restaurant instead of a main course—not a bad idea for weight-loss dieters—and I serve them at most dinners—not just those for company—in my own home. It's a shame that many home cooks seem loath to undertake what they see as the added work and time of preparing a first course. They are perfectly happy eating them in restaurants. Properly chosen and with the aid of a microwave oven, first courses can be simply and quickly prepared.

By nature and history, they are usually pointedly seasoned, which need not mean burning hot. This fullness of flavor makes me less avid for a main course; I eat less and the meal is more gracious for everybody—the antithesis of on-the-run eating and a meal from a can. Pleasure is important and a microwave oven makes it quickly, leanly possible.

On page 24 of Being Healthy and Slim, I have run on as to the reasons why even non-voluptuaries ought to change eating habits: to increase the number of courses in a meal and to prepare first courses, whether they be those in this chapter, or in Soups (pages 114–147), or in Good Grains and Other Starches (pages 148–225). I won't repeat myself, but will suggest that you think of adding first courses to your repertoire if they are not already a standard in your life.

Here is a collection of delicious, easily prepared first courses that are low in animal fat and cholesterol and rich in nutrition. Those who do not need to lose weight may well want to increase portion size. Some are appropriate for every day, others require more work and probably will be saved for parties, when we are more likely to think of festive first courses. Some of these do have fish or meat. Indulgence on special occasions is not a disaster if it is not excessive. Also, on days when breakfasts and lunches are quite low in protein, it may be desirable to increase the protein in our dinner with a more substantial first course.

With a microwave oven, first courses take very little time, especially when you consider that they can turn a quick meal into an event. Many can be made ahead, and they make happy dividends of leftovers to have as a light lunch the day after. Several of these recipes can also be the salvation of a cocktail party or reception.

Some dishes, such as pastas and risottos (see Good Grains and Other Starches)—noodle and rice first courses in Italy—will be used by Americans as main courses in larger quantities. Many first-course dishes become happy lunches, freshly prepared or left over.

The first course should complement the tastes and nutritional profile of the main course. In the healthy diet, this often means that animal protein is kept to a minimum. Many of the dishes are vegetarian, and a vegetarian can assemble complementary groups of these dishes in order to make a meal. Additionally, the recipes become a source of accompaniment dishes for main courses if you prefer to serve them that way.

It pays to be sensible when making a menu. If the main course is to be curried, choose a cooler flavor for your first course. If you are making a main course of a robust soup, you probably can have a first course with some animal protein. Even with a strong desire to up your carbohydrates, you probably won't want to serve a pasta before a paella. Color contrast is a good thing to keep in mind. The more senses that are pleased by a meal, the less any eater is liable to feel deprived.

If you choose a first course with significant protein, such as meat or cheese, follow it with an ample salad (pages 388–419), a big soup (pages 114–147) or a main course with less protein than most, such as Creamy Baked Shrimp with Peppers (page 276). The other option is to choose a lunch and breakfast that are essentially vegetarian. See pages 16 and 340 if you are curious about the reasons for limiting animal protein, even in a weight-loss diet.

First courses are also a particularly good way to add flavor to an otherwise extremely simple meal, grilled fish or meat (pages 347–348), for example. As with desserts, some of these can be kept on hand to ease the work of the week— a few even freeze.

If you really don't like to serve a separate first course, you will find that many of the vegetable-based dishes can be used equally well as accompaniments to a simple main course.

Once you get in the habit of adding first courses to your meals, develop a repertoire that gives you pleasure. In our zeal to lose weight and be healthy, we must not forget that pleasure is an important part of the equation.

To Begin

The chapter starts with cold first courses. Of course, this often means you must think ahead—make the dish the day before so that it has a chance to get cold. This section starts with dishes simple and quick enough for daily use and with no fish or meat and ends with others that are more complicated. It is only the last part of this group that is not totally vegetarian.

The next group of recipes is for hot beginners—food, not people. They are good for a cold day, a hot day when you will serve a cold main course or a day when you haven't had time to cook ahead.

Cold First Courses

Some cold first courses can and need to be made ahead, which eases the last-minute tensions of dinner preparation. Other cold first courses can be quickly put together. Do look at the chapters on Salads and Vegetables and Soups for other cold first-course suggestions. You will have great flexibility in tossing together first-course salads if you make some of the dressings in Basics, Sauces and Snacks or keep a selection of store-bought diet dressings on hand. Do remember that many such dressings may be heavy in salt and cholesterol. Be careful. Look at the section on pages 28–44 on a healthy-diet larder. It may suggest ideas for good foods to incorporate in these first courses.

ASPARAGUS: FIRST, LAST AND IN BETWEEN

Of course, asparagus is a vegetable and can be eaten cozying up to your main course. Alternatively, it is one of the quickest and easiest first courses—in the microwave oven—for a minimal amount of calories and a good boost of iron. Four average spears cost fifteen calories. There is another advantage to asparagus as a first course; eating them slows you down before you go on to something more substantial. Asparagus can be eaten hot or cold with a simple spritz of lemon or with one of the dressings on pages 486–499. Orange-Yogurt Dressing (page 494) is particularly good. Asparagus are low enough in calories that you can have a few first even if you plan to have a soup and a main course.

The nice thing about asparagus in the microwave oven is that they require no water unless the covering is not tightly sealed, stay bright green, retain all their vitamins, don't have to be bunched since they're not floating around, and the cooking time is by weight, not number of pieces. Further, it doesn't matter if that weight is composed of trimmed or untrimmed stalks, or fat or thin stalks.

When buying asparagus, remember that you will lose approximately half their total weight when you snap off the woody ends and peel them. For instance, one pound (450 g) from the store will give you about eight ounces (227 g) trimmed. Thick asparagus are defined as about twelve to the pound; medium, eighteen to the pound; and thin, thirty-two to the pound.

BASIC COOKING TIMES FOR ASPARAGUS

PER 4-SPEAR (2-OUNCE; 56-G) SERVING OF THIN ASPARAGUS: 15 calories; 0 milligrams cholesterol; 1 gram fat; 3 milligrams sodium. Double these figures for the commonly available medium asparagus.

Trim stalks by snapping off woody ends and peel with a vegetable peeler, if desired. Arrange 2 or 3 deep in a dish just large enough to hold them. Cover tightly with micro-wave plastic wrap or lid and cook at 100%.

¼ *pound (113.5 g)*	1 *pound (450 g)*
650- to 700-watt oven: 2 min.	650- to 700-watt oven: 4 minutes 15 sec.
400- to 500-watt oven: 4 min.	400- to 500-watt oven: Not recommended
½ *pound (227 g)*	2 *pounds (900 g)*
650- to 700-watt oven: 2 min. 30 sec.	650- to 700-watt oven: 7 min.
400- to 500-watt oven: 5 min.	400- to 500-watt oven: Not recommended

CELERY ROOT RÉMOULADE

*T*his is a classic of French cooking. If you cannot find celery root, substitute daikon radish or jicama. It makes a good first course on its own, or a small portion—say a tablespoon (20 calories)—can be served to accompany another vegetable first course, such as Carrots and Mushrooms with Cumin (page 82). At a large party, try it with Gravlax with Dill Buttermilk Sauce (page 90). It is also a perfect counterpoint for cold fish or chicken, or for grilled meats or fish.
SERVES 4

Per ½-cup (120-ml) serving: 116 calories; 0 milligrams cholesterol; 10 grams fat; 398 milligrams sodium; 1 gram protein (3% RDA); 8 grams carbohydrate

RDA: phosphorus 9%; vitamin C 13%

1 celery root (about ¾ pound; 340 g), trimmed and peeled	1 tablespoon Dijon mustard
¼ cup (60 ml) Egg White Mayonnaise (page 482), or bottled diet mayonnaise	1 tablespoon fresh lemon juice
	½ teaspoon kosher salt

1. Coarsely shred celery root in the food processor or julienne by hand.
2. Place celery root in a 10-inch (25.5-cm) quiche dish or pie plate. Cover tightly with microwave plastic wrap. Cook at 100% for 2 minutes in a 650- to 700-watt oven. Prick plastic to release steam.
3. Remove from oven and uncover. Stir in remaining ingredients and chill before serving.

To serve 8. Use 1½ pounds (680 g) celery root, ½ cup (120 ml) mayonnaise, 2 tablespoons each mustard and lemon juice and 1 teaspoon kosher salt. Prepare celery root as in Step 1. Cook as in Step 2 for 5 minutes. Finish recipe as in Step 3.

FOR 400- TO 500-WATT OVENS

To serve 4. Cook celery root as in Step 2 for 5 minutes. Finish recipe as in Step 3.

I SAY IT'S SPINACH AND I LOVE IT

It's hard to understand how spinach—especially with Popeye as a spokesper-son—got such a bad rap. Maybe it's because we recoil from being told constantly how good it is for us even though that is the truth. Badly overcooked and canned spinach are indeed rather repulsive, and very small children may have a problem with this vegetable's acidity. Adults usually love, as I do, well-prepared leaf spin-ach, Creamed Spinach (page 435) and Oriental Spinach Salad (opposite page).

It does take some time to stem and wash spinach. I find the quickest way is to run a sinkful of very cold water. As the water runs, I stem the spinach and tear off any nasty pieces and put the good stuff in the water. I swish it around and let it soak for a few minutes. Then I lift it, letting the water run through my fingers and being careful not to stir up the dirt and sand in the bottom of the sink, and put it in a colander. If it's still gritty, I just repeat the procedure in a cleaned sink with clean water.

Even though the iron in spinach is less available to the body than that in red meat, it is still plentiful. When you discover how good it tastes and looks when cooked in a microwave oven, you will find it useful not only as a vegetable but also as a component in many dishes, such as Gala Meat Loaf (page 352).

When buying spinach, figure that three quarters of a pound (340 g) of raw spinach with stems will yield about four and a half cups (1,100 ml) of stemmed, raw, loosely packed spinach, which makes 1 cup (240 ml) of cooked spinach.

BASIC COOKING TIMES FOR SPINACH

Spinach may be cooked in a microwave oven either in a container large enough to hold it, uncovered, or in a loosely knotted, microwave-safe plastic bag. The re-sults and timings differ. Spinach cooked in a bag cooks much more rapidly, needs to be drained (none of the considerable amount of water it releases evaporates) and turns a brighter green. It also has a slightly stronger flavor and scent. Slash the plastic bag with a knife. Empty the spinach out of the bag into a strainer and press out water.

Spinach that is cooked uncovered takes longer, evaporates much of the spinach water into the air and is slightly milder in flavor and darker in color. The choice is yours. In each recipe, I have suggested the method that I found preferable for the dish; but you can switch.

Spinach weights are for unstemmed, uncleaned, fresh-from-the-store spinach. Stem spinach, wash it well and then place it in the specified dish or bag. If it seems too voluminous for the dish, remember, it will drastically reduce during cooking. This equals two 10-ounce (284 g) packages of frozen spinach.

¼ pound (113.5 g), about 1½ cups (355 ml) raw. 10-inch (25.5-cm) quiche dish or pie plate, uncovered.
650- to 700-watt oven: 1 min. 30 sec.
400- to 500-watt oven: 4 min.

½ pound (227 g), about 3 cups (705 ml) raw. 10-inch (25.5-cm) quiche dish or pie plate, uncovered.
650- to 700-watt oven: 4 min.
400- to 500-watt oven: 6 min.

¾ pound (340 g), about 4½ cups (1.1 l) raw. Loosely knotted, microwave-safe plastic bag.
650- to 700-watt oven: 2 min.
400- to 500-watt oven: 4 min.

1 pound (450 g), about 6 cups (1.5 l) raw. 10-inch (25.5-cm) quiche dish or pie plate, uncovered.
650- to 700-watt oven: 5 min. 30 sec.
400- to 500-watt oven: 10 min.

1½ pounds (680 g), about 9 cups (2.2 l) raw. 9 × 13 × 2-inch (23 × 33 × 5-cm) glass or ceramic oval dish, uncovered.
650- to 700-watt oven: 7 min.
400- to 500-watt oven: 12 min.

2 pounds (900 g), about 12 cups (3 l) raw. Loosely knotted, microwave-safe plastic bag.
650- to 700-watt oven: 5 min. 30 sec.
400- to 500-watt oven: Not recommended

2½ pounds (1.15 kg), about 15 cups (3.75 l) raw. Loosely knotted, microwave-safe plastic bag.
650- to 700-watt oven: 7 min. 30 sec.
400- to 500-watt oven: Not recommended

ORIENTAL SPINACH SALAD

In a Japanese meal it is hard to know what precedes what as most dishes are usually eaten at the same time. I like to serve this slightly astringent and attractive salad at the beginning of a meal. If you have trouble finding fresh daikon radish, substitute peeled and grated plain white radish, or a slightly smaller amount of unpeeled and shredded red radish or peeled, shredded black radish. Nori, the flat black sheets of Japanese seaweed, is worth finding since it keeps virtually indefinitely.

It is easy to multiply this recipe. Timings for other quantities of spinach are given above. Multiply the other ingredients accordingly and follow all the recipe steps. Serve the salad in individual bowls with a fork or chopsticks. If chopsticks slow you down a little, by all means use them.

This salad is filling, and has lots of flavor and nutritional value—iron, vitamin C, vitamin A and calcium—and a minimum of calories. It requires a few preparatory steps; but all of them can be done ahead. *SERVES 4*

(continued)

Per ¾-cup (180-ml) serving of spinach with ½ ounce (14 g) daikon: 44 calories; 0 milligrams cholesterol; 1 gram fat; 129 milligrams sodium; 4 grams protein (10% RDA); 6 grams carbohydrate

RDA: calcium 16%; phosphorus 8%; iron 23%; 836 milligrams potassium; vitamin A 188%; thiamin 8%; riboflavin 15%; vitamin C 71%

2 ounces (56 g) daikon radish, peeled and finely minced (¼ cup; 60 ml)

2 tablespoons rice wine vinegar

2½ pounds (1.15 kg) spinach, washed and stemmed (about 2 bunches or 15 loosely packed cups; 3.75 l)

2 teaspoons sesame seeds

1 sheet nori (.04 ounce; 1 g)

1 teaspoon sesame oil

½ teaspoon tamari soy

1. Place daikon and vinegar in a small bowl and allow to marinate for at least 30 minutes or, covered and refrigerated, up to several days.

2. Place spinach leaves in a microwave-safe plastic bag. Cook at 100% for 7 minutes 30 seconds in a 650- to 700-watt oven. Prick plastic to release steam. Remove from oven and uncover. Allow to cool, then drain well.

3. Spread sesame seeds evenly on a dinner plate. Cook uncovered for 4 minutes or until lightly toasted, stirring once. Remove from oven and allow to cool.

4. Place sheet of nori in microwave and cook for 5 minutes, turning once. Remove from oven. Cut in half, then fold each half widthwise into quarters. With scissors, cut across to make strips ¼-inch (.5 cm) wide. Reserve.

5. Drain daikon, reserving liquid. Stir sesame oil and soy into daikon liquid. Pour dressing over spinach and toss to coat.

6. Divide spinach evenly among 4 small bowls. Sprinkle each bowl with a quarter of the daikon, sesame seeds and nori strips.

CAPRESE SALAD

This classic Italian summer salad comes originally from the isle of Capri and flaunts the colors—green, white and red—of the Italian flag. Made in moments, it is best when the tomatoes are ripest, the basil the most pungent. The calories are reduced by using skim-milk mozzarella. If your tomatoes aren't really ripe, you may want to add a little lemon juice. Italians believe that ripe tomatoes have enough good fruit acid on their own. For more portions, multiply the ingredients by the number of eaters, or make a big platterful for a buffet.

This salad provides a lot of calcium, vitamin A, vitamin C and phosphorus. It has a substantial amount of protein, so put it before a whole-meal soup, pasta dish or other main course with a low protein value. It also makes an excellent

light lunch accompanied by Oat Bran Wafers (page 161) and a portion of fruit, Cranberry Kissel (page 565), diet sorbet (pages 552–556) or store-bought.
SERVES 4

Per serving: 147 calories; 25 milligrams cholesterol; 9 grams fat; 205 milligrams sodium; 11 grams protein (25% RDA); 6 grams carbohydrate

RDA: calcium 33%; phosphorus 22%; iron 8%; vitamin A 25%; riboflavin 9%; vitamin C 23%

6 ounces (170 g) part-skim mozzarella, cut into 8 slices

2 medium tomatoes (each 5 ounces; 142 g), cut into 12 slices

12 large basil leaves, washed and dried

2 teaspoons olive oil

Freshly ground black pepper, to taste

1. On each of 4 salad plates arrange cheese, tomatoes and basil so that the pieces overlap slightly.

2. Pour ½ teaspoon olive oil over each serving and sprinkle with pepper, to taste.

SUMMER VEGETABLE JAMBOREE

Many of the best vegetable dishes are well cooked to blend their flavors rather than served raw. As a first course, serve this cool or at room temperature. There will be enough juices so that you can put some lettuce under it for looks. Also think of it as a topping—warm or hot—for Basic Soft Polenta (page 215) or pasta. Then it makes a delicious luncheon that even leaves enough calories for some fruit or a piece of cheese.

This attractive combination of flavors and colors can be used as a side dish. Serve about one-half cup (120 ml) per person with a simple grilled fish or meat. This dish will give you 85 percent of your vitamin C for the day. If you have leftovers, think of this as a filling for an omelette if you don't have to worry about cholesterol, or have a cup (240 ml) for lunch along with Tabbouleh (page 195), low-fat cottage cheese or a warm pita bread. You can still have a portion of fruit or a low-calorie dessert such as Tricky Chocolate Pudding (page 572).   *SERVES 6*

Per 1-cup (240-ml) serving: 109 calories; 0 milligrams cholesterol; 5 grams fat; 312 milligrams sodium; 3 grams protein (7% RDA); 15 grams carbohydrate

RDA: iron 8%; vitamin A 17%; thiamin 7%; riboflavin 6%; niacin 7%; vitamin C 85%

(continued)

10-ounce (284-g) box frozen artichoke hearts, defrosted in a sieve under warm running water, or 10 cooked fresh artichoke hearts (page 100)

8 ounces (227 g) new potatoes, cut into 1-inch (2.5-cm) cubes (about 1½ cups; 355 ml)

6 ounces (170 g) green beans, tipped, tailed and halved crosswise (about 1⅓ cups; 320 ml)

¼ cup (60 ml) water

1 medium yellow pepper (about 6 ounces; 170 g), stemmed, seeded and diced (about 1 cup; 240 ml)

1 large tomato (about 8 ounces; 227 g), seeded and diced (about 1½ cups; 360 ml)

2 tablespoons chopped fresh parsley

1 tablespoon chopped fresh tarragon

2 tablespoons olive oil

2 teaspoons tarragon vinegar

1 teaspoon kosher salt

1 tablespoon drained capers, rinsed and chopped

1. Place artichoke hearts or quartered bottoms in a 2½-quart (2.5-l) soufflé dish or casserole with a tightly fitted lid. Place potatoes on top of artichokes around the inside edge of dish and beans in the center. Pour water over all. Cover tightly with microwave plastic wrap or lid. Cook at 100% for 5 minutes in a 650- to 700-watt oven. If using plastic wrap, prick to release steam.

2. Remove from oven and uncover. Stir well and re-cover. Cook for 5 minutes. If using plastic wrap, prick.

3. Remove from oven and uncover. Add remaining ingredients and stir well to combine. Transfer to a serving dish and garnish with additional tarragon sprigs, if desired. Serve at room temperature or chilled.

FOR 400- TO 500-WATT OVENS

To serve 6. Cook vegetables as in Step 1 for 8 minutes. Continue with Step 2 and cook for 8 minutes more. Finish as in Step 3.

CARROTS AND MUSHROOMS WITH CUMIN

I have made one version or another of this over the years since a Moroccan friend served the two vegetables separately with toothpicks as a light hors d'oeuvre with wine. It can still be served that way. Be careful not to have more than about ten pieces. One at a time, they should keep you going for quite a while. As a first course, you will find these vegetables rich in taste and very satisfying. In addition, one serving has almost one and a half times the needed vitamin A. It will make only a two-calorie difference if you use the alternate dressing at the end of the recipe.

This dish can be successfully frozen in one-cup (240-ml) quantities. Defrost for 1 minute 30 seconds to 2 minutes. *SERVES 8*

Per ½-cup (120-ml) serving: 44 calories; 0 milligrams cholesterol; 1.6 grams fat; 105 milligrams sodium; 2 grams protein (5% RDA); 7 grams carbohydrate

RDA: phosphorus 10%; iron 8%; vitamin A 144%; thiamin 7%; riboflavin 23%; niacin 19%; vitamin C 10%

4 medium carrots (about ½ pound; 227 g), trimmed and peeled
2 teaspoons olive oil
1½ teaspoons ground cumin
1½ pounds (680 g) fresh mushrooms, wiped clean with a damp cloth

1½ teaspoons fresh lemon juice
½ teaspoon kosher salt
Pinch freshly ground black pepper

1. If carrots are thick, cut them in half lengthwise so that no piece is wider than ½ inch (1 cm). Cut carrots into 2-inch (5-cm) lengths.

2. In the center of a 5-quart (5-l) soufflé dish or casserole with a tightly fitted lid, combine oil and cumin to make a paste. Cook, uncovered, at 100% for 1 minute 30 seconds in a 650- to 700-watt oven.

3. Add the carrots to the cumin mixture and toss to coat. Cover tightly with microwave plastic wrap or casserole lid and cook for 7 minutes. If using plastic wrap, prick to release steam.

4. Remove from oven and uncover. Stir in the mushrooms and cook, uncovered, for 6 minutes, or until carrots and mushrooms are tender.

5. Remove from oven and stir in lemon juice, salt and pepper. Serve hot, warm or chilled.

VARIATION. To serve as a warm or chilled salad, drain and reserve the cooking liquid from the carrots and mushrooms. To ½ cup (120 ml) reserved liquid, add ½ teaspoon salt, ½ teaspoon Oriental sesame oil, 1½ teaspoons lemon juice and freshly ground black pepper to taste. Pour over carrot mixture and toss to coat.

To serve 4. Use 2 carrots, 1 teaspoon olive oil, ¾ teaspoon cumin, ¾ pound (340 g) mushrooms, ¾ teaspoon lemon juice, ¼ teaspoon salt, and freshly ground pepper to taste. Cook oil and cumin as in Step 2 for 1 minute 30 seconds. Continue with Step 3 and cook carrots for 5 minutes. Follow Step 4 and cook for 4 minutes. Finish as in Step 5.

FOR 400- TO 500-WATT OVENS

To serve 4. Cook oil and cumin as in Step 2 for 3 minutes. Continue with Step 3 and cook for 8 minutes. Stir in mushrooms and cook for 7 minutes.

TOMATO RICE SALAD

*I*nto every life leftovers fall. Instead of being tempted to eat more than you should of a yummy risotto, turn it into a light and healthy salad for an opening to the next day's dinner or as a light lunch accompanied by Salade Niçoise (page 91). Having something to look forward to may encourage you to save leftovers for a special use instead of overeating, especially when you know you will be getting one third of your vitamin C.   *SERVES 6*

Per generous ¼-cup (60-ml) serving: 99 calories; 0 milligrams cholesterol; 2 grams fat; 70 milligrams sodium; 2 grams protein (5% RDA); 18 grams carbohydrate

RDA: iron 6%; vitamin A 12%; vitamin C 35%

1½ cups (355 ml) Fat-free Risotto
  (page 187), or boiled rice
2 ounces (56 g) red pepper, stemmed,
  seeded, deribbed and diced (¼ cup;
  60 ml)

1 stalk celery (3 ounces; 85 g), peeled
  and diced (¼ cup; 60 ml)
2 tablespoons Skinny Tomato Dressing
  (page 496)
2 tablespoons water

1. Combine all ingredients in an attractive serving bowl. Serve chilled.

BELL PEPPERS AND SARDINES WITH BALSAMIC VINEGAR

I'm not at all sure that I can convince myself or you to eat the bones of the sardines; but my more robust friends assure me that they provide a rich source of calcium. They also provide the good kind of fish oil.

The sardines used in this recipe are rather small and often come ten to a can. If using large sardines—four to a can—use only half a sardine in each portion. Use leftover sardines in the Fennel Sardine Sauce (page 170) or Sardine Dip (page 521).

This first course feels right served before a pasta main course such as spaghettini with Tomato Sauce Casalinga (page 167), especially when you consider the dividends: all of your vitamin A and masses of vitamin C, as well as potassium, phosphorus, iron and calcium. It's also easy to make if you habitually keep the pepper strips on hand.   *SERVES 4*

Per 3-pepper strip and 1-sardine serving: 117 calories; 34 milligrams cholesterol; 8 grams fat; 124 milligrams sodium; 7 grams protein (15% RDA); 6 grams carbohydrate

RDA: calcium 12%; phosphorus 14%; iron 13%; vitamin A 109%; niacin 9%; vitamin C 295%

1 recipe (2-pepper version) Silky
   Pepper Strips (page 472)
4 whole sardines (each about ½ ounce;
   14 g) packed in oil, split and boned
   or left whole
4 basil sprigs

4 teaspoons oil from sardine can
4 teaspoons balsamic vinegar
1 small clove garlic, smashed, peeled
   and minced
Freshly ground black pepper, to taste

1. Prepare Silky Pepper Strips and divide among four small serving plates, arranging the strips overlapping.
2. Separate each sardine into 2 fillets. Discard the bones and wipe away any scales. Arrange 2 fillets skin side up on each plate and garnish with basil sprigs.
3. Whisk together sardine oil, vinegar and garlic in a small bowl. Drizzle over sardines and peppers and sprinkle with pepper.

THE SLENDER GREEK

I'm not so sure how Greek this salad is anymore; but a much more fattening version of it has become vastly popular in America. Those who don't need to lose weight can double it without harm, as can any happy luncher. Multiplication is no problem; just use a larger recipe of Silky Pepper Strips and more of each ingredient. If you don't need to worry about salt, you can use the traditional Greek feta cheese, which adds about fifty milligrams of sodium to each portion but decreases the calories by about ten. Similarly, the purple-black Kalamata olives that are packed in red wine vinegar have about sixty-three milligrams of sodium, and weight losers need to remember that each olive has about seven calories although it has no cholesterol and barely a hint of fat. I love them and often indulge in a few.   *SERVES 6*

Per 1-cup (240-ml) serving: 110 calories; 10 milligrams cholesterol; 7 grams fat; 254 milligrams sodium; 4 grams protein (8% RDA); 7 grams carbohydrate

RDA: iron 10%; vitamin A 92%; thiamin 6%; niacin 6%; vitamin C 222%

(continued)

1 recipe (2-pepper version) Silky
    Pepper Strips (page 472)
⅓ head iceberg lettuce, cut into ¾-inch
    (2-cm) strips (about 4 cups, 1 l)
2 ounces (56 g) Montrachet or other
    mild goat cheese, cut into ½-inch (1-
    cm) cubes

2 small tomatoes (each 4 ounces; 113.5
    g), cored and cut into sixths (about
    2 cups; 470 ml)
¼ cup (60 ml) Garlic Oregano Dressing
    (page 489)
4 anchovy fillets

1. Toss all ingredients, except anchovy fillets, together in a large mixing bowl until coated with dressing. Divide salad among four serving plates and top each with an anchovy fillet.

VEGETABLE TERRINE

*T*his layered terrine is based on an idea of Dominique Nahmias's. Her restaurant is the two-star Olympe in Paris. The luscious, bright vegetable layers make any company meal. Serve it at room temperature or chilled. Drizzle with olive oil if you're not trying too hard to lose weight or if your company isn't on a diet. Two tablespoons per portion of Fresh Tomato Purée (page 468) to use as a sauce for only ten calories is a pretty addition. I like to garnish each plate with a small sprig of mint.   *SERVES 8 AS A FIRST COURSE, 4 AS A LUNCHEON COURSE*

Per generous 1-inch (2.5-cm) slice (first-course serving): 44 calories; 0 milligrams cholesterol; 0.3 grams fat; 391 milligrams sodium; 2 grams protein (5% RDA); 10 grams carbohydrate

RDA: calcium 5%; vitamin A 22%; thiamin 9%; vitamin C 32%

1½ pounds (680 g) eggplant (2 small
    eggplants or 1 large), ends trimmed
    and cut lengthwise into ¼-inch (.5-
    cm) slices
2 teaspoons kosher salt
2 large tomatoes (each 8 ounces; 227
    g), cored and cut into ¼-inch (.5-
    cm) slices
3 stalks celery, peeled and thinly sliced
    on the diagonal (about ½ cup; 120
    ml)

Pinch freshly ground black pepper
¼ teaspoon ground cumin
2 medium zucchini (each 6–8 ounces;
    170–227 g), cut lengthwise into ¼-
    inch (.5-cm) slices (about 3 cups;
    705 ml)
24 fresh mint leaves
4 teaspoons fresh lemon juice

1. Layer eggplant slices in a $14 \times 11 \times 2$-inch ($35.5 \times 28 \times 5$-cm) dish. Sprinkle with 1 teaspoon of the salt. Cook, uncovered, at 100% for 2 minutes 30 seconds in a 650- to 700-watt oven. Remove from oven. Rinse well with cold water and pat dry.

2. Layer the vegetables in a $9 \times 5\frac{1}{2} \times 3$-inch ($23 \times 14 \times 7.5$-cm) glass or ceramic loaf pan, beginning with a layer of eggplant on the bottom, then half the tomatoes and all the celery. Sprinkle with salt, pepper and cumin. Cover with a layer of zucchini, half the mint, more salt and pepper, and half the lemon juice. Cover with another layer of eggplant and continue in this fashion until all vegetables are used, finishing with a layer of eggplant. Cook, uncovered, for 10 minutes.

3. Remove from oven. Cover with plastic wrap to prevent the terrine from drying out and let stand until cool. When cool, drain off the excess liquid and cover with a piece of cardboard cut to fit. Weight with coffee mugs, or other items of similar weight, and refrigerate overnight before serving.

EGGPLANT COOKING TIMES

In many dishes, eggplant has a meaty flavor that makes it particularly valuable in vegetarian dishes. See Stuffed Eggplant (page 456), Vegetable Couscous (page 452) and Eggplant Scaloppine (page 454). It also lends itself to many dishes in which it is cooked with other flavorful vegetables to a stewlike texture, such as the Summer Vegetable Jamboree in this chapter (page 81). Sometimes, however, we just need to cook eggplant to use in spreads, dips, sauces and other dishes. This the microwave oven does supremely well, leaving the eggplant pulp with the palest of green flesh rather than a nasty beige.

About 7 ounces (200 g) raw eggplant yields ½ cup (120 ml) cooked purée.

PER ½-CUP (120-ML) SERVING: 13 calories; 0 milligrams cholesterol; less than 1 gram fat; 2 milligrams sodium; less than 1 gram protein; 3 grams carbohydrate

To cook eggplant, prick each several times with the tip of a knife. Place whole on a double thickness of paper toweling and cook at 100% for the times indicated below. The weights given are for whole eggplant of the specified size. The eggplants will look like collapsed balloons when cooked. Old winter eggplants may sometimes take a little longer to cook. If they still look plump at the end of the specified cooking time, continue cooking about two minutes longer.

½ pound (227 g)
650- to 700-watt oven: 8 min.
400- to 500-watt oven: 11 min.

1 pound (450 g)
650- to 700-watt oven: 12 min.
400- to 500-watt oven: 16 min.

1½ pounds (680 g)
650- to 700-watt oven: 15 min.
400- to 500-watt oven: 20 min.

2 pounds (900 g)
650- to 700-watt oven: 19 min.
400- to 500-watt oven: 28 min.

2½ pounds (1.15 kg)
650- to 700-watt oven: 22 min.
400- to 500-watt oven: 35 min.

EGGPLANT PURÉE WITH TOMATO AND GREEN PEPPER

*T*his is one of my favorite first courses, with 40 percent of my daily vitamin C. I like to keep it on hand in the refrigerator, especially since one-third cup (80 ml), at about thirty calories, makes a quick sauce for each half-cup (120 ml) of cooked pasta (dry: 1 ounce; 28 grams); another good first course that can be multiplied for a main course. Remember that each half-cup (120 ml) of cooked pasta will add ninety-six calories. As a pasta-less first course, I add a wedge of lemon and put the whole thing on a lettuce leaf. Consider a double portion—one cup (240 ml)—of this for lunch along with a piece of fruit, some cheese and two Oat Bran Wafers (page 161).   *SERVES 4*

Per ½-cup (120-ml) serving: 48 calories; 0 milligrams cholesterol; 0.28 grams fat; 130 milligrams sodium; 2 grams protein (4% RDA); 11 grams carbohydrate

RDA: vitamin A 10%; thiamin 9%; vitamin C 42%

1¼ pounds (570 g) eggplant
2 ounces (56 g) finely diced, seeded
   green bell pepper (about ½ cup; 120
   ml)
1 small onion (2 ounces; 56 g), finely
   diced (about ½ cup; 120 ml)
4 ounces (113.5 g) drained, finely diced
   canned Italian plum tomatoes,
   (about ½ cup; 120 ml)

1 tablespoon tomato paste
½ clove garlic
¼ teaspoon kosher salt
Pinch freshly ground black pepper

1. Prick eggplant several times with the tip of a sharp knife. Set on a double thickness of paper towels and cook at 100% for 20 minutes in a 650- to 700-watt oven. Remove from oven and let cool to room temperature.

2. Mix pepper, onion, tomatoes, tomato paste and garlic in a 1-quart (1-l) soufflé dish or casserole with a tightly fitted lid. Cover tightly with microwave plastic wrap or casserole lid. Cook for 4 minutes. If using plastic wrap, prick to release steam. Remove from oven, uncover and let cool.

3. Remove stem from eggplant and cut in half lengthwise. Scoop out pulp and shred with two forks or give a few quick pulses in a food processor. Place in a mixing bowl. Add pepper mixture, salt and pepper and whisk until thoroughly blended. Serve at room temperature.

To serve 8. Use 2½ pounds (1.15 kg) eggplant, 1 cup (240 ml) finely diced green bell pepper, 1 cup (240 ml) finely diced onion, 1 cup (240 ml) finely diced canned plum tomatoes, 2 tablespoons tomato paste, 1 clove garlic, ½ teaspoon kosher salt and a generous pinch freshly ground black pepper. Cook eggplants as in Step 1 for 22 minutes. In Step 2, cook in a 2½-quart (2.5-l) soufflé dish for 6 minutes.

FOR 400- TO 500-WATT OVENS

To serve 4. Cook eggplant for 30 minutes. In Step 2, cook for 6 minutes.

To serve 8. Cook eggplant for 35 minutes. In Step 2, cook for 8 minutes.

EGGPLANT PURÉE WITH LEMON AND CHIVES

*E*ggplant is a revelation in the microwave oven. It is quick and keeps a delightful pale-green color. Think of this as a dip and serve it with some low-calorie raw vegetables. For four calories you can have one-quarter cup of sliced cucumber, for twelve calories one-half cup of broccoli florets and for six calories a stalk of celery. This is a good solution for a cocktail party; but put your amount of the dip and vegetables on a plate so you don't cheat by going back to the bowl too often.

As with the eggplant dish below, you can vary the amount by following the eggplant cooking chart on page 87 and multiplying or dividing the other ingredients accordingly.   *SERVES 6 AS A FIRST COURSE, 12–16 AS A DIP AT A BUFFET OR WITH COCKTAILS*

Per ½-cup (120-ml) serving: 82 calories; 0 milligrams cholesterol; 5 grams fat; 127 milligrams sodium; 1.8 grams protein (4% RDA); 15 grams carbohydrate

RDA: calcium 9%; phosphorus 8%; iron 7%; thiamin 13%; vitamin C 12%

2½ pounds (1.15 kg) eggplant
2 tablespoons olive oil
2 tablespoons fresh lemon juice
2 small cloves garlic, smashed, peeled
   and minced

½ teaspoon kosher salt
2 tablespoons minced fresh chives

1. Prick eggplants several times with the tip of a sharp knife. Set on a double thickness of paper towels and cook at 100% for 22 minutes in a 650- to 700-watt oven. Remove from oven and let cool to room temperature.

2. Remove stem and cut the eggplant in half lengthwise. Scoop out pulp and place in a mixing bowl. Add remaining ingredients and whisk until well blended. If the texture seems coarse, process in a food processor for a few seconds. Serve cool.

FOR 400- TO 500-WATT OVENS

To serve 6. Cook for 35 minutes.

GRAVLAX WITH DILL BUTTERMILK SAUCE

*T*his is a dish to make for a party either as an hors d'oeuvre—serve with Oat Bran Wafers (page 161)—or as a first course. If you have some left, have a double portion for lunch along with a Watercress, Fennel and Romaine Salad with Pernod Dressing (page 405) or a simpler green salad. For dinner on a hot night, have four ounces (113.5 g) of gravlax as a main course and begin with a filling soup such as Summer Borscht (page 143). Add a small hot boiled potato to eat with the gravlax and its sauce—very Scandinavian. Drink a glass of light beer if you want.   *SERVES 20*

Per 1-ounce (28-g) serving: 55 calories; 16 milligrams cholesterol; 2 grams fat; 587 milligrams sodium; 6 grams protein (14% RDA); 2 grams carbohydrate

RDA: vitamin A 11%; riboflavin 8%; niacin 12%; vitamin C 9%

FOR THE GRAVLAX

2 tablespoons coarsely chopped fresh
    dill
2 tablespoons kosher salt
½ teaspoon freshly ground black
    pepper
1 teaspoon granulated sugar
1¼ pounds (570 g) salmon fillets—flat
    pieces—in 2 equal pieces, skin left
    on

FOR THE SAUCE

¼ cup (60 ml) Dijon mustard
¾ cup (180 ml) buttermilk
¼ cup (60 ml) chopped fresh dill
¾ teaspoon granulated sugar

FOR PLATED FIRST COURSE

1 ounce (28 g) field salad, washed, per
    portion

1. Start the gravlax 2 days before it will be served. Combine dill, salt, pepper and sugar in a bowl. With tweezers, a small pair of pliers or your fingernails, carefully remove all pin bones from the salmon fillets. Rub mixture on both sides

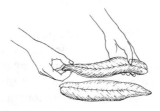

*Sandwich fillets with the sides that had the skin out,
topping thin and thick ends and
reversing positions so that a belly flap tops a thick long edge.*

of the salmon and sandwich the two pieces together with skin sides out. Place in a 9-inch (23-cm) pie plate or quiche dish and cover with plastic wrap. Weight with cans or similarly weighted item and place in the refrigerator for 2 days.

2. To serve, stir together sauce ingredients. Place 1 ounce (28 g) field lettuce on a salad plate with 1 ounce (28 g) thinly sliced gravlax. Spoon over 2 teaspoons sauce per person.

SALADE NIÇOISE

In Nice or anyplace nearby on the French Riviera, you can start a serious argument by simply listing what you believe to be the ingredients of a salade Niçoise. I have seen recipes that include cooked or raw artichokes. I have heard people make passionate repudiations of tomatoes. The inclusion of lettuce is pretty generally considered inauthentic. I have concluded that no recipe can be called right and most versions are acceptable.

As a first course have this before a simple fish dish like Scrod with Broccoli (page 239) or an ample pasta like Lean Bolognese (page 174). Alternatively precede it with Riviera Fish Soup (page 138) and you'll really think you are in the south of France.   *SERVES 6 AS A FIRST COURSE, 4 AS A MAIN COURSE*

Per 1½-cups (355-ml) first-course serving, including lettuce: 214 calories; 107 milligrams cholesterol; 12 grams fat; 168 milligrams sodium; 15 grams protein (34% RDA); 13 grams carbohydrate

RDA: calcium 5%; phosphorus 15%; iron 15%; vitamin A 25%; thiamin 6%; riboflavin 6%; niacin 6%; vitamin C 26%

8 ounces (227 g) green beans, tipped, tailed and halved crosswise (about 1½ cups; 355 ml)

3 small new potatoes (each 3 ounces; 85 g), washed and cut into 1-inch (2.5-cm) cubes (about 1½ cups; 355 ml)

8 ounces (227 g) tomato, cored and cut into 1-inch (2.5-cm) cubes (about 1¼ cups; 300 ml)

2 ounces (56 g) red onion, peeled and thinly sliced (about ⅔ cup; 160 ml)

8 ounces (227 g) water-packed canned tuna, flaked with a fork

2 tablespoons red wine vinegar

4 tablespoons olive oil

6 ounces (170 g) assorted lettuce (4 cups; 1 l)

2 hard-boiled eggs, quartered

1. Place green beans in a 1½-quart (1.5-l) soufflé dish or casserole with a tightly fitted lid. Cover tightly with microwave plastic wrap or casserole lid. Cook at 100% for 5 minutes, or until tender, in a 650- to 700-watt oven. If using plastic wrap, prick to release steam.

(continued)

Salade Niçoise (cont.)

2. Remove from oven and uncover. Rinse beans in cold water and drain. Place in a large bowl and reserve. Place potatoes in soufflé dish or casserole. Cover with cold water and cover tightly. Cook for 7 minutes or until tender. Prick plastic wrap.

3. Remove from oven and uncover. Rinse potatoes in cold water. Drain and add to green beans. Add tomato, onion and tuna to bowl. Stir together vinegar and oil, pour over salad and stir to combine. Place lettuce in a large serving bowl. Arrange salad on top of greens and place quartered eggs around the outside. Serve at room temperature.

FOR 400- TO 500-WATT OVENS

To serve 6. Cook beans as in Step 1 for 8 minutes. In Step 2, cook potatoes for 12 minutes. Finish as in Step 3.

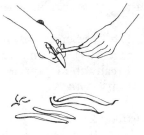

Tip and tail with a knife.

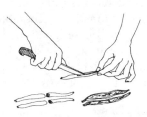

Halving green beans lengthwise or crosswise

MARINATED SHRIMP, MUSSEL AND ARTICHOKE SALAD

*T*his picture-perfect pink and white and green dish can start any party, find a home on any buffet. Do be careful about what you eat at lunch since this contains 27 percent of your day's protein.
SERVES 8 AS A FIRST COURSE, 16 AS PART OF A BUFFET

Per 1-cup (240-ml) serving: 106 calories; 59 milligrams cholesterol; 3 grams fat; 425 milligrams sodium; 12 grams protein (27% RDA); 9 grams carbohydrate

RDA: calcium 7%; phosphorus 25%; iron 19%; niacin 10%; vitamin C 15%

12 ounces (340 g) medium shrimp, shelled and deveined

18 large mussels (about 1½ pounds; 680 g), scrubbed and debearded

3 ribs celery (about 6 ounces; 170 g), trimmed, peeled and cut into ¼-inch (.5-cm) slices (about 1 cup; 240 ml)

3 ounces (85 g) onion, quartered and thinly sliced (about ½ cup; 120 ml)

2 boxes (each 10 ounces; 284 g) frozen artichoke hearts, defrosted in a sieve under warm running water

1 tablespoon olive oil

2 tablespoons fresh lemon juice

Scant teaspoon kosher salt

Pinch freshly ground black pepper

Lettuce leaves

1. Place shrimp in a 1½-quart (1.5-l) soufflé dish or casserole with a tightly fitted lid. Cover tightly with microwave plastic wrap or lid. Cook at 100% for 2 minutes 30 seconds, or until cooked through, in a 650- to 700-watt oven. If using plastic wrap, prick to release steam. Remove from oven and uncover.

2. Arrange mussels, hinge end down, in a 2-quart (2-l) soufflé dish or casserole. Cover and cook for 5 minutes, or until all mussels are open. If using plastic wrap, prick.

3. Remove from oven and uncover. When cool enough to handle, remove mussel meat from shells and reserve meat. Strain the juices through a cloth-lined sieve and reserve 4 tablespoons.

4. Combine shrimp, mussels, celery, onions and artichoke hearts in a bowl.

5. Whisk together remaining ingredients and mussel juice and pour over salad. Toss well to combine. Cover loosely and refrigerate.

FOR 400- TO 500-WATT OVENS

To serve 8. Cook shrimp as in Step 1 for 5 minutes. In Step 2, cook mussels for 9 minutes.

CORAL SCALLOP TERRINE

*T*his brilliantly colored terrine is the perfect start for a festive dinner. No one will believe that it is diet food and easy to make. For even more color, serve on individual plates that have been lightly coated with two tablespoons Rich Watercress Sauce for just twenty-six extra calories. Top with a sprig of watercress where the two slices of terrine come together. You can follow the terrine with a virtually vitaminless, but hearty, meat dish such as Jambalaya (page 323), since the terrine provides scads of vitamin C and a day's worth of vitamin A—that's without the sauce.

Remember, this must be made ahead, up to two days, but then you have nothing to do just before dinner except assemble it on plates.   *SERVES 8*

(continued)

Per 2½-inch (1-cm) slice serving: 74 calories; 19 milligrams cholesterol; 2 grams fat; 211 milligrams sodium; 6 grams protein (18% RDA); 6 grams carbohydrate

RDA: phosphorus 12%; iron 7%; vitamin A 107%; vitamin C 295%

2 pounds (900 g) red bell peppers,
    stemmed, seeded and deribbed
¾ pound (340 g) sea scallops, small
    external muscle removed, rinsed
2 tablespoons heavy cream

¾ teaspoon kosher salt
1 recipe Rich Watercress Sauce (page
    506), optional
8 sprigs watercress, optional

1. Place peppers in a 2½-quart (2.5-l) soufflé dish or casserole with a tightly fitted lid. Cover securely with microwave plastic wrap or casserole lid. Cook at 100% for 15 minutes in a 650- to 700-watt oven. If using plastic, prick to release steam.

2. Remove from oven and uncover. Pass peppers through the medium disc of a food mill and reserve.

3. Purée scallops in a food processor. Add reserved red pepper purée, cream and salt. Process until well combined. Scrape mixture into a 9 × 5 × 3-inch (23 × 12.5 × 7.5-cm) glass or ceramic loaf pan, preferably with a release coating, and smooth the top. Cook, tightly covered, for 5 minutes. Prick plastic wrap.

4. Remove from oven. Let stand until cool and refrigerate until chilled, preferably overnight. To unmold, uncover; drain off any liquid that has accumulated in the bottom of the dish (there will be quite a bit). Unmold onto a serving platter; wipe up any additional liquid with paper toweling. This is a fragile mixture. Handle carefully.

5. To serve as a first course, make 16 ½-inch (1-cm) crosswise slices. Put 2 tablespoons Rich Watercress Sauce on each of 8 first-course plates. Lay 2 slices of terrine next to each other on the sauce. Garnish with watercress, if desired.

FOR 400- TO 500-WATT OVENS

To serve 8. Cook peppers as in Step 2 for 22 minutes. Continue with Step 3. In Step 4, cook terrine for 7 minutes. Finish as in Step 5.

Warm and Hot First Courses

Oddly enough, warm and hot first courses often require less forethought than cold ones. They don't have to be made ahead, and with a microwave oven they can be made quickly. A warm beginning to a meal can seem especially welcoming. Most of the dishes that follow take so little time, it isn't worth thinking about making them ahead and then reheating. Some can easily be made ahead and then reheated. Where that works well I have given the proper method. Unlike the meat and chicken dishes or the soups, most of these should not be frozen. The big exception to this rule is the pasta sauces. I tend to make them in quantity, freeze them in small amounts and then defrost for about five minutes toward the end of the pasta-cooking time.

From the dieter's point of view, these can be used to make the virtually ideal first course rich in flavor and poor in calories and cholesterol. They are also blessedly quick. If your main course doesn't have many calories or a starch, consider serving the mushrooms over a slice of whole wheat toast or one-half cup (120 ml) of Basic Soft Polenta (page 215). That way, you will only add about forty-seven calories per person.

Dried shiitake or Japanese or Chinese mushrooms are more available than the fresh; but the fresh yield more sauce. That is why I have given recipes for both kinds.

DRIED SHIITAKE WITH PARSLEY

One advantage of the dried shiitake, besides availability, is that they can be easily cooked in the microwave oven in larger quantities than the fresh. They come in cellophane packages holding one ounce (28 g). The sizes may vary so you will have to eyeball the servings. When cooking, if some of the mushrooms are much larger than others, put them toward the edge of the cooking dish.   *SERVES 8*

Per ½-cup (240-ml) serving: 51 calories; 0 milligrams cholesterol; 0 grams fat; 173 milligrams sodium; 2 grams protein (4% RDA); 12 grams carbohydrate

RDA: riboflavin 11%; niacin 11%; vitamin C 9%

4 ounces (113.5 g) dried shiitake mushrooms	4 teaspoons tamari soy
	Generous pinch freshly ground pepper
1⅓ cups (320 ml) water	½ cup (120 ml) chopped parsley,
4 tablespoons rice wine vinegar	packed
8 cloves garlic, smashed, peeled and sliced	

1. Rinse mushrooms thoroughly and remove stems.
2. Combine water, vinegar, garlic, tamari and pepper in a 13×9×2-inch (33×23×5-cm) oval dish. Cover tightly with microwave plastic wrap. Cook at 100% for 3 minutes in a 650- to 700-watt oven. Prick plastic to release steam.
3. Remove from oven and uncover. Layer mushrooms in dish and cover tightly. Cook for 6 minutes, stirring twice.
4. Stir in parsley and serve hot.

To serve 2. Use 1 ounce (28 g) mushrooms, ⅓ cup (80 ml) water, 1 tablespoon rice wine vinegar, 2 cloves garlic, 1 teaspoon tamari soy, a tiny pinch of pepper

(continued)

Dried Shiitake with Parsley (cont.)

and 2 tablespoons chopped parsley. Follow Step 1. In Step 2, combine ingredients in a 10-inch (25.5-cm) quiche dish or pie plate and cook, covered, for 2 minutes. In Step 3, add mushrooms and cook 2 minutes, stirring once. Finish as in Step 4.

FOR 400- TO 500-WATT OVENS

To serve 8. Cook liquids as in Step 2 for 6 minutes. In Step 3, add mushrooms and cook for 10 minutes, turning mushrooms twice. Finish as in Step 4.

To serve 2. Cook liquids as in Step 2 for 4 minutes. In Step 3, add mushrooms and cook for 3 minutes, turning once. Finish as in Step 4.

FRESH SHIITAKE SAUTÉ

*F*resh shiitake are a great treat when available, and you will get all the good sauce that the mushrooms provide. Because of the way they are farmed, they are seldom dirty and will only require the removal of their woody stems and being wiped with your palm.   *SERVES 2*

Per 3-mushroom serving: 49 calories; 0 milligrams cholesterol; 0.15 gram fat; 371 milligrams sodium; 2 grams protein (4% RDA); 12 grams carbohydrate

RDA: riboflavin 10%; niacin 10%; vitamin C 14%

¼ cup (60 ml) finely chopped fresh
   parsley
¼ cup (60 ml) water
3 cloves garlic, smashed, peeled and
   sliced
6 large fresh shiitake mushroom caps,
   stemmed, each 3–4 inches (7–10
   cm) in diameter (each 2–3 ounces;
   56–85 g)

½ teaspoon kosher salt
Pinch freshly ground black pepper

1. Combine parsley, water and garlic in a 14 × 11 × 2-inch (35.5 × 28 × 5-cm) dish. Cover tightly with microwave plastic wrap. Cook at 100% for 2 minutes in a 650- to 700-watt oven. Prick plastic to release steam.
2. Remove from oven and uncover. Arrange mushrooms in dish, stem side down, without touching one another. Sprinkle with salt and pepper. Cover and cook for 5 minutes. Prick plastic to release steam.
3. Remove from oven, uncover and serve hot.

To serve 1. Use 1½ tablespoons parsley, 1½ tablespoons water, 2 cloves garlic, 3 large shiitake mushroom caps, scant ¼ teaspoon kosher salt and a small pinch freshly ground pepper. Combine parsley, water and garlic in a 10-inch (25.5-cm) quiche dish or pie plate. Cook as in Step 1 for 1 minute 30 seconds. Finish as in Steps 2 and 3, cooking for 3 minutes 30 seconds.

FOR 400- TO 500-WATT OVENS

To serve 1. Cook parsley, water and garlic for 3 minutes. Add mushrooms and cook for 5 minutes.

HERB-STUFFED MUSSELS

*T*his is served lukewarm, not hot, so you can make it just before you want to eat or before your guests come. Hazelnut oil is costly; little is used and it adds so much flavor for no cholesterol that it may be worth the indulgence. Walnut, peanut or Oriental sesame oil could be substituted.

We don't make mussels enough in this country, which is a shame. They are relatively inexpensive and rich in minerals such as iron, phosphorus and potassium. I think the problem has always been that they were difficult to clean. These days they are being farmed in Maine and come very clean if slightly more expensive. I find that the simplest way to clean them is with a plastic pot scrubber under cold running water. Store in the refrigerator, but not in water, which dilutes the flavor.

Another good thing about mussels for the dieter is that removing each one from its shell—often with a very small fork—and then licking the remaining good flavors from the shell takes time and provides satisfaction. The spinach provides iron and more than half of your vitamin A. *SERVES 4*

Per first-course (5-mussel) serving: 85 calories; 17 milligrams cholesterol; 4 grams fat; 202 milligrams sodium; 8 grams protein (19% RDA); 5 grams carbohydrate

RDA: calcium 6%; phosphorus 14%; iron 20%; vitamin A 55%; vitamin C 20%

½ pound (220 g) spinach, stemmed
   and washed (about 3 cups [705 ml]
   lightly packed leaves)
2 tablespoons chopped fresh tarragon

2 shallots, peeled and minced
2 pounds (900 g) mussels, scrubbed
   and debearded
2 teaspoons hazelnut or vegetable oil

1. Place spinach, tarragon and shallots in the bottom of a 2½-quart (2.5-l) soufflé dish or casserole with a tightly fitted lid. Arrange mussels, hinge end down, on top of spinach and cover tightly with microwave plastic wrap or lid.

(continued)

Cook at 100% for 7 minutes, or until all mussels open, in a 650- to 700-watt oven. If using plastic, prick to release steam.

2. Remove from oven and uncover. Transfer mussels to another bowl and reserve. Place spinach mixture in a food processor. Add oil and process until smooth.

3. Remove mussels from shells and replace each in half a shell. Spoon 1 tablespoon of sauce over each mussel and serve.

To serve 2. Use ¼ pound (113.5 g) spinach, 1 tablespoon chopped fresh tarragon, 1 minced shallot, 1 pound (450 g) mussels and 1 teaspoon oil. Cook as in Step 1 in a 1½-quart (1.5-l) soufflé dish for 3 minutes. Finish recipe as in Steps 2 and 3.

FOR 400- TO 500-WATT OVENS

To serve 4. Cook for 11 minutes.

To serve 2. Cook for 6 minutes.

STUFFED PEPPERS

*T*his is a pretty dish with the bright red pepper shell holding a green speckled stuffing. It is vegetarian and filling as well. A double portion makes a light main course at dinner. A single serving is the heart of a satisfying lunch. The peppers are meant to be served hot, but are also good cold, making ideal leftovers. If you prefer, heat your leftovers at home or at the office in a microwave oven for about three minutes. Add one-half cup (120 ml) of Lentil Salad (page 209) and some greens for a healthy, satisfying meal that is rich in vitamins B, C and A.
SERVES 4 AS A FIRST COURSE, 2 AS A MAIN COURSE

Per first-course (½-pepper) serving: 142 calories; 0 milligrams cholesterol; 4 grams fat; 6 milligrams sodium; 4 grams protein (9% RDA); 46 grams carbohydrate

RDA: calcium 7%; phosphorus 18%; iron 18%; vitamin A 95%; thiamin 35%; riboflavin 26%; niacin 26%; vitamin C 263%

¼ pound (113.5 g) domestic mushrooms, wiped clean and cut into quarters
½ pound (227 g) onions, peeled and cut into quarters
2 cloves garlic, smashed and peeled
1 tablespoon olive oil
½ cup (120 ml) packed, coarsely chopped watercress
½ cup (120 ml) pastina (see page 31)
3 tablespoons water
2 red bell peppers, cut in half crosswise and seeded
Kosher salt, to taste
Freshly ground black pepper, to taste

1. Place mushrooms, onions and garlic in a food processor. Process until finely chopped.

2. Place oil in a 9-inch (23-cm) pie plate or quiche dish and add chopped vegetables. Cook, uncovered, at 100% for 3 minutes in a 650- to 700-watt oven.

3. Stir in watercress, pastina and 1 tablespoon of the water. Fill peppers with stuffing, mounding lightly.

4. Arrange peppers, evenly spaced, around the inside edge of the pie plate or quiche dish. Pour remaining water in bottom of dish. Sprinkle with salt and pepper, if desired. Cover tightly with microwave plastic wrap and cook for 10 minutes. Prick plastic to release steam.

5. Remove from oven and serve hot.

To serve 2. Use 2 ounces (56 g) mushrooms, ¼ pound (113.5 g) onions, 1 clove garlic, ½ tablespoon olive oil, ¼ cup (60 ml) packed chopped watercress, ¼ cup (60 ml) pastina, 1 tablespoon plus 2 teaspoons water and 1 red bell pepper. Proceed as in Steps 1 and 2, cooking vegetables for 2 minutes. Add remaining ingredients and 1 tablespoon of the water. Fill peppers, mounding lightly. Finish as in Step 4 and cook for 5–6 minutes.

FOR 400- TO 500-WATT OVENS

To serve 4. Cook as in Step 2 for 5 minutes. In Step 4, cook for 15 minutes.

To serve 2. Cook as in Step 2 for 2 minutes 30 seconds. In Step 4, cook for 5 minutes 30 seconds to 6 minutes.

BASIC INSTRUCTIONS FOR COOKING ARTICHOKES

Artichokes are one of the dieter's best friends even though they have a fairly high calorie count. Make one and eat it warm or cold at the beginning of a meal. By the time the leaves are peeled and gnawed one by one after a light dip in a fragrant bath and the bottom is carefully exposed by scraping away the hairy choke and eaten in small, sauce-sprinkled pieces, I often find that my appetite has diminished mightily. Balsamic vinegar makes a virtually noncaloric dip, or you can choose instead two tablespoons of any of the dressings on page 392.

Keep cooked artichokes on hand and eat half of one as a satisfying snack instead of a more quickly consumed fruit. The cooked and cleaned bottoms can be kept on hand covered with water to make the base of several good dishes. While canned artichoke bottoms can be bought, they are expensive; I find that they have a nasty taste from the can and they are invariably salt-laden. Besides, artichokes cooked in the microwave oven are greener and less water-logged than those cooked any other way.

PER GLOBE ARTICHOKE: 166 calories; 0 milligrams cholesterol; 1 gram fat; 260 milligrams sodium; 8 grams protein

With a serrated knife, cut off the top 1½ inches (4 cm) of each artichoke. Cut or break off the stems flush with the bottoms and remove the outer two rows of leaves. Rub cut surfaces with a lemon half as you work. Place trimmed artichokes in a container just large enough to hold them in a nontouching circle. Cover tightly with microwave plastic wrap, or sprinkle with one tablespoon of water per artichoke and cover with a tightly fitting lid. It is better to cook artichokes on a carrousel (see page 27).

LARGE (GLOBE) ARTICHOKES: 8 to 12 ounces (227 to 340 g) each; about 1½ to 2 per pound (450 g).

One artichoke
650- to 700-watt oven: 7 min.
400- to 500-watt oven: 12 min.

Four artichokes
650- to 700-watt oven: 15 min.
400- to 500-watt oven: Not recommended

Two artichokes
650- to 700-watt oven: 10 min.
400- to 500-watt oven: 20 min. on a
  wind-up carousel

Six artichokes
650- to 700-watt oven: 19 min.
400- to 500-watt oven: Not recommended

ARTICHOKE BOTTOMS STUFFED WITH DUXELLES

*T*his is a delicious reward for preparing ahead staples such as cooked artichoke bottoms and duxelles. Even if you haven't, the microwave oven makes short work of the whole thing and provides you with a gala first course. If you are making this for a party, prepare the recipe ahead through Step 3. If the stuffed artichoke hearts have been refrigerated, cook for three minutes in Step 4.

By using the times given for artichoke cooking above, it is easy to multiply or divide this recipe. Allow one and a half tablespoons of duxelles and one and a half teaspoons of Parmesan cheese per serving.   *SERVES 4*

Per artichoke-heart serving: 86 calories; 2 milligrams cholesterol; 1 gram fat; 251 milligrams sodium; 5 grams protein (11% RDA); 16.6 grams carbohydrate

RDA: calcium 11%; phosphorus 15%; iron 14%; vitamin A 9%; thiamin 9%; riboflavin 12%; niacin 11%; vitamin C 31%

4 artichokes (each 10 ounces; 284 g)
1 teaspoon fresh lemon juice
½ cup (120 ml) Diet Duxelles (page 477)

2 tablespoons freshly grated Parmesan cheese

1. Cut or break off each artichoke stem flush with the bottom of the artichoke and remove 1½ inches (4 cm) from the tps. Rub cut surfaces with lemon juice. Place in a nontouching circle in a dish just large enough to hold them, such as a 2½-quart (2.5-l) soufflé dish. Sprinkle with 4 tablespoons water if covering with a lid, or cover tightly with microwave plastic wrap. Cook at 100% for 15 minutes in a 650- to 700-watt oven. If using plastic wrap, prick to release steam.

2. Remove from oven and uncover. Let stand until cool enough to handle. Remove outer leaves and scrape out the choke with a spoon.

3. Combine duxelles and cheese in a small bowl. Divide mixture among artichoke bottoms. Place in a circle on a dinner plate or 10-inch (25-cm) quiche dish. Cover.

4. Cook for 1 minute. Prick plastic wrap if using. Remove from oven and uncover. Serve on a bed of watercress tossed with balsamic vinegar, if desired.

FOR 400- TO 500-WATT OVENS

To serve 2. Use 2 globe artichokes, ¼ cup (60 ml) duxelles, and 1 tablespoon Parmesan cheese. Follow Step 1 and cook artichokes for 18 minutes. Continue with Step 2. Finish as in Step 4, cooking duxelles and artichoke hearts for 2 minutes.

Place four artichokes inside the rim of a 2½-quart (2.5-l) soufflé dish or casserole.

To prepare artichoke bottoms, pull off leaves and scrape out choke with a small spoon.

ARTICHOKES BARIGOULE

As you look through this book, you may guess that I have a passion for the cooking of the south of France. This is another dish that has a myriad of variations in the area. This particular version was inspired by Alain Ducasse at the Louis XV in Monaco. When he made it, it was richer and I don't think he was concerned with the delightful news that a serving provides three times the vitamin A you need for a day. Don't be surprised that the artichokes take longer to cook than when cooked alone; it's all those other vegetables.   *SERVES 4*

Per scant 1-cup (240-ml) serving: 88 calories; 0 milligrams cholesterol; 1 gram fat; 147 milligrams sodium; 2 grams protein (5% RDA); 18 grams carbohydrate

RDA: calcium 7%; phosphorus 7%; iron 7%; vitamin A 305%; vitamin C 30%

4 large globe artichokes (each about 12 ounces; 340 g)
1 lemon, cut in half
3 medium carrots (each 4 ounces; 113.5 g), peeled, trimmed and diagonally sliced ¼-inch (.5-cm) thick (about 2¼ cups; 530 ml)
2 cups (470 ml) frozen white pearl onions, defrosted in a sieve under warm running water

2 tablespoons Basic Chicken Broth (page 460), or unsalted or regular canned chicken broth
2 teaspoons balsamic vinegar
2 cloves garlic, smashed, peeled and finely sliced
1 teaspoon olive oil
¼ teaspoon kosher salt
Freshly ground black pepper, to taste

1. With a serrated knife, cut off the top 1½ inches (4 cm) of each artichoke. Cut or break off the stems flush with the bottoms and remove the outer two rows of leaves. Rub cut surfaces with a lemon half as you work.

2. Arrange the carrot slices in a ring around the bottom of a 5-quart (5-l) soufflé dish or casserole with a tightly fitted lid. Place onions in the center and set artichokes stem side down on top of the vegetables. Cover tightly with microwave plastic wrap or casserole lid. Cook at 100% for 25 minutes in a 650- to 700-watt oven, or until tender. If using plastic wrap, prick to release steam.

3. Remove from oven and let stand 2 minutes. Uncover and let stand until the artichokes are cool enough to handle.

4. Pull off and discard the leaves. Scrape out the choke with a spoon and trim the bottoms. Cut artichoke bottoms in half and then into wedges no thicker than ½ inch (1 cm) at their widest point.

5. Drain liquid from vegetables in dish. Add artichoke wedges and stir in remaining ingredients.

6. Cover and cook for 4 minutes. Prick plastic to release steam. Remove from oven and let stand 1 minute, then uncover. Serve hot, warm or cool.

One of the nicest ways of starting dinner or a party is with a light individual vegetable mold often held together like a custard and served warm. Usually this means lots of cream and egg yolks and a mildly dangerous, but certainly sloppy, hot water bath. These versions need no messy hot water bath, nor do they use egg yolks or heavy cream. You will probably find them so easy that you will not save them for special occasions. That's why there is a version for four as well as one for eight—as at a dinner party. Think of them not only when you are starting from scratch but also when you find yourself with some leftover cooked vegetables.

"Timbale" and "ramekin" are two very confusing words for most cooks. They are the names of cooking-container shapes most often used to cook foods that will retain the shape of the container when unmolded. Timbales are usually shaped like cones whose tips have been flattened. Most timbales are small so that their contents make an individual portion of a side course or a first course. Sadly, timbale molds are generally metal and are unsuitable for use in a microwave oven. I have substituted small custard cups and demitasse cups quite happily and gotten prettily shaped portions. More conventional cooking containers would come under the vague heading of ramekins. Ramekins are small soufflé dishes made either of porcelain with a square corner where the edge meets the bottom or of glass with a rounded profile. Both of these are often used in conventional cooking to make individual soufflés. In the three recipes that follow, it is not overwhelmingly important which shape you use, although I prefer the more cone-shaped look. What is important is that the fluid contents be about 4 ounces (120 ml). The ramekins or miniature soufflés should be about 3½ inches (9 cm) in diameter by about 1½ inches (4 cm) high. You don't want a pancake.

Once you have the container, the next thing to know is that these timbales all use a purée of cooked vegetables. Instead of using a one-vegetable mixture for each timbale, layer different kinds as long as the flavors and colors go well together.

Timbales go well with a light sauce made with another vegetable purée. It can be as easy as Fresh Tomato Purée (page 468), or, only slightly fancier, Tomato Sauce Casalinga (page 167). Ruby Beet Sauce (page 503) goes well with Cauliflower Timbale, Mushroom Sauce (page 169) or Fennel Sauce (page 501) with Carrot, and try Red Pepper Purée (page 500) with the Broccoli Timbale. Mix and match as you wish, knowing that you will be having lots of flavor, color and vitamins with few calories.

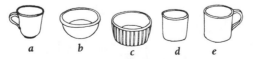

Demitasse cups, glass bowls, ramekins and timbale molds, each with ½-cup (120-ml) capacity, from left to right: a. 3 × 2½-inch (7.5 × 6-cm) demitasse cup; b. 3½ × 2-inch (9 × 5-cm) glass bowl; c. 3½ × 1½-inch (9 × 4-cm) ramekin; d. 2½ × 2-inch (6 × 5-cm) metal timbale mold for cold molds and conventional cooking; e. 3 × 2¾-inch (7.5 × 7-cm) demitasse cup

BROCCOLI TIMBALE

*T*o be honest, I had never cooked broccoli with these seasonings before; but it worked out wonderfully. Really, it's sometimes hard to know where the ideas come from. With 80 percent of the day's vitamin C, this is a diet bargain considering the low calorie count.   *SERVES 4*

Per ½-cup (120-ml) serving: 55 calories; 6 milligrams cholesterol; 2 grams fat; 260 milligrams sodium; 6 grams protein (14% RDA); 4 grams carbohydrate

RDA: calcium 9%; vitamin A 18%; riboflavin 9%; vitamin C 80%

½ pound (227 g) broccoli, stems
  peeled, cut into coins and florets
  (about 3¼ cups; 765 ml)
1 bay leaf
⅓ cup (80 ml) part-skim ricotta cheese

3 egg whites
3 leaves fresh or dried rosemary,
  optional
½ teaspoon kosher salt

  1. Place broccoli and bay leaf in a 4-cup (1-l) glass measure. Cover tightly with microwave plastic wrap. Cook at 100% for 4 minutes in a 650- to 700-watt oven. Prick plastic wrap to release steam.

  2. Remove from oven; uncover and remove bay leaf. Place ricotta in a food processor and process until smooth. Add cooked broccoli and remaining ingredients and process until smooth.

  3. Spray ramekins with a nonstick vegetable spray. Divide mixture evenly among ramekins. Cook, uncovered, at 50% for 10 minutes.

To serve 8. Place 1 pound (450 g) broccoli and 1 bay leaf in an 8-cup (2-l) glass measure. Cook, covered, for 6 minutes. Purée ⅔ cup (160 ml) ricotta as in Step 2, and add cooked broccoli, 6 egg whites, 6 leaves fresh or dried rosemary and 1 teaspoon kosher salt. Divide equally among 8 ½-cup (120-ml) ramekins. Finish as in Step 3, and cook at 50% for 14 minutes.

FOR 400- TO 500-WATT OVENS

To serve 4. Cook broccoli as in Step 1 for 6 minutes. Continue with Step 2. Divide among 4 ½-cup (120-ml) ramekins and cook, uncovered, at 100% for 10 minutes.

CARROT TIMBALE

Wow! Beauty, flavor and almost three times the daily requirement of vitamin A—that's almost perfection.   *SERVES 4*

Per ½-cup (120-ml) serving: 62 calories; 6 milligrams cholesterol; 2 grams fat; 171 milligrams sodium; 5 grams protein (12% RDA); 6.5 grams carbohydrate

RDA: calcium 7%; vitamin A 289%; riboflavin 8%; vitamin C 8%

½ pound (227 g) carrots, peeled, trimmed and cut into 1-inch (2.5-cm) rounds
⅓ cup (80 ml) part-skim ricotta cheese

¼ teaspoon kosher salt
1¼ teaspoons chopped fresh dill
3 egg whites

1. Place carrots in a 9-inch (23-cm) quiche dish or pie plate. Cover tightly with microwave plastic wrap. Cook at 100% for 6 minutes 30 seconds in a 650- to 700-watt oven. Prick plastic to release steam.

2. Remove from oven and uncover. Place ricotta in a food processor and process until smooth. Add cooked carrots and remaining ingredients. Process until smooth.

3. Divide mixture evenly among ramekins. Cook, uncovered, at 50% for 6 minutes.

To serve 8. Use 1 pound (450 g) carrots, ⅔ cup (160 ml) ricotta, ½ teaspoon kosher salt, 2½ teaspoons chopped fresh dill and 6 egg whites. Place carrots in a 10-inch (25.5-cm) quiche dish or pie plate. Cook as in Step 1, covered, for 10 minutes. Continue with Step 2. Divide among 8 ½-cup (120-ml) ramekins. Cook as in Step 3 for 11 minutes.

FOR 400- TO 500-WATT OVENS

To serve 4. Cook carrots for 10 minutes. Purée ricotta and remaining ingredients and divide among 4 ½-cup (120-ml) ramekins. Cook as in Step 3 at 100% for 8 minutes.

CAULIFLOWER TIMBALE

*T*his would be good served with two tablespoons of Rich Watercress Sauce (page 506), Paprika Lemon Béchamel (511) or Green Sauce (page 506).   *SERVES 4*

Per ½-cup (120-ml) serving: 54 calories; 6 grams cholesterol; 2 grams fat; 6 grams protein (13% RDA); 4 grams carbohydrate

RDA: calcium 8%; vitamin C 68%

½ pound (227 g) cauliflower florets
  (about 2½ cups; 590 ml)
⅓ cup (80 ml) part-skim ricotta cheese
3 egg whites

¼ teaspoon ground cardamom
¼ teaspoon kosher salt
Freshly ground black pepper, to taste

   1. Place cauliflower in a 2½-quart (2.5-l) soufflé dish or casserole with a tightly fitted lid. Cover tightly with microwave plastic wrap or casserole lid. Cook at 100% for 5 minutes in a 650- to 700-watt oven. If using plastic wrap, prick to release steam.
   2. Remove from oven and uncover. Transfer cauliflower to the food processor. Add remaining ingredients and purée. Divide mixture among 4 ½-cup (120-ml) ramekins. Space ramekins evenly in the oven. Cook, uncovered, at 50% for 6 minutes.
   3. Remove from oven and unmold onto a serving plate or onto four individual plates. Serve hot or warm.

To serve 8. Use 1 pound (450 g) cauliflower, ⅔ cup (160 ml) ricotta, 6 egg whites, ½ teaspoon cardamom, ½ teaspoon salt and a pinch black pepper. Cook cauliflower as in Step 1 for 8 minutes. Cook timbales as in Step 2 at 50% for 9 minutes.

FOR 400- TO 500-WATT OVENS

To serve 4. Cook cauliflower as in Step 1 at 100% for 7 minutes. Cook timbales as in Step 2 at 100% for 6 minutes.

SPINACH ROULADE

Roulades are rectangular soufflés made to fall flat on purpose. Then they are spread with a filling and rolled up, starting with a long edge—like a jelly roll. Even with the aid of a microwave oven they take some work. However, they are easier and more reliable than when made in a conventional oven. Made as they are here they are substantial but with few calories. The spinach layer can be made ahead as well as the filling, and then the whole thing rolled up and reheated as your guests are sitting down. Don't mention that this is good-for-them food. They'll never know.

This is just as good when two thicker slices of roulade come out as a main course, or a mini-roulade slice comes out as elegant cocktail-party food.

There are three different versions here. Once you get the basic spinach-roll technique down pat, you will want to serve it often. Vary each kind with different sauces by choosing a recipe from Basics, Sauces and Snacks (pages 458–529).

SPINACH ROULADE WITH DUXELLES

*T*his vegetarian roulade can be set off on a bed of Fresh Tomato Purée (page 468) or Red Pepper Purée (page 500). Even without those additions you get all of your vitamin A, one third of your vitamin C and 12 percent of your calcium.
SERVES 12 AS A FIRST COURSE, 4 AS A MAIN COURSE, 24 AS AN HORS D'OEUVRE

Per 1¼-inch (3-cm) crosswise slice, first-course serving: 47 calories; 2 milligrams cholesterol; 1 gram fat; 313 milligrams sodium; 5 grams protein (11% RDA); 5 grams carbohydrate

RDA: calcium 12%; iron 15%; vitamin A 112%; riboflavin 16%; vitamin C 45%

SPINACH ROLL

3 pounds (1.4 kg) spinach, stemmed and washed (12 tightly packed cups; 3 l)
1 teaspoon vegetable oil
1 tablespoon Fromage Blanc (page 518), or store-bought (page 44)
1 tablespoon skim milk
1 teaspoon kosher salt
¼ teaspoon freshly ground black pepper

¼ teaspoon freshly grated nutmeg
¼ cup (60 ml) freshly grated Parmesan cheese
4 egg whites
Pinch cream of tartar

1 cup (240 ml) Diet Duxelles (page 477)

1. Place spinach in a 14 × 11 × 2-inch (35.5 × 28 × 5-cm) rectangular dish. Cook, uncovered, at 100% for 9 minutes in a 650- to 700-watt oven. Remove from oven. As soon as spinach is cool enough to handle, remove from dish and squeeze out as much water as possible.

2. Clean cooking dish, brush with oil and reserve.

3. Place spinach in food processor and process until finely chopped. Add Fromage Blanc, milk, salt, pepper, nutmeg and Parmesan and pulse to combine. Transfer to a mixing bowl.

(continued)

4. In a clean bowl, with a whisk or mixer, beat egg whites with cream of tartar until soft peaks form. Fold into spinach mixture, making sure the mixture is thoroughly combined. Spread evenly into prepared dish. Cover tightly with microwave plastic wrap. Cook for 10 minutes. Prick plastic to release steam.

5. Remove from oven and uncover. Cover loosely with a kitchen towel and let stand 5 minutes. Uncover the roulade, loosen the bottom with a spatula and turn out onto a piece of parchment paper slightly larger than the cooking dish.

6. If you intend to serve the roulade as a first course, lift one of the long sides of the parchment paper and let the roulade roll onto itself. If the roulade will be used as an hors d'oeuvre, first cut the roulade in half crosswise before rolling each half. (The roulade can be made ahead up to this point if rolled between two pieces of parchment paper and wrapped tightly in plastic wrap and refrigerated. When ready to serve, bring roulade and filling to room temperature; unroll roulade and continue with recipe.)

7. Spread evenly with duxelles, or another desired filling (see below).

8. Leaving the roulade on the parchment paper, put an edge of the paper over the serving dish and roll roulade onto the dish. Reheat, uncovered, for 1 to 2 minutes or until hot. Using a serrated knife, cut across into 1¼-inch (3-cm) slices and serve.

Rolling a whole roulade:
Lift one of the long sides of the
parchment paper and let the roulade
roll onto itself.

To make a half roulade:
Halve roulade lengthwise and roll
each half, starting with a long side,
to make small roulades for first
courses or hors d'oeuvres.

SPINACH ROULADE WITH CHEESE FILLING

*T*his is the same spinach roulade as above, but filled with a cheese mixture. It too is vegetarian. It seems to work best in smaller rounds, which means that the roll is cut in half to form two smaller rectangles. When serving it as a first course, set off the spiral-colored rounds with 24 Karat Sauce (page 504) or Ruby Beet Sauce (page 503).

Calcium, phosphorus, iron, vitamin C and vitamin A (100 percent) are all in rich supply. *SERVES 12 AS A FIRST COURSE, 24 AS AN HORS D'OEUVRE.*

Per first-course serving of 2 ⅞-inch (2.25-cm) crosswise slices: 78 calories; 8 milligrams cholesterol; 3 grams fat; 370 milligrams sodium; 8 grams protein (19% RDA); 6 grams carbohydrate

RDA: calcium 18%; phosphorus 13%; iron 15%; vitamin A 114%; riboflavin 18%; niacin 7%; vitamin C 45%

1 recipe Spinach Roll (page 107),
   cooked and halved crosswise

CHEESE FILLING

½ cup (120 ml) Fromage Blanc (page
   518), or part-skim ricotta cheese

1 cup (240 ml) grated part-skim
   mozzarella (4 ounces; 113.5 g)
Pinch cayenne pepper

1. Combine Fromage Blanc, mozzarella and cayenne pepper in a mixing bowl. Divide mixture evenly between both halves of the spinach roll and spread smoothly. Roll according to directions in Spinach Roulade with Duxelles (opposite page).

2. Slice each roulade half into 12 even slices. Serve 2 slices per person as a first course, 1 slice as an hors d'oeuvre.

SPINACH ROULADE WITH SHRIMP FILLING

*P*ut this hearty first course with its attractive contrast of pink and green before a light or vegetarian main course, even a salad. As a sauce, try Red Pepper Purée (page 500).

Even without the main course, you will have had all your vitamin A, almost half of your vitamin C and good wallops of iron and calcium.
SERVES 12 AS A FIRST COURSE, 4 AS A MAIN COURSE

(continued)

Per 1¼-inch (3-cm) crosswise slice, first-course serving: 86 calories; 48 milligrams cholesterol; 2 grams fat; 377 milligrams sodium; 12 grams protein (26% RDA); 7 grams carbohydrate

RDA: calcium 15%; phosphorus 16%; iron 19%; vitamin A 113%; riboflavin 18%; niacin 11%; vitamin C 46%

1 recipe cooked Spinach Roll (page 107)

SHRIMP FILLING

1 pound (450 g) shrimp, peeled and deveined
½ cup (120 ml) Béchamel (page 508)

½ teaspoon Dijon mustard
1 teaspoon chopped fresh dill
1 teaspoon fresh lemon juice
Pinch kosher salt
Pinch freshly ground black pepper

1. Place shrimp in a 1½-quart (1.5-l) soufflé dish or casserole with a tightly fitted lid. Cover tightly with microwave plastic wrap or casserole lid. Cook at 100% for 2 minutes 30 seconds in a 650- to 700-watt oven. If using plastic wrap, prick to release steam.

2. Remove from oven and uncover. Drain shrimp and chop finely. Place in a metal bowl. Add Béchamel, mustard, dill, lemon juice, salt and pepper. Stir to combine. Spread mixture evenly on spinach roll and roll according to the directions for Spinach Roulade with Duxelles (page 108). Reheat, uncovered, for 1 to 2 minutes if desired and serve.

GREEN TERRINE

*T*his warm fish and spinach loaf is a brilliant shade of green. It's quick to make and so low in calories you can set it on a bed of dressed salad greens—very French—or a pool of Red Pepper Purée (page 500), Fresh Tomato Purée (page 468) or Ruby Beet Sauce (page 503). If you want to avoid the Christmas colors, try Rich Watercress Sauce (page 506). *SERVES 8*

Per generous 1-inch (2.5-cm) slice serving: 60 calories; 25 milligrams cholesterol; 1 gram fat; 255 milligrams sodium; 11 grams protein (25% RDA); 2 grams carbohydrate

RDA: calcium 6%; phosphorus 14%; iron 6%; vitamin A 42%; vitamin C 16%

¾ pound (340 g) spinach, stemmed,
   washed and tightly packed (3 cups;
   720 ml)
1 pound (450 g) cod fillet, cut into 2-
   inch (5-cm) chunks

1 teaspoon kosher salt
Large pinch nutmeg
Pinch freshly ground black pepper
½ cup (120 ml) buttermilk

1. Place spinach in a 13 × 9 × 2-inch (33 × 23 × 5-cm) oval dish. Cover tightly with microwave plastic wrap. Cook at 100% for 4 minutes in a 650- to 700-watt oven. Prick plastic to release steam.

2. Remove from oven and uncover. When spinach is cool enough to handle, squeeze well to remove excess liquid. Place in a food processor. Add remaining ingredients and purée until very smooth (no traces of white fillet should be visible in the mixture).

3. Scrape spinach mixture into a 9 × 5 × 3-inch (23 × 12.5 × 7.5-cm) glass loaf pan, preferably with a release coating. Smooth the top. Cook for 5 minutes or until firm to the touch.

4. Remove from oven. Drain off any liquid. Cover with a piece of cardboard cut to fit and weight with soup cans or an item of similar weight for about 5 to 10 minutes. Serve warm.

FOR 400- TO 500-WATT OVENS

To serve 8. Cook spinach as in Step 1 for 6 minutes. Continue with Step 2. In Step 3, cook for 7 minutes 30 seconds. Finish as in Step 4.

MUSSELS STUFFED WITH TABBOULEH

While slightly more fattening than most of the first courses, this is so good I couldn't omit it. I first had something similar at an Armenian restaurant, where it was much richer; but I don't think you'll feel deprived with this slimmer version, and you can feel enriched by the 23 percent of your daily iron that you're getting as well as the sensational mildly sweet flavor.

SERVES 4 AS A FIRST COURSE, 6 AS AN HORS D'OEUVRE

Per first-course (3-mussel) serving: 104 calories; 16 milligrams cholesterol; 2 grams fat; 167 milligrams sodium; 8 grams protein (18% RDA); 18 grams carbohydrate

RDA: phosphorus 21%; iron 23%

(continued)

1½ cloves garlic, smashed, peeled and minced

½ teaspoon ground cumin

1 dozen large mussels (1½–2 pounds; 680–900 g), washed and cleaned (pages 263–264)

¼ cup (60 ml) unseasoned tabbouleh

1 tablespoon raisins

1½ teaspoons pine nuts

1 teaspoon thinly sliced scallion greens

12 leaves fresh coriander

1. Place garlic, cumin and mussels (hinge end down) in a 2½-quart (2.5-l) soufflé dish or casserole with a tightly fitted lid. Cover tightly with microwave plastic wrap or casserole lid. Cook at 100% for 6 minutes, or until mussels open, in a 650- to 700-watt oven. If using plastic wrap, prick to release steam.

2. Remove from oven and uncover. Transfer mussels with a slotted spoon to another bowl and reserve. Strain liquid into a 4-cup (1-l) measure, reserving garlic. Leave ½ cup (120 ml) of mussel liquid in measure and set remaining liquid aside. Stir in tabbouleh, reserved garlic, raisins and pine nuts. Let stand for 20 minutes to absorb liquid. Add scallion greens.

3. To assemble, remove mussels from shells and reserve half of each shell. Place 1 tablespoon of tabbouleh in shell. Cover with mussel and arrange a coriander leaf over mussel. Place around a 12-inch (30.5-cm) platter. If the mixture seems dry, dribble over some of the reserved mussel liquid. Cover and cook for 1 minute to reheat. Serve hot.

FOR 400- TO 500-WATT OVENS

To serve 4. Follow Step 1 and cook for 8 minutes. Continue with Step 2. Reheat assembled mussels as in Step 3 on a 10-inch (25.5-cm) quiche dish or pie plate for 2 minutes 30 seconds.

SCALLOPS WITH FENNEL

*T*his is a stolen idea; it is probably too odd for me to have thought up on my own; but once I ate it, oh my, I had to try and do it to share. The oddness consists not in the pairing of scallops and fennel, but in cooking them in veal broth. The chef is Giles Épié, of Miraville, in Paris. He is not responsible for my results. I hope you will like them. It is a sophisticated dish for company and too much work to do for yourself alone. To cook evenly it requires a carrousel. Offer guests a spoon as well as a fork. They will want all the heavenly sauce.   *SERVES 6*

Per serving: 43 calories; 14 milligrams cholesterol; 0.4 grams fat; 106 milligrams sodium; 7 grams protein (17% RDA); 2 grams carbohydrate

RDA: phosphorus 10%; vitamin A 8%

9 ounces (255 g) bay scallops
6 ounces (170 g) fennel, peeled, cored and cut into thin strips (about 2½ cups; 590 ml)

1 cup plus 2 tablespoons (270 ml) Rich Veal Broth (page 464), or unsalted or regular canned chicken broth
1½ tablespoons chopped fennel sprigs
Freshly ground pepper, to taste

1. Divide scallops and fennel slices equally among 6 10-ounce (284-g) soup bowls. Add 3 tablespoons broth to each bowl and top with chopped fennel sprigs and a pinch of black pepper. Cover tightly with microwave plastic wrap.

2. Place bowls around the edge of the carrousel and cook for 3 minutes at 100% in a 650- to 700-watt oven. If all six bowls will not fit around edge, place one bowl in the center and allow an extra 50 seconds of cooking time for that bowl. Prick plastic to release steam.

3. Remove from oven and uncover. Allow bowls to stand for 1 minute for flavors to develop before serving.

To serve 4. Use 6 ounces (170 g) scallops, 4 ounces (113.5 g) fennel, ¾ cup (180 ml) veal broth, 1 tablespoon chopped fennel leaves, and a pinch pepper. Follow Step 1. Cook as in Step 2 for 4 minutes.

FOR 400- TO 500-WATT OVENS

To serve 4. Cook for 6 minutes.

Cut off the tops with a knife. Reserve tops.

Remove the core by cutting a deep cone in the base of the fennel.

Peel fennel bulb with a vegetable peeler.

Slice across the bulb into thin strips.

Cut fronds from tops to use as a garnish or flavoring.

SOUPS

Saved by Soup

Now, it may seem odd that while I am encouraging you to go on a diet, lose weight if necessary, get healthy, avoid temptation, minimize your time in the kitchen, I am also suggesting that you make soup, that I am providing you with a dazzling array of festive and homey, hot and cold, big-enough-to-be-a-meal, dainty-to-start-with, clear and creamy, peasant and elegant soups. Well, it isn't odd at all. Soup is one of the best friends the health-conscious dieter has.

Sure, I can hear you thinking, I can have all the clear, saltless, hospital-style broth I want. If you want to, you can; but there are very good reasons to have wonderful, as-good-as-any soups as well.

There is no doubt that it takes more time to make two courses instead of one; but soup reheats well, freezes well and can make a whole meal at lunch another day. Even so, why bother? Most important, soup is love. If we feel loved, we are less liable to make ourselves feel good by overeating.

The dividends for the extra work are enormous. Eating your meal in a number of satisfying courses slows you down. Soup gives time for your stomach to send a signal to your brain that something lovely is happening, that it is getting fed. This means you will eat less of a protein- and cholesterol-rich main course. You will get more different flavors out of the meal, which satisfies your taste buds. Even if your main course is just a piece of grilled meat, the proper choice of soup will provide you with lots of healthy vegetables and vitamins.

There is some proof that a salty liquid (not too salty) at the beginning of a meal will help you feel satiated so you are less liable to gorge.

If your day is a little light in calcium, choose a soup bound with a dietetic cheese. Is it low in fiber, iron or carbohydrates? Choose a soup with chick-peas or beans. Unless you are having the soup as a whole meal or as a starter before a vegetarian pasta or meatless salad, it will never have too little protein; but if you are having it before a meat, fish or poultry main course, you need to pick a soup that is not high in protein. I have only listed the amount of protein when it would make a significant difference to your total diet.

Make soups to have on hand so that instead of picking up a salt-laden or fattening frozen meal or snack food when you're tired, you have something healthy and homemade to defrost or heat quickly. Add a salad and bread, even some dessert or a portion of fruit (see pages 532–533 for menu suggestions), and you have an almost-no-work meal.

You have no time to make lunch, or lunch is at work, joylessly out of a vending machine or from the tired take-out menu. Take your cup of soup with *you and heat it in that dinky office microwave machine or heat it at home. Stop what you're doing and relax. The world will look different and there is less chance of hideous snacks from a passing cart.*

Oh, yes, soup is worth the effort and, as Mother said, it's good for you.

Soup

For me it is soup not sleep that knits the raveled sleave of care. Nothing is more comforting than a bowl of homemade soup, hot in winter and cool, perhaps, in summer. Soup can be a first course, a lunch or a whole meal; see menu ideas on pages 46–73. Watch your portion size—given in each recipe in cup (ml) measure—so that the amount you eat goes with the meal and nutrition count you want.

To choose a recipe, you may want to note that the recipes in this chapter move from simpler to more complex to cold. If you are looking for more substantial soups—the kind that are almost always a meal—look at pages 130–139, or, for others not in this chapter, look in the Index under "soup" and discover old friends like Chicken in the Pot (page 327).

A few of these recipes are vegetarian, but substituting vegetarian broth for a meat broth will make many of the recipes attractive to vegetarians.

While some soups can be made with water, most are tastier made with a broth or stock. Fortunately, the microwave oven has come along to make soup a reasonable proposition with broths or stocks that take anywhere from twenty to forty minutes (see Basic Broths, pages 460–462), instead of the many hours I used to invest in them. For short-order occasions you can substitute canned broth or dissolved stock (bouillon) cubes. Beware the salt.

COMPARISON OF CALORIE AND SODIUM CONTENT

	CAL.	SOD. (mg)
Chicken-flavored bouillon cube and water (6 oz.; 180-ml)	9	1,152
Chicken broth, canned (6 oz.; 180 ml)	29	582
Basic Chicken Broth (page 460) (6 oz.; 180 ml)	23	40

In some places, you can find canned broth that is made without salt; but I find the taste less than rewarding. In the long run, it is just as easy to make your broth ahead and freeze it in one-cup or smaller quantities to use as needed. See the next page for defrosting times.

There are other prepared ingredients, such as canned tomatoes, chick-peas and beans, that have a rather high amount of salt. To reduce the sodium content of soups with these ingredients, make some of them as staples. Tomato products freeze and defrost well. Cooked legumes and beans (pages 200–202) can be kept on hand by refrigerating covered with cold water. Change the water daily and they will stay good for a week.

Cooked soups are among the few things—other than basics—that I think really freeze well. Freeze leftovers, intentional or otherwise, in one-cup (240-ml) portions. Defrost and heat in the microwave oven in one procedure as needed. I love leftover soup. If you don't, or don't want to be tempted, you will find that many of the soups give variations for one or two servings.

When developing your own recipes, you may find this hint useful. Cook your solid ingredients—vegetables, meat, etc.—in a minimum of liquid. Add the remaining amount of desired liquid toward the end of the cooking time. This will be just long enough to get it hot. If you start with the full amount of liquid, your soup will take longer to cook. If the soup is to be served cold, don't cook the final amount of liquid at all. You will just be heating it so that you can chill it—a waste of time in my book.

You will find other soups in Good Grains and Other Starches (pages 148–225); see Index.

DEFROSTING TIMES FOR CLEAR SOUPS OR BROTHS

Remove lid of freezing container; cover tightly with microwave plastic wrap; defrost at 100%.

½ cup (120 ml)
650- to 700-watt oven: 2 min.
400- to 500-watt oven: 3 min.

2 cups (470 ml) in 2 separate containers
650- to 700-watt oven: 5 min.
400- to 500-watt oven: 10 min.

1 cup (240 ml)
650- to 700-watt ovens: 4 min.
400- to 500-watt oven: 5 min. 30 sec.

DEFROSTING AND HEATING TIMES FOR HEARTY SOUPS

Remove lid of freezing container; cover tightly with microwave plastic wrap; defrost at 100%.

1 cup (240 ml)
650- to 700-watt ovens: 3 min.
400- to 500-watt oven: 7 min.

THICKENING YOUR SOUPS

Thick and creamy soups are luxurious and sustaining as well as traditionally fattening. It is possible, however, to make soups that are creamy and wonderful without being fattening. Soups can be thickened in several ways. If you are making a vegetable soup, remove some of the vegetables with a slotted spoon and place in the food processor or blender. Purée and whisk back into the soup.

Part-skim ricotta cheese or Fromage Blanc (page 518) make great substitutes for heavy cream and can make a soup surprisingly rich and delicious. Place the cheese in a blender and blend until completely smooth. If you have trouble getting it smooth, add some of the cooked-soup liquid and continue to blend until smooth. Whisk into desired soup and reheat to serve hot or serve chilled. You can further reduce the calories, cholesterol and fat of recipes thickened with part-skim ricotta cheese by substituting an equal amount of all-skim-milk ricotta cheese if you can find it. For each cup (240 ml) substituted, you will reduce your recipe by 20 calories, 36 milligrams cholesterol and 3 grams fat. If you can find or make Fromage Blanc, substituting it for part-skim ricotta will reduce your recipe, for each cup (240 ml) substituted, by 188 calories, all the cholesterol and almost all the fat.

Potatoes are good for adding substance to soups. Simply boil or bake (see pages 219–220 for timings) the desired amount of potato (keeping in mind the calories). Place in a food processor or blender with some of the liquid from the soup. Purée until smooth and whisk back into the soup.

CARBOHYDRATES FOR YOUR SOUP

Now that we all know we should eat more carbohydrates, adding them to our broths is a good way to enjoy them. Their use also makes many of the soups substantial enough to be a meal when followed by a serving of fruit, or a salad topped with one of my special salad dressings. When broth is left from making a soup or a stew, think of making the broth into soup for lunch the next day by adding one of the following carbohydrates and a sprinkling of fresh herbs. (See pages 148–225 for cooking instructions.)

For an additional hundred calories or so—fine for active people, large people or when the soup is to become the entire meal—you can add substance to soup with a grain, pasta or potato. Given below are calorie counts for boiled rice (without butter or salt), boiled pasta and boiled or baked potato.

If you want to cook the pasta in the broth, see Chicken Soup with Orzo (page 122) as an example.

Brown long-grain rice: 116 calories per ½-cup serving

Instant long-grain rice: 60 calories per ½-cup serving

White enriched long-grain rice: 111 calories per ½-cup serving

Parboiled long-grain rice: 63 calories per ½-cup serving

Enriched macaroni: 96 calories per ½-cup serving

Egg noodles: 100 calories per ½-cup serving

Enriched spaghetti: 96 calories per ½-cup serving

Potato: 119 calories per 5-ounce (135-g) potato

Kidney beans (canned): 95 calories per ½-cup serving

Kidney beans (homemade): 109 calories per ½-cup serving

Pinto beans (canned): 83 calories per ½-cup serving

Kasha, before cooking: 95 calories per 1 ounce

Pearl barley, before cooking: 100 calories per 1 ounce

Bulgur, unseasoned: 114 calories per ½-cup serving

Not everyone at the table may be on a weight-loss diet. Some may not even need to watch their salt. They can add:

Parmesan cheese, grated: 23 calories per tablespoon; 93 milligrams sodium

Olive oil: 119 calories per tablespoon; 0 milligrams sodium

Croutons: 70 calories per ½ ounce; 210 milligrams sodium

GARLIC ESCAROLE SOUP

*T*his light and delicious soup has Italian antecedents and an unusual balance of flavors between the slight bitterness of the crunchy, clean-colored escarole, the nutty sweetness of the garlic and the light acid bite of the vinegar. It is as pleasant on a hot summer night as it is on a cold winter night.

The combination of escarole and garlic makes it very healthful. It is high in potassium and vitamin A and even has a wallop of iron. No salt is added and it is not missed due to the pepper and vinegar.

Adding one of the carbohydrates from the list on page 117 would go a long way to making this a whole meal. In any case, if this, with a slice of bread, is lunch, sprinkle on some good Parmesan cheese for more Italian flavor and to boost the protein content, as long as you don't have to worry about salt.

SERVES 4

Per 1-cup (240-ml) serving: 39 calories; 0 milligrams cholesterol; 1.5 grams fat; 60 milligrams sodium; 3 grams carbohydrate

RDA: vitamin A 12%; niacin 8%

4 cups (1 l) Basic Chicken Broth (page 460), or unsalted or regular canned chicken broth

3 cloves garlic, smashed and peeled

¼ pound (113.5 g) escarole, washed and cut into thin strips across the ribs (about 1 packed cup; 240 ml)

1 tablespoon balsamic vinegar

Pinch freshly ground black pepper, or to taste

1. Combine broth, garlic and escarole in a 2½-quart (2.5-l) soufflé dish. Cover tightly with microwave plastic wrap. Cook at 100% for 8 minutes in a 650- to 700-watt oven. Prick plastic to release steam.

2. Remove from oven and uncover. Stir in vinegar and pepper and serve.

To serve 2. Use 2 cups (470 ml) broth, 2 cloves garlic, 2 ounces (56 g) escarole, 1 teaspoon vinegar and pepper to taste. Cook in a 1½-quart (1.5-l) soufflé dish as in Step 1 for 5 minutes.

FOR 400- TO 500-WATT OVENS

To serve 4. Cook for 14 minutes.

To serve 2. Cook for 7 minutes.

To make a chiffonade of any leafy vegetable, cut across leaves and their ribs into narrow strips.

FENNEL SOUP

*T*he fresh, mild licorice taste of the fennel bulb is pleasantly pungent. This would be a good first course before Orange Pepper Fish (page 243), seafood or pasta. Again, no salt added or needed; the lemon juice and garlic do the trick. There are good quantities of vitamin C.   *SERVES 4*

Per ¾-cup (180-ml) serving: 34 calories; 0 milligrams cholesterol; 1 gram fat; 81 milligrams sodium; 3 grams carbohydrate

RDA: iron 6%; vitamin C 11%

½ pound (227 g) fennel, peeled, cored and thinly sliced across the bulb (about 1½ cups; 355 ml); save tops for garnish, if desired
3 cloves garlic, peeled and cut in slivers

3 cups (705 ml) Basic Chicken Broth (page 460), or unsalted or regular canned chicken broth
1 tablespoon fresh lemon juice

1. Combine fennel, garlic and broth in a 2½-quart (2.5-l) soufflé dish. Cover tightly with microwave plastic wrap. Cook at 100% for 7 minutes in a 650- to 700-watt oven. Prick plastic to release steam.

(continued)

2. Remove from oven and uncover. Stir in lemon juice and sprinkle each serving with a sprig of the fennel top, if desired.

To serve 2. Use ¼ pound (113.5 g) fennel, 2 cloves garlic, 2 cups (470 ml) broth and 2 teaspoons lemon juice. Cook in a 4-cup (1-l) glass measure as in Step 1 for 6 minutes. Finish as in Step 2.

To serve 1. Use 2 ounces (56 g) fennel, 1 clove garlic, 1 cup (240 ml) broth and 1 teaspoon lemon juice. Cook in a 4-cup (1-l) glass measure for 4 minutes. Finish as in Step 2.

FOR 400- TO 500-WATT OVENS

To serve 4. Cook soup for 13 minutes.

To serve 2. Cook soup for 9 minutes.

To serve 1. Cook soup for 7 minutes.

CHICKEN SOUP

Basic Chicken Broth is good; but what most of us mean by chicken soup is this vegetable-laden, pasta-enriched, dill-sparked golden soup that reassures many of us when we are sick. It can be just as good when we need soothing after a hard day. It is the optimal family soup. Sometimes I like to add a clove of finely sliced garlic along with the other vegetables and squirt in some lemon juice just before serving. Other fresh herbs can be substituted for the dill. Thyme, tarragon and coriander are particularly good. If you are using coriander, try adding two slices of fresh ginger and a pinch of hot pepper flakes.

Happily, chicken soup turns out to be very rich in vitamin A, and good in vitamin C, iron and niacin—all that and it tastes good.   SERVES 4

Per 1-cup (240-ml) serving: 97 calories; 0 milligrams cholesterol; 2 grams fat; 82 milligrams sodium; 4 grams protein (10% RDA); 16 grams carbohydrate

RDA: iron 10%; vitamin A 71%; niacin 13%; vitamin C 12%

½ small turnip (3 ounces; 85 g), peeled and cut into ¼-inch (.5-cm) wedges (about ¼ cup; 60 ml)

1 small carrot (2 ounces; 56 g), peeled and cut into ¼-inch (.5-cm) rounds (about ¼ cup; 60 ml)

1 rib celery, peeled and cut into ½-inch (1-cm) slices (about ¼ cup; 60 ml)

1 leek (4 ounces; 114 g), trimmed, washed and whites cut across into ¼-inch (.5-cm) slices (about ¼ cup; 60 ml)

4 cups (1 l) Basic Chicken Broth (page 460), or unsalted or regular canned chicken broth

⅓ cup (80 ml) pastina

2 tablespoons chopped fresh dill

1. Place vegetables (you will have 1 cup; 240 ml), 2 cups (470 ml) of the broth, pastina and dill in a 2½-quart (2.5-l) soufflé dish. Cover tightly with microwave plastic wrap. Cook at 100% for 12 minutes in a 650- to 700-watt oven, or until carrots are tender when pierced with a knife. Prick plastic to release steam.

2. Remove from oven and uncover. Add remaining chicken broth and re-cover. Cook at 100% for 2 minutes or until hot. Prick plastic to release steam.

3. Remove from oven, uncover and serve.

To serve 2. Use ½ cup (120 ml) of combined vegetables, 2 cups (470 ml) broth, 2½ tablespoons pastina and 1 tablespoon dill in a 4-cup (1-l) glass measure. Cook as in Step 1 for 8 minutes. Continue as in Step 2, cooking for 2 minutes.

To serve 1. Use ¼ cup (60 ml) of combined vegetables, 1 cup (240 ml) broth, 1½ tablespoons pastina and 1½ teaspoons dill in a 2-cup (470-ml) glass measure. Cook as in Step 1 for 6 minutes. Continue as in Step 2, cooking for 1 minute.

FOR 400- TO 500-WATT OVENS

To serve 4. Cook as in Step 1 for 18 minutes. Cook as in Step 2 for 4 minutes.

To serve 2. Cook as in Step 1 for 16 minutes. Cook as in Step 2 for 4 minutes.

To serve 1. Cook as in Step 1 for 10 minutes. Cook as in Step 2 for 2 minutes.

CHICKEN SOUP WITH ORZO

I love Maurice Sendak's little book *Chicken Soup with Rice,* but I prefer eating chicken soup with the rice-shaped pasta called orzo. I will often make myself a portion mid-afternoon as a soothing pick-me-up. For large quantities, I still suggest cooking the pasta on top of the stove and then adding it to the hot soup; but small quantities cook successfully and quickly in the microwave oven. Remember that the boiling time for the liquid is included in the microwave recipe. After you eat this, you will have had 15 percent of your niacin.   *SERVES 1*

Per 1-cup (240-ml) serving: 123 calories; 0 milligrams cholesterol; 2 grams fat; 54 milligrams sodium; 5 grams protein (12% RDA); 20 grams carbohydrate

RDA: iron 9%; thiamin 16%; riboflavin 9%; niacin 15%

1 cup (240 ml) Basic Chicken Broth   2 tablespoons dry orzo pasta
   (page 460), or unsalted or regular
   canned chicken broth

  1. Combine broth and orzo in a 4-cup (1-l) glass measure. Cover tightly with microwave plastic. Cook at 100% for 13 minutes in a 650- to 700-watt oven. Prick plastic to release steam.
  2. Remove from oven and uncover. Serve hot.

FOR 400- TO 500-WATT OVENS

To serve 1. Cook for 17 minutes.

CELERY SOUP

*T*his soup is a perfect example of why we should all keep Basic Chicken Broth on hand. Vegetarians may want to substitute Vegetarian Broth I or II (pages 465–466). A few simple additions turn it into a surprisingly good soup that has a cool light-green color provided by microwave-oven-cooked celery. It's a calorie bargain and provides vitamin C. Have it as a light start before a large salad or sandwich at lunch, or grilled fish or meat at dinner. As with all celery dishes, it has sodium.   *SERVES 4*

Per 1-cup (240-ml) serving: 56 calories; 0 milligrams cholesterol; 1 gram fat; 130 milligrams sodium; 3 grams protein (7% RDA); 9 grams carbohydrate

RDA: calcium 5%; iron 7%; vitamin C 18%

3 cups (705 ml) Basic Chicken Broth (page 460), or unsalted or regular canned chicken broth
1 pound (450 g) celery ribs (6–7 ribs), trimmed, peeled and cut into ½-inch (1-cm) pieces (about 2 cups; 470 ml)

2 medium onions (½ pound; 227 g), peeled and chopped (about 2 cups; 470 ml)

1. Combine 1 cup (240 ml) broth with the celery and onions in a 2½-quart (2.5-l) soufflé dish. Cover tightly with microwave plastic wrap and cook at 100% for 10 minutes in a 650- to 700-watt oven. Prick plastic to release steam.
2. Remove from oven and uncover. Place the mixture in a food processor and purée. Scrape mixture back into casserole. Add remaining broth and cover tightly with microwave plastic wrap. Cook for 3 minutes or until hot. Prick plastic to release steam.
3. Remove from oven and uncover. Serve hot.

FOR 400- TO 500-WATT OVENS

To serve 4. Cook as in Step 1 for 14 minutes. Cook as in Step 2 for 5 minutes.

MUSHROOM SOUP

This rich-tasting soup is so satisfying that it really makes you want to eat less food after it. You get iron, riboflavin, niacin and almost half of your vitamin C for the day. It's really a good-health brew. I don't think you'll miss the fattening cream that so often goes into mushroom soups. If you have Diet Duxelles (page 477) on hand, omit the first seven ingredients and the first two steps of the recipe. Vegetarians can also make this with Vegetarian Broth I (page 465).
SERVES 2

Per 1-cup (240-ml) serving: 90 calories; 0 milligrams cholesterol; 2 grams fat; 468 milligrams sodium; 6 grams protein (13% RDA); 14 grams carbohydrate

RDA: calcium 7%; phosphorus 15%; iron 21%; 718 milligrams potassium; vitamin A 17%; thiamin 12%; riboflavin 35%; niacin 32%; vitamin C 43%

(continued)

½ pound (227 g) mushrooms, wiped
  clean and stems trimmed
¼ pound (113.5 g) yellow onions,
  peeled and quartered
½ cup (120 ml) parsley leaves
2 ribs celery, peeled and cut into 2-inch
  (5-cm) lengths (about ½ cup;
  120 ml)

1 teaspoon fresh lemon juice
½ teaspoon kosher salt
Freshly ground black pepper, to taste
2 cups (470 ml) Basic Chicken Broth
  (page 460), or unsalted or regular
  canned chicken broth
1½ tablespoons chopped fresh dill

1. Coarsely chop mushrooms, onions, parsley and celery in food processor. Spread mixture evenly in a 10-inch (25.5-cm) quiche dish. Cover tightly with microwave plastic wrap. Cook at 100% for 10 minutes in a 650- to 700-watt oven. Prick plastic to release steam.

2. Leaving dish in oven, uncover and cook 5 minutes longer. Remove from oven and stir in lemon juice, salt and pepper.

3. Scrape mixture into a 4-cup (1-l) glass measure and stir in broth. Cover and cook for 4 minutes. Prick plastic to release steam.

4. Remove from oven and uncover. Sprinkle with dill and serve.

FOR 400- TO 500-WATT OVENS

To serve 2. Cook as in Step 1 for 15 minutes. Continue as in Step 2, cooking for 10 minutes. Cook as in Step 3 for 6 minutes.

JADE SOUP

*O*ne of the prettiest kinds of jade is called spinach jade by the Chinese. I thought I would return the favor by naming the soup for the jewel. It is also a nutritional jewel, providing calcium, iron, vitamins A and C, and a fair amount of phosphorus and riboflavin as well. *SERVES 3*

Per 1-cup (240-ml) serving: 73 calories; 9.5 milligrams cholesterol; 209 milligrams sodium; 6.75 grams protein (15% RDA); 7 grams carbohydrate

RDA: calcium 17%; phosphorus 9%; iron 19%; vitamin A 148%; riboflavin 16%; vitamin C 56%

2 shallots, peeled and sliced
1 pound (450 gm) fresh spinach,
  stemmed and washed (about 6
  loosely packed cups; 2 l)
¼ cup (60 ml) part-skim ricotta cheese

1½ cups (355 ml) Basic Chicken Broth
  (page 460), or unsalted or regular
  canned chicken broth
1 tablespoon fresh lemon juice
Freshly ground black pepper, to taste

1. Place shallots in an 8-cup (2-l) glass measure. Pack spinach into measure and cover tightly with microwave plastic wrap. Cook at 100% for 4 minutes 30 seconds in a 650- to 700-watt oven. Prick plastic to release steam.

2. Remove from oven. Uncover and scrape into a food processor. Add ricotta and process until smooth.

3. Return spinach mixture to measure and stir in broth. Cook, uncovered, for 1 minute or until hot. Remove from oven. Stir in lemon juice and pepper and serve.

FOR 400- TO 500-WATT OVENS

To serve 3. Follow Step 1 and cook for 6 minutes. Proceed as in Steps 2 and 3 and cook for 2 to 4 minutes or until hot.

ASPARAGUS SOUP

*T*he essence of spring, this thrifty soup seems very luxurious. It is thrifty because it can be made with just the stems of the asparagus while keeping the tips for another day's meal—for instance, A Spring Chicken (page 305). It also has the taste and texture of a cream soup; but it's cheating—it's light.   *SERVES 8*

Per ¾-cup (180-ml) serving: 68 calories; 10 milligrams cholesterol; 4 grams fat; 280 milligrams sodium; 7 grams protein (16% RDA); 12 grams carbohydrate

RDA: phosphorus 10%; iron 11%; vitamin A 31%; thiamin 13%; riboflavin 15%; niacin 15%; vitamin C 98%

2 pounds (900 g) asparagus stems, cut into 1-inch (2.5-cm) lengths (about 7 cups; 1.7 l); reserve tips for garnish, if desired
2½ cups (590 ml) Basic Chicken Broth (page 460), or unsalted or regular canned chicken broth

1 cup (240 ml) part-skim ricotta cheese
1 cup (240 ml) skim milk
1½ teaspoons kosher salt
Freshly ground black pepper, to taste

1. Combine asparagus stems and broth in a 2½-quart (2.5-l) soufflé dish. Cover tightly with microwave plastic wrap. Cook at 100% for 25 minutes in a 650- to 700-watt oven. Prick plastic to release steam.

2. Remove from oven. Uncover and transfer asparagus and broth to a food processor. Process until smooth.

3. Pass purée through a fine mesh sieve into a serving bowl. Whisk in remaining ingredients and serve warm or refrigerate and serve chilled.

(continued)

FOR 400- TO 500-WATT OVENS

To serve 2. Use ½ pound (227 g) asparagus, ¾ cup (180 ml) broth, ¼ cup (60 ml) ricotta and ¼ cup (60 ml) milk and ½ teaspoon salt. Follow Step 1, using a 4-cup (1-l) measure; cook for 15 minutes. Finish as in Steps 2 and 3.

QUICK TOMATO SOUP

*T*his is a quick and easy soup made from on-the-shelf or in-the-freezer ingredients. Add a large salad, two ounces (56 g) of mozzarella and a pita and you have a meal. The soup supplies plentiful vitamin C and a good amount of vitamin A as well. If you are restricting salt, try the Peasant Tomato Soup (opposite page). This soup is high in sodium because it uses bottled tomato juice.   *SERVES 2*

Per 1-cup (240-ml) serving: 48 calories; 0 grams cholesterol; 1 gram fat; 524 milligrams sodium; 8 grams carbohydrate

RDA: iron 8%; vitamin A 14%; vitamin C 40%

1 cup (240 ml) tomato juice
1 cup (240 ml) Basic Chicken Broth (page 460), or unsalted or regular canned chicken broth
½ teaspoon celery seed
2 cloves garlic, smashed, peeled and sliced

2 teaspoons Worcestershire sauce
Large pinch freshly ground black pepper
½ teaspoon fresh lemon juice, or to taste
Fresh basil, optional

1. Combine tomato juice, broth, celery seed, garlic and Worcestershire in a 4-cup (1-l) glass measure. Cover tightly with microwave plastic wrap. Cook at 100% for 12 minutes in a 650- to 700-watt oven. Prick plastic to release steam.
2. Remove from oven and uncover. Add pepper and lemon to taste and serve garnished with basil, if desired.

To serve 1. Use ½ cup (120 ml) tomato juice, ½ cup (120 ml) chicken broth, ¼ teaspoon celery seed, 1 clove garlic, 1 teaspoon Worcestershire, a pinch pepper and ¼ teaspoon lemon juice. Cook for 6 minutes.

FOR 400- TO 500-WATT OVENS

To serve 2. Cook for 14 minutes.

To serve 1. Cook for 8 minutes.

PEASANT TOMATO SOUP

*T*his is a hearty tomato soup, chunky with vegetables, and with a taste that hints of the Mediterranean. Those unconcerned with weight loss, but eager to reduce cholesterol, may add a delicious two teaspoons of extra olive oil for the group, or one-half teaspoon per person. The soup can be made with canned tomatoes; but that will virtually double the sodium. Canned broth will take it higher.   *SERVES 4*

Per 1-cup (240-ml) serving: 92 calories; 0 milligrams cholesterol; 2 grams fat; 246 milligrams sodium (422 if using canned tomatoes); 16 grams carbohydrate

RDA: calcium 7%; iron 7%; vitamin A 156%; niacin 12%; vitamin C 47%

2 medium carrots (¼ pound; 113.5 g), trimmed, peeled and cut into 2-inch (5-cm) lengths (about 1½ cups; 355 ml)

1 small yellow onion (¼ pound; 113.5 g), peeled and quartered

¼ pound (113.5 g) fennel bulb, peeled and trimmed

3 medium cloves garlic, smashed and peeled

1 teaspoon olive oil

2 cups (470 ml) Fresh Tomato Purée (page 468), or 1 1-pound can American tomatoes in thick purée

1 tablespoon cornstarch

2 cups (470 ml) Basic Chicken Broth (page 460), or unsalted or regular canned chicken broth

½ teaspoon kosher salt

1½ tablespoons fresh lemon juice

Fresh basil, washed and shredded, to taste

1. Coarsely chop carrots, onion, fennel and garlic in food processor. Stir together with oil in a 2½-quart (2.5-l) soufflé dish. Cook, uncovered, at 100% for 4 minutes in a 650- to 700-watt oven.

2. If using canned tomatoes, purée in food processor. Dissolve cornstarch in chicken broth. Add tomatoes and chicken broth to vegetables. Cover tightly with microwave plastic wrap. Cook at 100% for 7 minutes. Prick plastic to release steam.

3. Remove from oven and uncover carefully. Add salt, lemon juice and basil, if desired. Serve hot or cold.

FOR 400- TO 500-WATT OVENS

To serve 4. Cook as in Step 1 for 8 minutes. Continue cooking as in Step 2 for 10 minutes.

WINTER VEGETABLE SOUP

Mid-winter, vegetable soups that are vitamin-rich may be hard to make. This puréed soup fills the bill nicely, supplying almost two days' worth of vitamin A and 23 percent of your vitamin C. *SERVES 6*

Per generous 1-cup (240-ml) serving: 65 calories; 0 milligrams cholesterol; 1 gram fat; 84 milligrams sodium; 3 grams protein (7% RDA); 11 grams carbohydrate

RDA: iron 8%; vitamin A 196%; vitamin C 23%

6 ounces (170 g) chopped onions (about 1 cup; 240 ml)

½ pound (227 g) green beans, in 1-inch pieces (about 2 cups; 470 ml)

¼ pound (113.5 g) julienned celery root (about 1 cup; 240 ml)

4 ounces (113.5 g) peeled and chopped celery (about 1 cup; 240 ml)

½ pound (227 g) carrots, peeled and cut into matchsticks 2 × ⅛ × ⅛ inches (5 × .3 × .3 cm) (about 2 cups; 470 ml)

4 cups (1 l) Basic Chicken Broth (page 460), or unsalted or regular canned chicken broth

1. Place all vegetables in a 2½-quart (2.5-l) soufflé dish with the carrots on top. Add 2 cups (470 ml) broth and cover tightly with microwave plastic wrap. Cook at 100% for 15 minutes in a 650- to 700-watt oven. Prick plastic to release steam.

2. Remove from oven and uncover. Reserving liquids, transfer the solids, using a slotted spoon, to a food processor and chop well.

3. Return vegetables to dish with liquid; add remaining 2 cups (470 ml) broth. Cover and cook for 15 minutes. Prick plastic.

4. Remove from oven, uncover and serve.

FOR 400- TO 500-WATT OVENS

To serve 6. Follow Step 1 and cook for 25 minutes. Continue as in Steps 2 and 3, cooking for 20 minutes.

WATERCRESS SOUP

Watercress soup has a nice peppery bite and is easy to make. It offers a day's supply of vitamin A. It is good to have before a main course that doesn't offer any green vegetable, such as Meat and Potatoes on a Plate (page 298). It would make a very light lunch followed by some skim-milk cottage cheese, rye crackers and a portion of fruit.   *SERVES 4*

Per 1-cup (240-ml) serving: 46 calories; 0 grams cholesterol; 1.5 grams fat; 433 milligrams sodium; 3 grams protein (6% RDA)

RDA: vitamin A 111%; vitamin C 18%

3½ cups (825 ml) Basic Meat Broth (page 462), or unsalted or regular canned chicken broth

1 medium carrot (2 ounces; 56 g), peeled and thinly sliced (about ⅓ cup; 80 ml)

1 small onion (4 ounces; 113.5 g), peeled and chopped (about 1 cup; 240 ml)

1 cup (240 ml) packed watercress leaves, cleaned and dried

1 teaspoon kosher salt

1. Combine 1 cup (240 ml) of the broth with carrots and onions in a 2½-quart (2.5-l) soufflé dish. Cover tightly with microwave plastic wrap. Cook at 100% in a 650- to 700-watt oven for 7 minutes or until carrots are tender. Prick plastic to release steam.

2. Remove from oven and uncover. Stir in watercress. Re-cover and cook 2 minutes more. Prick plastic.

3. Remove from oven, uncover and add remaining 2½ cups (590 ml) broth. Cook, uncovered, for 2 minutes or until hot. Season with salt.

FOR 400- TO 500-WATT OVENS

To serve 4. Cook as in Step 1, covered, for 12 minutes. Continue to cook as in Step 2 for 4 minutes. Cook as in Step 3 for 3 minutes.

HEARTY VEGETABLE SOUP WITH PESTO

*T*his version of minestrone is so hearty and fresh that I don't think you will even notice that it is good for you. Leftovers make a perfect lunch.

Those not worried about salt or weight loss can stir in three tablespoons of good olive oil and four tablespoons of grated Parmesan cheese at the end, or if one person is a weight watcher and the others aren't, put the olive oil and cheese on the table for those who want them.

Even if you add the beans, you will have enough allowed calories remaining to have a salad, a small piece of cheese, a serving of fruit and bread to make a meal since the beans add some protein, iron and carbohydrate. If you are on a salt-restricted diet, watch out for canned beans since they more than double the amount of sodium. Use homemade beans if you have time or have them on hand.   *SERVES 8*

Per 1-cup (240-ml) serving: 70 calories (95 with beans); 0 milligrams cholesterol; 1 gram fat; 74 milligrams sodium with or without homemade beans, 184 with canned beans; 3 grams protein (6% RDA), 5 with beans (10% RDA); 13 grams carbohydrate, 17 with beans

RDA without beans: iron 9%; vitamin A 86%; vitamin C 35%

RDA with beans: calcium 6%; phosphorus 9%; iron 11%; vitamin A 86%; niacin 9%; vitamin C 36%

¾ pound (340 g) Idaho potatoes, peeled and cut into 1-inch (2.5-cm) pieces (about 1¾ cups; 410 ml)

¼ pound (113.5 g) turnips, peeled and cut into 1-inch (2.5-cm) pieces (about 1½ cups; 355 ml)

¼ pound (113.5 g) carrots, peeled and cut into 1-inch (2.5-cm) pieces (about 1 cup; 240 ml)

1 rib celery, peeled, and cut in 1-inch (2.5-cm) pieces (about ¼ cup; 60 ml)

½ cup (120 ml) sliced scallion whites (from 1 to 2 bunches scallions)

1 clove garlic, smashed and peeled

1 tablespoon chopped fresh parsley

3 cups (705 ml) Basic Chicken Broth (page 460), or unsalted or regular canned chicken broth

¼ pound (113.5 g) fresh tomatoes, cut into 1-inch (2.5-cm) cubes (about ½ cup; 120 ml)

¼ pound (113.5 g) zucchini, cut into 1-inch (2.5-cm) cubes (about ¾ cup; 180 ml)

¼ pound (113.5 g) green beans, tipped, tailed and cut in half (about ¾ cup; 180 ml)

4 tablespoons frozen peas, defrosted in a sieve under warm running water

1 cup (240 ml) homemade kidney beans or drained and rinsed canned beans, optional

3 tablespoons Diet Pesto Sauce (page 476)

1. Place potatoes, turnips, carrots, celery, scallions, garlic and parsley in a food processor. Pulse until coarsely chopped.

2. Scrape into a 2½ quart (2.5-l) soufflé dish and add 1½ cups (355 ml) broth. Cover tightly with microwave plastic wrap. Cook at 100% for 15 minutes in a 650- to 700-watt oven. Prick plastic to release steam.

3. Leaving dish in oven, uncover and add tomatoes, zucchini, green beans and remaining broth. Re-cover and cook for 10–12 minutes. Prick plastic. Test beans. If not tender, re-cover and cook 2 minutes longer.

4. Remove from oven and uncover. Stir in peas and kidney beans, if desired. Cook, uncovered, for 1 minute or until heated through. Remove from oven, stir in pesto and serve.

To serve 4. Use ½ pound (227 g) potatoes, 2 ounces (56 g) turnips, 2 ounces (56 g) carrots, ½ rib celery, ¼ cup (60 ml) scallions, 1 small clove garlic, 2 teaspoons parsley, 1½ cups (360 ml) broth, 2 ounces (56 g) each tomato, zucchini and green beans, 2 tablespoons peas, ½ cup (120 ml) beans, if desired, and 1½ table-spoons pesto. Prepare vegetables as in Step 1. Cook as in Step 2 with ¾ cup broth for 10 minutes. Continue with Step 3, cooking for 8 minutes more. Finish as in Step 4, cooking for 1 minute.

FOR 400- TO 500-WATT OVENS

To serve 4. Cook as in Step 2 for 15 minutes. Cook as in Step 3 for 12 minutes. Finish as in Step 4, cooking for 2 minutes.

*Peel celery rib with a
vegetable peeler.*

SPICY SOUTHWESTERN SOUP

*T*his is not a tomato soup. There is just a little tomato for sweetness and color. If you like really spicy food, double the chili pepper. It makes a satisfying lunch, contains 12 percent of the day's protein and leaves enough calories for a good-sized green salad and a portion of fruit. At dinner, enjoy it before a simple fish such as Scrod with Broccoli (page 239), knowing the soup alone gives lots of vitamin C.   *SERVES 5*

Per 1-cup (240-ml) serving: 106 calories; 0 milligrams cholesterol; 6 grams fat; 460 milligrams sodium if using canned beans (43 if using homemade beans); 5.5 grams protein (12% RDA)

RDA: phosphorus 10%; iron 10%; vitamin C 52%

1 cup (240 ml) canned pinto beans, rinsed and drained, or homemade beans
1 pound (450 g) tomatoes, peeled, seeded and chopped (about 2 cups; 470 ml)
Niblets from 2 ears fresh corn (about 1½ cups; 355 ml)
2 cloves garlic, smashed, peeled and chopped

3 tablespoons chopped fresh coriander leaves
1 jalapeño chili pepper, seeded, ribs removed and thinly sliced
3 cups (705 ml) Basic Chicken Broth (page 460), or unsalted or regular canned chicken broth
1 tablespoon fresh lime juice
½ teaspoon kosher salt, optional

1. Combine the beans, tomatoes, corn, garlic, coriander and pepper with 2 cups (470 ml) of the broth in a 2½-quart (2.5-l) soufflé dish. Cover tightly with microwave plastic wrap and cook for 7 minutes at 100% in a 650- to 700- watt oven. Prick plastic to release steam.

2. Remove from oven and uncover. Stir in remaining broth. With a slotted spoon, transfer 1 cup (240 ml) of the solids to a food processor and purée. Stir purée back into soup. Add lime juice and salt, if desired.

To serve 8–10. Use 2 cups (470 ml) beans, 2 pounds tomatoes, niblets from 4 ears corn, 4 cloves garlic, 6 tablespoons coriander leaves, 2 chili peppers, 6 cups (1.5 l) broth, 2 tablespoons lime juice and 1 teaspoon salt. Cook as in Step 1 for 12 minutes. Finish as in Step 2.

FOR 400- TO 500-WATT OVENS

To serve 5. Cook for 10 minutes.

CURRIED CABBAGE SOUP

*T*his is a homey winter soup. The unusual combination of cabbage and curry makes it hearty and filling. I'm delighted to have two portions, a large salad and a piece of cheese and call it dinner. It has health-giving quantities of vitamin C, potassium and iron.

Since there are a fair number of steps, it is not worth making for less than eight, which is an amount that is inefficient in a low-wattage oven. Serve at a party, or refrigerate leftovers and have them for lunch the next day with a portion of fruit, or freeze in batches to rejoice tired homecomings.   *SERVES 8*

Per 1-cup (240-ml) serving: 136 calories; 0 milligrams cholesterol; 3.5 grams fat; 57 milligrams sodium; 4.7 grams protein (11% RDA); 23 grams carbohydrate

RDA: phosphorus 7%; iron 13%; 682 milligrams potassium; niacin 13%; vitamin C 77%

2 pounds (900 g) potatoes, peeled and cut into 2-inch (5-cm) chunks (about 3½ cups; 825 ml)

3 tablespoons curry powder

1 tablespoon vegetable oil

6 cups (1.5 l) Basic Chicken Broth (page 460), or unsalted or regular canned chicken broth

1 medium onion (½ pound; 227 g), peeled and cut into 2-inch (5-cm) chunks (about 2½ cups, 590 ml)

1 pound (450 g) cabbage, cut into 2-inch (5-cm) chunks (about 4 cups; 1 l)

1. Place potatoes in a food processor and coarsely chop. Scrape into a 5-quart (5-l) casserole with a tightly fitted lid. Add curry powder, oil and 1 cup (240 ml) of the broth. Toss to coat. Cover casserole with lid. Cook at 100% for 10 minutes in a 650- to 700-watt oven.

2. Place onion and cabbage in the food processor and coarsely chop. Set aside.

3. Remove potatoes from oven. Uncover and stir in onion and cabbage mixture and 1 cup (240 ml) broth. Re-cover with lid and cook for 15 minutes.

4. Remove from oven and uncover carefully. Place entire contents in the food processor and process until very smooth. It may be necessary to do this step in batches.

5. Return to casserole; whisk in remaining 4 cups (1 l) broth. Reheat, covered, for 5 minutes or until hot, or, if serving cold, refrigerate until chilled.

GOULASH SOUP

*T*he clever Hungarians make this addictive dish, which is halfway between soup and stew. With 45 percent of your day's protein and more than a fourth of the calories, this is definitely a main-course soup. Have it with a piece of bread and a salad at dinner or on its own at lunch.   *SERVES 10*

Per 1-cup (240-ml) serving: 385 calories; 83 milligrams cholesterol; 29 grams fat; 276 milligrams sodium; 20 grams protein (45% RDA); 11 grams carbohydrate

RDA: phosphorus 21%; iron 17%; 630 milligrams potassium; vitamin A 29%; thiamin 9%; riboflavin 12%; niacin 17%; vitamin C 46%

2 tablespoons medium paprika (sweet-hot; if mild is all that is available, use it plus ¼ teaspoon cayenne pepper)
1 teaspoon vegetable oil
1 medium onion (8 ounces; 227 g), peeled and coarsely chopped (about 1 cup; 240 ml)
1 red bell pepper, stemmed, seeded, deribbed and cut into ¼-inch (.5-cm) cubes (about 1 cup; 240 ml)
3½ cups (825 ml) Basic Meat Broth (page 462), or unsalted or regular canned chicken broth

2½ pounds (1.2 kg) beef chuck, cut into ¼-inch (.5-cm) cubes
2 cloves garlic, smashed, peeled and chopped
1 pound (450 g) potatoes, peeled and cut into ¼-inch (.5-cm) cubes (about 1½ cups; 355 ml)
¼ teaspoon caraway seeds
½ cup (120 ml) Fresh Tomato Purée (page 468), or canned tomato purée
1 teaspoon kosher salt, optional

1. Make a small mound of the paprika in the center of a 5-quart (5-l) soufflé or casserole with a tightly fitted lid. Mix oil into the paprika. Cook, uncovered, at 100% for 2 minutes in a 650- to 700-watt oven.

2. Stir in onions and peppers to coat with paprika and oil mixture, spreading them over the bottom of the casserole. Cook, uncovered, for 3 minutes.

3. Add 1 cup (240 ml) of the broth and remaining ingredients except salt. Cover tightly with microwave plastic wrap or lid and cook for 15 minutes. If using plastic, prick to release steam.

4. Remove from oven and uncover. Pour in the remaining broth. Re-cover and cook for 10 minutes. Prick plastic, if using.

5. Remove from oven and uncover. Stir in salt, if desired.

To serve 4. Use 2 teaspoons paprika, 1 teaspoon oil, ¼ pound (113.5 g) onion, ½ red bell pepper, 1½ cups (355 ml) broth, 1 pound (450 g) beef chuck, 1 garlic clove, ½ pound (227 g) potatoes, ⅛ teaspoon caraway seeds, 3 tablespoons tomato purée and ½ teaspoon salt. Cook in a 2½-quart (2.5-l) soufflé as in Step 1 for 30 seconds. Continue with Step 2, cooking for 3 minutes. Cook as in Step 3 for 9 minutes. Cook as in Step 4 for 5 minutes.

FOR 400- TO 500-WATT OVENS

To serve 4. Cook oil and paprika as in Step 1 for 1 minute 30 seconds. Follow Step 2 and cook for 5 minutes. Cover and cook as in Step 3 for 15 minutes. Finish as in Step 4, cooking for 18 minutes.

*Mound paprika in the center
of the dish. Slowly stir in oil
to retain a mound.*

HEARTY CHICK-PEA SOUP

*T*his ample soup, with its combination of lamb and chick-peas, evokes the Middle East and makes a satisfying meal; and oh, it tastes good. For lunch, a cup followed by a salad and a portion of fruit is filling. At dinner, follow the soup with a light fish dish such as Paupiettes with Vegetables (page 251), salad and fruit or Peach Sorbet (page 554). Remember, this soup has lots of protein, so you don't want to follow it with a heavy meat dish. It is also rich in vitamin A, vitamin C and iron. Unfortunately, canned chick-peas have sodium.   SERVES 4

Per 1-cup (240-ml) serving: 197 calories; 0 grams cholesterol; 2 grams fat; 796 milligrams sodium; 8 grams protein (17% RDA); 37 grams carbohydrate

RDA: calcium 6%; phosphorus 14%; iron 11%; vitamin A 72%; vitamin C 21%

(continued)

1 turnip (4 ounces; 113.5 g), peeled and cut into 2-inch (5-cm) chunks (about 1 cup; 240 ml)

1 small onion (3 ounces; 85 g), peeled and cut into 2-inch (5-cm) chunks (about ½ cup; 120 ml)

1 small carrot (2 ounces; 56 g), peeled and cut into 2-inch (5-cm) chunks (about ⅓ cup; 80 ml)

4 cups (1 l) Basic Meat Broth (lamb) (page 462), or unsalted or regular canned chicken broth

½ bay leaf

1 teaspoon kosher salt

Pinch freshly ground black pepper

19-ounce (538-g) can chick-peas, rinsed and drained, or homemade chick-peas

1. Place turnip, onion and carrot in a food processor and coarsely chop. Scrape into a 2½-quart (2.5-l) soufflé dish. Add 2 cups (470 ml) of the broth, bay leaf, salt and pepper. Cover tightly with microwave plastic wrap. Cook at 100% in a 650- to 700-watt oven for 5 minutes. Prick plastic to release steam.

2. Remove from oven and uncover. Add 1 cup (120 ml) of the broth and the chick-peas. Re-cover and cook for 10 minutes. Prick plastic.

3. Remove from oven and uncover. With a slotted spoon, remove chick-peas and vegetables (discarding bay leaf) and place in a food processor. Process until vegetables are a smooth paste. Whisk mixture back into soup. Add remaining broth. Cook, uncovered, for 2 minutes or until hot.

To serve 2. Use ½ turnip (60 g), ½ small onion (1½ ounces; 42.5 g), ½ small carrot (1 ounce; 28 g), 2 cups broth (470 ml), a small piece of bay leaf, small pinches of kosher salt and black pepper and a 10-ounce (284-g) can chick-peas, rinsed and drained. Using 1 cup (240 ml) broth, cook as in Step 1 in a 2½-quart (2.5-l) soufflé dish for 3 minutes. Uncover carefully and stir in remaining broth and chick-peas. Re-cover and cook 5 minutes. Finish as in Step 3, reheating for 3–4 minutes.

FOR 400- TO 500-WATT OVENS

To serve 4. Cook as in Step 1 for 8 minutes. Add remaining broth and chick-peas and cook as in Step 2 for 15 minutes. Finish as in Step 3, reheating for 4 minutes.

To serve 2. Cook as in Step 1 for 6 minutes. Add remaining broth and chick-peas and cook as in Step 2 for 10 minutes or until vegetables and chick-peas are tender. Finish as in Step 3, reheating for 2 minutes.

MUSSEL SOUP

*I*t's hard to believe how much taste and protein and how few calories are in this festive soup for a party or as a substantial meal for two seafood lovers. The briny flavor permeates the potatoes.

When you're serving this as dinner, you will probably want a large salad afterward with a nice clear taste provided by Skinny Tomato Dressing (page 496). A glass of chilled white wine with ice and soda would go well also. Then round things off with a fruit sorbet, diet from the store, or Strawberry Sorbet (page 555). As a first course, this would do well before spaghettini with Tomato Sauce Casalinga (page 167). This dish is rich in iron, vitamin C and phosphorus.
SERVES 4 AS A FIRST COURSE, 2 AS A MEAL

Per first-course serving: 205 calories (410 each as a meal for 2); 28 milligrams cholesterol; 4 grams fat; 372 milligrams sodium; 16 grams protein (36% RDA); 27 grams carbohydrate

RDA: calcium 7%; phosphorus 26%; iron 34%; 1,004 milligrams potassium; niacin 14%; vitamin C 40%

1 pound (450 g) Idaho potatoes, peeled and cut into ¼-inch (.5-cm) slices
3 pounds (1.4 kg) mussels, scrubbed and debearded
½ cup (120 ml) white wine
2 ribs celery (about 6 ounces; 170 g), peeled and thinly sliced (about ½ cup; 120 ml)

¼ pound (113.5 g) leeks, cleaned and thinly sliced (about ¾ cup; 180 ml)
3 cups (705 ml) Basic Chicken Broth (page 460), or unsalted or regular canned chicken broth

1. Place potato slices on the bottom of a 2½-quart (2.5-l) soufflé dish. Arrange mussels, hinge end down, on top of potatoes. Add wine and cover tightly with microwave plastic wrap. Cook at 100% in a 650- to 700-watt oven for 9–10 minutes, or until mussels open. Prick plastic to release steam.

2. Remove from oven and uncover. Use a slotted spoon to transfer the mussels to another bowl and reserve. Add celery, leeks and 2 cups (470 ml) of broth to the potatoes. Cover and cook 20 minutes or until potatoes are easily pierced with a fork. While vegetables are cooking, shell mussels, reserve meat and discard shells.

3. Remove potato mixture from oven. Prick plastic and uncover. Place mixture in a blender (in two batches, if necessary) and blend until smooth. Stir in reserved mussels and remaining broth. Reheat, uncovered, for 1 minute, if necessary. Serve hot.

(continued)

To serve 2. Use 6 ounces (170 g) potatoes, 1 pound (450 g) mussels, 3 table-spoons wine, 1 rib celery, 2 ounces (56 g) leeks and 1 cup (240 ml) broth. Following Step 1, cook potatoes and mussels in a 1½-quart (1.5-l) soufflé dish for 3 minutes or until mussels open. Add wine, celery, leeks and ½ cup chicken broth. Re-cover and cook for 6 minutes. Finish as in Step 3, stirring in the remaining ½ cup (120 ml) broth and mussels. Reheat, uncovered, for 1 minute, if necessary.

FOR 400- TO 500-WATT OVENS

To serve 2. Follow Step 1 and cook, covered, for 6–7 minutes or until mussels open. Remove mussels and add remaining ingredients except half the broth. Cover and cook for 10 minutes. Finish as in Step 3.

RIVIERA FISH SOUP

*T*his is a typically Mediterranean robust soup, the kind of which I would eat two bowls as a meal. Most people will be happy having it as a first course before grilled chicken, fish or a vegetarian main course such as Polenta Lasagne (page 216). It's worth making the whole batch even if you don't need it; then you can freeze it and have it on hand. This classic soup is traditionally topped with thin croutons and Rouïlle (page 484), which is fine if you're not on an intense weight-loss diet. This soup will have very little sodium if you omit the salt. In any case, it is rich in vitamins A and C.   *SERVES 10*

Per 1-cup (240-ml) serving: 126 calories; 15 milligrams cholesterol; 6 grams fat; 468 milligrams sodium; 7 grams protein (17% RDA); 11 grams carbohydrate

RDA: phosphorus 11%; vitamin A 15%; vitamin C 27%

2 pounds (900 g) fish heads and bones from white-fleshed fish (not flounder, sole or other flat fish)
3 cups (705 ml) water
1 cup (240 ml) white wine
¼ cup (60 ml) olive oil
½ cup (120 ml) Pernod
1½ pounds (680 g) tomatoes, cored and cut into 1-inch (2.5-cm) chunks (about 3¾ cups; 885 ml)
20 cloves garlic

¾ pound (340 g) yellow onions, coarsely chopped (about 3 cups; 705 ml)
Large pinch saffron threads or knife-point powdered saffron
1 tablespoon kosher salt, optional
½–¾ pound (227–340 g) fish fillet (any firm white fish is fine)
¼ teaspoon cayenne pepper
1 tablespoon tomato paste, optional
1 teaspoon fresh lemon juice, optional

1. Combine all ingredients except cayenne, tomato paste and lemon juice in a 5-quart (5-l) soufflé dish or casserole. Cook, uncovered, at 100% in a 650- to 700-watt oven for 30 minutes.

2. Remove from oven. Prick plastic to release steam and uncover. Pass through the medium blade of a food mill. Add remaining ingredients. Serve hot.

SHRIMP GUMBO

*T*his is the kind of spicy food that has made New Orleans cooking so popular in recent years. The microwave oven is a better way to cook okra—it does not get slimy and stays green. The texture of fresh okra is better than frozen.

Like the Goulash Soup on page 134, this dish is halfway between a soup and a stew. One cup makes a perfect introduction to a light meal. Two cups plus one-half cup of boiled rice makes a satisfying meal for only 351 calories. This is not good for those who must keep their cholesterol and sodium firmly in mind. *SERVES 8*

Per 1-cup (240-ml) serving: 120 calories; 78 milligrams cholesterol; 3 grams fat; 580 milligrams sodium (661 if using canned tomatoes); 13 grams protein (29% RDA); 11 grams carbohydrate

RDA: calcium 10%; phosphorus 15%; iron 15%; vitamin A 60%; niacin 11%; vitamin C 105%

6 cloves garlic, smashed and peeled

1 small red bell pepper (6 ounces; 170 g), cut into 2-inch (5-cm) chunks (about 1 cup; 240 ml)

3 ribs celery (9 ounces; 255 g), peeled and cut into 2-inch (5-cm) chunks (about ¾ cup; 180 ml)

2 tablespoons chopped celery leaves

6 scallions, cut into 2-inch (5-cm) lengths

2 tablespoons chili powder (without cumin, if available; or substitute 2½ tablespoons chile powder with cumin)

1 teaspoon dried thyme

2 teaspoons vegetable oil

1 pound (450 g) large shrimp (20–24 per pound), peeled and deveined

8 ounces (227 g) fresh okra, trimmed and sliced into 1-inch- (2.5-cm-) thick rounds or 1 10-ounce (284-g) box frozen whole okra, defrosted in a sieve under warm water and sliced

2 cups (470 ml) Fresh Tomato Purée (page 468), or a 14½-ounce (220-ml) can tomatoes, drained and puréed in a food processor or blender

3 cups (705 ml) Basic Fish Broth (page 461)

2 teaspoons kosher salt, or to taste

(continued)

1. Place garlic, pepper, celery, celery leaves and scallions in a food processor. Process until coarsely chopped. Scrape vegetables into a 2½-quart (2.5-l) soufflé dish. Stir in chile powder, thyme and oil. Cover tightly with microwave plastic wrap. Cook at 100% for 5 minutes in a 650- to 700-watt oven. Prick plastic to release steam.

2. Remove from oven and uncover carefully. Mound vegetables in the center of the dish. Arrange shrimp around vegetables and place okra in the center, on top of the vegetables. Pour tomato purée over shrimp. Cover tightly with microwave plastic wrap. Cook for 3 minutes. Prick plastic.

3. Leaving dish in oven, stir ingredients well. Patch plastic and continue cooking for 2 minutes. Prick plastic.

4. Remove from oven. Uncover and add broth. Cook, uncovered, for 2 minutes or until hot. Stir in salt and serve.

Cut off stem of okra without exposing tubules.
When okra is sliced crosswise, tubules are exposed.

To serve 4. Use 3 cloves garlic, ½ small red bell pepper (3 ounces; 85 g), 1½ ribs celery (4½ ounces; 127 g), 1 tablespoon celery leaves, 3 scallions, 1 tablespoon chile powder, ½ teaspoon dried thyme, 1 teaspoon oil, ½ pound (227 g) shrimp, 4 ounces (113.5 g) fresh okra or ½ package frozen, 1 cup (240 ml) tomato purée, 1½ cups (360 ml) broth, and 1 teaspoon salt. Follow Step 1 and cook in a 2½-quart (2.5-l) soufflé dish for 3 minutes 30 seconds. Continue with Steps 2 and 3, cooking for 3 minutes, stirring ingredients after 2 minutes. Finish as in Step 4, cooking for 2 minutes or until hot.

FOR 400- TO 500-WATT OVENS

To serve 4. Prepare as in Step 1 and cook, covered, for 5 minutes. Follow Steps 2 and 3 and cook, covered, for 5 minutes, stirring after 3 minutes. Finish as in Step 4, cooking for 3 minutes or until hot.

Cold Soups

Cold soups are the traditional treats of summer and have usually meant lots of yummy cream and eggs, fat and cholesterol. It turns out that there are plenty of delicious ways to cheat and have the pleasure without the pain—a rare event. I find that with today's apartments and houses as warm in winter as in summer, I enjoy these at cold-weather meals. There are only two problems: They must be made four hours to a day ahead, and they do not travel well.

JELLIED FISH BROTH

*C*ome summer, I love jellied soups, even if they have to be made a day ahead. This has much more flavor than most cold soups. It is a perfect summer-meal starter, with a nice balance of acid and background flavors. Again, if you can afford the self-indulgence, Rouïlle (page 484) would be good on top. *SERVES 4*

Per 1-cup (240-ml) serving: 65 calories; 22 milligrams cholesterol; 0 grams fat; 330 milligrams sodium; 6 grams protein (14% RDA); 9 grams carbohydrate

RDA: vitamin C 12%

2¼ pounds (1 kg) fish bones and heads, cleaned of all blood and cut into 4-inch (10-cm) pieces
5 cups (1.2 l) water
Pinch saffron threads
⅓ cup (80 ml) white wine

2 ounces (56 g) canned American tomatoes packed in juice (about 1 tomato)
2 tablespoons tomato paste
7 cloves garlic, smashed and peeled
½ teaspoon ground fennel seeds

1. Place fish bones and water in a 5-quart (5-l) casserole. Cover tightly with microwave plastic wrap. Cook at 100% for 40 minutes in a 650- to 700-watt oven. Prick plastic to release steam.

2. Remove from oven and uncover. Let stand until room temperature. When cool, strain through a fine-meshed sieve lined with moistened cheesecloth. Rinse out casserole.

3. Combine saffron and wine in casserole. Cook, uncovered, for 30 seconds.

4. Place tomatoes, tomato paste, garlic and ¼ cup (60 ml) of the fish broth in a blender and blend until smooth. Stir into saffron-wine mixture and add remaining fish broth and ground fennel seeds. Cover and cook for 8 minutes. Prick plastic to release steam.

5. Remove from oven and uncover. Place soup in the refrigerator overnight or until well chilled and jelled.

CHILLED CUCUMBER SOUP

*T*his is fresh-tasting, cool and apparently creamy. A light soup for a summer meal, perfect before a salad or a substantial fish dish such as Fish Tagine (page 260) or Salmon in Red Wine (page 259). *SERVES 4*

Per 1-cup (240-ml) serving: 69 calories; 2 milligrams cholesterol; 1 gram fat; 281 milligrams sodium; 3.8 grams protein (8% RDA); 11 grams carbohydrate

RDA: calcium 9%; phosphorus 7%; riboflavin 9%; vitamin C 21%

2 cucumbers (about 1 pound; 450 g), peeled and seeded
2 cups (470 ml) Basic Chicken Broth (page 460), or unsalted or regular canned chicken broth

2 tablespoons cornstarch
1 cup (240 ml) buttermilk
½ teaspoon kosher salt, or to taste
1 tablespoon chopped fresh dill, optional

1. Thinly slice cucumbers and place in a 2½-quart (2.5-l) soufflé dish. Stir together ¼ cup (60 ml) broth and cornstarch to make a smooth slurry. Add to cucumbers with an additional ¾ cup (90 ml) broth. Cover tightly with microwave plastic wrap. Cook at 100% for 7 minutes in a 650- to 700-watt oven. Prick plastic to release steam.

2. Remove from oven and uncover carefully. Stir in remaining cup broth and buttermilk and refrigerate until chilled. Add salt to taste. Serve with dill sprinkled on top.

FOR 400- TO 500-WATT OVENS

To serve 4. Cook for 10 minutes.

SUMMER BORSCHT

This cold, sweet and sour Russian soup, with its brilliant magenta color, was one of my summer favorites when beets were young and sweet and when I was too. In those days, calories and cholesterol were far from my mind. I made it with heavy cream and devoured it with dollops of sour cream. Today, I make this version of borscht and enjoy it without guilt. The fat has gone, but the healthy calcium—almost one quarter of the RDA—and vitamin C linger on.   *SERVES 4*

Per 1-cup (240-ml) serving: 158 calories; 13 milligrams cholesterol; 3 grams fat; 380 milligrams sodium; 8 grams protein (18% RDA); 25 grams carbohydrate

RDA: calcium 23%; phosphorus 20%; iron 9%; 616 milligrams potassium; riboflavin 12%; vitamin C 71%

1 pound (450 g) beets, stems trimmed to 2 inches (5 cm) and scrubbed
1 cup (240 ml) apple juice (preferably without added sugar)
2 tablespoons plus 1 teaspoon cider vinegar
½ cup (120 ml) part-skim ricotta cheese
4 teaspoons fresh lemon juice
1½ cups (355 ml) buttermilk

½ teaspoon granulated sugar
½ teaspoon kosher salt, or to taste
1 cup (240 ml) water (approx.)
1⅓ ounces (40 g) white onion, peeled and chopped (about ⅓ cup; 80 ml)
1 cup (240 ml) peeled, seeded and chopped cucumber (about 1 pound; 450 g)
¼ cup (60 ml) chopped fresh dill

1. Place beets in a 3-inch- (7.5-cm) deep glass or ceramic dish large enough to hold them in a single layer. Cover tightly with microwave plastic wrap. Cook at 100% for 12 minutes in a 650- to 700-watt oven. Prick plastic to release steam.

2. Uncover carefully and test beets for tenderness. If a knife pierces them easily, they are done. If not, re-cover and cook 1–2 minutes longer or until tender.

3. When beets are cool enough to handle, peel and remove stems. Place in a blender or food processor. Add apple juice and vinegar and purée until very smooth. Remove all but ¼ cup (60 ml) of the mixture to a bowl. Add ricotta to the blender and blend until very smooth. Whisk into purée and add lemon juice, buttermilk, sugar, salt and enough water to thin soup to the desired consistency. Chill well, at least 4 hours.

4. Divide onion and cucumber among four serving bowls. Ladle soup over and sprinkle dill on top.

FOR 400- TO 500-WATT OVENS

To serve 4. Cook for 18 minutes.

24 KARAT SOUP

*F*rankly, I wasn't quite sure where to put this soup since it is as good hot as cold. Its color is radiant and it's quick and easy to make. With half a pita bread and a portion of fruit, it would make a good light lunch. Nevertheless, it is elegant enough to serve at any dinner. It is also a gold mine of vitamin A.   *SERVES 4*

Per 1-cup (240-ml) serving: 142 calories; 19 milligrams cholesterol; 9 grams fat; 255 milligrams sodium; 9 grams protein (21% RDA); 12.6 grams carbohydrate

RDA: calcium 20%; phosphorus 15%; iron 9%; vitamin A 433%; riboflavin 11%; niacin 9%; vitamin C 15%

¾ pound (340 g) carrots, peeled, trimmed and cut into 1-inch (2.5-cm) rounds (about 2 cups; 470 ml)
2¾ cups (650 ml) Basic Chicken Broth (page 460), or unsalted or regular canned chicken broth

1½ teaspoons ground cumin
1 cup (240 ml) part-skim ricotta cheese
½ teaspoon kosher salt, or to taste
1 tablespoon fresh lemon juice, or to taste

1. Place carrots, ¾ cup (180 ml) of the broth and cumin in a 9-inch (23-cm) pie plate. Cover tightly with microwave plastic wrap. Cook at 100% for 15 minutes in a 650- to 700-watt oven. Prick plastic to release steam.
2. Place ricotta and ¼ cup (60 ml) of broth in a blender. Blend until very smooth, about 1 minute.
3. Remove carrots from oven. Uncover and add to ricotta and broth in blender. Blend until very smooth. Remove to a serving bowl and add remaining ingredients (if you are serving the soup hot, do not add the lemon juice until after soup has been reheated). Refrigerate until chilled, or reheat, covered, for 4 minutes or until hot.

FOR 400- TO 500-WATT OVENS

To serve 4. Cook for 20 minutes. If serving hot, reheat for 5 minutes.

RED PEPPER SOUP

This soup is so simple, so good, so beautiful and so healthy, it seems like magic. The only catch is that it is really best made with a food mill to remove the pepper skin. You can purée the peppers coarsely in a food processor and then force them through a sieve; but that is much more work. This soup provides two days' worth of vitamin A and an astonishing seven days' worth of vitamin C. Surprisingly, it also has a substantial amount of iron.   *SERVES 4*

Per 1-cup (240-ml) serving: 74 calories; 0 grams cholesterol; 1 gram fat; 29 milligrams sodium (if no salt is added); 4 grams protein (8% RDA); 14.5 grams carbohydrate

RDA: calcium 7%; phosphorus 10%; iron 17%; 526 milligrams potassium; vitamin A 265%; thiamin 14%; riboflavin 10%; vitamin C 737%

2½ pounds (1.2 kg) red bell peppers (about 5 large peppers)	½ cup (120 ml) nonfat yogurt
2½ cups (590 ml) water	Kosher salt, to taste
	Freshly ground black pepper, to taste

1. Stem and seed and derib peppers. Place in a microwave plastic bag and loosely knot, or in a 2½-quart (2.5-ml) soufflé dish covered tightly with microwave plastic wrap. Cook at 100% for 15 minutes in a 650- to 700-watt oven. Prick plastic to release steam.
2. Remove from oven and uncover. Purée peppers in a food mill, using the medium disc.
3. Place red pepper purée in a mixing bowl and whisk in the water until well blended. Slowly whisk in the yogurt until smooth. Add salt and pepper to taste.
4. Chill in the refrigerator for three hours or overnight.

FOR 400- TO 500-WATT OVENS

To serve 4. Cook peppers for 25 minutes.

CHILLED CREAM OF TOMATO SOUP

*S*ummer provides a divine natural combination: basil and tomatoes. I grow basil plants between the tomato plants, which gives basil just enough shade so that it doesn't burn. You can serve this soup hot in mid-winter, but not if you must use dried basil. Increasingly, our markets carry fresh basil even in winter. I bring two plants into the house at the end of the summer, and that usually carries me through the better part of the winter. Canned tomatoes can be used, but remember, they will be salty. If serving hot, do not add lemon juice, and reheat, uncovered, for 1 minute. When hot, the soup will have tiny white flecks.

This fresh feast, perfect before an open sandwich or a plate of pasta with Diet Pesto (page 476), is also a gala of vitamin A, vitamin C, calcium, phosphorus and iron. *SERVES 4*

Per 1-cup (240-ml) serving: 131 calories; 7 milligrams cholesterol; 6 grams fat; 447 milligrams sodium (622 if using canned tomatoes); 6.5 grams protein (15% RDA); 15 grams carbohydrate

RDA: calcium 14%; phosphorus 13%; iron 11%; vitamin A 51%; thiamin 8%; riboflavin 11%; niacin 10%; vitamin C 64%

4 shallots (2 ounces; 56 g), peeled and thinly sliced (about ½ cup; 120 ml)
1 tablespoon olive oil
2 cups (470 ml) Fresh Tomato Purée (page 468), or a 1-pound (450-g) can tomatoes, puréed in the food processor
¼ cup (60 ml) shredded basil
Pinch powdered sage
1 teaspoon kosher salt

Pinch freshly ground black pepper
1½ cups (355 ml) Basic Chicken Broth (page 460), or unsalted or regular canned chicken broth
⅓ cup (80 ml) part-skim ricotta cheese, or Fromage Blanc (page 518)
⅓ cup (80 ml) nonfat yogurt, or buttermilk
Fresh lemon juice, to taste

1. Combine shallots and oil in a 2½-quart (2.5-l) soufflé dish. Cook, uncovered, at 100% for 2 minutes in a 650- to 700-watt oven.

2. Stir in ½ cup (120 ml) of the tomato purée, basil, sage, salt and pepper. Cook, uncovered, for 5 minutes. Remove from oven and stir in remaining purée and chicken broth.

3. Place ricotta in a blender. Add ¼ cup (60 ml) of the soup. Blend until smooth. Stir back into soup with yogurt and lemon juice. Chill until cool.

FOR 400- TO 500-WATT OVENS

To serve 4. Cook as in Step 1 for 3 minutes. Continue as in Step 2, cooking for 7 minutes. Finish as in Step 3.

SLIM VICHYSSOISE

I suppose that the dream of every cookery writer or chef is to create a dish that enters the culinary repertoire. With this cold variation on a French peasant classic, Louis Diat, once chef at New York's late, lamented Ritz Hotel, created a new classic. He might not have recognized this slim version; but I hope he might have liked it. I do. It keeps the sense of creamy luxury and the simplicity of the original, but cheats on the calories. What remains is protein, calcium, iron and vitamin C.

Vegetarians can use Vegetarian Broth I (page 465) instead of the chicken broth.   *SERVES 4*

Per 1-cup (240-ml) serving: 138 calories; 8 milligrams cholesterol; 7 grams fat; 285 milligrams sodium; 7 grams protein (15% RDA); 22 grams carbohydrate

RDA: calcium 13%; phosphorus 11%; iron 12%; niacin 10%; vitamin C 33%

¾ pound (340 g) potatoes, peeled and cut into 2-inch (5-cm) chunks (about 2 cups; 470 ml)

2 leeks (1 pound; 450 g), cleaned and cut across in 2-inch (5-cm) slices (about 1¼ cups; 300 ml)

2¼ cups (530 ml) Basic Chicken Broth (page 460), or unsalted or regular canned chicken broth

⅓ cup (80 ml) part-skim ricotta cheese

½ cup (120 ml) buttermilk

½ teaspoon kosher salt

2 tablespoons snipped fresh chives

1. Place potatoes and leeks in the work bowl of a food processor. Process until coarsely chopped. Scrape into a 2½-quart (2.5-l) soufflé dish. Add 1½ cups (355 ml) broth. Cover tightly with microwave plastic wrap. Cook at 100% for 10 minutes in a 650- to 700-watt oven. Prick plastic to release steam.

2. Remove from oven and uncover. Place ricotta in the work bowl of a food processor. Process until smooth. Add cooked potato mixture and ¼ cup (60 ml) broth and process until smooth.

3. Scrape into a serving bowl. Whisk in remaining broth, buttermilk and salt. Refrigerate until chilled. Serve with chives sprinkled on top.

FOR 400- TO 500-WATT OVENS

To serve 4. Cook for 20 minutes.

GOOD GRAINS AND OTHER STARCHES

*S*adly, *I hate being told what is good for me. I don't think I'm alone in that. Being told to stand up straight tends to send me into a slump. Being told to get more of my nutrition from carbohydrate sounds stodgy, until I realize that what is being talked about are some of my favorite foods: bread, pasta and noodles, risotto, baked potato, polenta, grits, beans and chick-peas. These are the foods that can make a meal and have in varying combinations for centuries, or they can fill out a meal, make it satisfying as well as good for us and keep us from feeling hungry.*

The Venetian favorite of a soupy risotto with peas, risi bisi, which has been expanded into a Green Risotto; the Southwestern combination of Chilied Red Beans with rice; and the Cuban Black Beans and Rice, are all good main courses, as, for me, are other risottos and the pastas. Many vegetarian dishes throughout the book, such as Summer Vegetable Jamboree (page 81) and Summer Vegetable Stew (page 449), can be made into main courses by using larger portions and pairing them with beans and pasta, or brown rice. Pasta dishes can open a meal or be it. So can bean soups, which are in this chapter rather than in Soups because they depend on basic bean-cooking times. Vary your recipes so you don't eat a potato with everything—good, but potentially boring.

Many of the starches in our lives turn up at breakfast. See pages 152–160 for recipes.

Carbohydrate

How much carbohydrate is enough? The same government that has not given an RDA for carbohydrate is telling us to eat more, and the figures change hourly and according to whatever group or agency you talk to. Even on a 1,200-calorie-a-day weight-loss diet, try to get 90 to 100 grams of carbohydrate a day; that's my best guess. As your diet increases in calories, so should the amount of carbohydrate you are getting. However, from the point of view of reducing cholesterol and feeling full, you cannot be hurt by getting yet more carbohydrate. If you follow the plans in Diets and Menus, you will be fine.

Vegetarians and vegans, who eat no milk or eggs, will be getting much more of their total calories and nutrition from carbohydrates. Different carbohydrate-rich foods have different amounts and kinds of protein that can complement each other to provide fairly full nutrition, especially in the vitamin-rich world of the vegetarian, who also drinks milk and eats cheese. No combination provides enough iron and B vitamins (see page 340 to see why spinach and grains will not do the job). For vegetarians and vegans, talking with their doctors or a licensed dietitian is the best thing to do.

While the bran and germ of grains such as wheat, oats and rice are higher in iron—10 to 16 percent of the RDA in a one-ounce (28 g) serving—than various flours, that same ounce also has eighty to one hundred calories, and the iron isn't the heme iron that you want.

FIBER

There is another element of the brans and germs that thrust them into our consciousness. It is their relatively high component of dietary fiber, of which the soluble part has been shown to reduce the clots in the blood vessels caused by cholesterol. Nonsoluble fiber or crude fiber has been recommended by various scientists concerned with cancer prevention as helpful in reducing the risk of bowel cancer, and by doctors in general to prevent diverticulitis and constipation. Both kinds of fiber are readily available in a well-balanced diet. Beneficial fibers are not the property of any one kind of grain. They are in beans, grains, legumes and many vegetables. It certainly will not hurt you to have a bowl of Oatmeal (page 158) or a whole-grain rice cereal for breakfast, as long as it isn't laden with fats and sugar, and it may provide some insurance against an unbalanced diet. If you refuse to eat starches and vegetables, I suppose sprinkling bran or germ on things will help; but it's hardly a good solution. Fads should not be taken too seriously.

Even pasta can be a source of fiber, particularly spinach and whole wheat, which have 10.6 grams and 11.8 grams per dry ounce (28 g), respectively, versus anywhere from 2.4 grams for spaghetti to 5.4 grams for udon. Conversely, oat bran has about 4.1 grams per ounce, and wheat bran, 10.8 grams per ounce. I'd rather have a bowl of pasta myself. As long as you eat your carbohydrates and vegetables, you shouldn't have any problem.

Don't go overboard. There is such a thing as too much fiber. It will push good things out of your system along with the bad.

Whole Grains Versus Polished and Ground Ones

Whole grains, seeds, beans and potatoes (with their skins left on and, when applicable, with their germs left in) are somewhat more nutritious than those that have been polished, such as white rice and pearled barley. However, many kinds of white rice are fortified to actually give them more of some nutrients than are found in the brown kind. This will matter to you primarily if you come from a culture whose nutritional mainstay is polished white rice. It will also matter to you if you are a vegetarian. Where else are you going to get your zinc?

MICROWAVE COOKING OF STARCHES

Here, unfortunately and literally, we come to the sticking point. While whole grains—rice, for example—and beans can be cooked very well in the microwave oven, flours and foods made with flour, such as pasta, do much less well. Some cooking times for starches appear to be no shorter than they are on top of the stove. Remember that the time to bring the water to the boil is not included in conventional recipes; but it is in microwave recipes. Even so, if you are serving your plain white or brown rice, boiled or steamed, as an accompaniment, it generally makes more sense to cook it on top of the stove, being sure to allow enough time so that your rapidly cooked main course isn't waiting and getting cold. An exception would be when you are serving rice with a bean dish or meat stew that has a standing time. The rice can be cooked while the other dish waits. Pasta almost always should be cooked on top of the stove.

Grits, breakfast cereals, risottos and polenta—cornmeal mush—are always worth doing in the microwave oven. They cook quickly and there are no lumps. Many potato dishes are very satisfactory. While dried beans take quite a while to cook, the time is considerably reduced from conventional cooking. Many people may be tempted to substitute canned beans for convenience, especially when they are just a side dish. Those who need to watch their sodium should beware (see page 19). Blanched or cooked beans keep well in the refrigerator, covered with liquid, and are nice to have on hand.

The dishes below that make full meals work very well in the microwave oven and will save you time.

Breads and Good-for-You Breakfasts

All over the Western world bread is the staff of life. That doesn't mean that nobody eats rice, pasta or other grains. However, rice is not the primary source of nutrition, which it is in the East. It is too bad that many of the breads we eat are poor sources of nutrition, including many of the breads advertised as low-calorie, since only bulk and air are increased.

If you don't have a good source of whole-grain bread available to you, it is well worthwhile making it yourself. It's even fun. Both of the whole-grain breads in this chapter keep well if wrapped in plastic wrap and refrigerated. If you find that too tempting—bread does have calories—slice the bread and wrap and freeze individual slices. Unwrap one and toast it, which will defrost it, to get a good start on the day.

The breads are baked in a conventional oven; but following them are numerous recipes for muffins and breakfast cereals that are cooked in the microwave oven. Although the breads are conventionally baked, the dough is forced—raised quickly—in a microwave oven. There is even a recipe for Oat Bran Wafers, in case you want to make, rather than buy, these crispy accompaniments to lunch.

Later in this chapter you will find recipes for Grits and Soft Polenta, which can clearly be used as breakfast cereal.

To pick the other foods in your breakfast you may want to know the relative nutrition of juices (page 73) and fruits (pages 532–533). You will find recipes for low-sugar—even vegetarian—jams on pages 587–594, and recipes for cottage-cheese spreads on pages 514–517. Start the day right.

Kneading bread by hand is a pleasure. However, you can do it quite well with a heavy-duty mixer or food processor. Glass or ceramic loaf pans can be used in both a microwave and a conventional oven. There are newly available glass loaf pans with release coatings on the inside. This saves greasing the pan, as well as fat and calories. If you are using an uncoated pan, spray the inside lightly with vegetable oil. The coated and uncoated pans are slightly different in size. This will make no difference to your results. Doughs can be risen in microwave ovens, but only in 650- to 700-watt ovens.

1. Mix dough until it absorbs most of the flour and pulls away from the sides of the bowl. Begin kneading.

2. If kneading by hand, rub hands with a little flour. Dust a work surface with flour. Form the dough into a ball. (As you knead, add as little flour as possible.) Push the ball of dough with the heel of your hand to flatten and stretch it. Fold flattened dough in half and turn it one quarter of a circle. Repeat until the sticky, shaggy blob of dough you started with is stretchy and smooth. The whole thing will take four to fifteen minutes. When the dough is sufficiently kneaded, blisters will break on its surface as you push. Press a finger into the dough. If it is springy and bounces back, it is ready.

OR

2. Dust with a little flour the large bowl of a mixer with a dough hook. Put in dough; mix at a low speed for four minutes, scraping down the sides of the bowl from time to time. Remove from bowl to floured surface and finish by hand.

3. Form dough into a ball and put in an ungreased bowl. Cover with two layers of paper towel, and let rise until doubled in bulk—looking twice as large. Allow forty-five minutes in a warm place.

OR

3. Place dough in bowl as above. Force—make it rise more quickly—in a microwave oven. Place covered bowl to one side of oven and a glass of water on the other side of oven. Rise dough at 10%—lowest setting—for 15 minutes.

4. When the dough has doubled in bulk, punch it down—deflate it by pushing your hand into it once or twice. Divide the dough into as many balls as the recipe makes loaves. Flatten each ball, fold the sides under and tuck in each end. Place each piece of dough in an oil-sprayed, or release-surface–lined, loaf pan and smooth the top of the dough with your hand.

5. Preheat conventional oven to 350°F (177°C).

6. Cover each pan with doubled paper toweling and let rise until doubled again, 30 minutes in a warm place. To force in a microwave oven, put covered pans in oven with a glass of water and rise at 10% for 10 minutes.

7. Bake in conventional oven as directed in recipe.

8. Test to see that loaves are done. They will sound hollow—top and bottom—when thumped with a knuckle.

9. Allow unmolded loaves to cool on racks.

MAJIC WHOLE GRAIN BREAD

I know "Majic" looks a little silly; but I wanted you to know that this highly nutritious bread tastes absolutely wonderful and lasts seemingly forever. I have kept it, well wrapped, in the refrigerator for up to two weeks without any problem. As with all dense or fragile breads, use a sharp serrated knife for cutting. The quarter-inch slice is rich and dense, not fluffy like the usual diet bread. It is filling. I like a little salt in my bread, but those who must avoid sodium as much as possible can simply omit it.   *MAKES 2 LOAVES, EACH YIELDING 32 ¼-INCH (.5-CM) SLICES; 64 PORTIONS*

Per 1-slice serving: 44 calories; 0 milligrams cholesterol; 0 grams fat; 70 milligrams sodium; 2 grams protein (4% RDA); 8 grams carbohydrate

RDA: phosphorus 6%; iron 3%; thiamin 6%; riboflavin 2%; niacin 3%

2 envelopes dry yeast
3 cups (705 ml) warm water (110°F; 43°C)
2 cups (470 ml) whole wheat flour
2 cups (470 ml) all-purpose flour
1 cup (240 ml) rye flour

1 cup (240 ml) oat bran
1 cup (240 ml) toasted unsweetened wheat germ
1 tablespoon kosher salt (2 teaspoons kosher salt if on a low-sodium diet)

1. Sprinkle yeast over 1 cup (240 ml) of the water in a small bowl. Stir and let stand until bubbling.

2. Combine dry ingredients in a large bowl. Thoroughly beat in yeast mixture. Add remaining 2 cups (470 ml) of water.

3. Knead and raise dough as in General Instructions (page 151).

4. Divide the dough into two equal pieces (each 1¾ pounds; 800 g). Put each half into a loaf pan and let rise as in General Instructions.

5. Bake in a preheated oven (350°F; 177°C) for 20 minutes. Sprinkle the tops of the loaves with warm water and bake 40 minutes more.

MULTI GRAIN BREAD

*T*his bread will only keep for a few days unless frozen. Defrost a whole loaf for six minutes at 100% in a 650- to 700-watt microwave oven. Then crisp in a preheated regular oven at 350°F (177°C). It is somewhat lighter in taste than Majic Whole Grain Bread and is paler (vaguely yellow if you use yellow cornmeal). I like it for sandwiches as well as for breakfast.

MAKES 2 LOAVES, EACH YIELDING 32 ¼-INCH (.5-CM) SLICES; 64 PORTIONS

Per serving: 47 calories; 0 milligrams cholesterol; 0 grams fat; 44 milligrams sodium; 1.5 grams protein (3% RDA); 9 grams carbohydrate

RDA: phosphorus 3%; iron 2%; thiamin 3%; riboflavin 2%; niacin 3%

2 packages active dry yeast
3 cups (705 ml) warm water (about 110°F; 43°C)
2 cups (470 ml) pumpernickel flour
1 cup (240 ml) cornmeal

2½ cups (590 ml) all-purpose flour plus ½ cup (120 ml) for kneading
2 cups (470 ml) quick-cooking oats
2 teaspoons kosher salt

1. Sprinkle yeast over 1 cup (240 ml) of the water in a small bowl. Stir and let stand until bubbling.
2. Combine dry ingredients in a large bowl. Thoroughly beat in yeast mixture. Add remaining 2 cups (470 ml) of water.
3. Knead and raise dough as in General Instructions (page 151).
4. Divide the dough into two equal pieces (each 1¾ pounds; 800 g). Put each half into a loaf pan and let rise as in General Instructions.
5. Bake in preheated oven (350°F; 177°C) for 20 minutes. Sprinkle the tops of the loaves with warm water and bake 40 minutes more.

BREAD CRUMBS

Since flour can be problematic in a microwave oven, it is sometimes better to start a recipe with bread crumbs. Most of us have leftover bread that can be turned into fresh crumbs and then batter. The number of calories, the nutritional advantages and the amount of bread you will have to start with will vary with the bread type. The crumbs used in the following recipes are based on ordinary commercial sliced bread. If using denser, more nutritious bread, the weight of bread needed for the crumbs, the calories and the nutrition will all increase slightly. The easiest way to make bread crumbs is to tear the bread into pieces and then chop in a food processor with on-off pulses until slightly coarse crumbs are formed.   *MAKES 1 CUP COARSE FRESH BREAD CRUMBS FROM:*

Just over two slices commercial white
    or whole wheat bread, or three one-
    inch-thick slices French or Italian
    bread (1.6 ounces; 45 g)
Two and a half slices Majic Whole
    Grain Bread (page 152) or Multi
    Grain Bread (page 153) (3.2 ounces;
    90 g)

Two slices dense commercial white
    bread (1.8 ounces; 50 g)

STEAMED BANANA MUFFINS

*T*hese are simply delicious, if rich, muffins that make part of a healthy breakfast. They will keep for several days after cooking, or the uncooked batter can be kept in the refrigerator until needed, which is why there are cooking times for small amounts of batter.   *MAKES 10 MUFFINS*

Per 1-muffin serving: 165 calories; 28 milligrams cholesterol; 8 grams fat; 217 milligrams sodium; 3 grams protein (6% RDA); 23 grams carbohydrate

RDA: calcium 3%; phosphorus 6%; iron 15%; vitamin A 6%; thiamin 6%; riboflavin 8%; niacin 7%; vitamin C 5%

1 cup (240 ml) fresh white bread crumbs, from about 1.6 ounces (45 g) bread
¾ cup (180 ml) finely ground bran flakes, from about 1½ cups (355 ml) bran flakes cereal
1½ teaspoons baking soda
2 tablespoons light brown sugar

2 large very ripe bananas (each about 8 ounces; 227 g), mashed with a fork (1½ cups; 355 ml)
⅓ cup (80 ml) buttermilk
⅓ cup (80 ml) vegetable oil
1 egg white
½ cup (120 ml) raisins

1. Combine bread crumbs, bran, baking soda and sugar in a large bowl.
2. Place mashed bananas in a small bowl. Stir in remaining ingredients. Add to the dry ingredients and stir with a fork just to mix.
3. Scoop batter into each of 10 3½ × 1½-inch (9 × 4-cm) ramekins. Place evenly spaced around the carrousel or directly on the bottom of the oven. Cook, uncovered, at 100% for 6 minutes in a 650- to 700-watt oven.
4. Remove from oven. Unmold muffins onto a plate and serve warm.

To serve 5. Use ½ cup (120 ml) bread crumbs, ⅓ cup (80 ml) bran flakes, ¾ teaspoon baking soda, 1 tablespoon sugar, 1 banana, 2 tablespoons buttermilk, 2 tablespoons oil, 1 egg white and ¼ cup (60 ml) raisins. Cook for 3 minutes.

To serve 2. Cook ½ cup batter in 2 ramekins for 1 minute 30 seconds.

To serve 1. Cook ¼ cup batter in 1 ramekin for 1 minute.

FOR 400- TO 500-WATT OVENS

To serve 4. Cook for 8 minutes.

To serve 2. Cook for 3 minutes 30 seconds.

To serve 1. Cook for 2 minutes.

APPLE OAT BRAN MUFFINS

*T*hese have fewer calories than the preceding muffins, and are just as sweet and good. The lower amount of calories means that you can have one at lunch with a salad.   *SERVES 8*

Per 1-muffin serving: 128 calories; 0 milligrams cholesterol; 5 grams fat; 155 milligrams sodium; 4 grams protein (8% RDA); 18 grams carbohydrate

RDA: calcium 2%; phosphorus 10%; iron 6%; thiamin 10%; riboflavin 4%; niacin 1%; vitamin C 25%

⅓ cup (80 ml) fresh whole wheat bread crumbs, from about .53 ounce (15 g) bread
1¼ cups (300 ml) unprocessed oat bran
1¼ teaspoons baking soda
4½ teaspoons light brown sugar
1 teaspoon cinnamon

1 cup (240 ml) Applesauce (page 548), or unsweetened canned
2 teaspoons fresh lemon juice
2 egg whites
¼ cup (60 ml) defrosted apple juice concentrate
2 tablespoons vegetable oil

1. Combine the bread crumbs, oat bran, baking soda, sugar and cinnamon in a mixing bowl.

2. Stir the remaining ingredients together in another bowl and add to the dry ingredients. Stir quickly with a fork just to mix.

3. Spoon ⅓ cup (80 ml) of batter into each of 8 3½ × 1½-inch (9 × 4-cm) ramekins and place evenly spaced around the carrousel or directly on the bottom of the oven. Cook, uncovered, at 100% for 8 minutes in a 650- to 700-watt oven.

4. Remove from oven. Turn muffins onto a plate and serve warm.

To serve 5. Use ¼ cup (60 ml) bread crumbs, ¾ cup (180 ml) oat bran, ¾ teaspoon baking soda, 1 tablespoon brown sugar, ¾ teaspoon cinnamon, ½ cup (120 ml) applesauce, 1 teaspoon lemon juice, 1 egg white, 2 tablespoons apple juice concentrate and 1 tablespoon oil. Cook for 6 minutes.

FOR 400- TO 500-WATT OVENS

To serve 5. Cook for 11 minutes.

PUMPKIN MUFFINS

*T*hese healthy muffins have a robust flavor—good on a winter morning. They are sweet enough that some of us might consider them dessert or a welcome snack. Since the batter doesn't hold well, make all the muffins at once. The muffins keep well refrigerated.   *SERVES 6*

Per serving: 113 calories; 0 milligrams cholesterol; 2 grams fat; 334 milligrams sodium; 3 grams protein (7% RDA); 21 grams carbohydrate

RDA: calcium 3%; phosphorus 3%; iron 5%; vitamin A 5%; riboflavin 5%; niacin 4%; vitamin C 2%

1 cup (240 ml) coarsely powdered
   graham crackers, about 7½ crackers
   (pulse in a food processor, or
   pulverize with a rolling pin)
½ cup (120 ml) whole wheat bread
   crumbs, from about .80 ounce (22.5
   g) bread
1¼ teaspoons baking soda

¾ teaspoon allspice
½ teaspoon nutmeg
1 teaspoon ginger
3 teaspoons molasses
¼ cup (60 ml) skim milk
2 egg whites
4 ounces (113.5 g) unsweetened
   pumpkin purée (½ cup; 120 ml)

1. Combine graham cracker crumbs, bread crumbs, baking soda and spices in a large mixing bowl. Combine remaining ingredients in a small bowl and add to the dry ingredients. Stir lightly with a fork just to mix.

2. Divide batter evenly among 6 3½ × 1½-inch (9 × 4-cm) ramekins. Place evenly spaced around the carrousel or directly on the bottom of the oven. Cook, uncovered, at 100% for 7 minutes 30 seconds in a 650- to 700-watt oven.

3. Remove from oven. Turn out onto a serving dish and serve warm or at room temperature.

OATMEAL

*T*here is no better way to start the day, particularly a cold one, than with a bowl of hot cereal. Top it off with some nonfat milk and half a banana, sliced, or with a little maple sugar.   *SERVES 1*

Per serving: 103 calories; 0 milligrams cholesterol; 2 grams fat; 89 milligrams sodium; 4 grams protein (9% RDA); 18 grams carbohydrate

RDA: phosphorus 13%; iron 6%; thiamin 13%

⅓ cup (80 ml) old-fashioned rolled oats   ¾ cup (180 ml) water
   (not "quick-cooking")   Pinch kosher salt

    1. Combine all ingredients in a 2-cup (470-ml) glass measure. Cover tightly with microwave plastic wrap. Cook at 100% for 1 minute in a 650- to 700-watt oven. Prick plastic to release steam.
    2. Remove from oven and uncover. Cook, uncovered, for 1 minute 30 seconds more.
    3. Remove from oven. Let stand for 1 minute and serve hot.

To serve 2–3. Use ⅔ cup (160 ml) oats, 1½ cups (355 ml) water and a pinch salt. Cook as in Step 1 in a 4-cup (1-l) glass measure for 2 minutes 30 seconds. Cook as in Step 2 for 1 minute. Finish as in Step 3.

FOR 400- TO 500-WATT OVENS

To serve 1. Cook as in Step 1 for 2 minutes. Cook as in Step 2 for 2 minutes.

To serve 2. Cook as in Step 1 for 4 minutes 30 seconds. Cook as in Step 2 for 2 minutes.

IRISH OATMEAL

*T*his is the coarse oatmeal with lots of texture. It's slightly more expensive and harder to find than rolled oats; but it's less caloric. You need a large container to cook this in, as otherwise it tends to boil over.   *SERVES 1*

Per serving: 78 calories; 0 milligrams cholesterol; 1 gram fat; 89 milligrams sodium; 3 grams protein (7% RDA); 14 grams carbohydrate

RDA: calcium 1%; phosphorus 10%; iron 5%; thiamin 9%

1 cup (240 ml) water   Pinch kosher salt
¼ cup (60 ml) Irish or Scotch oatmeal

   1.   Combine water and oatmeal in an 8-cup (2-l) glass measure. Cover tightly with microwave plastic wrap. Cook at 100% for 4 minutes 30 seconds in a 650- to 700-watt oven. Prick plastic to release steam.
   2.   Remove from oven and uncover. Cook, uncovered, for 5 to 6 minutes more.
   3.   Remove from oven. Stir in salt and serve hot.

To serve 2 or 3. Use 2 cups (470 ml) water, ½ cup (120 ml) oatmeal and salt to taste. Cook as in Step 1 for 5 minutes. Cook as in Step 2 for 8–9 minutes, stirring once halfway through cooking. Finish as in Step 3.

FOR 400- TO 500-WATT OVENS

To serve 1. Cook as in Step 1 for 7 minutes. Cook as in Step 2 for 12 minutes. Finish as in Step 3.

FARINA

*T*his is a quick and easy family breakfast with so few calories that they can still have toast and a portion of fruit. That should fill them all up. *SERVES 4*

Per serving: 81 calories; 0 milligrams cholesterol; 0 grams fat; 369 milligrams sodium; 2 grams protein (5% RDA); 17 grams carbohydrate

RDA: calcium 1%; phosphorus 2%; iron 5%; thiamin 8%; riboflavin 4%; niacin 4%

3 cups (705 ml) water 1 teaspoon kosher salt, or to taste
½ cup (120 ml) farina

    1. Place water in an 8-cup (2-l) glass measure or 2½-quart (2.5-l) soufflé dish. Heat, uncovered, at 100% for 6 minutes in a 650- to 700-watt oven.
    2. Add farina and salt and stir well to combine. Cook, uncovered, at 100% for 3 minutes. Remove from oven and serve hot.

To serve 2. Use 1½ cups (355 ml) water, ¼ cup (60 ml) farina and ½ teaspoon salt. Cook as in Step 1 in a 4-cup (1-l) glass measure for 3 minutes 30 seconds. Continue cooking as in Step 2 for 2 minutes.

To serve 1. Use ¾ cup (180 ml) water, 2 tablespoons farina and ¼ teaspoon salt. Cook as in Step 1 in a 2-cup (470-ml) glass measure for 2 minutes. Continue cooking as in Step 2 for 1 minute.

FOR 400- TO 500-WATT OVENS

To serve 4. Cook as in Step 1 for 9 minutes. Cook as in Step 2 for 5 minutes.

To serve 2. Cook as in Step 1 for 6 minutes. Cook as in Step 2 for 3 minutes.

To serve 1. Cook as in Step 1 for 3 minutes. Cook as in Step 2 for 2 minutes.

OAT BRAN WAFERS

*I*t's possible and easy to buy whole-grain flat breads, and some of them are low in calories. It's a lot cheaper to make them.   *MAKES 12 WAFERS*

Per wafer: 24 calories; 0 milligrams cholesterol; 0.3 grams fat; 0.3 milligrams sodium; 1 gram protein (2% RDA); 5 grams carbohydrate

RDA: phosphorus 3%; iron 2%; thiamin 3%; riboflavin 1%; niacin 1%

¼ cup (60 ml) plus 2 tablespoons
   warm (about 110°F; 43°C) water
½ teaspoon active dry yeast

¼ cup (60 ml) oat bran
½ cup (120 ml) whole wheat flour,
   plus additional for rolling

1. Place the water in a warm bowl. Sprinkle yeast over water and stir until completely dissolved. Let stand 5 minutes.

2. Stir in oat bran. Add whole wheat flour gradually, stirring continuously to form a stiff dough. Turn dough out onto a board and knead just until smooth.

3. Return dough to the cleaned bowl and cover with a kitchen towel. Let stand in a warm place for 1 hour. (There will not be much of an increase in the size of the dough.)

4. Turn out dough onto a board lightly floured with whole wheat flour. Roll dough into a rectangle approximately 12 × 8½ inches (30.5 × 21.5 cm) and ¹⁄₁₆-inch (.15-cm) thick, using additional flour as needed. Trim dough to an even rectangle and cut into pieces approximately 1¾ × 4 inches (4.5 × 10 cm). Prick each piece 12 times with the tines of a fork (3 rows of 4).

5. Line the carrousel of the oven with microwavable paper towels. Arrange as many of the dough pieces as possible without touching each other around the outside edge of the carrousel. Place remaining pieces in the center. Cook at 100% for 3 minutes 30 seconds in a 650- to 700-watt oven. Slightly longer cooking time may be necessary for the pieces in the center or during very humid weather. Remove wafers at once and let cool in a single layer.

FOR 400- TO 500-WATT OVENS

To make 12. Cook for 5 minutes.

Pasta Pleasure for Dieting

The world seems to be in the grip of noodle mania and pasta leads the hit parade, which is fine for your diet as long as you don't smother the noodles—as in fettuccine Alfredo—with heavy cream and cheese and even egg yolks. That wouldn't be so bad if it were all you ate; but following with meat and topping it off with zabaglione means trouble. The Italians really don't eat that way. Their pastas have a miniumum of highly flavored sauces. Pasta is not meant to swim in liquid unless it is soup.

They do use pastas and risottos as first courses and follow them with fish or meat; but typically the pasta will be light and the meat portion small and followed by a salad and perhaps fruit and cheese. Dessert is a rare festivity saved for special occasions.

The distinction in America between noodles and pasta has nothing to do with their country of origin. Flour and water and, optionally, vegetables and seasonings make pasta. When eggs or parts of eggs are added, pasta becomes noodles. The eggs don't add calories; they do add a small amount of fat and cholesterol. Technically, it doesn't matter what kind of grain is used; but it will make a difference to the flavor, texture and trace nutrients. Dry egg noodles typically swell up somewhat more in cooking than pastas do.

For those who are allergic to wheat, there are pastas made with artichokes or rice flour. Pasta may also be flavored or colored with tomatoes, carrots, squid or cuttlefish ink, dried mushrooms, spinach and even cocoa. Check the boxes for nutrition information.

The Chinese and Japanese have been using pasta and noodles for millennia. It sounds kind of dumb to call the Chinese products pasta; they are usually called noodles even if they are not made with eggs. The Chinese make their noodles both with and without eggs. Among the most available of Oriental pastas are brownish noodles with buckwheat, brittle white rice noodles, almost transparent mung bean noodles, wheat flour noodles and noodles with soy or seaweed. Orientals, including Thais, Vietnamese and Malaysians, are more likely to use their noodles as the base of a main course than in soup. They have cold noodle dishes, hot noodle dishes and fried noodle dishes.

Increasingly we in the West, even the Italians, are eating pasta as a main course; but it shows up as a first course, in soups, as a side dish and even in desserts.

PASTA PORTIONS

When you look at these recipes, you may think: Where's the pasta? While it's true that many of these sauces, especially Tomato Sauce Casalinga, are marvelous for other uses—to cook with, to put over other starches like polenta, to serve with plainly cooked fish, poultry, meat and vegetables—they are really meant to go over pasta. Pick your own favorite kind, although I make suggestions with each recipe.

While neither pasta nor these sauces is injurious to your health, too much pasta—rather than excess of these sauces—can easily add to your weight. Even an extra ounce of dry pasta will keep you from taking weight off. Most of the calories are in the pasta itself. Therefore, I recommend the following portions for those on weight-loss diets.

Allow yourself two ounces (57 g) of dry pasta for a first course; it will boil up to about three-quarters to one cup (180–240 ml). Allow three ounces (85 g), one to one and a half cups (240–355 ml) cooked, as a main course.

PASTA YIELDS

Before you think about making and serving pasta, you need to know how much you will want to cook per person and how much that will make as a serving.

Larger pasta shapes, such as shells, will take up more space when dry—for their weight—than small shapes; but small shapes will usually cook up to a somewhat greater volume. If the amount on your plate is more important to you than firm texture, cook the pasta longer and it will absorb more water.

ORZO (small, rice-shaped)

Dry:
2 ounces (56 g) or ⅓ cup (80 ml)
Cooked:
4½ ounces (128 g) or ¾ cup (180 ml)

Dry:
3 ounces (85 g) or ½ cup (120 ml)
Cooked:
6¾ ounces (191 g) or 1 cup plus 2 tablespoons (256 ml)

SHELLS, medium

Dry:
2 ounces (56 g) or 1 cup (240 ml)
Cooked:
5¼ ounces (149 g) or 1 cup (240 ml)

Dry:
3 ounces (85 g) or 1½ cups (355 ml)
Cooked:
7⅞ ounces (222 g) or 1 cup (240 ml)

LINGUINE

Dry:
2 ounces (56 g)
Cooked:
5 ounces (142 g) or ¾ cup (180 ml)

Dry:
3 ounces (85 g)
Cooked:
7½ ounces (213 g) or 1 cup plus 2 tablespoons (256 ml)

EGG NOODLES

Dry egg noodles tend to swell more in cooking by absorbing more water than the pastas. Three ounces (85 g) of dry egg noodles will cook up to make two cups (470 ml) and will have almost twice as many calories as three ounces of pasta. Start with one and a half ounces (43 g) of dry egg noodles to make a one-cup (240-ml) main-course portion, and start with three quarters of an ounce (21 g) of dry to make a half-cup (120-ml) first-course portion. Many egg noodles come in little circular nests that weight about .70 ounce (20 g). One of these nests can be used per person as a first course. Use two per person for a main course.

ADD PASTA NUTRITION TO SAUCE NUTRITION

Since neither pasta nor noodles is listed in the recipes, it is not included in the nutritional listings for the recipes. Look at Basic Pasta Nutrition below, and add the amount of calories for the quantity of pasta you are using to the amount for the sauce of your choice. The nutrition is always given for a main-course portion of sauce. If using less sauce for a first-course portion—usually half—reduce the calories and other nutritional information accordingly. Usually, you will halve these figures for a first-course serving.

BASIC PASTA NUTRITION

The mineral content of pasta is determined almost entirely by the grain or kind of wheat from which it is made. Semolina pasta contains iron, calcium, magnesium, phosphorus, potassium, sodium, zinc, copper and selenium. Two ounces (57 g) of dry pasta supply 10 percent of the RDA of iron.

PER SCANT ¾–1 CUP (180–240 ML) COOKED PASTA (FIRST-COURSE) SERVING, FROM 1½ OUNCES (43 G) DRY PASTA: 157 calories; 0 milligrams cholesterol; 0 grams fat; 1 milligram sodium; 5 grams protein (9% RDA); 32 grams carbohydrate

PER 1–1½ CUPS (240–355 ML) COOKED PASTA (MAIN-COURSE) SERVING, FROM 3 OUNCES (85 G) DRY PASTA: 314 calories; 0 milligrams cholesterol; 1 gram fat; 2 milligrams sodium; 11 grams protein (17% RDA); 64 grams carbohydrate

PER 1 CUP (240 ML) COOKED EGG NOODLES FROM 1½ OUNCES (43 G) DRY NOODLES: 165 calories; 0 milligrams cholesterol; 2 grams fat; 0 milligrams sodium; 6 grams protein (10% RDA); 30 grams carbohydrate

PER 2 CUPS (240 ML) COOKED EGG NOODLES FROM 3 OUNCES (85 G) DRY EGG NOODLES: 330 calories; 0 milligrams cholesterol; 3 grams fat; 0 milligrams sodium; 12 grams protein (19% RDA); 60 grams carbohydrate

Cooking Pasta

Bring a large pot of water to a boil on top of the stove. If you are on a salt-restricted diet, do not add salt to the water. If salt is not a problem, add about one teaspoon kosher salt for each quart (1 l) of water. With salt or without, a bay leaf in a large pot of water will give a lovely flavor to the pasta. When the water is boiling, add the pasta and stir until the water comes back to a boil. This keeps the strands or pieces of pasta from sticking. Cook the pasta to taste. The length of time will vary with the shape and age of the pasta, whether it is dry or not, what grains it is made from and your inclination. Most dry pastas take about seven minutes to cook to the chewy state Italians like; fresh ones cook in a minute or so, unless they are frozen. This is a situation in which tasting is appropriate.

Before you drain the pasta, ladle out some of the cooking liquid to use if you wish. Drain pasta; but do not rinse unless specially instructed. If you are on a weight-loss diet and need to keep the pasta from sticking, either toss with a spoon or so of the cooking liquid or an appropriate broth. If weight loss is not an issue, toss the pasta with a little olive oil.

You will usually need to bring the pasta water to a boil before you start making your sauce. That way both parts of the dish will be ready at the same time.

What to Serve with Pasta

Many of these sauces are vegetarian and low in protein. They are good with both first- and main-course pasta dishes. When used as the main course, precede with a high-protein first course, such as Caprese Salad (page 80) or Bell Peppers and Sardines with Balsamic Vinegar (page 84). As first courses, they make perfect beginnings for meals with plenty of protein but few calories and little carbohydrate. Look in The Fish and Shellfish Advantage (pages 226–288) and Perfectly Poultry (pages 289–339).

Other pasta sauces contain fish, shellfish or meat. They will have more protein and cholesterol. As first courses, pair them with some of the lower-cholesterol main courses. As main courses, they would go well with salads and desserts— very Italian if dessert is fruit and cheese.

The Oriental noodle dishes are intended as side dishes and should present no special problems.

Topping the Pasta

While you can use commercial pasta sauces, they usually are high in sodium and may be high in calories or cholesterol. Read labels. See page 467 for a comparison of store-bought and homemade tomato products. Whenever a commercial product is used in one of these recipes, you can lower the sodium dramatically by substituting a homemade staple. See Basics, Sauces and Snacks (page 458–529).

In most of the sauce recipes in this chapter, I have kept the fat, cholesterol and sodium way down. Those who do not need to lose weight may well want to indulge by adding some olive oil to a dish of pasta. It's monounsaturated and rather good for you. Again, use the best; you're going for flavor, not grease. One tablespoon of olive oil adds 120 calories, and it won't add any less because it is "light" olive oil. It will just have less taste.

You can make any of these sauces ahead; reheat the desired amount as the pasta is draining and have just as many portions as you want. If the sauce is frozen, it can easily be defrosted and heated in the microwave oven while the pasta cooks. Freeze the sauce in half-cup (120-ml) or cup (240-ml) amounts— the most usual quantities for first- and main-course portions—in containers that are microwave-safe and enough larger than the amount of sauce so that the sauce will not boil over when reheated. Pull off the lid; cover with microwave plastic wrap; arrange evenly spaced in the oven and heat. Prick plastic wrap to release steam; remove from oven; uncover and stir.

¼ cup (60 ml) liquid sauce such as Tomato Sauce Casalinga
650- to 700-watt oven: 2 min.
400- to 500-watt oven: 3 min.

¼ cup (60 ml) thick sauce such as Lean Bolognese
650- to 700-watt oven: 2 min.
400- to 500-watt oven: 3 min.

½ cup (120 ml) liquid sauce such as Tomato Sauce Casalinga
650- to 700-watt oven: 3 min.
400- to 500-watt oven: 4 min.

½ cup (120 ml) thick sauce such as Lean Bolognese
650- to 700-watt oven: 5 min.
400- to 500-watt oven: 5 min. 30 sec.

1 cup (240 ml) liquid sauce such as Tomato Sauce Casalinga
650- to 700-watt oven: 7 min.
400- to 500-watt oven: 10 min.

1 cup (240 ml) thick sauce such as Lean Bolognese
650- to 700-watt oven: 8 min.
400- to 500-watt oven: 10 min.

2 cups (470 ml) are heated in two containers, each with 1 cup (240 ml) frozen sauce
2 cups (470 ml) liquid or thick sauce
650- to 700-watt oven: 11 min.
400- to 500-watt oven: 13 min.

GRATED CHEESE

The Italians do not put cheese on every pasta. It is almost never used with a seafood sauce, for example. If you want to add cheese, the problem is not so much one of calories—twenty-three calories for a tablespoon of grated Parmesan—but one of salt, if it bothers you. That same tablespoon has ninety-three milligrams of sodium. Romano cheese is slightly less caloric and has less sodium. My feeling about these things is to get the best—aged imported Parmesan in a chunk for grating—and to use it sparingly. The flavor will be better. You will also get more flavor for your calories if you toss the pasta with the cheese before adding the sauce. If some people at the table really cannot have the cheese, pass it separately. I usually put it next to the olive oil and pepper mill.

Rotary cheese graters can be bought with several cylinders.
The one with small holes is good for grating hard cheeses
such as Parmesan. The one with medium holes is used for
onions and ginger, and the one with large holes is
for soft cheeses such as mozzarella.

TOMATO SAUCE CASALINGA (HOME-STYLE)

*T*his is my everyday tomato sauce; its basic idea was contributed by Chris Styler, a wonderful Italian cook, co-worker and friend. I suggest making the largest version you possibly can in your oven and keeping it on hand not only for a quick, comforting, slimming and filling bowl of pasta but also to have for almost any kind of simply cooked chicken, fish or meat (I wouldn't put it on beef). Keep some in the freezer and some in the refrigerator. The whole recipe would make a good buffet dish.

As a pasta sauce, I like it with spaghettini. If you have fresh basil, by all means toss some in when you mix the pasta with the sauce. While these quantities look huge, I normally make the sauce and then use it as I need it.

This sauce has so few calories that you can freely increase the amount you put on the pasta if you prefer. *MAKES 4½ CUPS (1,065 ML) SAUCE FOR 30 OUNCES (851 G) DRY PASTA, COOKED. SERVES 18 AS A MAIN COURSE, 36 AS A FIRST COURSE*

Per ¼ cup (60 ml) sauce for 3 ounces (85 g) dry pasta: 23 calories; 0 milligrams cholesterol; 1 gram fat; 173 milligrams sodium; 1 gram protein (2% RDA); 3 grams carbohydrate

RDA: vitamin A 24%; vitamin C 16%

1 tablespoon olive oil
4 cloves garlic, smashed, peeled and finely chopped
1 small onion (2 ounces; 56 g), peeled and finely chopped (about ½ cup; 120 ml)
1 small carrot (1½ ounces; 43 g), peeled and finely chopped (about ¼ cup; 60 ml)
1 small rib celery (1½ ounces; 43 g), peeled and finely chopped (about ¼ cup; 60 ml)

2 medium domestic mushrooms (about 4 ounces; 113.5 g), trimmed and thinly sliced (about 1 cup; 240 ml)
35-ounce (992-g) can Italian plum tomatoes, packed in juice, or Fresh Tomato Purée (page 468)
½ teaspoon dried oregano
½ teaspoon dried basil
1 tablespoon fresh lemon juice
1 teaspoon kosher salt
Pinch freshly ground black pepper

1. Combine olive oil and 2 of the garlic cloves in the center of a 2½-quart (2.5-l) soufflé dish or casserole. Cook, uncovered, at 100% for 2 minutes in a 650- to 700-watt oven. Add onion, carrot, celery and mushrooms and cook, uncovered, for 5 minutes.

2. Stir in tomatoes and their liquid, oregano, basil and remaining garlic cloves. Cook, uncovered, for 15 minutes, stirring twice. Remove from oven and let stand until cool.

(continued)

3. Add lemon juice, salt and pepper. Working in batches, process the sauce in a blender at low speed until smooth. Refrigerate, covered, for up to 7 days or freeze for up to 6 months.

To make 9 cups (2,129 ml). Use 2 tablespoons olive oil, 8 cloves garlic, 2 small onions, 2 small carrots, 2 small ribs celery, 8 ounces (227 g) mushrooms, 70 ounces (1,984.5 g) canned plum tomatoes, 1 teaspoon each dried oregano and dried basil, 2 tablespoons lemon juice, 2 teaspoons kosher salt, and black pepper to taste. Follow Step 1 and cook oil and garlic in a 5½-quart (5.5-l) casserole for 3 minutes. Stir in onion, carrot, celery and mushrooms and cook uncovered for 8 minutes. Continue with Step 2 and cook uncovered for 23 minutes. Finish as in Step 3.

FOR 400- TO 500-WATT OVENS

To make 4 cups. Follow Step 1 and cook oil and garlic for 3 minutes. Add onion, carrot, celery and mushrooms and cook for 8 minutes. Continue with Step 2 and cook for 25 minutes. Finish as in Step 3.

SWEET AND SPICY PEPPER SAUCE

*T*his hot and sweet sauce should be made in summer, when tomatoes are wonderful. It can be modified to your taste by increasing or decreasing the amount of jalapeños. I like this sauce over linguine.   MAKES 2½ CUPS (590 ML) SAUCE FOR 15 OUNCES (425 G) DRY PASTA, COOKED. SERVES 5 AS A MAIN COURSE, 10 AS A FIRST COURSE

Per ½ cup (120 ml) sauce for 3 ounces (85 g) dry pasta: 94 calories; 0 milligrams cholesterol; 6 grams fat; 230 milligrams sodium; 2 grams protein (4% RDA); 10 grams carbohydrate

RDA: calcium 4%; phosphorus 5%; iron 10%; vitamin A 104%; thiamin 8%; riboflavin 3%; niacin 6%; vitamin C 272%

12 ounces (340 g) red bell pepper, stemmed, seeded, deribbed and cut into 2 × ¼ × ¼-inch (5 × .5 × .5-cm) strips (about 3¼ cups; 885 ml)
1 ounce (28 g) fresh jalapeños, or Pickled Jalapeño Peppers (page 473), or canned jalapeños
2 tablespoons olive oil
6 cloves garlic, smashed, peeled and minced

5 tomatoes (each 4 ounces; 113.5 g), cored and cut into 1-inch (2.5-cm) chunks (about 3¼ cups; 885 ml)
¼ cup (60 ml) thin strips (chiffonade) fresh basil
½ teaspoon kosher salt
⅛ teaspoon freshly ground black pepper

1. Combine sweet peppers, fresh jalapeños (if using), oil and garlic in a 13 × 9 × 2-inch (33 × 23 × 5-cm) oval dish. Cook at 100%, uncovered, for 2 minutes in a 650- 700-watt oven.

2. Leaving dish in oven, stir and cook for 5 minutes more.

3. Stir in tomatoes and pickled jalapeños, if using. Cook for 5 minutes more, uncovered.

4. Remove from oven and add basil chiffonade, salt and pepper.

FOR 400- TO 500-WATT OVENS

To serve 5. Cook as in Step 1 for 4 minutes. Cook as in Step 2 for 10 minutes. Cook as in Step 3 for 10 minutes. Finish as in Step 4.

MUSHROOM SAUCE

I like this on medium egg noodles. If you use egg noodles you may want to decrease slightly the dry quantity with which you start. This is a quick light sauce that is best fresh, so I serve it as an easy main course for two or as a first course for four. Larger quantities follow.   *MAKES SCANT 1 CUP (240 ML) SAUCE FOR 6 OUNCES (170 G) DRY PASTA, COOKED, AS A MAIN COURSE. SERVES 2 AS A MAIN COURSE, 4 AS A FIRST COURSE*

Per scant ½ cup (120 ml) sauce for 3 ounces (85 g) dry pasta: 114 calories; 1 milligram cholesterol; 7 grams fat; 32 milligrams sodium; 3 grams protein (7% RDA); 10 grams carbohydrate

RDA: calcium 5%; phosphorus 10%; iron 6%; riboflavin 16%; niacin 14%

1 tablespoon olive oil
3 cloves garlic, smashed, peeled and
  minced
4 ounces (113.5 g) domestic
  mushrooms, trimmed and thinly
  sliced (about 1 cup; 240 ml)
½ cup (120 ml) Basic Chicken Broth
  (page 460), or unsalted or regular
  canned chicken broth

¼ cup (60 ml) skim milk
1 tablespoon cornstarch
¼ teaspoon ground cardamom
Pinch freshly ground black pepper

1. Combine oil and garlic in the center of a 2½-quart (2.5-l) soufflé dish or casserole. Cook uncovered at 100% for 2 minutes in a 650- to 700-watt oven.

2. Add mushrooms and stir to coat with oil and garlic. Spread out in dish or casserole. Cook, uncovered, for 6 minutes.

(continued)

Mushroom Sauce (cont.)

3. Combine broth, milk, cornstarch, cardamom and pepper in a small bowl and whisk until smooth. Stir into mushroom mixture and cook, uncovered, for 3 minutes.

4. Pour mushroom sauce over cooked pasta and toss to coat.

To serve 4. Use 2 tablespoons oil, 6 cloves garlic, 8 ounces (227 g) mushrooms, 1 cup (240 ml) broth, ½ cup (120 ml) milk, 2 tablespoons cornstarch, ½ teaspoon cardamom, and pinch black pepper. Cook as in Step 1 for 2 minutes. Add mushrooms as in Step 2 and cook for 8 minutes. Continue with Step 3, cooking for 6 minutes. Finish as in Step 4.

FOR 400- TO 500-WATT OVENS

To serve 2. Cook oil and garlic as in Step 1 for 3 minutes. Follow Step 2 and cook for 10 minutes. Continue with Step 3 and cook for 5 minutes. Finish as in Step 4.

To serve 4. Cook oil and garlic as in Step 1 for 3 minutes. Follow Step 2 and cook for 12 minutes. Continue with Step 3 and cook for 9 minutes. Finish as in Step 4.

FENNEL-SARDINE SAUCE

*I*n Sicily, they make rich, layered pastas with unusual combinations of flavors. This low-calorie version is more to my taste. Nevertheless, the sauce is robust and I prefer it on a substantial pasta such as rigatoni. This is a good sauce to make the day after you make Bell Peppers and Sardines with Balsamic Vinegar (page 84) to use up the remaining sardines. If you're not on a weight-loss diet, sprinkle some pignoli on top. *MAKES 2¼ CUPS (530 ML) SAUCE FOR ¾ POUND (340 G) DRY PASTA, COOKED, AS A MAIN COURSE. SERVES 4*

Per generous ½ cup (120 ml) sauce for 3 ounces (85 g) dry pasta: 138 calories; 51 milligrams cholesterol; 8 grams fat; 347 milligrams sodium; 11 grams protein (25% RDA); 5 grams carbohydrate

RDA: calcium 21%; phosphorus 24%; iron 14%; 658 milligrams potassium; vitamin A 5%; thiamin 5%; riboflavin 7%; niacin 14%; vitamin C 24%

1½ pounds (680 g) fennel, peeled, cored and cut into 1-inch (2.5-cm) chunks (about 4 cups; 1 l), tops finely chopped and reserved
¾ cup (180 ml) Basic Chicken Broth (page 460), or unsalted or regular canned chicken broth

3 cloves garlic, smashed and peeled
1 teaspoon fennel seeds
1 tablespoon olive oil
6 sardines (1½ ounces; 43 g) packed in olive oil, split and boned
1 teaspoon drained capers
Freshly ground black pepper, to taste

1. Combine fennel, chicken broth, garlic, and fennel seeds in a 2½-quart (2.5-l) soufflé dish or casserole with a tightly fitted lid. Cover tightly with plastic wrap or lid. Cook at 100% for 13 minutes in a 650- to 700-watt oven. If using plastic wrap, prick to release steam.

2. Remove from oven and uncover. Remove half of the fennel from the dish with a slotted spoon and reserve. Process the remaining fennel, broth, garlic and fennel seeds in the food processor with the olive oil and sardines.

3. Scrape the mixture into a bowl. Stir in reserved fennel, capers, fennel tops and pepper to taste. Serve over cooked pasta.

FOR 400- TO 500-WATT OVENS

To make 2¼ cups (530 ml). Cook for 20 minutes.

BEST RED CLAM SAUCE

Old-style Italian restaurants in America used to make this dish. I still do. It is quickly made even if you cannot buy shucked clams. Open them by cooking, tightly covered, for eight to nine minutes in a 650- to 700-watt oven or just until opened. See pages 274-275 for other quantities and for 400- to 500-watt ovens.

MAKES 2 CUPS (470 ML) SAUCE FOR 12 OUNCES (340 G) DRY PASTA, COOKED. SERVES 4 AS A MAIN COURSE, 8 AS A FIRST COURSE

Per ½ cup (120 ml) sauce for 3 ounces (85 g) dry pasta: 91 calories; 15 milligrams cholesterol; 4 grams fat; 215 milligrams sodium; 7 grams protein (15% RDA); 8 grams carbohydrate

RDA: calcium 7%; phosphorus 11%; iron 41%; vitamin A 25%; riboflavin 6%; niacin 8%; vitamin C 33%

1 tablespoon olive oil
4 cloves garlic, smashed, peeled and minced
1 cup (240 ml) shucked clams with their juice—16 clams, each 2½ inches (6 cm) across (total weight in shell about 2½ pounds; 1.1 kg)
2 tablespoons tomato paste

½ cup (120 ml) canned tomato purée, or Fresh Tomato Purée (page 468)
2 scallions, white and green parts, finely sliced across (about ½ cup; 120 ml)
⅓ cup (80 ml) fresh basil leaves thinly sliced (chiffonade), loosely packed
Freshly ground black pepper, to taste

1. Combine oil and garlic in 2½-quart (2.5-l) soufflé dish or casserole. Cook, uncovered, at 100% for 1 minute 30 seconds in a 650- to 700-watt oven.

2. Remove from oven. Drain clams and add their juice to casserole with tomato paste and pureé. Cook uncovered for 5 minutes.

(continued)

3. Add sliced scallions and basil chiffonade. Cook for 4 minutes more.
4. Add clams and pepper. Cook for 30 seconds.
5. Remove from oven and pour over cooked pasta. Toss to coat.

FOR 400- TO 500-WATT OVENS

To serve 4. Cook as in Step 1 for 2 minutes 30 seconds. In Step 2 cook for 7 minutes 30 seconds. Continue with Step 3 and cook for 6 minutes. In Step 4 cook for 2 minutes 30 seconds.

SHRIMP PASTA SAUCE

*T*his chunky, colorful sauce does well on a substantial pasta like cooked shells. The sauce is high in sodium because it was developed for harried cooks. If you have Fresh Tomato Purée in the freezer, the sodium will go way down.   *MAKES 3½ CUPS (825 ML) SAUCE FOR 12 OUNCES (340 G) DRY PASTA, COOKED. SERVES 4 AS A MAIN COURSE, 8 AS A FIRST COURSE*

Per generous ¾ cup (180 ml) sauce for 3 ounces (85 g) dry pasta: 158 calories; 122 milligrams cholesterol; 2 grams fat; 642 milligrams sodium; 20 grams protein (44% RDA); 18 grams carbohydrate

RDA: calcium 18%; phosphorus 34%; iron 33%; 934 milligrams potassium; vitamin A 77%; thiamin 41%; riboflavin 19%; niacin 40%; vitamin C 105%

2 cups (470 ml) canned tomato purée,
    or Fresh Tomato Purée (page 468)
2 teaspoons tomato paste
1 cup (240 ml) thinly sliced fresh basil
    leaves (chiffonade)
1⅓ cups (320 ml) thinly sliced across
    scallions, white and green parts
    (about 1½ bunches)

14 ounces (395 g) shrimp (about 20),
    peeled and deveined
Kosher salt, to taste
Freshly ground black pepper, to taste

1. Mix together tomato purée and tomato paste in a 2½-quart (2.5-l) soufflé dish or casserole. Cook at 100%, uncovered, for 4 minutes in a 650- to 700-watt oven.
2. Add basil and scallions and cook, uncovered, for 1 minute.
3. Add shrimp and cook, uncovered, for 4 minutes 30 seconds, stirring twice.
4. Remove from oven and add salt and pepper to taste. Toss together with cooked pasta and reheat, uncovered, for 4 minutes, or until hot.

To serve 2. Use 1 cup (240 ml) tomato purée, 1 teaspoon tomato paste, ½ cup (120 ml) basil chiffonade, ⅔ cup (160 ml) thinly sliced scallions, 10 shrimp and salt and pepper to taste. Cook as in step 1 for 3 minutes. Add basil and scallions as in Step 2 and cook for 1 minute. Continue with step 3, cooking for 2 minutes 30 seconds. Reheat with pasta for 1 minute, or until hot.

To serve 1. Use ½ cup (120 ml) tomato purée, ½ teaspoon tomato paste, ¼ cup (60 ml) basil chiffonade, ⅓ cup (80 ml) thinly sliced scallions, 3 ounces (85 g) shrimp and salt and pepper to taste. In a 1-quart (1-l) soufflé dish, cook tomato purée and tomato paste as in Step 1 for 2 minutes. Follow Step 2 and cook for 45 seconds. Continue with Step 3 and cook for 2 minutes. Reheat with cooked pasta for 1 minute.

FOR 400- TO 500-WATT OVENS

To serve 2. In Step 1 cook for 4 minutes. Cook basil and scallions as in Step 2 for 2 minutes. Continue with Step 3 and cook for 5 minutes. Serve over pasta.

To serve 1. In Step 1 cook for 3 minutes. Cook basil and scallions as in Step 2 for 1 minute 30 seconds. Continue with Step 3; cook for 3 minutes. Serve over pasta.

WHITE SEAFOOD SAUCE

*T*his apparently creamy sauce tasting of briny seas is really light as air. At lunch have the same amount of sauce on two ounces (56 g) of dry pasta, cooked, and have some fruit or a salad.   *MAKES 2 CUPS (470 ML) SAUCE FOR 12 OUNCES (340 G) DRY PASTA, COOKED. SERVES 4 AS A MAIN COURSE, 8 AS A FIRST COURSE*

Per ½ cup (120 ml) sauce for 3 ounces (85 g) dry pasta: 63 calories; 14 milligrams cholesterol; 1 gram fat; 156 milligrams sodium; 7 grams protein (15% RDA); 3 grams carbohydrate

RDA: calcium 5%; phosphorus 12%; iron 14%

½ cup (120 ml) dry white wine	¼ cup (60 ml) skim milk
½ cup (120 ml) water	1 tablespoon cornstarch
3 cloves garlic, peeled and sliced	½ cup (120 ml) chopped fresh parsley
16 medium mussels (about 1½ pounds; 680 g), scrubbed and debearded	2 teaspoons fresh lemon juice
	Pinch freshly ground black pepper

1. Cook pasta while preparing the sauce. Reserve ⅓ cup (80 ml) of pasta cooking liquid.

(continued)

2. Combine wine, water and garlic in a 2½-quart (2.5-l) soufflé dish or casserole with a tightly fitted lid. Cook, uncovered, at 100% for 10 minutes in a 650- to 700-watt oven.

3. Add mussels to garlic liquid. Cover tightly with microwave plastic wrap or casserole lid. Cook for 2 minutes or until mussels open. If using plastic wrap, prick to release steam.

4. Remove from oven and uncover. Transfer mussels with a slotted spoon to a mixing bowl. Combine milk and cornstarch, stirring until smooth. Stir cornstarch mixture into mussel liquid. Add parsley and cook, uncovered, for 3 minutes.

5. Remove mussels from shells. Stir mussels into sauce with lemon juice and pepper.

6. Return pasta to the pot with reserved cooking liquid and sauce. Over low heat, toss to coat.

FOR 400- TO 500-WATT OVENS

To serve 4. Follow Step 1. In Step 2, cook for 15 minutes. Continue with Step 3 and cook for 5 minutes, or until mussels are open. In Step 4, cook for 7 minutes. Finish as in Steps 5 and 6.

LEAN BOLOGNESE

*B*olognese is usually made with more caloric meats. This version still tastes delicious and lightens things up considerably. Don't use this on fresh pasta or a flimsy pasta like angel hair. Most other pastas will go well, making a substantial main course that can easily be topped with cheese and preceded or accompanied by a low-calorie vegetable dish or salad. Wind up with some fruit or a low-calorie dessert.   *MAKES 2½ CUPS (590 ML) SAUCE FOR 15 OUNCES (425 G) DRY PASTA, COOKED. SERVES 5 AS A MAIN COURSE*

Per ½ cup (120 ml) sauce for 3 ounces (85 g) dry pasta: 120 calories; 24 milligrams cholesterol; 3 grams fat; 455 milligrams sodium; 11 grams protein (25% RDA); 13 grams carbohydrate

RDA: calcium 7%; phosphorus 15%; iron 12%; 676 milligrams potassium; vitamin A 109%; thiamin 17%; riboflavin 10%; niacin 27%; vitamin C 53%

1 half-breast chicken, skinned, boned and trimmed of all fat (4 ounces; 113.5 g)

3 ounces (85 g) trimmed pork tenderloin

2 teaspoons olive oil

1 small carrot (3 ounces; 85 g), peeled, trimmed and cut into 2-inch (5-cm) lengths

1 small rib celery (2 ounces; 56 g), peeled and cut into 2-inch (5-cm) lengths

1 small onion (2 ounces; 56 g), peeled and cut into chunks

2 medium domestic mushrooms (about 3 ounces; 85 g), trimmed and quartered

4 cloves garlic, smashed, peeled and minced

28 ounces (794 g) canned Italian plum tomatoes, drained, and ½ cup (120 ml) liquid reserved

¼ cup (60 ml) chopped fresh parsley

1 teaspoon dried basil

1 teaspoon tomato paste

Large pinch dried sage

1 tablespoon cornstarch

½ teaspoon kosher salt

1. Cut chicken and pork into 1-inch (2.5-cm) cubes. Arrange in a layer on a plate and place in the freezer for 15 minutes or in the refrigerator for 30 minutes.

2. Drizzle olive oil over the meats. Transfer to a food processor and process until finely ground. Scrape meat into a 2½-quart (2.5-l) soufflé dish or casserole and spread evenly over the bottom of the dish. Cook, uncovered, at 100% for 4 minutes in a 650- to 700-watt oven.

3. Finely chop the carrot, celery, onion, mushrooms and garlic in the food processor. Stir the vegetables into the cooked meats, stirring vigorously to break up the lumps. Cook, uncovered, for 4 minutes.

4. Stir the drained tomatoes, parsley, basil, tomato paste and sage into the meat mixture, breaking the tomatoes into a coarse purée. Cook, uncovered, for 20 minutes, stirring once to break up the tomatoes.

5. Dissolve cornstarch in the reserved tomato juice and stir into the sauce. Cook for 4 minutes. Remove from oven; add salt. Serve hot over cooked pasta.

FOR 400- TO 500-WATT OVENS

To make 2½ cups. Follow Steps 1 and 2 and cook meats for 6 minutes, stirring once. Stir in vegetables as in Step 3 and cook for 6 minutes, stirring once. Continue with Step 4, cooking for 30 minutes, stirring once. Finish as in Step 5, cooking for 5 minutes.

Puncture canned tomatoes with your thumb.

Having squeezed tomato to remove juice and seeds, squeeze further to purée.

COUNTRY MACARONI WITH POTATOES AND PESTO

*T*his delicious dish made with a sort of pesto is an ample dinner for vegans or vegetarians as well as people who don't have such an idea in their head. It is ideally made at the end of fall, when there is a plethora of basil. You can make the sauce in the time of abundance (through Step 3) and freeze it for a winter meal. The absence of nuts and cheese improves the keeping quality. You can, of course, sprinkle the whole thing with freshly grated Parmesan and even include pignoli; but I don't think it's necessary. It will only make the dish more expensive and caloric.

You can have a substantial first course with this since the modest number of calories includes those in the pasta, unlike the other recipes in this chapter. It's a very good dish to add to a buffet.   *SERVES 10*

Per 1-cup (240-ml) serving: 211 calories; 0 milligrams cholesterol; 3 grams fat; 441 milligrams sodium; 7 grams protein (16% RDA); 40 grams carbohydrate

RDA: calcium 17%; phosphorus 13%; iron 25%; 617 milligrams potassium; vitamin A 54%; thiamin 23%; riboflavin 11%; niacin 18%; vitamin C 35%

¾ pound (340 g) small elbow macaroni (about 2⅔ cups; 630 ml)
1 pound (450 g) new potatoes, washed and cut into ¼-inch (.5-cm) dice (about 3 cups; 710 ml)
2 tablespoons water

1 pound (450 g) spinach, washed and stemmed (about 5 cups; 1.2 l)
1 cup (240 ml) Diet Pesto (page 476)
2 teaspoons kosher salt, or to taste
Freshly ground black pepper, to taste

1. Bring 6 quarts (1.5 l) of water to a boil on top of the stove. Add macaroni and cook for 5 minutes. Drain in a colander and reserve.

2. Arrange potatoes around the inside edge of a 10-inch (25.5-cm) quiche dish. Sprinkle with 2 tablespoons water. Cover tightly with microwave plastic wrap. Cook at 100% for 5 minutes in a 650- to 700-watt oven. Prick plastic and remove from oven. Mound spinach in the middle, re-cover and cook for 5 minutes more. Prick plastic to release steam.

3. Remove from oven and uncover. Add cooked spinach to a food processor with pesto and process until smooth.

4. Toss potatoes and reserved macaroni with sauce. Adjust seasonings and serve warm or cold.

FOR 400- TO 500-WATT OVENS

To serve 10. Follow Step 1. In Step 2, cook potatoes for 5 minutes, add spinach and cook 10 minutes more. Finish as in Steps 3 and 4.

There are almost as many kinds of Japanese, Chinese, Korean, Thai, Indonesian and Vietnamese noodle dishes as there are Italian. I'm afraid that for most of them, and many are delicious, you will need to look in appropriate cookbooks. If the recipes are authentic, they should be low in cholesterol; but considerable fat may be added in stir-frying sauces or in the deep-fat frying of the noodles themselves. Many of the dishes will contain fish sauce and soy, which are high in sodium. Be an intelligent judge and have fun experimenting.

The few recipes I have included here are for side dishes. All are vegetarian. Unfortunately, the nutritional information is missing because I have been unable to get reliable information for the noodles themselves.

SOBA NOODLES

*T*his can be served as either a first course or a side dish and warm or cold. It would be good with fish, instead of rice, and does equally well with simple chicken dishes. *SERVES 2*

¼ sheet nori, optional
2 ounces (56 g) Japanese soba noodles
1 large dried shiitake mushroom, stemmed and broken into small pieces

½ teaspoon Oriental sesame oil
2 drops chili oil, or to taste
1½ teaspoons tamari soy
2 teaspoons rice wine vinegar
3 tablespoons water

1. Bring a large pot of water to the boil on top of the stove.
2. If using nori, place in microwave oven and cook at 100% for 2 minutes in a 650- to 700-watt oven. Remove from oven and cut into ¼ × 2-inch (.5 × 5-cm) strips. Reserve.
3. Place soba in water and cook for 7 minutes or until tender. While soba is cooking, place remaining ingredients except 2 tablespoons of the water in a 2-cup (470-ml) glass measure. Cover tightly with microwave plastic wrap. Cook at 100% for 1 minute in a 650- to 700-watt oven. Prick plastic to release steam.
4. Remove from oven and uncover. Drain soba and add to measure, stirring to coat. Stir in remaining tablespoon water and divide between two serving bowls. Sprinkle with reserved nori.

FOR 400- TO 500-WATT OVENS

To serve 2. Cook nori as in Step 2 for 3 minutes. Cook as Step 3 for 2 minutes. Finish as in Step 4.

MUNG BEAN NOODLES

Mung bean noodles sound awful, but they become transparent when cooked and have a delightfully slippery consistency that makes this as fine a cold dish as it is a hot one. Peanut butter in a pasta sauce may sound equally weird, but the flavor and nutrition are great. You may want to garnish the serving dish with extra sprigs of fresh coriander. Think of it for picnics.   *SERVES 6*

½ teaspoon chili oil, or more if you like spicy food

½ cup (120 ml) Peanut Butter (page 478), or commercial peanut butter

1 cup (240 ml) Vegetarian Broth II (page 466)

4 ounces (113.5 g) dried mung bean noodles, soaked in warm water to cover until transparent (20–30 minutes), drained (3 cups; 705 ml)

¼ cup (60 ml) coarsely chopped fresh coriander leaves

2 cloves garlic, smashed, peeled and chopped

1 tablespoon peanut oil

1. Mash together oil and peanut butter in a small bowl. Stir in broth. Combine noodles, coriander leaves and garlic in a 2½-quart (2.5-l) soufflé dish or casserole with a tightly fitted lid. Pour in peanut-butter mixture, and toss until well coated.

2. Cover tightly with microwave plastic wrap or lid. Cook at 100% for 8 minutes, or until all liquid is absorbed, in a 650- to 700-watt oven. If using plastic wrap, prick to release steam. Remove from oven.

3. Uncover. Toss noodles with peanut oil until well coated. Serve hot, or . . .

4. If serving cool, spread noodles on a platter. When cool, toss with fingers to separate strands.

FOR 400- TO 500-WATT OVENS

To serve 6. Cook for 14 minutes.

RICE NOODLES

I love this dish hot or cold and make it often. *SERVES 4*

Per ½-cup (120-ml) serving: 165 calories; 0 milligrams cholesterol; 4 grams fat; 263 milligrams sodium; 3 grams protein (7% RDA); 30 grams carbohydrate

RDA: calcium 3%; phosphorus 4%; iron 7%; vitamin A 49%; thiamin 3%; riboflavin 3%; niacin 3%; vitamin C 28%

1 tablespoon vegetable oil
1 tablespoon tamari soy
3 scallions, white and green parts cut into 2-inch (5-cm) lengths and thinly sliced lengthwise (1 cup; 240 ml)
1½ tablespoons salted black beans, optional
1 cup (240 ml) Vegetarian Broth II (page 466), or Basic Chicken Broth (page 460), or unsalted or regular canned chicken broth

3 cloves garlic, smashed, peeled and sliced
4 ounces (113.5 g) dried rice noodles, soaked in warm water to cover until transparent (about 20–30 minutes), drained (3 cups; 705 ml)

1. Combine all ingredients in a 2½-quart (2.5-l) soufflé dish or casserole with a tightly fitted lid. Cover tightly with microwave plastic wrap or lid. Cook at 100% for 8 minutes in a 650- to 700-watt oven. If using plastic, prick to release steam.

2. Remove from oven and uncover. Serve warm.

FOR 400- TO 500-WATT OVENS

To serve 4. Cook for 12 minutes.

COUSCOUS NUTRITION

The nutrition for instant couscous and regular couscous is the same.

PER ½ CUP (120 ML) COOKED COUSCOUS: 109 calories; 0 milligrams cholesterol; 0 grams fat; 5 milligrams sodium; 4 grams protein (8% RDA); 24 grams carbohydrate

RDA: thiamin 7%; niacin 5%

BASIC COUSCOUS COOKING TIMES

There are no small-oven timings because it takes the same amount of time to do it on the top of the stove.

TO MAKE INSTANT COUSCOUS

MAKES 3½ CUPS (825 ML)

1½ cups (355 ml) water   1 cup (240 ml) instant couscous

   1. Place water in a 2½-quart (2.5-l) soufflé dish. Cover tightly with microwave plastic wrap. Cook at 100% in a 650- to 700-watt oven for 4 minutes. Prick plastic to release steam.
   2. Remove from oven and uncover. Stir in couscous. Cover loosely with paper toweling or a kitchen towel. Let stand for 7 minutes.
   3. Uncover couscous and fluff with a fork to remove lumps.

To make 1¼ cups (300 ml) couscous. Use ¾ cup (180 ml) water and ½ cup (120 ml) instant couscous. Cook as in Step 1 for 2 minutes. Allow mixture to stand for 5 minutes as in Step 2. Finish as in Step 3.

To make 5½ cups (1.3 ml) couscous. Use 2¼ cups (530 ml) water and 1½ cups (355 ml) instant couscous. Cook as in Step 1 for 5 minutes. Allow mixture to stand for 9 minutes as in Step 2. Finish as in Step 3.

To make 7 cups (1.7 l) couscous. Use 3 cups (705 ml) water and 2 cups (470 ml) instant couscous. Cook as in Step 1 for 6 minutes in a 13×10×2-inch (33×25.5×5-cm) oval dish. Allow mixture to stand for 10 minutes as in Step 2. Finish as in Step 3.

TO MAKE REGULAR COUSCOUS

TO MAKE 3½ CUPS (825 ML) COUSCOUS

2 cups (470 ml) water   1 cup (240 ml) regular couscous

1. Combine water and couscous in a 13 × 10 × 2-inch (33 × 25.5 × 5-cm) oval dish. Cover tightly with microwave plastic wrap. Cook at 100% in a 650- to 700-watt oven for 4 minutes. Prick plastic to release steam.
2. Remove from oven and uncover. Stir mixture well. Re-cover and cook for 4 minutes longer. Prick plastic to release steam.
3. Remove from oven and uncover. Fluff with a fork to remove lumps.

Rice, Pilaf and Risotto

Rice is the staple food of more people in the world than any other grain. Unfortunately, most of it is eaten as polished white rice, which has nutritional disadvantages (see Nutritional Comparison of Various Types of Rice, page 183). In this country, there are rices that are white and polished but which have been enriched to supply more of the important nutritional elements. We get many of the Oriental rice varieties as brown whole-grain rice. I often enjoy brown basmati rice or boiled long-grain brown rice with Indian-style curries or Chinese- or Japanese-inspired dishes. No one from any of these countries would tolerate that.

Brown rice is not applicable to every kind of dish and it has one distinct disadvantage—it takes a long time to cook. Once the liquid (water or broth) boils, the rice is stirred in and the water comes back to the boil, the pot is covered and the heat reduced to a simmer. From that point, it takes at least forty-five minutes for the rice to cook.

If you like brown rice but seldom have the time to make it, there is a nice microwave trick. Cook a good quantity of brown rice, say two cups in ten cups water, in the usual way on top of the stove. Rinse through a sieve with cold water. Drain. Allow rice to cool. Refrigerate it in half-cup (120-ml) and one-cup (240-ml) quantities in microwavable containers. When you want to serve some rice, take the container or containers out of the refrigerator. Remove the lid; add the amount of liquid indicated in the chart; cover tightly with microwave plastic wrap and cook at 100%.

While I don't usually bother with this precooking for white rice, it can be done. Bring eight cups (2 l) of water to the boil. Stir in four cups (1 l) rice. Return to the boil. Reduce heat to a simmer. Cover pot. Cook for fifteen minutes. Drain and rinse with cold water.

Large-Quantity, Top-of-the-Stove Yields for Brown and White Rice

2 cups brown rice cooked and rinsed make 7 cups
2 cups white rice cooked and rinsed make 11 cups

TIMES FOR REHEATING COOKED BROWN OR WHITE RICE
IN THE MICROWAVE OVEN

Reheat rice tightly covered with the specified amount of water in a 2½-quart (2.5-l) soufflé dish.

1 cup (240 ml) cooked brown rice with 2 tablespoons water
650- to 700-watt oven: 2 min.
400- to 500-watt oven: 3 min.

4 cups (1 l) cooked brown rice with 1 cup (80 ml) water
650- to 700-watt oven: 6 min.
400- to 500-watt oven: 8 min.

2 cups (470 ml) cooked brown rice with ¼ cup (60 ml) water
650- to 700-watt oven: 5 min.
400- to 500-watt oven: 7 min.

MICROWAVE COOKING TIMES FOR LONG-GRAIN RICE

I usually cook plain rice, boiled or steamed, on top of the stove and save the microwave for more interesting work. The advantages of cooking it in the microwave oven are reliable results, the bottom of the rice will not scorch and boiling of the water is achieved more rapidly. If your main course takes five minutes or less to cook, this is a valid way to cook rice as it will be ready at the same time as the dish it is to accompany.

Rice may be cooked in the same way in any liquid that has almost the consistency of water. All the Basic Broths (pages 460– 462) can be used. Combine quantities of rice and liquid specified below. Cover tightly with casserole lid and cook according to the times given. Plastic wrap is less desirable since it may cause the rice to boil over. If you are using it due to the lack of a lid, make a hole, which will act as a steam vent, in the center of the wrap with a sharp knife. Remove from oven. Let rest for 5 minutes. Uncover and fluff with a fork before serving.

As you look at the chart below, you may realize that the cooking times are odd compared to most microwave cooking times. When cooking rice, quantity has a very small influence on the cooking time. The timing difference between quantities and ovens has to do only with the amount of time needed to bring the liquid to a boil. Once it is boiling the times are the same. This is equally true when cooking rice on top of the stove.

1 cup (240 ml) rice with 1½ cups (355 ml) liquid in a 2½-quart (2.5-l) soufflé or casserole with a tightly fitted lid. Yield: 3½ cups (825 ml) rice
650- to 700-watt oven: (5 min. to boil) 18 min. total cooking time plus 5 min. standing time
400- to 500-watt oven: (8 min. to boil) 21 min. total cooking time and 5 min. standing time

2 cups (470 ml) rice with 3¼ cups (765 ml) liquid in a 5½-quart (5.5-l) soufflé dish or casserole with a tightly fitted lid. Yield: 6 cups (1,460 ml) rice
650- to 700-watt oven: (7 min. to boil) 18 min. total cooking time plus 5 min. standing time
400- to 500-watt oven: (15 min. to boil) 24 min. total cooking time plus 5 min. standing time

NUTRITIONAL COMPARISON OF VARIOUS TYPES OF RICE

Note: All data are for ½ cup (120 ml) plain cooked rice, served hot. The chart won't show the advantages of brown rice, which are its generous supply of B vitamins, calcium and phosphorus. Once again, that's the way the USDA supplies information. Wild rice, which is not really a rice at all but a grass, is much more nutritious than white or brown rice, with twice the protein, four times the phosphorus, eight times the thiamin, and twenty times the riboflavin. It is also multiply more expensive. For basic cooking times, see *Microwave Gourmet.*

TYPE	CAL.	PROT. (g)	CARB. (g)	IRON (mg)	POT. (mg)
Arborio rice	N/A	N/A	N/A	N/A	N/A
Brown rice					
Long	116	3	25	0.5	69
Short	110	2	23	0.36	
Enriched white rice, long grain (parboiled), usually in the market as "converted"	96	2	22	0.80	41
Instant rice	90	2	20	0.65	N/A

Types of White Rice and How They Are Cooked

The microwave cooking times above are valid only for long-grain (Carolina) rice simply boiled. Other kinds of white rice when boiled or steamed will take different amounts of time depending on the length and starchiness of the grain and the amount of water that you want to use to get a specific texture, from sticky rice to have with Chinese food to splendidly separate firm grains of rice to have with Southern American food.

While the microwave oven has no part in that cooking, it can be very helpful with several festive and special rice preparations. It has taken some finagling to reduce the fat in some of my favorites—risottos and pilafs—and still get good results. Even so, not all of the lower-calorie versions will work in every quantity or in all wattages of ovens. Those who are not worried about weight can look in *Microwave Gourmet* for non-calorie-saving versions; but they may want to substitute oil for all or part of the butter in the recipes.

To make the weight-loss versions, I have developed a technique of slightly parching the grains in an uncovered dish in the microwave oven. The dried grains are slowed in their absorption of the liquid that is then added. It is a tricky business but can give a delightful result.

PILAF

India, Turkey, Iran, Afghanistan and many European countries, among them Spain, Bulgaria and Portugal, all make versions of a basic rice preparation variously called pilaf, pillaf, piloo and pilau. For some of these versions, the rice is washed frequently before cooking; in others, not at all. Either before liquid is added to the rice or at the same time, a fairly substantial amount of fat is stirred in. The rice is then cooked in a tightly covered container with or without a whole range of seasonings, fruits and nuts.

The rice used for pilaf is one variety or other of patna rice, a white long-grain with pointy ends that does not split when cooked. Basmati rice is the most expensive, elegant and aromatic of these. While excellent, brown basmati, grown in this country, is never used in traditional dishes.

RISOTTO

Not only do I love the taste of risotto, the creamy rice dish of Italy's Veneto, but I also owe it a debt. More people with serious doubts about the gastronomic validity of microwave cooking—my editor, Ann Bramson, included—became converts because of risotto. For them, I was no longer among the philistines. What we enjoy is not so much the decrease in cooking time, but the ease and perfection of preparation, the lack of standing on our feet while constantly stirring.

Slimmed, I still love risotto. There are main-course risotto dishes in this book.

Those of you who can afford the fat and calories can look in *Microwave Gourmet* for a largish group of rich risottos. I give one here, stripped of its butter but resplendent in olive oil. Make your own decision. The other risottos in this book pretty much avoid fat. The technique of parching of the grain is carried out and then the risotto is cooked. I normally keep extra broth on the side to stir into the risotto after it comes out of the oven or just before serving. Slimmed risottos tend to need more broth since they don't have the silkiness of the fat. In any case, it's your decision. There seem to be as many ideas as to just how creamy-liquid a risotto should be as there are cooks and eaters.

The rice used in risotto is the rice of the Veneto's Po Valley—most often arborio, occasionally its cousin, ambra. Arborio is a short-grain white rice with a characteristic white dot in the center. It is rather starchy but does not break apart in cooking. Ambra is similar except that it is pale gold in color and slightly less starchy. It is usually used for seafood risottos.

OTHER COMPOSED RICE DISHES

Rice dishes in this book that are not either pilafs or risottos are made with white long-grain (Carolina) rice. If you are using converted rice and cooking it in the microwave oven, increase cooking time slightly.

PARSLEY PILAF

*T*his green, light pilaf goes well with all curries except those that are themselves green; but don't stop there. Think of this as an alternate any time you want a simple variation on rice with dinner. Vegetarians should use a vegetarian broth. *SERVES 10*

Per ½-cup (120-ml) serving: 111 calories; 0 milligrams cholesterol; 0 grams fat; 10 milligrams sodium; 2 grams protein (5% RDA); 24 grams carbohydrate

RDA: iron 7%; vitamin A 3%; thiamin 8%; niacin 6%; vitamin C 6%

3 shallots, peeled and chopped (about ½ cup; 120 ml)
½ cup (120 ml) finely chopped fresh parsley
1½ cups (360 ml) white rice

1¼ cups (300 ml) Basic Chicken Broth (page 460), or Vegetarian Broth II (page 466), or unsalted or regular canned chicken broth
1¼ cups (300 ml) water

1. Combine shallots and parsley in a 13×9×2-inch (33×23×5-cm) oval dish and cover tightly with microwave plastic wrap. Cook at 100% for 2 minutes in a 650- to 700-watt oven. Prick plastic wrap to release steam.

2. Remove from oven and uncover. Add rice and cook, uncovered, for 1 minute. Stir in broth and water. Re-cover and cook for 18 minutes. Prick plastic.

3. Remove from oven and uncover. Season to taste and serve hot.

FOR 400- TO 500-WATT OVENS

To serve 10. Follow Step 1 and cook shallots and parsley, tightly covered, for 3 minutes. Add rice and cook for 2 minutes, uncovered. Add liquids and cook, covered, for 28 minutes. Finish as in Step 3.

CURRIED PILAF

I wouldn't use this with a curry; but it's delicious with simply cooked chicken and fish.   *SERVES 6*

Per ½-cup (120-ml) serving: 187 calories; 0 milligrams cholesterol; 3 grams fat; 17 milligrams sodium; 4 grams protein (8% RDA); 31 grams carbohydrate

RDA: iron 11%

1½ teaspoons vegetable oil
1 tablespoon curry powder
1 teaspoon ground cumin
4 ounces (113.5 g) onion, peeled and minced (½ cup; 120 ml)
4 cloves garlic, smashed, peeled and minced
2 tablespoons slivered almonds (about ½ ounce; 14 g)

2 tablespoons dried currants
1 cup (240 ml) rice
1½ cups (360 ml) Basic Chicken Broth (page 460), or unsalted or regular canned chicken broth
Freshly ground black pepper, to taste
1 teaspoon grated orange zest
2 teaspoons chopped fresh parsley

   1. Combine oil, curry powder and cumin in the bottom of a $13 \times 9 \times 2$-inch ($33 \times 23 \times 5$-cm) oval dish. Cook, uncovered, at 100% for 1 minute 30 seconds in a 650- to 700-watt oven.
   2. Remove from oven. Add onion, garlic, almonds, currants and rice and stir to coat with the spices. Cook, uncovered, for 4 minutes.
   3. Remove from oven and stir in broth. Cover tightly with microwave plastic wrap. Cook for 15 minutes. Prick plastic to release steam.
   4. Remove from oven and uncover. Stir in remaining ingredients and serve.

FOR 400- TO 500-WATT OVENS

To serve 6. Cook as in Step 1 for 2 minutes 30 seconds. Cook as in Step 2 for 6 minutes. Continue as in Step 3, cooking for 25 minutes.

FAT-FREE RISOTTO

Here it is, risotto in which you will not miss the fat or the sodium. Unfortunately, it does not work well in a low-wattage oven. *SERVES 4 AS A FIRST COURSE, 6 AS A SIDE DISH*

Per ³⁄₄-cup first-course serving: 200 calories; 0 milligrams cholesterol; 1 gram fat; 43 milligrams sodium; 5 grams protein (11% RDA); 40 milligrams carbohydrate

RDA: calcium 2%; phosphorus 5%; iron 11%; thiamin 15%; riboflavin 4%; niacin 14%; vitamin C 4%

½ cup (120 ml) minced yellow onion
   (about ¼ pound; 113.5 g)
1 cup (240 ml) arborio rice
3 cups (705 ml) Basic Chicken Broth
   (page 460), or unsalted or regular
   canned chicken broth

¼ cup (60 ml) chopped fresh herbs,
   optional

1. Place onions in an 11 × 8½ × 2-inch (28 × 21.5 × 5-cm) dish. Cook, uncovered, at 100% for 2 minutes in a 650- to 700-watt oven. Stir in rice and cook, uncovered, for 1 minute, or until rice is milky-white but not browned.
2. Stir in broth. Cook, uncovered, for 9 minutes. Stir and cook for 9 to 11 minutes more, or until rice is al dente. Remove from oven. Add herbs, if desired. Cover with a kitchen towel and let stand for 5 minutes, or until rice absorbs excess liquid.

To serve 8 as a first course. Use 1 cup (240 ml) minced onion, 2 cups (470 ml) rice, 6 cups (1,460 ml) broth, and ½ cup (120 ml) chopped fresh herbs. Cook onion in a 14 × 11 × 2-inch (35.5 × 28 × 5-cm) dish, uncovered, for 3 minutes. Stir in rice and cook, uncovered, for 4 minutes. Stir in broth. Cook, uncovered, for 12 minutes. Stir and cook for 12 minutes more, or until rice is tender.

To serve 2 as a first course. Use ¼ cup (60 ml) onion, ½ cup (120 ml) rice, 1½ cups (355 ml) broth and 2 tablespoons chopped fresh herbs (optional). Cook onion in a 9-inch (23-cm) pie plate or quiche dish, uncovered, for 2 minutes. Add rice and cook, uncovered, for 1 minute. Stir in broth. Cook, uncovered, for 9 minutes. Stir and cook for 4–5 minutes more, or until rice is tender.

RISOTTO—THE OTHER WAY

*T*his is the other kind of risotto, fine for the health-conscious but not for the weight-loss dieter. It works well in many quantities and in low-wattage as well as full-wattage ovens. *SERVES 4 AS A FIRST COURSE, 6 AS A SIDE DISH*

Per ¾-cup (180-ml) serving: 320 calories; 0 milligrams cholesterol; 15 grams fat; 780 milligrams sodium; 5 grams protein (11% RDA); 40 grams carbohydrate

RDA: iron 12%; thiamin 15%; niacin 14%

¼ cup (60 ml) olive oil
½ cup (120 ml) minced yellow onion
  (about ¼ pound; 113.5 g)
1 cup (240 ml) arborio rice
3 cups (705 ml) Basic Chicken Broth
  (page 460), or unsalted or regular
  canned chicken broth

2 teaspoons kosher salt
Freshly ground black pepper, to taste
Freshly grated Parmesan cheese,
  optional

1. Heat olive oil in a 10-inch (25.5-cm) quiche dish or pie plate, uncovered, at 100% for 2 minutes in a 650- to 700-watt oven. Add onion and stir to coat. Cook, uncovered, for 4 minutes. Add rice and stir to coat. Cook, uncovered, for 4 minutes more.

2. Stir in broth. Cook, uncovered, for 18 minutes, stirring once halfway through cooking.

3. Remove from oven. Let stand, uncovered, for 5 minutes to let rice absorb remaining liquid, stirring several times. Stir in salt, pepper and cheese, if desired.

To serve 2. Use 2 tablespoons oil, ¼ cup (60 ml) onion, ½ cup (120 ml) rice, 1½ cups (355 ml) broth, 1 teaspoon salt, pinch pepper and cheese, if desired. Heat oil as in Step 1 for 2 minutes. Add onion and cook for 2 minutes. Add rice and cook for 2 minutes more. Finish as in Steps 2 and 3, cooking for 18 minutes.

To serve 1. Use 1 tablespoon oil, 1 tablespoon onion, ¼ cup (60 ml) rice, 1¼ cups (300 ml) broth, salt, pepper and cheese, if desired. Heat oil as in Step 1 for 2 minutes in a 9-inch (23-cm) pie plate. Add onion and rice and cook for 2 minutes. Finish as in Steps 2 and 3, cooking for 12 minutes.

FOR 400- TO 500-WATT OVENS

To serve 4. Cook as in Step 1; heat oil for 7 minutes, cook rice and onion for 7 minutes. Finish as in Steps 2 and 3, cooking for 24 minutes, stirring twice.

To serve 2. Cook as in step 1; heat oil for 5 minutes, cook rice and onion for 5 minutes. Finish as in Steps 2 and 3, cooking for 22 minutes, stirring twice.

To serve 1. Cook as in Step 1; heat oil for 4 minutes, cook rice and onion for 4 minutes. Finish as in Steps 2 and 3, cooking for 18 minutes, stirring twice.

RISOTTO WITH WILD MUSHROOMS

Back to fat-free risottos. This is festive—the dried wild mushrooms are expensive—and I save it for parties when this largish version is appropriate. Since the dried mushrooms are plumped as the rice cooks, more liquid is needed than in a plain risotto. The risotto will be colored and perfumed by the mushrooms.
SERVES 3 AS A FIRST COURSE, 6 AS A SIDE DISH

Per ¾-cup (180-ml) first-course serving: 287 calories; 0 milligrams cholesterol; 2 grams fat; 70 milligrams sodium; 8 grams protein (17% RDA); 58 grams carbohydrate

RDA: calcium 3%; phosphorus 8%; iron 21%; vitamin A 5%; thiamin 21%; riboflavin 8%; niacin 23%; vitamin C 13%

½ cup (120 ml) minced yellow onion (about ¼ pound; 113.5 g)
1 cup (240 ml) arborio rice
3½ cups (825 ml) Basic Chicken Broth (page 460), or unsalted or regular canned chicken broth
½ cup (120 ml) plus 2 tablespoons dried mushrooms (such as porcini, cepes, tree ears or straw mushrooms), or a mixture
Freshly ground black pepper, to taste
¼ cup (60 ml) finely minced parsley

1. Place onion in an 11 × 8½ × 2-inch (28 × 21.5 × 5-cm) dish. Cook, uncovered, at 100% for 2 minutes in a 650- to 700- watt oven. Stir in rice and cook, uncovered, for 1 minute. Add broth and stir well. Cook, uncovered, for 9 minutes.
2. Add dried mushrooms. Cook, uncovered, for 9 minutes. Stir well and cook for 5 minutes more.
3. Remove from oven and stir in black pepper and parsley. Cover with a kitchen towel and let stand for 5 minutes or until rice absorbs excess liquid.

To serve 6 as a first course. Use 1 cup (240 ml) minced onion, 2 cups (470 ml) arborio rice, 7 cups (1.7 l) broth, ¾ cup (180 ml) mixed dried mushrooms, freshly ground pepper to taste and ½ cup (120 ml) minced parsley. Cook onion in a 14 × 11 × 2-inch (35.5 × 28 × 5-cm) dish for 3 minutes. Stir in rice and cook,

(continued)

uncovered, for 3 minutes. Add broth, stir well and cook, uncovered, for 12 minutes. Add dried mushrooms and cook, uncovered, for 12 minutes. Stir well and cook for 3 minutes more. Remove from oven and stir in black pepper and parsley. Finish as in Step 3.

To serve 2 as a first course. Use ¼ cup (60 ml) minced onion, ½ cup (120 ml) arborio rice, 1¾ cups (410 ml) broth, ⅓ cup (80 ml) mixed dried mushrooms, freshly ground pepper to taste and 2 tablespoons minced parsley. Cook onion in a 9-inch (23-cm) pie plate or quiche dish, uncovered, for 2 minutes. Stir in rice and cook, uncovered, for 1 minute. Add broth, stir well and cook, uncovered, for 9 minutes. Add dried mushrooms and cook, uncovered, for 4–5 minutes. Stir well and cook for 5 minutes more. Remove from oven and stir in black pepper and parsley. Finish as in Step 3.

SEAFOOD RISOTTO

This satisfying and pretty, low-calorie and low-fat risotto can be introduced by Caprese Salad (page 80), Bell Peppers and Sardines with Balsamic Vinegar (page 84) or Coral Scallop Terrine (page 93). All of which goes well with cold white wine. Enjoy a luscious dessert.   *SERVES 4 AS A MAIN COURSE, 8 AS A FIRST COURSE*

Per main-course serving: 269 calories; 53 milligrams cholesterol; 2 grams fat; 198 milligrams sodium; 18 grams protein (39% RDA); 42 grams carbohydrate

RDA: calcium 6%; phosphorus 23%; iron 23%; vitamin A 1%; thiamin 14%; niacin 15%

¼ pound (113.5 g) chopped yellow onion

1 cup (240 ml) arborio rice

1½ cups (360 ml) Basic Fish Broth (page 461), Basic Chicken Broth (page 460), or unsalted or regular canned chicken broth

½ cup (120 ml) white wine

½ teaspoon dried thyme

¾ teaspoon dried tarragon

1 tablespoon finely chopped fresh parsley

¼ pound (113.5 g) sea scallops—any scallops larger than 1 inch (2.5 cm)—cut in half

¼ pound (113.5 g) shrimp, peeled, deveined and cut in half crosswise

1 pound (450 g) mussels, scrubbed and debearded

1. Place onion in a 12 × 9½ × 2-inch (30.5 × 24 × 5-cm) oval dish. Cook, uncovered, at 100% for 2 minutes in a 650- to 700-watt oven. Add rice and cook, uncovered, for 1 minute.

2. Add broth, wine, thyme, tarragon and parsley. Cook, uncovered, for 9 minutes. Stir in scallops and shrimp and arrange mussels on top of mixture around the inside edge of the dish. Cook, uncovered, for 9 minutes more.

3. Remove from oven. Let stand, covered with a kitchen towel, for 5 minutes. Stir well and serve.

GREEN RISOTTO

*T*his nonfat risotto is a greener version of the Venetian risi bisi. If you want to make it even more Venetian, add an extra one-third cup (94 ml) of broth per person. Vegetarian Broth I (page 465) substituted for chicken broth makes this a good vegetarian dish. With cheese sprinkled on top and a salad, this makes a good lunch.   SERVES 4

Per ¾-cup first-course serving: 273 calories; 0 milligrams cholesterol; 2 grams fat; 106 milligrams sodium; 11 grams protein (25% RDA); 52 grams carbohydrate

RDA: calcium 12%; phosphorus 15%; iron 32%; vitamin A 142%; thiamin 29%; riboflavin 18%; niacin 24%; vitamin C 111%

1 cup (240 ml) arborio rice
4 cups (1 l) Basic Chicken broth (page 460), or unsalted or regular canned chicken broth
2 cups (470 ml) spinach leaves, packed (about ½ pound; 227 g)
2 tablespoons fresh parsley leaves

½ pound (227 g) scallions cut into 2-inch (5-cm) lengths, whites and half the greens (about 6 scallions)
1½ cups (355 ml) shelled peas, fresh or frozen, defrosted in a sieve under warm running water (8 ounces; 227g)

1. Place rice in an 11 × 9 × 2-inch (28 × 23 × 5-cm) oval dish. Cook, uncovered, at 100% for 2 minutes in a 650- to 700-watt oven. Stir in broth and cook, uncovered, for 9 minutes. Stir well and cook, uncovered, for 9 minutes more, or until rice is al dente.

2. While rice is cooking, place spinach, parsley and scallions in a food processor. Process until finely chopped. Reserve.

3. Stir chopped greens and peas into rice. Cook, uncovered, for 3 minutes. Remove from oven. Cover with a kitchen towel and let stand for several minutes or until liquid is absorbed.

To serve 8 as a first course. Use 2 cups (470 ml) arborio rice, 8 cups (2 l) broth, 4 cups (950 ml) spinach leaves, ¼ cup (60 ml) fresh parsley, 1 pound (450 g) scallions and 3 cups (705 ml) peas. Cook rice as in Step 1 in a 14 × 11 × 2-inch

(continued)

(35.5 × 28 × 5-cm) casserole, uncovered, for 3 minutes. Stir in broth and cook, uncovered, for 12 minutes. Stir well and cook, uncovered, for 12 minutes more, or until rice is al dente. Follow Step 2. In Step 3, cook for 5 minutes more and finish as directed.

To serve 2 as a first course. Use ½ cup (120 ml) arborio rice, 2 cups (470 ml) broth, 1 cup (240 ml) spinach leaves, 1 tablespoon fresh parsley, ¼ pound (113.5 g) scallions and ¾ cup (180 ml) peas. Cook rice as in Step 1 in a 9-inch (23-cm) pie plate or quiche dish, uncovered, for 2 minutes. Stir in broth and cook, un-covered, for 9 minutes. Stir well and cook, uncovered, for 6 minutes more, or until rice is al dente. Follow Step 2. In Step 3, cook for 2 minutes more and finish as directed.

CREOLE RICE

*T*his very American, brightly colored side dish is starch and vegetable all in one and goes well with fish and chicken. Those who like their Creole spicy can dou-ble the amount of the hot pepper sauce.   *SERVES 8 AS A SIDE DISH*

Per ½-cup (120-ml) serving: 116 calories; 0 milligrams cholesterol; 1 gram fat; 114 milligrams sodium; 2 grams protein (5% RDA); 23 grams carbohydrate

RDA: calcium 3%; iron 7%; vitamin A 21%; thiamin 9%; niacin 7%; vitamin C 56%

4 ounces (113.5 g) red pepper, stemmed, seeded, deribbed and diced (⅔ cup; 160 ml)
4 ounces (113.5 g) onion, peeled and diced (¾ cup; 180 ml)
2 ribs celery, peeled and diced (½ cup; 120 ml)
3 cloves garlic, smashed, peeled and sliced
2 teaspoons vegetable oil

1 cup (240 ml) long-grain rice
2 cups (470 ml) canned Italian plum tomatoes with juice, roughly chopped
½ teaspoon hot red pepper sauce
1 cup (240 ml) water
2 teaspoons fresh lemon juice
Freshly ground black pepper, to taste

1. Place red pepper, onion, celery, garlic and vegetable oil in a 13 × 9 × 2-inch (33 × 23 × 5-cm) oval glass dish and stir to combine. Cook, uncovered, at 100% for 4 minutes in a 650- to 700-watt oven.
2. Remove from oven, stir in rice, tomatoes with juice, hot pepper sauce and water. Cook, uncovered, for 25 minutes, stirring 3 times.
3. Remove from oven. Stir in lemon juice and black pepper to taste. Serve hot.

To serve 4. Use 2 ounces (56 g) red pepper, 2 ounces (56 g) onion, 1 rib celery, 2 small cloves garlic, 1 teaspoon oil, ½ cup (120 ml) rice, 1 cup (240 ml) tomatoes, ¼ teaspoon hot pepper sauce, ½ cup (120 ml) water, 1 teaspoon lemon juice and pepper to taste. Cook as in Step 1 for 2 minutes. Continue with Step 2, cooking for 15 minutes, stirring 3 times.

FOR 400- TO 500-WATT OVENS

To serve 4. Use ingredients to serve 4 plus an additional ¼ cup (60 ml) water. Cook as in Step 1 for 5 minutes. Cook as in Step 2 for 35 minutes, stirring 3 times.

VEGETABLE FRIED RICE

Let's be honest; this isn't fried. What it is is a very good imitation of the fried rice served as a side dish in Chinese restaurants.   *SERVES 9 AS A SIDE DISH*

Per ½-cup (120-ml) serving: 98 calories; 0 milligrams cholesterol; 0 grams fat; 126 milligrams sodium; 3 grams protein (6% RDA); 20 grams carbohydrate

RDA: iron 6%; thiamin 8%; niacin 7%; vitamin C 10%

1 cup (240 ml) long-grain rice
4 radishes, trimmed and sliced (½ cup; 120 ml)
1 teaspoon rice wine vinegar
3 cloves garlic, smashed, peeled and minced
1 teaspoon Oriental sesame oil
4 scallions, sliced (½ cup; 120 ml)

4 ounces (113.5 g) mushrooms, thinly sliced (about 1⅓ cups; 320 ml)
3 ounces (85 g) frozen peas, defrosted in a sieve under warm running water
2 ounces (56 g) water chestnuts, sliced (about ⅓ cup; 80 ml)
1 tablespoon tamari soy

    1. Cook rice either on top of the stove or in the microwave (see page 182). Drain and reserve.

    2. Combine radishes with rice wine vinegar in a small bowl and reserve.

    3. Place garlic and sesame oil in 13×9×2-inch (33×23×5-cm) oval dish. Cook, uncovered, at 100% for 2 minutes in a 650- to 700-watt oven.

    4. Remove from oven and stir in scallions and mushrooms. Cook, uncovered, for 4 minutes.

    5. Remove from oven and add reserved rice and radishes and remaining ingredients. Stir to combine and cook, uncovered, for 4 minutes or until hot.

    6. Remove from oven. Serve hot.

(continued)

Vegetable Fried Rice (cont.)

To serve 4. Use ½ cup (120 ml) rice, 2 radishes, ½ teaspoon vinegar, 2 small cloves garlic, ½ teaspoon oil, 2 scallions, 2 ounces (56 g) mushrooms, 1½ ounces (42 g) peas, 1 ounce (28 g) water chestnuts and 1½ teaspoons tamari soy. Cook rice as in Step 1. Cook as in Step 3 for 1 minute. Cook as in Step 4 for 2 minutes. Continue with Step 5, cooking for 3 minutes.

FOR 400- TO 500-WATT OVENS

To serve 4. Cook as in Step 3 for 3 minutes. Cook as in Step 4 for 5 minutes. Continue with Step 5, cooking for 4 minutes.

Other Grains

When we look for something to go with our main course, the immediate ideas tend to be potatoes—more later—rice and noodles. There are lots of other possibilities. If we are going to increase the amount of carbohydrate in our diets without boredom, we are going to have to venture beyond the usual. Here are a few ideas.

BASIC NUTRITION FOR UNSEASONED TABBOULEH

PER ½-CUP (120-ML) SERVING SWELLED TABBOULEH: 78 calories; 0 milligrams cholesterol; <1 gram fat; <1 milligram sodium; 2 grams protein (4% RDA); 19 grams carbohydrate

TABBOULEH

*T*abbouleh doesn't even need to be cooked. It can be served hot; but I like it best as a salad with cold food or as a light first course. This is a good dish for a buffet.   SERVES 8

Per generous ½-cup (120-ml) serving: 126 calories; 0 milligrams cholesterol; 4 grams fat; 172 milligrams sodium; 3 grams protein (6% RDA); 21 grams carbohydrate

RDA: calcium 4%; iron 20%; vitamin A 23%; thiamin 4%; niacin 8%; vitamin C 46%

FOR THE TABBOULEH

1 cup (240 ml) tabbouleh
5 cups (1,220 ml) water

FOR THE SALAD

¾ pound (340 g) radishes, stemmed, tailed, halved and sliced thin (about 2 cups; 240 ml)
¼ cup (60 ml) rice wine vinegar
4 ribs celery, peeled and cut into 1-inch (2.5-cm) lengths

1 bunch scallions (about 6 ounces; 170 g), green and white parts, cut into 1-inch (2.5-cm) lengths
1 Pickled Jalapeño Pepper (page 473), or canned jalapeño pepper
2 tablespoons olive oil
3 cloves garlic, smashed, peeled and minced

1. Put tabbouleh in a large bowl; bring water to a simmer on the stove. Stir 3 cups (705 ml) of the simmering water into the tabbouleh. Keep remaining water simmering. Let tabbouleh sit for 15 minutes. Drain. Add the remaining 2 cups (470 ml) water and let sit for 10 minutes more. Drain well.

2. While tabbouleh is sitting, combine radishes with vinegar in a small bowl. Place celery, scallions, and jalapeño in a food processor and process until finely chopped.

3. Thoroughly toss tabbouleh with olive oil. Stir in remaining ingredients. Let sit at room temperature for 30 minutes before serving.

BARLEY NUTRITION

PER ½-CUP (120-ML) COOKED PEARL BARLEY SERVING: 114 calories; 0 milligrams cholesterol; 0 grams fat; 3 milligrams sodium; 4 grams protein (8% RDA); 24 grams carbohydrate

RDA: PHOSPHORUS 8%; IRON 6%; VITAMIN A 7%; THIAMIN 5%; NIACIN 8%; VITAMIN C 6%

BASIC BARLEY COOKING TIMES

*B*arley is a side dish with a grainy texture and a nutty taste. It can be flavored in many ways and added, cooked, to soups and stews. See nutrition above.
YIELDS 3 CUPS (705 ML)

1 cup (240 ml) pearl barley   4 cups (1 l) water

   1. Place barley and water in a 2½-quart (2.5-l) soufflé dish or casserole. Cover with a lid and cook at 100% for 30 minutes in a 650- to 700-watt oven. Remove lid.
   2. Remove from oven and drain.

To make 6 cups (1.5 l). Use 2 cups (470 ml) barley and 2 quarts (2 l) water. Cook as in Step 1 in a 5-quart (5-l) casserole for 45 minutes. Finish as in Step 2.

FOR 400- TO 500-WATT OVENS
To make 3 cups (705 ml). Cook for 40 minutes.

UPBEAT BARLEY

*B*arley heated with a few vegetables makes an attractive accompaniment to pork stews and simple microwave-cooked meats.   *SERVES 6*

Per ½-cup (120-ml) serving: 119 calories; 0 milligrams cholesterol; 0 grams fat; 192 milligrams sodium; 4 grams protein (9% RDA); 25 grams carbohydrate

RDA: iron 6%; thiamin 5%; niacin 8%

3 cups (705 ml) cooked barley
¼ cup (60 ml) Vegetarian Broth II
   (page 466)
¼ cup (60 ml) chopped fresh parsley

¼ cup (60 ml) peeled and chopped
   celery (about 1½ ribs)
½ teaspoon kosher salt
Freshly ground black pepper, to taste

   1. Stir together all ingredients in a 1½-quart (1.5-l) soufflé dish. Cover tightly with microwave plastic wrap. Cook for 5 minutes at 100% in a 650- to 700-watt oven. Prick plastic wrap with the tip of a sharp knife to release steam.
   2. Remove from oven and serve.

FOR 400- TO 500-WATT OVENS

To serve 6. Cook for 8 minutes.

HEARTY BARLEY SOUP

A cup of this is lunch or a great start to a winter meal. If you like garlic as much as I do, stir in Garlic to Go which will also give the dish a somewhat smoother texture.   *SERVES 6*

Per 1-cup (240-ml) serving: 148 calories; 0 milligrams cholesterol; 1 gram fat; 15 milligrams sodium; 5 grams protein (11% RDA); 31 grams carbohydrate

RDA: calcium 3%; phosphorus 11%; iron 9%; thiamin 6%; riboflavin 9%; niacin 13%

4 ounces (113.5 g) fresh mushrooms, sliced (1 cup; 240 ml)

1 small onion (4 ounces; 113.5 g), peeled and diced (½ cup; 120 ml)

1 rib celery, peeled and diced (⅓ cup; 80 ml)

3 cloves garlic, smash, peeled and minced

1 cup (240 ml) barley, cooked and drained (page 196)

½ ounce (14 g) dried boletus mushrooms, broken into small pieces, or shiitake mushrooms, stems removed and broken into small pieces

4 cups (1 l) Basic Meat Broth (page 462), or unsalted or regular canned chicken broth

¼ cup (60 ml) chopped fresh dill

Kosher salt, to taste

Freshly ground black pepper, to taste

1 tablespoon Garlic to Go (page 470), optional

1. Combine fresh mushrooms, onion, celery and garlic in a 2½-quart (2.5-l) soufflé dish. Cook, uncovered, at 100% for 4 minutes in a 650- to 700-watt oven.

2. Remove from oven. Stir in remaining ingredients. Cover tightly with microwave plastic wrap. Cook for 10 minutes. Prick plastic to release steam.

3. Remove from oven and uncover. Serve hot.

Kasha Cooking Times

Combine kasha and water in a 2½-quart (2.5-l) soufflé dish or casserole with a tightly fitted lid. Cook for time specified below, uncover and fluff with a fork, then cook uncovered for second time specified.

1 CUP (240 ML) DRY KASHA YIELDS 3 CUPS (705 ML) COOKED KASHA

PER ¾ CUP (180 ML) COOKED KASHA SERVING: 145 calories; 3 grams protein (4% RDA); 30 grams carbohydrate

RDA: iron 8%; thiamin 1.2%; riboflavin 3%; niacin 4%

¼ cup (60 ml) kasha and ¾ cup (180 ml) water
650- to 700-watt oven: 3 min. covered;
   2 min. more uncovered
400- to 500-watt oven: Same as for 650-
   to 700-watt oven

1 cup (240 ml) kasha and 3 cups (705 ml) water
650- to 700-watt oven: 10 min. covered;
   4 min. more uncovered
400- to 500-watt oven: Same as for 650-
   to 700-watt oven

½ cup (120 ml) kasha and 1½ cups (355 ml water
650- to 700-watt oven: 8 min. covered;
   3 min. more uncovered
400- to 500-watt oven: Same as for 650-
   to 700-watt oven

Millet Cooking Times

Millet isn't used much anymore. It's a tiny grain that can be found in specialty and health-food stores and is a nice change. The grains stay separate when properly cooked. Use as is or add butter, or oil, and salt.

Combine millet with water in specified dish. Cover tightly with microwave plastic wrap and cook at 100%.

1 CUP (240 ML) DRY MILLET YIELDS 4 CUPS (1 L) COOKED MILLET

PER ½-CUP (120 ML) SERVING COOKED MILLET: 75 calories; 0 milligrams cholesterol; <1 gram fat; <1 milligram sodium; 2 grams protein (5% RDA); 17 grams carbohydrate

RDA: phosphorus 7%; iron 9%; thiamin 11%

1 cup (240 ml) millet with 2 cups (470 ml) water in a 2½-quart (2.5-l) soufflé dish
650- to 700-watt oven: 15 min.
400- to 500-watt oven: 22 min.

2 cups (470 ml) millet with 4 cups (1 l) water in a 14 × 11 × 2-inch (35.5 × 28 × 5-cm) dish
650- to 700-watt oven: 20 min.
400- to 500-watt oven: Not recommended

Beans and Legumes

Beans and legumes are the heart of the vegan's diet. Combined with rice, wheat, corn and potatoes, they come close to making a nutritional whole when supplemented by fresh fruits and vegetables. However, iron, zinc and some of the B vitamins remain problematic, especially for those who eat no milk or cheese.

All of us need to learn to get more of our nutrition from these fiber-rich foods. While getting them out of a can may be easy, it is not a good idea if we are trying to limit our salt intake (see opposite page).

These foods do not cook instantaneously in a microwave oven. Including the soaking, you need to allow about two hours for most dried beans. The top-of-the-stove cooking is even longer, about four and a half hours. It's worthwhile soaking some beans or cooking them ahead. Store them in the refrigerator, either in their own cooking liquid or covered with water. They will keep for about a week, and you can use them as you need them. Soaked beans will give you more flexibility in the seasoning of your recipe than fully cooked beans. I usually keep them soaked.

NUTRITIONAL COMPARISON OF BEANS AND OTHER LEGUMES

The following data are based on ½ cup (120 ml) cooked, drained beans and legumes. (They have been cooked without salt.)

VARIETY	CAL.	PROT. (g)	CARB. (g)	CALC. (mg)	IRON (mg)	SOD. (mg)	POT. (mg)
Great Northern	106	7	19	45	2	7	375
Kidney, red	109	7	20	35	2	3	315
Lima, Fordhook	131	8	25	28	3	2	582
Lima, baby	94	6	18	25	2	26	370
Pea beans, navy	112	8	20	48	3	7	395
Broad	28	3	5	9	2	21	97
Green peas	63	4	11	19	1	70	134

Nutritional data for the following legumes exist only for the dried state. Hence, data are given for 1 ounce (28 g) of each variety. After cooking, this amount will yield approximately ½ cup (120 ml). "N/A" indicates data not available at the time this book went to press.

VARIETY	CAL.	PROT. (g)	CARB. (g)	CALC. (mg)	IRON (mg)	SOD. (mg)	POT. (mg)
Black turtle	95	7	18	N/A	N/A	8	N/A
Blackeye peas	35	7	18	N/A	N/A	<1	N/A
Chick-peas	100	6	18	N/A	N/A	8	N/A
Lentils, green	95	7	18	N/A	N/A	8	N/A
Lentils, red	98	7	17	N/A	N/A	9	N/A
Pinto	100	7	18	N/A	N/A	3	N/A
Split peas	100	7	18	N/A	N/A	13	N/A

For the purposes of cooking, dried beans are divided into two groups by size. Although it would seem logical for large beans to take longer to cook and to give a larger yield when cooked, the reverse is true as more small beans can fit in a cup than large beans.

LARGE DRIED BEANS blackeye peas, cannellini, kidney beans, red beans, pink beans, pinto beans

SMALL DRIED BEANS flageolets, navy beans, white beans, turtle beans

LEGUMES broad (fava) beans, chick-peas, lentils, lima beans, split peas

Yield when soaked
1 cup (240 ml) large dried beans yields 2 cups (470 ml)
1 cup (240 ml) small dried beans yields 2½ cups (600 ml)

Yield when cooked
1 cup (240 ml) large dried beans yields 2½ cups (600 ml)
1 cup (240 ml) small dried beans yields a scant 3 cups (705 ml)

SODIUM CONTENT

The sodium content of canned beans is very high. I have given a few samples for you to compare with the median sodium content of freshly cooked dried beans. Now you know why they are worth cooking if you want to observe any salt restrictions in your diet.

Canned beans, drained (1 cup; 240 ml)
8 ounces (227 g) turtle beans: 810 mg sodium
8 ounces (227 g) cannellini: 717 mg sodium

8 ounces (227 g) chick-peas: 691 mg sodium

Freshly cooked beans from 2 ounces (56 g) dry, 1 cup (240 ml) cooked (8 ounces; 227 g): median sodium 15 mg

TO SOAK (PARCOOK) DRIED BEANS AND LEGUMES

To soak 1 or 2 cups of dried beans of any size or legumes, place in a 5-quart (5-l) casserole with a tightly fitted lid with 2 cups (470 ml) water. Cook at 100% for 15 minutes in a 650- to 700-watt oven. Remove from oven and let stand, covered, for 5 minutes. Uncover and add 2 cups very hot tap water. Re-cover and let stand for 1 hour. Drain.

To Cook Dried Beans and Legumes After Soaking

Put presoaked (see above) beans and fresh water in a 5-quart (5-l) casserole with tightly fitted lid.

LARGE BEANS

1 cup (240 ml) presoaked beans with 3 cups (1 l) warm water
650- to 700-watt oven: 35 min., rest 20 min.
400- to 500-watt oven: 55 min., rest 20 min.

2 cups (470 ml) presoaked beans with 6 cups (1.5 l) warm water
650- to 700-watt oven: 45 min., rest 20 min.
400- to 500-watt oven: Not recommended

SMALL BEANS

1 cup (240 ml) presoaked beans with 4 cups (1 l) warm water
650- to 700-watt oven: 40 min., rest 30 min.
400- to 500-watt oven: 70 min., rest 30 min.

2 cups (470 ml) presoaked beans with 4 cups (1 l) warm water
650- to 700-watt oven: 40 min., rest 30 min.
400- to 500-watt oven: Not recommended

CHICK-PEAS Presoak chick-peas as for dried beans (see above). Remove the skins; drain, rinse and return to casserole. Cover tightly.

1 cup (240 ml) presoaked chick-peas with 4 cups (1 l) water
650- to 700-watt oven: 35 min.
400- to 500-watt oven: Not recommended

2 cups (470 ml) presoaked chick-peas with 6 cups (1.5 l) water
650- to 700-watt oven: 45 min.
400- to 500-watt oven: Not recommended

GREEN OR BROWN LENTILS

1 cup (240 ml) lentils with 4 cups (1 l) water
650- to 700-watt oven: 35 min.
400- to 500-watt oven: 45 min.

2 cups (240 ml) lentils with 6 cups (1.5 l) water
650- to 700-watt oven: 35 min.
400- to 500-watt oven: 45 min.

REHEATING COOKED BEANS

It is often convenient to cook a quantity of beans when you have the time and keep them in the refrigerator, covered with their cooking liquid or drained and covered with fresh water. They can then be used in salads or reheated as needed. Reheat as much as you need covered with cooking liquid or fresh water and tightly covered with microwave plastic wrap. As an example, it will take you 17 minutes at 100% in a 650- to 700-watt oven, stirring twice, to reheat 3 cups (705 ml) beans with 1½ cups (355 ml) cooking liquid.

BLACK BEAN SALAD

This is a nice addition to a buffet for a party. The beans are spicy and satisfying. At lunch, you could have a portion of bean salad with some low-fat cottage cheese and some juicy wedges of orange or some Orange and Red Onion Salad (page 402). This large-scale recipe will not work in a small oven. You can make less by using the cooking times for small beans above and reducing the other ingredients proportionately. If you cook all the beans, but don't need all of them for salad, you can make the soup below with the remainder.   *SERVES 10*

Per scant ½-cup (120-ml) serving: 170 calories; 1 milligram cholesterol; 1 gram fat; 344 milligrams sodium; 10 grams protein (21% RDA); 32 grams carbohydrate

RDA: calcium 8%; phosphorus 17%; iron 12%; thiamin 26%; riboflavin 6%; niacin 4%; vitamin C 37%

2 cups (470 ml) dried black (turtle) beans, presoaked (see opposite page), to make 5 cups (1.2 l)

4 cups (1 l) water

2 cups (470 ml) orange juice

5 cloves garlic, smashed, peeled and minced

2 teaspoons kosher salt

1 teaspoon ground coriander seed

½ teaspoon crushed red pepper

1 large onion (1 pound; 450 g), finely chopped (about 1¾ cups; 410 ml)

1–2 teaspoons minced Pickled Jalapeño Peppers (page 473), or canned jalapeño peppers

½ cup (120 ml) Orange Yogurt Dressing (page 494)

¼ cup (60 ml) chopped fresh coriander leaves

1. Combine beans with water, orange juice, garlic, salt, ground coriander seed and red pepper in a 5-quart (5-l) casserole with a tightly fitted lid. Cover tightly with lid and cook, at 100%, 45 minutes or until beans are tender in a 650- to 700-watt oven.

2. Remove from oven and let stand, covered, for 20 minutes. Uncover and drain thoroughly.

3. Stir onion and jalapeño into the beans. Let cool to room temperature. Just before serving, toss together with dressing and fresh coriander.

VARIATION. Instead of the Orange Yogurt Dressing, combine 1 tablespoon orange juice, 2 tablespoons lemon juice and 1 teaspoon olive oil. Toss with the bean mixture to coat.

BLACK BEAN SOUP

*O*nce you know how to make beans, it is easy to turn them into soup. If you like, add a splash of sherry to this at the table. If you make all the beans for the previous recipes, but only sauce half of them, you can make this soup without any additional water by using all the cooking liquid with the remaining half of the beans.   *SERVES 10*

Per 1-cup (240-ml) serving: 163 calories; 0 milligrams cholesterol; 1 gram fat; 304 milligrams sodium; 9 grams protein (20% RDA); 31 grams carbohydrate

RDA: calcium 6%; phosphorus 15%; iron 12%; 707 milligrams potassium; thiamin 26%; riboflavin 5%; vitamin C 36%

1 recipe Black Bean Salad (page 203), without dressing	1⅓ cups (320 ml) Vegetarian Broth I or II (pages 465–466), or water

1. Prepare Black Bean Salad as in Step 1.
2. Let beans stand as in Step 2. Do not drain. Place beans and their cooking liquid in the food processor and purée until smooth, or put through a food mill. Scrape back into casserole. Add broth or water. Cook at 100% for 15 minutes or until hot.

CUBAN BLACK BEANS AND RICE

*T*he food of people in poor countries can sometimes be the most delicious, the healthiest and the most satisfying. All this needs is a Chunky Tomato Basil Salad (page 407), Salsa (page 522), crusty bread, some fruit and a glass of cold beer.
SERVES 6 AS A MAIN COURSE, 12 AS A SIDE DISH

Per generous 1-cup (240-ml) serving: 262 calories; 0 milligrams cholesterol; 3 grams fat; 534 milligrams sodium; 10 grams protein (23% RDA); 49 grams carbohydrate

RDA: calcium 9%; phosphorus 17%; iron 18%; vitamin A 26%; thiamin 29%; riboflavin 5%; niacin 10%; vitamin C 16%

6 ounces (170 g) onion, peeled and chopped (about 1½ cups; 355 ml)
3 ribs celery (6 ounces; 170 g), trimmed, peeled and cut across into ¼-inch (.5-cm) slices (¾ cup; 180 ml)
2 cups (470 ml) chopped spinach (about 12 ounces; 340 g)
4 cloves garlic, smashed and peeled
1 tablespoon olive oil

1 cup (240 ml) dried black (turtle) beans, presoaked (page 202), to make 2½ cups (600 ml)
4 cups (1 l) water
1 cup (240 ml) long-grain rice
2 teaspoons kosher salt
Freshly ground black pepper, to taste
3 drops hot red pepper sauce, or to taste

1. Place onion, celery, spinach, garlic and oil in a 2½-quart (2.5-l) soufflé dish with a tightly fitted lid. Cook, uncovered, at 100% for 5 minutes in a 650- to 700-watt oven.

2. Remove from oven and stir in presoaked beans and water. Cover with lid and cook for 20 minutes. Uncover and stir in rice. Re-cover and cook for 15 minutes.

3. Remove from oven. Let stand, covered, for 30 minutes. Uncover and stir in salt, pepper and pepper sauce.

VARIATION WITH CANNED BEANS. If using canned beans, the yield will be 5 cups (1,220 ml). Follow Step 1 and cook for 5 minutes. Add rice and 1½ cups (355 ml) water. Cover and cook for 10 minutes. Add 1 cup (240 ml) canned beans, re-cover and cook for 5 minutes. Let stand, covered, for 15 minutes. Finish as in Step 3.

FOR 400- TO 500-WATT OVENS

To serve 6. Use canned black beans instead of presoaked. Follow Step 1 and cook for 8 minutes. Add rice and 1½ cups (355 ml) water. Cover and cook for 15 minutes. Add 1 cup (240 ml) canned beans, re-cover and cook for 8 minutes. Let stand, covered, for 15 minutes. Finish as in Step 3.

BLACK BEAN AND TOMATO SALAD

If you cook black beans and keep them on hand, they are a splendid addition to this salad, which doesn't even need a dressing and can be a satisfying lunch, a first course, go with cold chicken or fish, or be combined with other salads and some hot tacos to make a vegetarian dinner. If you use canned beans, there will be lots more sodium. The recipe multiplies easily and is good at parties—say, with outdoor grilling.   SERVES 3

Per ½-cup (120-ml) serving: 87 calories; 3 milligrams cholesterol; 0 grams fat; 3 milligrams sodium; 5 grams protein (12% RDA); 16 grams carbohydrate

RDA: iron 8%; thiamin 10%; vitamin C 13%

6 ounces (170 g) presoaked and cooked black beans (page 202), or 10½-ounce (298-g) can black beans, drained and rinsed

1 medium tomato (3 ounces; 85 g), cored and diced

½ small red onion (about 2 ounces; 56 g), peeled and diced (¼ cup; 60 ml)

2 tablespoons chopped fresh coriander leaves

1 tablespoon fresh lime juice

Freshly ground black pepper, to taste

1. Mix all ingredients together in a medium bowl.

CHILIED RED BEANS

*T*his dish is a freewheeling invention based on nothing but the fact that all the ingredients are used in the same parts of America and Mexico. Serve over one-half cup (120 ml) cooked rice for dinner with a salad. *SERVES 10*

Per ½-cup (120-ml) serving of beans: 179 calories; 0 milligrams cholesterol; 4 grams fat; 212 milligrams sodium; 10 grams protein (22% RDA); 28 grams carbohydrate

RDA: calcium 9%; phosphorus 19%; iron 29%; vitamin A 22%; thiamin 15%; riboflavin 6%; niacin 7%; vitamin C 24%

2 tablespoons olive oil
6 cloves garlic, smashed, peeled and
   minced
2 medium onions, peeled and chopped
   (about 2 cups; 470 ml)
3 tablespoons chile powder
4 tablespoons ground cumin

2 cups (470 ml) tomato juice
4 cups (1 l) water
2 cups (470 ml) dried red kidney beans
   (see page 202), presoaked to make 4
   cups (1 l)

1. Combine oil, garlic, onion, chile powder and cumin in a 5-quart (5-l) casserole with a tightly fitting lid. Cover tightly with lid. Cook at 100% for 5 minutes in a 650- to 700- watt oven.
2. Remove from oven and uncover. Stir in tomato juice, water and beans. Recover and cook for 55 minutes.
3. Remove from oven and let stand, covered, for 45 minutes to allow beans to absorb liquid. Serve warm. (Note: Once refrigerated, beans can be reheated by cooking, covered, for 15 minutes, stirring twice.)

To make 3 cups (705 ml) beans with 1½ cups (355 ml) cooking liquid. Use 1 tablespoon oil, 3 cloves garlic, 1 onion, 1½ tablespoons chile powder, 2 tablespoons cumin, 1 cup (240 ml) tomato juice, 2 cups (470 ml) water and 2 cups (470 ml) presoaked beans. Combine ingredients in a 2½-quart (2.5-l) soufflé dish or casserole as in Step 1. Cook for 4 minutes. Continue with Step 2, cooking for 45 minutes. Let stand for 20 minutes.

FOR 400- TO 500-WATT OVENS
To make 3 cups (705 ml) beans with 1½ cups (355 ml) cooking liquid. Cook as in Step 1 for 6 minutes. Continue with Step 2, cooking for 55 minutes. Let stand for 20 minutes.

CHILIED RED BEAN SOUP

As with cooked and seasoned black beans, it is easy to turn the seasoned beans in the previous recipe into a spicy soup.   SERVES 8

Per generous 1-cup (240-ml) serving: 224 calories; 0 milligrams cholesterol; 5 grams fat; 265 milligrams sodium; 13 grams protein (28% RDA); 35 grams carbohydrate

RDA: calcium 12%; phosphorus 23%; iron 37%; 928 milligrams potassium; vitamin A 27%; thiamin 18%; riboflavin 7%; niacin 9%; vitamin C 29%

1 recipe Chilied Red Beans (page 207),   3⅓ cups (785 ml) water
   puréed in blender

   1. Combine bean purée and water. Cover tightly with microwave plastic wrap. Cook at 100% for 15 minutes, or until hot, in a 650- to 700-watt oven.

FOR 400- TO 500-WATT OVENS

To serve 8. Combine bean purée and water. Cover tightly with microwave plastic wrap. Cook at 100% for 17 minutes, or until hot.

CANNELLINI BEANS WITH GARLIC

This is one of my favorite emergency rations. I serve it with roast leg of lamb or roast chicken. There is only one problem. Since the dish is made with canned beans, it's high in sodium. If you have the time and sodium is a problem, replace the canned beans with two cups (470 ml) home-cooked cannellini beans.
SERVES 6 AS A SIDE DISH

Per ⅓-cup (80-ml) serving: 118 calories; 0 milligrams cholesterol; 5 grams fat; 313 milligrams sodium; 5 grams protein (11% RDA); 15 grams carbohydrate

RDA: calcium 3%; phosphorus 10%; iron 7%; thiamin 6%

2 tablespoons olive oil   ¼ cup (60 ml) fresh parsley or basil
6 cloves garlic, smashed and peeled   leaves, finely chopped
19-ounce (535-g) can cannellini beans,
   drained and rinsed

1. Combine olive oil and garlic in a 2½-quart (2.5-l) soufflé dish or casserole with a tightly fitted lid. Cover tightly with microwave plastic wrap or lid. Cook at 100% for 1 minute in a 650- to 700-watt oven. If using plastic, prick.

2. Remove from oven and uncover. Stir in beans and cook, uncovered, for 3 minutes. Stir in chopped parsley or basil and cook for 1 minute, or until hot.

FOR 400- TO 500-WATT OVENS

To serve 6. Cook oil and garlic as in Step 1 for 1 minute 30 seconds. Continue with Step 2, cooking beans for 5 minutes. Add parsley or basil and cook for 1 minute, or until hot.

LENTIL SALAD

This is a good dish for a summer buffet, or add some Black Bean Salad (page 203), a green salad with cheese, bread and dessert.   *SERVES 12*

Per ½-cup (120-ml) serving: 136 calories; 0 milligrams cholesterol; 2 grams fat; 29 milligrams sodium; 10 grams protein (22% RDA); 21 grams carbohydrate

RDA: calcium 3%; phosphorus 16%; iron 18%; vitamin A 49%; thiamin 10%; riboflavin 5%; niacin 7%; vitamin C 8%

2 medium carrots (about 4 ounces; 113.5 g), peeled and cut into small dice (about ¾ cup; 180 ml)
1 medium onion, peeled and cut into small dice (about 1 cup; 240 ml)
1 tablespoon olive oil
2 cups (470 ml) dried brown lentils
3 cups (705 ml) Basic Chicken Broth (page 460), or unsalted or regular canned chicken broth

3 cups (705 ml) water
2 cups (470 ml) chopped fresh coriander leaves, loosely packed
2 ribs celery, peeled and cut into small dice (about 1 cup; 240 ml)
¼ cup (60 ml) Garlic Oregano Dressing (page 489)

1. Combine chopped carrot, onion and olive oil in a 5-quart (5-l) soufflé dish or casserole with a tightly fitted lid. Cook at 100%, uncovered, for 3 minutes in a 650- to 700-watt oven.

2. Remove from oven. Stir in lentils, broth and water. Cover tightly with microwave plastic wrap or casserole lid and cook for 30 minutes. If using plastic, prick to release steam.

3. Remove from oven and uncover. Drain lentils and return to 5-quart (5-l) casserole. Allow to cool.

4. Add coriander, celery and dressing. Mix well and serve.

SPICY LENTIL DAL

Dal is usually eaten in small quantities as an accompaniment to curries. That's why there are so many portions. This takes a long time to cook in a low-wattage oven and is therefore not recommended. If you do not have a full-power oven, cook lentils on top of the stove according to directions on bag. *SERVES 12*

Per 2-tablespoon serving: 43 calories; 0 milligrams cholesterol; 0 grams fat; 95 milligrams sodium; 3 grams protein (8% RDA); 7 grams carbohydrate

RDA: phosphorus 6%; iron 7%; thiamin 4%; niacin 2%

1 cup (240 ml) dried brown lentils
½ teaspoon turmeric
1 teaspoon cumin
3½ cups (825 ml) water

1 tablespoon grated fresh ginger
1 Pickled Jalapeño Pepper (page 473),
   or canned jalapeño pepper, chopped
1 teaspoon kosher salt

1. Place lentils, turmeric, cumin and 3 cups (705 ml) of the water in a 2½-quart (2.5-l) soufflé dish or casserole with tightly fitted lid. Cover tightly with microwave plastic wrap or lid. Cook at 100% for 20 minutes in a 650- to 700-watt oven. If using plastic, prick to release steam.

2. Remove from oven and uncover. Stir in remaining ingredients except ½ cup (120 ml) water. Re-cover and cook for 10 minutes, stirring once halfway through cooking. Prick plastic, if using.

3. Remove from oven and uncover. Scrape mixture into a food processor. Add remaining water and process until smooth. Add additional water, if necessary, to make a smooth, slightly liquid purée. This may be served immediately or reheated later. It will thicken upon standing and may need additional water stirred in before reheating.

HUMMUS

I tend to use this as a dip at cocktail parties with lots of raw crisp vegetables. It can be used the same way as a first course. As a cold side dish it is good with grilled and cold meats along with Summer Vegetable Jamboree (page 81).
SERVES 6 AS A DIP OR SIDE DISH

Per ¼-cup (60-ml) serving: 121 calories; 0 milligrams cholesterol; 6 grams fat; 126 milligrams sodium; 5 grams protein (11% RDA); 16 grams carbohydrate

RDA: calcium 4%; phosphorus 10%; iron 10%; thiamin 4%

2 cups (470 ml) presoaked, skinned
   and cooked chick-peas (page 202),
   or 1 19-ounce (535-g) can chick-
   peas, drained and rinsed
2 tablespoons fresh lemon juice
2 cloves garlic, smashed and peeled

½ teaspoon kosher salt
½ teaspoon Oriental sesame oil
1 tablespoon olive oil
2 teaspoons sesame seeds
1 tablespoon chopped fresh mint
¼ cup (60 ml) water

1. Place chick-peas, lemon juice, garlic, salt, sesame oil and olive oil in a food processor. Purée until smooth.

2. Remove from processor and stir in remaining ingredients. Serve at room temperature or warm. If serving warm, place in a 4-cup (1-l) glass measure. Cover tightly with microwave plastic wrap. Cook at 100% for 2 minutes in a 650- to 700-watt oven.

CORIANDER CHICK-PEA SALAD

*T*his is another quick recipe with somewhat high sodium due to using a canned ingredient. Chick-peas are one of the few things I regularly use canned; they are a bother to cook and skin. This is good at lunch with some nonfat cottage cheese, a green salad and a piece of fruit.   *SERVES 4*

Per ½-cup (120-ml) serving: 156 calories; 0 milligrams cholesterol; 4 grams fat; 329 milligrams sodium; 6 grams protein (12% RDA); 12 grams carbohydrate

RDA: phosphorus 10%; vitamin C 11%

3 cloves garlic, smashed and peeled
2 teaspoons Oriental sesame oil
½ teaspoon cumin
¼ teaspoon dried coriander
2 cups (470 ml) presoaked, skinned
   and cooked chick-peas (page 202),
    or 1 15½-ounce (439-g) can chick-
    peas, drained and rinsed

1 tablespoon fresh lemon juice
1 tablespoon chopped fresh coriander

1. Place garlic, oil, cumin and dried coriander in a 2½-quart (2.5-l) soufflé dish. Cook, uncovered, at 100% for 2 minutes in a 650- to 700-watt oven. Stir in chick-peas and cook, uncovered, for 1 minute more.

2. Remove from oven. Stir in remaining ingredients. Place in the refrigerator to chill. Serve cold or at room temperature.

FOR 400- TO 500-WATT OVENS

To serve 4. Cook garlic, oil, cumin and dried coriander as in Step 1 for 3 minutes. Add remaining ingredients and cook for 3 minutes more.

CORN

When the Spaniards and the Portuguese came to Central and South America, they found vines of beans growing up around corn stalks. It made the best use of the land; but it is also an ideal nutritional combination that is perpetuated to this day in dishes like corn tacos with beans. Corn is at its best freshly picked in summer. In winter, substitute vacuum-packed corn niblets.

As corn was a staple, many ways were devised to dry it for winter use. The two most common corn products today are meal and grits. Meal is simply the dried corn ground to make a flour. It may be white or yellow and varies in fineness. The Italians use a relatively coarse grind to make polenta. I find that polenta works equally well with the finer American grind. Americans used to call it corn-meal mush until we all got so sophisticated. I suppose mush doesn't sound as attractive as polenta. If you think of it as mush, maybe you will think of it as a hot cereal to serve with maple syrup, especially since it is so quickly made, without any lumps, in a microwave oven.

Grits are made from kernels of corn that have been treated so that they swell and break their skin, and then are dried and ground. The best are black-heart, or speckled-heart, grits that have the germ left in. Grits can be used at breakfast and as a side dish. In the South, grits takes the singular verb: Grits is good.

CORN NUTRITION

PER 1-EAR-OF-CORN SERVING: 123 calories; 0 milligrams cholesterol; 0 grams fat; 6 milligrams sodium; 4 grams protein (8% RDA); 29 grams carbohydrate

Cooking Times for Corn on the Cob

Arrange ears of corn, with silk and husks intact, in a single layer on a carrousel or platter. Cook, uncovered, for the time specified. There are 2–3 ears of corn per pound (450 g); 1 ear yields ½ cup (120 ml) kernels.

1 ear
650- to 700-watt oven: 2 min.
400- to 500-watt oven: 7 min.

2 ears
650- to 700-watt oven: 5 min.
400- to 500-watt oven: 12 min.

4 ears
650- to 700-watt oven: 9 min.
400- to 500-watt oven: 18 min.

6 ears
650- to 700-watt oven: 14 min.
400- to 500-watt oven: Not recommended

CORN AND BEANS

*H*ere is a modern, fresh version of that Guatemalan classic. The sharp color contrast of pink, yellow and green should brighten up any plate. If you don't have cooked pinto beans on hand, substitute any cooked beans you do have. If you like coriander, use it instead of the parsley. Those who like spicy food can shake on some hot red pepper sauce; but remember, those sauces are high in sodium.
SERVES 5

Per ½-cup (120-ml) serving: 92 calories; 0 milligrams cholesterol; 1 gram fat; 9 milligrams sodium; 4 grams protein (10% RDA); 19 grams carbohydrate

RDA: calcium 2%; phosphorus 10%; iron 9%; 337 milligrams potassium; vitamin A 17%; thiamin 10%; riboflavin 3%; niacin 5%; vitamin C 60%

1 cup (240 ml) presoaked and cooked pinto beans (page 202), or canned pinto beans, drained and rinsed
1½ cups (355 ml) corn kernels, from about 3 ears corn (page 213), or 1 15-ounce (425-g) can corn niblets, drained

¼ cup (60 ml) chopped fresh parsley

1. Place all ingredients in a 1½-quart (1.5-l) soufflé dish or casserole with a tightly fitted lid. Cover tightly with microwave plastic wrap or lid. Cook at 100% for 4 minutes in a 650- to 700-watt oven. If using plastic wrap, prick to release steam.

2. Remove from oven and uncover. Stir and serve.

FOR 400- TO 500-WATT OVENS

To serve 5. Cook for 7 minutes.

To remove corn niblets, or kernels, from a shucked ear, stand ear on end and slice down firmly with a knife.

BASIC SOFT POLENTA

Soft polenta is used as a cereal—cornmeal mush—or as a side dish. It can be mixed with butter, a soft cheese such as Monterey Jack, cream and jalapeños if you can afford the calories and cholesterol and like the heat. Otherwise, think of it as a variation on mashed potatoes and serve it with a stew or main courses with lots of sauce. For vegetarians, it goes well with spicy bean dishes.   *SERVES 8*

Per ½-cup (120-ml) serving: 47 calories; 0 milligrams cholesterol; 0 grams fat; 184 milligrams sodium; 1 gram protein (2% RDA); 10 grams carbohydrate

RDA: traces of many things, a substantial amount of none

4 cups (1 l) water
¾ cup (340 ml) yellow or white
   cornmeal

1 teaspoon kosher salt
⅛ teaspoon freshly ground black
   pepper

1. Combine water, cornmeal and salt in a 2½-quart (2.5-l) soufflé dish or casserole. Cook, uncovered, at 100% for 6 minutes in a 650- to 700-watt oven. Stir well, cover loosely with paper toweling and cook for 6 minutes more.

2. Remove from oven. Uncover and stir in pepper. Let stand for 3 minutes. Serve hot.

FOR 400- TO 500-WATT OVENS

To serve 8. Cook as in Step 1 for 9 minutes, cover loosely and cook for 9 minutes more. Finish as in Step 2.

BASIC FIRM POLENTA

When ground cornmeal is cooked and allowed to cool, it becomes firm and is cut in pieces for sautéing, grilling or, as in the Polenta Lasagne (below), made into more complicated dishes. This way of cooking polenta is perfect for those uses.
SERVES 8

Per serving: 79 calories; 0 milligrams cholesterol; 0 grams fat; 275 milligrams sodium; 2 grams protein (4% RDA); 17 grams carbohydrate

RDA: iron 3%; thiamin 6%; riboflavin 3%; niacin 4%

4 cups (1 l) water
1¼ cups (300 ml) yellow or white
   cornmeal

1 teaspoon kosher salt
⅛ teaspoon freshly ground black
   pepper

1. Combine water, cornmeal and salt in a ½-quart (2.5-l) soufflé dish or casserole. Cook, uncovered, at 100% for 12 minutes in a 650- to 700-watt oven, stirring once.
2. Remove from oven, add pepper and let stand for 3 minutes.
3. Lightly coat a 7×4×2-inch (18×10×5-cm) loaf pan with nonstick vegetable spray if not using treated pan (page 35). Pour polenta into pan. Let stand until cool.
4. Cover and refrigerate until chilled. To serve, slice the polenta about ½-inch (1-cm) thick and fry or grill.

FOR 400- TO 500-WATT OVENS
To serve 8. Reduce water to 3½ cups (825 ml). Cook as in Step 1 for 20 minutes.

POLENTA LASAGNE

This is a perfect lunch with a salad. It's a good vegetarian first course with a light main course, and an excellent main course—a double portion—if you are not on the lowest-calorie weight-loss diet. You won't miss the meat and the cholesterol.   SERVES 5

Per serving: 243 calories; 22 milligrams cholesterol; 8 grams fat; 942 milligrams sodium; 9 grams protein (21% RDA); 33 grams carbohydrate

RDA: calcium 17%; phosphorus 17%; iron 9%; 276 milligrams potassium; vitamin A 17%; thiamin 13%; riboflavin 10%; niacin 9%; vitamin C 21%

FOR THE FILLING

2 ounces (56 g) onion, cut into 1-inch (2.5-cm) pieces (about 1 cup; 240 ml)

1 clove garlic, smashed and peeled

2 teaspoons olive oil

2 ounces (56 g) eggplant, cut into 1-inch (2.5-cm) pieces (about ½ cup; 120 ml)

4 ounces (113.5 g) zucchini, cut into 1-inch (2.5-cm) pieces (about 1 cup; 240 ml)

½ cup (120 ml) Fresh Tomato Purée (page 468), or canned tomato purée

Pinch dried oregano

Pinch dried thyme

1 teaspoon kosher salt

Pinch freshly ground black pepper

1 tablespoon chopped fresh basil

FOR THE LASAGNE

1 recipe Basic Firm Polenta (page 216)

5 ounces (142 g) part-skim mozzarella, cut into 5 slices

1. Finely chop onion and garlic in a food processor. Scrape into a 10-inch (25.5-cm) quiche dish or pie plate and add oil. Stir to coat. Cook, uncovered, at 100% for 2 minutes in a 650- to 700-watt oven.

2. While onion and garlic are cooking, finely chop eggplant and zucchini in the food processor. Stir into onion mixture. Cook, uncovered, for 4 minutes.

3. Leaving dish in oven, add purée, oregano, thyme and salt. Cook, uncovered, for 3 minutes. Remove from oven. Stir in pepper and basil.

4. Place half the polenta slices spoke-fashion in a $14 \times 11 \times 2$-inch ($35.5 \times 28 \times 5$-cm) dish. Divide filling equally among the polenta slices. Top each with a piece of mozzarella and another slice of polenta. Cook, uncovered, for 5 minutes.

FOR 400- TO 500-WATT OVENS

To serve 5. Cook onion, garlic and oil as in Step 1 for 3 minutes. Follow Step 2 and cook for 6 minutes. Continue with Step 3 and cook for 6 minutes. Assemble lasagne as in Step 4. Place 3 of the prepared slices in a 10-inch (25.5-cm) quiche dish or pie plate. Cover with a sheet of microwavable paper toweling. Cook for 11–12 minutes or until hot and cheese is melted. Remove to a plate and cover with foil to keep warm. Place remaining slices in the dish and cook, uncovered, for 8 minutes.

GRITS

I'm the original mashed-potato freak; but grits will do me very well. If I've been bad, I omit the butter and salt and just top with stew or sauce—still good.
SERVES 8 AS A SIDE DISH OR FOR BREAKFAST

Per ½-cup (120-ml) serving: 85 calories; 4 milligrams cholesterol; 2 grams fat; 92 milligrams sodium; 2 grams protein (4% RDA); 15 grams carbohydrate

RDA: iron 4%; thiamin 8%; riboflavin 4%; niacin 5%

1 cup (240 ml) grits (not quick-
   cooking)
5 cups (1,220 ml) water

½ teaspoon kosher salt
Freshly ground black pepper, to taste
1 tablespoon unsalted butter, optional

1. Combine grits and water in an 8-cup (2-l) glass measure. Cook, uncovered, at 100% for 15 minutes in a 650- to 700-watt oven.

2. Remove from oven and stir until smooth. Stir in salt, pepper and butter, if desired, and serve.

To serve 1. Use 3 tablespoons grits, 1 cup (240 ml) water, a pinch salt and pepper and ½ teaspoon butter, if desired. Cook as in Step 1 for 4 minutes. Finish as in Step 2.

FOR 400- TO 500-WATT OVENS

To serve 4. Cook for 25 minutes.

To serve 1. Cook for 7 minutes.

POTATOES

There used to be fifty varieties of potatoes on the American market at any one time. In recent years, there have been very few. I see a few hopeful signs that some of the old and a few new varieties are finding their way back. Potatoes divide into two groups for cooking purposes: mealy and firm. A typical mealy potato is an Idaho baking potato. A typical firm potato is a red new potato. Mealy potatoes are best for baking and mashing; firm potatoes are best for boiling, sautéing and salads. Potatoes with their skins on are more nutritious than those without.

POTATO NUTRITION

These figures are for boiled potatoes. A baking potato weighs about 8 ounces (227 g), which is about 1½ cups (360 ml) of nonmashed or puréed potato.

PER ½ CUP (120 ML) COOKED FLESH (WITHOUT SKIN): 67 calories; 0 milligrams cholesterol; <1 gram fat; 3 milligrams sodium; 1 gram protein (2% RDA); 16 grams carbohydrate; 256 milligrams potassium

PER ½ CUP (120 ML) COOKED FLESH AND SKIN (THIS IS A COMPOSITE FIGURE; DIFFERENT KINDS OF POTATOES HAVE MORE OR LESS SKIN): 66 calories; 0 milligrams cholesterol; 0 grams fat; 5 milligrams sodium; 1 gram protein (3% RDA); 15 grams carbohydrate; 232 milligrams potassium

Baking Potatoes

When I want an old-fashioned baked potato with a really crisp skin and fluffy insides, I still bake it in a 450°F–500°F (232°C–260°C) oven for 45 minutes to an hour. Sometimes I want a cooked baking potato and don't have the time to bake it in the oven. That's when I use the microwave oven. Baking potatoes cooked in the microwave oven are also ideal for mashing. Prick each potato (8 ounces; 227 g) several times with a fork. Place directly on the bottom of the oven or on a double thickness of paper toweling.

1 potato
650- to 700-watt oven: 7 min.
400- to 500-watt oven: 10 min.

2 potatoes
650- to 700-watt oven: 11 min.
400- to 500-watt oven: 18 min.

3 potatoes
650- to 700-watt oven: 16 min.
400- to 500-watt oven: 25 min.

4 potatoes
650- to 700-watt oven: 20 min.
400- to 500-watt oven: Not recommended

Sweet Potatoes

Per ½ cup (120 ml) cooked flesh (without skin): 103 calories; 0 milligrams cholesterol; 1 gram fat; 10 milligrams sodium; 2 grams protein (6% RDA); 24 grams carbohydrate

Prick each potato (8 ounces; 227 g) several times with a fork. Place directly on the bottom of the oven or on a double thickness of paper toweling.

1 potato
650- to 700-watt oven: 7 min.
400- to 500-watt oven: 10 min.

2 potatoes
650- to 700-watt oven: 11 min.
400- to 500-watt oven: 18 min.

3 potatoes
650- to 700-watt oven: 16 min.
400- to 500-watt oven: 25 min.

4 potatoes
650- to 700-watt oven: 20 min.
400- to 500-watt oven: Not recommended

New Potatoes

New potatoes can be steamed in the microwave oven with minimal liquid. Without liquid, they tend to wrinkle and look unattractive. Try to buy potatoes that are all close to the same size. Place in the dish indicated below and cover tightly with microwave plastic wrap.

¼ pound (113.5 g) new potatoes with 1 tablespoon water in a 9-inch (23-cm) pie plate
650- to 700-watt oven: 3 min.
400- to 500-watt oven: 4 min.

½ pound (227 g) new potatoes with 2 tablespoons water in a 1½-quart (1.5-l) soufflé dish
650- to 700-watt oven: 4 min.
400- to 500-watt oven: 7 min.

1 pound (450 g) new potatoes with ¼ cup (60 ml) water in a 1½-quart (1.5-l) soufflé dish
650- to 700-watt oven: 7 min.
400- to 500-watt oven: 14 min.

2 pounds (900 g) new potatoes with ½ cup (120 ml) water in a 1½-quart (1.5-l) soufflé dish
650- to 700-watt oven: 14 min.
400- to 500-watt oven: 20 min.

OLIVE OIL MASHED POTATOES

This is absolute heaven. Nothing is better with meat loaf and its juices. If I'm not on a weight-loss diet, I can eat the whole thing myself. To multiply quantities, see basic baking potato timings above.   *SERVES 4*

Per ⅓-cup (80-ml) serving: 127 calories; 0 milligrams cholesterol; 7 grams fat; 5 milligrams sodium; 2 grams protein (4% RDA); 15 grams carbohydrate

RDA: iron 4%; 462 milligrams potassium; thiamin 5%; niacin 6%; vitamin C 28%

2 baking potatoes (each about 8
   ounces; 227 g)
2 tablespoons olive oil

Kosher salt, to taste
Freshly ground black pepper, to taste

  1. Prick potatoes several times with a fork. Place on a piece of paper toweling and cook at 100% for 11 minutes, or until tender, in a 650- to 700-watt oven.
  2. Remove potatoes from oven. When cool enough to handle, halve each potato and scoop out flesh with a spoon. Pass through a ricer or place in a bowl and mash with a potato masher. Stir in oil and salt and pepper to taste. Serve hot.

FOR 400- TO 500-WATT OVENS

To serve 4. Cook potatoes as in Step 1 for 18 minutes. Finish as in Step 2.

Ricer for mashed potatoes

FENNEL AND POTATO PURÉE

*T*his pale-green purée goes well with fish and chicken dishes. It's moist enough so that it doesn't need a sauce or gravy as a topping.   *SERVES 6*

Per scant ½-cup (120-ml) serving: 55 calories; 3 milligrams cholesterol; 1 gram fat; 240 milligrams sodium; 3 grams protein (7% RDA); 8 grams carbohydrate

RDA: calcium 6%; phosphorus 6%; iron 4%; 322 milligrams potassium; vitamin C 16%

8 ounces (227 g) fennel, tops trimmed, cored and cut into large dice (about 2 cups; 470 ml)

1 baking potato (10 ounces; 284 g), peeled, diced and covered with ice water to prevent discoloring (about 1¼ cups; 300 ml)

1 cup (240 ml) Basic Chicken Broth (page 460), or unsalted or regular canned chicken broth

¼ cup (60 ml) part-skim ricotta cheese

¼ cup (60 ml) skim milk

¾ teaspoon kosher salt

Freshly ground black pepper, to taste

1. Combine fennel, potato and broth in a 2½-quart (2.5-l) soufflé dish or casserole with a tightly fitted lid. Cover tightly with microwave plastic wrap or lid. Cook at 100% for 13 minutes in a 650- to 700-watt oven.

2. Remove from oven. Prick plastic to release steam and uncover. Pour fennel, potato and broth into a food processor. Add remaining ingredients and process until smooth. Serve hot.

FOR 400- TO 500-WATT OVENS

To serve 6. Cook for 20 minutes.

GARLIC POTATOES

My once and future favorites, newly slimmed for a new world. Serve these with roasted or grilled meats. If no one is losing weight, I double the portions. See new-potato cooking times (page 220) to increase the quantity. Cold leftovers have a way of disappearing.   *SERVES 4*

Per 4-ounce (113.5-g) serving: 130 calories; 0 milligrams cholesterol; 4 grams fat; 193 milligrams sodium; 3 grams protein (6% RDA); 22 grams carbohydrate

RDA: phosphorus 7%; iron 5%; 424 milligrams potassium; thiamin 7%; niacin 11%; vitamin C 32%

1 pound (450 g) small new potatoes
  (each about 2 ounces; 56 g)
6 large cloves garlic, smashed and
  peeled

1 tablespoon olive oil
½ teaspoon kosher salt
Freshly ground black pepper, to taste

   1. Place potatoes in a 1½-quart (1.5-l) soufflé dish or casserole with a tightly fitted lid. Add remaining ingredients and stir to coat. Cover tightly with microwave plastic wrap or casserole lid. Cook at 100% for 9 minutes, or until potatoes are tender, in a 650- to 700-watt oven. If using plastic, prick to release steam.
   2. Remove from oven and uncover. Serve hot.

FOR 400- TO 500-WATT OVENS

To serve 4. Cook for 15 minutes, or until potatoes are tender.

NEW POTATO SALAD

This is a European-style potato salad that is good with our Skinny Burger (page 302) or with cold food. *SERVES 4*

Per ½-cup (120-ml) serving: 61 calories; 0 milligrams cholesterol; 1 gram fat; 178 milligrams sodium; 1 gram protein (3% RDA); 11 grams carbohydrate

RDA: calcium 1%; phosphorus 3%; iron 3%; vitamin A 8%; thiamin 3%; riboflavin 2%; niacin 6%; vitamin C 21%

8 ounces (227 g) new potatoes, thinly sliced
⅓ cup (80 ml) thinly sliced scallions, white and green parts (about 2 scallions)
5 tablespoons white wine

2 tablespoons white wine vinegar
1 teaspoon olive oil
¼ teaspoon kosher salt
Freshly ground black pepper, to taste
1 teaspoon Dijon mustard

1. Combine potatoes, wine and vinegar in a 10-inch (25.5-cm) quiche dish. Cover tightly with microwave plastic wrap. Cook at 100% for 8 minutes, or until tender, in a 650- to 700-watt oven. Prick plastic to release steam.
2. Remove from oven and uncover. Stir in remaining ingredients and let stand until cool. Serve at room temperature.

FOR 400- TO 500-WATT OVENS
To serve 4. Cook for 14 minutes, or until tender.

ALL-AMERICAN POTATO SALAD

*T*his is the picnic-, barbecue-, Grandma-style potato salad. The jazzing-up is done to bring the calories and the cholesterol down. The flavor stays high.
SERVES 4

Per ½-cup (120-ml) serving: 113 calories; 0 milligrams cholesterol; 7 grams fat; 37 milligrams sodium; 2 grams protein (4% RDA); 12 grams carbohydrate

RDA: iron 5%; vitamin A 33%; thiamin 5%; niacin 5%; vitamin C 113%

1 large potato (8–10 ounces; 227–284 g), peeled and cut into 1-inch (2.5-cm) cubes (about 1¼ cups, 300 ml)

1 cucumber (6 ounces; 170 g), peeled, quartered, seeded and cut into 1-inch (2.5-cm) chunks (about 1 cup; 120 ml)

1 rib celery, peeled, halved lengthwise and cut into ½-inch (1-cm) pieces

4 ounces (113.5 g) Silky Pepper Strips (page 472), cut into 1-inch (2.5-cm) squares, or 2 teaspoons white vinegar

3 tablespoons Egg White Mayonnaise (page 482), or bottled diet mayonnaise

1. Place potato and enough water to cover, about 1 cup (240 ml), in a 2½-quart (2.5-l) soufflé dish or casserole with a tightly fitted lid. Cover tightly with microwave plastic wrap or casserole lid. Cook at 100% for 10 minutes, or until tender, in a 650- to 700-watt oven. If using plastic, prick to release steam.

2. Remove from oven and uncover. Drain potatoes and let cool. Combine potatoes with remaining ingredients and let stand 30 minutes to allow flavors to combine.

FOR 400- TO 500-WATT OVENS

To serve 4. Cook as in Step 1 for 13 minutes. Finish as in Step 2.

THE FISH AND
SHELLFISH ADVANTAGE

*T*he only way I know that anybody could have predicted when I was growing up that I was going to be a food writer was that I liked fish and mussels when red meat was the American norm; but I was a little odd.

By now, all adults in America must be convinced that they would live forever if they could only get themselves to live on fish. While only the most polar of Eskimos seem to be really trying, fish consumption has gone up enormously. There are real advantages to eating many kinds of fish; but much depends on preparation as well as that boring oldy, menu balance. Before we fall into the pit of thinking that if we eat fish we are eating healthy, we must beware the enormous salad trap.

The salad trap often catches those of us who lunch. Confronted by the temptations of the menu, we say: "I'll just have a salad." We eat it with a radiant sense of virtue that is unimpeded by the amount of rich dressing, salt and indeed cholesterol in the form of the eggs and meat it may include. Then, we feel entitled to the reward of dessert.

The fish-equivalent is to eat enormous portions happily—after all, it's fish— and not to worry that it was cooked with fats and sauces. At dinner, we may combine a large salad and fish with the perfect serenity of a deed well done. Cook that fish in butter, dip pieces of a two-pound lobster—high in cholesterol—in melted butter or indulge in rich sauces and you have taken away much of the cause for triumph.

Fish and shellfish are good if you are reasonable. As well as the pleasures of a varied diet and fabulous flavors, there are nutritional benefits from increasing the amount of seafood that we eat. While all protein contains the same amount of calories by weight, which is hard to judge since the foods we eat also contain water and fat, fish is usually less fatty than meat and cheese and therefore less caloric. Additionally, the fat in fish, especially that from cold-water fish, tends to be high in the Omega-3 fatty acid group—you've heard of fish oils—which is good for us (see page 15). Incidentally, studies have shown that fish farmed inland, such as trout, are even higher in Omega-3 than those in the wild. Maybe, as with people, it's a question of less exercise. What is known is that fish that live in icy water need these fats that stay liquid at extremely cold temperatures to protect their bodies. Then they protect ours.

The recommendation to help keep our arteries clean is to eat such fish three times a week—so we need lots of good recipes if we are not to get bored.

Different fish that we call by the same name will vary in the amount of fat and hence calories they provide. Coho salmon is quite a bit less fatty and therefore less caloric than Atlantic salmon. Don't worry about it. We have chosen an average value for salmon and, unless you eat it daily, the caloric difference won't really trouble you.

All the sea-dwellers tend to be rich in minerals and provide the iodine that we don't get if we use—as I do—kosher salt. By combining fish and shellfish with vegetables, these recipes increase the nutritional benefits of dinner. Almost all the dishes are low in sodium and fat. Those who have no trouble with sodium may want to use more salt. Those who do not need to shed pounds may want to add some olive oil to a few of these dishes for flavor. See page 34 to see how fish compares to other meats in iron, zinc, cholesterol, fat and calories.

Choosing Your Denizen of the Deep

There are negative as well as positive health considerations when deciding to eat fish and seafoods, since parasites, bacteria and residues of man's waste-disposal habits turn up in their flesh. We have all been alarmed by dire warnings of red tides, mercury and hepatitis epidemics. The Dutch no longer permit their traditional green herrings to be sold for raw eating unless they have been commercially frozen. Many of my friends, doctors among them, will no longer eat raw seafood. The fact remains that proper cooking will kill only the nasty parasites, and then only if the internal temperature of the fish is sufficiently elevated (see page 230 for proper temperatures and precautions). Commercial freezing produces the same results. If you cook seafood long enough to kill anything else unpleasant, you will have clams that bounce, oysters to use as rubber bands and sawdust fish.

The real protection is to buy only the best seafood from legal waters. The federal and local governments do a good job of testing the waters around us. They also check our lakes. The famous Lake Superior whitefish is, for the time being, a thing of the past; but we can eat whitefish from other lakes.

Search out stores that specialize in fish. They may be supermarkets. Since they sell more of it, they buy better fish, and it is usually fresher. There is also a greater variety from which to choose. A fishman should be as good as a butcher in providing you with special services: properly filleted and cut fish, portion sizes you want, and, because he butchers whole fish, heads and bones for broths.

When at all possible, ask for the heads and bones of the fish you are buying. You are paying for their weight when you buy steaks (thick slices across the fish with or without the bones, depending on the size of the fish—salmon steaks usually have bones, swordfish do not) and fillets (boneless, lengthwise sides of fish with or without skin). These heads and bones may be used to make Basic

Fish Broth (page 461), and as a dividend for soups and stews, if you have enough bones. To amass enough, keep a bag in the freezer, add cleaned heads and bones to it as you get them and make broth when you have enough. Don't bother with the heads and bones from flat fish such as sole and flounder, since they make a bitter broth and your fishman probably gets these fish already filleted. Keep the bones from dark and oily fish such as salmon, sturgeon and mackerel separately, since these will make dominating, colored broths useful in preparing the same fish varieties. All the heads and bones from white-fleshed fish other than the flat fish can be used together.

The rules for selecting good fish remain the same. A first and foremost criterion is the lack of any fishy smell. Buying fish that is shrink-wrapped may make it difficult to smell the fish. If you're sensitized to off smells, you can probably pick up strong smells through the packaging. Otherwise, insist on unwrapped fish. When buying whole fish, check that the eyes are not sunken, that the gills are red, not brown, and that when you poke the skin of the fish the indentation doesn't remain. The same poking test is valid for pieces of fish; they should not be mushy. If you can see the flesh of the fish, look to see that there are no minuscule white dots—opaque rather than translucent; they indicate parasites.

When buying frozen fish—a good safety measure and, in the case of fish caught far out at sea during a prolonged voyage, a flavor measure as well— look for individually wrapped and frozen fillets or whole fish. Fish frozen this way will not be embedded in blocks of water. Portions can be separated and defrosted in the amounts needed. See opposite page for defrosting information.

Unless you frequent a truly special fish market or live in an area where shrimp are caught, don't believe that the shrimp you see reposing on the ice are really fresh. They have been defrosted. It is cheaper to buy block-frozen shrimp. Pick up the unwrapped block of shrimp in towels or potholders and smack it sharply on the edge of your counter. A piece will break off. With a little practice you will be able to estimate just where you want to whack the block to get the amount of shrimp you want. Wrap and freeze the portion you do not need. Defrost by placing shrimp in a sieve under warm running water. Do not defrost the whole block in the microwave oven, or the outside pieces will cook before the inside of the block is defrosted.

Portion Size

Most of the recipes in this chapter are based on a four-ounce (113.5-g) serving of fish or shellfish in order to give us all a good chance of eating a reasonable proportion of animal protein with its cholesterol each day (see page 16 for the whys). If you eat little animal protein during the day or one of the eaters is a large, active person, look for recipes that give larger portions, or increase the serving size to six ounces (170 g) or more. Look at the cooking charts on pages 232–234 to upscale the recipes, or simply serve more.

Until you are thoroughly familiar with what a four-ounce (113.5-g) portion of fish looks and feels like, you may do better cooking previously portioned fish or fillets of the right size. There are many such recipes.

Microwave Cooking of Fish

Fish and other seafood cook better in a microwave oven than any other place. The only time I would cook them another way is when cooking out-of-doors, either on a grill or in an iron skillet next to a stream. The joy of cooking fish in the microwave oven is that it cooks evenly—no more powdery outside and raw fish in the center. Moreover, those sensitive to the smell of cooking fish will find it sharply diminished when the fish is tightly covered in the enclosed environment of the oven. If your oven develops an odor, see page 601 for the solution.

Some people are still not comfortable cooking fish. The microwave oven will help. The recipes are as close to foolproof as you can get, if you follow them exactly.

Cooking seafood in the microwave oven eliminates the need for adding fat, which is valuable on a weight-loss diet and for general nutrition as well. Fat, when added, is primarily for flavor. Often, I will select olive oil, Oriental sesame oil (dark brown due to toasted nuts) or nut oils, all of which are unsaturated or monounsaturated. Since these oils will be used in small quantities for flavor, choose the best available.

Since fish and shellfish cook so rapidly in the microwave oven, it is generally not reasonable to cook them ahead. The exceptions are the big dishes like Green Shrimp Curry and Fish Couscous. When planning to cook and reheat, do not add fresh herbs and acid such as lemon juice until the final reheating for maximum freshness of taste.

Fish and seafood are generally low in calories. Many of these dishes permit you to have multiple courses for dinner, or, if you are not having much animal protein during the day, to increase your portion. Look at the Basic Cooking Times for Fish (pages 231–234) for how long to cook different numbers and sizes of portions.

To further vary the flavor of your seafood dishes, particularly when using bland fish, flavorings can be kept on hand. Herbs, spices—not salt—and lemon juice can be added virtually ad lib. Then you can add a sauce or dressing from Basics, Sauces and Snacks (pages 458–529) and a side dish from Good Grains and Other Starches (pages 148–225) or Salads and Vegetables (pages 388–457). These charts will also permit you to vary the amount you cook for a given recipe. Increase or decrease the other ingredients accordingly.

Since fish can easily be bought in individual portions, you will find many recipes in this chapter that can be prepared for varying numbers of eaters, from one up.

It seems better to defrost the individually frozen fillets in the refrigerator—putting them there in the morning if you want them for dinner—than to add the defrosting time to the cooking time. If defrosting time is added to the cooking time, the finished dish will tend to be too watery and the fish texture may be compromised. Frozen fish normally comes in such small pieces that it is virtually impossible to defrost them without cooking them. If caught short, add about two and a half minutes at 50 percent power to the cooking time of each fillet if cooking from frozen; continue to cook at 100 percent power for the normal recipe timing. Check to make sure that the fish is thoroughly cooked. If not, add more time in thirty-second spurts.

Individually frozen fillets will never be as good as the best fresh fish you can buy, so use them in preparations with sauces or spices that will mask imperfections. However, those using commercially frozen fish do not have to worry about parasites. Those who home-freeze fish do not have the same reassurance, as a home freezer does not get cold enough to kill the monsters reliably.

Because fish cooks extremely quickly, it is more important than with most foods to arrange it properly in the cooking dish. When possible, arrange single pieces of fish so that they are in an even layer in the dish. When arranging multiple fillets, follow the illustrations on page 232.

Ordinarily, we consider that fish and other seafoods are fully cooked when they are totally opaque rather than translucent. If you want to make sure that your fish and seafood are cooked to the point at which any parasites are killed, you can insert an instant-read thermometer into various places in the food, either directly through the plastic or with the food uncovered. The thermometer should read at least 140°F (60°C). If the seafood needs to continue cooking, re-cover or patch the holes in the plastic with little pieces of plastic wrap and cook in thirty-second increments until you get a proper reading. A single thin fillet may require about one minute more cooking time to get to the recommended temperature.

Since seafood cooks so quickly, it is often convenient to cook one or two portions on the dishes from which they will be eaten. If you are using a microwave plastic wrap that should not touch the hot food (see information on the box), or for general safety, use dinner plates with deep wells or sharply angled rims. If you don't have such plates, substitute a quiche dish or pie plate. You will have to transfer the food to a plate with a large offset spatula, the kind that often comes with barbecue sets.

By and large, I have used widely available varieties of fish and other seafood; but you can substitute regionally available delicacies as long as you keep to the timings. Shellfish recipes are found toward the end of the chapter. The recipes

Poke an instant-read thermometer into cooked meat in several places—do not touch bone or dish—to determine the internal temperature so as to assure safety and desired degree of doneness.

start with simple everyday dishes and move on to those special enough for larger groups and entertaining. These days, you may find that your guests are as eager to eat healthy food as you are. Many of them may be avoiding red meat. It is nice to have a repertoire of festive meals for these situations. Most portions are based on four ounces (113.5 g) of protein. For parties, you may want to prepare a few more portions than the number of guests so that you can offer seconds.

Many of these dishes include enough vegetables to make dinner, though they may be lacking a starch. Having the vegetable in the dish makes life easier. If you want a starch other than bread, look on pages 162–198 and 219–225, or be sure to bring water to the boil on top of the stove for rice, noodles or potatoes so that they can cook while you are making the main course. Otherwise, make the starch dish first in the microwave oven. Fish cooks so quickly that the starch should be hot enough if kept covered to be at a good eating temperature when the fish dish is ready. Don't make the fish dish wait: Fish will continue to cook until it gets cold after cooking, and that's unpleasant.

If there is to be a first course, I often get the seafood dish ready for its final or only cooking in a dish in the oven with the time set so that I can punch "start" just as I serve the first course.

I hope that in this chapter you will find dishes so irresistible that the recommended three servings per week will be a delight and not a punishment.

Basic Cooking Times for Fish

Many times you will want to cook a piece of fish simply, just seasoning it. Lemon juice, vinegar, olive oil, fresh herbs, spices, salt and pepper are the easiest seasonings for quick additions. For many people, fish is most readily available in fillets. When using the timing chart for fillets that follow, remember that you need to pay attention to both the weight and thickness of the piece or pieces of fish. Also, look at page 232 for the arrangement in the cooking dish. If you want to cook fish steaks—with or without the bone—see page 233.

Arrange fish fillets for even cooking and for maximum spatial efficiency. It requires looking at your piece or pieces of fish to determine whether there is one end that is much smaller than the other. Then look at the accompanying drawings to see how you should arrange it or them.

PER 4-OUNCE (113.5 G) FILLET (UNCOOKED WEIGHT), SUCH AS FLOUNDER OR SOLE: 90 calories; 57 milligrams cholesterol; less than 1 gram fat; 90 milligrams sodium; 19 grams protein (40% RDA)

Fish such as salmon, tuna, swordfish and halibut are higher in calories, varying from Atlantic salmon at 248 calories for a 4-ounce (113.5 g) boneless portion to 119 calories for the same portion of halibut.

½-INCH (1-CM) THICK FILLETS, 4 OUNCES (113.5 G) EACH: Place fish fillets in the dish specified and cover tightly with microwave plastic wrap. For four to six fillets, arrange spoke-fashion with thin ends toward center and thick ends turned under.

1 fillet in a 10-inch (25.5-cm) quiche dish or pie plate
650- to 700-watt oven: 1 min.
400- to 500-watt oven: 1 min. 30 sec.

2 fillets in a 10-inch (25.5-cm) quiche dish or pie plate
650- to 700-watt oven: 2 min. 15 sec.
400- to 500-watt oven: 3 min. 30 sec.

4 fillets in a 10-inch (25.5-cm) quiche dish or pie plate
650- to 700-watt oven: 4 min.
400- to 500-watt oven: 6 min.

6 fillets in a 9 × 13 × 2-inch (23 × 33 × 5-cm) oval dish
650- to 700-watt oven: 6 min.
400- to 500-watt oven: 7 min. 30 sec.

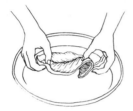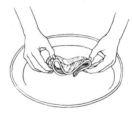
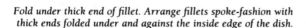

Fold under thick end of fillet. Arrange fillets spoke-fashion with thick ends folded under and against the inside edge of the dish.

Fold under both ends of fillet to create an even thickness.

½-INCH (1-CM) THICK FILLETS, 6–8 OUNCES (170–227 G) EACH

1 fillet in a 10-inch (25.5-cm) quiche dish or pie plate
650- to 700-watt oven: 2 min.
400- to 500-watt oven: 3 min. 30 sec.

2 fillets in a 10-inch (25.5-cm) quiche dish or pie plate
650- to 700-watt oven: 2 min. 30 sec.
400- to 500-watt oven: 4 min.

4 fillets in a 13 × 9 × 2-inch (33 × 23 × 5-cm) oval dish
650- to 700-watt oven: 5 min.
400- to 500-watt oven: 7 min.

6 fillets in a 13 × 9 × 2-inch (33 × 23 × 5-cm) oval dish
650- to 700-watt oven: 7 min.
400- to 500-watt oven: 8 min. 30 sec.

1-INCH (2.5-CM) THICK FILLETS, 6–8 OUNCES (170–227 G) EACH

1 fillet in a 10-inch (25.5-cm) quiche dish or pie plate
650- to 700-watt oven: 3 min.
400- to 500-watt oven: 4 min. 30 sec.

2 fillets in a 10-inch (25.5-cm) quiche dish or pie plate
650- to 700-watt oven: 4 min. 30 sec.
400- to 500-watt oven: 6 min.

4 fillets in a 13 × 9 × 2-inch (33 × 23 × 5-cm) oval dish
650- to 700-watt oven: 6 min.
400- to 500-watt oven: 8 min.

6 fillets in a 13 × 9 × 2-inch (33 × 23 × 5-cm) oval dish
650- to 700-watt oven: 8 min. 30 sec.
400- to 500-watt oven: 11 min.

Steaks

½-INCH (1-CM) THICK STEAKS, 4 OUNCES (113.5 G) EACH Place steaks in the dish specified and cover tightly with microwave plastic wrap. For 4 to 6 steaks, arrange spoke-fashion with pointed ends toward center of dish.

1 steak in a 10-inch (25.5-cm) quiche dish or pie plate
650- to 700-watt oven: 1 min. 30 sec.
400- to 500-watt oven: 2 min. 30 sec.

2 steaks in a 10-inch (25.5-cm) quiche dish or pie plate
650- to 700-watt oven: 2 min.
400- to 500-watt oven: 3 min. 30 sec.

4 steaks in a 13 × 9 × 2-inch (33 × 23 × 5-cm) oval dish
650- to 700-watt oven: 3 min.
400- to 500-watt oven: 7 min.

6 steaks in a 13 × 9 × 2-inch (33 × 23 × 5-cm) oval dish
650- to 700-watt oven: 5 min.
400- to 500-watt oven: 9 min.

1-INCH (2.5-CM) THICK STEAKS, 4 OUNCES (113.5 G) EACH

1 steak in a 10-inch (25.5-cm) quiche dish or pie plate
650- to 700-watt oven: 2 min.
400- to 500-watt oven: 3 min.

2 steaks in a 10-inch (25.5-cm) quiche dish or pie plate
650- to 700-watt oven: 3 min.
400- to 500-watt oven: 4 min. 30 sec.

4 steaks in a 13 × 9 × 2-inch (33 × 23 × 5-cm) oval dish
650- to 700-watt oven: 4 min.
400- to 500-watt oven: 6 min.

6 steaks in a 13 × 9 × 2-inch (33 × 23 × 5-cm) oval dish
650- to 700-watt oven: 6 min.
400- to 500-watt oven: 9 min.

Arrange two steaks thin end to thick end.

Arrange four steaks spoke-fashion with wide ends against the inside edge of the dish.

Whole Fish

Cook whole fish with or without head and tail as indicated below. Sprinkle herbs and chopped vegetables inside cavity, if desired. Place on dish indicated and cover tightly with microwave plastic wrap.

1½ pounds (680 g) fish, head and tail on, in a 13 × 10 × 2-inch (33 × 25.5 × 5-cm) dish
650- to 700-watt oven: 8–10 min.
400- to 500-watt oven: 12 min.

2 pounds (900 g) fish, head and tail on, in a 13 × 10 × 2-inch (33 × 25.5 × 5-cm) dish
650- to 700-watt oven: 11 min.
400- to 500-watt oven: 14 min.

2½ pounds (1.14 kg) fish, head and tail on, in a 14 × 11 × 2-inch (35.5 × 8 × 5-cm) dish
650- to 700-watt oven: 14 min.
400- to 500-watt oven: Not recommended

3 pounds (1.4 kg) fish, head and tail on, in a 14 × 11 × 2-inch (35.5 × 28 × 5-cm) dish
650- to 700-watt oven: 16 min.
400- to 500-watt oven: Not recommended

6 pounds (2.72 kg) fish, head removed, cooking weight 4½ pounds (2 kg), in a 14 × 11 × 2-inch (35.5 × 28 × 5-cm) dish
650- to 700-watt oven: 18 min.
400- to 500-watt oven: Not recommended

8 pounds (3.6 kg) fish, head and tail removed, cooking weight 6 pounds (2.8 kg), on a 17-inch (43-cm) platter
650- to 700-watt oven without a
   carrousel: 22 min.
400- to 500-watt oven: Not recommended

SAUCY FISH WITH ASPARAGUS

Coming home tired and wanting a quick complete dinner that doesn't speak of diets and self-deprivation, you will find this a perfect solution, with an intimation of cream that is soothing. Make the sauce after you come in the door and arrange everything on your plate. Now, get into something comfortable; turn on some music; open a chilled bottle of white wine that you thoughtfully put in the refrigerator in the morning and pour out a glass to sip as you wash some salad greens, cut up a tomato and take your pre-prepared diet salad dressing (pages 483–499) out of the refrigerator. Cut yourself two slices of Majic Whole Grain Bread (page 152) or French or Italian bread. Now, press the start button on your microwave oven; toss the salad; take the fish from the oven and relax.

This pleasing but very dietetic meal—just consider that its main course has only 162 calories for all the nutrition in the RDA listing—can even be yours after lunching at a restaurant or on a Beef Sandwich (page 71) or Tuna Salad sandwich (page 70). *SERVES 1*

Per plated serving of fish fillet with 8 stalks asparagus and ¼ cup (60 ml) sauce: 162 calories; 56 milligrams cholesterol; 2 grams fat; 217 milligrams sodium; 27 grams protein (60% RDA); 10 grams carbohydrate

RDA: calcium 12%; phosphorus 33%; 888 milligrams potassium; vitamin A 38%; thiamin 16%; riboflavin 19%; niacin 24%; vitamin C 70%

4 ounces (113.5 g) sole fillet or other
   firm white fish fillet, about ½-inch
   (1-cm) thick
8 stalks asparagus, trimmed and peeled
   (about 4 ounces; 113.5 g)

¼ cup (60 ml) Paprika-Lemon
   Béchamel (page 511)
Freshly ground black pepper, to taste

1. Place fillet in the center of a dinner plate or 10-inch (25.5-cm) quiche dish, folding an end under if necessary to create an even thickness. Place 4 stalks asparagus on either side of the fish. Pour the sauce over the fillet. Cover tightly with microwave plastic wrap. Cook at 100% for 3 minutes in a 650- to 700-watt oven. Prick plastic to release steam.
2. Remove from oven and uncover. Sprinkle on pepper and serve.

FOR 400- TO 500-WATT OVENS

To serve 1. Cook for 5 minutes.

FISH WITH SPINACH AND TOMATO SAUCE

*I*f you have tomato sauce on hand—substituting bottled sauce will add sodium and calories, but can be done—the only real work here is stemming and washing the spinach, and that's not much. Then you will have a delicious dinner full of health—169 percent RDA of vitamin A, 64 percent of vitamin C, 23 percent of niacin and 21 percent of iron—that tastes good and is vivid with color and flavor. Have linguine with Mushroom Sauce (page 169) to begin and Creamy Custard (page 570) or a diet sorbet for dessert. You still have calories left for a little bread and a glass of wine, even on a weight-loss diet. Others can double the serving of pasta and add a salad.   *SERVES 1*

Per plated serving of fish fillet with ⅓ cup (80 ml) cooked spinach and 3 tablespoons sauce: 145 calories; 54 milligrams cholesterol; 2 grams fat; 312 milligrams sodium; 25 grams protein (56% RDA); 6.5 grams carbohydrate

RDA: calcium 15%; phosphorus 30%; iron 21%; 1,159 milligrams potassium; vitamin A 169%; thiamin 13%; riboflavin 19%; niacin 23%; vitamin C 64%

⅓ pound (150 g) spinach leaves, washed, stemmed and thoroughly dried (loosely packed, about 2 cups; 470 ml)

4 ounces (113.5 g) flounder fillet or other firm white fish fillet

Freshly ground black pepper, to taste

3 tablespoons Tomato Sauce Casalinga (page 167), or bottled tomato sauce

1. Mound spinach leaves in the center of a dinner plate or 10-inch (25.5-cm) quiche dish. Cook, uncovered, at 100% for 1 minute in a 650- to 700-watt oven.

2. Remove from oven. Push spinach to the edges of the plate to form a ring. Place fillet in the center. Sprinkle lightly with pepper. Pour tomato sauce over fillet. Cover tightly with microwave plastic wrap. Cook for 2 minutes 30 seconds. Prick plastic to release steam.

3. Remove from oven and uncover. Serve hot.

FOR 400- TO 500-WATT OVENS

To serve 1. Cook spinach as in Step 1 for 2 minutes. Cook as in Step 2 for 3 minutes 30 seconds, or until fish is cooked through.

FISH FILLETS WITH TONNATO SAUCE

I first tasted a more fattening version of this delicious dish at San Domenico, an elegant new-Italian-cooking restaurant in New York. It is an imaginative variation on the classic *vitello tonnato,* although warm rather than cold and a lot cheaper to make. This healthy version tastes as good as the original. You can make more or fewer portions by referring to the Basic Cooking Times for Fish Fillets (pages 232–233) and using two tablespoons of sauce for each. The parsley adds vitamins and some color to a basically white dish. If possible, choose a brightly patterned or colored plate to set it off.

Since there is an absence of green or red vegetables in this dish, add a large salad or start the meal with Oriental Spinach Salad (page 79). Don't put a vegetable on the same plate; it will mess up the elegant sauce. If you haven't had enough carbohydrates in the day, a good way to start the meal would be spaghettini with Tomato Sauce Casalinga (page 167).   *SERVES 4*

Per 4-ounce (113.5-g) serving of fish with 2 tablespoons sauce: 246 calories; 59 milligrams cholesterol; 17 grams fat; 164 milligrams sodium; 20 grams protein (43% RDA); 0 grams carbohydrate

RDA: phosphorus 23%; niacin 12%

4 firm white fish fillets (each 4 ounces; 113.5 g), such as scrod, flounder or cod, cooked according to chart on page 232
Freshly ground black pepper, to taste

½ cup (120 ml) Tonnato Sauce (page 484)
Fresh minced parsley, to taste

1. Sprinkle fish fillets with pepper and place, spoke-fashion, in a 10-inch (25.5-cm) quiche dish or pie plate. Cover tightly with microwave plastic wrap. Cook at 100% for 4 minutes or until cooked through in a 650- to 700-watt oven. Prick plastic to release steam.

2. Remove from oven and uncover. Spoon 2 tablespoons Tonnato Sauce around each fillet and sprinkle with minced parsley.

CHINESE-STYLE FISH FILLETS

*T*he Chinese, particularly the Cantonese, are very good at making simple fish preparations extremely savory. While I would follow their lead and serve rice, I would change it to a cup of brown rice, something they abhor. I would probably have a glass of beer and a piece of melon or some cut-up ripe pineapple. *SERVES 1*

Per plated serving of fish fillet with ¾ cup (180 ml) bok choy and sauce: 167 calories; 46 milligrams cholesterol; 4 grams fat; 489 milligrams sodium; 24 grams protein (53% RDA); 8 grams carbohydrate

RDA: calcium 15%; 666 milligrams potassium; vitamin A 87%; vitamin C 98%

4 ounces (113.5 g) Napa cabbage or
  bok choy, shredded (about 2 cups;
  470 ml)
1 tablespoon peeled and slivered fresh
  ginger
4 ounces (113.5 g) skinned sea bass or
  black bass fillet, ½-inch (1-cm) thick
  (if unavailable, substitute any good-
  quality fillet)
2 tablespoons water

¼ teaspoon cornstarch
1 scallion, trimmed, whites and greens
  thinly sliced
1 teaspoon tamari soy
1 teaspoon mirin
1 teaspoon rice wine vinegar
1 clove garlic, smashed, peeled and
  minced
¼ teaspoon chili oil

1. Toss bok choy and ginger together until ginger is evenly distributed. Arrange in the center of a dinner plate. Score the skin side of the fish fillet with slashes ⅛ inch (.25 cm) deep about 1 inch (2 cm) apart. Place fish, skin side up, over the greens.

2. Stir water and cornstarch together until smooth. Stir in remaining ingredients and pour over fish. Cover tightly with microwave plastic wrap. Cook at 100% for 3 minutes in a 650- to 700-watt oven. Prick plastic to release steam.

3. Remove from oven, uncover and serve hot.

To serve 2. Use 8 ounces (227 g) bok choy, 2 tablespoons ginger, 2 fish fillets, 2 tablespoons water, ½ teaspoon cornstarch, 2 scallions, 2 teaspoons each soy, mirin and vinegar, 2 cloves garlic and ½ teaspoon oil. Arrange ingredients as in Steps 1 and 2. Cook in an 11 × 7 × 2-inch (28.5 × 18 × 5-cm) rectangular dish for 6 minutes. Remove greens and stir before serving.

To serve 4. Use 1 pound (450 g) bok choy, 4 tablespoons ginger, 4 fish fillets, 4 tablespoons water, 1 teaspoon cornstarch, 4 scallions, 4 teaspoons each soy, mirin and vinegar, 4 cloves garlic and 1 teaspoon oil. Arrange ingredients as in Steps 1 and 2. Cook in an 11 × 7 × 2-inch (28.5 × 18 × 5-cm) rectangular dish for 9 minutes. Remove greens and stir before serving.

FOR 400- TO 500-WATT OVENS

To serve 1. Cook for 5 minutes 30 seconds.

To serve 2. Cook for 4 minutes. Uncover and turn fish over. Cook for 6 minutes.

SCROD WITH BROCCOLI

*T*his is the simplest dish to make and very good too. You can even top it with some olive oil or a tablespoon of a diet dressing if you keep some in the refrigerator (pages 483–499). Add some Oat Bran Wafers (page 161) or a slice of whole wheat toast for a satisfying lunch that also provides 64 percent of your vitamin C. Since it is also low in protein, it is an ideal main course after a first course that has some protein in it. Make sure you serve a carbohydrate with this. *SERVES 1*

Per 3-ounce (85-g) fish serving: 86 calories; 37 milligrams cholesterol; 1 gram fat; 58 milligrams sodium; 17 grams protein (38% RDA); 3 grams carbohydrate

RDA: vitamin A 17%; vitamin C 64%

3 ounces (85 g) scrod or cod fillet
2 ounces (56 g) broccoli florets, cut
    into 2-inch (5-cm) lengths (about
    1⅓ cups; 320 ml)

    1. Place scrod in the center of a dinner plate or a 10-inch (25.5-cm) quiche dish. Arrange broccoli around fish with stem ends pointing in. Cover tightly with microwave plastic wrap. Cook at 100% for 2 minutes in a 650- to 700-watt oven. Prick plastic to release steam.
    2. Remove from oven and uncover. Serve hot.

FOR 400- TO 500-WATT OVENS

To serve 1. Cook for 3 minutes.

SALMON WITH CUCUMBERS AND DILL

*T*his attractive pink-and-green dinner for two has a mildly Scandinavian aura, fragrant with dill. The salmon is rich in Omega-3 fatty acids. If you add the yogurt, each portion increases by only twelve calories. Follow Scandinavian tradition and serve this with steamed new potatoes (page 220). For a gala summer dinner, start with Red Pepper Soup (page 145). Finish up with your dessert of choice.   SERVES 2

Per 4-ounce (113.5-g) fish serving: 194 calories; 62 milligrams cholesterol; 7 grams fat; 245 milligrams sodium; 24 grams protein (54% RDA); 7 grams carbohydrate

RDA: calcium 11%; phosphorus 28%; iron 20%; 926 milligrams potassium; vitamin A 46%; thiamin 21%; riboflavin 31%; niacin 46%; vitamin C 52%

6 scallions
½ pound (227 g) cucumber, trimmed, peeled, halved, seeded and cut across into ⅛-inch (.3-cm) slices (about ½ cup; 120 ml)
½ pound (225 g) skinless salmon fillet, halved lengthwise and each half cut across into six slices

¼ cup (60 ml) packed chopped fresh dill
¼ teaspoon kosher salt
2 tablespoons nonfat yogurt, optional

1. Trim white part of scallions to 2 inches (5 cm). Thinly slice scallion greens to make ¼ cup (60 ml). Reserve.
2. Arrange cucumbers in a ring around inside edge of a 10-inch (25.5-cm) quiche dish. Place scallion whites over cucumbers.
3. Arrange salmon pieces in a single layer in the center of the dish. Sprinkle on scallion greens, dill and salt. Cover tightly with microwave plastic wrap. Cook at 100% for 2 minutes 15 seconds in a 650- to 700-watt oven. Prick plastic to release steam.
4. Remove from oven and uncover. Serve with a tablespoon of yogurt on each portion, if desired.

FOR 400- TO 500-WATT OVENS

To serve 2. Cook for 5 minutes.

SALMON WITH VEGETABLES AND ORZO

This hearty dish is a nice way to treat yourself when alone and hurried for a good hot meal. The fish and vegetables give off a lovely, light aromatic juice that moistens the orzo. If the orzo seems like extra work, sop up the goodness with a slice of French bread. Add a dessert and a glass of wine and you're all fixed.
SERVES 1

Per plated serving containing 4 ounces (113.5 g) of fish: 471 calories; 62 milligrams cholesterol; 17 grams fat; 66 milligrams sodium; 31 grams protein (67% RDA); 48 grams carbohydrate

RDA: iron 25%; phosphorus 37%; 1,163 milligrams potassium; vitamin A 81%; thiamin 55%; riboflavin 41%; niacin 65%; vitamin C 194%

¼ cup (60 ml) dry orzo (very small rice-shaped pasta)

2 ounces (56 g) zucchini, halved lengthwise and cut across into ¼-inch (.5-cm) slices (½ cup; 120 ml)

1 small tomato (4 ounces; 113.5 g), cored, halved across and cut into ¼-inch (.5-cm) slices (½ cup; 120 ml)

2 ounces (56 g) red bell pepper, stemmed, seeded, deribbed and thinly sliced (⅓ cup; 80 ml)

4 ounces (113.5 g) salmon fillet

2 teaspoons olive oil

2 teaspoons fresh lemon juice

2 tablespoons chopped fresh dill

1. Bring 2 cups (470 ml) of water to the boil on top of the stove. Add orzo and cook until al dente. Drain and keep warm.

2. Arrange vegetables in two rows on either side of a 10-inch (25.5-cm) quiche dish or pie plate. Alternate slices of zucchini, tomato and pepper and slightly overlap them so that they all fit on the plate. Place salmon in the middle of the dish.

3. Drizzle oil and lemon juice over fish and vegetables. Sprinkle dill over all. Cover tightly with microwave plastic wrap. Cook at 100% for 3 minutes 30 seconds to 4 minutes, or until salmon is cooked through and opaque, in a 650- to 700-watt oven. Prick plastic to release steam.

4. Remove from oven and uncover. Spoon cooked orzo onto empty space on plate and serve.

FOR 400- TO 500-WATT OVENS

To serve 1. Cook orzo as in Step 1. Cook fish and vegetables as in Step 3 for 5 minutes 30 seconds.

FESTIVE FISH FILLETS

*T*his dinner for two is festive because it tastes so good and is so colorful—red, white and green—and mildly Mexican with the hot pepper and the coriander; think fun and lots of vitamins. Black beans or Chilied Red Beans (page 207) would be a happy accompaniment if rice seems boring.   *SERVES 2*

Per plated serving containing 4 ounces (113.5 g) of fish: 200 calories; 82 milligrams cholesterol; 3 grams fat; 154 milligrams sodium; 35 grams protein (77% RDA); 9 grams carbohydrate

RDA: phosphorus 37%; iron 14%; 985 milligrams potassium; vitamin A 151%; niacin 29%; vitamin C 426%

2 firm white fish fillets (each 4 ounces, 113.5 g)
½ teaspoon fresh lemon juice
1 cup (240 ml) diced red bell pepper (about 8 ounces; 227 g)
2 tablespoons snipped fresh chives

Pinch hot red pepper flakes
1 tablespoon chopped fresh coriander
4 ounces (113.5 g) broccoli florets, cut into 1-inch (2.5-cm) pieces (2½ cups; 590 ml)
Kosher salt, to taste

1. Place one fillet in the center of each of two dinner plates or 10-inch (25.5-cm) quiche dishes. Sprinkle with lemon juice.
2. Stir together bell pepper, chives, pepper flakes and coriander in a small bowl. Spoon half this mixture down the center of each fillet.
3. Place broccoli on either side of the fillets. Cover tightly with microwave plastic wrap. Cook at 100% for 3 minutes, using a rack and switching plates after 1 minute 30 seconds, in a 650- to 700-watt oven. Prick plastic to release steam.
4. Remove from oven and uncover. Serve immediately.

To serve 1. Use 1 fillet, ¼ teaspoon lemon juice, ½ cup (120 ml) bell pepper, 1 tablespoon chives, pinch red pepper flakes, 1½ teaspoons coriander, 2 ounces (56 g) broccoli and a pinch salt. Arrange as in Steps 1–3. Cook for 2 minutes 15 seconds.

FOR 400- TO 500-WATT OVENS

To serve 2. Cook for 5 minutes, switching plates after 2 minutes 30 seconds.

To serve 1. Cook for 3 minutes 15 seconds.

ORANGE PEPPER FISH

*S*lightly exotic in flavor, with hints of sweet, sour and spicy, this is a beautiful dish of red, orange and white. For even more color and vitamins and a few extra calories, you can surround each portion—if doing one on a plate—or the group of portions with two ounces (56 g) tipped and tailed green beans (multiply this by the number of portions). Even without the beans, you are already providing two days' worth of vitamin C and half a day's worth of vitamin A. You are, however, also providing a good deal of protein, making this a perfect dinner for a day with a big salad for lunch. At dinner, choose a high-carbohydrate, low-protein first course such as linguine with Mushroom Sauce (page 169), and have a portion of fruit or a diet sorbet (pages 552–557).   *SERVES 4 AS A MAIN COURSE*

Per 7-ounce (200-g) off-the-bone serving: 280 calories; 0 milligrams cholesterol; 8 grams fat; 109 milligrams sodium; 36 grams protein (81% RDA); 14 grams carbohydrate

RDA: vitamin A 58%; 1,137 milligrams potassium; vitamin C 223%

1 tablespoon vegetable oil
¼ teaspoon hot red pepper flakes
2 tablespoons fresh lemon juice
2 tablespoons fresh orange juice
3½-pound (1.6-kg) whole white-fleshed fish such as sea bass, rockfish, tilefish or weakfish, without head

2 juice oranges (each 8 ounces; 227 g), 1½ thinly sliced and ½ chopped
1 large red bell pepper (8 ounces; 227 g), thinly sliced
2 tablespoons chopped fresh coriander

1. Combine oil and pepper flakes on a 16 × 10-inch (40.6 × 25.5-cm) platter. Cook, uncovered, at 100% for 30 seconds in a 650- to 700-watt oven. Remove from oven and add lemon juice and orange juice. Cook for 30 seconds more.

2. Remove from oven. Roll fish in the mixture and remove to another plate. Arrange half of the orange and pepper slices overlapping on the platter. Fill the cavity of the fish with the chopped orange.

3. Place fish on the platter diagonally, on top of the oranges and peppers. Arrange remaining orange and pepper slices on top of fish. Cover tightly with microwave plastic wrap and cook for 15 minutes. Prick plastic to release steam.

4. Remove from oven and uncover carefully. Sprinkle with coriander and serve hot.

To serve 1. Use 1 teaspoon oil, a pinch pepper flakes, 2 teaspoons each lemon and orange juice, 4 ounces (113.5 g) fish fillet, 1 small juice orange (about 4 ounces; 113.5 g) thinly sliced, 2 ounces (56 g) red bell pepper, and 1 teaspoon coriander.

(continued)

Place oil and pepper flakes on a dinner plate. Cook oil and pepper flakes as in Step 1 for 30 seconds. Add lemon and orange juice and cook for 30 seconds more. Continue with Step 2. Arrange vegetables and fish as in Step 3 on a dinner plate or 10-inch (25.5-cm) quiche dish and cook for 2 minutes.

FOR 400- TO 500-WATT OVENS

To serve 1. Cook oil, pepper flakes, lemon and orange juice as in Step 1 for 1 minute 30 seconds. Continue as in Steps 2 and 3, cooking fish for 3 minutes 30 seconds.

ORIENTAL FISH SALAD

*F*ish makes as good a cold main course as it does a hot one. This tasty salad can also be made with leftover fish. With only 219 calories, you are left with plenty of room for complementary courses or wine; but watch out! This dish provides 85 percent of your protein. Be mildly vegetarian for the rest of the day. Have a large salad for lunch; but have a piece of cheese for the calcium.

Though you may have to watch your protein, in return you get walloping amounts of vitamins C and A along with some iron. It's not just another pretty plate. For other quantities, multiply or divide the other ingredients to match your amount of cooked fish. Consider Mung Bean Noodles (page 178) as a go-along.

SERVES 4 AS A MAIN COURSE

Per plated serving containing 5 ounces (142 g) of fish: 219 calories; 96 milligrams cholesterol; 4 grams fat; 473 milligrams sodium; 38 grams protein (85% RDA); 8 grams carbohydrate

RDA: iron 21%; 1,174 milligrams potassium; vitamin A 173%; niacin 22%; vitamin C 200%

FOR THE DRESSING

2 tablespoons rice wine vinegar
1 tablespoon tamari soy
1 teaspoon Oriental sesame oil
Freshly ground black pepper, to taste

FOR THE SALAD

1½ pounds (680 g) spinach, washed
   and stemmed (about 6 cups; 1.5 l)

1¼ pounds (570 g) cooked fish (any
   firm-fleshed white fish, such as
   flounder or cod, is fine; see pages
   232–233 for cooking times)
4 endive (each 3½ ounces; 90 g),
   trimmed and quartered lengthwise
1 large red pepper (about 8 ounces; 227
   g), thinly sliced
¼ cup (60 ml) thinly sliced scallion

1. In a small bowl, whisk together ingredients for the dressing.

2. Toss spinach with 2 tablespoons of dressing. Divide evenly among four dinner plates. Divide fish evenly among the plates, placing it in the center over the spinach. Arrange endive spoke-fashion around the fish. Divide pepper rings evenly among the four portions and arrange on top of fish. Scatter scallion over each, drizzle with remaining dressing and serve.

SWORDFISH WITH PESTO

*F*resh and light, this is as easily made for one as for four, especially if you keep the Diet Pesto on hand. That pesto is a clue that you might want to serve a pasta (see page 164 for dietary information) with a little extra pesto as a side dish, or choose a complementary vegetable such as Chunky Tomato Basil Salad (page 407).

Serve a first course or a soup and feel free to add some crusty whole wheat bread to sop up the juices, as this is low in calories. You can even have a light dessert, or substitute a glass of wine such as a crisp chardonnay for one of the courses. Since the swordfish contains only half of your animal protein allotment for the day, your first course can have another 25 percent, which still leaves 25 percent for the rest of the day.   *SERVES 4*

Per 1 swordfish-steak serving: 199 calories; 39 milligrams cholesterol; 8 grams fat; 309 milligrams sodium; 22 grams protein (49% RDA); 10 grams carbohydrate

RDA: calcium 24%; phosphorus 33%; iron 29%; 676 milligrams potassium; vitamin A 21%; niacin 52%

¾ cup (180 ml) Diet Pesto Sauce (page 476)

4 1-inch (2.5-cm) thick swordfish steaks (each 4 ounces; 113.5 g)

1. Spread pesto on the bottom of a 10-inch (25.5-cm) quiche dish or pie plate. Arrange swordfish on pesto with any thinner or narrower parts pointing toward the center of the dish. Cover tightly with microwave plastic wrap. Cook at 100% for 4 minutes in a 650- to 700-watt oven. Prick plastic to release steam.

2. Remove from oven, uncover and serve.

To serve 2. Use ¼ cup (60 ml) pesto and 2 swordfish steaks. Arrange as in Step 1 and cook for 3 minutes.

(continued)

Swordfish with Pesto (cont.)

To serve 1. Use 3 tablespoons pesto and 1 swordfish steak. Arrange as in Step 1 and cook for 2 minutes.

FOR 400- TO 500-WATT OVENS

To serve 2. Cook for 5–6 minutes.

To serve 1. Cook for 3 minutes 30 seconds.

DIET SALAD BAR FISH

I've said it before and no doubt will say it again: The salad bar of the local store is one of the best friends the harried dieter can have since it is easy to pick up a selection of cut-up vegetables cleaned and in just the sizes you want. Carefully avoid vegetables in dressings or sauces and try to pick uncooked vegetables. If you must make do with a cooked vegetable, advance its place in the arrangement to front and center, in the middle of the fish.

Have an artichoke to begin and a dessert of your choice. Add a glass of wine if you wish, or have a snack later in the evening.   *SERVES 1*

Per plated serving containing 4 ounces (113.5 g) of fish: 228 calories; 44 milligrams cholesterol; 9 grams fat; 130 milligrams sodium; 26 grams protein (58% RDA); 11 grams carbohydrate

RDA: iron 12%; 769 milligrams potassium; vitamin A 186%; niacin 64%; vitamin C 104%

4 ounces (113.5 g) boneless swordfish or tuna steak, about ½-inch (1-cm) thick

1 ounce (28 g) mushrooms, wiped clean with a damp cloth and thinly sliced through the stem (about ½ cup; 120 ml)

½ cup (120 ml) broccoli florets (about ¾ ounce; 21 g)

1 ounce (28 g) green beans, trimmed and each quartered crosswise (about ⅓ cup; 80 ml)

1 ounce (28 g) carrot, cut into 2 × ⅛ × ⅛-inch (5 × 3 × 3-cm) matchsticks (about ⅓ cup; 80 ml)

1 tablespoon fresh lemon juice

1 teaspoon olive oil

Freshly ground black pepper, to taste

1. Place fish in the center of a dinner plate or 10-inch (25.5-cm) quiche dish. Top with mushrooms and broccoli. Arrange green beans and carrots around fish.

2. Mix lemon juice, oil and pepper together in a small bowl. Pour over fish and vegetables. Cover tightly with microwave plastic wrap. Cook at 100% for 2 minutes in a 650- to 700-watt oven. Prick plastic to release steam.

3. Remove from oven and uncover. Serve hot.

To serve 2. Use 8 ounces (227 g) fish, 2 ounces (56 g) mushrooms, 1 cup (240 ml) broccoli florets, 2 ounces (56 g) beans, 2 ounces (56 g) carrot, 2 tablespoons lemon juice, 2 teaspoons oil and a pinch black pepper. Divide ingredients between two dinner plates or quiche dishes. Arrange as in Step 1. Cook for 4 minutes using a rack, and switch plates after 2 minutes.

FOR 400- TO 500-WATT OVENS

To serve 1. Cook for 3 minutes.

TUNA WITH TOMATOES

This is a quick, easy and good way to serve a large crowd. If there are leftovers, they will be good on the day after cooking as a cold lunch or dinner if kept refrigerated. If your weight-loss needs aren't severe, drizzle a little olive oil over the fish. You can even make it ahead and plan to serve it cold on its own or as Tuna Salad (page 70). Curried Cabbage Soup (page 133) or Summer Vegetable Jamboree (page 81) to begin, and Summer Fruit Compote (page 540) or Peaches with Cherry Sauce (page 547) to sum up, and with chunky Italian bread on the side, turn this into a party.   *SERVES 12*

Per serving: 181 calories; 43 milligrams cholesterol; 6 grams fat; 48 milligrams sodium; 27 grams protein (60% RDA); 2.6 grams carbohydrate

RDA: vitamin A 62%; niacin 51%

2 large tomatoes (each 10 ounces; 284 g), each cut into six slices
3 pounds (1.4 kg) tuna steak, 1 inch (2.5 cm) thick
2 teaspoons olive oil
2 teaspoons fresh lemon juice
Kosher salt, to taste
Freshly ground black pepper, to taste
16 large fresh basil leaves

1. Arrange tomato slices in a 14 × 11 × 2-inch (35.5 × 28 × 5-cm) dish in a single layer. Arrange fish over tomatoes. Drizzle with oil and lemon juice, and sprinkle with salt and pepper. Scatter basil over all. Cover tightly with microwave plastic wrap. Cook at 100% for 9 minutes in a 650- to 700-watt oven. Prick plastic to release steam.

2. Remove from oven. Let stand, covered, for 2 minutes. Uncover and serve hot.

To serve 2 to 3. Use 4 slices tomato, ¾ pound (340 g) tuna, ½ teaspoon oil, ½ teaspoon lemon juice, pinch salt, pinch pepper and 4 basil leaves. Cook as in Step 1 on a dinner plate or 10-inch (25.5-cm) quiche dish for 4 minutes.

FISH WITH TOMATOES AND CUCUMBER

*T*his is a version of a recipe I first published in *Food for Friends*. There, it is a recipe for a whole fish. This recipe is simplified and lightened. If you cannot find bass, snapper or rockfish, use the ubiquitous sole or flounder fillets.

Start with Carrot Timbale (page 105). Let some steamed new potatoes (page 220) bathe in the fragrant cooking liquid.   *SERVES 6*

Per serving containing 4½ ounces (128 g) of fish: 191 calories; 90 milligrams cholesterol; 7 grams fat; 105 milligrams sodium; 26 grams protein (58% RDA); 5 grams carbohydrate

RDA: calcium 19%; phosphorus 30%; iron 23%; 715 milligrams potassium; vitamin C 17%

4 firm, white, skinless fish fillets (each 7 ounces; 200 g), such as black bass, pin bones removed with a tweezers or needle-nosed pliers
1 Kirby cucumber, cut into ⅛-inch (.3-cm) slices; if using other cucumbers, peel, halve and seed before slicing (¾ cup; 180 ml)

1 medium tomato (6 ounces; 170 g) cored, seeded and cut into ¼-inch (.5-cm) slices (¾ cup; 180 ml)
½ cup (120 ml) coarsely chopped fresh dill
2 tablespoons fresh lemon juice
1 tablespoon olive oil
Freshly ground black pepper, to taste

1. Arrange two of the fillets, skin side (the shiny one) down, side by side and head to tail in an 11 × 9 × 2-inch (28 × 18 × 5-cm) dish. Arrange cucumber slices, slightly overlapping, over the fish. Repeat with tomato slices.

2. Sprinkle dill on tomato. Drizzle with lemon juice, oil and pepper. Top with remaining fillets, matching thin and thick ends. Cover tightly with microwave plastic wrap. Cook at 100% for 8 minutes in a 650- to 700-watt oven. Prick plastic to release steam.

3. Remove from oven and uncover. Slice each fillet "sandwich" across into three equal slices. Serve with some of the cooking liquid spooned over.

To serve 1. Use 4 ounces (113.5 g) fillet, 2 slices each cucumber and tomato, 2 tablespoons dill, 1 teaspoon lemon juice, ½ teaspoon olive oil and pinch pepper. Place fillet skin side down on a work surface. Cover the thin end of the fillet with overlapping slices of cucumber and tomato. Sprinkle over remaining ingredients. Fold fillet in half to cover stuffing. Place in the center of a dinner plate or quiche dish. Cover and cook for 2 minutes 30 seconds.

FOR 400- TO 500-WATT OVENS

To serve 1. Cook for 3 minutes 30 seconds.

FLOUNDER WITH CREAMED SPINACH

*T*here are times when I crave an old-fashioned gooey dish, when nothing will satisfy except something that seems to be creamy. This is a version of what is known in French menu circles as Florentine, which refers to the creamed spinach. After making this, I got to thinking that perhaps the old dishes of the fifties were better than we remember. Certainly, when trimmed down to a good calorie and cholesterol size, they can make us feel indulged and virtuous at the same time. If you prefer to substitute fresh spinach, see pages 78–79 for cooking directions. Start with about six ounces (170 g) raw, untrimmed spinach.   *SERVES 4*

Per 1-fillet serving: 156 calories; 56 milligrams cholesterol; 2 grams fat; 367 milligrams sodium; 26 grams protein (58% RDA); 9 grams carbohydrate

RDA: calcium 20%; phosphorus 32%; 771 milligrams potassium; vitamin A 114%; vitamin C 33%

1¼ cup (300 ml) skim milk
1 tablespoon cornstarch
½ teaspoon kosher salt
1 tablespoon fresh lemon juice
Large pinch freshly ground nutmeg
Pinch freshly ground black pepper

10-ounce (284-g) box frozen spinach, defrosted in a sieve under warm running water
4 flounder fillets (each 4 ounces; 113.5 g)

1. Combine milk, cornstarch and salt in a 4-cup (1-l) glass measure. Cover tightly with microwave plastic wrap. Cook at 100% for 4 minutes, or until boiling and thickened, in a 650- to 700-watt oven. Prick plastic to release steam.

2. Remove from oven and uncover. Stir in lemon juice, nutmeg and pepper. Squeeze as much water from the spinach as possible and stir into sauce.

3. Roll the fillets into paupiettes and lay them down in an 8-inch (20-cm) square dish. Pour the sauce over the fish. Cover tightly with microwave plastic wrap. Cook at 100% for 6 minutes. Prick plastic to release steam.

4. Remove from oven and uncover. Serve each fillet with some of the sauce spooned over.

FOR 400- TO 500-WATT OVENS

To serve 4. Cook the sauce as in Step 1 for 8 minutes, stirring after 4 minutes. Proceed with recipe as in Steps 2 and 3. Cook for 12 minutes on a wind-up carrousel or turn the dish once or twice.

Paupiettes

This festive way to serve fish consists of strips or fillets that are rolled up, often around a stuffing. When stuffed, they are usually cooked standing on end to present an attractive pinwheel. Whole fillets are generally not rolled around a stuffing and are cooked with the roll lying flat.

The most commonly used and least fattening fish strips are made by halving fillets of sole or flounder lengthwise. Often the two halves can be pulled apart along the center membrane. If this doesn't work, lay the fillet flat and run a sharp knife on either side of the membrane to separate the two halves. If you have pulled the halves apart, pull off the strip of membrane.

Strips of a similar size can be made from skinned and filleted salmon; but attractive as their pink color is, they will be significantly more expensive and caloric. Don't substitute salmon in farces—the purée of fish stuffings—or they will be grainy.

Once you have your halved fillets or other strips, lay them on your work counter skin side down (that is, where the skin was). This will be the shinier, firmer side of the strip. Roll from the thick end to the thinner end to obtain a neat shape.

Halve fillets along the membrane.

Pull off membrane.

To roll a half-fillet or a whole fillet to make paupiettes, start with the fat end and roll toward the thin end.

PAUPIETTES WITH VEGETABLES

*T*his is an extremely pretty dish, with the white fish surrounding yellow, green, red and orange vegetable strips. Set each portion off on a little green bed of Watercress Sauce. Cutting up those vegetables is a certain amount of work, so I make it for parties. If it's one of my very weight-conscious days, I stick to the two-paupiette serving; but I can have as many as four pieces with a light first course such as Fresh Shiitake Sauté (page 96) and a starch such as rice and some fruit for dessert. That would make this a dish for two.   *SERVES 4 AS A MAIN COURSE, 8 AS A FIRST COURSE*

Per 2-paupiette main-course serving: 114 calories; 54 milligrams cholesterol; 1 gram fat; 279 milligrams sodium; 22 grams protein (48% RDA); 2 grams carbohydrate

RDA: phosphorus 22%; vitamin A 66%; niacin 18%; vitamin C 50%

FOR THE STUFFING

1½ ounces (42.5 g) carrot, trimmed, peeled and cut into 2-inch matchsticks (about ⅓ cup; 150 ml)

2½ ounces (71 g) zucchini, trimmed, halved lengthwise and cut into 2-inch (5-cm) matchsticks (½ cup; 120 ml)

1½ ounces (42.5 g) red bell pepper, stemmed, seeded, deribbed and cut into 2-inch (5-cm) matchsticks (⅓ cup; 150 ml)

1½ ounces (42.5 g) yellow bell pepper, stemmed, seeded, deribbed and cut into 2-inch (5-cm) matchsticks (⅓ cup; 150 ml)

4 sole fillets (each 4 ounces; 113.5 g), each halved lengthwise

½ teaspoon kosher salt

1 recipe Watercress Sauce (page 505), optional

1. Place vegetables in a $13 \times 10 \times 2$-inch ($33 \times 25.5 \times 5$-cm) oval dish. Cover tightly with microwave plastic wrap. Cook at 100% for 1 minute 30 seconds in a 650- to 700-watt oven. Prick plastic to release steam.

2. Remove from oven and uncover. Arrange 2 or 3 pieces of each vegetable across the wide end of each half fillet. Starting with the wide ends, roll the half fillets and secure each roll (paupiette) with a toothpick. Space paupiettes evenly around the inside rim of the dish. Cover and cook for 5 minutes. Prick wrap.

3. Remove from oven, uncover and sprinkle with salt. Serve hot with watercress sauce.

FOR 400- TO 500-WATT OVENS

To serve 4 as a main course. Follow Step 1 and cook for 2 minutes 15 seconds. Continue with Step 2 and cook, covered, for 7 minutes 30 seconds. Finish as in Step 3.

PAUPIETTES WITH PARSLEY STUFFING

*B*ecause of the fish in the bright-green stuffing, this is a slightly more substantial main course than the last one. Larger or more active eaters can still have a double portion. Small ones like me can have the four pieces if they have a salad, rice and fruit for dessert and not much else.

SERVES 4 AS A MAIN COURSE, 8 AS A FIRST COURSE

Per 2-paupiette main-course serving: 142 calories; 65 milligrams cholesterol; 2 grams fat; 307 milligrams sodium; 26 grams protein (58% RDA); 4 grams carbohydrate

RDA: phosphorus 27%; vitamin A 158%; niacin 21%; vitamin C 27%

FOR THE STUFFING

4 ounces (113.5 g) carrot, trimmed, peeled and sliced into ½-inch (5-cm) rounds (1 cup; 240 ml)

3 ounces (85 g) sole fillet

1 cup (240 ml) fresh parsley leaves

2 shallots, trimmed and peeled

½ teaspoon kosher salt

⅛ teaspoon freshly ground black pepper

4 sole fillets (each 4 ounces; 113.5 g), each halved lengthwise

1 recipe Watercress Sauce (page 505), optional

1. Place carrots in a 2-cup (470-ml) glass measure. Cover tightly with microwave plastic wrap. Cook at 100% for 1 minute in a 650- to 700-watt oven. Prick plastic to release steam.

2. Remove from oven, uncover and transfer to a food processor. Add the 3 ounces (85 g) of sole, parsley, shallots, salt and pepper and process until smooth. You will have about 1 cup (240 ml) of stuffing.

3. Divide stuffing among the fillet halves, mounding it on the wider end of each fillet. Beginning with the wide end, roll the fillets around the stuffing. As each paupiette is rolled, set it in a 13 × 10 × 2-inch (33 × 25.5 × 5-cm) glass or ceramic dish with its loose end against the side of the dish. Space paupiettes evenly around the dish. Cover and cook for 5 minutes. Prick plastic wrap.

4. Remove from oven and uncover. Serve hot with watercress sauce.

FOR 400- TO 500-WATT OVENS

To serve 4 as a main course. Follow Step 1; cook for 1 minute 30 seconds. Continue with Step 2. In Step 3 cook for 7 minutes 30 seconds. Finish as in Step 4.

CARROT-STUFFED PAUPIETTES WITH CARROT SAUCE

*T*his is a spectacular-looking dish—tastes good too—whose portions can easily be doubled if the rest of the meal is lean. Do try to have some carbohydrate with this; bread will do. If you want to fill the paupiettes and make the sauce ahead of time, reheat the sauce briefly before cooking the paupiettes.   *SERVES 4 AS A MAIN COURSE, 8 AS A FIRST COURSE*

Per 2-paupiette main-course serving: 193 calories; 78 milligrams cholesterol; 4 grams fat; 174 milligrams sodium; 31 grams protein (69% RDA); 6 grams carbohydrate

RDA: phosphorus 34%; vitamin A 217%; niacin 23%

6 ounces (170 g) carrot, trimmed, peeled and cut across into 1-inch (2.5-cm) rounds (about 1⅓ cups; 410 ml)

½ cup (120 ml) Basic Chicken Broth (page 460), or unsalted or regular canned chicken broth

¾ teaspoon ground cumin

½ cup (120 ml) part-skim ricotta cheese

Kosher salt, to taste

5 sole fillets (each 4 ounces, 113.5 g)

1. Stir together carrots, broth and cumin in a 9-inch (23-cm) pie plate. Cover tightly with microwave plastic wrap. Cook at 100% for 10 minutes, or until carrots are tender, in a 650- to 700-watt oven. Prick plastic to release steam.

2. Remove from oven and uncover. Place ricotta in a blender or food processor and process until smooth. Add carrot mixture and process until very smooth. Add salt if desired.

3. Remove half the carrot mixture and reserve. Add 1 sole fillet, cut into 1-inch (2.5-cm) chunks, to mixture in processor. Process until smooth.

4. Cut remaining 4 fillets in half lengthwise. Place, skin side down, on a work surface. Spread 1 tablespoon of carrot mixture on each half, leaving 1 inch (2.5 cm) at each end of fillet. Carefully roll up fillets starting with the thicker end and place around the inside edge of a 13×9×2-inch (33×23×5-cm) oval dish with the loose end against the side of the dish. Cover tightly with microwave plastic wrap. Cook at 100% for 5 minutes. Prick plastic to release steam.

5. Remove from oven and uncover. Divide reserved carrot sauce among four dinner plates. Place two paupiettes on each plate and serve immediately.

FOR 400- TO 500-WATT OVENS

To serve 4. Cook carrots, broth and cumin as in Step 1 for 15 minutes. Cook fish for 7 minutes 30 seconds.

HALIBUT WITH SPRING VEGETABLES

*T*his makes a complete main course, with all the vegetables charmingly arrayed in their tender spring colors. The radishes are soaked in the vinegar partly for flavor and partly to keep the red color of the skins.

Begin your dinner perhaps with bowls of Mushroom Soup (page 123) or Caprese Salad (page 80). Serve a crusty Italian bread. Add a little cheese if you're not starting with the salad, and finish with Peppered Strawberries (page 535) and Oat Bran Crisps (page 574). Accompany with a cold white wine.   *SERVES 6*

Per generous 5-ounce boned-fish serving with a fair share of vegetables: 292 calories; 49 milligrams cholesterol; 8 grams fat; 222 milligrams sodium; 35 grams protein (78% RDA); 18 grams carbohydrate

RDA: phosphorus 41%; iron 14%; vitamin A 131%; niacin 55%; vitamin C 47%

10 medium radishes, trimmed, washed and cut into ¼-inch (.5-cm) slices (2 cups; 470 ml)

2 tablespoons red wine vinegar

2½ pounds (1.15 kg) halibut steaks, about ¾-inch (2 cm) thick

12 baby carrots, peeled (about 5 ounces; 142 g)

1 pound (450 g) new potatoes, scrubbed and cut into 1-inch (2.5-cm) pieces (about 3 cups; 705 ml)

14 ounces (395 g) asparagus, woody ends snapped off, peeled and cut into thirds (about 3 cups; 705 ml)

2 tablespoons olive oil

½ teaspoon kosher salt

Freshly ground black pepper, to taste

2 teaspoons celery seeds

2 tablespoons minced fresh parsley

Snap off the woody ends.

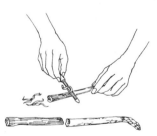

If desired, peel stems with a vegetable peeler.

1. Place radishes in a small bowl with vinegar.

2. Place fish steaks in the center of a 14 × 11 × 2-inch (35.5 × 28 × 5-cm) dish. Arrange carrots around fish, and potatoes on top of carrots. Place asparagus over fish in a ring toward the edge of the dish.

3. Remove radishes from vinegar with a slotted spoon. Place on center of fish inside asparagus ring.

4. Add remaining ingredients to vinegar and stir to combine. Drizzle over fish and vegetables. Cover tightly with microwave plastic wrap. Cook at 100% for 11 minutes, or until fish and vegetables are cooked through, in a 650- to 700-watt oven. Prick plastic to release steam.

5. Remove from oven and uncover. Serve hot.

FOR 400- TO 500-WATT OVENS

To serve 3 to 4. Use 5 medium radishes, 1 tablespoon vinegar, 1½ pounds (680 g) fish, 6 carrots, ½ pound (225 g) potatoes, 7 ounces (200 g) asparagus, 1 tablespoon oil, ¼ teaspoon salt, pinch black pepper, 1 teaspoon celery seed and 1 tablespoon parsley. Arrange as in Steps 1–4 in a 13 × 9 × 2-inch (33 × 23 × 5-cm) oval dish. Cook for 20 minutes, or until fish and vegetables are cooked through.

ANNA'S FISH WITH BLACK BEAN SAUCE

*O*ver the years, I've worked with many assistants. One of the most talented has been Anna Brandenburger, who helped with the work on parts of this book. This is her recipe and delicious it is. At a party, begin with Vegetable Terrine (page 86). Family dinner could start with Spicy Southwestern Soup (page 132). End with Raspberry Poached Pears (page 545).   *SERVES 4*

Per fillet with ¼-cup sauce serving: 173 calories; 42 milligrams cholesterol; 3 grams fat; 104 milligrams sodium; 25 grams protein (56% RDA); 11 grams carbohydrate

RDA: phosphorus 26%; niacin 8%

6 sprigs fresh coriander
8 cloves garlic, smashed and peeled
2 ounces (56 g) fresh ginger, peeled
  and cut into 8 slices
2 tablespoons salted Chinese black
  beans
4 tablespoons rice wine vinegar

⅔ cup (160 ml) white wine
2 teaspoons sesame seeds
1 cup (240 ml) water
2 teaspoons honey
4 red snapper fillets (each 4 ounces;
  113.5 g)

1. Remove coriander leaves from stems. Coarsely chop leaves and reserve. Place stems in a 10-inch (25.5-cm) quiche dish or pie plate. Add remaining ingre-

(continued)

dients except honey and fish. Cover tightly with microwave plastic wrap. Cook at 100% for 8 minutes in a 650- to 700-watt oven. Prick plastic wrap to release steam.

2. Remove from oven and uncover. Remove and discard ginger slices. Purée mixture in a food processor or blender until smooth. Add honey.

3. Pour sauce back into the quiche dish or pie plate, spreading it evenly on the bottom of the dish. Place fillets over sauce. Cover tightly and cook for 6 minutes, or until fish is cooked through and opaque. Prick plastic wrap.

4. Remove from oven and uncover. Sprinkle with reserved chopped coriander leaves and serve.

FOR 400- TO 500-WATT OVENS

To serve 4. Reduce water to ½ cup (120 ml). Follow Step 1 and cook sauce ingredients for 15 minutes. Continue with Steps 2 and 3 and cook fish fillets for 8 minutes. Finish as in Step 4.

SWEET AND SOUR FISH

Remember the good old days before we knew about regional Chinese food— Hunan, Szechuan and the like—when we had a local Chinese nondenominational restaurant that we really liked? Sometimes I crave food just like that and this Sweet and Sour Fish is that kind of dish, meant to be eaten with a pile of white rice (one-half cup for 116 calories), tea and chopsticks. The fish tends to be flaky. If you like firm fish, substitute similarly chunked pieces of tuna, swordfish or even shrimp for the scrod. That makes it more up-to-date—better I'm not clear about.

One change has been made to protect our lives. The fish is not battered and deep-fried before cooking in the sauce. Yes, there is less crunch; but there is also less fat.   *SERVES 4*

Per 1-cup (240-ml) serving: 204 calories; 49 milligrams cholesterol; 1 gram fat; 316 milligrams sodium; 22 grams protein (48% RDA); 28 grams carbohydrate

RDA: phosphorus 26%; 753 milligrams potassium; vitamin A 56%; vitamin C 177%

20-ounce (570-g) can pineapple slices packed in juice, no added sugar
1 tablespoon plus 1 teaspoon cornstarch
¼ teaspoon hot red pepper flakes
1 tablespoon tamari soy
1 red bell pepper (8 ounces; 227 g), cored, seeded and cut into 1¼-inch (3-cm) cubes (about 1½ cups; 360 ml)

1 pound (450 g) scrod fillets, cut into 1-inch (2-cm) cubes
2 tablespoons fresh lemon juice

1. Drain the pineapple slices, reserving 1 cup (240 ml) of juice. Cut pineapple rings into quarters.

2. Combine cornstarch and red pepper flakes in a small bowl. Slowly whisk in reserved juice and continue whisking until cornstarch is completely dissolved. Stir in soy.

3. Pour cornstarch mixture into a 2½-quart (2.5-l) soufflé dish or casserole with a tightly fitted lid. Add red pepper and pineapple pieces. Cover tightly with microwave plastic wrap or casserole lid. Cook at 100% for 8 minutes in a 650- to 700-watt oven. If using plastic wrap, prick to release steam.

4. Remove from oven and uncover. Add fish chunks; do not stir; re-cover and cook for 2 minutes 30 seconds. If using plastic wrap, prick.

5. Remove from oven and gently stir in lemon juice.

FOR 400- TO 500-WATT OVENS

To serve 4. Cook as in Step 3 for 15 minutes, stirring halfway through. Add fish, re-cover and cook for 4 minutes more.

STEAMED WHOLE FISH

This is about as simple as a fish and vegetable dish can be. When you have a good fish, you don't need anything else. The vegetables should be divided between two happy eaters to provide masses of vitamin A, some vitamin C, phosphorus, calcium and iron. Serve a low-protein first course such as Eggplant Purée with Tomato and Green Pepper (page 88); accompany the fish with steamed potatoes and follow it with a salad (Orange and Red Onion Salad [page 402] would add on all the vitamin C you could want) and dessert—Peaches with Cherry Sauce (page 547) in summer, Cranberry Kissel (page 565) in winter. Have a glass of wine if you want to. You can even add a light soup and still stay within a 619- to 632-calorie range. All that food because the fish has only 165 calories; so there to frozen diet entrées. To make a larger fish for a party, see page 234 for additional timings. *SERVES 2 AS A MAIN COURSE*

Per half-fish—4 ounces (113.5 g) of cooked meat—serving: 165 calories; 40 milligrams cholesterol; 2 grams fat; 137 milligrams sodium; 24 grams protein (53% RDA); 13 grams carbohydrate

RDA: phosphorus 27%; 863 milligrams potassium; vitamin A 428%; vitamin C 21%; calcium 9%; iron 9%

1½ pounds (680 g) fish, head and tail
   on (red snapper or striped bass)
¼ teaspoon thyme
¼ teaspoon oregano
½ bay leaf
1 carrot (about 6 ounces; 170 g), peeled
   and cut into 2 × ¼ × ¼-inch
   (5 × .5 × .5-cm) sticks (about ⅔ cup;
   160 ml)

2 stalks celery, cut into 2 × ¼ × ¼-inch
   (5 × .5 × .5-cm) sticks
¼ pound (113.5 g) white part of leek,
   cleaned and chopped (about ½ cup;
   120 ml)

1. Arrange fish diagonally in a 13 × 10 × 2-inch (33 × 25.5 × 5-cm) dish. Sprinkle thyme, oregano and bay leaf in the cavity of the fish. Strew carrots and celery around the fish and scatter leeks over the top. Cover tightly with microwave plastic wrap. Cook at 100% for 8 to 10 minutes, or until done, in a 650- to 700-watt oven. Prick plastic to release steam.

2. Remove from oven and uncover. Serve hot.

FOR 400- TO 500-WATT OVENS

To serve 2. Follow Step 1 and arrange fish in a 13 × 10 × 2-inch (33 × 25.5 × 5-cm) oval dish. Cook for 12 minutes.

SALMON IN RED WINE

*T*his was devised as a cold dish for an elegant summer party; but you can serve it hot. The microwave oven's prowess at cooking fish is shown off here, with the fish fully cooked but moist throughout. Start with a cold soup like Slim Vichyssoise (page 147); add a big Black Bean Salad (page 203)—the black is beautiful against the salmon—and finish with Summer Fruit Compote II (page 541). If you don't mind going over your six hundred calories, you can add a salad with a light dressing (pages 486–499).   *SERVES 12*

Per plated serving of a ¾- to 1-inch (2–2.5-cm) wide slice salmon with 2 tablespoons sauce: 204 calories; 73 milligrams cholesterol; 8 grams fat; 80 milligrams sodium; 27 grams protein (59% RDA); 3.5 grams carbohydrate

RDA: vitamin A 72%; thiamin 21%; riboflavin 30%; niacin 53%

4 cloves garlic, smashed and peeled
6 ounces (170 g) onion, peeled and cut
 into 2-inch (5-cm) chunks
6 ounces (170 g) carrot, peeled and cut
 into ½-inch (1- cm) pieces
3 cups (705 ml) dry red wine (such as
 zinfandel)

Pinch clove
Pinch nutmeg
Pinch mace
½ teaspoon tamari soy
2 center-cut fillets of salmon (each 1¾
 pounds; 800 g)

1. Coarsely chop garlic, onion and carrots in the food processor or by hand. Spread vegetables in a 14 × 11 × 2-inch (35.5 × 28 × 5-cm) dish. Add wine, spices and soy. Cook, uncovered, at 100% for 10 minutes in a 650- to 700-watt oven.

2. Remove from oven. Strain mixture through a fine sieve and return to dish. Let stand until cool.

3. When liquid is cool, place one piece of salmon, skin side down, on top. Place second piece on top of first piece, skin side up, with the belly flap side directly over the meaty side of the bottom fillet. The assembled fillets will be of even thickness. Cover tightly with microwave plastic wrap. Cook at 100% for 5 minutes. Prick plastic to release steam.

4. Remove from oven and uncover. Using two wide spatulas, carefully turn over fish fillets. Re-cover and cook for 5 minutes more. Prick plastic to release steam.

5. Remove from oven and uncover. Let stand until cool enough to handle. Gently remove skin from top piece of salmon. Transfer salmon to a platter and refrigerate until well chilled, several hours or overnight. Reserve liquid to serve as a sauce.

6. To serve, slice across into 12 equal slices and serve with 2 tablespoons of sauce per person.

FISH TAGINE

Whenever I have a taste for things Moroccan, I turn to Paula Wolfert's *Couscous and Other Good Foods from Morocco*; it's my guide. Now, Paula doesn't always agree with me or I with her, and I am sure she would never make a tagine (the name of a cooking pot and the food cooked in it) in a microwave oven, so this is not an authorized version. It is my real-life homage to a cook I admire. The flaws in the recipe are mine, the virtues hers.

While such dishes normally cook for a long time at a low heat, I find that the rapidity of microwave cooking, with its characteristic ability to get spices to reveal all their energy, allows the fish to be eaten before it is overcooked. There will be lots of delicious sauce—more than a quarter-cup per person—that you can soak up with bread in traditional fashion, or serve a half-cup (120 ml) of cooked rice. To keep that sauce under control, serve the fish in a rimmed soup dish with a big spoon. I would add a salad and some Tangerine Pudding (page 563). Consider mint tea as a drink.

This makes a festive dinner but may be too much work for everyday cooking, so there is no small-serving version. Leftovers are good cold.   *SERVES 6*

Per plated serving of 1 fillet with a generous ½ cup (120 ml) sauce: 164 calories; 54 milligrams cholesterol; 4 grams fat; 455 milligrams sodium; 23 grams protein (51% RDA); 9 grams carbohydrate

RDA: phosphorus 25%; iron 11%; vitamin A 30%; niacin 22%; vitamin C 42%

FOR THE CHARMOULA

¼ cup (60 ml) fresh cilantro leaves
2 cloves garlic, smashed and peeled
1 tablespoon white wine vinegar
2 teaspoons fresh lemon juice
½ teaspoon paprika
½ teaspoon ground cumin
2 tablespoons water

FOR THE TAGINE

6 flounder fillets (each 4 ounces; 113.5 g), no more than ½-inch (1 cm) at the thickest point
1 tablespoon olive oil

2 teaspoons paprika
1 teaspoon ground cumin
3 cloves garlic, smashed, peeled and minced
Large pinch cayenne
4 stalks celery, trimmed, peeled and cut into 1½ × ¼ × ¼-inch (4 × .5 × .5-cm) julienne (about 1 cup; 240 ml)
1 can (28 ounces; 790 g) Italian plum tomatoes with liquid, coarsely chopped
½ teaspoon kosher salt
1 tablespoon fresh lemon juice

1. Combine the charmoula ingredients in a food processor and chop coarsely. Transfer to a nonmetal dish. Rub the fillets on all sides with the charmoula and let stand while preparing the rest of the recipe.

2. Stir together oil, paprika, cumin, garlic and cayenne in a small bowl to make a paste. Place in the center of an $11 \times 9 \times 2$-inch ($28 \times 23 \times 5$-cm) oval dish. Cook, uncovered, at 100% for 1 minute in a 650- to 700-watt oven.

3. Add celery and stir to coat with the spice mixture. Cook, uncovered, for 5 minutes. Stir in tomatoes and salt and cook, uncovered, for 8 minutes.

4. Roll the marinated fillets into paupiettes. Lay the paupiettes down spoke-fashion (see illustration below), on top of the vegetables. Cover tightly with microwave plastic wrap. Cook for 7 minutes, or until fish is cooked through and opaque. Prick plastic to release steam.

5. Remove from oven and uncover. With a slotted spoon, remove fillets to a shallow serving bowl or individual plates. Stir lemon juice into sauce and spoon over fish.

FOR 400- TO 500-WATT OVENS

To serve 6. Follow Step 1. In Step 2, cook spice mixture uncovered for 2 minutes. Continue with Step 3 and cook celery for 7 minutes. Add tomatoes and salt and cook for 12 minutes. In Step 4 cook paupiettes for 9 minutes. Finish as in Step 5.

Arrange paupiettes made with half-fillets standing up around the inside rim of the dish with loose ends against the edge of the dish.

Arrange paupiettes made with whole fillets lying down, spoke-fashion, around the inside rim of the dish with loose ends tucked under.

FISH COUSCOUS

*T*his ample dish also has Moroccan influence behind it. After you fill up with pleasure, you can note that this has a moderate amount of protein and little fat, so it could make a very special party by starting with Coral Scallop Terrine (page 93) and ending with Gingered Oranges (page 534).   *SERVES 6*

Per serving of ¾ cup (180 ml) fish and vegetables with 1 cup (240 ml) couscous: 289 calories; 30 milligrams cholesterol; 3 grams fat; 433 milligrams sodium; 19 grams protein (43% RDA); 49 grams carbohydrate

RDA: iron 13%; thiamin 17%; niacin 17%; vitamin C 49%

⅛ teaspoon cinnamon
¼ teaspoon cayenne
1 teaspoon ground coriander
1 teaspoon cumin
2 teaspoons vegetable oil
10 ounces (284 g) baking potatoes, peeled and cut into 1- inch (2-cm) cubes (about 2 cups; 470 ml)
8 ounces (227 g) onion, peeled and cut into 1-inch (2.5 cm) pieces (about 2 cups; 480 ml)
1½ cups (355 ml) Basic Fish Broth (page 461)
1 teaspoon kosher salt
Freshly ground black pepper, to taste

2 zucchini (each 8 ounces; 227 g), cut into rounds ½-inch (1-cm) thick (about 3 cups; 705 ml)
12 ounces (340 g) scrod fillets, cut into 1-inch (2.5-cm) chunks
6 ounces (170 g) canned chick-peas, rinsed and drained
1 lemon, cut into 16 wedges, pits removed
1 tablespoon chopped fresh coriander leaves
1¼ cups (300 ml) water
1¾ cups (410 ml) instant couscous; or regular couscous (see page 181 for cooking instructions)

1. Combine cinnamon, cayenne, ground coriander, cumin and oil in a 13×9×2-inch (33×23×5-cm) oval dish. Cook at 100%, uncovered, for 1 minute in a 650- to 700-watt oven.
2. Remove from oven and add potatoes, onion, ½ cup (120 ml) of the fish broth, ½ teaspoon salt and pepper to taste. Cover tightly with microwave plastic wrap. Cook 9 minutes, or until potatoes are tender. Prick plastic to release steam.
3. Remove from oven and uncover. Place zucchini slices over potato mixture. Re-cover and cook for 2 minutes. Prick plastic and uncover. Arrange fish around the inside edge of the dish with chick-peas in the center in a single layer. Scatter lemon wedges over all, then re-cover and cook for 3 minutes. Prick plastic wrap.
4. Remove from oven and uncover. Sprinkle chopped coriander over all and gently stir to combine. Keep warm while preparing couscous.

5. Combine water with remaining fish broth and ½ teaspoon salt in an 11×8×2-inch (28×20×5-cm) rectangular glass or ceramic dish. Cover and cook for 4 minutes 30 seconds. Prick plastic wrap. Remove from oven and uncover. Add instant couscous and re-cover. Allow to stand for 10 minutes, or until all liquid has been absorbed, or use hot liquid to cook regular couscous as on page 180.

6. To serve, fluff couscous with a fork to remove lumps. Mound couscous in a ring on a serving platter, with fish and vegetables in the center.

FOR 400- TO 500-WATT OVENS

To serve 6. Cook spices as in Step 1 for 2 minutes. In Step 2 cook for 15 minutes. Add zucchini, re-cover and cook for 4 minutes more. Prick plastic wrap and add fish, chick-peas and lemon wedges. Re-cover and cook for 7 minutes 30 seconds. Continue as in Step 5, boiling liquid on top of the stove and preparing couscous according to package directions.

Microwave Cooking of Shellfish

Shellfish cook as well as fish in the microwave oven. They are a good bet for the weight-loss dieter because they are low in calories. Nevertheless, they shouldn't be eaten in overwhelming quantities since they tend to be relatively high in cholesterol. Relative, that is, to their weight. They don't weigh terribly much. If you follow these recipes, you won't have any problems and you will benefit from many minerals. They won't all show up in the listings, since—I'm sorry to say—there aren't RDAs for all of them; but the seas are full of minerals that pass through the shellfish.

It is important to buy good shellfish. See page 227 for possible health hazards. Their quality will also influence the way they taste. Pick and choose.

MUSSELS

Mussels from various parts of the world have different-colored shells, from brown to black to purple and even green. They also come in many sizes. To tell you the sizes used in the recipes, I describe how many there are to a pound. If your mussels are smaller, they may take a little less time to open; if they are larger, they may take a little longer. You will be able to watch them through the plastic wrap or through a glass lid; when they open they are cooked. If they are not open, let them cook a minute or so longer. If one or two fail to open, discard them.

When you buy mussels, they should be tightly closed, or when you squeeze them shut they should close tightly and stay that way when the shell halves are pinched together. Discard any that are open and any that feel weirdly heavy; they may contain sand. The best mussels—worth paying extra for—are farmed and come to you very clean. If you cannot get clean mussels and cannot convince the fish person to clean them for you, wash them one by one under cold running water and scrub with a plastic scrubbing pad or a stiff brush. If there is a fibrous beard sticking out of the shell, scrape it off by running the blade of a sharp paring knife along the edge of the shell and giving the beard a sharp tug between your fingers and the knife blade when you get to the sticking point.

Always refrigerate mussels until you cook them. Even if they are already cleaned, do not refrigerate them covered with water as they will lose flavor. Instead, put them in a bowl and cover them lightly with a damp towel—it can be paper.

A large quantity of mussels should be cooked by standing them on their hinge ends in a container just large enough to hold them with just enough space around each one so that they can open. A lesser amount of mussels can be cooked lying flat. Liquid may or may not be added to the cooking dish, as you wish. When the mussels are cooked, if you want to serve the liquor, strain it through a damp cheesecloth-lined sieve.

It is hard to give exact yields for mussel meat, and hence nutritional values. A large shell may contain a small mussel while a smaller shell is bursting with meat; but mussels are so low in calories that a little miscalculation will not hurt.

PER 4-OUNCE (113.5-G) SERVING OF MUSSELS, MEAT ONLY: 109 calories; 57 milligrams cholesterol; 2 grams fat; 330 milligrams sodium; 16 grams protein (33% RDA)

YIELD: Each 2 pounds (900 g) of mussels in the shell will give about 1 cup (240 ml) mussel liquid and 1½ cups (355 ml) chopped mussel meat.

There are many other mussel recipes in this book. Look in the Index for ideas. Most mussel dishes can be served as either a first course or a main course, depending on the size of the portion.

Scrape beards from scrubbed mussels,
tugging firmly with a knife.
Arrange mussels hinge end down in
the dish.

Cook mussels (16–18 per pound; 450 g) standing up, hinge end down; cover tightly with microwave plastic wrap.

1 pound (450 g) mussels, in a 2½-quart (2.5-l) soufflé dish
650- to 700-watt oven: 3 min.
400- to 500-watt oven: 6 min.

2 pounds (900 g) mussels with ¾ cup (180 ml) liquid in a 2½-quart (2.5-l) soufflé dish
650- to 700-watt oven: 8 min.
400- to 500-watt oven: 12 min.

2 pounds (900 g) mussels, in a 2½-quart (2.5-l) soufflé dish
650- to 700-watt oven: 7 min.
400- to 500-watt oven: 10 min.

4 pounds (1.8 kg) mussels, in a 5-quart (5-l) casserole
650- to 700-watt oven: 15 min.
400- to 500-watt oven: Not recommended

CLAMS

Clams come in all sizes, from the tiniest of Atlantic Coast cherrystones to the giant geoduck clams of the Pacific. Manila clams in Seattle have pretty striped shells, as do the small Capri clams used for making pasta alla vongole; but the Italian clams are smaller, the shells flatter. There are also soft-shell clams, mainly used for steaming. They have long black siphons sticking out of their shells.

Hard-shell clams are cleaned and stored as mussels are (above); but they have no beards to remove. Raw clams are delicious once you have learned how to open them, or if you can find a nearby source for opened clams. Clams spoil quickly when opened and should be kept in the refrigerator packed on top of ice. I prefer smaller clams for eating raw. Avoid salty cocktail sauces. Try them with just a squeeze of lemon juice, or add a dollop of horseradish, freshly grated or prepared, or combine a little red wine vinegar with some finely chopped shallots and freshly ground black pepper.

Atlantic hard-shell clams are graded by size. Littlenecks, the smallest hard-shell clams, are young and ideally should be no more than 1½ inches (4 cm) across, but you will find them up to 2 inches. Save the very smallest to eat raw—they are too good to cook. The medium-sized, middle-aged cherrystones are about 3 inches (7.5 cm) across.

Steamers must be washed in several changes of cold water.

PER 4-OUNCE (113.5-G) SERVING OF CLAMS, MEAT ONLY: 91 calories; 57 milligrams cholesterol; 1 gram fat; 233 milligrams sodium; 13 grams protein 27% RDA)

YIELDS: 1½ pounds (680 g) steamers give ⅓ to ½ cup (80 to 120 ml) meat; 3 pounds (1.4 kg) littlenecks give ¾ cup (180 ml) meat; 5 pounds (2.3 kg) cherrystones give 1¾ cups (410 ml) meat.

Cook clams in a single layer, placed hinge-end down in a dish 2 inches (5 cm) deep. Cover tightly with microwave plastic wrap. Clams are cooked as soon as they open; they don't have to gape. If using a 400- to 500-watt oven, cook in batches of no more than 14 clams.

STEAMERS, 12 PER POUND (450 G) If using a 400- to 500- watt oven, cook in batches of no more than 14 clams.

14 clams
650- to 700-watt oven: 4 min.
400- to 500-watt oven: 6 min.

36 clams
650- to 700-watt oven: 6 min.
400- to 500-watt oven: Not recommended

18 clams
650- to 700-watt oven: 4 min.
400- to 500-watt oven: Not recommended

36 clams on two dishes, using a rack
650- to 700-watt oven: 8 min.
400- to 500-watt oven: Not recommended

LITTLENECKS, 8 TO 10 PER POUND (450 G)

6 clams
650- to 700-watt oven: 2 min. 30 sec. to 3
   min. 30 sec.
400- to 500-watt oven: 4 min.

24 clams, 3 pounds (1.4 kg)
650- to 700-watt oven: 7 min.
400- to 500-watt oven: 10 min.

12 clams, 1½ pounds (680 g)
650- to 700-watt oven: 4 min.
400- to 500-watt oven: 6 min.

48 clams, 6 pounds (2.8 kg)
650- to 700-watt oven: 11 min.
400- to 500-watt oven: Not recommended

SHRIMP

For notes on buying shrimp, see page 228. Seafood vendors estimate large shrimp as coming twenty to twenty-four to the pound in the shell. Medium shrimp come twenty-four to twenty-eight to the pound. Smaller shrimp can be used as well. Jumbo shrimp will require different cooking times. All the weights in these recipes are given on the basis of shrimp in the shell. If you are buying shelled shrimp, remember that each half-pound—eight ounces (227 g)—in the shell is only seven ounces (200 g) shelled.

If you buy shrimp in the shell, most of these recipes other than that for Cajun Shrimp Boil require that you shell them. Rarely will you get shrimp with the heads on. If you do, pull the heads off first and rinse them well and set them aside; they are too good to waste. The heads can be frozen if you don't have time to deal with them. Hold a shrimp between the fingers and elongated thumb of one hand with the frondy bottoms facing out. With your other hand, grasp the fronds the same way and pull them off, starting at the head end and moving toward the tail. Now it will be easy to pull off the shells. You can remove the tail portion or not, as you wish.

The shells and heads, if you have them, can be frozen or cooked immediately to make shrimp broth which is wonderful in seafood soups.

Most people prefer to remove the sometimes dark strip that lies under the skin along the back of the shrimp. With a small sharp knife, make an incision the whole length of the back of the shrimp. A thumbnail or the tip of the knife can easily scrape off the thin dark line.

Some recipes call for butterflying the shrimp. They will cook more quickly and look bigger, which may be desirable to the weight-loss dieter. Lay the shelled shrimp, tail on, flat on its side on a work surface. Hold the shrimp flat with your extended fingers. With a sharp knife cut the shrimp almost in half with the knife held parallel to the work surface. Cut from the head end toward the tail end. Leave the shrimp just sufficiently attached at the tail so that the two sides can open out like a book but remain attached only at the end.

Shrimp can also be grilled, broiled and boiled, either in or out of the shell. To boil, bring a large amount of either plain water or seasoned liquid to a boil. Put in the shrimp all at once. Stir; bring liquid back to a boil; cover the pot; turn off the heat and allow to sit for at least five minutes, until pink. Do not use salt, which will toughen the shrimp. Grill shrimp either whole in the shell or butterflied in the shell, shell side down. The shells help protect the shrimp. Broil shrimp as you grill them; but in the case of shrimp butterflied in the shell, have the meat face the flame so that all the juices are retained. Shrimp to be grilled or broiled may be brushed with a little olive oil, lemon juice and garlic.

PER 4 OUNCES (113.5 G) SHELLED SHRIMP: 104 calories; 171 milligrams cholesterol; 2 grams fat; 251 milligrams sodium; 21 grams protein (47% RDA)

Shrimp Cooking Times

When cooking shrimp en masse, not arranged on a plate in a single layer, shake the cooking dish halfway through the cooking time to redistribute them for even cooking. Cover the dish tightly with microwave plastic wrap.

SHRIMP IN THE SHELL

¼ pound (113.5 g), in a 9-inch (23-cm) pie plate
650- to 700-watt oven: 1 min.
400- to 500-watt oven: 1 min. 30 sec.

½ pound (227 g), in a 9-inch (23-cm) pie plate
650- to 700-watt oven: 2 min.
400- to 500-watt oven: 2 min. 30 sec.

¾ pound (340 g), in a 1½-quart (1.5-l) soufflé dish
650- to 700-watt oven: 3 min. to 3 min. 30 sec.
400- to 500-watt oven: 4 min. 30 sec.

1 pound (450 g), in a 2½-quart (2.5-l) soufflé dish
650- to 700-watt oven: 3 min., stirring twice
400- to 500-watt oven: 7 min., stirring twice

2 pounds (900 g), in a 14 × 11 × 2-inch (35.5 × 28 × 5-cm) rectangular dish
650- to 700-watt oven: 5 min.
400- to 500-watt oven: Not recommended

6 pounds (2.8 kg), in a 5-quart (5-l) soufflé dish
650- to 700-watt oven: 20 min., stirring 3 times
400- to 500-watt oven: Not recommended

SHELLED SHRIMP

¼ pound (113.5 g), in a 9-inch (23-cm) pie plate
650- to 700-watt oven: 1 min.
400- to 500-watt oven: 1 min. 30 sec.

½ pound (227 g), in a 9-inch (23-cm) pie plate
650- to 700-watt oven: 2 min.
400- to 500-watt oven: 3 min., stirring twice

¾ pound (340 g), in a 1½-quart (1.5-l) soufflé dish
650- to 700-watt oven: 2–3 min.
400- to 500-watt oven: 4 min., stirring twice

1 pound (450 g), in a 2½-quart (2.5-l) soufflé dish
650- to 700-watt oven: 3 min.
400- to 500-watt oven: 5 min., stirring twice

2 pounds (900 g), in a 14 × 11 × 2-inch (35.5 × 28 × 5-cm) dish
650- to 700-watt oven: 3–4 min.
400- to 500-watt oven: Not recommended

BUTTERFLIED SHRIMP

¼ pound (113.5 g), in a 9-inch (23-cm) pie plate
650- to 700-watt oven: 25–30 sec.
400- to 500-watt oven: 45 sec.

½ pound (227 g), in a 9-inch (23-cm) pie plate
650- to 700-watt oven: 1 min. to 1 min. 30 sec.
400- to 500-watt oven: Not recommended

¾ pound (340 g), in a 1½ quart (1.5-l) soufflé dish
650- to 700-watt oven: 2–3 min.
400- to 500-watt oven: Not recommended

If using shrimp whole, make a slit down the back to remove vein.

Pull out vein.

With shrimp on a flat surface, hold lightly with fingers and cut parallel to work surface, leaving shrimp intact at tail end. Spread halves apart to butterfly.

SCALLOPS

Unfortunately we buy most of our scallops out of their beautiful shells, which are the symbol of Catholic pilgrims. If you do find scallops in the shell, wash them well and place them in the microwave oven just until they open. They can be freed from the shell with a small knife. Both the white-to-beige meat and quarter-moon-shaped pink-to-coral roe are delicious.

The scallops that we get out of the shell are commonly called sea or bay. However, scallops are of many different kinds and qualities. Although similar in size, the fingernail-sized white bay scallops of the north Atlantic are infinitely more tender and delicate in flavor than the beige calico scallops. Sea scallops also vary in size. The best are translucent, white and about one and a half inches in diameter.

Note that scallops rarely have a fishy smell; but they will develop an overly sweet smell if they are overage.

Even though the scallops that we get out of the shell are cleaned and, sadly, most have had their roes removed, there remains one small chore that is not essential but is preferable for the very best results. If you look at a scallop carefully, you will notice a thin strip of muscle running down the side. This strip has a tougher texture than that of the main muscle. Pull it off.

Scallops are also often eaten raw although marinated in an acid—lemon or lime juice—or wine long enough so that they appear to be cooked. They turn from translucent to opaque. Seviche (page 415) is one of the most common preparations.

PER 4 OUNCES (113.5 G) SCALLOPS: 128 calories; 61 milligrams cholesterol; 1 gram fat; 303 milligrams sodium; 26 grams protein (58% RDA)

CRABS

I am, unfortunately, extremely allergic to crab. Based on memories of a time when I could still eat crab, I can develop recipes; but I must depend on others to taste them. Since they are very expensive, I feel a little less sheepish about giving you so few recipes.

The very largest crabs have meat in their legs; smaller crabs, such as the Maryland blue crabs, don't. Crabs can be bought whole and as crabmeat. The best meat is fresh, vacuum-packed and refrigerated; but it can also be bought frozen or canned. All picked crabmeat should be rinsed and carefully gone over with the fingers to remove any remaining shell and cartilage.

Some whole crabs can be bought in their adolescent state; that is, before the shell has hardened. They are called soft-shell crabs. Other crabs are bought whole—in their hard shell—or only as legs. Do not let a store confuse you with imitation crab legs made from a ground-up fish paste called surimi.

Try to get the fish seller to clean the crabs for you. If you must do it yourself, consult a good manual. Do not discard the eggs, which are a prized enricher of sauces.

Simply cooked and spiced hard-shell crabs—best cooked in the microwave oven without water—can make a crab feast. Serve at an informal gathering. Provide sheets of newspaper on which each person can crack and pick their crabs. Provide hammers for cracking the shells and picks for getting at the meat. Serve with Egg White Mayonnaise (page 482) or Rouïlle (page 484), wedges of lemon and Coleslaw (page 394). Light beer and damp towels for hand-wiping are a good idea.

PER 4 OUNCES (113.5 G) CRABMEAT: 105 calories; 114 milligrams cholesterol; 2 grams fat; 239 milligrams sodium; 20 grams protein (43% RDA)

YIELD: One 4-ounce (113.5-g) hard-shell crab gives 0.6 ounce (16 g) meat.

Hard-shell Crab Cooking Times

WHOLE HARD-SHELL CRABS, 3 TO 4 PER POUND (450 G) Cook at 100% in a knotted microwave plastic bag.

6 crabs
650- to 700-watt oven: 9 min.
450- to 500-watt oven: 14 min.

12 crabs
650- to 700-watt oven: 15 min.
450- to 500-watt oven: 20 min.

24 crabs
650- to 700-watt oven: 25 min.
450- to 500-watt oven: 33 min. (Take bag out of oven and shake it gently after cooking for 15 min. Return to oven and finish cooking for 18 min. more.)

LOBSTER

People seem to have serious problems with the cooking of live lobsters, which is the best way to cook them. I have read dozens of differing suggestions about the kindest way of proceeding. Some people suggest starting the lobsters in cold water and slowly bringing it to a boil. This is odd when you consider that lobsters drown in fresh water. Others say to plunge the lobster headfirst into boiling water. Somewhere an article appeared saying that by stroking the top of the lobster's shell, the lobster is soothed into a sleepy and less-anguished state. The French and Chinese regularly stick a knife or skewer between the lobster's eyes or sever the head from the body with a knife. I have done this and can, but consider it unpleasant, as the extremely primitive lobster keeps on wiggling.

After consulting with experts at many aquariums, it seems clear that, while no one knows how a lobster feels, the quickest death is deemed to be preferable. Consequently, knowing full well that some will be offended, I offer suggestions for the microwave cooking of lobsters. They stop moving and turn red much more quickly than with any other cooking method that I know. Despite my admitted prejudice and many people's revulsion, this is probably the kindest way to go about the whole thing. Lobsters may vary in color when alive; but all are red when cooked.

The microwave oven is not a suitable place to cook large lobsters or many lobsters for a large lobster dinner. You will choose your own way; but do not overcook the lobsters since they dry out and toughen.

These recipes and cooking times were developed for *Homarus gammarus* or *Homarus americanus,* the so-called Maine lobster or Atlantic lobster. Spiny lobsters will take longer because of their harder shells.

PER 4 OUNCES (113.5 G) LOBSTER, MEAT ONLY: 104 calories; 88 milligrams cholesterol; 2 grams fat; 240 milligrams sodium; 19 grams protein (42% RDA)

YIELD: Each 1¼-pound (570-g) lobster will give about ¼ pound (113.5 g) of meat at 104 calories.

Lobster Cooking Times

Place in microwavable plastic cooking bags and knot loosely. Cook at 100% power. Remove bag from oven. Slit the bag with a sharp knife or cut with a scissors. Remove lobsters. They will be very hot.

One lobster (1¼ pounds; 570 g)
650- to 700-watt oven: 5 min.
400- to 500-watt oven: 8 min.

Two lobsters (each 1¼ pounds; 570 g)
650- to 700-watt oven: 8 min.
400- to 500-watt oven: Not recommended

Three lobsters (each 1¼ pounds; 570 g)
650- to 700-watt oven: 11 min.
400- to 500-watt oven: Not recommended

Once lobster is cooked, it can be served with a variety of sauces. Take your pick of those on pages 500–506 or serve it with melted butter and wedges of lemon. Butter may be disappearing from our lives; but lobster is not an everyday occurrence and it does taste wonderful with butter.

SHELLING LOBSTER

If you don't want to serve lobster in the shell, which is messy, the meat will have to come out of it. All this can be done ahead of time and the final cooking done just before you are ready to serve. Taking the meat out of the shell permits you to serve less than a whole lobster per person, which is good for reducing weight, cholesterol and expense.

Pick up the cooked lobster. If you are shelling a hot lobster, hold it in a cloth. Work over a bowl to catch juices. Hold the back of the body in one hand and the back of the head in the other. Twist hands in opposite directions while pulling to separate the head from the tail.

With a heavy, sharp kitchen shears, cut the tail in half lengthwise from the head end to the tail end. The meat can now be pulled out easily with a fork. If you are lucky, or know how to pick female lobsters—their top pair of tiny legs at the head end of the tail will be crossed demurely and are soft—there may well be a bright red strip of cooked roe. Alternatively, the tail meat can, with a little practice, be removed whole. Twist off the center pieces of the fan at the end of the tail. This will expose the flesh, which can be pushed out with a finger toward the open head end of the tail. Reserve the tail meat.

Again working over a bowl, twist off the claws from the head. Twist off the small part of the claw, which looks like a thumb. Twist off the two small segments of claw, the knuckles, which are attached to the head. If they won't come off, you may have to cut them off. Move the claw to a cutting board. With a heavy knife or a nutcracker, crack the shell of each part of the claw. Remove the meat. Feel the largest claw piece for the large flat piece of cartilage. Remove it, trying not to break up the meat too much. Reserve the claw meat.

Now pick up the head and again work over your bowl. Hold the smooth, bright-red part of the head shell in one hand. With the other hand pull out the bottom of the head. The shell part will contain the green tomalley and a creamy white substance. Do not discard these. Scrape them out into a bowl with a spoon. The only thing that isn't edible is a grit sac at the very top of the head shell. Don't worry, it's hard to get out; but don't try.

The remaining feathery inside of the other half of the head and the small claws are not usually thought to be edible. When I get a whole lobster, they are my favorite part of the lobster. I tear them apart and suck them to get really sensational flavors. Do this only with true lobster aficionados. They will be doing the same thing.

Cooks who do not worry about their diets make lobster butter and bisque with the chopped or ground-up shells. The shells are simmered with butter or cream for about thirty minutes; the mixture is then put through a fine sieve. The shells are discarded and the rich sauce is kept. I warned you.

MUSSELS IN WINE

This is a very light main course, light in calories and protein. That should be your clue to serve a substantial first course such as The Slender Greek (page 85), and to eat some good whole wheat bread. Slim as this meal may be, it provides lots of iron, phosphorus and substantial potassium. If you can buy clean farm mussels, this is a very quick meal with a robust flavor. To clean mussels, see pages 263–264.   *SERVES 2 AS A MAIN COURSE*

Per 15-mussel serving (about 1 pound; 450 g) with ½ cup (120 ml) sauce: 127 calories; 37 milligrams cholesterol; 3 grams fat; 381 milligrams sodium; 16 grams protein (36% RDA); 8 grams carbohydrate

RDA: phosphorus 28%; iron 33%; 512 milligrams potassium

2 pounds (900 g) small mussels, scrubbed and debearded (about 15 mussels per pound)
½ cup (120 ml) white wine

4 cloves garlic, smashed and peeled
¾ teaspoon dried tarragon
¼ teaspoon dried thyme

1. Place mussels, hinge end down, in a 2½-quart (2.5-l) soufflé dish or casserole with a tightly fitted lid. Add remaining ingredients. Cover tightly with microwave plastic wrap or casserole lid. Cook at 100% for 8 minutes, or until mussels open, in a 650- to 700-watt oven. If using plastic wrap, prick to release steam.

2. Remove from oven. Uncover and remove mussels to a serving dish. Strain liquid through a fine sieve. Pour over mussels and serve.

FOR 400- TO 500-WATT OVENS

To serve 2. Cook as in Step 1 for 12 minutes or until mussels open.

CLANS IN TOMATO SAUCE

*T*his Neapolitan-style dish used to be a hallmark of American Italian restaurants before we got so sophisticated. It is practically instantaneous if you keep the tomato sauce on hand. If you like your food spicier, add two smashed, peeled and chopped cloves of garlic and a sprinkling of hot red pepper flakes. See page 000 for buying and cleaning clams.

This makes a simple main course for one or more. Extremely high in iron and suitably accompanied by vitamin C, it is low in calories and protein and even cholesterol. The clams can be preceded by Artichoke Bottoms Stuffed with Duxelles (page 100) and served with crusty bread to mop up the sauce. This is the day to choose a festive dessert or to eat a piece of cheese with your fruit. Enjoy a glass of red or white wine if you like. Larger and more active people and those not trying to lose weight can add extra bread, a Watercress, Fennel and Romaine Salad with Pernod Dressing (page 405) and Meringue Clouds (page 585) to go with the fruit.   *SERVES 1 AS A MAIN COURSE, 2 AS A FIRST COURSE*

Per 12-clam serving with ½ cup (120 ml) sauce: 179 calories; 61 milligrams cholesterol; 4 grams fat; 448 milligrams sodium; 24 grams protein (54% RDA); 11.5 grams carbohydrate

RDA: calcium 12%; phosphorus 35%; iron 145%; riboflavin 26%; niacin 23%; vitamin C 31%

1 dozen littleneck clams, shells intact   ½ cup (120 ml) Tomato Sauce
   (about 1½ pounds; 680 g)   Casalinga (page 167)

1. Combine clams and sauce in a 2½-quart (2.5-l) soufflé dish or casserole with a tightly fitted lid. Cover tightly with microwave plastic wrap or casserole lid. Cook at 100% for 4 minutes in a 650- to 700-watt oven. If using plastic wrap, prick to release steam.
2. Remove from oven and uncover. Serve hot.

To serve 2 as a main course, 4 as a first course. Use 2 dozen littleneck clams (3 pounds; 1.4 kg) and 1 cup (240 ml) sauce. Combine clams and sauce in a 2½-quart (2.5-l) soufflé dish or casserole. Cook as in Step 1 for 7 minutes, stirring once.

To serve 4 as a main course, 8 as a first course. Use 4 dozen littleneck clams (6 pounds; 2.8 kg) and 2 cups (470 ml) sauce. Combine clams and sauce in a 14 × 11 × 2-inch (35.5 × 28 × 5-cm) rectangular dish. Cook as in Step 1 for 11 minutes, stirring twice.

To serve 1. Cook for 6 minutes, stirring once.

To serve 2. Cook for 10 minutes, stirring once.

CLAMS WITH BLACK BEANS

I've had this dish many times in Chinese restaurants. It's one of my favorites and makes a good diet main course as well. Serve with one-half cup (120 ml) of cooked white rice per person for a happy, iron-rich evening. If salt is not a problem, I suggest you double the black beans.

Since this dish is not heavy in protein, you could start the meal with Hearty Chick-pea Soup (page 135) or a simple salad. Even if you add a dessert, this will make a light meal, so it's a good choice for a day when work or pleasure may have provided a large lunch.   *SERVES 1 AS A MAIN COURSE, 2 AS A FIRST COURSE*

Per 12-clam serving with ⅔ cup (160 ml) sauce: 109 calories; 36 milligrams cholesterol; 1 gram fat; 209 milligrams sodium; 15 grams protein (34% RDA); 9 grams carbohydrate

RDA: calcium 10%; phosphorus 21%; iron 88%; vitamin A 54%; vitamin C 44%

1 teaspoon salted Chinese black beans
3 scallions, trimmed and sliced (⅓ cup; 80 ml)
¼ cup (60 ml) fresh coriander leaves, coarsely chopped
3 cloves garlic, smashed, peeled and chopped

2½-inch (9-cm) strip lemon zest
¼ cup (60 ml) water
Freshly ground black pepper, to taste
1 dozen littleneck clams (about 1½ pounds; 680 g), scrubbed

1. Place black beans, scallions, coriander, garlic, lemon zest, water and pepper in a 2½-quart (2.5-l) soufflé dish or casserole with a tightly fitted lid. Stir to combine. Arrange clams, hinge end down, over mixture. Cover tightly with microwave plastic wrap or casserole lid. Cook at 100% for 4 minutes in a 650- to 700-watt oven. If using plastic wrap, prick to release steam.
2. Remove from oven and uncover. Serve in a wide soup bowl.

To serve 2 as a main course, 4 as a first course. Use 2 teaspoons salted Chinese black beans, 6 scallions, ½ cup (120 ml) chopped fresh coriander leaves, 6 cloves garlic, 2 strips lemon zest, ½ cup (120 ml) water, freshly ground pepper to taste and 2 dozen littleneck clams (3 pounds; 1.4 kg). Follow Step 1 and cook for 7 minutes, stirring once.

(continued)

To serve 4 as a main course, 8 as a first course. Use 4 teaspoons salted Chinese black beans, 12 scallions, 1 cup (240 ml) chopped fresh coriander leaves, 12 cloves garlic, 4 strips lemon zest, 1 cup (240 ml) water, freshly ground pepper to taste and 4 dozen littlenecks (6 pounds; 2.8 kg). Follow Step 1 and cook for 11 minutes, stirring once.

FOR 400- TO 500-WATT OVENS

To serve 1. Cook for 6 minutes, stirring once.

To serve 2. Cook for 10 minutes, stirring once.

CREAMY BAKED SHRIMP WITH PEPPERS

*T*hese attractive individual portions of shrimp are an alternative to a frozen diet main course, take no more time than defrosting one and are better for you. Consider starting with Celery Soup (page 122) or a cooked artichoke (page 99). Lemon Bavarian (page 561) or fruit finishes up the meal, which has few enough calories so that you can have some wine or a snack before dinner.   SERVES 2

Per serving: 177 calories; 149 milligrams cholesterol; 4 grams fat; 251 milligrams sodium; 25 grams protein (55% RDA); 9 grams carbohydrate

RDA: calcium 22%; phosphorus 33%; iron 16%; vitamin A 31%; niacin 13%; vitamin C 116%

2 teaspoons cornstarch
½ cup (120 ml) skim milk
¼ teaspoon fennel seeds
¼ teaspoon kosher salt
¼ teaspoon hot red pepper sauce
1½ ounces (42.5 g) green bell pepper strips (about ⅓ cup; 80 ml)
1½ ounces (42.5 g) red bell pepper strips (about ⅓ cup; 80 ml)

8 ounces (227 g) large shrimp, peeled, deveined and halved lengthwise (see illustration on page 268)
1 ounce (28 g) part-skim mozzarella, grated (¼ cup; 60 ml)
1 teaspoon fresh lemon juice

1. Combine cornstarch and milk in a 4-cup (1-l) glass measure, stirring well to dissolve cornstarch completely. Stir in fennel seeds, salt, pepper sauce and green and red pepper strips. Cover tightly with microwave plastic wrap. Cook at 100% for 3 minutes in a 650- to 700-watt oven, stirring once halfway through cooking. Prick plastic to release steam.

2. Remove from oven and uncover. Add shrimp and cheese and stir well to combine. Divide mixture between two round 5 × 1-inch (12.5 × 2.5-cm) minia-

ture quiche dishes. Place on either side of the oven and cook uncovered for 2 minutes 30 seconds, rotating the dishes by 180° halfway through cooking.

3. Remove from oven. Stir ½ teaspoon lemon juice into each dish and let stand for several minutes before serving.

To serve 1. Use 1 teaspoon cornstarch, ¼ cup (60 ml) skim milk, pinches of fennel seeds and salt, dash hot red pepper sauce, ¾ ounce (21 g) green bell pepper strips, ¾ ounce (21 g) red bell pepper strips, 4 ounces (113.5 g) medium shrimp, ½ ounce (14 g) part-skim mozzarella (about 1 tablespoon), and ½ teaspoon lemon juice. Combine cornstarch and milk in a 2-cup (470-ml) glass measure. Cook, covered, as in Step 1 for 1 minute. Follow Step 2 and pour into a round 5 × 1-inch (12.5 × 2.5-cm) miniature quiche dish. Place in center of oven and cook, uncovered, for 1 minute. Finish as in Step 3.

FOR 400- TO 500-WATT OVENS

To serve 2. Follow Step 1 and cook for 5 minutes. Continue with Step 2 and cook for 5 minutes, rotating dishes after 2 minutes 30 seconds. Finish as in Step 3.

To serve 1. Follow Step 1 and cook for 3 minutes. Continue with Step 2 and cook for 2 minutes 30 seconds to 3 minutes, or until shrimp are cooked through. Finish as in Step 3.

Peel pepper with a vegetable peeler.

Remove core with a knife.

Cut out ribs.

Slice into strips.

ORIENTAL SHRIMP

If you make Oriental Glaze, it keeps virtually indefinitely if refrigerated and can be used on any simple fish. Here, it is used to cook quickly some tasty shrimp. Add one cup of cooked rice, a salad and some fruit for a gratifying dinner. Use cooking times for butterflied shrimp (page 268) to prepare this recipe for more than one, and use one tablespoon of glaze for each portion.   *SERVES 1*

Per 4-ounce (113.5-g) serving shrimp with 1 tablespoon glaze: 119 calories; 171 milligrams cholesterol; 2 grams fat; 663 milligrams sodium; 19 grams protein (43% RDA); 4 grams carbohydrate

RDA: phosphorus 20%; iron 13%; niacin 13%

4 ounces (113.5 g) large shrimp, 1 tablespoon Oriental Glaze (page 512)
   shelled, deveined and butterflied

1. Combine shrimp and glaze in a small bowl and toss to coat.
2. Place shrimp in a single layer on a deep rimmed dinner plate or pie plate and cover tightly with microwave plastic wrap. Cook at 100% for 1 minute in a 650- to 700-watt oven. Prick plastic wrap to release steam.
3. Remove from oven and serve hot.

FOR 400- TO 500-WATT OVENS

To serve 1. Cook for 2 minutes.

SHRIMP MEXICAN

*I*f you have Red Pepper Purée on hand, this is a virtually instantaneous dish—two and a half minutes to cook and no more than five minutes to prepare. If you want to serve rice with this (one-half cup [120 ml] per person), make sure to start it well before the shrimp. The rice will wait; the shrimp won't. If you need to make Red Pepper Purée, allow six to seven minutes more time. You will have a half-cup (120-ml) dividend for another meal. *SERVES 2*

Per 6- to 9-shrimp—depending on size—serving with ¼ cup (60 ml) sauce: 151 calories; 186 milligrams cholesterol; 2 grams fat; 191 milligrams sodium; 26 grams protein (57% RDA); 6 grams carbohydrate

RDA: phosphorus 27%; iron 22%; 410 milligrams potassium; vitamin A 91%; niacin 18%; vitamin C 248%

½ cup (120 ml) Red Pepper Purée
  (page 500)
4 drops hot red pepper sauce, or to
  taste
⅔ pound (300 g) extra-large (18–20
  count) or large (20–24 count)
  shrimp, peeled and deveined

10 leaves fresh coriander
1½ teaspoons fresh lime juice

1. In a 9-inch (23-cm) quiche dish or pie plate, stir together pepper purée and hot pepper sauce. Arrange shrimp on the sauce with tails pointing toward the center. Strew coriander over the shrimp and sprinkle with lime juice. Cover tightly with microwave plastic wrap.

2. Cook at 100% for 2 minutes 30 seconds, or until shrimp are pink, in a 650- to 700-watt oven. Prick plastic to release steam. Remove from oven and serve immediately.

FOR 400- TO 500-WATT OVENS

To serve 2. Cook for 4 minutes 30 seconds.

CHINESE SHRIMP AND BROCCOLI

*T*his is not trendy, specific Chinese, but rather an anybody-can-like-it, light but copious Chinese dish. It may not be ideal for salt-watchers. Serve one-half cup (120 ml) of rice per person to catch all the good sauce. Remember, chopsticks will slow the eaters down. Consider Eggplant Purée with Lemon and Chives (page 89) as a first course. Fresh fruit with a piece of cheese or Creamy Custard (page 510) makes a calcium-rich dessert to balance the meal.   *SERVES 4*

Per 1¼-cup (300-ml) serving: 176 calories; 140 milligrams cholesterol; 4 grams fat; 656 milligrams sodium; 22 grams protein (50% RDA); 13 grams carbohydrate

RDA: phosphorus 26%; iron 17%; 490 milligrams potassium; niacin 20%; vitamin C 65%

1 ounce (28 g) dried shiitake
   mushrooms, stems removed
1½ cups (355 ml) water
1 ounce (28 g) peeled ginger, grated (2
   tablespoons)
4 cloves garlic, smashed and peeled
2 teaspoons vegetable oil

½ pound (225 g) broccoli florets (about
   5½ cups; 1.3 l)
2 teaspoons cornstarch
¼ cup (60 ml) rice wine vinegar
2 tablespoons tamari soy
1 pound (450 g) large shrimp (20–24
   count), peeled and deveined

1. Place shiitakes and ½ cup (120 ml) of the water in a 2½-quart (2.5-l) soufflé dish or casserole with a tightly fitted lid. Cover tightly with microwave plastic wrap or casserole lid. Cook at 100% for 3 minutes in a 650- to 700-watt oven, stirring once halfway through cooking. If using plastic wrap, prick to release steam.

2. Remove from oven and uncover. Drain mushrooms, rinse and cut into ¼-inch (.5-cm) strips. Reserve.

3. Place ginger, garlic and oil in the soufflé dish or casserole. Cook, uncovered, for 3 minutes. Add broccoli and toss to coat. Cover tightly and cook for 2 minutes. Prick plastic wrap.

4. Remove from oven and uncover. Stir together cornstarch, remaining 1 cup (240 ml) of the water, vinegar and soy in a small bowl. Stir into broccoli mixture along with reserved mushrooms. Scatter shrimp on top. Cover tightly and cook for 5 minutes, stirring mixture twice during cooking. Prick plastic wrap.

5. Remove from oven and uncover. Serve hot.

FOR 400- TO 500-WATT OVENS

To serve 4. Follow Step 1 and cook for 5 minutes. Continue with Step 2. In Step 3, cook ginger, garlic and oil, uncovered, for 5 minutes. Add broccoli, toss to coat and cook, covered, for 4 minutes. Follow Step 4 and cook for 8 minutes.

CAJUN SHRIMP BOIL

An advantage of serving shrimp in the shell is that the time needed for peeling slows everybody down while the full flavor fills them up. The disadvantage is that there are people who are uncomfortable eating with their hands. So know your guests before you serve this. It's a terrific party dish and goes well with beer, so a variation is given for six pounds—a big party's worth. Be sure to have a bowl or a bucket around for the shells. This is also a good addition to a picnic or other outdoor party; but if you're having some barbecued meat, just taste a shrimp or two.

The obvious buddies for this are Coleslaw (page 394) and All-American Potato Salad (page 225). I would probably add Chunky Tomato Basil Salad (page 407) or Oriental Spinach Salad (page 79). Then you can put out Summer Fruit Salad (page 537) or Gingered Oranges (page 534) and Oat Bran Crisps (page 574). You can still have some light beer or Black Bean Salad (page 203).

If you have a full portion of shrimp, you will get substantial phosphorus, iron and niacin. Other nutrients will have to come from the salads and fruit or lunch and breakfast.   SERVES 4

Per 5- to 6-shrimp (113.5-g) serving: 153 calories; 210 milligrams cholesterol; 3 grams fat; 212 milligrams sodium; 28 grams protein (63% RDA); 2.5 grams carbohydrate

RDA: phosphorus 29%; iron 21%; niacin 18%

1½ teaspoons chili powder	2 cloves garlic, smashed, peeled and
½ teaspoon celery seeds	sliced
½ teaspoon oregano	Small piece bay leaf
½ teaspoon cayenne	1 pound (450 g) large shrimp (20–24
½ teaspoon paprika	count)
¼ teaspoon dried thyme	1 teaspoon kosher salt, optional
Pinch ground allspice	

1. Combine all ingredients in a 2½-quart (2.5-l) soufflé dish or casserole with a tightly fitted lid. Cover tightly with microwave plastic wrap or lid. Cook at 100% for 3 minutes in a 650- to 700-watt oven, stirring twice. If using plastic, prick to release steam.

2. Remove from oven and uncover. Serve hot or warm.

To serve 24. Use 3 tablespoons chili powder, 1 tablespoon celery seeds, 1 tablespoon oregano, 1 tablespoon cayenne, 1 tablespoon paprika, 1½ teaspoons

(continued)

thyme, 1 teaspoon ground allspice, 12 cloves garlic, 1 bay leaf, 6 pounds medium shrimp and 2 tablespoons kosher salt, optional. Toss all ingredients together in a 5-quart (5-l) soufflé dish or casserole with a tightly fitted lid. Cover and cook for 20 minutes, stirring 3 times.

FOR 400- TO 500-WATT OVENS

To serve 4. Cook for 7 minutes, stirring twice.

GREEN SHRIMP CURRY

I like this for parties and entertaining. It is mouth-fillingly spicy. If you prefer a less fiery taste, reduce the red pepper. The ingredient list is long; but the recipe isn't. I have one person in my family who hates coriander, and I have successfully made this with flat-leaf parsley and fresh mint substituting for the coriander.

Instead of making many courses, serve this Indian-style with some accompaniments, such as one-half cup (120 ml) brown rice and one-half cup (120 ml) Lentil Salad (page 209) per person, Pear Chutney (page 524), some raisins and slivered almonds and a tablespoon of nonfat yogurt. I put all the accompaniments into attractive bowls and let guests serve themselves. I just watch out for my portions. This is a very filling meal that I find leaves no room for anything but fruit. Iced tea with lemon juice and mint or beer are good drinks.   *SERVES 8*

Per 1⅓-cup (320-ml) serving: 220 calories; 140 milligrams cholesterol; 4 grams fat; 607 milligrams sodium; 24 grams protein (54% RDA); 23 grams carbohydrate

RDA: calcium 16%; phosphorus 30%; iron 29%; 994 milligrams potassium; vitamin A 86%; thiamin 14%; niacin 21%; vitamin C 71%

6 small onions (about ¾ pound; 340 g), peeled and quartered through the root

8 cloves garlic, smashed, peeled and slivered

4 dried red chili peppers, crumbled, or ½ teaspoon crushed red pepper flakes

½ teaspoon ground cumin

½ teaspoon ground cardamom

½ teaspoon celery seeds

½ teaspoon hot mustard powder

Large pinch ground cinnamon

1 tablespoon olive oil

¾ pound (340 g) Idaho potatoes, peeled and cut into ½-inch (1-cm) cubes (1½ cups; 355 ml)

1 cup (240 ml) plus 3 tablespoons water

¾ pound (340 g) zucchini, washed, trimmed and cut into ½-inch (1-cm) slices (about 2½ cups; 590 ml)

2 pounds (900 g) large (20–24 count) shrimp, shelled and deveined (about 28 ounces; 794 g)

1¼ pounds (570 g) fresh spinach, stemmed and washed (about 8 cups; 2 l) finely chopped in the food processor

3 ribs celery, peeled and cut across into ½-inch (1-cm) slices (1½ cups; 355 ml)

3 tablespoons cornstarch

10-ounce (284-g) box frozen peas, defrosted in a sieve under warm running water

6 ounces (170 g) fresh coriander leaves, stems removed, finely chopped (about 1 cup [240 ml] loosely packed)

6 tablespoons fresh lime or lemon juice

2 teaspoons kosher salt

1. Place onions and garlic in a 5-quart (5-l) casserole with a tightly fitted lid. Sprinkle over spices and oil. Stir to coat. Cook, uncovered, at 100% for 5 minutes in a 650- to 700-watt oven.

2. Add potatoes and 1 cup (240 ml) of the water. Cover with lid and cook for 10 minutes, stirring once after 5 minutes.

3. Add zucchini, cover and cook for 5 minutes, stirring once halfway through.

4. Stir in shrimp, spinach and celery. Combine cornstarch with remaining 3 tablespoons water in a small bowl. Stir into dish, making sure ingredients are well combined. Cover with lid and cook for 5 minutes.

5. Stir in peas and coriander. Cover and cook for 3 minutes. Remove from oven. Stir in lime or lemon juice and salt.

To serve 4. Use 3 small onions (each 2 ounces; 56 g), 4 cloves garlic, 2 dried red chilies or ¼ teaspoon crushed red pepper, ¼ teaspoon cumin, ¼ teaspoon cardamom, ¼ teaspoon celery seeds, ¼ teaspoon hot mustard powder, a pinch ground cinnamon, 1½ teaspoons olive oil, 1 medium potato (about 6 ounces; 170 g), ½ cup (120 ml) plus 4½ teaspoons water, 6 ounces (170 g) zucchini, 1 pound (450 g) shrimp, 10 ounces (284 g) fresh spinach, 1½ ribs celery, 4½ teaspoons cornstarch, 5 ounces (142 g) frozen peas, 3 ounces (85 g) fresh coriander leaves (about ½ cup [120 ml] loosely packed), 3 tablespoons lime or lemon juice and 1 teaspoon kosher salt. Combine onions, garlic, spices and oil in a 2½-quart (2.5-l) soufflé dish as in Step 1, and cook uncovered for 3 minutes. Follow Step 2, adding potatoes and ½ cup (120 ml) of the water. Cover tightly and cook for 5 minutes, stirring once. Continue with Step 3 and cook for 3 minutes. In Step 4, cook for 4 minutes. Finish as in Step 5 and cook for 1½ minutes.

FOR 400- TO 500-WATT OVENS

To serve 4. Follow Step 1 and cook for 4 minutes 30 seconds. In Step 2, cook for 7 minutes 30 seconds. In Step 3 cook for 4 minutes 30 seconds. Continue with Step 4 and cook for 6 minutes 30 seconds. Finish as in Step 5 and cook for 2 minutes 15 seconds.

SCALLOPS SORRENTO

I don't have too many scallop recipes in this book, since really good scallops are hard to find. If you do find some, then this is immediate gratification. If you don't have Tomato Sauce Casalinga on hand, you can make this with a bottled tomato sauce; but it will have more salt and slightly more calories.

This is a quick dinner. The easiest way to round it out is to put one ounce of dry linguine that has been cooked and tossed with one-half teaspoon of olive oil in the center of each dish of scallops before cooking. Follow with a large green salad tossed with one tablespoon per person of Garlic Oregano Dressing (page 489). Finish up with a good dessert like Honey Baked Apples (page 551), which can cook while you eat. Since this is skinny in calories and moderate in protein, if you are planning to make it for lunch or dinner, you can have a more substantial than usual meal at the other time, or make this a day with a substantial snack such as a bowl of soup.   *SERVES 2*

Per plated serving of 4–5 scallops with ¼ cup (60 ml) sauce: 125 calories; 37 milligrams cholesterol; 2 grams fat; 357 milligrams sodium; 20 grams protein (44% RDA); 7 grams carbohydrate

RDA: phosphorus 27%; 568 milligrams potassium; vitamin A 26%; vitamin C 17%

½ cup (120 ml) Tomato Sauce
   Casalinga (page 167), or bottled
   tomato sauce
2 tablespoons shredded fresh basil
   leaves

½ pound (227 g) fresh sea scallops,
   external muscle removed (about
   8–10 scallops)

1. Stir together tomato sauce and basil. Divide between two deep, rimmed soup dishes or 9-inch (23-cm) quiche dishes or pie plates, spreading the sauce to make a puddle about 6 inches (15 cm) across.

2. On each dish, arrange half the scallops in a ring about 2 inches (5 cm) from the center of the puddle. Make sure there is a small space between the scallops to assure even cooking. Cover each plate tightly with microwave plastic wrap. Using a rack, cook at 100% for 3 minutes in a 650- to 700-watt oven, switching plates halfway through the cooking. Prick plastic to release steam.

3. Remove from oven, uncover and serve immediately.

FOR 400- TO 500-WATT OVENS

To serve 2. Cook for 5 minutes, switching plates halfway through.

SOFT-SHELL CRABS

Soft-shell crabs are expensive and have a short season; but when they're available, they are a great delicacy and are a healthy self-indulgence. If you serve them as a first course or a luncheon dish, you can share them. Usually when made on top of the stove, they are sautéed in so much butter that their nutritional benefits are submerged. Here, with their bed of greens, they provide lots of vitamins and minerals with few calories. Choose for today Skinny Chili (page 357) or some other filling lunch. Complete dinner with Hearty Vegetable Soup with Pesto (page 130) or Curried Cabbage Soup (page 133) and Mango Mousse (page 564). You stay thin and happy at the same time; but don't have this if salt is a serious problem.   *SERVES 1 AS A MAIN COURSE, 2–4 AS A FIRST COURSE*

Per plated main-course serving of 4 crabs with 4 cups (470 ml) of raw greens (about 1½ cups cooked): 116 calories; 24 milligrams cholesterol; 3 grams fat; 814 milligrams sodium; 18 grams protein (40% RDA); 5 grams carbohydrate

RDA: calcium 17%; 672 milligrams potassium; vitamin A 156%; thiamin 18%; riboflavin 19%; niacin 29%; vitamin C 97%

4 soft-shell crabs (each 3–4 ounces; 85–113.5 g)

4 cups (1 l) loosely packed arugula (or any other tender, slightly bitter spring green, such as dandelion), stems removed, cut into bite-sized pieces

4 tablespoons raspberry vinegar

½ teaspoon kosher salt

Large pinch freshly ground black pepper

1. Rinse crabs and arugula and pat dry. Spread arugula leaves on a 12-inch (30.5-cm) platter. Place crabs on top of leaves with front legs pointing toward the center. Sprinkle with remaining ingredients. Cover tightly with microwave plastic wrap. Cook at 100% for 4 minutes in a 650- to 700-watt oven. Prick plastic to release steam.

2. Remove from oven and uncover. Serve hot.

To serve 2 as a first course. To serve two plated servings, divide ingredients between 2 10-inch (25.5-cm) quiche dishes or pie plates. Cover and cook on a rack for 5 minutes, switching plates after 3 minutes.

To serve 1 as a first course. Use 2 crabs, 2 cups (470 ml) arugula, 2 tablespoons raspberry vinegar, ¼ teaspoon salt and pepper to taste. Follow Step 1 and arrange greens and crabs on a dinner plate. Cover tightly and cook for 2 minutes.

(continued)

FOR 400- TO 500-WATT OVENS

To serve 2 as a first course. Arrange arugula and crabs on 2 10-inch (25.5-cm) quiche dishes or pie plates. Cover tightly. Using a rack, cook for 7 minutes, switching dishes after 3 minutes 30 seconds.

To serve 1 as a first course. Cook for 3 minutes 30 seconds.

LOBSTER À LA NAGE

*I*f you are uncomfortable cooking lobsters in the microwave oven (see pages 270–271), steam or boil as you prefer and continue with Step 2. This is festive enough for a small dinner party and not as expensive as it appears, since you are only serving half a lobster to each person. The calories are so skinny and the protein so minimal that you could start your party with Coral Scallop Terrine (page 93) made ahead or Artichokes Barigoule (page 102) made ahead and heated just before dinner. You can serve some rice—one-half cup per person—or steamed potatoes (page 220) with the lobster and still have salad, cheese, dessert and a small glass of white wine.   SERVES 4

Per generous ¾-cup (180-ml) serving: 97 calories; 45 milligrams cholesterol; 1 gram fat; 625 milligrams sodium; 15 grams protein (34% RDA); 8 grams carbohydrate

RDA: phosphorus 17%; 546 milligrams potassium; vitamin A 114%; vitamin C 42%

2 small live lobsters (each 1¼ pounds; 570 g)
1 cup (240 ml) water
½ cup (120 ml) dry white wine
½ teaspoon loosely packed saffron threads
1 carrot, trimmed, peeled and cut into 2 × ¼ × ¼-inch (5 × .5 × .5-cm) sticks (about ⅔ cup; 160 ml)
1 stalk celery, trimmed, peeled and cut into 2 × ¼ × ¼-inch (5 × .5 × .5-cm) sticks (about ½ cup; 120 ml)

1 large leek, white part only, cleaned and cut into 2 × ¼-inch (5 × .5-cm) strips (about ¾ cup; 180 ml)
½ teaspoon kosher salt
1 bunch thin asparagus, tips removed and stems reserved for another use (about ¾ pound; 340 g)
1 teaspoon fresh lemon juice

1. Place lobsters head to tail in a microwave plastic bag. Loosely knot end. Cook at 100% for 8 minutes in a 650- to 700-watt oven. Remove from oven and leave in bag until cool enough to handle.
2. Combine water, wine and saffron in a 2½-quart (2.5-l) soufflé dish or casserole with a tightly fitted lid. Cook, uncovered, for 10 minutes.

3. Open the bag with lobsters over a bowl to catch any liquid. Working over the bowl, twist tails from lobsters, allowing liquid and the greenish tomalley to drip into bowl. Remove meat from the tail and slice into ¼-inch (.5-cm) rounds. Remove meat from the claws and claw joints and leave it whole.

4. Whisk lobster liquid and tomalley into saffron mixture. Add carrots, celery and leeks. Cover tightly with microwave plastic wrap or casserole lid and cook for 8 minutes. If using plastic wrap, prick to release steam.

5. Uncover and stir in salt, lobster meat and asparagus tips. Cook, uncovered, for 2 minutes. Stir in lemon juice. Divide among four warmed soup dishes.

To serve 6. Use 3 lobsters (each 1¼ pounds; 570 g), 1½ cups (355 ml) water, ¾ cup (180 ml) wine, ¾ teaspoon saffron, 1½ carrots, 1½ stalks celery, 1½ leeks, ¾ teaspoon salt, tips from 1 pound (450 g) thin asparagus and 1½ teaspoons lemon juice. Cook lobsters as in Step 1 for 11 minutes. Cook water, wine and saffron as in Step 2 for 12 minutes. Continue with recipe as in Steps 3 and 4, cooking mixture for 10 minutes. Finish as in Step 5, cooking for 3 minutes.

FOR 400- TO 500-WATT OVENS

To serve 4. Cook lobsters one at a time as in Step 1 for 8 minutes each. Cook water, wine and saffron as in Step 2 for 15 minutes. Continue with recipe as in Steps 3 and 4, cooking mixture for 12 minutes. Finish as in Step 5, cooking for 4 minutes.

LOBSTER SUCCOTASH SALAD

*L*obster is as good cold as it is hot. If you want some warmth in the meal, start with Peasant Tomato Soup (page 127). If the day is too steamy for hot soup, try Chilled Cream of Tomato Soup (page 146) or Summer Borscht (page 143). If you didn't plan ahead, begin with some quickly cooked asparagus (page 76). Asparagus are skinniest, Borscht the roundest in flavor and most caloric. The already-lean should add extra bread and even an extra first course. Finish off with a fresh sorbet (pages 552–556), or store-bought diet sorbet. You can have a wine spritzer and two slices of Majic Whole Grain Bread (page 152) or two slices of Italian bread.   *SERVES 2*

Per 1½-cup (355-ml) serving: 253 calories; 41 milligrams cholesterol; 10 grams fat; 491 milligrams sodium; 17 grams protein (38% RDA); 26 grams carbohydrate

RDA: phosphorus 20%; 617 milligrams potassium; vitamin C 30%

(continued)

1 small live lobster (1¼ pounds; 570 g)

½ cup (120 ml) frozen baby lima beans, defrosted in a sieve under warm running water

½ cup (120 ml) frozen pearl onions, defrosted in a sieve under warm running water

½ cup (120 ml) frozen corn niblets, defrosted in a sieve under warm running water, or fresh corn, cooked (page 213)

⅓ cup (80 ml) Skinny Tomato Dressing (page 496)

Lettuce, if desired, for garnish

1. Place lobster in a microwave-safe plastic bag. Loosely knot bag and place in the center of the oven. Cook at 100% in a 650- to 700-watt oven for 5 minutes. Remove from oven and leave in bag until cool enough to handle.

2. While lobster is cooling, place lima beans in a 1½-quart (1.5-l) soufflé dish or casserole with a tightly fitted lid. Cover tightly with microwave plastic wrap or casserole lid. Cook for 2 minutes. If using plastic wrap, prick plastic to release steam.

3. Remove from oven and uncover. Stir in onions, re-cover and cook for 1 minute. Prick plastic wrap.

4. Remove from oven and uncover. Drain and reserve.

5. Remove lobster from plastic bag. Twist off tail and spoon tomalley into a small bowl. Whisk in dressing and reserve.

6. Remove meat from tail and cut across into ¼- inch (.5-cm) rounds. Remove meat from claws and joints, leaving claw meat whole for garnish, and cut remaining meat into ¼-inch (.5-cm) slices. Stir together lobster meat except claws, vegetables including corn and dressing in a large bowl. Divide between two dinner plates, serving on lettuce leaves if desired. Garnish with the whole claws.

FOR 400- TO 500-WATT OVENS

To serve 2. Cook lobster as in Step 1 for 8 minutes. Proceed with Step 2, cooking lima beans for 3 minutes. Add onions as in Step 3 and cook for 2 minutes. Finish as in Steps 4 through 6.

PERFECTLY POULTRY

令

*I*f you are on some kind of diet—particularly weight-loss or low-cholesterol—and are not a vegetarian, poultry can seem the answer to a prayer, especially since it is inexpensive. Many people have switched from red meat to poultry for its seeming benefits. Beware. Leaving the skin on poultry will increase the amount of calories in a portion by more than 25 percent. Poultry is good for you and your diet if it is skinned and you limit the amount per serving at your main meal to about four ounces (113.5 g). If you are a large and/or active person or not on a weight-loss diet, increase to about six ounces (170 g) or double the portion in the recipes. While this will increase your protein for the day beyond the RDA, that is not a major problem (see page 16). The problem will be cholesterol if you plan to have a lunch containing meat, poultry or fish.

Animal protein contains the same amount of calories ounce-for-ounce no matter what its color. Nevertheless, poultry does not have as much fat and therefore calories as red meats and most cuts of pork. On the other hand, it does not have as much iron either. See page 341 for a comparison of iron and zinc.

Keeping this in mind, it is preferable to remove the skin of all poultry and to observe the basic rule of dietary sanity: Vary your diet.

Fortunately, there is a virtual infinity of ways to prepare poultry to give variety to our meals. Since the microwave oven does not brown foods, the skin of chicken can be abandoned without regret. Except for occasional self-indulgence, fried chicken should be consigned to the past. Roast chicken and turkey have wonderful flavor and are easily cooked; but it requires real self-discipline to remove the tantalizing browned skin. Duck with a crisp and crackling skin is but a memory for the dieter.

Skinless halves, quarters and portions of birds—with or without bone—can be grilled or broiled. Either brush or spray your broiler pan or the grid on your grill with a minimum of neutral oil and cook away. Do not marinate or baste with oily or heavily salted mixtures that would defeat your attempts at virtue. Do look at Basics, Sauces and Snacks (pages 458–529) for alternative marinades and basting and accompanying sauces.

When planning your meals based on a poultry main course, think about adding vegetables (pages 388–457) and starches from Good Grains and Other Starches (pages 148–225), or beginning with a soup or first course. Many of the dishes in this chapter include their own vegetables to make a more complete main course. Many of these composite dishes will surprise you by the generosity of the portion; but the poultry itself will be kept to a modest amount. If you are *a large and/or active person, or you are cooking for one, it is better to add more grains, beans or bread and even courses to the meal rather than increasing the amount of poultry.*

Since most of your daily allotment—about 60 percent—of protein is used up by some of the dishes in this chapter, it is important to keep in mind that your other meals should be low in meat protein. Look at Good Grains and Other Starches for breakfast suggestions. Look at the menus in Diets and Menus (pages 46–73) for lunch and snack suggestions. You may find some helpful ideas in Salads and Vegetables (pages 388–457) for vegetarian dinners or lunches, or in Soups (pages 114–147) for soup lunches—even Riviera Fish Soup (page 138)—which are low in protein and are happily, fillingly rounded out by a salad or a piece of fruit.

Once again, don't omit the recommended bread, rice, pasta, etc., from your menu. Meat doesn't provide much in the way of carbohydrate. Some dishes, like Meat and Potatoes on a Plate (page 298), have more than twenty grams of carbohydrate; but that is the potatoes, not the chicken, talking.

Hints for Microwave Cooking of Poultry

It remains true that poultry does not roast well in the microwave oven. This is not a ghastly deprivation. Anyhow, all that crisp but fatty skin just isn't good for anyone, no matter how wonderful it tastes. When holidays that seem to require a roasted bird roll around, just plunk your bird in the conventional oven your kitchen no doubt has. Use your microwave oven for the vegetables and accompaniments. It will be fully occupied.

The rest of the year, there are a myriad of good and easy dishes that can be cooked in healthful fashion in the microwave oven. To cook the bird unadorned or to develop your own recipes with a sauce or liquid, follow the timings in the charts on pages 294–295. Place pieces to be cooked in a dish just large enough to hold them and, preferably, high enough so that plastic wrap (cling film) will not touch the food while cooking.

As with almost all foods, fresh is best. If you must use frozen, try to defrost overnight in the refrigerator. Cooking raw fowl directly from the frozen state seems to yield a tougher bird. You can defrost in the microwave oven as part of the cooking time. Chicken pieces are best defrosted in their cooking liquid. See page 296.

Recent reports have scared many of us about the possibility of being attacked by salmonella due to eating infected and undercooked poultry. It is comforting to know that salmonella die at 128°F–130°F (54°C). At this temperature the poultry will also be attractively cooked and still moist. You can easily test the temperature of your poultry with an instant-read thermometer. Simply poke the thermometer through the plastic into the thickest part of the meat—poke in a couple of places if you are anxious—making sure not to touch any bone or the plate. If the poultry is not cooked enough, patch the hole(s) with a small piece of fresh plastic wrap and cook for an additional minute or until it tests done.

For proper cooking, it is important that the poultry be at room temperature before cooking and to arrange the pieces of meat properly and to be sure that they are of the indicated weight. This is also important to the accuracy of the dietary information given with each recipe.

A microwave oven cooks—like a cake in your conventional oven—from the outside of the dish toward the center. In order to cook evenly, the chicken must be arranged in such a way that thicker or dark-meat pieces face toward the edge of the dish, and thinner or white-meat pieces are in the center. When a bird is whole, the thickest edges of the two half-breasts meet; when the breast halves are separated for cooking, their positions should be reversed, so that the two thin long edges are next to each other in the center of the dish. Numerous half-breasts should be arranged like the petals of a daisy or the spokes in a wheel, with the

Arranging several half-breasts:
Place skinned and halved breasts
around the dish spoke-fashion.

Arranging two half-breasts: Split whole skinned and boned chicken breasts down the center. Reverse position
so thin edges of breast are next to each other in dish.

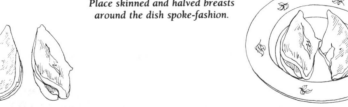

Arranging a chicken cut in pieces: Place dark-meat pieces around the bottom of the dish with heaviest
parts toward the edge. Place breast halves with the thin edges together in the center
of the dish over dark-meat sections.

thicker ends toward the edge of the dish and the thinner points toward the center. See the accompanying illustrations for all poultry-in-parts arrangements.

Almost all the following recipes call for skinned poultry parts due to the high calorie content of poultry skin. (See page 341 for the gruesome details.) Skinned and boned chicken breasts and skinless turkey cutlets can usually be bought. Whole birds and other-than-breast cuts usually do not come skinned. You can try seducing the butcher. If this isn't feasible, there is no avoiding it: You will have to learn to skin the bird yourself. Have courage; it isn't even hard. It is usually best to start with the cut-up bird. You can buy it that way or do it as follows:

Once the bird is cut up, skinning it is easy. You can usually pull the skin off with your hands. At most, you will have to cut through a very light membrane that attaches the skin to the bird. When you get to the bone, cut off the skin. Trim off any surface fat with a sharp knife.

Once you have your skinned and boned breasts, you may want to butterfly them. This gives a much larger-looking portion—important for kidding your eyes—and makes for a more even piece for grilling, broiling or even some microwave recipes.

Hold breast flat with your hand and cut almost in half with knife parallel to work surface to butterfly; open out like a book and flatten.

Some of the recipes in this chapter call for making brochettes. You will find that birds presented this way make a nice change and look like much more food. Do not use metal skewers. Wooden or bamboo ones can be easily found. If you plan to grill a brochette either for the entire cooking time or after microwave cooking in order to brown the food, soak the skewers thoroughly in water before using so that they do not burn.

Many of these recipes call for Basic Chicken Broth (page 460). While canned broth—you can even use stock (bouillon) cubes dissolved in water—is a suggested alternative, look at page 115 to see how much sodium you will be adding to the dish. Even if you are not salt-sensitive, homemade Basic Chicken Broth tastes much better, particularly better than the salt-free canned broths available, and cooks very quickly in the microwave oven. Freeze it to have on hand and defrost as needed (page 116). You may find that you want to add a few tablespoons of broth to cooked noodles—rather than butter or oil (lots of calories)—to keep them from sticking.

If you want a more intense taste in your sauces, consider making Basic Glaze (page 466) and keeping it on hand; add one teaspoon to a dish for two, one tablespoon to a dish for four.

The recipes within each section of this chapter—chicken, turkey and duck—are arranged by the number of people served by the principal recipe, going from one to eight. Normally, most recipes will have other quantities given so that you can cook just what you need or enough to provide leftovers for lunch or another meal. Some of the more elaborate recipes do not have versions for a single or small number of servings. It just seems like too much work. If you must freeze leftovers, do so in single-serving amounts for good portion control.

It is often convenient when cooking for one or two people to cook directly on the plates on which you wish to serve. I find that the old-fashioned wide-rimmed soup dishes with deep center wells contain the food nicely and keep the plastic off the food. If you want to use a dinner plate, try to find one on which the edge or rim is substantially higher than the center of the plate. To cook two portions in this fashion, use a plastic rack, which is easily found in a hardware store. Switch the plate on top of the rack with the one underneath it about halfway through the cooking time in order to achieve even cooking. If the recipe time is not already given for two plates, add thirty seconds to the timing for a portion for two to allow for the second plate.

Chicken

In order for chicken to cook evenly, the pieces must be arranged in the way described and illustrated on page 291, with thicker or dark-meat pieces toward the edge of the dish.

While every chicken recipe gives as best as I can an indication of how much is intended as a portion—either in cups or in number of pieces to be served—since portion is such an important element of diet, it may not be a bad idea to state what is generally intended as a portion. A portion is not your piece of chicken plus more than your fair share of the vegetables, rice or sauce. Don't cheat. If you forget how many people the recipe was intended to serve, base your portion on the amount of chicken intended as a healthy portion.

There is a lot of confusion about what is meant by a half-breast. A chicken has one whole breast. For cooking, this breast is usually divided into two pieces along the breastbone. One of the two resulting pieces is what is meant as a half-breast in this book.

PORTION PER PERSON OF CHICKEN 1 half-breast, skinned and boned (4 ounces; 113.5 g), or skinned but on the bone as in a stew (7 ounces; 200 g)

A leg and a thigh or two legs or two thighs, skinned and boned (4 ounces; 113.5 g), or skinned but on the bone as in a stew (8 ounces; 227 g)

COMPARISON BETWEEN LIGHT AND DARK PIECES OF CHICKEN

PORTION	CAL.	CHOL. (mg)	IRON (mg)	ZINC (mg)
Light meat, skinned, boned and stewed (4 oz.; 113.5 g)	182	88	1	1.12
Dark meat, skinned, boned and stewed (4 oz.; 113.5 g)	219	101	2	N/A

All chicken, except where indicated, is skinned. The skin adds a substantial amount of calories to a portion—roughly forty-eight—and does not add much in the way of flavor in the microwave oven.

BASIC COOKING TIMES FOR CHICKEN

Chicken Pieces

The following times will be useful when you find a recipe that you like, but wish to increase or decrease the number of portions that are given in the recipe. Look at pages 291 and 296 to see how to arrange the pieces that you have and then follow the guidelines below for the wattage of your oven and the amount of other stuff in the dish. Where a time is not given—usually for cooking in a low-wattage oven—it indicates that I didn't find it feasible, whether because of the dish size, the unevenness of the cooking or the overall time involved.

CHICKEN BREASTS skinned, boned and split, each half- breast weighing about four ounces (113.5 g), on a dish just large enough to hold them, covered tightly with microwave plastic wrap. Cook at 100% power.

One half-breast on a dinner plate
650- to 700-watt oven: 2 min. 30 sec.
400- to 500-watt oven: 3 min.

Two half-breasts on a dinner plate
650- to 700-watt oven: 3 min. 30 sec.
400- to 500-watt oven: 4 min.

Four half-breasts in a 10-inch (25.5-cm) round dish
650- to 700-watt oven: 5 min.
400- to 500-watt oven: 7–8 min. on a wind-up carrousel, or turning the dish once

Four half-breasts with 1½ cups (360 ml) vegetables in a 2-quart (2-l) soufflé dish
650- to 700-watt oven: 9 min.
400- to 500-watt oven: Not recommended

Six half-breasts in a 12 × 10 × 2-inch (30.5 × 25.5 × 5-cm) glass or ceramic dish
650- to 700-watt oven: 6 min.
400- to 500-watt oven: Not recommended

Eight half-breasts with ¼ cup (60 ml) broth in a 14 × 11 × 2-inch (35.5 × 28 × 5-cm) ceramic dish
650- to 700-watt oven: 8 min.
400- to 500-watt oven: Not recommended

CHICKEN LEGS AND THIGHS with or without skin, bone in, drumsticks cut around the thin end to release tendons, on a dish just large enough to hold them. Cover tightly and cook at 100%. Each thigh will weigh about 4 ounces (113.5 g) and each leg (drumstick) will weigh about 4 ounces (113.5 g). Legs and thighs may be used interchangeably.

1 whole leg or 2 pieces on a dinner plate
650- to 700-watt oven: 4 min.
400- to 500-watt oven: 7 min. 30 sec.

1 whole leg or 2 pieces with ¼ cup (60 ml) broth or light sauce on a dinner plate
650- to 700-watt oven: 5 min.
400- to 500-watt oven: 7 min. 30 sec.

1 whole leg or 2 pieces with ¾ cup (60 ml) liquid and ½ cup (120 ml) vegetables in a 1½-quart (1.5-l) soufflé dish
650- to 700-watt oven: 7 min.
400- to 500-watt oven: 9 min.

2 whole legs or 4 pieces in a 10-inch (25.5-cm) round dish
650- to 700-watt oven: 7 min. 30 sec.
400- to 500-watt oven: 9 min.

2 whole legs or 4 pieces with ¼ cup (60 ml) broth or coated with sauce in a 10-inch (25.5-cm) round dish
650- to 700-watt oven: 7 min. 30 sec.
400- to 500-watt oven: 9 min.

4 whole legs or 8 pieces with ¼ cup (60 ml) broth or sauce in a 12 × 10 × 2-inch (30.5 × 25.5 × 5-cm) dish
650- to 700-watt oven: 11 min.
400- to 500-watt oven: Not recommended

Whole Chicken in Parts

WHOLE CHICKENS cut into serving pieces, with or without skin, pieces arranged inside a 2½-quart (2.5-l) soufflé dish, with dark-meat pieces toward the edge and breast pieces in the center. Larger chickens or two chickens should be arranged in a large dish, either a 14 × 11 × 2-inch (35.5 × 28 × 5-cm) or a 13 × 9 × 2-inch (33 × 28 × 5-cm) oval. Chickens can be layered in a large 5-quart (5-l) casserole; but they will take longer to cook, need to be stirred and usually cook less evenly. They are cooked tightly covered at 100%. If they are covered with microwave plastic wrap, prick plastic before removing from oven.

2½-pound (1.2-kg) bird with 1 cup (240 ml) liquid, or 1 cup (240 ml) liquid and 1½ pounds (680 g) vegetables
650- to 700-watt oven: 15 min.
400- to 500-watt oven: 22 min.

3-pound (1.4-kg) bird with ½ cup (120 ml) liquid and 1 pound (450 g) vegetables
650- to 700-watt oven: 17 min.
400- to 500-watt oven: Not recommended

4-pound (1.8-kg) bird or two 2½-pound (1.2-kg) birds with 2 cups (470 ml) liquid, or 2 cups (470 ml) liquid and 1 pound (450 g) vegetables
650- to 700-watt oven: 22 min.
400- to 500-watt oven: Not recommended

Arrange dark-meat pieces of two birds around the inside edge of the dish and white-meat pieces in the center with the thin edges coming together.

Parcooking Times for Chicken

There will be times when you don't want to cook your chicken all the way through. You simply want to parcook it so that it can be brushed with or marinated in sauce before broiling or grilling. Cooking times are for dishes tightly covered with microwave plastic wrap at 100% power.

*4-pound (1.8-kg) bird in a 2½-quart (2.5-l)
soufflé or casserole*
650- to 700-watt oven: 10 min., turn
    breast pieces, cook 3 min. more
400- to 500-watt oven: 18 min., turn
    breast pieces, cook 3 min. more

Cook at 100% tightly covered with microwave plastic wrap. For skinned, boned and halved frozen breasts:

Cooking of Frozen Chicken Breasts

Two half-breasts, in ½ cup (120 ml) liquid (and ¼–½ cup [60–120 ml] vegetables, if desired) Arrange pieces in an 8½ × 6½ × 2-inch (21.5 × 16.5 × 5-cm) dish.
650- to 700-watt oven: 8 min., turning
    pieces and re-covering after 5 min.
400- to 500-watt oven: 27 min., turning
    pieces and re-covering after 19 min.

Four half-breasts, in 2 cups (470 ml) broth or light sauce (and ½–1 cup [120–240 ml] vegetables, if desired) Arrange pieces in an 11 × 8 × 2-inch (28 × 20 × 5-cm) dish.
650- to 700-watt oven: 9 min., turning
    pieces and re-covering after 5 min.
400- to 500-watt oven: Not recommended

BARBECUED CHICKEN

*T*his is a mildly spicy quick dish for one or a family. It is given here in a quantity for one since it is just the kind of messy, satisfying dinner food I like when I am alone, and it is most easily made in a microwave oven. Since the timing is the same as that for chicken legs and thighs with up to one-quarter cup sauce (page 295), it easily multiplies.

This is not a crispy, crunchy barbecued chicken with a darkened skin. Indeed, it is skinless; but it can have a crusty top if you preheat the broiler before you start assembling the chicken for the microwave oven. After the chicken cooks in the microwave oven, put it in a broiler pan and let it brown. A vegetable soup, such as Hearty Vegetable Soup with Pesto (page 130) or Winter Vegetable Soup (page 128), would be a good beginning. A microwave-cooked baking potato (page 219) and an iron-rich salad such as Oriental Spinach Salad (page 79) will fill up a hungry eater and give as much pleasure as it does rounded nutrition. Healthy eaters who don't need to lose weight could have the Olive Oil Mashed Potatoes (page 221) with sumptuous pleasure.

This dish is rich in niacin and has good amounts of phosphorus, riboflavin and iron.   *SERVES 1*

Per serving: 274 calories; 104 milligrams cholesterol; 15 grams fat; 233 milligrams sodium; 30 grams protein (66% RDA); 3 grams carbohydrate

RDA: phosphorus 20%; iron 11%; riboflavin 14%; niacin 36%

1 chicken leg (8 ounces; 227 g), cut into drumstick and thigh pieces and skinned	1 tablespoon Quick Barbecue Sauce (page 513)

1. Using a pastry brush, coat chicken with the sauce. Place on a dinner plate. Cover tightly with microwave plastic wrap. Cook at 100% for 5 minutes in a 650- to 700-watt oven. Prick plastic to release steam.

2. Remove from oven and uncover.

FOR 400- TO 500-WATT OVENS

To serve 1. Cook for 7 minutes 30 seconds or until chicken is cooked through.

MEAT AND POTATOES ON A PLATE

The day is sure to come when you walk in the door and feel like a simple meat-and-potatoes dinner. It cooks so quickly because the half-breast is butterflied (see illustration page 292). The red peppers and scallions are not merely decorative. They make this a fairly complete meal; but you are still entitled to a bowl of soup or a big salad and a dessert as well. This is a happy solution when you are avoiding cholesterol, and it provides you with iron, thiamin and large amounts of vitamin C, niacin and vitamin A. Blessings on potatoes.   *SERVES 1*

Per serving: 221 calories; 68 milligrams cholesterol; 2 grams fat; 85 milligrams sodium; 30 grams protein (67% RDA); 20 grams carbohydrate

RDA: phosphorus 30%; iron 14%; 928 milligrams potassium; vitamin A 80%; thiamin 14%; niacin 74%; vitamin C 223%

3 ounces (85 g) red new potatoes, scrubbed and cut into ¼-inch (.5-cm) slices (about 1 cup; 240 ml)

1 large clove garlic, smashed, peeled and cut into slivers

1 tablespoon water

2 ounces (56 g) red bell pepper, stemmed, seeded, deribbed and thinly sliced lengthwise (about ¼ cup; 60 ml)

1 half-breast chicken (4 ounces; 113.5 g), skinned, boned and butterflied

1 scallion, cut into thin rounds

Kosher salt, to taste

Freshly ground black pepper, to taste

Pinch dried tarragon, optional

1. Arrange potato slices, without overlapping, in the center of a dinner plate, making a disc the size of the chicken piece. Sprinkle with garlic and water and cover tightly with microwave plastic wrap. Cook at 100% for 4 minutes in a 650- to 700-watt oven. Prick plastic to release steam.

2. Remove from oven and uncover carefully. Scatter peppers over potatoes, saving several slices for the top of the chicken. Lay the chicken on the vegetables. Sprinkle with scallions, salt and pepper, remaining pepper strips and tarragon, if desired. Cover and cook for 1 minute 30 seconds, or until chicken is opaque. Prick plastic.

3. Remove from oven. Uncover carefully and serve.

To serve 2. Use 6 ounces (170 g) potatoes, 2 cloves garlic, 2 tablespoons water, 4 ounces (113.5 g) bell pepper, 2 half-breasts (each 4 ounces; 113.5 g) and 2 scallions. Arrange potatoes as in Step 1 on two dinner plates. Cook, using a rack, for 6 minutes, switching plates after 3 minutes. Continue as in Step 2 and cook for 3 minutes 30 seconds, switching plates after 2 minutes.

To serve 1. Cook as in Step 1 for 6 minutes. Cook as in Step 2 for 2 minutes 30 seconds to 3 minutes, or until chicken is opaque throughout.

To serve 2. Arrange as in Step 1 on two dinner plates and cook for 8 minutes, switching plates after 4 minutes. Cook as in Step 2 for 5–6 minutes, switching plates after 3 minutes.

CURRIED CHICKEN BREAST

*T*he French love the taste of curry powder, but not the complexity and exoticism of a real Indian dish. If you want a traditionally Indian, delicious dish best made for a crowd, look at Chicken Curry for Real (page 321). French-style curry is perfect in this skinny version for a night with little time, but with the desire for a gratifyingly definite taste. Add rice, simply boiled on top of the stove (about one-half cup [120 ml] cooked), or a similar amount of Parsley Pilaf (page 185). The sauce is too good to waste. You will still have almost three hundred calories to allocate as you will: a glass of wine and Grated Carrot Salad (page 395), and a first course or a dessert; but lunch should probably be vegetarian—a big salad and some low-fat cottage cheese or skim-milk yogurt for calcium.   *SERVES 1*

Per serving: 221 calories; 68 milligrams cholesterol; 2 grams fat; 85 milligrams sodium; 30 grams protein (67% RDA); 13 grams carbohydrate

RDA: calcium 11%; phosphorus 31%; iron 10%; niacin 67%

¼ cup (60 ml) skim milk
1½ teaspoons cornstarch
1 clove garlic, smashed, peeled and sliced
¼ cup (60 ml) Fromage Blanc (page 518) (available at specialty stores), or part-skim ricotta cheese

1½ teaspoons curry powder
½ teaspoon vegetable oil
1 half-breast chicken (4 ounces; 113.5 g), skinned and boned
¼ teaspoon fresh lemon juice

1. Combine milk and cornstarch in a 1-cup (240-ml) glass measure. Stir well, making sure there are no lumps. Stir in garlic and cover tightly with microwave plastic wrap. Cook at 100% for 2 minutes in a 650- to 700-watt oven. Prick plastic to release steam.
2. Remove from oven and uncover. Remove garlic with a spoon; whisk in Fromage Blanc. Reserve.

(continued)

3. On a deep-rimmed dinner plate or in a 10-inch (25.5-cm) quiche dish or pie plate, combine curry powder and oil. Cook, uncovered, for 30 seconds.

4. Remove from oven. Stir reserved milk mixture into curry powder. Place chicken on top of sauce and turn to coat well. Cover and cook for 3 minutes. Prick plastic.

5. Remove from oven and uncover. Add lemon juice and serve.

To serve 2. Use ½ cup (120 ml) skim milk, 1 tablespoon cornstarch, 2 cloves garlic, ½ cup (120 ml) Fromage Blanc, 1 tablespoon curry powder, 1 teaspoon vegetable oil, 2 half-breasts chicken (each 4 ounces; 113.5 g) and ½ teaspoon lemon juice. Cook as in Step 1 in a 2-cup (470-ml) glass measure for 3 minutes 30 seconds. Continue with Step 2. Cook as in Step 3 for 30 seconds. Continue as in Steps 4 and 5, cooking for 4 minutes, or until chicken is cooked through.

FOR 400- TO 500-WATT OVENS

To serve 1. Cook sauce as in Step 1 for 3 minutes. Cook curry and oil for 40 seconds. Combine ingredients as in Step 4 and cook for 4 minutes 30 seconds.

To serve 2. Cook sauce as in Step 1 for 3 minutes 30 seconds. Cook curry and oil for 45 seconds. Combine ingredients as in Step 4 and cook for 6 minutes.

CHICKEN WITH PEPPERS

*T*his chicken dish, with its Italian colors of red, white and green, is good on its own or cooked on top of one-half cup of previously cooked pasta—linguine or orzo would be good. The tomatoes and peppers make a light sauce for the pasta. The cooking time doesn't change as long as the pasta is still warm. You will need to add about one hundred calories for the pasta to your calculations. Add Spinach, Mushroom and Celery Salad (page 401) and Chocolate Tapioca Pudding (page 568) or a portion of fruit and cheese for a hearty meal. The chicken dish offers three days' worth of vitamin C, a day's worth of vitamin A, and almost a day's needs of niacin.   *SERVES 1*

Per serving: 162 calories; 66 milligrams cholesterol; 2 grams fat; 81 milligrams sodium; 28 grams protein (61% RDA); 8 grams carbohydrate

RDA: phosphorus 26%; iron 13%; vitamin A 119%; niacin 68%; vitamin C 314%

4 ounces (113.5 g) red bell pepper, stemmed, seeded, deribbed and cut into thin strips (½ cup; 120 ml)

1 small clove garlic, smashed, peeled and chopped

⅓ medium tomato (2 ounces; 56 g), roughly chopped (about ½ cup; 120 ml)

1 half-breast chicken (4 ounces; 113.5 g), skinned, boned and cut on the diagonal into strips

Pinch freshly ground black pepper

1 teaspoon chopped fresh basil, optional

½ cup (120 ml) cooked pasta, optional

1. Toss together all ingredients except the black pepper, basil and pasta either directly in a soup plate or on top of pasta in a soup plate. Cover tightly with microwave plastic wrap. Cook at 100% for 3 minutes in a 650- to 700-watt oven. Prick plastic to release steam.

2. Remove from oven. Uncover, stir in black pepper and sprinkle over basil, if desired.

To serve 2. Use 8 ounces (227 g) red pepper, 2 cloves garlic, ⅔ medium tomato (4 ounces; 113.5 g), 2 half-breasts chicken (each 4 ounces; 113.5 g), large pinch black pepper, 2 teaspoons fresh basil and 1 cup (240 ml) cooked pasta, if desired. Divide between two soup plates and arrange as in Step 1, or place all ingredients in a 9-inch (23-cm) pie plate. Cook, using a rack if food is in two plates, at 100% for 5 minutes, switching plates after 2 minutes 30 seconds.

FOR 400- TO 500-WATT OVENS

To serve 1. Cook for 4 minutes 30 seconds.

To serve 2. Arrange as in Step 1 on one or two plates. Cook, using a rack if desired, for 6 minutes. Switch plates after 3 minutes if using a rack.

SKINNY BURGER

*T*his heart-healthy burger will make you forget the beef. If you want ketchup, fine; but remember, you are adding 18 calories and 180 milligrams of sodium per tablespoon. Instead try Chinese Stewed Tomatoes (page 442), Early American Tomato Ketchup (page 469) or Tomato Braised Onions (page 528). Even at lunch, you can have a slice of toast and a serving of fruit. At dinner, you can have a vegetable first course such as Stuffed Peppers (page 98)—save the extras for the next day's lunch—or Artichokes Barigoule (page 102), and Lemon Bavarian (page 561) or Rice Pudding (page 566) for dessert. No need to lose weight, serve with a microwave-cooked baking potato. If you like this so much you want to serve it to more people, double the ingredients, cook the spinach for four minutes, and cook in a ten-inch (25.5-cm) quiche dish the way you would Crunchy Vegetable and Chicken Loaf (page 313).

This dish has good amounts of iron, and sensational amounts of vitamins C and A. You don't have to worry too much about balancing items at this night's dinner. *SERVES 1*

Per serving: 172 calories; 68 milligrams cholesterol; 2 grams fat; 233 grams sodium; 31 grams protein (70% RDA); 8 grams carbohydrate

RDA: phosphorus 32%; iron 24%; vitamin A 148%; niacin 72%; vitamin C 80%

¼ pound (113.5 g) fresh spinach, stemmed and washed (loosely packed, about 1½ cups; 360 ml)

2 scallions, cut into 1-inch (2.5-cm) lengths

¼ pound (113.5 g) zucchini, halved lengthwise and cut across into ½-inch (1-cm) slices (about ⅓ cup; 80 ml)

1 half-breast chicken (4 ounces; 113.5 g), skinned, boned and cut into chunks

¼ teaspoon summer savory

Pinch kosher salt

Pinch freshly ground black pepper

1. Place spinach in a 9-inch (23-cm) pie plate. Cook, uncovered, at 100% for 2 minutes in a 650- to 700-watt oven.

2. Remove from oven. Let spinach stand until cool enough to handle. Using your hands, squeeze out as much water as possible. Place in the work bowl of a food processor. Add scallions and half the zucchini. Process until coarsely chopped and scrape into a small bowl.

3. Place the chicken in the food processor and process until finely chopped but not completely smooth. Add to the chopped vegetables. Stir in savory, salt and pepper and stir until well combined.

4. In the center of a dinner plate, shape mixture into a ½-inch (1-cm) thick disc. Surround with remaining zucchini slices. Cover tightly with microwave plastic wrap. Cook at 100% for 2 minutes 30 seconds or until the burger reaches 130°F (54.5°C) on an instant-read thermometer inserted in several places. Prick plastic to release steam.

5. Remove from oven and uncover. Serve hot.

To serve 2. Use ½ pound (230 g) spinach, 4 scallions, ½ pound (230 g) zucchini, 2 half-breasts chicken (each 4 ounces [113.5 g]), ½ teaspoon savory, ⅛ teaspoon salt and ⅛ teaspoon pepper. Cook spinach as in step 1 for 3 minutes. Continue with steps 2 and 3. In step 4, divide ingredients between two dinner plates. Cook, using a rack, at 100% for 7 minutes, switching plates after 4 minutes, or until chicken reaches an internal temperature of 130°F (54.5°C).

FOR 400- TO 500-WATT OVENS

To serve 1. Cook spinach as in Step 1 for 3 minutes. Cook chicken as in Step 4 for 5 minutes, or until it reaches an internal temperature of 130°F (54.5°C).

To serve 2. Cook spinach as in Step 1 for 5 minutes. Divide ingredients between two dinner plates. Cook, using a rack, for 10 minutes, switching plates after 5 minutes, or until chicken reaches an internal temperature of 130°F (54.5°C).

CHICKEN BREASTS WITH SPINACH AND GINGER

This quickie is a pleasure for those who like Oriental flavors. The iron, vitamin A, vitamin C and niacin in this dish make it a diet bargain that still leaves 328 calories to splurge on a first course or soup and a dessert. If you are watching your sodium intake, avoid this dish or substitute 1½ teaspoons tamari soy for the salt to decrease the sodium by 382 milligrams per serving. Even if you are alone, make both portions. Mix the second serving with its rice and eat cold for lunch on a bed of lettuce.   SERVES 2

Per ½-breast serving with ½ cup rice: 272 calories; 66 milligrams cholesterol; 2 grams fat; 901 milligrams sodium if using kosher salt, 529 if using tamari soy; 32 grams protein (71% RDA); 32 grams carbohydrate

RDA: calcium 16%; phosphorus 32%; iron 27%; 988 milligrams potassium; vitamin A 151%; thiamin 17%; riboflavin 19%; niacin 73%; vitamin C 74%

(continued)

8 ounces (227 g) fresh spinach, stemmed and washed (about 4 cups; 1 l)

1½ teaspoons peeled and grated fresh ginger

3 cloves garlic, smashed and peeled

1 teaspoon kosher salt, or 1½ teaspoons tamari soy

Pinch freshly ground black pepper

2 half-breasts chicken (each 4 ounces; 113.5 g), skinned and boned

2 thin slices lemon with rind

1 cup cooked white or brown rice (page 182), optional

1. Place spinach, ginger, garlic, salt and pepper in a food processor. Process until coarsely chopped. Divide mixture evenly between two dinner plates or 10-inch (25.5-cm) quiche dishes, pressing it into a round.

2. Center one half-breast over each spinach round. Place a slice of lemon on each breast. Cover tightly with microwave plastic wrap. Using a rack, cook at 100% for 6 minutes in a 650- to 700-watt oven, switching plates after 3 minutes. Prick plastic to release steam.

3. Remove from oven and uncover. Spoon ½ cup (120 ml) rice onto dish to absorb juices.

FOR 400- TO 500-WATT OVENS

To serve 2. Cook for 9 minutes, switching plates after 4 minutes 30 seconds.

A SPRING CHICKEN

The bright green of spring asparagus and the freshness of dill and lemon make this a vernal treat rich in iron, vitamins A and C and niacin. Start the meal with an artichoke (page 99) with Egg White Mayonnaise (page 482). Sop up the sauce with a couple of slices of crusty French bread or give each person one-half cup (120 ml) cooked spinach pasta, and finish the meal with Rummy Baked Pineapple (page 543) or seasonal strawberries with Whipped Ricotta Topping (page 581). Have a glass of wine and serve a couple of Meringue Clouds (page 585) with your dessert. You still have enough calories left for a salad and a piece of cheese.
SERVES 2

Per ½-breast serving: 158 calories; 68 milligrams cholesterol; 2 grams fat; 85 milligrams sodium; 30 grams protein (66% RDA); 5 grams carbohydrate

RDA: phosphorus 27%; vitamin A 14%; niacin 71%; vitamin C 45%

¼ cup (60 ml) Basic Chicken Broth (page 460), or unsalted or regular canned chicken broth
1½ teaspoons cornstarch, dissolved in 1 tablespoon cold water
2 half-breasts chicken (each 4 ounces; 113.5 g), skinned and boned

10 medium stalks asparagus, woody ends snapped off and peeled
1½ teaspoons fresh lemon juice
1½ teaspoons minced fresh dill
Kosher salt, to taste
Freshly ground black pepper, to taste

1. Stir together broth and cornstarch in a 1-cup (240-ml) glass measure. Cover tightly with microwave plastic wrap. Cook at 100% for 2 minutes in a 650- to 700-watt oven. Prick plastic to release steam.

2. Remove from oven and uncover. Reserve.

3. Arrange chicken breasts on a dinner plate with the thin ends toward the center of the plate. Leave about 2 inches (5 cm) between them. Place asparagus spears in the space between the breasts. Cover tightly with microwave plastic wrap. Cook at 100% for 3 minutes 30 seconds. Prick plastic to release steam.

4. Remove from oven and uncover. Carefully pour cooking juices into reserved sauce. Whisk in remaining ingredients. Pour over chicken and asparagus and serve.

FOR 400- TO 500-WATT OVENS

To serve 2. Prepare sauce as in Step 1, cooking for 3 minutes. Arrange chicken and asparagus as in Step 3. Cook for 4 minutes 40 seconds. Finish recipe as in Step 4.

CHICKEN WITH HERB CREAM

*T*his bright-green sauce has a delicate flavor and a creamy texture that gives an illusion of calories; but it is so light in calories you can still have one-half cup (120 ml) cooked rice or cooked noodles, a first course of Peasant Tomato Soup (page 127), Fennel and Red Onion Salad (page 400) and Strawberry Sorbet (page 555) or store-bought diet sorbet. Large and/or active people or those not trying to lose weight should have an ample lunch; they probably can eat more than this for dinner, doubling the main-course portion; but be careful with the day's cholesterol if that is a concern. Instead of doubling the main-course portion, add a banana and some cookies as a snack and increase the amount of rice. I would like a chilly glass of gewürztraminer or chardonnay myself.   *SERVES 2*

Per ½-breast serving: 193 calories; 73 milligrams cholesterol; 3 grams fat; 368 milligrams sodium; 32 grams protein (70% RDA); 9 grams carbohydrate

RDA: calcium 16%; phosphorus 32%; iron 13%; 662 milligrams potassium; vitamin A 58%; riboflavin 16%; niacin 68%; vitamin C 27%

½ small shallot, peeled and quartered
¼ pound (115 g) spinach, stemmed
    and washed (packed, about 1 cup;
    240 ml)
1 tablespoon cornstarch
½ cup (120 ml) buttermilk
1 tablespoon part-skim ricotta cheese
1 tablespoon dill sprigs
1 tablespoon parsley leaves
1 tablespoon Basic Chicken Broth (page
    460), or unsalted or regular canned
    chicken broth or water

1 teaspoon fresh lemon juice
2 drops hot red pepper sauce
¼ teaspoon kosher salt
2 half-breasts chicken (each 4 ounces;
    113.5 g), skinned and boned
1 cup (240 ml) cooked rice or orzo,
    optional
2 tablespoons chopped parsley, optional

1. Place shallot and spinach in a 2½-quart (2.5-l) soufflé dish. Cook, uncovered, at 100% for 2 minutes in a 650- to 700-watt oven. Remove from oven and reserve.

2. Combine cornstarch and buttermilk thoroughly in a 2-cup (470-ml) glass measure. Cover tightly with microwave plastic wrap. Cook for 3 minutes. Prick plastic to release steam.

3. Remove from oven and uncover. Stir well, making sure to stir in any undissolved cornstarch. Scrape into a blender. Add reserved spinach and remaining ingredients except chicken. Blend until smooth.

4. Place each half-breast in the center of a dinner plate or 10-inch (25.5-cm)

quiche dish. Cover each tightly with microwave plastic wrap. Using a rack, cook for 3 minutes. Switch plates and cook for 1 minute more. Prick plastic.

5. Remove from oven and uncover. Spoon ¼ cup (60 ml) sauce to one side of each breast. Return to oven and cook, uncovered, using the rack, for 1 minute.

6. Remove from oven and serve with ½ cup (120 ml) cooked rice or orzo mixed with 1 tablespoon chopped parsley for each person, if desired.

FOR 400- TO 500-WATT OVENS

To serve 2. Cook as in Step 1 for 5 minutes. Cook buttermilk and cornstarch as in Step 2 for 5 minutes. Continue with Step 3. Cook chicken as in Step 4 for 3 minutes. Switch plates and cook for 2 minutes more. Finish as in Step 5, cooking for 2 minutes.

ORIENTAL CHICKEN STEW

*T*he small quantity of vinegar gives the dish piquancy. Light as the stew may be, its cabbage, mushrooms and sesame seeds provide as much nutrition as they do flavor. Serve each portion over a cup of cooked brown rice. Begin dinner with Oriental Spinach Salad (page 79) or Carrot Timbale (page 105)—have the leftovers for lunch. Finish off with Apple Snow (page 549) or a piece of fruit—a glass of wine. Have a late-evening snack.   *SERVES 2*

Per ½-breast serving: 265 calories; 69 milligrams cholesterol; 5 grams fat; 286 milligrams sodium; 33 grams protein (73% RDA); 23 grams carbohydrate

RDA: calcium 18%; phosphorus 36%; iron 18%; 1,002 milligrams potassium; vitamin A 41%; thiamin 14%; riboflavin 25%; niacin 85%; vitamin C 80%

¾ ounce (21 g) dried shiitake
   mushrooms (4 or 5 mushrooms),
   stems removed, broken into pieces
½ ounce (14 g) dried tree ears (about
   ⅓ cup; 80 ml)
¾ pound (340 g) Chinese cabbage,
   washed and finely shredded across
   the leaves (about 3 cups; 705 ml)
2 half-breasts chicken (each 4 ounces;
   113.5 g), skinned, boned and each
   half sliced diagonally into 3 pieces

2 teaspoons sesame seeds
½ teaspoon Chinese five-spice powder
1 tablespoon cornstarch
½ teaspoon Oriental sesame oil
1 tablespoon rice wine vinegar
1 teaspoon tamari soy
¾ cup (180 ml) Basic Chicken Broth
   (page 460), or unsalted or regular
   canned chicken broth

(continued)

1. Place shiitakes and tree ears in a $13 \times 9 \times 2$-inch ($33 \times 23 \times 5$-cm) oval glass dish. Spread cabbage over mushrooms and place chicken pieces around the inside edge of the dish.

2. Stir together sesame seeds, spice powder and cornstarch in a 2-cup (470-ml) glass measure. Add remaining ingredients to measure and stir to combine. Pour mixture over chicken and cabbage. Cover tightly with microwave plastic wrap. Cook at 100% for 6 minutes, or until chicken is opaque and cooked through, in a 650- to 700-watt oven. Prick plastic to release steam.

3. Remove from oven and uncover. Serve hot or at room temperature.

FOR 400- TO 500-WATT OVENS

To serve 2. Cook for 9 minutes 30 seconds. Serve hot or at room temperature.

GILDED CHICKEN

*T*he carrot sauce for this dish is the most beautiful color and gives the dish enormous amounts of vitamin A and niacin and some calcium. That's not bad for a sauce so creamy no one will believe this is diet food. It comes with its own zucchini. Add some Garlic Potatoes (page 223) or bread if you want. Begin with Hearty Vegetable Soup with Pesto (page 130) and finish up with Peach Sorbet (page 554) or Mango Mousse (page 564), depending on the season. Add a glass of white wine or some Oat Bran Crisps (page 574).   SERVES 4

Per ½-breast serving: 201 calories; 78 milligrams cholesterol; 4 grams fat; 320 milligrams sodium; 32 grams protein (71% RDA); 7 grams carbohydrate

RDA: calcium 12%; phosphorus 32%; vitamin A 221%; niacin 70%; vitamin C 17%

4 small zucchini (about 8 ounces; 227 g)

4 half-breasts chicken (each 4 ounces; 113.5 g), skinned and boned

1 cup (240 ml) 24 Karat Sauce (page 504)

1. Cut each zucchini on the diagonal into six thin slices. Holding your knife on the diagonal, make four lengthwise cuts in each breast, cutting almost completely through the meat. Place a slice of zucchini between each cut and one at both ends of the breast.

2. Cut a piece of aluminum foil long enough to fit around a 10-inch (25.5-cm) quiche dish. Fold foil in half lengthwise and wrap around the outside of the dish, folding excess over the rim to create a ledge. Spread carrot sauce on the bottom of the dish.

3. Using a spatula, place each breast on the sauce with the thickest end toward the edge of the dish. Cover tightly with microwave plastic wrap. Cook at 100% for 5 minutes, or until chicken is opaque and cooked through, in a 650- to 700-watt oven. Prick plastic to release steam.

4. Remove from oven, uncover and serve.

To serve 2. Use 2 zucchini, 2 half-breasts chicken and ½ cup (120 ml) sauce. Cook for 3 minutes 30 seconds.

To serve 1. Use 1 zucchini, 1 half-breast chicken and ¼ cup (60 ml) sauce. Cook for 2 minutes 30 seconds.

FOR 400- TO 500-WATT OVENS

To serve 4. Prepare as above, cooking for 7–8 minutes on a wind-up carrousel.

To serve 2. Cook for 4 minutes.

To serve 1. Cook for 3 minutes.

*Arrange chicken studded with vegetables
on sauce in a shielded dish.*

SPICY BROCHETTES

*T*his spicy and festive dish is a treat for a family of four or a single hungry diner. You will find it hard to believe that you can eat this on a diet and get lots of vitamin A and niacin and a mammoth amount of vitamin C. Serve with one-half cup per person of cooked white or brown rice (one hundred calories more) set between the two skewers to soak up the sauce. You need a 650- to 700-watt oven to make this for more than one; additional portions cook unevenly in a low-wattage oven. The brochettes can be prepared and put in the refrigerator to marinate the night or morning before you want to eat them. Just remember to bring them to room temperature before cooking.   *SERVES 4*

Per 2-brochette serving: 261 calories; 68 milligrams cholesterol; 7 grams fat; 106 grams sodium; 29 grams protein (64% RDA); 22 grams carbohydrate

RDA: calcium 4%; phosphorus 27%; iron 14%; 616 milligrams potassium; vitamin A 72%; riboflavin 10%; niacin 71%; vitamin C 190%

8 ounces (227 g) red bell pepper, stemmed, seeded and deribbed, cut into 24 squares (about 1½ cups; 355 ml)

4 half-breasts chicken (each 4 ounces; 113.5 g), skinned and boned, each cut into 6 pieces

8 ounces (227 g) canned (packed in unsweetened juice) or fresh pineapple, cut into 24 chunks (about 1½ cups; 355 ml)

4 teaspoons vegetable oil

4 teaspoons chili powder (without cumin), or 2 tablespoons chile powder (with cumin)

1 teaspoon cumin, if you are using pure chili powder

4 cloves garlic, smashed, peeled and minced

4 teaspoons fresh lemon juice

¼ cup (60 ml) unsweetened pineapple juice (if using canned pineapple, use its juice)

2 cups (470 ml) cooked rice, optional

1. On each of eight 6-inch (15-cm) wooden skewers, place a slice of pepper, then a piece of chicken and a pineapple chunk. Continue in this manner, dividing ingredients equally among the skewers.

2. In a small bowl, combine remaining ingredients, mashing them together with a small fork or spoon. Spread mixture on the brochettes, making sure all sides are covered with it. Arrange the skewers in a 13×9×2-inch (33×23×5-cm) glass oval dish. Cover tightly with microwave plastic wrap and let stand for 3 hours at room temperature or refrigerate overnight.

3. Leaving brochettes in same dish and covered, cook at 100% for 4 minutes in a 650- to 700-watt oven. Prick plastic to release steam.

4. Remove from oven and uncover. Turn skewers over; re-cover and cook 1 minute 30 seconds more. Prick plastic wrap.

5. Remove from oven and uncover. Let stand several minutes to cool slightly and serve with ½ cup (120 ml) cooked white or brown rice per person, if desired.

To serve 2. Use 4 ounces (113.5 g) red pepper, 2 half-breasts chicken (each 4 ounces; 113.5 g), 4 ounces (113.5 g) pineapple, 2 teaspoons vegetable oil, 2 teaspoons chili powder, ½ teaspoon cumin, 2 cloves garlic, 2 teaspoons lemon juice and 2 tablespoons pineapple juice. Prepare as in Steps 1 and 2, dividing ingredients among 4 skewers. Arrange on two dinner plates and let stand. Cook, using a rack, at 100% for 3 minutes, switching plates after 1 minute 30 seconds.

To serve 1. Use 2 ounces (56 g) red pepper, 1 half-breast chicken (4 ounces; 113.5 g), 2 ounces (56 g) pineapple, 1 teaspoon vegetable oil, 1 teaspoon chili powder, ¼ teaspoon cumin, 1 clove garlic, 1 teaspoon lemon juice and 1 tablespoon pineapple juice. Arrange on two skewers; cook for 1 minute 30 seconds to 2 minutes, or until opaque.

FOR 400- TO 500-WATT OVENS

To serve 1. Cook for 3 minutes or until chicken is opaque.

WARM CHICKEN SALAD ORIENTAL

*I*t takes longer to list the ingredients in this recipe than it does to cook it. Its low-calorie count makes it a perfect choice for lunch accompanied by some Oat Bran Wafers (page 161). If you're having it as a light meal for a hot summer day's dinner, you can double the portion and still be in good shape. I don't think you will need to; it's filling. Take advantage of its lightness to have on the day before or after a larger-than-usual feed—a summer wedding, or, with leftover turkey substituted, Thanksgiving. In hot weather, try a hearty chilled soup such as Slim Vichyssoise (page 147) and feel free to indulge in dessert. Plum Timbales (page 562), even with a topping of one tablespoon of whipped cream, would be fine. A small (8 ounces; 240 ml) glass of light beer would probably go better than wine. *SERVES 2 AS A MAIN COURSE, 4 AS A FIRST COURSE*

Per 1-cup (240-ml) serving: 220 calories; 66 milligrams cholesterol; 6 grams fat; 136 milligrams sodium; 30 grams protein (66% RDA); 6 grams carbohydrate

RDA: phosphorus 14%; vitamin A 13%; niacin 35%; vitamin C 16%

(continued)

1½ ounces (42.5 g) peeled and grated
   fresh ginger
3 cloves garlic, smashed and peeled
Pinch hot red pepper flakes
2 teaspoons rice wine vinegar
8 sprigs fresh coriander, leaves chopped
   and stems reserved
1 cup (240 ml) Basic Chicken Broth
   (page 460), or unsalted or regular
   canned chicken broth
½ pound (227 g) cucumber, peeled,
   halved lengthwise, seeded and cut
   across into ¼-inch (.5-cm) slices (1
   cup; 240 ml)

2 half-breasts chicken (each 4 ounces;
   113.5 g), skinned, boned and cut
   into 1-inch (2.5-cm) chunks
¼ cup (60 ml) sliced water chestnuts
1 tablespoon thinly sliced scallion
   greens
¼ teaspoon Oriental sesame oil
1 teaspoon vegetable oil
⅛ teaspoon tamari soy
Boston lettuce leaves, optional

1. Combine ginger, garlic, pepper flakes, vinegar, coriander stems and broth in a 2½-quart (2.5-l) soufflé dish. Cover tightly with microwave plastic wrap. Cook for 5 minutes at 100% in a 650- to 700-watt oven. Prick plastic to release steam.

2. Remove from oven and uncover. Add cucumber slices to broth. Re-cover and cook for 3 minutes. Prick plastic.

3. Remove from oven and uncover. With a slotted spoon, remove cucumber to a medium bowl. Add chicken to broth. Re-cover and cook for 2 minutes. Prick plastic.

4. Remove from oven and uncover. Take out chicken with a slotted spoon and add to cucumbers along with water chestnuts. Place 1 tablespoon of the cooking liquid in a small bowl and discard remaining liquid. Add chopped coriander leaves and remaining ingredients. Pour over chicken mixture and serve at room temperature on leaves of Boston lettuce, if desired.

FOR 400- TO 500-WATT OVENS

To serve 2. Combine broth ingredients as in Step 1. Cook for 8 minutes. Add cucumbers and cook for 5 minutes. Remove cucumber and stir in chicken as in Step 3. Cook for 3 minutes. Finish as in Step 4.

CRUNCHY VEGETABLE AND CHICKEN LOAF

This is a meat loaf with better-for-you chicken. It may not look like a loaf since it is cooked in a ring. It cooks more evenly in that shape in a microwave oven. I think you will find it as delicious a family staple as regular meat loaf. With its flecks of red and green, it is certainly prettier, and the serving is large enough so that you will feel full. Even on a weight-loss diet, consider adding Garlic Spinach (page 434), a good salad and Raspberry Poached Pears (page 545) for dessert. Add some Light White Ice Cream (page 558) to the pears for those who don't have to lose weight. If you don't have time to boil brown rice—which can be made ahead—substitute white rice. It is quicker-cooking, but less nutritious.
SERVES 4

Per ¼-ring serving: 186 calories; 68 milligrams cholesterol; 2 grams fat; 260 milligrams sodium; 29 grams protein (64% RDA); 12 grams carbohydrate

RDA: vitamin A 37%; niacin 69%; vitamin C 102%

4 ounces (113.5 g) red onion, cut into chunks (1 cup; 240 ml)
4 ounces (113.5 g) red bell pepper, cut into chunks (1½ cups; 355 ml)
¼ cup (60 ml) parsley leaves
4 half-breasts chicken (each 4 ounces; 113.5 g), skinned and boned

½ teaspoon kosher salt
Pinch cayenne pepper
⅔ cp (160 ml) cooked brown rice (page 182)
Additional parsley sprigs, if desired

1. Coarsely chop onion, pepper and parsley in a food processor. Scrape into a small bowl.

2. Place breast meat in the food processor and process until finely chopped but not completely smooth. Stir into vegetables along with salt, cayenne pepper and brown rice.

3. Pack mixture loosely into a 9-inch (23-cm) glass ring mold if you have one. If not, place in a 10-inch (25.5-cm) quiche dish and form mixture into a 9-inch (23-cm) ring about 2 inches (5-cm) wide. Place additional parsley over the top, if desired. Cover tightly with microwave plastic wrap. Cook at 100% in a 650- to 700-watt oven for 6 minutes if in a ring mold, 5 minutes if free form, or until the food reaches a temperature of at least 130°F (54.5°C). Prick plastic to release steam.

4. Remove from oven and uncover. There will be liquid in the quiche dish that will be absorbed if the loaf sits.

(continued)

To serve 2. Use 2 ounces (56 g) red onion, 2 ounces (56 g) red pepper, 2 table-spoons parsley leaves, 1 whole breast chicken, skinned and boned (about 8 ounces; 227 g), ¼ teaspoon kosher salt, a small pinch of cayenne and ⅓ cup (80 ml) cooked brown rice. Prepare as in Steps 1 and 2. Shape mixture into 2 oval loaves. Place a loaf on either side of a quiche dish or a 9-inch (23-cm) pie plate. Cover tightly and cook for 3 minutes 30 seconds to 4 minutes, or until the food reaches a temperature of at least 130°F (54.5°C).

FOR 400- TO 500-WATT OVENS

To serve 4. Cook for 8 minutes.

To serve 2. Cook for 6 minutes.

*Make a 2-inch (5-cm) wide ring
with the mixture 1 inch (2.5 cm)
from the edge of the dish.*

CHICKEN WITH CELERY

*T*his simple, rapidly cooked family dinner is surprisingly pretty and has more flavor than you would think. It makes a lovely sauce that would be complemented by one-half cup (120 ml) of cooked brown rice for each person. That makes only 262 calories for the main course, leaving plenty of leeway for a first course such as Mussels Stuffed with Tabbouleh (page 111) or spaghettini with Tomato Sauce Casalinga (page 167) and a serving of fruit or a dessert like Pumpkin Pudding (page 571). This dish provides almost two-thirds your niacin and vitamin A for the day.

In spring, if you have a garden, you can make a delicious version, Chicken with Lovage and Spring Onions. Substitute one-half ounce lovage leaves cut into chiffonade (one-quarter cup; 60 ml) and four spring onions sliced in half lengthwise for vegetables below. If you haven't planted lovage, it's worth finding some in a garden center; but be warned, in a few years, it will make a large clump, five feet across and over six feet high. If you cut off the flower heads before they bloom, you will have fresh leaves all summer long. Lovage always reassures me. It's the first green to come back from seeming death in the spring.   *SERVES 4*

Per half-breast serving: 146 calories; 66 millligrams cholesterol; 2 grams fat; 281 milligrams sodium; 27 grams protein (60% RDA); 4 grams carbohydrate

RDA: phosphorus 24%; vitamin A 62%; niacin 65%; vitamin C 14%

4 half-breasts chicken (each 4 ounces; 113.5 g), skinned and boned

4 stalks celery (8 ounces; 227 g), peeled and sliced with leaves (about ½ cup [120 ml] stalk and about ½ cup [120 ml] leaves)

⅓ cup (80 ml) sliced scallion whites and greens (about 6 scallions)

½ medium carrot (2 ounces; 56 g), cut into 2 × ¼ × ¼-inch (5 × .5 × .5-cm) matchsticks (about ⅓ cup; (80 ml)

½ cup (120 ml) Basic Chicken Broth (page 460), or unsalted or regular canned chicken broth

½ teaspoon kosher salt

Pinch freshly ground black pepper

1 tablespoon cornstarch

1. Arrange chicken breasts spoke-fashion, with the thick ends toward the edge of a 10-inch (25.5-cm) quiche dish or pie plate. Sprinkle with vegetables, ¼ cup (60 ml) of the broth, salt and pepper. Cover tightly with microwave plastic. Cook at 100% for 4 minutes in a 650- to 700-watt oven. Prick plastic to release steam.

2. While the chicken is cooking, combine remaining broth and cornstarch and stir until smooth.

3. Remove dish from oven and uncover. Turn breasts over and stir in broth and cornstarch mixture. Re-cover and cook for 2 minutes more. Prick plastic wrap.

4. Remove from oven and uncover. Stir well and serve immediately.

FOR 400- TO 500-WATT OVENS

To serve 4. Follow Step 1 and cook chicken for 6 minutes. Continue as in Steps 2 and 3; cook for 5 minutes. Finish as in Step 4.

CHICKEN PISTOU

*P*istou is the French version of Italian pesto, the smooth, basil-scented, garlic-sharpened sauce. It's usually very fattening. I'm so proud of my Diet Pesto that I make large batches of it and stir it into all sorts of dishes. While we may be mostly familiar with pesto as a pasta sauce—very good too—in its homeland, the sunny French and Italian Rivieras, it is also stirred into bean or vegetable soups to make them rich and fragrant. Here, it is the pleasurable difference in a soupy chicken stew thick with vegetables that makes a whole meal and gets much of its healthy protein from chick-peas. It's pretty too. Those on a low-salt diet should take the time to make basic chick-peas (page 202).

I find that a salad and a piece of low-cholesterol cheese completes this meal; but hearty eaters not needing to lose weight can serve this over one-half cup (120 ml) of cooked orzo and sprinkle grated Parmesan on top. Happily, weight-losers get plenty of carbohydrate even without the orzo, in addition to iron and vitamin A. Give everybody a glass of red wine. Serve in soup dishes with big spoons.
SERVES 4

Per 1-cup (240-ml) serving: 345 calories; 66 milligrams cholesterol; 5 grams fat; 587 milligrams sodium; 35 grams protein (78% RDA); 40 grams carbohydrate

RDA: calcium 15%; phosphorus 39%; iron 26%; 839 milligrams potassium; vitamin A 212%; niacin 71%; vitamin C 28%

2 medium carrots, trimmed, peeled, cut in half lengthwise and thinly sliced across (1 cup; 240 ml)

2 ounces (56 g) green beans, cut into ½-inch (1-cm) pieces (½ cup; 120 ml)

½ small yellow onion, peeled and chopped (¼ cup; 60 ml)

1 stalk celery, peeled, trimmed and thinly sliced (½ cup; 120 ml)

1¼ cups (300 ml) Basic Chicken Broth (page 460), or unsalted or regular canned chicken broth

4 half-breasts chicken (each 4 ounces; 113.5 g), skinned, boned and cut into quarters

1 19-ounce (535-g) can chick-peas, drained and rinsed, or cooked chick-peas (page 202)

¼ cup (60 ml) Diet Pesto Sauce (page 476)

Kosher salt, to taste

Freshly ground black pepper, to taste

1. Arrange carrots and green beans around the inside edge of a 13 × 9 × 2-inch (33 × 23 × 5-cm) oval glass dish. Place the onions and celery in the center and pour over chicken broth. Cover tightly with microwave plastic wrap. Cook at 100% for 8 minutes in a 650- to 700-watt oven. Prick plastic to release steam.

2. Remove from oven and uncover. Stir in chicken and chick-peas. Re-cover and cook for 4 minutes. Prick plastic wrap.

3. Remove from oven and uncover. Stir in pesto and salt and pepper, if desired. Serve hot.

FOR 400- TO 500-WATT OVENS

To serve 4. Combine vegetables and broth as in Step 1 and cook for 15 minutes. Follow Step 2; cook for 8 minutes, or until chicken is opaque and cooked through. Stir in remaining ingredients and serve hot.

CHICKEN AND FENNEL STEW

A light cornstarch-thickened broth binds this comforting stew. The slight licorice flavor of the fennel makes it a nice change from regular fare. Although I use little butter for the recipes in this book, I really like the flavor in this dish. If you are on a very tightly controlled low-cholesterol diet, substitute olive oil.

Serve this with some steamed new potatoes, or one-half cup (120 ml) of boiled rice or noodles per person. At a party, begin with Vegetable Terrine (page 86); family dinner can start with an artichoke (pages 99–100). Follow the stew with Chunky Tomato Basil Salad (page 407) and wind up with fruit or dessert.

SERVES 4

Per ¼ chicken or half-breast serving: 231 calories; 103 milligrams cholesterol; 8 grams fat; 377 milligrams sodium; 31 grams protein (69% RDA); 8 grams carbohydrate

RDA: calcium 7%; phosphorus 29%; iron 13%; thiamin 10%; riboflavin 12%; niacin 60%; vitamin C 25%

1 tablespoon unsalted butter
1 pound (450 g) fennel bulb, trimmed, peeled and cut into 1-inch wedges (about 5 cups; 1.2 l)
½ pound (227 g) onion, root trimmed, peeled and cut into wedges (about 2½ cups; 600 ml)
2½-pound (1.15-kg) chicken, cut into serving pieces and skinned, or 4 half-breasts chicken (each 4 ounces; 113.5 g), skinned and boned

¼ cup (60 ml) white wine
¾ cup (180) ml) Basic Chicken Broth (page 460), or unsalted or regular canned chicken broth
½ teaspoon kosher salt
Pinch freshly ground black pepper
1 tablespoon cornstarch

1. Heat butter, uncovered, in a 2½-quart (2.5-l) soufflé dish or casserole with a tightly fitted lid at 100% for 2 minutes in a 650- to 700-watt oven. Make a ring

(continued)

of the fennel with the root ends against the edge of the dish. Put onion pieces in the center. Cook, uncovered, at 100% for 2 minutes. Remove from oven.

2. Arrange chicken on top of vegetables. Place dark-meat pieces around the inside edge of the dish and breast pieces—thin edges toward the center of the dish—in the middle. Pour over wine and broth. Sprinkle with salt and pepper. Cover with microwave plastic wrap or casserole lid and cook for 10 minutes. If using plastic, prick to release steam.

3. Remove from oven. Uncover and remove ¼ cup (60 ml) of the liquid. Add cornstarch and stir until smooth. Pour back into cooking dish and stir to combine. Re-cover and cook for 5 minutes more, or until chicken juices run clear and sauce has thickened.

FOR 400- TO 500-WATT OVENS

To serve 4. Follow Step 1 and heat butter for 3 minutes; cook vegetables for 4 minutes. Continue with Step 2 and cook for 15 minutes. Add cornstarch as in Step 3 and cook for 7 minutes more, or until chicken juices run clear and sauce has thickened.

CHICKEN PAPRIKÁS

*T*here was a time in America when food was routinely sprinkled with paprika. We didn't really think about the flavor; we were using it for color. Now that we have learned that food can be beautiful on its own, we seem to have forgotten how good paprika can taste. It is historically a South American flavoring, the sweet version of chili—pod peppers dried and ground to a fine powder. Early in the history of European involvement in the Americas, the Spaniards discovered just how good this flavoring could be and took it home with them. For dynastic reasons, they owned Hungary at that time and took their new seeds there. Hungarian soil seemed the perfect location for the red peppers used to make paprika, and Hungarians took to the new seasoning with glee. They have three different kinds: hot—close to our pure chili powder without cumin; medium—half hot and half sweet; and sweet, which is the kind to which we are most accustomed. Paprika is also rich in vitamin C, so this dish provides more than a third of your daily needs.

Don't tell anyone that this light version of a scrumptious Hungarian classic is a diet dinner; they'll never guess that the fragrant, pale-salmon-colored sauce isn't full of weight-producing sour cream. I like to stir in two cups of cooked orzo (the rice-shaped pasta), which makes it seem even less dietetic, but only adds forty-eight calories per person. Best of all, this festive dish is easy to make. By taking the half-breast-and-wing serving, you cut calories even further. This meal should have only the lightest of first courses; it is that filling. Try Eggplant Purée with Lemon and Chives. (page 89). Have tea, coffee or soothing chamomile with some Oat Bran Crisps (page 574) or a diet sorbet for dessert.   *SERVES 4*

Per ¼-chicken serving: 252 calories; 97 milligrams cholesterol; 8 grams fat; 518 milligrams sodium; 32 grams protein (72% RDA); 13 grams carbohydrate

RDA: calcium 9%; phosphorus 31%; iron 14%; 602 milligrams potassium; vitamin A 43%; thiamin 11%; riboflavin 18%; niacin 61%; vitamin C 27%

2 teaspoons vegetable oil
2 tablespoons sweet paprika
1 pound (450 g) yellow onions, peeled and thinly sliced (2 cups; 470 ml)
2½ pounds (1.15 kg) chicken, cut into serving pieces and skinned
⅔ cup (160 ml) Basic Chicken Broth (page 460), or unsalted or regular canned chicken broth

½ cup (120 ml) buttermilk
1 tablespoon cornstarch
1 teaspoon kosher salt
1 tablespoon fresh lemon juice
Freshly ground black pepper, to taste
2 cups (470 ml) cooked orzo, optional

1. Mix oil and paprika together in the center of a 2½-quart (2.5-l) soufflé dish or casserole with a tightly fitted lid. Cook, uncovered, at 100% for 1 minute in a 650- to 700-watt oven. Add onions and stir to coat. Cook, uncovered, for 6 minutes.

2. Remove from oven. Arrange chicken pieces on top of onions, with dark-meat pieces around the inside edge of the dish and breast pieces in the center. Pour chicken broth over all. Cover tightly with microwave plastic wrap or lid. Cook for 12 minutes, turning chicken pieces over after 6 minutes. If using plastic, prick to release steam.

3. Remove from oven and uncover. Stir together buttermilk and cornstarch, making sure there are no lumps. Stir ¼ cup (60 ml) of the cooking liquid into cornstarch mixture and stir back into dish with chicken. Cook, uncovered, for 3 minutes.

4. Remove from oven. Add salt, lemon juice and pepper and stir well. Stir in cooked orzo, if desired. Serve hot.

FOR 400- TO 500-WATT OVENS

To serve 4. Follow Step 1 and cook oil and paprika for 1 minute 30 seconds; cook onions for 10 minutes. Continue as in Step 2 and cook for 15 minutes, turning pieces over after 7 minutes. Finish as in Steps 3 and 4; cook for 4 minutes 30 seconds.

HOMEY WINTER STEW

*T*his cozy dish is just the kind of thing that would have sustained many of our ancestors on cold winter evenings when most of the vegetables came from a root cellar. Even in today's odd world of strawberries in winter, it is a delight and provides more iron and vitamins than we might think comes from wintery stuff. I think I would serve it with a half-cup (120 ml) of cooked old-fashioned broad egg noodles per person, which would add about a hundred calories. Another option would be to cook two Idaho potatoes (page 219) and add a half-cup of peeled one-inch cubes to each portion. That would be a good dinner for me with a salad and a glass of wine; but if you have a large man or ravenous child at the table, add bread and dessert and some milk for the child.   *SERVES 4*

Per ¼-chicken serving: 242 calories; 95 milligrams cholesterol; 5 grams fat; 372 milligrams sodium; 32 grams protein (70% RDA); 16 grams carbohydrate

RDA: phosphorus 31%; iron 14%; riboflavin 15%; niacin 63%; vitamin C 29%

1 turnip (4 ounces; 113.5 g), peeled and cut into ½-inch (1-cm) wedges (about 1 cup; 240 ml)

4 ounces (113.5 g) parsnip, peeled and cut across into ½-inch (1-cm) rounds (about 1 cup; 240 ml)

5 ounces (142 g) celery root, peeled and cut into 2 × ½ × ½-inch (5 × 1 × 1-cm) sticks (about 1¼ cups; 300 ml)

2 leeks (each 3 ounces; 85 g), trimmed, cleaned and cut across into ½-inch (1-cm) slices (about 1 cup; 240 ml)

2 cups (470 ml) Basic Chicken Broth (page 460), or unsalted or regular canned chicken broth

¼ teaspoon summer savory

¼ teaspoon dried thyme

Large pinch dried rosemary

2½ pounds (1.15 k) chicken, cut into serving pieces and skinned

2 tablespoons cornstarch

½ teaspoon kosher salt

1. In a 2½-quart (2.5-l) soufflé dish or casserole with a tightly fitted lid, arrange vegetables, with turnips, parsnips and celery root around the inside edge and leeks in the center. Pour chicken broth over, and sprinkle with herbs. Cover tightly with microwave plastic wrap or lid. Cook at 100% for 10 minutes in a 650- to 700-watt oven. If using plastic, prick to release steam.

2. Remove from oven and uncover. Place chicken pieces over vegetables with dark-meat pieces around the outside and breast pieces in the center. Cover and cook for 10 minutes. If using plastic, prick.

3. Remove from oven and uncover. Remove ½ cup (120 ml) of the liquid and add cornstarch. Stir well to combine, making sure there are no lumps. Stir back into stew along with the salt. Cook, uncovered, for 3 minutes or until liquid is boiling and thickened.

FOR 400- TO 500-WATT OVENS

To serve 4. Combine vegetables and broth as in Step 1; cook for 18 minutes, or until vegetables are tender. Follow Step 2 and cook for 15 minutes; uncover and turn pieces over; re-cover and cook for 5 minutes more. Add cornstarch as in Step 3 and cook for 5 minutes, or until liquid is boiling and thickened.

CHICKEN CURRY FOR REAL

I can't tell you what the Indians would call this—certainly not curry. What they would recognize is the combination of spices and flavorings that fills every corner of the mouth with sensation. It's not really hot; but does it taste good. You'll notice that it accomplishes that without any salt—a good thing to remember when seasoning your own salt-free foods. With enough well-balanced seasonings, including the front-of-your-mouth sparkle of acid and the mellow background flavor of well-cooked garlic, you will never miss salt.

There are many acidic flavors from which to choose in Western cooking; but Indian cooking provides an even greater group, typically acids that don't fade with the longer cooking of most Indian dishes. Even though microwave cooking takes much less time, ordinary acids tend to wilt. Besides, the Indian ones provide some interesting flavors worth trying. Mango powder is one. Tamarind is used here. If you substitute fruit juice or vinegar in Indian recipes, remember to add it at the end.

This is a good dish for a party. You can serve Parsley Pilaf (page 185) and surround it with any number of those little dishes of condiments that led to the English describing a curry as a four- (or more) boy curry; a different serving person passed each condiment. Plumped raisins (soaked in water and drained), grated unsweetened coconut, sliced bananas mixed with a little lemon juice to prevent discoloration, toasted raw peanuts or cashews and chutney are all very nice; but watch out—they all contain calories. Mint Yogurt Dressing (page 494) and Pear Chutney (page 524) won't hurt too much, and a half-cup (120 ml) of Parsley Pilaf will add only 111 calories, which will still let you join your guests in dessert; but if you're trying to lose weight, avoid the nuts and raisins unless it's been a low-calorie day. If you've been saving calories in anticipation, then raisins will add iron, bananas will add potassium.   *SERVES 6*

(continued)

Per 1-cup (240-ml) serving: 221 calories; 67 milligrams cholesterol; 3 grams fat; 113 milligrams sodium; 30 grams protein (67% RDA); 18 grams carbohydrate

RDA: calcium 13%; phosphorus 32%; vitamin A 23%; niacin 66%; vitamin C 65%

FOR THE SPICE MIXTURE

1 dried red chili pepper
Pinch nutmeg
⅛ teaspoon anise seeds
¼ teaspoon ground cumin
½ teaspoon turmeric
⅛ teaspoon ground cardamom
¼ teaspoon ground ginger
Pinch dry mustard
¼ teaspoon ground coriander

FOR THE CURRY

1 teaspoon vegetable oil
½ pound (225 g) yellow onions, peeled and coarsely chopped (2 cups; 470 ml)
5 cloves garlic, smashed, peeled and sliced
1 teaspoon black mustard seeds
2 tablespoons tamarind liquid or 2 tablespoons lime juice if unavailable

½ cup (120 ml) Basic Chicken Broth (page 460), or unsalted or regular canned chicken broth
¼ cup (60 ml) raisins
1 underripe (green) papaya, peeled, seeded and cut into 1-inch (1-cm) chunks (4 cups; 950 ml), and tossed with:
2 tablespoons fresh lemon juice
6 half-breasts chicken (each 4 ounces; 113.5 g), skinned, split and cut into 1-inch (1-cm) chunks
1 tablespoon peeled and grated fresh ginger
Kosher salt, to taste
Freshly ground black pepper, to taste
1 cup (240 ml) nonfat yogurt

1. Place ingredients for spice mixture in spice grinder or clean coffee grinder and grind to a powder.

2. Combine spice mixture with oil in the center of a 13×9×2-inch (33×23×5-cm) glass oval dish and stir to form a paste. Cook, uncovered, at 100% for 1 minute in a 650- to 700-watt oven.

3. Add onions and garlic and toss to coat with spice mixture. Cook, uncovered, for 2 minutes. Add mustard seeds and cook, uncovered, for 1 minute.

4. Stir in tamarind liquid, if using, and chicken broth. Cook, tightly covered with microwave plastic wrap, for 2 minutes. Prick plastic to release steam.

5. Remove from oven and uncover. Stir in raisins, papaya and chicken pieces. Cover and cook 5 minutes, stirring once.

6. Remove from oven and uncover. Add ginger with salt and pepper to taste, then stir in yogurt and lime juice, if using.

To serve 6. Prepare as in Steps 1 and 2 and cook, uncovered, for 2 minutes. Follow Step 3 and cook, uncovered, for 3 minutes. Add mustard seeds and cook, uncovered, for 1½ minutes. Add tamarind liquid and chicken broth and cook, covered, for 3 minutes. Follow Step 5 and cook 10 minutes, stirring once.

JAMBALAYA

This down-home Cajun recipe is good and inexpensive for a party or a larger family dinner. Leftovers, if there are fewer than six in your group, reheat marvelously, and I have even been known to eat them cold. There is only one problem. This dish would take forever to make in a low-wattage oven; don't bother.

I must say that when I first thought of doing this dish I was stymied by the traditional inclusion of tasso, a very spicy, salty and generally unavailable, New Orleans cured ham. I have resolved this problem by spicing ham in the microwave oven. It works well and is much less salty. Try this method in recipes of your own that call for tasso.

Clever cooks will realize that the seasonings and method are not wildly different from the paella recipe that follows. The Spanish tradition worked out similar recipes in similar places; but this is much less expensive. This filling dish only needs something like Bibb and Tarragon Salad (page 393) and a portion of fruit for dessert, which still leaves enough calories for a small glass of beer or a glass of wine. While jambalaya is healthy, supplying almost a quarter of your iron needs for the day, along with two thirds of the niacin and substantial vitamin C, it is best avoided by the very salt-sensitive except for a special party.   *SERVES 6*

Per 1½-cup (355-ml) serving: 383 calories; 63 milligrams cholesterol; 7 milligrams fat; 742 milligrams sodium; 31 grams protein (69% RDA); 48 grams carbohydrate

RDA: phosphorus 32%; iron 23%; 735 milligrams potassium; vitamin A 30%; thiamin 45%; riboflavin 13%; niacin 69%; vitamin C 11%

(continued)

2 bay leaves
6 dried chili peppers
1 teaspoon dried thyme
1 teaspoon freshly ground black pepper
½ teaspoon cayenne pepper
½ teaspoon sage
½ teaspoon mustard powder
½ pound (227 g) smoked ham, cut into
  ½-inch (1-cm) cubes
½ pound (227 g) onion, peeled and
  chopped (about 1 cup; 240 ml)
2 stalks celery, peeled and chopped
  (about ½ cup; 120 ml)

½ pound (227 g) green bell pepper,
  stemmed, seeded, deribbed and
  chopped (about 1 cup; 240 ml)
1 tablespoon vegetable oil
1½ cups (355 ml) white rice
1 14½ ounce (409-g) can peeled
  tomatoes in juice
2½ cups (590 ml) Basic Chicken Broth
  (page 460), or unsalted or regular
  canned chicken broth
4 half-breasts chicken (each 4 ounces;
  113.5 g), skinned, boned and cut
  into 1-inch (2.5-cm) cubes

1. Finely grind all spices in a spice grinder or clean coffee grinder. Transfer spice mixture to a 9-inch (23-cm) pie plate or quiche dish. Add ham and toss to coat evenly with the spices. Cover loosely with paper toweling. Cook 5 minutes at 100% in a 650- to 700-watt oven.

2. Remove from oven, uncover and reserve.

3. Place onion, celery, pepper and oil in a 13×9×2-inch (33×23×5-cm) oval dish. Cook, uncovered, for 6 minutes. Stir in rice and cook, uncovered, for 2 minutes.

4. Stir in tomatoes and broth. Cook, uncovered, for 9 minutes. Stir and cook 10 minutes more, or until rice is cooked.

5. Remove from oven. Place chicken around the inside edge of the dish, on top of rice. Place reserved ham in the center, scraping up any spices on the bottom of the pie plate. Cover tightly with microwave plastic wrap and cook for 5 minutes, or until chicken is cooked through. Prick plastic to release steam.

6. Remove from oven and uncover. Stir well and serve.

PAELLA

*T*his is another rice-based peasant dish; but by American standards, this Spanish version with saffron and seafoods is festive enough for a party. It makes a whole meal with a green salad. You probably should have a breakfast and lunch without meat or fish. Consider Steamed Banana Muffins (page 155) with diet jam—Strawberry Jam (page 590) would be good—for breakfast and Black Bean and Tomato Salad (page 206) or a large bowl of Spicy Southwestern Soup (page 132) with warm pita bread and a portion of fruit for lunch. Don't do in a low-wattage oven.

Even though you are eating light other meals, don't be concerned; this dish comes up with a wallop of nutrition. *SERVES 6*

Per 2-cup (470-ml) serving: 439 calories; 147 milligrams cholesterol; 9 grams fat; 219 milligrams sodium; 42 grams protein (93% RDA); 45 grams carbohydrate

RDA: calcium 8%; phosphorus 41%; iron 44%; vitamin A 18%; thiamin 21%; riboflavin 16%; niacin 64%; vitamin C 29%

2 medium tomatoes, diced (about 2 cups; 470 ml)
2 small onions, peeled and chopped (about 1 cup; 240 ml)
8 cloves garlic, smashed, peeled and sliced
2 teaspoons vegetable oil
1½ cups (355 ml) white rice
2 cups (470 ml) Basic Chicken Broth (page 460), or unsalted or regular canned chicken broth
½ teaspoon saffron threads

1 ounce (28 g) chorizo sausage, cut into ⅛-inch (.3-cm) slices
3 pounds (1.4 k) chicken, skinned and cut into 6 pieces
10 littleneck clams, scrubbed
10 mussels, scrubbed and debearded
10 large shrimp, peeled (tails left on) and deveined
2 tablespoons chopped fresh parsley
Kosher salt, to taste
Freshly ground black pepper, to taste

1. Place tomatoes, onions, garlic and oil in a 5-quart (5-l) soufflé dish or casserole with a tightly fitted lid. Cook, uncovered, at 100% for 4 minutes in a 650- to 700-watt oven. Stir in rice, toss to coat and cook, uncovered, for 2 minutes.

2. Remove from oven. Stir in broth and saffron. Cook, uncovered, for 9 minutes. Stir and cook, uncovered, for 5 minutes more.

3. Remove from oven. Stir in chorizo. Arrange chicken on top of rice with dark-meat pieces around the inside edge of the dish and breast pieces in the center. Cover tightly with microwave plastic wrap or lid. Cook for 4 minutes. If using plastic wrap, prick to release steam.

4. Remove from oven and uncover. Turn chicken pieces over and place around the inside edge of the dish. Place clams, hinge end down, in the center. Re-cover and cook for 3 minutes. If using plastic wrap, prick to release steam.

5. Remove from oven and uncover. Place clams on top of chicken pieces. Arrange mussels in the center of the dish, hinge end down, and place shrimp over mussels. Cover and cook for 4 minutes, or until shrimp is opaque. If using plastic wrap, prick.

6. Remove from oven and uncover. Add parsley and salt and pepper to taste. Stir and serve.

CHICKEN IN RHUBARB CREAM

*T*his is a perfect springtime company dinner, and as such deserves homemade chicken broth, which will give it not only better flavor but also better texture. The Basic Glaze gives a slightly sweet, intense flavor that balances the acidity of the pink-red rhubarb; but it can be omitted.

You can have the secret satisfaction of knowing you are giving yourself and your guests a healthy meal, with two thirds of their niacin, more than a quarter of their vitamin C and phosphorus for the day and a light dose of calories, even with the heavy cream. If they are hearty eaters, you may want to allow two half-breasts for each. You can even indulge yourself that far if you are not on a low-cholesterol diet and eat lightly at lunch. I would serve a half-cup (120 ml) of cooked egg noodles per person, which adds about one hundred calories. When the noodles are cooked and drained—four cups—add one-half cup of Basic Chicken Broth to keep them separated. Start with Carrots and Mushrooms with Cumin (page 82) and finish with Peppered Strawberries (page 535). *SERVES 8*

Per half-breast serving: 210 calories; 86 milligrams cholesterol; 8 grams fat; 386 milligrams sodium; 28 grams protein (62% RDA); 6 grams carbohydrate

RDA: calcium 7%; phosphorus 25%; vitamin A 18%; niacin 67%; vitamin C 28%

2 cups (470 ml) Basic Chicken Broth (page 460), canned will not be good
5 tablespoons Basic Glaze (page 466), optional
8 half-breasts chicken (each 4 ounces; 113.5 g), skinned and boned
¼ cup (60 ml) red wine vinegar
1½ teaspoons kosher salt
Pinch freshly ground black pepper

½ cup (120 ml) heavy cream
1½ tablespoons cornstarch
1⅓ cups (320 ml) sliced-crosswise rhubarb (about 9 ounces; 225 g)
1 cup (240 ml) sliced scallion whites and greens—2 bunches (about 8 ounces; 225 g)
1 cup (240 ml) thinly sliced radish (about 8–10 ounces; 225 g)

1. Combine broth and glaze in a 14×11×2-inch (35.5×28×5-cm) dish. Cook, uncovered, at 100% for 10 minutes in a 650- to 700-watt oven.

2. Leaving dish in oven, place chicken spoke-fashion in dish, with thick ends toward the rim. Add vinegar, salt and pepper. Cover tightly with microwave plastic wrap and cook for 5 minutes. Prick plastic to release steam.

3. Combine cream and cornstarch and stir until smooth.

4. Remove dish from oven and uncover. Stir in cream mixture and remaining ingredients. Re-cover and cook for 3 minutes 30 seconds. Prick plastic wrap.

5. Remove from oven, uncover and serve immediately.

To serve 4. Use 1 cup (240 ml) broth, 3 tablespoons glaze, 4 half-breasts chicken, 2 tablespoons vinegar, ¾ teaspoon salt, pinch pepper, ¼ cup (60 ml) cream, 1 tablespoon cornstarch, ¾ cup (180 ml) rhubarb, ½ cup (120 ml) scallions and ½ cup (120 ml) radishes. Cook as in Step 1 in an 11 × 8 × 2-inch (28 × 20 × 5-cm) dish for 6 minutes. Continue with Step 2, cooking for 3 minutes. Cook as in Step 4 for 2 minutes.

FOR 400- TO 500-WATT OVENS

To serve 4. Cook as in Step 1 for 10 minutes. Cook as in Step 2 for 5 minutes. Continue with Steps 3 and 4, cooking for 5 minutes, or until chicken is cooked through.

CHICKEN IN THE POT

Old-fashioned and cozy, this can feed a family or be frozen in individual portions for later use. Defrost and cook a single portion for seven minutes at 100 percent power. If you are freezing part or all of this dish, don't add noodles to the portions you are freezing until after defrosting. Since this is a whole meal, you can afford the calories that come from the chicken skin; but if your cholesterol is high, you should really skin the bird. That simple step will let you have one of the diet Desserts (pages 530–596).

When I have people over informally, I am glad to serve this from a tureen into big, old-style rimmed soup dishes.

Your family will get a lot of vitamins—A, B and C—and minerals. Grandma knew something.   SERVES 8

Per ¼-chicken serving: 689 calories (409 if chicken is skinned); 186 milligrams cholesterol (132 is chicken is skinned); 279 milligrams sodium; 48 grams protein (108% RDA); 43 grams carbohydrate

RDA: calcium 11%; phosphorus 46%; iron 29%; 924 milligrams potassium; vitamin A 293%; thiamin 36%; riboflavin 26%; niacin 93%; vitamin C 51%

(continued)

2 chickens (each 2½–3 pounds; 1.1–1.4 kg), cut into serving pieces

¾ pound (340 g) onions, cut into 1- to 2-inch (2.5–5-cm) chunks (about 4 cups; 1 l)

4 small carrots (each 3–4 ounces; 85–115 g), peeled and cut into 1-inch (2.5-cm) chunks (about 1 cup; 240 ml)

½ pound (227 g) turnips, peeled, quartered and cut into ½-inch (1-cm) slices (about 2 cups; 470 ml)

½ pound (227 g) parsnips, peeled and cut into ½-inch (1-cm) dice (about 2 cups; 470 ml)

5¾ cups (1.4 l) Basic Chicken Broth (page 460), or unsalted or regular canned chicken broth

2 leeks (8 ounces; 227 g), cleaned and cut into ⅛-inch (.3-cm) slices (about 1¼ cups; 300 ml)

8 ounces (227 g) fine egg noodles

½ cup (120 ml) coarsely chopped fresh dill

1 10-ounce (284-g) box frozen tiny peas, defrosted in a sieve under warm running water

1. In a 5-quart (5-l) soufflé dish or casserole with a tightly fitted lid, arrange chicken with legs and thighs around the inside edge of the dish and wings and breasts in the center. Place onions over breasts and carrots, turnips and parsnips around the inside rim of the dish. Pour over 4¾ cups (1.2 l) of the broth. Cover tightly with microwave plastic wrap or lid. Cook at 100% for 35 minutes in a 650- to 700-watt oven. If using plastic wrap, prick to release steam.

2. Remove from oven, uncover and sprinkle leeks on top. Re-cover and cook for 5 minutes more. If using plastic wrap, prick.

3. Meanwhile, bring a large pot of water to boil on top of the stove. Cook noodles. Just before noodles are done, drain. Toss with dill, peas and remaining cup broth.

4. Remove chicken from oven and uncover. Stir in noodle mixture and serve in a large soup tureen, or serve noodles separately.

CHICKEN IN RED WINE

What is remarkable about the microwave oven is the way it extracts flavors from ingredients to enrich sauces. This is a diet version of a basic coq au vin recipe that I have been making for years. Gradually, I have adapted it for the young American chickens. Here, the calories are stripped way down; but I think you will be as pleased as I am by the richness of the flavor to be enjoyed without guilt.

Serve each portion with half a cup of cooked rice or noodles or half of a large Idaho potato cooked in the microwave oven and add one hundred calories, or follow with a salad and serve guests an impressive first course such as Polenta

Lasagne (page 216) and a fruit dessert, perhaps Minted Melon (page 536) in summer or Winter Fruit Compote (page 542) in winter. Red wine is the drink.

This party dish has good amounts of vitamins B and C and some iron; but also enough sodium so that you should have it rarely.   *SERVES 8*

Per ¼-chicken serving: 231 calories; 95 milligrams cholesterol; 537 milligrams sodium; 5 grams fat; 31 grams protein (70% RDA); 14 grams carbohydrate

RDA: phosphorus 30%; iron 14%; riboflavin 20%; niacin 64%; vitamin C 20%

1 teaspoon vegetable oil
½ pound (227 g) mushrooms, cleaned and sliced with stems attached (about 2 cups; 470 ml)
½ pound (227 g) pearl onions, peeled, or frozen pearl onions defrosted in a sieve under warm running water
2 chickens (each 2½ pounds; 1.1 kg), cut into serving pieces and skinned
¼ cup (60 ml) brandy
¼ cup (60 ml) Basic Glaze (page 466), optional
2 tablespoons red wine vinegar

3 tablespoons tomato paste
½ teaspoon dried thyme
1½ bay leaves
2 teaspoons kosher salt
16 large garlic cloves, smashed and peeled
1 cup (240 ml) Basic Chicken Broth (page 460), or unsalted or regular canned chicken broth
2 cups (470 ml) good-quality red wine
⅓ cup (80 ml) cornstarch
Freshly ground black pepper, to taste

1. Put vegetable oil into the bottom of a $14 \times 11 \times 2$-inch ($35.5 \times 28 \times 5$-cm) dish. Add mushrooms to fat and toss. Mound in the center of the dish. Place onions around the inside edge of dish.

2. Place chicken breasts, meaty side up, in center of dish on top of mushrooms. Put legs, thighs, wings and the 2 meatiest pieces of the back around breasts. Pour brandy, meat glaze (if using), vinegar and tomato paste over chicken. Add thyme, bay leaves and salt. Tuck garlic between chicken pieces. Pour broth and wine over chicken. Cover tightly with microwave plastic wrap. Cook at 100% for 22 minutes in a 650- to 700-watt oven. Prick plastic wrap to release steam.

3. Remove from oven and uncover. Remove chicken pieces to a serving platter and keep warm.

4. In a small bowl stir ½ cup (120 ml) of the cooking liquid into the cornstarch. Stir back into liquid in dish. Add pepper. Cook, uncovered, for 5 minutes.

5. Remove from oven. Stir well and stir chicken pieces back into sauce. Serve immediately.

Speedy Turkey Dinners

Turkey is the Thanksgiving bird even with today's smaller families. When the time comes, turn your conventional oven up to 500° F (260° C) and roast a fifteen-pound (4.5 kg) bird for about two hours unstuffed or two to two-and-a-half hours stuffed. Oddly, a twelve-pound (5.5-kg) bird, even stuffed, will take only about an hour and twenty minutes if you preheat your oven well, just as hot as it will go. Save your microwave oven for the other parts of the dinner. It will be fully occupied and everything will turn out better.

Today, even at Thanksgiving, a whole bird may be too much turkey for most families. Few households are going to make a whole turkey the rest of the year. Fortunately, this most American of birds need not disappear from our tables. The markets and the breeders have reacted to the change in family size by providing us with pieces and slices of bird meat. I find that the easiest cut to work with is thin slices of breast called cutlets—they should be raw and not breaded or prepared. They weigh about three ounces (85 g) per slice and have no surface fat or skin. They look just like a scaloppine of veal. Try to find them fresh; they will be much better than frozen.

There are many easy, delicious ways to serve these cutlets. You can make a sauce such as Tomato Sauce Casalinga (page 167), Diet Pesto Sauce (page 476) or Tonnato Sauce (page 484); or, even simpler, use tomato sauce from a jar. Then too, a few slices of vegetable per person, or a reasonable amount of a prepared stuffing, as in Turkey Duxelles (page 332), will not change the cooking times. Invent; this convenient, inexpensive, low-calorie, low-cholesterol meat is too good to waste. One drawback: Cooked without vegetables or sauce these cutlets get tough. Therefore, I have provided no basic cooking times.

TURKEY PARMESAN

*T*his very Italian, light and inexpensive version of scaloppine of veal Parmesan is a cook's reward for having had the foresight to make and freeze sauces ahead, since it is much better and has less sodium made with Fresh Tomato Purée (page 468) than with store-bought. Either way, it makes a satisfying meal. You can cook some pasta and put it on the plate without changing the cooking time; but you will up the calorie count by seventy-eight calories per half-cup (120 ml) of cooked pasta—no change in the cholesterol. I like to serve a half-cup (120 ml) of Garlic Spinach (page 434) with this, adding 138 calories per person. If you have just cooked the spinach, put it right on the plate with the turkey; it won't change the cooking time.

Serve a slice of bread and, filled with virtue, eat a dessert you love. You will be filled with virtue because you have had so few calories and 20 percent of your iron, a third of your phosphorus, a fifth of your calcium, almost a third of your vitamin C and lots of your niacin for the day. Even large men and starving teenagers should be happy. They could eat a double portion in terms of calories, but should be careful the rest of the day about cholesterol, as they will be getting 138 milligrams out of their suggested 300-milligram allowance.   *SERVES 4*

Per 1-slice serving: 190 calories; 69 milligrams cholesterol; 6 grams fat; 288 milligrams sodium; 28 grams protein (62% RDA); 6 grams carbohydrate

RDA: calcium 21%; phosphorus 33%; vitamin A 27%; riboflavin 13%; niacin 29%; vitamin C 30%

4 turkey cutlets (each 3 ounces; 85 g)	Pinch freshly ground black pepper
1 cup (240 ml) Fresh Tomato Purée (page 468), or canned tomato purée	4 ounces (113.5 g) coarsely grated part-skim mozzarella (1 cup; 240 ml)
½ teaspoon dried thyme	4 ounces (113.5 g) dried pasta such as
½ teaspoon dried oregano	linguine, cooked on top of the stove,
¼ teaspoon kosher salt	drained and kept warm, optional

1. Place turkey slices around the inside edge of a 13 × 9 × 2-inch (33 × 23 × 5-cm) oval glass dish.

2. In a small bowl, combine tomato purée with thyme, oregano, salt and pepper. Spread mixture over turkey, dividing it equally among the four slices. Sprinkle each with grated cheese. Cover tightly with microwave plastic wrap. Cook at 100% for 4 minutes in a 650- to 700-watt oven. Prick plastic wrap to release steam.

3. Remove from oven and uncover. Serve with pasta, if desired.

(continued)

To serve 2. Use 2 turkey cutlets (each 3 ounces; 85 g); ½ cup (120 ml) tomato purée; ¼ teaspoon thyme; ¼ teaspoon oregano, pinches of kosher salt and pepper and 2 ounces (56 g) grated mozzarella. Cook 2 ounces (56 g) pasta, if using. Arrange turkey and other ingredients as in Steps 1 and 2, dividing ingredients between two dinner plates. Cook, using a rack, 3 minutes, switching plates after 1 minute 30 seconds.

To serve 1. Use 1 turkey cutlet (3 ounces; 85 g); ¼ cup (60 ml) tomato purée; pinch each thyme and oregano, a small pinch each kosher salt and pepper and 1 ounce (28 g) grated mozzarella. Cook 1 ounce (28 g) pasta, if using. Arrange turkey and other ingredients as in Steps 1 and 2 on a dinner plate. Cook 2 minutes.

FOR 400- TO 500-WATT OVENS

To serve 4. Cook for 8 minutes.

To serve 2. Cook on two plates for 4 minutes, switching after 2 minutes.

To serve 1. Cook on a dinner plate for 3 minutes.

TURKEY DUXELLES

*T*his is a French-style recipe that tastes creamy and rich. It's another reward for forward planning; if you have the duxelles on hand, it goes very quickly.   *SERVES 4*

Per 1-slice serving: 304 calories; 69 milligrams cholesterol; 7 grams fat; 403 milligrams sodium; 33 grams protein (72% RDA); 28 grams carbohydrate

RDA: calcium 25%; phosphorus 44%; vitamin A 28%; thiamin 25%; riboflavin 33%; niacin 47%; vitamin C 33%

2 cups (470 ml) watercress sprigs, washed
4 turkey cutlets (each 3 ounces; 85 g)
1 cup (240 ml) Diet Duxelles (page 477)

4 ounces (113.5 g) coarsely grated part-skim mozzarella (1 cup; 240 ml)
4 ounces (113.5 g) dried linguine, cooked

   1. Place watercress on a dinner plate or a 9-inch (23-cm) pie plate. Cover tightly with microwave plastic wrap. Cook at 100% in a 650- to 700-watt oven for 1 minute 30 seconds. Prick plastic to release steam.
   2. Remove from oven and uncover. Reserve.
   3. Arrange turkey slices in a 13 × 9 × 2-inch (33 × 23 × 5-cm) oval glass dish. Spread ¼ cup (60 ml) of duxelles over each slice and divide the cheese evenly

among the slices. Cover tightly with microwave plastic wrap and cook for 4 minutes. Prick plastic wrap.

4. While turkey is cooking, toss reserved watercress with cooked pasta.

5. Remove turkey from oven and uncover. Place cooked pasta in center of dish and serve.

To serve 2. Use 1 cup (240 ml) watercress, 2 turkey cutlets (each 3 ounces; 85 g), ½ cup (120 ml) duxelles, 2 ounces (56 g) grated mozzarella, and 2 ounces (56 g) dried linguine, cooked. Cook watercress on a dinner plate, covered as in Step 1, for 50 seconds. Continue with Step 2. Following Step 3, divide turkey cutlets and duxelles between two dinner plates and cook for 3 minutes, using a rack and switching the plates once. Finish as in Steps 4 and 5.

To serve 1. Use ½ cup (120 ml) watercress, 1 turkey cutlet (3 ounces; 85 g), ¼ cup (60 ml) duxelles, 1 ounce (28 g) grated mozzarella, and 1 ounce (28 g) dried linguine, cooked. Cook watercress on a dinner plate, covered as in Step 1, for 30 seconds. Continue with Step 2. Follow Step 3 and cook, covered, on a dinner plate for 2 minutes. Finish as in Steps 4 and 5.

FOR 400- TO 500-WATT OVENS

To serve 4. Cook watercress for 6 minutes. Cook turkey and duxelles for 8 minutes.

To serve 2. Cook watercress for 3 minutes. Using a rack, cook turkey and duxelles for 4 minutes, switching plates after 2 minutes.

To serve 1. Cook watercress for 2 minutes. Cook turkey and duxelles for 3 minutes.

TURKEY HASH

If you have made a Thanksgiving turkey, you are going to have leftovers. How nice to have them in a satisfying and light new disguise. This dish is so good I also make it from scratch with turkey cutlets. Add a big green salad, bread and cheese and finish up with seasonal Pumpkin Pudding (page 571); but I don't make this in a low-wattage oven. It doesn't cook evenly.

This easy dish provides more than two days' worth of vitamin C, half a day's vitamin A, and iron and calcium. *SERVES 4*

Per ¾ cup serving: 314 calories; 55 milligrams cholesterol; 4 grams fat; 487 milligrams sodium; 27 grams protein (59% RDA); 42 grams carbohydrate

RDA: calcium 15%; phosphorus 35%; iron 17%; 1,231 milligrams potassium; vitamin A 49%; thiamin 17%; riboflavin 16%; niacin 37%; vitamin C 231%

FOR THE BÉCHAMEL

1½ cups (355 ml) skim milk
6 tablespoons cornstarch
1 teaspoon kosher salt
¼ teaspoon freshly ground black pepper
1 bay leaf

FOR THE HASH

¼ pound (113.5 g) onion, peeled and cut into ½-inch (1-cm) dice (about ¾ cup; 180 ml)
2 cloves garlic, smashed, peeled and sliced
2 teaspoons vegetable oil
1 pound (450 g) new potatoes, cut into ½-inch (1-cm) dice (3½ cups; 825 ml)

¼ cup (60 ml) Basic Chicken Broth (page 460), or unsalted or regular canned chicken broth
6 ounces (170 g) green bell pepper, stemmed, seeded, deribbed and cut into ¼-inch (.5-cm) dice (about ⅔ cup; 160 ml)
6 ounces (170 g) red bell pepper, stemmed, seeded, deribbed and cut into ¼-inch (.5-cm) dice (about ⅔ cup; 160 ml)
4 turkey cutlets (each 3 ounces; 85 g), or leftover skinless turkey, cut into 1-inch (2.5-cm) squares
2 tablespoons chopped fresh parsley

1. Combine milk and cornstarch in an 8-cup (2-l) glass measure and stir thoroughly to combine. Stir in salt, pepper and bay leaf. Cover tightly with microwave plastic wrap. Cook at 100% for 5 minutes in a 650- to 700-watt oven. Prick plastic to release steam.

2. Remove from oven and uncover. Stir well to remove any lumps and reserve.

3. Toss together onion, garlic and oil in a $13 \times 9 \times 2$-inch ($33 \times 23 \times 5$-cm) oval glass dish. Cook, uncovered, for 2 minutes. Add potatoes and broth. Cover and cook for 8 minutes. Prick plastic wrap.

4. Remove from oven and uncover. Stir in peppers. Re-cover and cook for 3 minutes. Prick plastic and uncover. Stir in turkey, re-cover and cook for 3 minutes. Prick plastic.

5. Remove from oven and uncover. Drain liquid from mixture and stir into béchamel. Reserve ½ cup (120 ml) of sauce. Stir remaining sauce and parsley into hash. Transfer to a broiling pan and spread reserved béchamel on top. Broil 3 inches from heat for 6–8 minutes, or until evenly browned.

TURKEY SALAD GALA

Come a hot summer night, you will love this recipe, coolly prepared in your microwave oven and set out in a large bowl. A pitcher of cold soup to pour into mugs, such as Chilled Cucumber Soup (page 142) can be made ahead. Serve crunchy bread and a bowl of Strawberry Sorbet (page 555) with a platter of Oat Bran Crisps (page 574). The crowd will not know they have lost weight, and you can have all the food done ahead. Very cold white wine (try a riesling) spritzers would be perfect; but have some diet soda on hand for the alcohol-free and the thirsty. *SERVES 8*

Per ¾-cup serving: 208 calories; 69 grams cholesterol; 6 grams fat; 86 milligrams sodium; 28 grams protein (62% RDA); 11 grams carbohydrate

RDA: phosphorus 27%; iron 12%; vitamin A 23%; riboflavin 11%; niacin 40%; vitamin C 39%

2½ pounds (1.15 k) fresh half-breast turkey, skinned and boned

½ cup (120 ml) Basic Chicken Broth (page 460), or unsalted or regular canned chicken broth

½ pound (227 g) small red new potatoes, cut into 2-inch (5-cm) chunks (about 1½ cups; 355 ml)

1 pound (450 g) ripe tomatoes, cored and cut in 2-inch (5-cm) chunks (about 3 cups; 705 ml)

½ cup (120 ml) thinly sliced scallions, both white and green parts

1 cup (240 ml) Green Bean Frappé (page 502)

Kosher salt, to taste

Freshly ground black pepper, to taste

Assorted salad greens, washed and dried, optional

1. Place turkey in a $9 \times 5 \times 3$-inch ($23 \times 12.5 \times 7.5$-cm) loaf pan. Add broth. Cover tightly with microwave plastic wrap. Cook at 100% for 6 minutes in a 650- to 700-watt oven. Prick plastic to release steam.

(continued)

2. Remove from oven and uncover. Turn over breast. Re-cover and cook for 6 minutes longer. Prick plastic. Remove from oven and uncover. Turn breast over again. Re-cover and cook for 3 minutes, or until turkey reaches an internal temperature of 160°F (71°C) on an instant-read thermometer. Prick plastic.

3. Remove from oven and uncover. Remove breast to a plate. Add potatoes to cooking liquid. Cover and cook for 6 minutes.

4. Remove from oven and uncover. With a slotted spoon, remove potatoes to a large serving bowl. Cut reserved turkey into 2-inch (5-cm) chunks and add to potatoes. Stir in ¼ cup (60 ml) of the cooking liquid and remaining ingredients. Serve at room temperature on lettuce, if desired.

FOR 400- TO 500-WATT OVENS

To serve 8. Cook turkey as in Steps 1 and 2 for 30 minutes, or until done. Continue with recipe as in Step 3, cooking potatoes for 10 minutes. Finish as in Step 4.

Duck

Normal American- or Czech-style duck, crisply roasted, is never diet food. Who would make it and discard the skin? When one thinks of all the delicious French duck preparations, with duck simmering away in a rich gravy, one realizes that something else is possible. If the duck is skinned, duck can become a party dish of distinction and virtue all at once.

Once again, fresh is better than frozen. If you must use frozen ducks, defrost for twenty-four hours in the refrigerator, or place in a microwave-safe plastic bag, loosely knotted, and defrost at 30% power for 20 minutes in a 650- to 700-watt oven. Turn bird over and defrost at 30% for 20 minutes more.

DUCK AND TURNIP STEW

Allard, once one of Paris's best-known bistros, was famous for its canard aux navets, made only in the spring with tiny turnips that were deep-fried until golden and crisp on the outside, melting on the inside. These turnips were then stirred into a duck stew. While I can no longer deep-fry my turnips in good conscience, I can re-create this happy marriage of flavors in a stew elegant enough for company.   *SERVES 4*

Per ½-breast serving: 236 calories; 109 milligrams cholesterol; 9 grams fat; 176 milligrams sodium; 28 grams protein (62% RDA)

RDA: phosphorus 32%; iron 24%; thiamin 35%; riboflavin 39%; niacin 42%; vitamin C 42%

3 medium turnips (about 12 ounces; 340 g), peeled, halved and cut into ¼-inch (.5-cm) slices (3 cups; 705 ml)
6 cloves garlic, smashed and peeled
1 bay leaf
1¾ cups (410 ml) Basic Chicken Broth made with duck bones (page 460), or unsalted or regular canned chicken broth
⅛ teaspoon dried sage

⅛ teaspoon dried thyme
½ teaspoon celery seeds
1 tablespoon cornstarch
3 red radishes, stem and root end removed, thinly sliced
1 tablespoon red wine vinegar
4 half-breasts duck (each 5 ounces; 140 g), skinned and boned
Kosher salt, to taste
Freshly ground black pepper, to taste

1. Place turnips, garlic, bay leaf, sage, thyme and celery seeds and 1½ cups (355 ml) of the broth in a 13×9×2-inch (33×23×5-cm) oval dish. Cover

(continued)

tightly with microwave plastic wrap. Cook at 100% for 15 minutes, or until turnips are tender and translucent, in a 650- to 700-watt oven. Prick plastic to release steam.

2. While turnips are cooking, combine remaining ¼ cup (60 ml) broth with cornstarch in a 1-cup (120-ml) glass measure, making sure there are no lumps. Toss radishes with vinegar in a small bowl.

3. Remove turnips from oven and uncover. Thoroughly stir in cornstarch mixture and scatter radishes on top. Arrange duck over vegetables spoke-fashion, with thick ends toward the edge of the dish and thin ends toward the center. Cover and cook for 3 minutes. Prick plastic wrap.

4. Remove from oven and uncover. With a slotted spoon, remove breasts to a plate and keep warm. Continue cooking vegetables and sauce, uncovered, for 2 minutes.

5. Remove from oven. Add salt and pepper to taste. To serve, using a slotted spoon divide vegetables among four plates. Thinly slice each breast on the diagonal and place slices over vegetables. Spoon some sauce over each breast.

FOR 400- TO 500-WATT OVENS

To serve 4. Cook as in Step 1 for 25 minutes. Continue with Step 2. Cook for 5 minutes in Step 3. Continue cooking vegetables and sauce as in Step 4 for 3 minutes.

DUCK AND ASPARAGUS

Here, the rich flavor of duck is combined with the crunch, flavor and color of asparagus in a recipe for a small party. It is best made in the spring, when ducks can be bought fresh and the asparagus are slim and crisp (just like us). Serve a half-cup (120 ml) of noodles with the duck. This is such a slimming and healthful dish that you can start with Bell Peppers and Sardines with Balsamic Vinegar (page 84) or Herb-Stuffed Mussels (page 97). You can still have Watercress Soup (page 129) or Peasant Tomato Soup (page 127) along with a slice of Italian bread. Finish up with Strawberry Bavarian (page 560) or another dessert that you like and that fits the season. Have a chilled Beaujolais or a bigger red wine.   *SERVES 4*

Per half-breast serving: 178 calories; 87 milligrams cholesterol; 7 grams fat; 64 milligrams sodium; 23 grams protein (51% RDA); 5 grams carbohydrate

RDA: phosphorus 26%; iron 19%; vitamin A 10%; thiamin 29%; riboflavin 34%; niacin 35%; vitamin C 37%

4 half-breasts duck (each 5 ounces; 140 g), skinned, boned and thinly sliced on the diagonal
½ pound (227 g) asparagus, ends snapped off and peeled
½ cup (120 ml) thinly sliced scallion whites and greens
¾ cup (180 ml) Basic Chicken Broth made with duck bones (page 460), or unsalted or regular canned chicken broth

½ teaspoon cumin
2 cloves garlic, smashed and peeled
2 teaspoons tamari soy
1 tablespoon cornstarch
Pinch cayenne pepper

1. Arrange duck slices around the bottom of a 11×8×2-inch (28×20×5-cm) oval dish. Lay asparagus on top of duck and sprinkle scallions over all. Add broth, cumin, garlic and soy. Cover tightly with microwave plastic wrap. Cook at 100% in a 650- to 700-watt oven for 7 minutes. Prick plastic to release steam.

2. Remove from oven and uncover. Remove ¼ cup (60 ml) of broth and stir the cornstarch into it, making sure there are no lumps. Stir back into cooking dish and add cayenne. Cover and cook for 3 minutes. Prick plastic wrap.

3. Remove from oven and uncover. Stir well and serve.

FOR THE CARNIVORE

Why and How to Be a Carnivore

*I*t is not pandering to the American life-style to give recipes for meat, including what has become a bogeyman to scare your children—red meat. There
are sound nutritional reasons for eating meat; you just shouldn't eat too much,
which is more than four to six ounces (113.5–170 g) for your main meal. The
portion size, smaller than the American norm, relates to the amounts of saturated fat, cholesterol and calories in most meats. Also, you still need vegetables,
grains and dairy products for good nutritional balance. If you eat too much
meat plus all the other things, you will be getting too many calories overall,
particularly if you are on a weight-reduction diet.

The most common dietary deficiency in America is iron. Despite the favorable
publicity for the iron in leafy green vegetables, they don't have enough and they
don't have the good heme iron, found only in meat, that our bodies can absorb
readily. Despite meat's recent fall from favor, it is the best source of iron.

Three times as much of the iron in meat is absorbed by our bodies as of the
same amount of the kind found in grains and beans. We'll leave out the similar
iron in eggs, since we would have to eat a truly taboo number. Heme iron is six
times as absorbable as the kind found in spinach. No one can eat that many
leafy greens. Now that most cooks use iron pots rarely if at all, the iron that
leached from those cooking pots into the cooked food is almost gone.

You can substitute iron tablets. I, for one, get nauseated when I take them. It
is not clear whether our systems absorb the iron found in pills, usually ferrous
iron, as they do the iron in meat. Iron in pill form is better with a balance of
minerals and vitamins and not taken at mealtime. Vitamin C helps its absorption; but iron blocks zinc. Increased zinc and vitamin C are needed. In food
terms, this means that you should, for instance, have some vitamin C–rich broccoli along with your meat. The zinc in its most absorbable form will come from
the meat. All of which adds up to your eating more meat than you may have
thought was good for you; but probably not as much as you used to eat.

That frail flower of young womanhood who is wolfing down a hamburger or
cutting up a steak is not mad. She needs more iron than the large young man
with her does, or, for that matter, than I do. She may want to eat meat more
often than the thrice weekly recommended for basic, sound nutrition. However,
if one of those meat meals is a giant prime steak, she should not have red meat
again during the week. If she wants to trim her weight, she will have to slim
down the rest of her meals for a couple of days. Eating liver once a week does
the trick.

Slimming down the meals will be a question of balancing out the cholesterol and saturated fat that she gets along with her meat. If she is virtuous, she will trim off all the fat she can get at before eating the meat. I, unfortunately, love the crisp fat on a good steak or chop. If I can't resist, I make up for it by eating fewer calories and lots of carbohydrates on other days.

Understanding Meats and Their Nutritional Offerings

Not all meats provide the same amounts of nutrients. As you look at the charts on the next few pages, you may be in for a few surprises. Don't worry. Vary your diet and don't exaggerate the portions. It may help to know that the RDA of iron is ten milligrams for men and eighteen milligrams for women. The RDA of zinc is fifteen milligrams for both men and women.

These comparisons are not cut-by-cut and grade-by-grade. Instead, they are what are called composite figures, a sort of averaging of the different cuts of meat. Fish are so various that it is impossible to know anything from an average, so the iron content is given for some of the more common kinds. Except where noted, these comparisons are based on four ounces (113.5 g) of trimmed raw meat. While they will not tell you how much iron or other nutrients you are getting from any given piece of food, they will permit you to balance the advantage of high iron content against increased fat (for weight-losers), saturated fat and cholesterol (for the health conscious). Since data are unavailable for raw lamb, veal, tuna and sardines, figures for cooked or canned have been substituted. A sad blank space means that as of now there are no known figures in that category. All poultry is skinned—flesh only.

MEAT	IRON (mg)	ZINC (mg)	FAT (g)	SAT. FAT (g)	CAL.	CHOL. (mg)
Beef (lean choice)	2.57	4.94	7.5	2.9	169	68
Lamb (cooked)	2.32	6.08	11	3.45	235	104
Pork	1.16	2.78	8	2.65	167	74
Veal (cooked)	1.49	6.13	6.3	1.53	209	171
Chicken	1.01	1.75	3.5	0.9	135	79
Turkey	1.47	2.79	3	1.01	133	77
Duck (domestic)	2.72	2.15	7	2.63	150	87
Tuna (canned, drained)						
Light, in oil	1.58	1.02	9.3	1.74	225	20
Light, in water	3.63	0.50	0.57	.18	149	N/A
White, in water	0.68	N/A	2.8	.74	154	48
Swordfish	0.92	1.3	4.55	1.25	137	44
Salmon, Atlantic	0.91	N/A	7	1.11	161	62
Halibut	0.95	0.48	3	.37	125	36
Sole and flounder	0.41	0.51	1	.32	103	54
Monkfish	0.36	0.46	2	N/A	86	28
Sardines (canned, drained)	3.31	1.49	13	1.74	236	161

The iron-searcher can substitute game such as venison or buffalo for beef steak if it's available. Game is quite a bit lower in fat and calories than domesticated animals, and toward the low end in cholesterol content compared to other red meats. Yet it still has high levels of iron, zinc and the B vitamins. Lean venison has only 140 calories in 4 ounces (113.5 g), and only 74 milligrams of cholesterol.

There are organically raised cattle whose feed has been adjusted to produce leaner, although high-quality, meat. It is hard to find and expensive. If you really love beef, you may want to locate this special kind to reduce residual hormones and antibiotics in your diet as well as calories and cholesterol.

It's clear that meat should be trimmed of all surrounding fat before cooking. Also, the less fancy the grade of meat, the less internal fat, marbling, and calories it will have. The following charts are based on simply, conventionally cooked—roasted or simmered—meats with all the external fat removed and no fat added, rather than on microwave-cooked meats. The numbers are absolutely valid only for conventional cooking. Microwave cooking is different since all the meat juices—along with the nutrients they contain—are retained in the finished dish. The relationship of one cut to another in the charts holds true no matter what the cooking method. If you use a more caloric cut or grade, it will be more caloric no matter how you cook it. The same holds true for cholesterol.

It is important to notice that cholesterol does not vary in step with fat and calories. Leaner meat such as veal may well have more cholesterol per ounce than a well-marbled cut of beef. Indicated portions are based on cholesterol and fat considerations as well as calories.

The nutritional information for beef recipes in this book is based on choice-grade meat. If you substitute prime, the calories and fat will increase. If you substitute select, the calories and fat will go down.

You will notice that select-grade cuts have fewer calories even though the cholesterol is the same. Select-grade cuts will be tougher and have somewhat less flavor. They are most suitable for stewing and for grinding into ground beef or hamburger. Even though I personally use select-grade top round for ground beef, the calories and cholesterol in the recipes are based on store-bought lean ground beef, since it is easier to find. If you buy what I buy, your calorie and cholesterol counts will go down below those given.

COMPARISON OF CALORIES AND CHOLESTEROL
OF VARIOUS MEATS BY GRADE AND CUT

BEEF All data, except those for ground meat, are based on 4 ounces (113.5 g) of trimmed, lean boneless meat cooked without added fat to yield a 3-ounce (85-g) portion.

CUT	GRADE	CAL.	CHOL. (mg)
Filet (tenderloin)	Prime	217	73
	Choice	189	73
	Select	177	73
Rib, small end (aka N.Y. Strip)	Prime	259	68
	Choice	191	68
	Select	178	68
Sirloin, wedgebone, meat only	Prime	201	76
	Choice	180	76
	Select	170	76
Top loin	Prime	208	65
	Choice	176	65
	Select	162	65
Chuck blade	Prime	270	90
	Choice	234	90
	Select	218	90
Top round	Prime	208	65
	Choice	176	65
	Select	162	65
Brisket, flat half	None given	223	77

GROUND BEEF OR HAMBURGER I generally specify the cut that I want to have ground—usually select-grade top round—and ask that it be trimmed of all fat before grinding. If you do this, the nutrition specifications can be found in the chart above. If you buy already-ground meat, the values below, which are for 4 ounces (113.5 g) of raw meat, are the standard.

CUT	GRADE	CAL.	CHOL. (mg)
Ground beef, regular (27% fat)	None given	352	96
Ground beef, lean (21% fat)	None given	299	85
Ground beef, extra lean (17% fat)	None given	265	78

LAMB All data are based on 4 ounces (113.5 g) of trimmed, lean boneless meat cooked to yield 3 ounces (85 g).

CUT	GRADE	CAL.	CHOL. (mg)
Leg	None given	158	85
Loin chop	None given	160	85
Rib chop	None given	179	85
Lean stew meat	Data not available as such; use value of cut being used.		
Shoulder	None given	174	85

PORK All data are based on 4 ounces (113.5 g) of trimmed, lean boneless meat cooked to yield 3 ounces (85 g).

CUT	GRADE	CAL.	CHOL. (mg)
Tenderloin	Not given	188	105
Loin chop	Not given	275	72
Leg (aka fresh ham)	Not given	185	78

VEAL All data are based on 4 ounces (113.5 g) of trimmed, lean boneless meat braised to yield 3 ounces (85g).

CUT	GRADE	CAL.	CHOL. (mg)
Rib chop	None given	229	86
Loin	None given	199	86
Scaloppine (round with rump; leg cutlets)	None given	184	86
Chuck cuts and boneless, for stew	None given	200	86

INNARDS

Even though innards, liver, kidneys and the like are very iron-rich, you should make eating them a once-a-week event at most. Innards are as rich in cholesterol as they are in iron, even though they are fairly low in calories.

COMPARISON OF INNARDS BY ANIMAL

Beef and pork innard data are based on 3 ounces (85 g) of boneless meat, simmered or braised, unless otherwise noted. Veal innard data are based on 3.5 ounces (100 g) of cooked meat unless otherwise noted. Some of the figures for veal innards are given for raw meat. The weight is still 3.5 ounces (100 g). Don't blame me; that's the way the USDA gives it out.

MEAT	CHOL. (mg)	CAL.	IRON (mg)
BEEF			
Brain	1,746	136	1.88
Heart	164	148	6.38
Kidneys	329	122	6.21
Liver	331	137	5.75
Tongue	91	241	2.88
PORK			
Liver	302	141	15.23
VEAL			
Brain (raw)	2,286	143	2.74
Liver (raw)	343	160	10.06
Sweetbreads:			
Pancreas (raw)	286	184	3.20
Thymus	466	168	1.60

Man does not live by minerals alone. Those who don't eat meat or eggs or consume dairy products—in other words, vegans or overzealous dieters—may be deficient in vitamin B_{12}, and there go their nerves. Meat is a good source of the other B vitamins as well.

Nonmicrowave Cooking of Meat

It is at this point that I must stress that many cuts of meat are not at their best when cooked in the microwave oven. Yes, it can be done, but why? The rest of your kitchen hasn't died. Grill, broil or pan broil your steaks and chops—other than pork, which cooks brilliantly in a microwave oven. Roast in a conventional oven unless you are really braising or pot-roasting, in which case it's back to the microwave. What the microwave does not do well is to brown and firm up the surface of the meat. I find this to be true even with convection-microwave (combination) ovens.

I hope that the conventional cooking methods given below will also be helpful for rapid preparation of poultry and fish, even though they do very well in the microwave oven. Sometimes we want a change.

If you want browned surfaces on microwave-cooked foods, see page 350.

TO GRILL THE MEAT

If you live in a part of the country where grilling goes on all year, or if you leap at an opportunity to grill when you can, don't give it up; but do follow special rules and techniques to avoid extra fat. First, remove all the external fat from the meat. Second, make sure that your grill has gotten very hot; the meat will be less likely to stick. Rub the grill surface with brown paper—such as a paper bag—on which you have put some neutral oil, or use olive oil for chicken, fish, veal and steak if you like the flavor. Once you have placed the meat on the grill, let it stay in one position long enough to sear or the flesh will tear and juice will be lost.

If you want to marinate the meat before grilling or roasting on a spit, avoid marinades with fat and excessive salt—which probably means you will have to make your own. Both Quick Barbecue Sauce (page 513) and Oriental Glaze (page 512) will do well. To avoid fats, you can rub the meat with a dry marinade such as Spice Mix (page 475), or any mixture of spices that pleases you. The spices can be mixed with a little water, wine, lemon or vinegar if you prefer to use a paste, or use some prepared mustard (not too much; it has salt). If you are using a commercial mixture, make sure it doesn't contain sodium if salt is a problem for you. You can also rub one-half teaspoon of an oil-based salad dressing such as Garlic Oregano Dressing (page 489) on both sides of a portion of red meat, or Spicy Buttermilk Dressing (page 495) on chicken and fish.

You can also vary the flavor of simply grilled foods with a sauce from Basics, Sauces and Snacks (pages 458–529). Since any juices that come out of the meat will be lost to the fire, you cannot make a deglazing sauce. The potential loss of meat juices—rich in nutrients—is the reason it is better to eat meat on the rare side.

An instant-read thermometer (page 25) is a great aid to all but the experienced griller, who can touch the meat and feel how done it is. Remember, the internal temperature of pork should reach at least 140°F (60°C), as should that of fish, while chicken should reach at least 128°F (53°C). The temperature to which you cook beef and lamb depends on taste rather than safety. Very rare beef will be cooked at 120°F (49°C), medium rare at 140°F (60°C). Small, thin cuts of steak may need to be cooked to an even lower temperature if they are to be rare.

BROILING

Broiling is very much like grilling, but it is done inside your oven, the heat is above the food rather than underneath and you usually will not need to oil the pan. The same rules apply; but there is one additional caution. The broiler pans that come with your oven often do not allow all the fat that comes out of the meat to drip off. I find that a stainless steel cake-cooling grid works very well when placed over the bottom of the broiler pan, which will catch the fat.

When you have finished broiling, you can take the broiler pan and grid out of the oven. Remove the grid. Pour or spoon off all the fat in the broiler pan. Then you can put the broiler pan on top of a burner, pour in a little wine or an appropriate basic broth (pages 460–462) and scrape the pan vigorously with a wooden spoon. You will reclaim all the pan juices to make a little deglazing sauce that can be seasoned to taste with pepper and salt if you wish.

For timings and seasonings, see To Grill the Meat (opposite page).

PAN BROILING, SAUTÉING AND BROWNING

These are the ways that various meats, chicken and fish are cooked on top of the stove with a minimum of sauce. In pan broiling, the meat is usually in one piece and no vegetables are included. In sautéing, the meat is in smaller pieces and is often accompanied by vegetables cut to the same size. "Sauté," in French, means to jump. The idea is to keep the food moving in the pan by shaking it vigorously back and forth. Sautéing may be followed by stewing, humid cooking. When a large piece of meat such as a pot roast is browned prior to subsequent humid cooking, it is properly called just that, browning, not sautéing. Although for dieters, the same problems and solutions exist whatever the name.

All three of these usually imply the presence of fat in the cooking pan. The fat may either be added or, as with a roast, be present on the outside of the meat. It is the hot fat that keeps the meat from sticking to the pan, and that aids in the browning. If this is a technique you enjoy and wish to use, you might consider trimming the fat from the meat and using an unsaturated vegetable oil—for instance, canola oil—or monounsaturated oil—usually olive oil—to avoid the extra cholesterol of animal fat. Olive oil is better for health reasons (see page 15) than a polyunsaturated oil; but it may taste too strong on some meats. After the browning has been accomplished, extra fat can be poured off before serving or continuing with other parts of the recipes. You may diminish the flavor slightly, and you shouldn't kid yourself—you won't get rid of all the fat you added.

Moderately successful pan broiling and sautéing can be done in a nonstick pan. It will be hard to get quite the degree of rapid browning that you get with fat. The same pan surface that keeps the food from sticking keeps it from browning uniformly; but for quick, everyday cooking, these pans can be a real boon.

It is even harder to brown a large piece of meat successfully in these nonstick pans. You may want to save your pot roasts and daubes for days when you are not on a weight-loss or low-cholesterol diet, or trim meat of all fat and use olive oil, which is fine for many hearty Mediterranean dishes. I find that the smother-pot roasting technique in the microwave oven is a very successful and much lower fat alternative. It is also much more rapid.

In days of yore and recently in my kitchen, pan broiling has been done in cast-iron skillets heated to the maximum and then liberally sprinkled with kosher salt and coarsely ground black pepper. The meat is placed on the seasoning layer, which—at that heat—keeps the meat from sticking. This is not a technique for those on salt-restricted diets. It's my guess that the original steak au poivre came from this technique. It is a technique that does well with chicken and fish too.

STIR-FRYING

Stir-frying is a technique generally associated with Oriental cooking. It is very similar to sautéing, except that the pan is not moved. Instead the food is rotated against the hot surfaces by being fairly continuously tossed with cooking spoons or spatulas. If the pan is hot enough, we don't need very much fat. At the end of the stir-frying, any visible fat can be poured off before serving or adding the sauce ingredients.

ROASTING

I love to roast. I like the way the food tastes and smells and I like the easy rapidity of roasting for entertaining. However, even today, when I keep at a fairly reasonable weight, I don't roast very often. Partly it's a matter of dietary and economic sanity. I find it hard to get myself to remove cracklings, skins and surface fat; but you may be brave. Cuts or whole birds to be roasted must be of the best—read expensive—kind and must have a fairly high fat content to roast well. The fat can be on the skin of a bird, or be a thin outer layer such as that on a leg of lamb, or it may be applied to the outside in thin sheets, often of pork fat. This is called barding. Larding is the insertion of thin strips of fat into lean meats such as venison to increase their juiciness.

Roasting can be done in one or two ways. The original method, long before there were ovens, was spit-roasting, which was done in front of or over a fire. Today, most roasting is done in the more humid environment of an oven. These ovens are typically heated from the bottom, whereas earlier brick and cast-iron ovens radiated heat more evenly from all sides.

I find that roasting is most successfully done at high temperatures, around 475°F–500°F (246°C–260°C), as it is done in most restaurants. There will be more shrinkage—less meat to eat than you buy—and a dirtier oven, which meant more to me before self-cleaning ovens. The results will be superior to roasting at medium heat. In *Food for Friends,* an earlier book of mine, I discuss roasting at some length.

The only thing I would add today, from a health-conscious point of view, is that I have joined Jim Beard in recommending the use of a rack in a roasting pan. This permits the fat to fall away from the meat as it cooks. The pan juices can then be skimmed as with broiling (see above) juices. If you are watching weight and cholesterol, try to make yourself remove the skin of birds and the visible fat from meat.

POT-ROASTING AND BRAISING

The line between these two cooking methods is very fuzzy, to the point of nonexistence. Both require that the food be seized (the outer layer heat-set but not browned) or browned and then cooked with a small amount of liquid, which may be provided by vegetables in a tightly covered pot either in the oven or on top of the stove. Braising was originally done either in the coals of a fire, on top of the stove or in a low-heat baker's oven; today it is usually done in the oven. The term "pot-roasting" is used for foods cooked in similar fashion on top of the stove. While seizing and browning are done at high heat, the subsequent cooking is usually done at very low heat.

Pot-roasting is always done with a large piece of meat. Braising may be done with a large or small pieces of meat, as in stewing.

The healthiness of this kind of cooking will depend on the fattiness of the meat, the amount and kind of fat used for the initial seizing or browning and the thoroughness with which the richly flavored sauce that is produced is degreased (see below) at the end of the cooking.

When the food is browned before further cooking, a dark sauce or stew will result. When the meat is seized rather than browned before further cooking, the result is usually a fricassée or blanquette.

These are preparations that are extremely well paralleled with much less fat in the microwave oven. See Microwave Cooking of Meat on the next page.

STEWING

Stewing is essentially the same as braising, except that the quantity of liquid is greater and the meat is generally cut into smaller pieces. The same specifications as to health and microwave cooking apply.

DEGREASING

When foods are conventionally cooked, the juices, sauces and gravies they make are often laden with fat. In the case of braises, pot roasts and stews, fat can be skimmed from the top of the food at the end of the cooking. It can also be skimmed from the surface of the food as it cooks. To degrease cooking juices, see Broiling and Pan Broiling on page 347.

When foods are slow-cooked on top of the stove, it is important that they not boil vigorously. This tends to emulsify the fat with the acid and protein—which makes it impossible to skim the fat. Sometimes it helps to move the cooking pan to one side of the heat as it simmers. This will cause the fat to collect in one place and it will be easier to remove.

Foods that reheat well, such as stews and braises, can be allowed to cool or be refrigerated. The fat will come to the top and can be skimmed off. If any bits of fat remain, they can be easily removed with a wad of paper towel used as a blotter.

Microwave Cooking of Meat

People who like to cook with a microwave oven often find that they get good results with fish, poultry and vegetables; but they have less success or disasters with beef, pork, lamb and veal. Microwave writers, on the other hand, are often given to claiming that a microwave oven can do anything. I find that for me the results lie somewhere in between.

As I have indicated at the beginning of this chapter, there are many ways other than cooking in a microwave oven to cook meat, and some of them cannot, in my opinion, be duplicated well or at all in the microwave oven. It does not roast, give crisp and brown skin or fat. It does not broil, grill or brown. These are procedures that should be carried out elsewhere.

If you want browned meat, you can sauté the meat before putting it in the dish for microwave cooking. You will be adding fat. Alternatively, food previously cooked in a microwave oven can be placed under the broiler for surface browning.

The microwave oven can be used to stew, poach, steam, braise, pot-roast and boil. The major problem that cooks encounter when they try to prepare meat in these ways is the toughening of protein and fiber. Some experts propose the solution of cooking meat at less power for a longer period of time. I don't find that this helps. Instead, it prolongs cooking to or beyond conventional timings.

The answer, for me, is to use the proper cut of meat and not to overcook it. As with salt, you can always add time; but you can't take it away. Some dishes call for standing time, during which the meat continues to cook. Therefore, it may seem undercooked when it comes out of the oven. Recipes that suggest this waiting time—such as my risotto recipes—will stay hot long enough so that they are still good to eat.

Since one of the advantages of microwave cooking to the healthy eater or someone on a weight-loss diet is the microwave oven's ability to cook foods without any surface fat, added fat, and with minimal internal fat, it seems unfortunate to negate its strengths. The following dishes seem to me robust enough in flavor that you will not miss the fat and the browning.

You will also get a plus in that the flavors and nutrients in the meat juices will remain in the dish instead of draining off.

Naturally tender meats such as tenderloin of beef, often served as filet mignon, and tenderloin of pork are both tender and low in fat and in cholesterol, making them triply desirable. Ground meats are tenderized by the grinding, which breaks down their fibers. If you cannot buy stew meat that is trimmed of all fat, you may be better off buying a solid piece and trimming and cutting it yourself. This has the additional advantage of allowing you to divide the meat into separate muscles, as is done in European butchering. Then, when you cut the meat into the proper-size cubes, the grain will not be going in two different ways.

Since the meat juices retained in microwave cooking provide broths or sauces even when the dish is not a stew, you should regularly think about adding some noodles, rice or potatoes or serving some bread. See Good Grains and Other Starches (pages 148–225) for nutritional information.

Beef

Beef is the reddest of the red, practically an iron curtain Communist if you go by what many people say about it today. Yet, as I noted above, it has many nutritional virtues. In addition, it tastes good. I am one of the American generation raised on beef, from hamburgers to steak to roasts, and there are days when I crave its flavor. Not every day.

The simplest, quickest way to cook beef always involves the most expensive cuts. Beef tenderloin—filet mignon—cooks rapidly, evenly and moistly. It also comes to you without any fat. This is a reminder that you should buy your beef trimmed as much as possible of all surface fat. If you cannot get the butcher to do it, buy a whole piece of meat, trim it of fat and cut it up into even pieces for stewing. Generally, chuck stews better than other cuts. When it comes to ground meat, don't buy something called hamburger. Buy lean ground top round. It will be more expensive; but it will have much less fat.

When cooking stews, you may find that the beef doesn't seem entirely cooked when it comes out of the oven. Stir it well; cover lightly with a kitchen towel, and after the waiting time for the stew is up the meat will be thoroughly cooked and tender.

When it comes to steaks and roasts, retreat to your stove. See Nonmicrowave Cooking of Meats (pages 346–349).

GALA MEAT LOAF

*T*his meat loaf is gala because it tastes so good and looks attractive, with the green-spinach splashes throughout. I serve it to guests with Olive Oil Mashed Potatoes (page 221) and Red Pepper Purée (page 500). They love it; but it's basic enough to be family fare. Leftovers are good cold and make great sandwiches. At a party, serve Dried Shiitake with Parsley (page 95) as a first course. Add a salad and a light sorbet or other dessert. This dish has that good-for-you combination of substantial iron and enough vitamin C to help you absorb it.   SERVES 6

Per 1¼-inch (3-cm) serving: 353 calories; 86 milligrams cholesterol; 24 grams fat; 513 milligrams sodium; 24 grams protein (52% RDA); 9 grams carbohydrate

RDA: phosphorus 21%; iron 22%; vitamin A 73%; riboflavin 21%; niacin 31%; vitamin C 28%

1 pound (450 g) fresh spinach, washed and stemmed (6 loosely packed cups; 1.5 l), or 2 10-ounce (284-g) boxes frozen spinach, defrosted in a sieve under warm running water
1 medium onion, about 6 ounces (170 g), peeled and quartered

3 cloves garlic, smashed and peeled
1½ cups (360 ml) fresh bread crumbs
2 tablespoons tamari soy
Freshly ground black pepper, to taste
1½ pounds (680 g) lean ground beef, preferably top round

1. Place spinach in a 10-inch (25.5-cm) quiche dish or pie plate. Cook, uncovered, at 100% for 5 minutes 30 seconds in a 650- to 700-watt oven. If using frozen spinach, omit this step.

2. Remove from oven and let stand until cool. Coarsely chop spinach in a food processor. Transfer to a mixing bowl and reserve.

3. Finely chop onion and garlic in a food processor and add to spinach. Add bread crumbs, soy, pepper and ground beef to spinach mixture and mix well.

4. Transfer mixture to a 9×5×3-inch (23×12.5×7.5-cm) glass loaf pan, making sure there are no air pockets. Cook, uncovered, for 14 minutes.

5. Remove from oven and let stand, covered with a kitchen towel, for 10 minutes. Serve hot or cold.

FOR 400- TO 500-WATT OVENS

To serve 6. If using fresh spinach, follow Step 1 and cook for 10 minutes. If using frozen, omit Step 1. Continue with Step 2. In Step 4, cook for 24 minutes.

QUICK BEEF STEW

*T*his is a family dinner especially if you add the potatoes (eighty calories per portion). Serve a big green salad with a diet dressing (pages 486–499), or store-bought, and add some fruit and even some cookies. You will feel full and happy. Those who do not need to lose weight or are large or active can have a cup and a half (355 ml) of stew.   *SERVES 4*

Per 1-cup (240-ml) serving: 396 calories; 83 milligrams cholesterol; 28 grams fat; 311 milligrams sodium; 21 grams protein (47% RDA); 15 grams carbohydrate

RDA: phosphorus 24%; iron 23%; 800 milligrams potassium; vitamin A 176%; vitamin C 45%

1 pound (450 g) trimmed beef chuck, cut into 1-inch (2.5-cm) cubes

4 ounces (113.5 g) carrot, trimmed, peeled and cut across into ¼-inch (.5-cm) slices (about ¾ cup; 180 ml)

4 ounces (113.5 g) celery, peeled and cut across into ¼-inch (.5-cm) slices (about ½ cup; 120 ml)

4 ounces (113.5 g) leek (white only), cut across into ¼-inch (.5-cm) slices (about ¾ cup; 180 ml)

2 cups (470 ml) canned tomatoes with juice, smashed

5 cloves garlic, smashed, peeled and sliced

¼ teaspoon dried thyme

¼ teaspoon dried oregano

1½ bay leaves

Pinch freshly ground black pepper

1 cup (240 ml) water

2 small potatoes (each 6 ounces; 170 g), optional

1. Place meat around the inside edge of a 2½-quart (2.5-l) soufflé dish. Place carrots on top of meat and celery in the center of the dish.

2. Except for the potatoes, scatter remaining ingredients, but only ⅓ cup (80 ml) of the water, over meat and vegetables. Cover tightly with microwave plastic wrap. Cook at 100% for 8 minutes in a 650- to 700-watt oven. Prick plastic to release steam.

3. Uncover and stir in remaining water. Patch hole with a fresh piece of plastic. Cook at 100% for 3 minutes. Prick plastic to release steam.

4. Remove from oven. Let stand, uncovered, for 10 minutes. While stew is standing, cook potatoes in the microwave oven (see page 220), if desired.

To serve 2. Use ½ pound (225 g) beef, 2 ounces (56 g) each carrot, celery and leek, 1 cup (240 ml) tomatoes, 3 cloves garlic, ⅛ teaspoon each thyme and oregano, 1 bay leaf, ½ cup (120 ml) water and 1 potato. Cook as in Step 2 with ¼ cup (60 ml) water in a 1½-quart (1.5-l) soufflé dish for 4 minutes. Continue with Step 3, adding remaining water and cooking for 2 minutes more. Let stand for 5 minutes. *(continued)*

Quick Beef Stew (cont.)

To serve 1. Use ¼ pound (113.5 g) beef, 1 ounce (28 g) each carrot, celery and leek, ½ cup (120 ml) tomatoes, 1 large clove garlic, a pinch each thyme and oregano, ½ bay leaf, ¼ cup (60 ml) water and ½ potato. Cook as in Step 2 in a 1½-quart (1.5-l) soufflé dish for 5 minutes. Remove from oven and let stand for 5 minutes before serving.

FOR 400- TO 500-WATT OVENS

To serve 4. Cook as in Step 2 for 13 minutes. Cook as in Step 3 for 3 minutes more. Let stew stand for 10 minutes.

To serve 2. Cook as in Step 2 for 8 minutes. Cook as in Step 3 for 3 minutes more. Let stew stand for 5 minutes.

To serve 1. Cook as in Step 2 for 7 minutes. Let stew stand for 5 minutes.

BEEF IN RED WINE

*T*his is a skinny version of the Burgundian French dish Boeuf Bourguignon. I find it every bit as good as the original, and it takes only eighteen minutes to cook enough for a dinner party's worth. If the beef doesn't seem fully cooked to you when it comes out of the oven, don't worry. By the time you have stirred it and allowed it to sit for ten minutes, it will have finished cooking.

Serve it with some steamed new potatoes (page 220) or broad egg noodles. Begin with Green Terrine (page 110); follow with Bibb and Tarragon Salad (page 393) and Purple Pudding (page 569). Serve a nice red wine. Once again, the large and the active and those not needing to lose weight can increase their portions.

SERVES 8

Per generous ¾-cup (180-ml) serving: 256 calories; 77 milligrams cholesterol; 12 grams fat; 190 milligrams sodium; 24 grams protein (54% RDA); 15 grams carbohydrate

RDA: phosphorus 31%; iron 23%; niacin 32%

2 teaspoons vegetable oil

10 ounces (284 g) pearl onions, peeled (if frozen, defrosted in a sieve under warm running water)

1½ pounds (680 g) mushrooms, wiped clean and quartered

¼ cup (60 ml) plus 2 tablespoons Basic Chicken Broth (page 460), or unsalted or regular canned chicken broth

2 pounds (900 g) lean beef chuck, cut into 1½-inch (4-cm) cubes

½ cup (120 ml) red wine

1 bay leaf

½ teaspoon dried thyme

1 teaspoon granulated sugar

Freshly ground black pepper, to taste

½ teaspoon kosher salt

9 cloves garlic, smashed and peeled

3 tablespoons cornstarch

1. Place oil in a 2½-quart (2.5-l) soufflé dish or casserole with a tightly fitted lid. Cook, uncovered, at 100% for 2 minutes in a 650- to 700-watt oven. Stir in onions and mushrooms and cook, uncovered, for 4 minutes.

2. Stir in ¼ cup (60 ml) of the broth and remaining ingredients except cornstarch. Cover tightly with microwave plastic wrap or casserole lid and cook for 8 minutes. If using plastic wrap, prick to release steam and remove dish from oven.

3. Combine remaining broth with cornstarch in a small bowl, stirring until completely smooth. Stir into meat mixture and cook, uncovered, for 4 minutes more.

4. Remove from oven and let stand, loosely covered, for 10 minutes before serving.

FOR 400- TO 500-WATT OVENS

To serve 8. Follow Step 1 and cook oil for 3 minutes. Add onions and mushrooms. Cover and cook for 9 minutes. Uncover and cook for 5 minutes more. Continue with Step 2, cooking for 12 minutes. Add cornstarch mixture as in Step 3 and cook for 6 minutes. Finish as in Step 4.

TOMATO-BEEF CURRY

*T*he discovery of America added some wonderful ingredients to the world's cooking, notably pod peppers and tomatoes. This recipe adds their red goodness to a beef curry. The obvious accompanying dish is rice. Parsley Pilaf (page 185) would add a green and tempting note. Make the pilaf ahead. After the curry is cooked, add one-quarter cup (60 ml) of water to the pilaf; stir and reheat for three minutes. Since this is not a conventional curry, I wouldn't add a lot of side dishes. I would begin with Jade Soup (page 124) and end with Pineapple Sorbet (page 556). *SERVES 6*

Per 1-cup (240-ml) serving: 320 calories; 98 milligrams cholesterol; 18 grams fat; 250 milligrams sodium; 31 grams protein (68% RDA); 8 grams carbohydrate

RDA: phosphorus 32%; iron 26%; 754 milligrams potassium; niacin 21%; vitamin C 27%

½ teaspoon black mustard seeds
½ teaspoon fennel seeds
4 teaspoons vegetable oil
½ ounce (14 g) peeled fresh ginger, grated
½ teaspoon turmeric
1 teaspoon ground cardamom
⅛ teaspoon ground cloves
½ teaspoon paprika
1 teaspoon ground cumin

¼ teaspoon cayenne
2 medium onions (each 6 ounces; 170 g), peeled and cut into ½-inch (1-cm) cubes (about 1 cup; 240 ml)
8 cloves garlic, smashed, peeled and sliced
2 cups (470 ml) canned Italian tomatoes packed in juice, coarsely chopped
2 pounds (900 g) lean beef chuck, cut into ½-inch (1-cm) cubes
1 tablespoon fresh lime juice

1. Combine mustard and fennel seeds with 1 teaspoon of the oil in a 2½-quart (2.5-l) soufflé dish or casserole with a tightly fitted lid. Cook, uncovered, at 100% for 2 minutes in a 650- to 700-watt oven. Add remaining oil, all the spices and ginger and cook, uncovered, for 2 minutes.

2. Add onion and garlic and toss to coat. Cover tightly with microwave plastic wrap or casserole lid. Cook for 5 minutes, stirring once. If using plastic, prick to release steam.

3. Remove from oven and uncover. Stir in tomatoes and their liquid and place beef on top. Cover and cook for 5 minutes. Stir, re-cover and cook for 4 minutes more. Prick plastic.

4. Remove from oven and uncover. Stir in lime juice and serve.

To serve 6. Follow Step 1 and cook, uncovered, for 3 minutes. Add remaining 3 teaspoons oil, spices and ginger and cook, uncovered, for 3 minutes. Continue with Step 2 and cook, covered, for 7 minutes 30 seconds, stirring twice. In Step 3, add tomatoes and beef, cover tightly and cook for 6 minutes. Stir, re-cover and cook for 6 minutes more. Finish as in Step 4.

SKINNY CHILI

Chili is a great Southwestern classic, and it would be too bad if the traditionally fatty recipes for chili prevented the healthy and the weight-loss dieters from eating it. Here is a recipe that has all the traditional flavor, but cuts the fat and cholesterol to a minimum. You can serve this with cooked beans (page 202), black or pinto; but I like it over half of a cooked baking potato—sort of an adult sloppy joe. Top each portion with nonfat yogurt for only nine more calories per tablespoon. Leftovers make a delicious lunch with a nice salad.

This makes a good, informal dinner. I like it for an easy party that is low in calories, protein and cholesterol; you might want to start with Salade Niçoise (page 91), or, in fancier fashion, with Carrot Timbale (page 105). Make Apricot Soufflé (page 584) for dessert, or have Creamy Custard (page 570) with Cherry Sauce (page 577). *SERVES 8*

Per ½-cup (120-ml) serving: 186 calories; 43 milligrams cholesterol; 12 grams fat; 244 milligrams sodium; 11 grams protein (25% RDA); 7 grams carbohydrate

RDA: vitamin A 47%; vitamin C 110%

½ pound (227 g) red bell pepper, stemmed, seeded and deribbed
½ pound (227 g) yellow onions, peeled and cut into 2-inch (5-cm) chunks
2 cloves garlic, smashed and peeled
2 cups (470 ml) canned Italian tomatoes with liquid
1 pound (450 g) lean ground beef

2 teaspoons ground cumin
2 teaspoons oregano
1 tablespoon chili powder
¼ teaspoon hot red pepper sauce
½ teaspoon kosher salt, optional
2 teaspoons cider vinegar
Freshly ground black pepper, to taste

1. Finely chop pepper, onion and garlic in the food processor. Scrape into a 13 × 10 × 2-inch (33 × 25.5 × 5-cm) oval dish and stir in tomatoes, breaking up any whole tomatoes. Cover tightly with microwave plastic wrap. Cook at 100% for 9 minutes in a 650- to 700-watt oven. Prick plastic to release steam.

(continued)

2. Remove from oven. Uncover carefully and stir in beef and remaining ingredients except vinegar and black pepper. Cover tightly with microwave plastic wrap. Cook at 100% for 5 minutes. Prick plastic.

3. Remove from oven and uncover. Stir in vinegar and pepper to taste. Stir well, breaking up any large chunks of beef. Serve over baked potatoes or rice.

To serve 4. Use ¼ pound (113.5 g) each pepper and onion, 1 clove garlic, 1 cup (240 ml) tomatoes, ½ pound (227 g) beef, 1 teaspoon each cumin and oregano, 1½ teaspoons chili powder, ⅛ teaspoon red pepper sauce, ¼ teaspoon salt, 1 teaspoon vinegar and pepper to taste. Cook as in Step 1 in a 2½-quart (2.5-l) soufflé dish for 6 minutes. Cook as in Step 2 for 3 minutes more.

FOR 400- TO 500-WATT OVENS

To serve 4. Cook as in Step 1 for 9 minutes. Cook as in Step 2 for 5 minutes.

Beef filet—tenderloin—cooks so well in a microwave oven that I have given you lots of different timings and quantities and even portions so that you can decide how much beef to eat based on your size, activity and whether you want to lose weight. Since the beef doesn't brown, you may want to slice it before serving to show off the beautiful color of the rare meat evenly cooked throughout. It cooks to perfection—not black and blue—to develop maximum flavor. The technique is based on the classic French boeuf à la ficelle, which means beef on a string. In that recipe, the beef is tied up in cheesecloth and poached in a simmering broth. This microwave version is easier.

I discovered this way of cooking beef when I was talking to French chefs in highly esteemed restaurants about how they used the microwave oven. Two chefs—José Lampreia of Maison Blanche in Paris and Bernard Robin of Restaurant Bernard Robin in Bracieux—both cook beef this way. Their recipes make for festive dinner parties. The simpler version makes a good dinner to treat yourself well. Choose a sauce from Basics, Sauces and Snacks (pages 458–529); add a vegetable such as Fennel and Potato Purée (page 222) or Ratatouille (page 450) for sybaritic satisfaction.

PER 4 OUNCES (113.5 G) RAW BEEF TENDERLOIN, COOKED TO YIELD A 3-OUNCE (85-G) SERVING: 174 calories; 72 milligrams cholesterol; 8 grams fat; 54 milligrams sodium; 24 grams protein (53% RDA)

Cooking times for beef filet in the microwave oven

FOUR-OUNCE (113.5-G) PORTIONS OF 1-INCH (2.5-CM) THICK BEEF FILET Arrange room temperature filets on a 10-inch (25-cm) quiche dish or pie plate. Cover tightly with microwave plastic wrap.

One 4-ounce (113.5-g) slice filet
650- to 700-watt oven: 1 min. 30 sec.
400- to 500-watt oven: 2 min. 30 sec.

Four 4-ounce (each 113.5-g) slices filet
650- to 700-watt oven: 4 min. 30 sec.
400- to 500-watt oven: not recommended

Two 4-ounce (each 113.5-g) slices filet
650- to 700-watt oven: 2 min. 30 sec.
400- to 500-watt oven: 4 min.

SIX-OUNCE (170-G) PORTIONS OF 1½-INCH (4-CM) THICK BEEF FILET Arrange room temperature filets on a 10-inch (25-cm) quiche dish or pie plate. Cover tightly with microwave plastic wrap.

One 6-ounce (170-g) slice filet
650- to 700-watt oven: 2 min. 30 sec.
400- to 500-watt oven: 4 min.

Four 6-ounce (each 170-g) slices filet
650- to 700-watt oven: 6 min.
400- to 500-watt oven: Not recommended

Two 6-ounce (each 170-g) slices filet
650- to 700-watt oven: 3 min. 30 seco.
400- to 500-watt oven: 6 min.

JOSÉ LAMPREIA'S POACHED BEEF

Chef Lampreia of Maison Blanche in Paris obviously uses the rich stock to make his dish. He also adds a buttery sauce. I find that a quick and very satisfactory version can be made using water instead of stock. Make this dish up to three hours ahead. Cover and reheat for three minutes before serving.

You could begin this dinner party with Artichokes Barigoule (page 102) and accompany the meat with some horseradish, mustard or Rouïlle (page 484). Serve a good red wine, a Burgundy or a cabernet sauvignon, salad and a light dessert. Give those who aren't trying to lose weight some bread and provide spoons for the broth.

Considering that this is basically a meat dish, it is remarkably well balanced nutritionally, with vitamins and minerals of every sort. *SERVES 4*

Per 6-ounce (170-g) serving: 480 calories; 137 milligrams cholesterol; 23 grams fat; 219 milligrams sodium; 47 grams protein (104% RDA); 19 grams carbohydrate

RDA: calcium 8%; phosphorus 48%; iron 37%; 1,258 milligrams potassium; vitamin A 271%; thiamin 17%; riboflavin 22%; niacin 39%; vitamin C 31%

2 carrots (about 5 ounces; 142 g), peeled, halved lengthwise and quartered

1 turnip (4 ounces; 113.5 g), peeled and cut into 8 wedges

2 leeks (each 4 ounces; 113.5 g), cleaned, dark green removed, halved lengthwise and quartered

1 rib celery (2 ounces; 56 g), peeled, halved lengthwise and quartered

Bouquet garni (1 bay leaf, parsley stems from 1 bunch parsley and ½ teaspoon dried thyme)

2½ cups (590 ml) Rich Beef Broth (page 463), or water

1½ pounds (1.6 kg) filet of beef, cut into 4 equal tournedos and tied with string

3 cloves garlic, smashed and peeled

Beef tournedos tied with butcher's string

1. Arrange vegetables in a 5-quart (5-l) casserole, placing carrots and turnips around the inside edge and leeks and celery in the center. Add bouquet garni and enough broth just to cover the vegetables (about 2½ cups; 590 ml). Cover tightly with microwave plastic wrap and cook at 100% for 9 minutes in a 650- to 700-watt oven. Prick plastic to release steam.

2. Remove from oven and uncover. Place each of the tournedos in a corner of the casserole on top of the vegetables. They should not be covered with broth. Add garlic. Cover and cook for 5 minutes 30 seconds or until beef is just rare. Prick plastic.

3. Remove from oven and uncover. Remove meat and vegetables from broth. Remove strings from the meat and place each piece in the center of a large soup dish. Divide broth and vegetables among the four bowls and serve hot.

To serve 2. Use 1 carrot, ½ turnip, 1 leek, ½ rib celery, bouquet garni, 1¼ cups (300 ml) broth, ¾ pound (340 g) beef, and 2 small cloves garlic. Arrange ingredients as in Step 1 in a 2½-quart (2.5-l) soufflé dish. Cook, covered, for 6 minutes. Continue with Step 2, cooking for 3 minutes 15 seconds, or until beef is just rare. Finish as in Step 3.

FOR 400- TO 500-WATT OVENS

To serve 2. Cook as in Step 1 for 15 minutes. Continue with Step 2, cooking for 9 minutes. Finish as in Step 3.

BEEF FILET WITH SPINACH AND MUSHROOMS

*T*his is a party dish with no holds barred. If you like wine, now is the time to break out your best Burgundy, pinot noir, Bordeaux or cabernet sauvignon. Since you shouldn't be drinking too much, go for quality. If you avoid meat, chicken and fish at lunch, consider Coral Scallop Terrine (page 93) as a first course. Serve some potatoes and a good dessert. *SERVES 6*

Per 4-ounce (113.5-g) filet and ⅓-cup (80 ml) vegetable serving: 258 calories; 67 milligrams cholesterol; 13 grams fat; 168 milligrams sodium; 27 grams protein (60% RDA); 10 grams carbohydrate

RDA: calcium 13%; phosphorus 33%; iron 35%; vitamin A 152%; thiamin 15%; riboflavin 33%; niacin 31%; vitamin C 59%

6 ounces (170 g) shallots, peeled and sliced (about 1½ cups; 355 ml)
2 teaspoons vegetable oil
8 ounces (227 g) mushrooms, wiped clean and thinly sliced (about 2 cups; 240 ml)

1 pound (450 g) spinach, washed and stemmed (about 6 packed cups; 1.5 l)
1½ pounds (680 g) trimmed beef filet in 1 piece
Freshly ground black pepper, to taste

1. Place shallots and oil in a 13 × 9 × 2-inch (33 × 23 × 5-cm) oval dish. Cook, uncovered, at 100% for 8 minutes in a 650- to 700-watt oven, stirring three times.
2. Remove from oven. Place mushrooms in an even layer on top of shallots and mound spinach over all. Cook, uncovered, for 4 minutes. Stir well and cook, uncovered, for 4 minutes more.
3. Sprinkle beef with pepper and place on top of vegetables. Cover tightly with microwave plastic wrap. Cook for 4 minutes. Prick plastic to release steam.
4. Remove from oven and uncover. Turn filet over. Re-cover and cook for 3 minutes more for rare beef. If you like your beef medium, cook for an additional 1–2 minutes. Prick plastic to release steam.
5. Remove from oven and uncover; slice across into 1½- to 1¾-inch (3.8- to 4.5-cm) thick servings. The size of the slice will depend on the shape of the piece of filet, but what you want are 6 even slices.

To serve 2. Use 2 ounces (56 g) shallots, 1 teaspoon vegetable oil, 2 ounces (56 g) mushrooms, 2 cups (470 ml) spinach, 8 ounces (227 g) beef filet and freshly ground black pepper to taste. Cook shallots and oil as in Step 1 for 1 minute 30 seconds. In Step 2 cook for 1 minute 30 seconds, uncovered. Stir together and cook 1 minute 30 seconds more. Follow Step 3 and cook for 3 minutes 30 seconds. Remove to a serving dish, turning the meat over as you do so. Finish as in Step 5.

To serve 1. Use 1 ounce (28 g) shallots, ½ teaspoon vegetable oil, 1 ounce (28 g) mushrooms, 1 cup (240 ml) spinach, 4 ounces (113.5 g) 1-inch (2.5-cm) thick beef filet and freshly ground black pepper to taste. Cook shallots and oil as in Step 1 for 1 minute. In Step 2 cook for 1 minute, uncovered. Stir together and cook 1 minute more. Follow Step 3 and cook for 1 minute 30 seconds. Remove to a serving dish, turning the meat over as you do so. Finish as in Step 5.

FOR 400- TO 500-WATT OVENS

To serve 6. Cook as in Step 1 for 12 minutes, stirring three times. In Step 2, layer mushrooms on top of shallots with spinach mounded over all. Cook for 6 minutes, stir together and cook for an additional 6 minutes. Sprinkle beef with pepper and place on vegetables. Cover and cook for 7 minutes. Prick plastic and uncover. Turn filet over and cook for 6 minutes more. Finish as in Step 5.

To serve 2. Cook as in Step 1 for 2 minutes, stirring three times. In Step 2, layer mushrooms on top of shallots with spinach mounded over all. Cook for 2 minutes, stir together and cook for an additional 2 minutes. Sprinkle beef with pepper and place on vegetables. Cover and cook for 5 minutes. Prick plastic and uncover. Remove to a serving dish, turning the meat over as you do so. Finish as in Step 5.

To serve 1. Cook as in Step 1 for 1 minute 30 seconds, stirring three times. In Step 2, layer mushrooms on top of shallots with spinach mounded over all. Cook for 1 minute 30 seconds, stir together and cook for an additional 1 minute 30 seconds. Sprinkle beef with pepper and place on vegetables. Cover and cook for 3 minutes 30 seconds. Prick plastic and uncover. Remove to a serving dish, turning the meat over as you do so. Finish as in Step 5.

Wipe mushrooms clean with the palm of your hand or a damp paper towel.

Snap off stems.

Slice mushrooms through the stem.

PORK

You will notice that all the pork recipes are for pork tenderloin. Ever since Lynne Hill, who did the nutritional analyses for this book, pointed out to me that pork tenderloin has only one gram more fat and two milligrams more cholesterol per three and one half ounces (100 g) than skinned white meat of chicken, I have been using it with gusto and pleasure. The pork, however, has 52 percent more iron, 204 percent more zinc and 9 percent more cholesterol than chicken.

I think you will be surprised at the elegant taste of this cut of pork. When I serve it, people almost always assume that it is veal. The price is much lower.

Pork tenderloin can be bought in Cryovac (air-tight plastic) packages at many supermarkets and comes trimmed of any surface fat. In many instances, you may want to portion the meat before cooking it for exactness of portion and ease of service. Cooking times in the chart may not be the same as those in recipes due to the added ingredients in the recipes. To cut four-ounce (113.5-g) slices, cut three-inch (7.5-cm) long slices from the thick end and four-inch (10-cm) long slices from the thin. I usually get three portions from each strip, or six from a package. I flatten individual portions to make even pieces. Pork tenderloin is so tender that it can be easily flattened by pressing it gently with the heel of your hand.

Since pork tenderloin comes in largish amounts, it is nice to know that it can be portioned, tightly wrapped in individual portions, frozen and then quickly cooked—as many portions at a time as you need—from the frozen state. Unwrap each portion, put on a dish large enough to hold the number you are making and use the following charts to determine cooking times.

Cooking Times for Frozen Pork Tenderloin in the Microwave Oven

Cook pork on dish specified, covered tightly with microwave plastic wrap.

One 4-ounce (113.5-g) piece on a dinner plate
650- to 700-watt oven: 4 min.
400- to 500-watt oven: 4 min.

Four 4-ounce (113.5 g) pieces on a 10-inch (25.5-cm) quiche dish or pie plate
650- to 700-watt oven: 9 min.
400- to 500-watt oven: Not recommended

Two 4-ounce (113.5 g) pieces on a 10-inch (25.5-cm) quiche dish or pie plate
650- to 700-watt oven: 5 min. 30 sec.
400- to 500-watt oven: 9 min.

If you can't find pork tenderloin, you can use the meat from the loin—where the chops are—and trim it down to the center round of meat. This may seem wasteful; but it eliminates most of the fat. Still, you will be adding about 90 calories, 5 grams of fat and 5 milligrams of cholesterol to each three-and-a-half-ounce (99-g) cooked portion.

Since pork tenderloin is so lean, you may want to increase serving sizes for those who do not need to lose weight or who are large and/or active. I would keep the maximum portion between six and eight ounces (170–227 g).

Good sauces to serve with simply cooked pork tenderloin are Tomato Sauce Casalinga (page 167), Green Salsa Dressing (page 497), Ruby Beet Sauce (page 503), 24 Karat Sauce (page 504) and Red Pepper Purée (page 500). Cooking the pork brushed with Oriental Glaze (page 512) or on a bed of Diet Duxelles (page 477) works very well.

Leftover pork stews make good lunches. You may want to reduce the portion to three quarters of a cup and add a salad or a piece of fruit. The stews can be easily reheated in a microwave oven at home or at the office.

It is important that the pork be at room temperature before cooking or cooking times will be longer. All pork should be cooked, tightly covered to reduce evaporation and even out cooking temperatures, until it reaches at least 140°F (60°C) to 160°F (71°C). Test it with an instant-read thermometer. It will keep on cooking after you take it out of the oven. Once you have tried some of these dishes, I think you will start inventing your own.

Cooking Times for Raw Pork Tenderloin in the Microwave Oven

Cut across into 4-ounce (113.5-g) pieces. Upend pieces and flatten each with the palm of your hand to a thickness of 1½ inches (4 cm). Place in a 10-inch (25.5-cm) quiche dish and cover tightly with microwave plastic wrap. Cook until the pork registers 140°F (60°C) on an instant-read thermometer.

4 ounces (113.5 g) pork tenderloin
650- to 700-watt oven: 1 min. 30 sec.
400- to 500-watt oven: 3 min.

8 ounces (227 g) pork tenderloin, placed on either side of the dish
650- to 700-watt oven: 2 min. 30 sec.
400- to 500-watt oven: 5 min.

16 ounces (453 g) pork tenderloin, placed around the inside rim of the dish
650- to 700-watt oven: 4 min.
400- to 500-watt oven: 7 min.

*Slices of pork loin lightly flattened with the palm of your hand
into small tournedos about 1½ inches (3.8 cm) thick, or smaller slices
flattened into scaloppines, about ¼ inch (.5 cm) thick*

INSTANT PORK DINNER

Since pork cooks so quickly and so well, individual portions are as amenable to the salad-bar treatment as fish and chicken are. When you are in a hurry, the cleaned and sliced vegetables can be picked up at a salad bar—no waste, less work. The seasonings are slightly Oriental.

You can easily have a soup to begin—something made on another day—a slice of French bread or Majic Whole-Grain Bread (page 152), a piece of cheese and a piece of fruit. There is no need to feel deprived. Even if you consume a portion for two all by yourself, you can still have a nice large salad with a diet dressing (pages 486–499) and some whole-grain bread. However, that would not be a day to have a meat sandwich for lunch. Stick to a salad or another vegetarian or almost-vegetarian lunch. *SERVES 1*

Per serving: 196 calories; 74 milligrams cholesterol; 5 grams fat; 415 milligrams sodium; 28 grams protein (62% RDA); 9 grams carbohydrate

RDA: phosphorus 37%; iron 18%; 1,081 milligrams potassium, vitamin A 83%; thiamin 83%; riboflavin 32%; niacin 41%; vitamin C 66%

4 ounces (113.5 g) pork tenderloin, flattened with your palm to a 1½-inch (4-cm) thickness
1½ ounces (42.5 g) asparagus tips (about ⅓ cup; 80 ml)
1½ ounces (42.5 g) broccoli florets (about 1 cup; 240 ml)
1 ounce (28 g) carrot, cut into 2 × ¼ × ¼-inch (5 × .5 × .5-cm) matchsticks (about ¼ cup; 60 ml)
½ ounce (14 g) sliced mushrooms (about 2 cups; 470 ml)

1 teaspoon tamari soy
½ teaspoon Oriental sesame oil
½ teaspoon mirin
1 tablespoon Basic Meat Broth made with pork bones (page 462), or Basic Chicken Broth (page 460), or unsalted or regular canned chicken broth, or water
Freshly ground black pepper, to taste

1. Place pork in the center of a deep-rimmed dinner plate, soup plate or 10-inch (25.5-cm) quiche dish or pie plate. Arrange vegetables around pork, placing asparagus closest to the meat, then broccoli and carrots. Scatter mushrooms over pork.

2. Combine remaining ingredients in a small bowl. Pour over meat and vegetables. Cover tightly with microwave plastic wrap. Cook at 100% for 3 minutes 30 seconds in a 650- to 700-watt oven. Prick plastic to release steam.

3. Remove from oven and uncover. Serve hot.

To serve 2. Use 8 ounces (227 g) pork, 3 ounces (85 g) each asparagus and broccoli, 2 ounces (56 g) carrot, 1 ounce (28 g) mushrooms, 2 teaspoons soy, 1 teaspoon each sesame oil and mirin, 2 tablespoons broth and black pepper to taste. Divide ingredients between two dinner plates or 10-inch (25.5-cm) quiche dishes. Arrange as in Step 1. Continue with Step 2. Cook, using a rack, for 6 minutes, changing plates after 3 minutes.

FOR 400- TO 500-WATT OVENS

To serve 1. Cook for 6 minutes.

To serve 2. Cook for 12 minutes, changing plates after 6 minutes.

BRAISED PORK AND VEGETABLES

Many recipes in *Microwave Gourmet* are perfectly suitable for those who want to lose weight and select a healthier way of eating, as many readers have discovered. Some of the recipes are richer, less suitable. Some need to be adapted. This is a diet adaptation of Smothered Pork Roast, one of my favorite recipes in *Microwave Gourmet*. I was pleasantly surprised that the flavor of this version does so well in comparison. This dish is a large piece of tenderloin to be sliced for company dinner.

Adding potatoes to make a delicious purée will increase your calories per portion to 245; but it makes no difference to the cholesterol and fat and adds 11 grams of carbohydrate. Oddly, adding the potatoes doesn't increase the one-third-cup (80-ml) serving of vegetables. They take up less space when puréed. A large or active person could increase the portion size to six ounces (170 g). Small people who are not losing weight can do the same.

Even a small person on a weight-loss diet who has added the potatoes will still have enough calories left to start with Mushroom Soup (page 123), Jade Soup (page 124), Quick Tomato Soup (page 126) or many of the others. Have a salad. Spinach, Mushroom and Celery Salad (page 401) would be nice if you're not having Jade Soup. Chunky Tomato Basil Salad (page 407) would be delicious if you're not having Quick Tomato Soup. Either would round out your vitamins nicely. Have a dessert, or skip the dessert and have a glass of wine.   *SERVES 6*

Per 4-ounce (113.5-g) pork with generous ⅓-cup (80 ml) vegetable serving, excluding optional potatoes: 196 calories; 68 milligrams cholesterol; 9 grams fat; 106 milligrams sodium; 24 grams protein (54% RDA); 4 grams carbohydrate

RDA without potatoes: phosphorus 28%; thiamin 77%; riboflavin 20%; niacin 32%; vitamin C 11%

(continued)

¼ cup (60 ml) Basic Meat Broth made
with pork bones (page 462), or Basic
Chicken Broth (page 460), or
unsalted or regular canned chicken
broth

8 ounces (227 g) onion, peeled and
sliced (about 2 cups; 470 ml)

2 ribs celery, peeled and sliced (about
¾ cup; 180 ml)

½ fennel bulb (about 4 ounces; 113.5
g), peeled and sliced (1 cup; 240 ml)

1½ pounds (680 g) trimmed pork
tenderloin, cut across into 2 equal
halves

Freshly ground black pepper, to taste

2 potatoes (each 8 ounces; 227 g),
baked (page 219), peeled and diced,
optional

1. Combine broth and onion in a 13 × 9 × 2-inch (33 × 23 × 5-cm) oval glass or ceramic dish. Cover tightly with microwave plastic wrap. Cook for 3 minutes at 100% in a 650- to 700-watt oven. Prick plastic to release steam.

2. Remove from oven and uncover. Stir in celery and fennel. Sprinkle black pepper over both pieces of pork. Arrange on top of vegetables with the thin ends next to the thick ends. Cover and cook for 5 minutes. Prick plastic wrap.

3. Remove from oven and uncover. Turn tenderloins over and re-cover. Cook for 6 minutes more, or until temperature of meat reaches 140°F–160°F (60°C–71°C) while inside oven.

4. Remove from oven and uncover. Transfer meat to a serving platter and let stand, covered loosely with aluminum foil, while finishing the vegetables.

5. Transfer vegetables to a food processor along with diced potatoes, if using. Purée until smooth.

6. To serve, slice pork and divide among 6 plates. Place a generous ⅓ cup (80 ml) vegetable purée on each plate.

VARIATION Omit potatoes and do not purée vegetables. Serve a generous ⅓ cup braised vegetables with the meat.

FOR 400- TO 500-WATT OVENS

To serve 6.   Follow Step 1 and cook for 4 minutes 30 seconds. In Step 2, cook for 10 minutes. Cook as in Step 3 for 6 minutes (allow 8 minutes for well done). Finish as in Step 5.

PORK SCALOPPINE WITH MUSHROOMS AND NOODLES

*H*ere's a luscious simple dinner for a family, guests or on your own. It comes with its own noodles and generous helpings of iron and the B vitamins. Start with Oriental Spinach Salad (page 79), Caprese Salad (page 80) or Carrots and Mushrooms with Cumin (page 82). Feel free to add a salad, a piece of cheese with a portion of fruit, or a dessert. *SERVES 4*

Per serving: 259 calories; 100 milligrams cholesterol; 5 grams fat; 109 milligrams sodium; 29 grams protein (64% RDA); 24 grams carbohydrate

RDA: phosphorus 38%; iron 17%; thiamin 93%; riboflavin 39%; niacin 45%; vitamin C 14%

4 ounces (113.5 g) dried noodles or
   other pasta
8 ounces (225 g) mushrooms, wiped
   clean and sliced through the stem
   (about 2 cups; 470 ml)

4 teaspoons coarse mustard
3 tablespoons fresh lemon juice
1 pound (450 g) pork tenderloin, cut
   across into 16 slices
Freshly ground black pepper, to taste

1. Cook pasta on top of the stove. Drain and reserve.

2. Combine mushrooms, mustard and lemon juice in a small bowl. Flatten pork slices with the palm of your hand.

3. Arrange 4 pork slices and ¼ of the mushroom mixture in each corner of a 14×11×2-inch (35.5×28×5-cm) dish, alternating pork and mushrooms and slightly overlapping the pork slices.

4. Place pasta in the center of the dish and sprinkle pepper over all. Cover tightly with microwave plastic wrap. Cook at 100% for 5 minutes 30 seconds, or until pork reaches 160°F (71°C) on an instant-read thermometer, in a 650- to 700-watt oven. Prick plastic to release steam.

5. Remove from oven and let stand for 2 minutes. Uncover, divide among four dinner plates and serve.

*Arrange overlapped pork and mushroom portions
spoke-fashion around a 10-inch (25.5-cm) quiche dish.*

(continued)

Pork Scaloppine with Mushrooms and Noodles (cont.)

To serve 2. Use 2 ounces (56 g) pasta, 4 ounces (113.5 g) mushrooms, 2 teaspoons mustard, 4 teaspoons lemon juice, 8 ounces (225 g) pork, and black pepper to taste. In a 10-inch (25.5-cm) quiche dish, arrange as in Step 3, with the pork and mushrooms to either side of the dish and the noodles in the center. Cook for 3 minutes. Finish as in Step 5.

To serve 1. Use 1 ounce (28 g) pasta, 2 ounces (56 g) mushrooms, 1 teaspoon mustard, 2 teaspoons lemon juice, 4 ounces (113.5 g) pork, and black pepper to taste. In a 10-inch (25.5-cm) quiche dish, arrange as in Step 3, with the pork and mushrooms to one side of the dish and the noodles on the other side. Cook for 1 minute 30 seconds. Finish as in Step 5.

FOR 400- TO 500-WATT OVENS

To serve 2. Cook for 5 minutes.

To serve 1. Cook for 4 minutes.

WINTER PORK STEW

This robust stew is a complete main course, with potatoes and vegetables and their attendant vitamins. Rather than increasing the amount of this protein-rich stew when serving a large, active or non—weight-loss eater, add a big first course, such as an artichoke (pages 99–100) with Egg White Mayonnaise (page 482), and a salad and a dessert such as Tapioca Pudding (page 567). Weight losers can substitute asparagus (page 76) for the artichoke.   *SERVES 6*

Per generous 1-cup (240-ml) serving: 224 calories; 74 milligrams cholesterol; 4 grams fat; 91 milligrams sodium; 28 grams protein (62% RDA); 20 grams carbohydrate

RDA: phosphorus 37%; iron 18%; 1,081 milligrams potassium; vitamin A 147%; thiamin 83%; riboflavin 32%; niacin 41%; vitamin C 66%

2 baking potatoes (each 8 ounces; 227 g), peeled and cut into ½-inch (1-cm) cubes (about 2 cups; 470 ml)

1⅔ cups (400 ml) Basic Meat Broth made with pork bones (page 462), or Basic Chicken Broth (page 460), unsalted or regular canned chicken broth

6 ounces (170 g) carrot, trimmed, peeled, halved lengthwise and cut across into ¼-inch (.5-cm) slices (about 1 cup; 240 ml)

6 ounces (170 g) onion, peeled and cut into ½-inch (1-cm) pieces (about 1½ cups; 355 ml)

6 ounces (170 g) Brussels sprouts, trimmed and halved lengthwise

8 ounces (227 g) mushrooms, wiped clean and thinly sliced through the stem (about 2 cups; 470 ml)

2 teaspoons cornstarch

½ teaspoon oregano

½ bay leaf

1 teaspoon kosher salt

Freshly ground black pepper, to taste

1½ pounds (680 g) trimmed pork tenderloin, cut into 1-inch (2.5-cm) chunks

1. Place potatoes and ⅔ cup (160 ml) of the broth in a 2½-quart (2.5-l) soufflé dish. Cover tightly with microwave plastic wrap. Cook at 100% for 2 minutes in a 650- to 700-watt oven. Prick plastic to release steam.

2. Remove from oven and uncover. Add carrots and re-cover. Cook for 2 minutes. Prick plastic to release steam.

3. Uncover and stir in onions, Brussels sprouts and mushrooms. Re-cover and cook for 4 minutes. Prick plastic.

4. Remove from oven and uncover. Combine remaining broth with cornstarch in a small bowl, making sure there are no lumps. Stir oregano, bay leaf, salt and pepper into cornstarch mixture and stir into soufflé dish. Cover and cook for 3 minutes. Prick plastic.

5. Uncover and place pork on top of vegetables around the inside rim of the dish. Cover and cook for 3 minutes, or until pork is just pink and reaches 160°F (71°C) on an instant-read thermometer, stirring once halfway through cooking. Prick plastic.

6. Remove from oven. Uncover and remove bay leaf. Stir well; cover lightly and let rest 5 minutes; serve.

FOR 400- TO 500-WATT OVENS

To serve 6. Follow Step 1 and cook potatoes and broth for 8 minutes. Continue with Step 2 and cook for 4 minutes. Continue with Step 3 and cook for 6 minutes. In Step 4, cook for 5 minutes 30 seconds. In Step 5 cook for 9 minutes, stirring twice. Finish as in Step 6.

PORK WITH BRAISED RED CABBAGE

*T*his is another fine winter dish. I serve it with broad egg noodles or whole wheat noodles; a half-cup (120 ml) cooked per person adds on about one hundred calories. Bell Peppers and Sardines with Balsamic Vinegar (page 84) or Broccoli Timbale (page 104) with 24 Karat Sauce (page 504) adds more vitamins when used as starters. A good salad such as Bibb and Tarragon Salad (page 393) is always a nice addition. That would still leave room for Rice Pudding (page 566). Larger and/or more active people and those not losing weight can add more noodles, some bread and a piece of cheese. *SERVES 6*

Per 1-cup (240-ml) serving: 201 calories; 74 milligrams cholesterol; 5 grams fat; 312 milligrams sodium; 25 grams protein (57% RDA); 15 grams carbohydrate

RDA: phosphorus 32%; iron 12%; thiamin 76%; riboflavin 19%; niacin 27%; vitamin C 79%

6 ounces (170 g) onion, peeled and sliced
3 cloves garlic, smashed, peeled and sliced
2 teaspoons vegetable oil
1 pound (450 g) shredded red cabbage (about 6 cups; 1.5 l)
2 tablespoons red wine vinegar
1 tablespoon red wine
⅓ cup (80 ml) Basic Chicken Broth (page 460), or unsalted or regular canned chicken broth

¼ cup (60 ml) raisins
1 tablespoon light brown sugar, packed
5 juniper berries
1 bay leaf
Freshly ground black pepper, to taste
1 teaspoon kosher salt
1½ pounds (680 g) trimmed pork tenderloin, cut into 1½-inch (4-cm) cubes

1. Combine onion, garlic and oil in a 13×9×2-inch (33×23×5-cm) oval glass or ceramic dish. Cook at 100%, uncovered, for 3 minutes in a 650- to 700-watt oven.

2. Add cabbage and cover tightly with microwave plastic wrap. Cook for 6 minutes. Prick plastic to release steam.

3. Remove from oven and uncover. Combine remaining ingredients except pork in a small bowl. Pour over cabbage and mix well. Cover tightly and cook for 7 minutes. Prick plastic.

4. Remove from oven and uncover. Mound cabbage mixture in center of dish and arrange pork pieces around the inside edge of dish. Cover and cook for 3 minutes. Prick plastic to release steam.

5. Remove from oven and uncover. Stir well, re-cover and cook for 2 minutes more, or until the internal temperature of the pork reaches 160°F (71°C).

6. Prick plastic. Remove from oven and uncover. Stir and let stand for 5 minutes before serving.

FOR 400- TO 500-WATT OVENS

To serve 6. Follow Step 1 and cook, uncovered, for 4 minutes 30 seconds. In Step 2, cook for 9 minutes. Continue with Step 3 and cook for 10 minutes 30 seconds. In Step 4, cover and cook for 6 minutes 30 seconds. Finish as in Steps 5 and 6, cooking for 5 minutes.

Lamb

I love lamb. I know it's not the most popular American meat; but I think that if more people roasted it rare or had interesting and reliable recipes for preparing it in other ways, it would gain acclaim. Many people are unhappy when they roast lamb at home, although rack of lamb is one of the most popular restaurant dishes. I think this is a question of the smell. If lamb is roasted only until rare and is thoroughly trimmed of the fell—a thin membrane covering it—and fat, it won't smell strongly as it cooks. In stews and other, more complicated dishes—not complicated to make, but in taste—lamb adds a marvelously rich flavor to the sauces and finished dishes.

Leg of lamb is frequently bought frozen and stored that way as good emergency food for when company comes. It can be quickly defrosted in a microwave oven and then roasted briefly for a good main course. When you get your portion, try to eat only between four and six ounces (113.5–170 g)—211 to 316 calories. Trim off any visible fat. Serve with a Ratatouille (page 450) and Cannellini Beans with Garlic (page 208) for a happy meal tasting of Provence.

To Defrost a Leg of Lamb in the Microwave Oven and Then Roast It

TO DEFROST AND COOK A SHORT SPRING LEG OF LAMB (ABOUT 4 POUNDS; 1.8 KG): Place in a 14 × 11 × 2-inch (35.5 × 28 × 5-cm) dish. Shield shanks with aluminum foil. Cook, uncovered, at 100% for 15 minutes in a 650- to 700-watt oven. Remove foil and cook for 6 minutes more. Then season and cook for 20 minutes in a 500°F (260°C) oven for medium rare. Serves 6.

TO DEFROST AND COOK A WHOLE LEG OF LAMB (ABOUT 7 POUNDS; 3.2 KG): Place in a 14 × 11 × 2-inch (35.5 × 28 × 5-cm) dish. Shield shanks with aluminum foil. Cover tightly with microwave plastic wrap. Cook at 100% for 14 minutes in a 650- to 700-watt oven. Prick plastic and uncover. Remove foil. Re-cover and cook 14 minutes more. Season and cook for 20 minutes in a 500°F (260° C) oven for medium rare. Serves 10.

Wrap the shank bone with aluminum foil to shield.　　*Make an incision down to the bone with a knife.*　　*Cut off lamb steaks from the leg with a saw.*

LAMB MEAT LOAF

*T*his is an easy, delicious main course for two with lots of the B vitamins and a modest load of calories. Serve it with Olive Oil Mashed Potatoes (page 221) and have Summer Vegetable Salad (page 412) before or after it. Finish off with Peppered Strawberries (page 535) and an Oat Bran Crisp (page 574) for a well-rounded meal. Those who can eat more heavily can add another vegetable, such as Stewed Okra (page 444) or Oriental Carrots (page 437). Make all the side dishes and dessert ahead. Make the lamb at the last minute.

If you cannot buy ground lamb, buy the leanest lamb you can find and grind it in a food processor.   *SERVES 2*

Per serving: 240 calories; 81 milligrams cholesterol; 9 grams fat; 362 milligrams sodium; 24 grams protein (53% RDA); 13 grams carbohydrate

RDA: phosphorus 25%; iron 13%; thiamin 16%; riboflavin 20%; niacin 33%

¼ cup (60 ml) Bread Crumbs (page 154), or store-bought
¼ cup (60 ml) skim milk
1 clove garlic, smashed and peeled
3 slices peeled fresh ginger

2 ounces (56 g) onion, peeled and cut into 2-inch (5-cm) chunks
½ pound (225 g) lean ground lamb
¼ teaspoon kosher salt

1. Combine bread crumbs and milk in a large mixing bowl and reserve.
2. Finely chop garlic, ginger and onion in a food processor. Add to bread crumb mixture along with lamb and salt. Mix lightly with a fork or your fingertips to combine.
3. Shape mixture into two ovals and place on either side of a 10-inch (25.5-cm) quiche dish. Cover tightly with microwave plastic wrap. Cook at 100% for 3 minutes in a 650- to 700-watt oven. Prick plastic to release steam.
4. Remove from oven. Uncover and serve immediately.

FOR 400- TO 500-WATT OVENS

To serve 2. Cook for 7 minutes.

LAMB PROVENÇALE

When I buy a leg of lamb, I often ask the butcher to prepare it as a short leg and cut off the two steaks after the joint. I trim off all the fat and freeze the steaks, individually wrapped, for later use. If I have them on hand, this makes a quick dinner in summer when the tomatoes are really ripe. It's not worth making unless the tomatoes are good. Take the steaks out of the freezer and put them in the refrigerator in the morning. Take them out of the refrigerator before starting preparation. Don't defrost them in the microwave as they are thin and will cook rather than defrost.

Fennel Soup (page 119) or Watercress Soup (page 129) would start the meal off with pleasure. You can make some steamed new potatoes (page 220), Garlic Potatoes (page 223) or a baking potato (page 219) to accompany the lamb; but you might try something more unusual, such as couscous (page 180) or Grits (page 218). Have some spinach (page 78) on the side, or make a big green salad. Add a wedge of cheese or have Apple Snow (page 549) for dessert. You can still have a well-chilled glass of rosé wine.

Prepare the lamb. Cook the soup, vegetables and dessert, if you are having one. Prepare the salad and salad dressing before you cook the lamb. Re-heat the soup and serve it. Re-heat both vegetables for about a minute and cook the lamb. Eat. *SERVES 2*

Per serving: 167 calories; 79 milligrams cholesterol; 6 grams fat; 84 milligrams sodium; 23 grams protein (51% RDA); 3 grams carbohydrate

RDA: phosphorus 23%; iron 14%; vitamin A 14%; thiamin 15%; riboflavin 18%; niacin 34%; vitamin C 18%

½ pound (225 g) trimmed lamb steak, cut from a leg of lamb
¼ pound (115 g) fresh tomato, cored and cut into 1-inch (2.5-cm) chunks (about ¾ cup; 180 ml)
½ clove garlic, smashed, peeled and minced
1 tablespoon chopped fresh basil
Kosher salt, to taste
Freshly ground black pepper, to taste

1. Place lamb in the bottom of a 2½-quart (2.5-l) soufflé dish. Scatter remaining ingredients, except pepper, over lamb. Cover tightly with microwave plastic wrap. Cook at 100% for 3 minutes, or until just pink and tender in a 650- to 700-watt oven. Prick plastic to release steam.

2. Remove from oven and uncover. Sprinkle with black pepper, if desired, and serve.

FOR 400- TO 500-WATT OVENS

To serve 1. Cook for 5 minutes. Turn steak over and cook for 4 minutes more.

LAMB CURRY

*T*his is a very simple curry with few ingredients and is quickly cooked to make a warmly flavored main course that should be served with a half-cup (120 ml) of cooked rice per person. A good in-a-hurry first course would be Caprese Salad (page 80), or simply toss up a Cucumber Salad (page 403). If you serve fruit for dessert, you have dinner almost without work and can still have a glass of wine or light beer.   *SERVES 2*

Per serving: 244 calories; 79 milligrams cholesterol; 9 grams fat; 453 milligrams sodium; 24 grams protein (52% RDA); 17 grams carbohydrate

RDA: phosphorus 24%; iron 16%; thiamin 16%; riboflavin 16%; niacin 33%; vitamin C 16%

1 teaspoon vegetable oil
1½ teaspoons curry powder
4 ounces (113.5 g) onion, peeled and sliced (about 1⅓ cups; 320 ml)
4 ounces (113.5 g) green apple, cut into thin wedges (about ½ cup; 120 ml)

½ pound (227 g) lamb steak, cut into 2-inch (5-cm) cubes
1 tablespoon raisins
½ teaspoon kosher salt
4 drops hot red pepper sauce
2 teaspoons fresh lime juice

1. Stir together oil and curry powder in the bottom of a 2½-quart (2.5-l) soufflé dish. Add onion and apple and stir to coat. Cook, uncovered, at 100% for 2 minutes in a 650- to 700-watt oven.

2. Add lamb and raisins and stir to coat with the curry powder. Cover tightly with microwave plastic wrap. Cook at 100% for 2 minutes. Prick plastic to release steam.

3. Remove from oven and uncover. Stir in remaining ingredients and serve over rice, if desired.

FOR 400- TO 500-WATT OVENS

To serve 2. Cook as in Step 1 for 3 minutes. Continue with Step 2, cooking for 2 minutes.

SEMI-IRISH STEW

*T*his is semi-Irish because I add the pop and color of green peas and the flavor of mint. The Irish might well have mint with lamb, but not in stew. Even though there is a version for two people, it might be a good idea to make the larger version. It freezes very well. It can also be made the day before a party and reheated.

If you are making this as party food, contrast the flavors and style with a refined first course such as Coral Scallop Terrine (page 93). You can afford the protein because this dish has a moderate amount. Add a salad and finish up with Plum Timbales (page 562) or Chocolate Junket (page 572), depending on the season. If you are watching your sodium, eliminate the salt. *SERVES 8*

Per 1-cup (240-ml) serving: 362 calories; 68 milligrams cholesterol; 23 grams fat; 639 milligrams sodium; 18 grams protein (40% RDA); 20 grams carbohydrate

RDA: iron 18%; 778 milligrams potassium; vitamin A 157%; thiamin 17%; riboflavin 14%; niacin 30%; vitamin C 52%

2 pounds (900 g) lamb, bone in (stew meat), cut into 1-inch (2.5-cm) chunks

3 medium carrots (about 9 ounces; 255 g), cut into $2 \times \frac{1}{4} \times \frac{1}{4}$-inch ($5 \times .5 \times .5$-cm) pieces (about 3 cups; 705 ml)

½ pound (225 g) small white onions, peeled

1 pound (450 g) small new potatoes, scrubbed, any large ones cut in half

½ pound (225 g) small turnips, cut into ½-inch (1-cm) wedges (about 1½ cups; 355 ml)

1 tablespoon kosher salt

1½ cups (355 ml) water

Freshly ground black pepper, to taste

1 cup (240 ml) fresh shelled peas, or frozen peas defrosted in a sieve under warm running water

½ cup (120 ml) chopped fresh mint, or 1 tablespoon dried mint

1 tablespoon fresh lemon juice, optional

1. Place lamb around the inside edge of a 2½-quart (2.5-l) soufflé dish. Mound vegetables in the center.

2. Dissolve salt in water and pour over all. Grind pepper on top. Cover tightly with microwave plastic wrap. Cook at 100% for 20 minutes in a 650- to 700-watt oven. Prick plastic to release steam.

3. Leaving dish in oven, uncover and stir in peas and mint. Re-cover and cook at 100% for 5 minutes more.

4. Remove from oven and uncover. Add lemon juice, if desired, and stir well. Mellow overnight or serve immediately.

To serve 2. Use 8 ounces (225 g) lamb, 1 small carrot, 2 ounces (56 g) onion, 4 ounces (113.5 g) potatoes, 2 ounces (56 g) turnips, 1¾ teaspoons salt, ¼ cup (60 ml) plus 2 tablespoons water, pepper to taste, ¼ cup (60 ml) peas and 2 tablespoons mint. Prepare as in Steps 1 and 2 in a 1½-quart (1.5-l) soufflé dish. Cook for 5 minutes. Continue with Step 3, cooking for 5 minutes more. Finish as in Step 4 with ½ teaspoon lemon juice, if using.

FOR 400- TO 500-WATT OVENS

To serve 8. Cook as in Step 2 for 30 minutes. Continue as in Step 3, cooking for 8 minutes. Finish as in Step 4.

To serve 2. Cook as in Step 2 for 8 minutes. Continue with Step 3, cooking for 7 minutes. Finish as in Step 4.

RISOTTO WITH LAMB AND DILL

This risotto finds its home here because it is so substantial, a real main course. Unfortunately, as with the other slim risottos, it doesn't cook as well in a low-wattage oven. This has a wonderfully rich and creamy texture. All it needs is a large salad, a dessert and a glass of wine to make a soothing and nutritious meal. Those who are large and/or active or not on a weight-loss diet may well want to eat another half-portion. Leftovers are good cold or reheated for lunch.   *SERVES 4*

Per 1⅓-cup (320-ml) serving: 335 calories; 60 milligrams cholesterol; 6 grams fat; 102 milligrams sodium; 23 grams protein (51% RDA); 45 grams carbohydrate

RDA: phosphorus 25%; iron 24%; thiamin 27%; riboflavin 22%; niacin 44%; vitamin C 13%

½ pound (227 g) yellow onion, peeled and chopped (about 1 cup; 240 ml)
1 cup (240 ml) arborio rice
2¾ cups (650 ml) Basic Chicken Broth (page 460), or unsalted or regular canned chicken broth
¼ pound (113.5 g) mushrooms, cleaned and sliced through the stem (about 1 cup; 240 ml)

¾ pound (340 g) lean ground lamb
2 cloves garlic, smashed and peeled
¼ cup (60 ml) finely chopped fresh dill
1 tablespoon fresh lemon juice, or to taste
Freshly ground black pepper, to taste

1. Place onion in a 13×9×2-inch (33×23×5-cm) oval dish. Cook, uncovered, at 100% for 2 minutes in a 650- to 700-watt oven. Add rice and cook, uncovered, for 1 minute.

(continued)

2. Stir in broth. Cook, uncovered, for 9 minutes. Add mushrooms, lamb and garlic. Cook, uncovered, for 12 minutes more.

3. Remove from oven. Stir in dill. Cover with a towel and let stand for 5 minutes. Add lemon juice and pepper and serve.

To serve 2. Use ¼ pound (113.5 g) onion, ½ cup (120 ml) rice, 1¾ cups (410 ml) broth, 2 ounces (56 g) mushrooms, 6 ounces (170 g) lamb, 1 clove garlic, 2 tablespoons dill, 1½ teaspoons lemon juice and pepper to taste. Cook as in Step 1 in an 11 × 8½ × 2-inch (28 × 21.5 × 5-cm) dish for 1 minute 30 seconds. Add rice and cook for 1 minute. Continue with Step 2, cooking for 9 minutes. Stir in mushrooms, lamb and garlic and cook for 9 minutes more. Finish as in Step 3.

VEAL

The most serious problem with veal is its cost. It's a lovely meat often used with elegant sauces by the French. Italians are more likely either to simply sauté thin slices or to braise less expensive cuts like veal shanks in a deep, rich sauce. Thin cuts of the leg meat also grill very well as paillards.

The quality of veal will make a great difference in the cooking of roasts, scaloppines and paillards. Less marvelous veal may be used in stew, for braising and ground. The difficulty is in recognizing good veal. We have been trained by promotional campaigns to believe that the whitest veal is the best. Originally, veal was considered to be the flesh of very young animals. Today, we sometimes see huge legs of "veal" that we know cannot come from a very young animal. The color and tenderness of such large animals comes from being fed almost entirely with milk and being kept relatively immobile. You can still find in specialty meat stores and by mail order really young veal that is organically raised. It will have a darker color than the veal you are accustomed to seeing; but it will taste better.

One source of good veal is Summerfield Farms, SR 4, Box 195A, Brightwood, Virginia 22715 (Telephone: [703] 948-3100). From them you can also buy Veal Glaze, a veal stock so concentrated it is a solid jelly. It needs to be frozen or refrigerated. A very small amount added to stews and sauces will enrich them with a bundle of flavor. French chefs use it in stews and sauces, even with other meats. It has no added salt and no fat. You can also make it (page 466).

Veal is the source of the most delicately flavored innards: sweetbreads, liver and kidneys. While you might not want to eat them often, they are a good way to vary your diet and a rich source of iron. I generally prefer liver that is grilled or sautéed. Kidneys and sweetbreads cook extremely well in the microwave oven. Those of you who want to cook sweetbreads should look in *Microwave Gourmet*. I haven't included any recipes in this book because they are a poor nutritional bargain considering their high levels of cholesterol. Brains are worse.

POACHED VEAL

Because of its mild flavor, veal sets off sauces beautifully. Pale in color, it does well with sauces of any color, from Tonnato Sauce (page 484) to Rich Watercress Sauce (page 506) to Paprika-Lemon Béchamel (page 511), and vegetable sauces such as 24 Karat Sauce (page 504) and Red Pepper Purée (page 500). The best and least fattening way to cook veal simply is to poach it, which keeps it moist. Then it can be sliced and served with a sauce or Diet Duxelles (page 477) or a vegetable dish with its own sauce or a purée.

PER 4-OUNCE (113.5-G) SLICE: 265 calories; 115 milligrams cholesterol; 15 grams fat; 73 milligrams sodium; 29 grams protein (64% RDA)

1½ pounds (570 g) boneless veal loin in a
9 × 5 × 3-inch (23 × 12.5 × 5-cm) glass loaf
pan with ½ cup (120 ml) liquid, tightly
covered with microwave plastic wrap
650- to 700-watt oven: 6 min.
400- to 500-watt oven: 6 min., turn veal
  over and cook for 6 min. more

VEAL SAVARIN

A savarin is a circular mold usually used to make cakes, also called savarins. Here, the ring shape is formed by hand from a meat mixture. The shape is pretty, and also helps the food to cook more evenly.

One of the least expensive ways to use veal is ground. If you cannot buy ground veal, buy the leanest and least expensive cuts you can find, cut in smallish chunks, and chop them up to the texture of a medium grind in a food processor. Be careful that you do not overprocess this tender meat and make it mushy.

This nice way to treat yourself, or yourself and a friend, is also an extraordinary nutritional treat, with iron and vitamins of almost every kind. I sometimes put some cooked spinach (page 78) in the center of the cooked circle for lots of color. I would rather have bread than another starch with this. Start with a light soup—Garlic Escarole Soup (page 118), Celery Soup (page 122), or, if it's hot out, a chilled bowl of 24 Karat Soup (page 144) or Red Pepper Soup (page 145). Pick a light dessert and have a small glass of wine or a piece of cheese. *SERVES 2*

Per serving: 256 calories; 81 milligrams cholesterol; 12 grams fat; 845 milligrams sodium; 24 grams protein (54% RDA); 13 grams carbohydrate

RDA: phosphorus 33%; iron 27%; 873 milligrams potassium; vitamin A 102%; thiamin 18%; riboflavin 34%; niacin 52%; vitamin C 24%

(continued)

¼ pound (113.5-g) mushrooms, wiped
    clean, trimmed and quartered (about
    2 cups; 470 ml)
2 tablespoons fresh parsley leaves
4 shallots, peeled
½ teaspoon fresh lemon juice
½ pound (227 g) lean ground veal

1½ teaspoons kosher salt
½ teaspoon paprika
Freshly ground black pepper, to taste
6 ounces (170 g) carrot, trimmed,
    peeled and thinly sliced across or
    julienned (about 1 cup; 240 ml)

1. Finely chop mushrooms, parsley and shallots in the food processor. Scrape into a mixing bowl and add lemon juice, veal, salt, paprika and pepper. Stir well with a fork to combine.

2. Divide mixture in half and shape into donuts. Place each in the center of a dinner plate or a 10-inch (25.5-cm) quiche dish. Divide carrots between plates and arrange around veal. Cover tightly with microwave plastic wrap.

3. Using a rack, cook at 100% for 5 minutes, switching plates after 2 minutes 30 seconds, in a 650- to 700-watt oven. Prick plastic to release steam.

4. Remove from oven and uncover. Serve immediately.

To serve 1. Use 2 ounces (56 g) mushrooms, 1 tablespoon parsley, 2 shallots, ¼ teaspoon lemon juice, ¼ pound (113.5 g) veal, ¾ teaspoon salt, ¼ teaspoon paprika, pepper to taste and 3 ounces (85 g) carrot. Cook as in Step 3 for 2 minutes 45 seconds.

FOR 400- TO 500-WATT OVENS

To serve 2. Cook for 7 minutes 30 seconds, switching plates after 4 minutes.

To serve 1. Cook for 4 minutes.

VEAL WITH LETCHO

*H*ungarians love red bell peppers and paprika, which they make into a kind of sauce or side dish called letcho. They serve it with everything except dessert. They start pairing it with eggs in the morning and go on until late night. While I am perfectly happy eating it by the spoonful, I find this delicious with veal.
SERVES 8

Per serving: 253 calories; 81 milligrams cholesterol; 13 grams fat; 112 milligrams sodium; 23 grams protein (52% RDA)

RDA: phosphorus 26%; iron 24%; vitamin A 59%; thiamin 15%; riboflavin 18%; niacin 39%; vitamin C 161%

1 recipe Letcho (page 474)
2 pounds (900 g) lean stewing veal or
   veal shoulder, cut into 2-inch (5-cm)
   cubes

1. Place letcho in a 13 × 9 × 2-inch (33 × 23 × 2-cm) oval dish. Mound in the center of the dish. Arrange veal around the inside edge of the dish. Cover tightly with microwave plastic wrap. Cook at 100% for 10 minutes, or until veal is just pink, in a 650- to 700-watt oven. Prick plastic to release steam.

2. Remove from oven and uncover. Stir well to combine veal and letcho and serve.

VEAL STEW

*T*his is a perfectly normal stew that is given a kick of flavor by caraway seeds and lemon juice. It is terrific and terrifically good for you as well, with a wide distribution of vitamins and minerals. Those who are large or active or not on a weight-loss diet may want to increase their portion to one and a quarter cups (30 ml). If you don't increase the portion and this is a party dinner, serve Green Terrine (page 110) with Paprika-Lemon Béchamel (page 511) or Herb-Stuffed Mussels (page 97) as a first course, both of which can be made ahead. Add a green salad, or, in summer, a Chunky Tomato Basil Salad (page 407) and a little white wine. Wind up with a dessert and even some Oat Bran Crisps (page 574).

When making stew ahead, do not add lemon juice until it is time to reheat. The clear flavor of lemon tends to die with cooking and can discolor the vegetables. Serve with one-half cup (120 ml) cooked rice (112 calories for white, enriched long-grain rice; fewer calories for other types of rice), or one-half cup (120 ml) Basic Soft Polenta (page 215). A crisp white wine or a nice round red would go equally well. *SERVES 8*

Per generous ¾-cup (180-ml) serving: 273 calories; 81 milligrams cholesterol; 12 grams fat; 161 milligrams sodium; 25 grams protein (56% RDA); 15 grams carbohydrate

RDA: phosphorus 29%; iron 25%; vitamin A 184%; thiamin 19%; riboflavin 20%; niacin 43%; vitamin C 22%

3 large carrots (10 ounces; 284 g), peeled and cut into 2 × ¼ × ¼-inch (5 × .5 × .5-cm) matchsticks (about 3½ cups; 825 ml)

5 ounces (142 g) shallots, sliced (about 1 cup; 240 ml)

1⅔ cups (400 ml) Basic Meat Broth made with veal bones (page 462), or Basic Chicken Broth (page 460), or unsalted or regular canned chicken broth

2 pounds (900 g) lean stewing veal or veal shoulder, cut into 1- to 2-inch (2.5- to 5-cm) cubes

1½ teaspoons caraway seeds

3 tablespoons cornstarch

10 ounces (284 g) frozen peas, defrosted in a sieve under warm running water

4 ribs celery, trimmed, peeled and cut across the rib into ¼-inch (.5-cm) slices (about 1½ cups; 355 ml)

1½ tablespoons fresh lemon juice

Freshly ground black pepper, to taste

1. Combine carrots, shallots and ⅓ cup (80 ml) of the broth in a 2½-quart (2.5-l) soufflé dish or casserole with a tightly fitted lid. Cover tightly with microwave plastic wrap or lid. Cook at 100% for 3 minutes in a 650- to 700-watt oven. If using plastic wrap, prick to release steam.

2. Remove from oven and uncover. Add veal, remaining broth and caraway seeds. Cover tightly and cook for 5 minutes. Prick plastic and remove from oven.

3. Remove ½ cup (120 ml) cooking liquid and combine with cornstarch in a small bowl, stirring until completely smooth. Return liquid to stew along with peas and celery and mix well. Cover and cook for 7 minutes, stirring once. Prick plastic wrap.

4. Remove from oven and stir in lemon juice and pepper. Serve hot.

FOR 400- TO 500-WATT OVENS

To serve 6. Follow Step 1 and cook for 6 minutes 30 seconds. Stir together remaining broth with cornstarch and add with veal and caraway as in Step 2. Cook for 7 minutes 30 seconds. Continue with Step 3 and cook for 20 minutes, stirring once. Finish as in Step 4.

VEAL KIDNEYS

Kidneys—the most frequently used are veal and lamb—have a strong taste that is not to everybody's liking. As with other innards, they have recently acquired a bad reputation due to their high percentage of cholesterol. In any case, Americans have never been hearty consumers of innards. In the face of all this, I recommend cooking them and eating them. Served with an emphatic sauce such as Mustard Dressing (page 492), their strong taste blends into the total flavor and is delicious.

Nutritionally, there is a sound reason to eat kidneys: They contain lots of iron. Just do not eat them too often.

To be honest, I had never thought about cooking kidneys in a microwave oven. Correspondence with Roger Vergé, the three-star chef-owner of Moulin de Mougins in the south of France, who is a very prestigious and ardent exponent of microwave cooking, convinced me to try them following his guidelines. He actually wraps the kidneys in caul fat and cooks them whole. Caul fat is next to impossible to buy in the United States and adds substantial fat. If you can find the caul fat, you might want to try it.

I cut the kidneys in half lengthwise because—due to the high cholesterol—that seems the best way to get a reasonable portion. Also, it is much easier to clean them that way. I reassemble them before cooking to help them achieve rosy perfection. Overcooked kidneys are dry and leathery.

(continued)

Veal Kidneys (cont.)

Halve kidneys and clean with a kitchen scissors, removing all connective tissue but leaving kidneys intact. Place halves together and wrap in cheesecloth that has been soaked in 1 tablespoon of vegetable oil per whole kidney. Arrange in a 10-inch (25.5-cm) quiche dish and cook, uncovered, turning over once about half-way through cooking. Remove from oven and place on a rack set over a dish to catch the juices. Use the juices in your sauce, if you wish, or discard them. Each kidney weighs about ¾ pound (340 g) and makes two portions. USDA information on nutrition is not available.

One kidney
650- to 700-watt oven: 1 min. 45 sec., turn and cook 1 min. 30 sec.
400- to 500-watt oven: 3 min., turn and cook 1 min. 30 sec.

Two kidneys
650- to 700-watt oven: 3 min., turn and cook 2 min.
400- to 500-watt oven: 5 min., turn and cook 3 min.

RABBIT IN WILD MUSHROOM SAUCE

Rabbit is not an everyday food; but now that it is available frozen in super-markets, maybe it will be more popular. It is very lean. If you cannot abide the idea of rabbit or are afraid your guests will be squeamish, substitute skinless, boneless chicken breast halves. This is a meal for a big party and the quantity precludes its working in a low-wattage oven. If you are having nondieters, allow a double portion for them. Serve rice, noodles or steamed new potatoes (page 220).

Begin with a Vegetable Terrine (page 86) or Gravlax with Dill Buttermilk Sauce (page 90). Have a big salad after the main course with a wedge of cheese. That still leaves room for dessert and wine; but be careful to have only one portion, and limit yourself to a light lunch.   *SERVES 10*

Per serving: 240 calories; 83 milligrams cholesterol; 7 grams fat; 750 milligrams sodium; 30 grams protein (66% RDA); 14 grams carbohydrate

RDA: phosphorus 52%; iron 20%; 808 milligrams potassium; riboflavin 21%; niacin 94%

1 ounce (28 g) dried morel mushrooms
1 cup (240 ml) water
½ pound (227 g) domestic mushrooms, thinly sliced
2 teaspoons fresh lemon juice
2 fresh or frozen rabbits (each 1½–2 pounds; 680–900 g), trimmed of all visible fat

1 tablespoon minced shallot
3 tablespoons Basic Glaze (page 466), optional
3 tablespoons red wine
1 tablespoon Cognac
3 tablespoons minced fresh parsley

1 can (15 ounces; 425 g) straw
  mushrooms, drained (about 1 cup;
  240 ml)
2 ounces (56 g) dried shiitake
  mushrooms
1 ounce (28 g) dried cèpes mushrooms
⅓ cup (80 ml) dried tree ears (½
  ounce; 14 g)
2 cups (470 ml) Basic Chicken Broth
  (page 460), or unsalted or regular
  canned chicken broth

3½ tablespoons Dijon mustard
1 tablespoon kosher salt
1 teaspoon dried thyme
1 teaspoon dried summer savory
Freshly ground black pepper, to taste
5 cloves garlic, smashed and peeled
2 tablespoons cornstarch

1. Place morels in a 4-cup (1-l) glass measure with water and cover tightly with microwave plastic wrap. Cook at 100% for 3 minutes in a 650- to 700-watt oven. Prick plastic wrap to release steam.

2. Remove from oven. Let stand, covered, for 3 minutes. Uncover, remove mushrooms, rinse well and reserve. Strain liquid through a coffee filter into a clean measure and reserve.

3. Toss together domestic mushrooms and lemon juice in a 10-inch (25.5-cm) quiche dish. Cover tightly with microwave plastic wrap. Cook at 100% for 3 minutes. Prick plastic. Remove from oven, uncover and reserve.

4. Arrange rabbit in a single layer in a 14 × 11 × 2-inch (35.5 × 28 × 5-cm) dish. Combine reserved morels with liquid, domestic mushrooms and remaining ingredients except cornstarch. Pour over rabbit.

5. Cover tightly with microwave plastic wrap. Cook at 100% for 7 minutes. If you are using frozen rabbit, cook at 30% for 10 minutes, turning pieces once halfway through cooking. Turn pieces again and cook at 100% for 7 minutes. Prick plastic wrap.

6. Working quickly, remove dish from oven and uncover. Turn pieces over and move pieces from the outside into the center and those from the center to the outside. Re-cover and cook for 10 minutes more. If you are using frozen rabbit, cook for only 7 minutes more. Prick plastic wrap.

7. Remove from oven. Uncover and remove rabbit to a serving platter (some of the pieces may be underdone at this point). Remove ¼ cup (60 ml) of liquid and stir in cornstarch to make a smooth slurry. Stir back into liquid. Cook, uncovered, for 5 minutes.

8. Remove from oven. Place rabbit back into sauce to reheat, making sure any underdone pieces are around the inside edge of the dish, with the underdone side facing up. Cover tightly with microwave plastic wrap. Cook for 5 minutes. Prick plastic.

9. Remove from oven. Uncover and serve hot.

SALADS AND VEGETABLES, SMALL AND LARGE

I love growing vegetables and making still lives of them in baskets and bowls around my kitchen: piles of red, orange and yellow tomatoes—round, oval and miniature—in a blue and white spongeware bowl; glossy purple, lavender and white eggplants in wicker; the finger-size dark green zucchini that I find hiding under their large leaves, in a dark brown splotched Bennington cream separator; peppers of every degree of heat, from tiny red zingers and dark green jalapeños in custard cups to pointy red and yellow gypsy peppers in wooden bowls and large, smooth bell peppers, yellow and red, in wide-open trugs; bunches of tiny carrots with their tender, frondy leaves; and pitchers of every size and material stuffed with bunches of herbs, their feet in water. Later, there will be braids of onions, large baskets of acorn squash, firm heads of cabbage and prematurely dug tiny potatoes for simple steaming to sweet perfection.

Corn, string beans and peas aren't allowed to stay out of the garden long enough to make pictures. They are picked minutes before cooking.

From spring, with its first shoots of herbs coming back, bright red radishes peeking out of the ground and the early outside leaves plucked from lettuce to make tender salads, through late fall, with its fat leeks, fragrant parsnips and rounded pods of beans for shucking, vegetables make up a major part of my life and diet, particularly now that I have mastered my microwave oven. Sometimes the vegetables are washed and raw, other times they are cooked but still slightly crisp and sprinkled with diet dressing or a handful of chopped herbs; often they are combined for slightly longer cooking to develop into aromatic stews. Salads with leaves and vegetables, cooked and raw, change with every meal.

I don't have to give up on vegetables in winter, although I may back off a little. Winter vegetables used to take a long time to cook—no longer. In addition, good vegetables and salads come to us out of season from around the world. Watch out for those unseasonal tomatoes, though. They are of limited quality. I use them only when I cook them long enough so that a lot of their water evaporates and their flavor develops. Otherwise, I use canned tomatoes or tomatoes I had the forethought to prepare and freeze ahead.

I am not a vegetarian or a vegan, although I have friends who are and whom I entertain. For them, I combine a variety of vegetable dishes with grains and starches to make ample, colorful meals.

At other meals, vegetables and salads can be first courses, go-along-withs and followers of main courses. They fill us up at the same time that they give us vitamins, minerals and fiber. Very few of these recipes are for dishes containing cholesterol. Sometimes there will be a small amount of fat. It usually comes from the fruit or vegetable itself or is the monounsaturated kind and comes from olive oil.

Those of us who are concerned about pesticide and artificial fertilizer residues in our food will do well to grow our own, look for local growers whose agricultural habits we trust, or pay slightly more for organically grown fruits, salads and vegetables. Not only are they safer; they often taste better. They can look just as beautiful as nonorganic products; it's a question of care in the kind of seed planted and the growing.

Salads

I am a salad addict. Aside from breakfast (and it has been known to happen even then), I eat salads along with most meals, instead of meals and even as snacks. This means that I have had to develop a substantial group of dressings that will not turn my healthful salads into fatty nightmares. You will find them in Basics, Sauces and Snacks (pages 458–529). You can substitute commercially prepared diet dressings; but they tend to be higher in sodium and, sometimes, cholesterol.

It is often easy to multiply salad recipes to get more servings. Just multiply the ingredients and the amount of salad dressing by the number of people you want to serve.

Almost anything—except chocolate bars—can go into a salad: leftover fish, shellfish, chicken, meats and cheeses. Some salads with these in them—salads that make a meal—come at the end of this section. Salads for sandwiches—like tuna salad—are on pages 70–72. There are many starches that are good in salads: cooked pasta, grains, rice, potatoes and bread. You will find the predominantly carbohydrate salads in Good Grains and Other Starches (pages 148–225), or by looking in the Index for specifics—potato salad, for example. Starches will turn up in some of the more ample salads toward the end of this section. Lest we forget, cooked vegetables, raw fruits and nuts, in moderation, can all go in. If you want to know what you are adding by way of nutrition and calories, look up the ingredient in the Index.

Many of the salads require no cooking, although their dressings may. The actual recipes are given mainly as guidelines and ideas. I need lots since I eat salad so often. Almost any meal is improved—nutritionally as well as in pleasure—by a salad. They certainly help fill you up.

All the salads in this chapter include the calories that come from the dressings in Basics, Sauces and Snacks. If you don't have the dressing I suggest or like on hand, substitute another one or use a bottled diet dressing; but compare calories and sodium when you make the change to know what you are getting.

I do have friends and even one relative who are happy using some pepper and vinegar—a mild one such as rice wine vinegar or balsamic vinegar—or lemon juice on their salads and calling it a day. I'm greedier than that; but the dressings I have worked out are more full of flavor than of fat and calories.

The base of almost all salads—the little ones that start or go with a meal and the big ones that are a meal—are the salad greens and vegetables.

NUTRITIONAL DATA FOR COMMON SALAD INGREDIENTS

For a typical serving allow one cup (240 ml) of any leafy green or any raw or blanched vegetables, or a combination that pleases you and adds up to one cup (240 ml). Top with one tablespoon diet salad dressing, up to 85 calories. Some of my dressings are very low in calories, as you will see from the list below. You can increase the quantity you use of those, or just enjoy saving the calories. Obviously, these are only guidelines. Even if you had two cups of lettuce and two tablespoons of Spicy Buttermilk Dressing, you would still be under 45 calories for the whole thing.

Add up the calories from your ingredients and your dressing and there you are.

A few more examples: Using one cup (240 ml) of lettuce, one-half cup of sliced cucumbers, one tablespoon of chopped scallions and a tablespoon and a half of Skinny Tomato Dressing costs only 51 calories; one cup of chopped endive plus one-half cup of sliced raw mushrooms with one and a half tablespoons of Garlic Oregano Dressing is 95 calories; and a half-cup of chopped bell peppers, a half-cup of chopped broccoli, a half-cup of lettuce, a tablespoon of chopped red onion and one and a half tablespoons of Orange-Yogurt Dressing is just 49 calories (changing the dressing to Paprika Dressing ups the calories to 131 calories—still not bad for a cup and a half of salad). You get the idea.

Data are provided below for raw greens and vegetables commonly found in salad bars. Substituting other ingredients will give you slightly different values. If you use canned vegetables rather than fresh, the sodium component will increase mightily.

There may be days when you want to include frozen vegetables. See how to defrost them on page 420.

If you want to add potatoes, rice, pasta or other grains, see the nutritional information in Good Grains and Other Starches (pages 148–225). Once again, canned beans and chick-peas will add lots of sodium.

TYPE	CAL.	CARB. (g)	CALC. (% RDA)	IRON (% RDA)	SOD. (mg)	POT. (mg)	VIT. C (% RDA)	VIT. A (% RDA)

LEAFY GREENS Per 1 cup (240 ml), unless otherwise noted

TYPE	CAL.	CARB.	CALC.	IRON	SOD.	POT.	VIT. C	VIT. A
CABBAGE, shredded								
Cabbage, green (2½ oz.; 70 g)	16	4	0.3	2.2	12	172	56	2
Red cabbage (5¼ oz.; 150 g)	32	6	0.8	4.1	17	309	143	1
Savoy cabbage (2½ oz.; 70 g)	20	4	0.2	1.6	20	162	37	14
Garden cress (1¾ oz.; 50 g)	16	6	0.4	3.7	8	304	58	93
Endive, chopped (1¾ oz.; 50 g)	8	<1	0.3	2.3	12	158	8	0
LETTUCE								
Butterhead (8 leaves) (2 oz.; 60 g)	8	1	N/A	0.9	4	156	8	12
Romaine (2 oz.; 56 g)	8	<1	0.1	1.2	2	58	22	29
Iceberg (4 leaves) (2¾ oz.; 80 g)	12	<1	0.2	2.2	8	128	23	30
Loose-leaf (2 oz.; 56 g)	10	<1	0.4	4.3	6	148	17	21
SPINACH (2 oz.; 56 g)	12	<1	0.6	8.4	44	312	26	75

VEGETABLES Per 1 cup (240 ml) raw portion, unless otherwise noted

TYPE	CAL.	CARB.	CALC.	IRON	SOD.	POT.	VIT. C	VIT. A
BEAN SPROUTS								
Kidney	54	8	0.4	8.3	N/A	344	237	N/A
Mung	32	6	0.1	5.2	6	154	23	N/A
Navy	70	14	0.2	11.1	N/A	318	33	N/A
Bell peppers chopped (3½ oz.; 100 g)	24	6	0.1	7	4	196	213	11
Broccoli, chopped (3 oz.; 88 g)	24	4	0.4	4.3	24	286	132	26
Carrots, shredded (4 oz.; 110 g)	48	12	0.3	3	38	348	17	619
Cauliflower, pieces (3½ oz.; 100 g)	24	4	0.3	3.2	14	356	119	N/A
Celery, diced (4¼ oz.; 120 g)	18	4	0.4	3.2	106	340	13	3
Cucumber, sliced (3½ oz.; 104 g)	14	4	0.1	1.6	2	156	8	1
Mushrooms, white (2½ oz.; 70 g)	18	4	N/A	4.8	2	260	4	N/A
Tomatoes: American, chopped (6⅓ oz.; 180 g)	36	8	0.1	4.8	16	372	53	41
Zucchini, sliced (4½ oz.; 130 g)	18	4	0.2	3.1	4	132	20	9

SALAD ADDITIONS

There will be times when you want to sprinkle your salad with a bit of this or that. Watch out for commercially prepared products like imitation bacon bits. One teaspoon has more than two hundred milligrams of sodium, as does half an ounce (14 g) of commercially prepared croutons. See page 480 for Croutons.

TYPE	CAL.	CARB. (g)	CALC. (% RDA)	IRON (% RDA)	SOD. (mg)	POT. (mg)	VIT. C (% RDA)	VIT. A (% RDA)
Onions, chopped:								
white (1 tbsp.)	3	<1	N/A	0.2	0	16	1	N/A
spring (1 tbsp.)	2	<1	N/A	0.6	9	15	5	6
Radishes, sliced (¼ cup; 60 ml)								
(1 oz.; 28 g)	5	1	0.1	0.5	7	67	11	N/A

CALORIE COUNTS FOR DIET SALAD DRESSINGS FROM THIS BOOK

The calorie counts listed below are for one tablespoon of each dressing.

DRESSING	CAL.	PAGE
Aïoli	83	483
Avocado Dressing	14	493
Balsamic Dressing	31	486
Buttermilk Dressing	33	491
Creamy Italian Dressing	31	490
Curry Mayonnaise	62	485
Diet Pesto	26	476
Egg White Mayonnaise	82	482
Garlic Oregano Dressing	63	489
Green Salsa Dressing	22	497
Mint Yogurt Dressing	10	494
Mustard Dressing	9	492
Orange-Cumin Vinaigrette	28	487
Orange-Yogurt Dressing	9	494
Paprika Dressing	64	498
Pernod Dressing	57	487
Rouïlle	85	484
Saté Dressing	37	499
Sesame Dressing	69	488
Skinny Tomato Dressing	34	496
Spicy Buttermilk Dressing	10	495

BIBB AND TARRAGON SALAD

*T*his is one of my favorite salad combinations, based on a once-much-loved dish at Trader Vic's. I make it in summer, when the small Bibb lettuce and tarragon are in ample and not poisonously expensive supply. You can use one-third the quantity of dry tarragon if there is no alternative; but I really am not wild for it.

Growing your own helps. I think everyone, no matter how small their garden, should have a couple of tarragon plants. They can be grown in greenhouses and sunny windows as well; but they need frequent watering. I put mine in the middle of a flower bed near the kitchen door. That way I know they will get all the water they like and be readily available. I have a friend who had a pool when his children were young and grew his tarragon around it. The plants loved all the splashing. If you are going to plant tarragon, start with plants not seeds—hard to start. Make sure they are French tarragon. Russian tarragon has virtually no scent or flavor. If in doubt, rub a leaf between your fingers. The fragrance should be strong.

Since tarragon likes to be root-divided in the spring every other year, you will soon have enough plants for gifts.   *SERVES 1*

Per serving: 81 calories; 0 milligrams cholesterol; 8 grams fat; 39 milligrams sodium; 1 gram protein (2% RDA); 3 grams carbohydrate

RDA: calcium 5%; iron 5%; vitamin A 22%; vitamin C 18%

1 head Bibb lettuce (2 ounces; 56 g), or equal amount of Boston lettuce (about 1 cup; 240 ml), cored and leaves washed

1 teaspoon chopped fresh tarragon
1 tablespoon Sesame Dressing (page 488)
Pinch sesame seeds, optional

1. Combine all ingredients in a bowl and serve.

To serve 10. Use 10 heads Bibb lettuce (20 ounces; 566 g), 3 tablespoons tarragon and 1 recipe Sesame Dressing. Prepare as in Step 1.

COLESLAW

Coleslaw is the constant friend of barbecues and clambakes, barn raisings and church suppers. It goes well with sandwiches. Consider putting a tablespoon or two of leftover coleslaw on your sandwich to moisten it instead of a caloric spread; it will have more tang and texture. I regularly do this with meat and chicken sandwiches. Add a little mustard and I'm all set. Surprisingly, at least to me, coleslaw is also rich in vitamins. Although this first version is for two so you won't have leftovers if you don't want them, consider making a larger batch. It keeps well.   *SERVES 2*

Per generous ½-cup (120-ml) serving: 110 calories; 0 milligrams cholesterol; 9 grams fat; 46 milligrams sodium; 1 gram protein (3% RDA); 6 grams carbohydrate

RDA: calcium 4%; 232 milligrams potassium; vitamin A 104%; vitamin C 51%

1 cup (240 ml) thinly sliced cabbage
    (about 5 ounces; 140 g)
⅓ cup (80 ml) shredded carrot (about
    1 ounce; 28 g)
⅓ cup (80 ml) thinly sliced red onion
    (about 1 ounce; 28 g)

2 tablespoons Egg White Mayonnaise
    (page 482)
1 teaspoon celery seeds, optional

1. Place all ingredients in a small bowl and toss to coat. Allow to sit for at least 30 minutes. Serve at room temperature.

To serve 12. Use 6 cups (1.5 l) cabbage, 2 cups (470 ml) carrots, 1½ cups (355 ml) red onion, 1 recipe Egg White Mayonnaise and ¼ cup celery seeds, if desired. Stir together in a large bowl and let stand overnight in the refrigerator.

To serve 6. Use 3 cups (705 ml) cabbage, 1 cup (240 ml) carrots, ¾ cup (180 ml) onion, ¾ cup (180 ml) Egg White Mayonnaise and 2 tablespoons celery seeds, if desired. Prepare as in Step 1.

The Swiss love grated salads and often serve an assortment as a light meal at lunch accompanied by bread and cheese. If you want to do that, use a quarter-cup of each salad and arrange them in a circle on your plate. I like the look of this on a huge platter for a buffet.

You can grate your vegetables on an old four-sided grater. I often do when I'm not making a large salad, but a food processor with a grating disc makes things easier, especially in quantities for a crowd. Peel your vegetables when necessary; trim off any ugly or tough pieces and cut the pieces of vegetable so that they will just fit, on their sides, in the feed tube. Push down with the plunger on the food in the feed tube. Turn the machine on and grate away. Stop the machine between batches. When you turn the grated vegetables out into a bowl to mix them with the dressing, remove any large chunks that have slipped through.

GRATED CARROT SALAD

*I*t takes very little to make a carrot glamorous; but it's easier with younger, smaller carrots. There is a temptation to use large carrots—less peeling and easier grating—but they tend to have large cores that can be tough and bitter. There is a fancier and more caloric Cooked Carrot Salad with Raisins and Walnuts (page 000); but this simple salad is the one I use more often for salad assortments. Like all carrot dishes, it is stuffed with vitamin A.

You can make any quantity by allowing for each serving a half-cup (120 ml) of shredded carrots from one and a half ounces (42.5 g) whole peeled carrots and two teaspoons of the dressing.   *SERVES 10*

Per ½-cup (120-ml) serving: 59 calories; 0 milligrams cholesterol; 5 grams fat; 34 milligrams sodium; .5 grams protein (1% RDA); 4 grams carbohydrate

RDA: vitamin A 227%; vitamin C 7%

1 pound (450 g) carrots, peeled, trimmed and grated (about 5 cups; 1.2 l)

6 tablespoons Sesame Dressing (page 488)

1. In a large bowl mix together the carrots with the dressing. Let stand for 10 minutes.

GRATED ZUCCHINI SALAD

Grate your zucchini with the skins on for more color, crunch and vitamins. Small zucchini will have fewer formed seeds and a less pulpy inside. If you are stuck with giants, cut the zucchini into quarters and run a knife down the length of the strip to remove the pulp and seeds. Reweigh the zucchini and proceed.

You can make any quantity by allowing a half-cup (120 ml) of shredded zucchini from one and a half ounces (42.5 g) whole zucchini and one and a half teaspoons of the dressing.   *SERVES 10*

Per ½-cup (120-ml) serving: 38 calories; 0 milligrams cholesterol; 3 grams fat; 69 milligrams sodium; .5 grams protein (1% RDA); 2 grams carbohydrate

RDA: vitamin C 10%

1 pound (450 g) zucchini, trimmed and grated (about 5 cups; 1.2 l)

5 tablespoons Garlic Oregano Dressing (page 489)

1. In a large bowl mix together the zucchini with the dressing. Let stand for 10 minutes.

GRATED RED CABBAGE SALAD

It's amazing how the balsamic vinegar brightens the color and flavor of the cabbage to make a simple and exceptional salad with a very good vitamin C.

You can make any quantity by allowing for each serving a half-cup (120 ml) of grated cabbage from one and a half ounces (42.5 g) cored cabbage and one and a half teaspoons of the dressing.   *SERVES 10*

Per ½-cup (120-ml) serving: 25 calories; 0 milligrams cholesterol; 2 grams fat; 4 milligrams sodium; .5 grams protein (1% RDA); 2 grams carbohydrate

RDA: vitamin C 35%

1 pound (450 g) red cabbage, trimmed, cored and grated (about 5 cups; 1.2 l)

5 tablespoons Balsamic Dressing (page 486)

1. In a large bowl mix together the red cabbage with the dressing. Allow to stand 10 minutes.

GRATED TURNIP SALAD

Here, even more than in the other shredded salads, it is important to use young vegetables. Old, large turnips can have an unpleasantly sharp taste. Young ones will be mild and slightly sweet.

You can make any quantity by allowing for each serving a half-cup (120 ml) of shredded turnip from one and a half ounces (42.5 g) whole peeled turnip and two teaspoons of the dressing.   *SERVES 10*

Per ½-cup (120-ml) serving: 49 calories; 0 milligrams cholesterol; 4 grams fat; 52 milligrams sodium; 3 grams carbohydrate

RDA: vitamin C 14%

1 pound (450 g) turnips, peeled and
   grated (about 5 cups; 1.2 l)

6 tablespoons Paprika Dressing (page
   498)

1. In a large bowl mix together the turnips with the dressing. Allow to stand for 10 minutes.

*A four-sided grater is useful for larger pieces
of food or in place of a rotary grater.*

GRATED YELLOW SQUASH SALAD

*T*he flavor of yellow summer squash in salads is sadly underestimated. Treat very large yellow squash as you do large zucchini (page 428). Also, leave the attractive yellow skins on. If there are some brown spots—it often happens—just pry them out with the tip of a knife before grating.

You can make any quantity by allowing for each serving a half-cup (120 ml) of shredded squash from one and a half ounces (42.5 g) whole squash and two teaspoons of the dressing.   *SERVES 10*

Per ½-cup (120-ml) serving: 15 calories; 0 milligrams cholesterol; 0 grams fat; 6 milligrams sodium; .7 grams protein (1.5% RDA); 3 grams carbohydrate

RDA: vitamin A 10%; vitamin C 16%

1 pound (450 g) yellow squash, trimmed and grated (about 5 cups; 1.2 l)

6 tablespoons Spicy Buttermilk Dressing (page 495)

1. In a large bowl mix together the yellow squash with the dressing. Allow to stand for 10 minutes.

COOKED CARROT SALAD WITH RAISINS AND WALNUTS

*U*nlike the simpler Grated Carrot Salad (page 395), which is raw, this cooked salad doesn't multiply or divide easily. Like the simpler salad, it's loaded with vitamin A. It's good with simply broiled or grilled chicken and Curried Pilaf (page 186). If you have a portion left over, mix it with a half-cup of the leftover pilaf for a light lunch with some nonfat yogurt or low-fat cottage cheese and a small pita. *SERVES 5*

Per ½-cup (120-ml) serving: 90 calories; 0 milligrams cholesterol; 5 grams fat; 16 milligrams sodium; 1.5 grams protein (3% RDA); 11 grams carbohydrate

RDA: vitamin A 227%; 218 milligrams potassium; thiamin 5%; vitamin C 7%

8 ounces (227 g) carrots, trimmed, peeled and shredded (about 2½ cups; 590 ml)
¼ cup (60 ml) raisins
¼ cup (60 ml) coarsely chopped walnuts

2 tablespoons Balsamic Dressing (page 486)
Freshly ground black pepper, to taste

1. Place carrots in a 1½-quart (1.5-l) soufflé dish. Cover with microwave plastic wrap. Cook at 100% for 1 minute 30 seconds in a 650- to 700-watt oven. Prick plastic to release steam.
2. Remove from oven and uncover. Stir in raisins and let stand until cool.
3. Add walnuts, dressing and pepper and mix well to coat.

FOR 400- TO 500-WATT OVENS

To serve 5. Cook for 2 minutes 30 seconds.

FENNEL SALAD

*T*his crisp salad makes a good opener for a meal with pasta as a main course, or use it to follow a tomato-based fish or chicken dish. I also like it on a buffet—it's pretty and doesn't wilt. The recipe can easily be multiplied.   *SERVES 3*

Per 1-cup (240-ml) serving: 81 calories; 0 milligrams cholesterol; 5 grams fat; 122 milligrams sodium; 2 grams protein (4% RDA); 8 grams carbohydrate

RDA: calcium 7%; phosphorus 7%; iron 7%; 542 milligrams potassium; thiamin 5%; vitamin C 49%

1 fennel bulb (about 1 pound, 450 g), peeled, halved, cored and cut across into ⅛-inch (.3-cm) thick slices (about 3 cups; 705 ml)
2 tablespoons fresh lemon juice
3 ounces (85 g) red onion, peeled and cut across into ⅛-inch (.3-cm) thick slices (about 1 cup; 240 ml)

¼ cup (60 ml) fresh orange juice
4 teaspoons chopped fennel tops
1 tablespoon olive oil
Kosher salt, to taste
Freshly ground black pepper, to taste

1. In a large bowl toss the fennel with the lemon juice. Add the remaining ingredients and mix well to combine.

A whole bulb of fennel

SPINACH, MUSHROOM AND CELERY SALAD

This is a healthy, filling everyday salad. Have it at lunch as a main course with a carbohydrate-rich soup like Hearty Chick-Pea Soup (page 135) or Black Bean Soup (page 204), and add a piece of fruit. At dinner, serve this as a first course before broiled or grilled meat. The salad provides your vitamins. Have some potatoes or bread with the meat and enjoy a dessert. Unfortunately, this salad is not low in sodium, in part due to the celery; but I think it's well worth it for the ample nutrition.

Frozen spinach will not do. The salad needs to be crisp. See page 79 for cleaning spinach. Serve immediately after tossing, or the spinach will wilt. The ingredients can be prepared several hours ahead and the mushrooms mixed with the dressing up to an hour ahead. Finish just before serving. Multiply as often as you like; but make extra dressing.   *SERVES 4*

Per 1½-cup (355-ml) serving: 58 calories; 1 milligram cholesterol; 1 gram fat; 506 milligrams sodium; 4 grams protein (8% RDA); 9 grams carbohydrate

RDA: calcium 11%; phosphorus 11%; iron 13%; 596 milligrams potassium; vitamin A 77%; thiamin 6%; riboflavin 19%; niacin 12%; vitamin C 35%

6 ounces (170 g) mushrooms, cleaned and cut into ¼-inch (.5-cm) slices (about 2 cups; 470 ml)
⅔ cup (160 ml) Mustard Dressing (page 492)
4 cups (1 l) stemmed, washed and torn into pieces spinach leaves (about ¾ pound with stems; 340 g)

6 ribs celery (¾ pound; 340 g), trimmed, peeled and cut into ⅛-inch (.5-cm) slices (about 1½ cups; 355 ml)

1. Place mushrooms and dressing in a large bowl. Stir to coat mushrooms with the dressing and let stand while preparing rest of salad.
2. Stir in spinach and celery and toss well to coat. Serve immediately.

ORANGE AND RED ONION SALAD

At first this may seem like an odd salad; but it is very pretty and refreshing after a complex main course like one of the Moroccan-inspired fish dishes (pages 260–262) or Green Shrimp Curry (page 282). It makes an attractive first course, even before a substantial salad. On a buffet, a large round platter filled with concentric rings of the overlapping slices of a large amount of this salad is very dramatic. You can top it with a few small Nice olives, or a sprinkling of chopped fresh parsley or coriander for even more beauty. Don't gobble up all the olives.

This salad should be made with the thinnest-skinned juice oranges. If they are beautifully, uniformly orange, get suspicious. Ask if the skins have been dyed. If they have, remove the peel even though it's more work and less attractive. You can have this vitamin C–rich salad at lunch or dinner instead of the morning juice. *SERVES 2*

Per serving: 69 calories; 0 milligrams cholesterol; 3 grams fat; 46 milligrams sodium; 1 gram protein (2% RDA); 12 grams carbohydrate

RDA: calcium 5%; iron 4%; 191 milligrams potassium; thiamin 5%; vitamin C 67%

1 juice orange (8 ounces; 227 g), thinly sliced and seeded with skin left on
1 ounce (28 g) red onion, peeled and thinly sliced into rings (⅓ cup; 80 ml)

2 tablespoons Orange-Cumin Vinaigrette (page 487)

1. Arrange orange and onion slices overlapping on two salad plates or on a serving plate. Dribble dressing evenly over the slices. Refrigerate until well chilled.

To serve 8. Use 4 oranges (each 8 ounces; 227 g), 4 ounces (113.5 g) onion and ½ cup (120 ml) Orange-Cumin Vinaigrette. Prepare as in Step 1 on individual plates or in a large salad bowl.

CUCUMBER SALAD

This is not the traditional cucumber salad that is served with cold salmon, although you can use it that way. It is pleasantly minty and aromatic, like an Indian raita. It goes very well as a side dish with curry. *SERVES 4*

Per ½-cup (120-ml) serving: 37 calories; 1 milligram cholesterol; 0 grams fat; 310 milligrams sodium; 3 grams protein (7% RDA); 6 grams carbohydrate

RDA: calcium 10%; phosphorus 8%; iron 2%; 231 milligrams potassium; vitamin A 1%; thiamin 3%; riboflavin 6%; niacin 1%; vitamin C 17%

2 medium cucumbers (each 6 ounces; 170 g), peeled, seeded and shredded (about 2 cups; 470 ml)
2 cloves garlic, smashed, peeled and thinly sliced
2 tablespoons water
¾ cups (180 ml) nonfat yogurt
2 tablespoons chopped fresh mint
1½ teaspoons fresh lemon juice
½ teaspoon kosher salt
Freshly ground black pepper, to taste

1. Place shredded cucumber in a strainer set over a bowl. Let drain for at least 10 minutes.

2. Place garlic and water in a 1-cup (240-ml) glass measure. Cover tightly with microwave plastic wrap. Cook at 100% for 2 minutes in a 650- to 700-watt oven. Prick plastic to release steam.

3. Remove from oven, uncover and transfer to a medium bowl. Add remaining ingredients and mix well. Stir in drained cucumber and toss to coat.

FOR 400- TO 500-WATT OVENS

To serve 4. Cook for 3 minutes.

*Cut cucumber in half lengthwise
and scoop out seeds with a spoon.
Slice across into new moons.*

BEET AND ENDIVE SALAD

*T*his classic French salad is often used as a first course with a hint of sweetness and lots of color from the beets. It provides a little sweetness at the beginning of the meal, which may help to reduce appetite. Premicrowave, I would never have bothered with this salad since I don't like canned beets and they tend to have lots of sodium. In Europe, it's easy to buy baked beets, which can be substituted. Cooking beets the nonmicrowave way takes a long time. They are quicker and better in a microwave oven. Either wear rubber gloves when peeling the beets or scrub your hands with lemon juice afterward. Otherwise, you will look like Lady Macbeth.   *SERVES 4*

Per plated serving: 110 calories; 0 milligrams cholesterol; 7 grams fat; 71 milligrams sodium; 2 grams protein (4% RDA); 11 grams carbohydrate

RDA: phosphorus 6%; iron 6%; 403 milligrams potassium; thiamin 5%; riboflavin 5%; vitamin C 26%

4 medium beets (each about 4 ounces; 113.5 g), scrubbed and stems trimmed to ½ inch (1 cm)
2 tablespoons red wine vinegar

2 tablespoons water
2 tablespoons vegetable oil
Kosher salt, to taste
Freshly ground black pepper, to taste
4 heads endive (each 3½ ounces; 99 g)

1. Place beets in a shallow 11 × 7 × 2-inch (28 × 19 × 5-cm) dish. Cover tightly with microwave plastic wrap. Cook at 100% for 8 minutes in a 650- to 700-watt oven. Prick plastic to release steam.

2. Remove from oven and uncover. Let stand until cool enough to handle. Peel beets, slice into ⅓-inch (.75-cm) rounds and return to cooking dish.

3. Add vinegar, water, oil and salt and pepper to taste. Toss to coat well.

4. Cut each endive lengthwise into quarters and remove core. Cut each quarter in half again lengthwise.

5. Mix endive together with beets and dressing and divide among 4 salad plates.

FOR 400- TO 500-WATT OVENS

To serve 4. Cook beets for 12 minutes.

WATERCRESS, FENNEL AND ROMAINE SALAD
WITH PERNOD DRESSING

This is a terrific side salad or a salad to follow a rich meaty stew. It's another good one to multiply for a party since the resilient greens let it wait. *SERVES 5*

Per 1-cup (240-ml) serving of greens with 1 tablespoon dressing: 67 calories; 0 milligrams cholesterol; 6 grams fat; 191 milligrams sodium; 1 gram protein (3% RDA); 4 grams carbohydrate

RDA: calcium 5%; iron 4%; 281 milligrams potassium; vitamin A 32%; vitamin C 42%

FOR THE SALAD

1½ bunches watercress, stemmed
    (about 3 cups; 705 ml sprigs)
½ large head romaine lettuce, torn into
    small pieces (about 2 cups; 470 ml)
1 small head fennel, tops removed and
    thinly sliced across the bulb (about
    1½ cups; 355 ml)

FOR THE DRESSING

¼ cup (60 ml) fresh orange juice
¼ cup (60 ml) olive oil
1 tablespoon fresh lemon juice
1 teaspoon kosher salt
1¼ tablespoons Pernod
Freshly ground black pepper, to taste

1. Wash greens well and dry. Refrigerate in a large plastic bag if preparing ahead.

2. Whisk together dressing ingredients. Just before serving, place greens in a large salad bowl. Toss well to combine.

WALDORF SALAD

*I*n the 1930s and '40s in America, a very rich version of this salad, in imitation of that created at the famous New York hotel, turned up frequently at fancy dinners. I always thought it was rather gooey. Stripped of cholesterol and some of its fat, it's lighter and better, but still too rich for everyday as a side dish. Consider it for lunch with some low-fat cottage cheese and bread, as a first course on a bed of lettuce, or as a main course with fish cooked in the microwave or simply broiled.   *SERVES 4*

Per generous ½-cup (120-ml) serving: 158 calories; 0 milligrams cholesterol; 14 grams fat; 57 milligrams sodium; 1 gram protein (3% RDA); 9 grams carbohydrate

RDA: vitamin C 9%

4 ribs celery, peeled and cut into ¼-inch (.5-cm) dice (about 1 cup; 240 ml)

1 tart red apple (about 6 ounces; 170 g), cut into ¼-inch (.5-cm) dice (about 1 cup; 240 ml), tossed in

1 teaspoon fresh lemon juice

¼ cup (60 ml) coarsely chopped walnuts

¼ cup (60 ml) Egg White Mayonnaise (page 482)

1. Combine all ingredients in a medium bowl and toss until well combined.

CHUNKY TOMATO BASIL SALAD

This is one of my favorite salads in August, when tomatoes are ripe and basil is plentiful. If you are going to make the salad, use this as an opportunity to make large quantities of Diet Pesto to freeze for colder times.

Don't be surprised to find that this salad is full of juice. Dunk your bread in it, scoop it up with a spoon as I do, or use it as a cold sauce for a hot cup of cooked pasta as a main course light enough for lunch, followed by a piece of fruit. I like linguine with this sauce. A half-portion is also good mixed with a cooked half-breast of chicken cut in strips and served on top of lettuce as a main course. The same can be done with four ounces (113.5 g) of cooked fish or shrimp.

Multiply this vitamin-rich salad as many times as you want. If making a large quantity, allow to sit for fifteen minutes before serving. If you have leftovers, refrigerate them and purée them to add to a sauce.   *SERVES 4*

Per 1-cup (240-ml) serving: 46 calories; 0 milligrams cholesterol; 2 grams fat; 250 milligrams sodium; 2 grams protein (4% RDA); 8 grams carbohydrate

RDA: calcium 7%; iron 10%; 352 milligrams potassium; vitamin A 31%; vitamin C 39%

3 large ripe tomatoes (each 12 ounces; 340 g), cored

1 small red onion (4 ounces; 113.5 g), peeled and thinly sliced (about 1⅓ cups; 320 ml)

3 tablespoons Diet Pesto Sauce (page 476)

½ teaspoon kosher salt

Pinch freshly ground black pepper

Extra basil leaves, for topping, optional

1. Cut the tomatoes into 8 wedges each and cut each wedge in half crosswise. Toss all ingredients together to coat tomatoes with the pesto. Serve at room temperature, topped with additional basil leaves, if desired.

SHREDDED NAPA SALAD

Make this in winter when the selection of other greens is limited. It has a lightly Oriental flavor and is very pretty. Again, it's as good a first course as it is a side dish. It goes very well with fish dishes.   *SERVES 8*

Per ½-cup (120-ml) serving: 64 calories; 0 milligrams cholesterol; 5 grams fat; 30 milligrams sodium; 1 gram protein (2% RDA); 5 grams carbohydrate

RDA: vitamin A 12%; vitamin C 19%

1 ounce (28 g) dried shiitake
    mushrooms
⅓ cup (80 ml) rice wine vinegar
⅛ teaspoon hot red pepper sauce
½ cup (120 ml) water
Freshly ground black pepper, to taste
8 ounces (227 g) Napa cabbage,
    shredded (about 4 cups; 1 l)

3 scallions, green and white parts sliced
    (about ⅓ cup; 80 ml)
⅓ cup Sesame Dressing (page 488)
1 ounce (28 g) radish, washed, trimmed
    and cut into ⅛-inch (.3-cm) slices
    (about ¼ cup; 60 ml)

1. Combine mushrooms, vinegar, hot pepper sauce, water and black pepper in a 2½-quart (2.5-l) soufflé dish or casserole with a tightly fitted lid. Cover tightly with microwave plastic wrap or lid. Cook at 100% for 5 minutes in a 650- to 700-watt oven. If using plastic wrap, prick to release steam.

2. Remove from oven and uncover. Allow to stand until cool enough to handle. Using scissors, remove mushroom stems and discard. Cut mushroom into ½-inch (1-cm) strips.

3. In a large serving bowl, combine mushrooms with cabbage, scallions and dressing. Toss to coat and scatter radish slices over.

FOR 400- TO 500-WATT OVENS

To serve 8. Cook for 8 minutes.

GREEN PAPAYA SALAD

You may be surprised by the idea of fruit in a light, acidic salad. It and the following salad come from the Caribbean. Put it on the plate as a vitamin-rich accompaniment to broiled or grilled fish. Like all salads, it is easily multiplied. Don't use ripe papayas; they will be hard to grate, get mushy and have insufficient acidity.   *SERVES 4*

Per ½-cup (120-ml) serving: 74 calories; 0 milligrams cholesterol; 2.5 grams fat; .7 grams protein (1.6% RDA); 12 grams carbohydrate

RDA: 303 milligrams potassium; vitamin A 46%; vitamin C 123%

1 underripe papaya (1½ pounds; 680 g), peeled and seeded (shredded, makes about 3 cups; 705 ml)
5 teaspoons fresh lemon juice

1 tablespoon olive oil
¼ teaspoon kosher salt
12 drops hot red pepper sauce
Freshly ground black pepper, to taste

1. Grate papaya using the grating disc of a food processor or a hand grater. Transfer to a serving dish and stir in 2 teaspoons of the lemon juice to prevent discoloring.

2. Stir together remaining 3 teaspoons lemon juice with oil and salt and add to papaya with hot pepper sauce and black pepper. Stir to mix and let stand for 30 minutes to allow flavors to develop.

MANGO-TOMATO SALAD

*T*his is one of the most beautiful first-course salads I know, with the thin slices of golden-orange mango providing sweetness on top of the acid-sweet tomatoes. The basil tops it off with a sprinkle of green and a hint of pepper. Multiply as often as you want to spectacularly open a dinner party.   *SERVES 2*

Per serving: 104 calories; 0 milligrams cholesterol; 4 grams fat; 102 milligrams sodium; 1 gram protein (3% RDA); 19 grams carbohydrate

RDA: vitamin A 85%; vitamin C 73%

2 tomatoes (each about 7 ounces; 200 g), cut across into ¼-inch (.5-cm) slices
1 pound (450 g) mango, peeled and cut toward pit into ½-inch (1-cm) lengthwise slices (about 1½ cups; 355 ml) (peeled and pitted, about 9½ ounces; 269 g)

4 teaspoons fresh lemon juice
1 teaspoon finely shredded across the vein fresh basil leaves
1 tablespoon olive oil
2 tablespoons fresh lime juice
¼ teaspoon kosher salt
Freshly ground black pepper, to taste

1. Arrange tomato slices, slightly overlapping, in a circle on a dinner plate. Toss mango slices with ½ teaspoon of the lemon juice and fan over tomato slices. Sprinkle basil over all.

2. Stir together remaining lemon juice, oil, lime juice and salt. Pour over tomatoes and mango. Sprinkle pepper over and serve.

Peel mango. Cut toward the pit into slices that can be scraped from pit.

WINTER VEGETABLE SALAD

You must cook the vegetables to make this salad. So I make a lot while I'm at it. Many times I use it for a buffet, where it's perfect since the vegetables don't go limp with keeping. The salad also freezes and defrosts well, so you can have it on hand.   *SERVES 16*

Per ½-cup (120-ml) serving: 50 calories; 0 milligrams cholesterol; 3 grams fat; 103 milligrams sodium; 1 gram protein (2% RDA); 4 grams carbohydrate

RDA: 174 milligrams potassium; vitamin A 75%; vitamin C 41%

8 ounces (227 g) carrot, peeled and cut across into ¼-inch (.5-cm) slices (about 1½ cups; 355 ml)

10 ounces (284 g) medium cauliflower florets, about 1-pound (900-g) head (about 3 cups; 705 ml)

6 ounces (170 g) broccoli florets, about ½ bunch (about 4 cups; 1 l)

6 ounces (170 g) onion, peeled and cut into ½-inch (1-cm) chunks (about 2 cups; 470 ml)

1 cup (240 ml) Skinny Tomato Dressing (page 496)

1. Arrange carrot slices in a circle around the inside edge of a 13 × 10 × 2-inch (33 × 25.5 × 5-cm) oval dish. Place cauliflower florets inside carrots and place broccoli in the center. Scatter the onions over all. Cover tightly with microwave plastic wrap. Cook at 100% for 7 minutes in a 650- to 700-watt oven. Prick plastic to release steam.

2. Remove from oven and uncover. Transfer vegetables to a strainer. Rinse under cold running water and drain.

3. Return vegetables to cooking dish. Pour over dressing and toss well to coat.

FOR 400- TO 500-WATT OVENS

To serve 16. Cook for 10 minutes.

SUMMER VEGETABLE SALAD

*T*he vegetables in this salad are cooked to blend their flavors while still tasting sunny-fresh, with brilliant color and vitamins. For many people a half-cup will be enough; but the calorie count is low, the taste is good and it's filling.   *SERVES 4*

Per 1-cup (240-ml) serving: 44 calories; 0 milligrams cholesterol; .4 gram fat; 10 milligrams sodium; 3 grams protein (7.5% RDA); 8 grams carbohydrate

RDA: calcium 5%; phosphorus 7%; iron 8%; 410 milligrams potassium; vitamin A 22%; thiamin 9%; riboflavin 7%; niacin 5%; vitamin C 74%

1 small zucchini (about 5 ounces; 142 g), trimmed and cut across into ¼-inch (.5-cm) slices (about 1 cup; 240 ml)

1 small yellow squash (about 6 ounces; 170 g), trimmed and cut across into ¼-inch (.5-cm) slices (about 1 cup; 240 ml)

12 ounces (340 g) asparagus, ends snapped off, edible stalk cut into 2 pieces (about 3 cups; 705 ml)

4 ounces (113.5 g) snow peas, ends removed (about 1½ cups; 355 ml)

2 scallions, white and green parts, sliced

3 tablespoons Spicy Buttermilk Dressing (page 495)

1. Place zucchini and yellow squash in a circle around the inside edge of a 13 × 10 × 2-inch (33 × 25.5 × 5-cm) oval dish. Place asparagus tips inside squash and snow peas in the center. Sprinkle the scallion slices over all. Cover tightly with microwave plastic wrap. Cook at 100% for 5 minutes in a 650- to 700-watt oven. Prick plastic to release steam.

2. Remove from oven and uncover. Rinse vegetables under cold water and drain.

3. Return vegetables to dish and toss with dressing. Let stand for 5 minutes and serve at room temperature.

FOR 400- TO 500-WATT OVENS

To serve 4. Cook for 9 minutes.

String snow peas from both ends.

I can make a meal out of almost any salad if the portion is large enough. I add some cheese and bread and a piece of fruit. At most I might increase the meal by starting with a soup or a small portion of pasta. It's a healthy way to eat; but most people don't choose it. Enter the large salad with meat, cheese, fish or poultry—stage center.

The following large salads all contain enough protein so that they make good main courses. You will find others, based on beans and legumes, in Good Grains and Other Starches (pages 148–225).

SUMMER VEGETABLE SALAD WITH YOGURT AND DILL

I can eat this as a cooling whole meal during the hottest days of summer. At dinner, I double the portion and serve it with bread and a cup of skim-milk cottage cheese. I drink iced tea and finish up with a very cold piece of watermelon and a cookie. I get very full. Since I don't have a salt problem, I will sometimes up the salt slightly. Use your judgment, or add it at the table. To make a substantial lunch, serve with one-half cup low-fat cottage cheese, some Oat Bran Wafers (page 161) and a piece of fruit.

As a side salad or first course, half a portion will probably be enough; it's filling.

The vegetable part of this salad can be prepared up to two hours in advance and refrigerated. Add yogurt and toss just before serving. Since there's no cooking, this can be made in any quantity.   *SERVES 5*

Per 1-cup (240-ml) serving: 79 calories; 1 milligram cholesterol; 1 gram fat; 286 milligrams sodium; 6 grams protein (13% RDA); 14 grams carbohydrate

RDA: calcium 20%; phosphorus 16%; iron 12%; vitamin A 66%; riboflavin 15%; vitamin C 137%

(continued)

2 cucumbers (each about 8 ounces; 227 g), peeled

2 medium tomatoes (each about 8 ounces; 227 g), cored

½ teaspoon kosher salt

1 green bell pepper (9 ounces; 255 g), stemmed, seeded, deribbed and coarsely chopped (about 1 cup; 240 ml)

1 red bell pepper (9 ounces; 255 g), stemmed, seeded, deribbed and coarsely chopped (about 1 cup; 240 ml)

1 bunch scallions (white part only), chopped (about ½ cup; 120 ml)

½ cup (120 ml) loosely packed, coarsely chopped dill

1½ cups (355 ml) nonfat yogurt

Freshly ground black pepper, to taste

1. Halve cucumbers lengthwise and scoop out the seeds. Cut cucumbers and tomatoes into ½-inch (1-cm) dice. Toss in a bowl with the salt and let stand 30 minutes.

2. Add remaining ingredients and toss to coat. Serve at once.

SEVICHE

*S*eviche is a brilliant Mexican invention of raw fish that is cooked only by the acidity of the lime juice in which it marinates. If raw fish makes you queasy, skip this; but I promise it doesn't taste or feel raw. In this version, low-calorie cucumber has replaced the sometimes-used avocado. If you can afford the calories, by all means use avocado. It has lots of fat; but it's all unsaturated. If you like your food really spicy, double the amount of jalapeño.

When you have this as a main course, pick a smooth and soothing cold soup to go first. Put the salad on a bed of greens. Add some bread—hot grilled tortillas would be excellent. Dessert could be as easy as fresh berries or melon. A half-portion of seviche as a first course could go before an ample pasta dish like that served with Fennel Sardine Sauce (page 170) or the vegetarian Country Macaroni with Potatoes and Pesto (page 176). Try this as one of the dishes at a buffet where it will feed many. I have even served a tablespoon or so in well-washed clam shells as an hors d'oeuvre.

Since this is an uncooked dish, it can easily be multiplied for that large summer party.   *SERVES 4 AS A MAIN COURSE, 8 AS A FIRST COURSE*

Per 1½-cup (355-ml) serving: 150 calories; 54 milligrams cholesterol; 2 grams fat; 106 milligrams sodium; 23 grams protein (52% RDA); 11 grams carbohydrate

RDA: phosphorus 26%; vitamin A 31%; thiamin 13%; niacin 21%; vitamin C 75%

1 pound (450 g) sole fillets, cut into
    1½ × 1½-inch (4 × 4-cm) pieces
4 medium tomatoes (each about 5
    ounces; 142 g), cored and cut into
    ½-inch (1-cm) dice (3 cups; 705 ml)
4 ounces (113.5 g) red onion, peeled
    and cut into ¼-inch (.5-cm) dice (¾
    cup; 180 ml)
8 ounces (227 g) cucumber, peeled,
    seeded and cut into ½-inch (1-cm)
    dice (about ¾ cup; 180 ml)

⅓ cup (80 ml) fresh lime juice
2 tablespoons chopped fresh cilantro
½ ounce (14 g) Pickled Jalapeño
    Peppers (page 473) or canned
    jalapeño, stemmed, seeded and
    chopped (about half a jalapeño)
Freshly ground black pepper, to taste

1. Mix all ingredients together in a large bowl. Let stand 30 minutes to 1 hour. Serve at room temperature.

SHRIMP SALAD

Shrimp Salad can be multiplied to feed as many people as you want to by cooking the multiplied amounts of shrimp and broccoli separately. Multiply the other ingredients accordingly; toss and serve on a bed of lettuce if you wish. At lunch, all you need to add is a cracker or two. At a summer dinner, precede the salad with Chilled Cream of Tomato Soup (page 146) or Red Pepper Soup (page 145), and follow with Light White Ice Cream (page 558) or Summer Fruit Compote II (page 540). You can add a glass of wine or a cookie, or add a snack when hunger hits. *SERVES 2*

Per 1½-cup (300-ml) serving: 296 calories; 221 milligrams cholesterol; 17 grams fat; 301 milligrams sodium; 29 grams protein (65% RDA); 7 grams carbohydrate

RDA: calcium 7%; phosphorus 19%; iron 24%; 561 milligrams potassium; vitamin A 22%; niacin 29%; vitamin C 57%

2 ounces (56 g) broccoli stems, peeled and cut across into ¼-inch (.5-cm) slices (about ½ cup; 120 ml)

8 ounces (227 g) shelled shrimp, cooked (page 267), with their liquid

4 ounces (113.5 g) tomato, cored and cut into 16 wedges (about ⅔ cup; 160 ml)

1 small rib celery, peeled and cut across into ¼-inch (.5-cm) slices (about ¼ cup; 60 ml)

¼ cup (60 ml) unsalted peanuts

1 tablespoon chopped fresh parsley

1½ tablespoons Rouïlle (page 484)

1. Place broccoli stems in a 1-quart (1-l) soufflé dish. Cover tightly with microwave plastic wrap. Cook at 100% for 1 minute in a 650- to 700-watt oven. Prick plastic to release steam.

2. Remove from oven and uncover. Rinse broccoli under cold running water and drain. Place in a medium bowl. Add shrimp, reserving cooking liquid, tomato wedges, celery, peanuts and parsley.

3. In a small bowl, mix together the Rouïlle with 2 teaspoons of the reserved liquid from the shrimp. Pour over the salad and toss well to coat.

FOR 400- TO 500-WATT OVENS

To serve 2. Cook for 2 minutes 30 seconds.

CHOPPED SALAD

*H*ere's the main course of a party meal, loosely based on California's famous Cobb salad. At lunch, just add a whole wheat crisp or a piece of fruit. When it's the star of a warm evening's dinner, begin with a cold soup like Slim Vichyssoise (page 147) and end up with a slice of Angel Food Cake (page 582) and some strawberries. Add a spritzer or a glass of wine for well-fed company.   *SERVES 8*

Per 2-cup (470-ml) serving: 285 calories; 39 milligrams cholesterol; 22 grams fat; 212 milligrams sodium; 17 grams protein (38% RDA); 6 grams carbohydrate

RDA: calcium 25%; phosphorus 24%; iron 7%; 355 milligrams potassium; vitamin A 27%; riboflavin 10%; niacin 13%; vitamin C 29%

8 ounces (227 g) turkey breast cutlets
3 cloves garlic, smashed, peeled and sliced
½ cup (120 ml) Basic Chicken Broth (page 460), or unsalted or regular canned chicken broth
1 egg white
1 teaspoon Dijon mustard
1 tablespoon fresh lemon juice
Kosher salt, to taste
Freshly ground black pepper, to taste
½ cup (120 ml) vegetable oil

½ head iceberg lettuce (about 8 ounces; 227 g), cut into ½-inch (1-cm) cubes (9 cups; 2.25 l)
8 ounces (227 g) part-skim mozzarella cheese, cut into ¼-inch (.5-cm) cubes (about 2 cups; 470 ml)
2 large tomatoes (about 12 ounces; 340 g), cut into ¼-inch (.5-cm) cubes (1½ cups; 355 ml)
1 small onion (4 ounces; 113.5 g), peeled and chopped (½ cup; 120 ml)

1. Arrange pieces of turkey breast in an 8 × 8 × 2-inch (20 × 20 × 5-cm) glass or ceramic dish so that they do not overlap. Place garlic slices over the meat and cover with broth. Cover tightly with microwave plastic wrap. Cook at 100% for 4 minutes in a 650- to 700-watt oven. Prick plastic to release steam.

2. Remove from oven and uncover. Drain and reserve liquid. Transfer garlic to a food processor. Allow turkey to cool and cut into ¼-inch (.5-cm) cubes.

3. To garlic in food processor, add egg white, mustard, lemon juice and salt and pepper to taste. Process until well mixed. With motor running, pour oil in a thin stream through the feed tube. Add 2 tablespoons of the reserved cooking liquid and process to blend. Scrape dressing into a small bowl.

4. To serve, make a bed of the lettuce in a large open bowl. Arrange 4 separate piles of cubed turkey, cheese, tomato and onion on top of the lettuce. Serve the garlic dressing on the side. Or toss ingredients and serve on a bed of lettuce.

FOR 400- TO 500-WATT OVENS

To serve 8. Cook turkey, covered, as in Step 1 for 6 minutes.

CURRIED CHICKEN SALAD

Curried Chicken Salad is a fine main course for a dinner party or a brunch; but you would have to follow such a brunch with a light dinner if you are on a weight-loss diet. Consider beginning with Chilled Cucumber Soup (page 142), serving a small heated pita bread with the salad and having Creamy Custard (page 570) for dessert. Drink a light beer or chilled mint tea. Non–weight-losers can have more bread and Ginger Crisps (page 586) or Oat Bran Crisps (page 574) with dessert.   *SERVES 6*

Per generous 1-cup (240-ml) serving: 335 calories; 44 milligrams cholesterol; 18 grams fat; 156 milligrams sodium; 21 grams protein (46% RDA); 23 grams carbohydrate

RDA: phosphorus 22%; iron 10%; thiamin 11%; niacin 51%; vitamin C 31%

1 pound (450 g) new potatoes, cut into 1-inch (2.5-cm) cubes (about 3 cups; 705 ml)

⅓ cup (80 ml) Basic Chicken Broth (page 460), or unsalted or regular canned chicken broth

4 half-breasts chicken (each 4 ounces; 113.5 g), skinned, boned and cut into 1-inch (2.5-cm) chunks

3 ribs celery, peeled and cut crosswise into ½-inch (1-cm) slices (1½ cups; 355 ml)

9 ounces (255 g) unsweetened canned pineapple slices (about 6 slices), each cut into 6 pieces

¾ cup (180 ml) Curry Mayonnaise (page 485)

¼ cup (60 ml) walnut pieces

1 tablespoon chopped fresh coriander, optional

1. Place potatoes in a 13 × 10 × 2-inch (33 × 25.5 × 5-cm) dish. Pour broth over. Cover tightly with microwave plastic wrap. Cook at 100% for 10 minutes in a 650- to 700-watt oven. Prick plastic to release steam.

2. Remove from oven and uncover. Push potatoes to the sides of the dish. Place chicken in a single layer in the center of the dish. Cover tightly and cook for 6 minutes, stirring once halfway through cooking. Prick plastic to release steam.

3. Remove from oven and uncover. Let stand until cool. When cool, drain off liquid and discard. Transfer to a serving dish. Add celery, pineapple and mayonnaise and stir to coat. Scatter walnuts over all. Sprinkle with coriander, if desired.

FOR 400- TO 500-WATT OVENS

To serve 6. Cook potatoes as in Step 1 for 15 minutes. Continue cooking as in Step 2 for 11 minutes. Finish as in Step 3.

ROAST BEEF SALAD

*T*his salad—made with luscious leftovers of either basic poached beef (page 359), José Lampreia's Poached Beef (page 360) or store-bought roast beef trimmed of all fat—is substantial enough for a winter's day lunch with a small pita bread and a piece of fruit. Have it at dinner on a night when you have had more meat, fish or chicken at lunch than you ordinarily do. It might be a day when you have had lunch at a restaurant. Start with a soup like Chilled Red Bean Soup (page 208) and finish with a dessert you really like.

To multiply, use new potato cooking times on page 220.   *SERVES 1*

Per 1½-cup (360-ml) serving: 215 calories; 46 milligrams cholesterol; 5 grams fat; 272 milligrams sodium; 16 grams protein (43% RDA); 22 grams carbohydrate

RDA: calcium 4%; phosphorus 23%; iron 18%; 784 milligrams potassium; vitamin A 61%; thiamin 12%; riboflavin 15%; niacin 22%; vitamin C 138%

2 small new potatoes (2 ounces; 56 g), cut into quarters

2 ounces (56 g) lean and trimmed of all fat roast beef, in one ½-inch (1-cm) slice, or leftover poached beef (page 360), cut into strips ½ × ½ × 1½-inches (1 × 1 × 3 cm)

½ scallion, cut into ¼-inch (.5-cm) slices

1 ounce (28 g) red pepper, cut into thin slices

1 radish, trimmed and cut into thin slices (about ¼ cup; 40 ml)

1½ tablespoons Mustard Dressing (page 492)

4 leaves romaine lettuce, torn into 1-inch (2.5-cm) pieces

1. Place potatoes in a 1-quart (1-l) soufflé dish. Cover tightly with microwave plastic wrap. Cook at 100% for 2 minutes in a 650- to 700-watt oven. Prick plastic to release steam.

2. Remove from oven and uncover. Allow potatoes to cool.

3. In a small bowl combine potatoes with roast beef, scallion, red pepper and radish slices. Add dressing and toss well to coat.

4. Place torn lettuce leaves around inside edge of a dinner plate and mound salad in the center.

Vegetables

Of course, it's possible to solve the problem of what to serve with by defrosting vegetables; but that misses the pleasure of fresh. I do use frozen and peeled pearl onions, frozen baby lima beans, frozen artichoke hearts and frozen baby peas. Sometimes I resort to frozen spinach. If time is short and I am alone, the numerous salad bars with cleaned and cut-up vegetables can be a quick kitchen helper; but the best helpers of all are a microwave oven, a sharp paring knife and an inexpensive vegetable peeler that is reasonably new. They are cheap, so it's easy to buy one from to time.

When I use frozen vegetables, I seldom defrost them in the microwave oven. However, you can make them out of the package by putting them in a bowl or dish, covering them tightly and cooking them in a 650- to 700-watt oven at 100% for five minutes, or for eight minutes in a 400- to 500-watt oven. If they are not really hot, stir and cook a few more minutes. Then drain through a sieve to remove excess water.

What I do is to put the frozen block of vegetables in a sieve and then run warm water over them, stirring them with my hand from time to time until they are no longer cold. Then I can cook them any way I want to. I find that the flavor, color and evenness of cooking is improved. The only canned vegetables that I use with any regularity are vacuum-packed corn niblets, American and Italian, plum and regular tomatoes, both canned in juice, and dried beans and legumes such as chick-peas. I try not to use too many because of the heavy sodium content. I must admit a weakness, coming from childhood, for the tiny canned French-style peas; but that's the way other people feel about peanut butter and jelly.

Now that I've gotten frozen and canned vegetables out of the way, it is time to have fun. Look for basic cooking directions for vegetables other than those in this chapter in the Index. For instance, you will find that asparagus is in First Courses

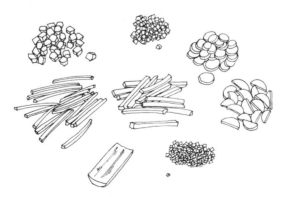

Vegetables listed clockwise from 12 o'clock: ½-inch (1-cm) dice, ½-inch (1-cm) coins, half-moons, ¼-inch (.5-cm) dice, lengthwise slices, 2 × ¼ × ¼-inch (5 × .5 .5-cm) julienne, 1-inch (2.5-cm) dice and 2 × ½ × ½-inch (5 × 1 × 1-cm) batonettes in center.

(pages 74–113) along with artichokes and spinach; potatoes, grains and legumes are in Good Grains and Other Starches (pages 148–225). Here, I start with some of the most common and nutritious vegetables and go on to vegetables you may only cook from time to time. Almost every vegetable is introduced by basic cooking times and nutritional values.

Some vegetables are notable for not being here even though they are occasional favorites, because they are high in calories. Green peas are here; but I don't give any special recipes. You almost need to think of them as a starch; use them instead of rice or potatoes. If you look at the nutrition chart, you'll see why. Look in *Microwave Gourmet*'s Dictionary for cooking times of other vegetables.

After all this brouhaha, you may ask why there aren't even more vegetable recipes. Simple—many of the main-course recipes include vegetables and don't need an extra. Also, many of the first courses are vegetable dishes that you can just as easily use as side dishes.

Many of these recipes can be multiplied or divided by using the basic cooking times for the appropriate vegetable. I will say which can be done that way. When reheating purées, allow from three to seven minutes, depending on the amount of purée and the wattage of the oven. You want a hot vegetable.

STRING BEANS

Smaller and fresher string beans—green beans—are better. While nobody wants them cooked until they are mushy and gray, they are frequently undercooked so that they have an unpleasantly raw taste. The cooking times given here will produce beans that are thoroughly cooked but still crisp.

PER 4 OUNCES (113.5 G) RAW GREEN BEANS: 35 calories; 0 milligrams cholesterol; .1 gram fat; 2 grams protein (4.6% RDA); 8 grams carbohydrate

RDA: calcium 4%; phosphorus 4%; iron 6.5%; 237 milligrams potassium; vitamin A 15%; thiamin 6%; riboflavin 7%; niacin 4%; vitamin C 31%

Tip and tail and arrange in dish specified below. Sprinkle with 1 tablespoon water. Cover tightly with microwave plastic wrap. Four ounces (113.5 g) raw green beans yields 1¼ cups (300 ml) tipped and tailed; ¾ cup (160 ml) cooked. Cup amounts of a given weight of raw and cooked beans will vary slightly with the size of the beans.

4 ounces (113.5 g) beans in a 1½-quart (1.5-l) soufflé dish
650- to 700-watt oven: 3 min. 30 sec.
400- to 500-watt oven: 5 min.

8 ounces (227 g) beans in a 1½-quart (1.5-l) soufflé dish
650- to 700-watt oven: 4 min. 30 sec.
400- to 500-watt oven: 6 min.

1 pound (430 g) beans in a 13 × 10 × 2-inch (33 × 25.5 × 5-cm) dish
650- to 700-watt oven: 7 min.
400- to 500-watt oven: 10 min.

1½ pounds (680 g) beans in a 13 × 10 × 2-inch (33 × 25.5 × 5-cm) dish
650- to 700-watt oven: 10 min.
400- to 500-watt oven: Not recommended

ITALIAN GREEN BEANS

Green beans and tomatoes make a wonderful combination. Try tossing cooked green beans with raw tomatoes and red onions with Mustard Dressing (page 492). Here, they are cooked with basic Italian herbs for a good and simple dish. You can multiply or divide this as much as you want by using the basic string bean cooking times above. *SERVES 4*

Per scant 1-cup (240-ml) serving: 76 calories; 0 milligrams cholesterol; 3 grams fat; 168 milligrams sodium; 3 grams protein (7% RDA); 13 grams carbohydrate

RDA: iron 11%; vitamin A 26%; vitamin C 55%

4 cloves garlic, smashed, peeled and chopped
2 teaspoons olive oil
½ teaspoon dried thyme
¼ teaspoon dried oregano
14 ounces (395 g) canned Italian plum tomatoes, drained

1 pound (450 g) green beans, tipped and tailed (about 5 cups; 1.2 l)
Freshly ground black pepper, to taste
1½ teaspoons fresh lemon juice

1. Place garlic and oil in a 13 × 10 × 2-inch (33 × 25.5 × 5-cm) oval dish. Cook, uncovered, at 100% for 3 minutes in a 650- to 700-watt oven.

2. Remove from oven. Stir in thyme, oregano and tomatoes. Cook, uncovered, for 2 minutes.

3. Remove from oven and stir in green beans and black pepper. Cover tightly with microwave plastic wrap and cook for 7 minutes. Prick plastic to release steam.

4. Remove from oven and uncover. Stir in lemon juice and serve.

FOR 400- TO 500-WATT OVENS

To serve 4. Cook as in Step 1 for 5 minutes. Cook as in Step 2 for 3 minutes. Continue with Step 3, cooking for 10 minutes.

GREEN BEANS AMANDINE

A classic of French cooking is quickly made with very little fat in the microwave oven. Once again, you can increase this recipe by using the basic cooking times above and multiplying the ingredients. *SERVES 2*

Per generous ⅓-cup (80-ml) serving: 38 calories; 0 milligrams cholesterol; 4 grams fat; 4 milligrams sodium; 2 grams protein (5% RDA); 5 grams carbohydrate

RDA: vitamin C 14%

1 tablespoon slivered almonds (½ ounce; 14 g)
¼ teaspoon vegetable oil
4 ounces (113.5 g) green beans, tipped and tailed (about 1¼ cups; 300 ml)

Pinch summer savory
Freshly ground black pepper, to taste

1. Place almonds and oil in 1½-quart (1.5-l) soufflé dish. Cook, uncovered, at 100% for 3 minutes in a 650- to 700-watt oven.

2. Remove from oven. Stir in remaining ingredients. Cover tightly with microwave plastic wrap. Cook for 3 minutes 30 seconds. Prick plastic to release steam.

3. Remove from oven, uncover and serve.

FOR 400- TO 500-WATT OVENS

To serve 2. Cook as in Step 1 for 6 minutes. Cook as in Step 2 for 5 minutes.

SZECHUAN GREEN BEANS

Well, if I weren't dieting I would make the version in *Microwave Gourmet;* but these are quite good. If you want to serve them cold, halve the amount of vinegar.   *SERVES 6*

Per ½-cup (120-ml) serving: 34 calories; 0 milligrams cholesterol; 1 gram fat; 110 milligrams sodium; 2 grams protein (4% RDA); 6 grams carbohydrate

RDA: vitamin A 19%; vitamin C 27%

4 cloves garlic, smashed, peeled and
    chopped
2 teaspoons peeled and grated ginger
1 teaspoon chili oil
1 pound (450 g) green beans, tipped
    and tailed (about 5 cups; 1.2 l)

4 scallions, green and white parts,
    trimmed and thinly sliced across
2 teaspoons Chinese salted black beans
1½ tablespoons rice wine vinegar
1 teaspoon tamari soy

1. Place garlic, ginger and chili oil in a 13 × 10 × 2-inch (33 × 25.5 × 5-cm) oval dish. Cook, uncovered, at 100% for 2 minutes in a 650- to 700-watt oven.

2. Remove from oven. Stir in green beans, scallions, black beans and rice wine vinegar. Cook, uncovered, for 12 minutes, stirring 3 times.

3. Remove from oven and stir in tamari soy. Serve hot.

FOR 400- TO 500-WATT OVENS

To serve 6. Cook as in Step 1 for 4 minutes. Cook as in Step 2 for 18 minutes, stirring 3 times during cooking. Finish recipe as in Step 3.

CAULIFLOWER

Cauliflower tends to get underused because the only thing that we can think of doing with it is to boil it and drench it in butter or cream sauce. Too bad, because it has few calories and lots of nutrition.

PER 4 OUNCES (113.5 G) RAW CAULIFLOWER: 27 calories; 0 milligrams cholesterol; .2 gram fat; 17 milligrams sodium; 2.3 grams protein (5% RDA); 6 grams carbohydrate

RDA: calcium 3%; phosphorus 5%; iron 4%; 403 milligrams potassium; thiamin 6%; riboflavin 4%; niacin 4%; vitamin C 135%

An average untrimmed head weighs 2 pounds (900 g). Cook florets in dish specified below, covered tightly with microwave plastic wrap. Eight ounces (227 g) cauliflower florets, from 12 ounces (340 g) of untrimmed head, yields 2 cups (470 ml) raw small florets (1½ × 1½ × 2½-inches; 4 × 4 × 6-cm), or 2¾ cups (650 ml) raw large florets (3 × 3 × 2½-inches; 7.5 × 7.5 × 6 cm). Both yield 2 cups (470 ml) cooked florets.

4 ounces (113.5 g) cauliflower florets in a 1½-quart (1.5-l) soufflé dish
650- to 700-watt oven: 2 min.
400- to 500-watt oven: 4 min.

8 ounces (227 g) cauliflower florets in a 1½-quart (1.5-l) soufflé dish
650- to 700-watt oven: 4 min.
400- to 500-watt oven: 6 min.

1 pound (450 g) cauliflower florets in a 13 × 10 × 2-inch (33 × 25.5 × 5-cm) dish
650- to 700-watt oven: 7 min.
400- to 500-watt oven: 10 min.

1½ pounds (680 g) cauliflower florets in a 13 × 10 × 2-inch (33 × 25.5 × 5-cm) dish
650- to 700-watt oven: 9 min.
400- to 500-watt oven: Not recommended

2 pounds (900 g) cauliflower florets in a 14 × 11 × 2-inch (35.5 × 28 × 5-cm) dish
650- to 700-watt oven: 11 min.
400- to 500-watt oven: Not recommended

Cut off outside leaves from head of cauliflower.

Core deeply with a small knife.

Cut into small florets (1½ × 1½ × 2½ inches; 4 × 4 × 6 cm) or large florets (3 × 3 × 2½ inches; 7.5 × 7.5 × 6 cm).

CAULIFLOWER GRATIN

*T*his is a dish to satisfy an old-fashioned taste—like mine—for creamy cauliflower dishes, but with new-fashioned amounts of fat and calories. Once again, you can multiply or divide the amount you make of this dish by using the basic cooking times on the preceding page and those on page 508 for the amount of béchamel you need.   *SERVES 4*

Per ¾-cup (180-ml) serving: 77 calories; 9 milligrams cholesterol; 2 grams fat; 99 milligrams sodium; 6 grams protein (14% RDA); 8 grams carbohydrate

RDA: calcium 16%; phosphorus 14%; vitamin C 102%

12 ounces (340 g) cauliflower in small florets (about 3 cups; 705 ml)
½ cup (120 ml) Béchamel (page 508)

2 ounces (56 g) part-skim mozzarella, grated (about ½ cup; 120 ml)
Freshly ground black pepper, to taste

1. Place cauliflower in a 9-inch (23-cm) pie plate. Cover tightly with microwave plastic wrap. Cook at 100% for 6 minutes in a 650- to 700-watt oven. Prick plastic to release steam.

2. Remove from oven and uncover. Preheat conventional broiler.

3. In a small bowl mix together béchamel, mozzarella and black pepper. Pour over cauliflower. Place under the broiler and cook for 5 minutes, or until cheese is browned and bubbly. Remove from broiler and serve hot.

FOR 400- TO 500-WATT OVENS

To serve 4. Cook as in Step 1 for 9 minutes. Finish recipe as in Steps 2 and 3.

CAULIFLOWER PURÉE

*T*his combination of flavors may seem odd until you think how much like cabbage cauliflower tastes. Caraway is often used with cabbage. This is a light and elegant purée, good enough for a party. You can expand it to the size of your party by using the basic cooking times above.   *SERVES 2*

Per generous ½-cup (120-ml) serving: 54 calories; 2 milligrams cholesterol; 1 gram fat; 81 milligrams sodium; 4 grams protein (10% RDA); 9 grams carbohydrate

8 ounces (227 g) cauliflower in large
   florets (about 2¾ cups; 650 ml)
½ cup (120 ml) buttermilk

½ teaspoon caraway seeds
Pinch freshly ground black pepper

1. Place cauliflower in a 1½-quart (1.5-l) soufflé dish. Cover tightly with microwave plastic wrap. Cook at 100% for 4 minutes in a 650- to 700-watt oven. Prick plastic to release steam.
2. Remove from oven and uncover. Place in a food processor and add buttermilk. Purée until smooth. Stir in caraway seeds.
3. Return mixture to soufflé dish. Re-cover and cook for 3 minutes, or until hot. Prick plastic to release steam.
4. Remove from oven and uncover. Stir in pepper and serve.

FOR 400- TO 500-WATT OVENS

To serve 4. In Step 1, cook for 6 minutes. Reheat in Step 3 for 6 minutes, or until hot.

The summer squashes come in all shades of yellow, white and green. They range from little scalloped pattypans to zucchini (courgettes) to the lemon yellow of what is actually called "summer squash." All are best young and small, when their seeds are unformed and their flesh is firm, not pulpy. All have edible skins that add color and nutrition.

The very smallest may be hard to find when they are growing, as they hide under the huge, dark green leaves and mimic the look of the stems. A few always get away from me and grow to an exaggerated size before discovery. If you are confronted with one of these, check the skin for blemishes and gouge them out with the tip of a sharp knife. Cut the squash lengthwise into quarters. Place each quarter skin side down and run your knife down its length to cut out the large seeds and pulpy interior, Proceed to cook as if you had a normal squash; but do check the weight.

PER 4 OUNCES (113.5 G) RAW SUMMER SQUASH: 23 calories; 0 milligrams cholesterol; .2 gram fat; 2 milligrams sodium; 1.3 grams protein (3% RDA); 5 grams carbohydrate

RDA: calcium 2%; phosphorus 4%; iron 3%; 221 milligrams potassium; vitamin A 4%; thiamin 4%; riboflavin 2%; niacin 3%; vitamin C 28%

Trim and cut across into ¼-inch (.5-cm) slices or 2½ × ¼-inch (6 × .5-cm) julienne. Place in dish specified below, covered tightly with microwave plastic wrap. Four ounces (113.5 g) squash yields about 1 cup (240 ml) raw squash cut in rounds or julienne and ½ cup (120 ml) cooked squash.

4 ounces (113.5 g) squash in a 1½-quart (1.5-l) soufflé dish
650- to 700-watt oven: 2 min. 30 sec.
400- to 500-watt oven: 3 min. 30 sec.

8 ounces (227 g) squash in a 1½-quart (1.5-l) soufflé dish
650- to 700-watt oven: 3 min. 30 sec.
400- to 500-watt oven: 5 min.

1 pound (450 g) squash in a 13 × 10 × 2-inch (33 × 25.5 × 5-cm) dish
650- to 700-watt oven: 5 min.
400- to 500-watt oven: 7 min. 30 sec.

1½ pounds (680 g) squash in a 14 × 11 × 2-inch (35.5 × 28 × 5-cm) dish
650- to 700-watt oven: 6 min. 30 sec.
400- to 500-watt oven: Not recommended

ZUCCHINI WITH DILL

This fresh, green vegetable goes well with simple fish or chicken. Salmon is particularly good with the dill here.

To divide or multiply this recipe, use the basic cooking times above in Step 2. Reheat from thirty seconds to three minutes. It is flexible.   *SERVES 4*

Per ½-cup (120-ml) serving: 24 calories; 0 milligrams cholesterol; 0 grams fat; 188 milligrams sodium; 1.4 grams protein (3% RDA); 5 grams carbohydrate

RDA: iron 5%; 294 milligrams potassium; vitamin C 16%

1 pound (450 g) zucchini, trimmed and cut into 3 × ¼ × ¼-inch (7.5 × .5 × .5-cm) julienne (about 4 cups; 1 l)

1 tablespoon cornstarch
¼ cup (60 ml) water
¼ cup (60 ml) minced fresh dill
½ teaspoon kosher salt

1. Place zucchini in a 2½-quart (2.5-l) soufflé dish or casserole with a tightly fitted lid.

2. Dissolve cornstarch in water in a small bowl and stir well, making sure there are no lumps. Stir into zucchini. Cover tightly with microwave plastic wrap or lid. Cook at 100% for 5 minutes in a 650- to 700-watt oven. If using plastic wrap, prick to release steam.

3. Uncover and stir in dill. Re-cover and cook for 1 minute longer. If using plastic wrap, prick to release steam.

4. Remove from oven and uncover. Add salt and serve.

FOR 400- TO 500-WATT OVENS

To serve 4. Cook for 7 minutes 30 seconds in Step 2. Cook for 1 minute 30 seconds in Step 3.

YELLOW SQUASH WITH TARRAGON

Well, I gave in and used some butter; but it really improves the taste of this dish, which is perfect with fish, chicken or veal. In return, I kept the sodium to almost nothing.

To multiply, use basic cooking times above less one minute in Step 1 and, no matter what the quantity, cook for one minute after adding tarragon.   *SERVES 4*

Per ½-cup (180-ml) serving: 49 calories; 8 milligrams cholesterol; 3 grams fat; 3 milligrams sodium; 1.2 grams protein (2.7% RDA); 5 grams carbohydrate

RDA: iron 4%; 257 milligrams potassium; vitamin A 10%; vitamin C 16%

1 pound (450 g) yellow squash,
   trimmed and cut across into ¼-inch
   (.5-cm) slices (about 4 cups; 1 l)

1 tablespoon unsalted butter, cut into
   small pieces
2 tablespoons fresh tarragon

1. Place squash in a 2½-quart (2.5-l) soufflé dish or casserole with a tightly fitted lid. Scatter over butter pieces. Cover tightly with microwave plastic wrap or casserole lid. Cook at 100% for 4 minutes in a 650- to 700-watt oven. If using plastic, prick to release steam.

2. Remove from oven and uncover. Stir in tarragon. Re-cover and cook for 1 minute. If using plastic, prick to release steam.

3. Remove from oven and uncover. Serve hot.

FOR 400- TO 500-WATT OVENS

To serve 4. Cook as in Step 1 for 6 minutes. Cook as in Step 2 for 1 minute 30 seconds.

BROCCOLI

Broccoli is a wonderful source of vitamin C with very few calories. It's easy to cook up enough just for yourself or for a group. I like to peel the stems when I'm making whole stalks. With a knife, cut up large heads into individual stalks with their florets. Cut off woody ends. Then peel stem ends with a potato peeler.

Stems and florets can also be cooked separately. Stems cut across into coins are a good addition to salads.

PER 4 OUNCES (113.5 G) RAW BROCCOLI: 32 calories; 0 milligrams cholesterol; .3 gram fat; 25 milligrams sodium; 3.5 grams protein (8% RDA); 6 grams carbohydrate

RDA: calcium 4%; phosphorus 6%; iron 4%; 280 milligrams potassium; vitamin A 33%; thiamin 4%; riboflavin 6%; niacin 3%; vitamin C 125%

Cut into florets or ¼-inch (.5-cm) coins or stalks with their florets cooked whole (see below). Place in dish specified below and cook, tightly covered with microwave plastic wrap. Four ounces (113.5 g) broccoli yields 1¼ cups (300 ml) raw florets and coins and a scant 1 cup (240 ml) cooked.

FOR FLORETS AND COINS

4 ounces (113.5 g) broccoli in a 1½-quart (1.5-l) soufflé dish
650- to 700-watt oven: 1 min. 30 sec.
400- to 500-watt oven: 3 min.

8 ounces (227g) broccoli in a 1½-quart (1.5-l) soufflé dish
650- to 700-watt oven: 3 min.
400- to 500-watt oven: 6 min.

1 pound (450 g) broccoli in a 13 × 10 × 2-inch (33 × 25.5 × 5-cm) dish
650- to 700-watt oven: 4 min.
400- to 500-watt oven: 8 min.

1½ pounds (680 g) broccoli in a 14 × 11 × 2-inch (35.5 × 28 × 5-cm) dish
650- to 700-watt oven: 6 min.
400- to 500-watt oven: Not recommended

WHOLE BROCCOLI STALKS WITH THEIR FLORETS: Cook in a single layer in a dish just large enough to hold them. Cover tightly.

½ pound (227 g) stalks with 1 tablespoon water
650- to 700-watt oven: 4 min.
400- to 500-watt oven: 6 min.

1 pound (470 g) stalks with 1½ tablespoons water
650- to 700-watt oven: 6 min.
400- to 500-watt oven: 8 min. 30 sec.

2 pounds (900 g) stalks with 3 tablespoons water
650- to 700-watt oven: 8 min.
400- to 500-watt oven: 10 min.

2½ pounds (1.15 kg) stalks with 4 tablespoons water
650- to 700-watt oven: 12 min.
400- to 500-watt oven: Not recommended

SESAME BROCCOLI SAUTÉ

*T*his is a practically perfect accompanying vegetable, with a round savor, low sodium, few calories and lots of vitamins. Multiply ingredients and cook by weight of broccoli in chart above.   *SERVES 4*

Per generous ¾-cup (180-ml) serving: 57 calories; 0 milligrams cholesterol; 3 grams fat; 70 milligrams sodium; 4 grams protein (8% RDA); 6 grams carbohydrate

RDA: calcium 7%; phosphorus 8%; iron 7%; 345 milligrams potassium; vitamin A 32%; thiamin 5%; riboflavin 7%; vitamin C 160%

1½ teaspoons Oriental sesame oil
1 tablespoon sesame seeds
1 pound (450 g) broccoli, trimmed,
   peeled and cut into florets and coins
   (about 5 cups; 1.2 l)

½ teaspoon tamari soy
1 teaspoon rice wine vinegar

1. Toss together oil, sesame seeds and broccoli in a 13 × 10 × 2-inch (33 × 25.5 × 5-cm) dish. Push the florets into the center of the dish and coins around the inside edge. Cover tightly with microwave plastic wrap. Cook at 100% for 4 minutes in a 650- to 700-watt oven. Prick plastic to release steam.

2. Remove from oven and uncover. Add soy and vinegar and toss to coat.

FOR 400- TO 500-WATT OVEN

To serve 4. Cook for 8 minutes.

BROCCOLI PURÉE

Broccoli purée can be a low-calorie stand-in for mashed potatoes. Serve it with meat loaf, burgers and stews as well as simpler meats.   *SERVES 10 AS A SIDE DISH*

Per ½-cup (120-ml) serving: 87 calories; 13 milligrams cholesterol; 4 grams fat; 81 milligrams sodium; 8 grams protein (18% RDA); 8 grams carbohydrate

RDA: calcium 16%; phosphorus 15%; 345 milligrams potassium; vitamin A 35%; riboflavin 12%; vitamin C 159%

2½ pounds (1.15 kg) broccoli (2 bunches), trimmed, stems peeled and cut into florets and coins (about 12½ cups; 3 l)

2 cups (470 ml) part-skim ricotta cheese (16 ounces; 450 g)
Kosher salt, to taste

1. Arrange broccoli in a 14×11×2-inch (35.5×28×5-cm) rectangular dish with florets in the center and coins around the inside edge. Cover tightly with microwave plastic wrap. Cook at 100% for 8 minutes in a 650- to 700-watt oven. Prick plastic to release steam.

2. Leaving dish in oven, uncover and stir. Re-cover and cook for 2 minutes more. Prick plastic wrap.

3. Remove from oven and uncover. Transfer to a food processor. Add ricotta and salt and process until smooth.

FOR 400- TO 500-WATT OVENS

To serve 6. Use 1¼ pounds (570 g) broccoli, 8 ounces (240 ml) ricotta and salt to taste. Follow Step 1 and cook in a 13×9×2-inch (33×23×5-cm) oval dish for 12 minutes. In Step 2 cook for 4 minutes. Finish as in Step 3.

Peel broccoli stems with a vegetable peeler or small knife.

Arrange broccoli cut into slim stalks in a dish so that floret ends are toward the center.

For basic cooking times and nutrition, see pages 78–79.

GARLIC SPINACH

One of my favorite spinach dishes in Italian restaurants used to be prepared aglio-olio, with garlic and olive oil. Once I figured out how many calories all that olive oil was costing me, I stopped ordering it. Instead, I perfected this microwave version. The recipe can be easily multiplied by using the cooking times for spinach and the timings for Garlic to Go. _SERVES 2_

Per ½-cup (120-ml) serving: 134 calories; 0 milligrams cholesterol; 10 grams fat; 314 milligrams sodium; 6 grams protein (12% RDA); 11 grams carbohydrate

RDA: calcium 19%; iron 26%; vitamin A 219%; riboflavin 19%; vitamin C 84%

1 pound (450 g) raw spinach, cooked (page 79), making about 1 cup (240 ml), or 2 10-ounce (284-g) packages frozen spinach, defrosted

⅓ cup (80 ml) Garlic to Go (page 470)

1. Place cooked spinach in a 1½-quart (1.5-l) soufflé dish. Pour over Garlic to Go and stir well to combine. Cook, uncovered, for 3 minutes or until hot in a 650- to 700-watt oven.
2. Remove from oven and serve hot.

FOR 400- TO 500-WATT OVENS

To serve 2. Cook for 5 minutes.

CREAMED SPINACH

I love the smoothness of creamed spinach; but usually it is laden with calories and cholesterol. This version is low in calories and other naughty things. Make as much or as little as you want by using the cooking times for spinach.   *SERVES 4*

Per generous ⅓-cup (80-ml) serving: 53 calories; 1.2 milligrams cholesterol; < 1 gram fat; 84 milligrams sodium; 4 grams protein (9% RDA); 9 grams carbohydrate

RDA: calcium 15%; phosphorus 9%; iron 8%; 331 milligrams potassium; vitamin A 112%; riboflavin 11%; vitamin C 30%

½ pound (340 g) fresh spinach, cooked (page 79) and drained, making about ½ cup (120 ml), or 1 10-ounce (284-g) package frozen spinach, defrosted in a sieve under warm running water and drained

1 cup (240 ml) Thick Béchamel (page 510)

1. Place spinach in a food processor and process until finely chopped. Stir in Béchamel and process until well combined.

2. Transfer mixture to a 1-quart (1-l) soufflé dish. Cook, uncovered, at 100% for 1 minute 30 seconds in a 650- to 700-watt oven.

FOR 400- TO 500-WATT OVENS

To serve 2. Cook for 3 minutes.

CARROTS

Carrots are the home of vitamin A in its best form, beta-carotene. They keep their texture without getting mushy with microwave cooking.

PER 4 OUNCES (113.5 G) RAW CARROTS: 49 calories; 0 milligrams cholesterol; .2 gram fat; 40 milligrams sodium; 1.2 grams protein (2.6% RDA); 11 grams carbohydrate

RDA: calcium 3%; phosphorus 5%; iron 3%; 366 milligrams potassium; vitamin A 638%; thiamin 7%; riboflavin 4%; niacin 5%; vitamin C 18%

Peel and cut into 2½ × ¼-inch (6 × .5-cm) julienne or into ¼-inch (.5-cm) rounds. Place in dish specified below and cover tightly with microwave plastic wrap. Eight ounces (227 g) carrots, trimmed and sliced into rounds or julienne, yields 1½ cups (355 ml) raw and a scant ½ cup (180 ml) cooked.

4 ounces (113.5 g) carrots in a 1½-quart (1.5-l) soufflé dish
650- to 700-watt oven: 4 min.
400- to 500-watt oven: 6 min.

8 ounces (227 g) carrots in a 1½-quart (1.5-l) soufflé dish
650- to 700-watt oven: 6 min. 30 sec.
400- to 500-watt oven: 9 min. 30 sec.

1 pound (450 g) carrots in a 13 × 10 × 2-inch (33 × 25.5 × 5-cm) dish
650- to 700-watt oven: 8 min.
400- to 500-watt oven: 12 min.

1½ pounds (680 g) carrots in a 13 × 10 × 2-inch (33 × 25.5 × 5-cm) dish
650- to 700-watt oven: 10 min.
400- to 500-watt oven: Not recommended

2 pounds (900 g) carrots in a 14 × 11 × 2-inch (35.5 × 28 × 2-cm) dish
650- to 700-watt oven: 11 min.
400- to 500-watt oven: Not recommended

ORIENTAL CARROTS

*T*his unusually flavored carrot dish is a good accompaniment to bland foods simply prepared or in cream sauce. You can multiply or divide the recipe by using the standard cooking times above.   *SERVES 4*

Per scant ½-cup (120-ml) serving: 65 calories; 0 milligrams cholesterol; 2 grams fat; 204 milligrams sodium; 1 gram protein (3% RDA); 11 grams carbohydrate

RDA: vitamin A 568%; vitamin C 16%

1 pound (450 g) carrots, peeled and cut
   on the diagonal into ⅛-inch (.5-cm)
   slices (about 1½ cups; 355 ml)
1 teaspoon grated fresh ginger

1½ teaspoons Oriental sesame oil
2 teaspoons tamari soy
1 teaspoon sesame seeds
1 teaspoon rice wine vinegar

1. Place carrots in a 2½-quart (2.5-l) soufflé dish. Add ginger, sesame oil, tamari and sesame seeds and stir to combine. Cover tightly with microwave plastic wrap. Cook at 100% for 8 minutes in a 650- to 700-watt oven, stirring once. Prick plastic to release steam.
2. Remove from oven and uncover. Stir in rice wine vinegar. Serve hot.

FOR 400- TO 500-WATT OVENS

To serve 2. Cook for 12 minutes.

CARROT PURÉE

*C*arrots make a rich and richly beautiful purée. Multiply or divide by using basic cooking times above.   *SERVES 4*

Per ⅓-cup (80-ml) serving: 118 calories; 19 milligrams cholesterol; 5 grams fat; 103 milligrams sodium; 8 grams protein (17% RDA); 11 grams carbohydrate

RDA: calcium 19%; phosphorus 15%; vitamin A 433%

¾ pound (340 g) carrots, trimmed, peeled and cut across into ¼-inch (.5-cm) rounds (about 2¼ cups; 530 ml)

1 cup (240 ml) part-skim ricotta cheese

1. Place carrots in a 9-inch (23-cm) pie plate. Cover tightly with microwave plastic wrap. Cook at 100% for 9 minutes in a 650- to 700-watt oven. Prick plastic to release steam.
2. Remove from oven and uncover. Reserve.
3. Place ricotta in work bowl of food processor and purée until completely smooth. Add carrots and process until combined.
4. Scrape mixture into a 2-cup (470-ml) glass measure. Cover with microwave plastic wrap and reheat for 3 minutes. Prick plastic to release steam.
5. Remove from oven and uncover.

FOR 400- TO 500-WATT OVENS

To serve 4. Cook as in Step 1 for 12 minutes. Proceed with Steps 2 and 3. Cook as in Step 4 for 6 minutes.

For basic tomato nutrition, see page 467.

BRAISED TOMATOES

*C*lassically American, but not requiring the traditional addition of sugar since the intensity of microwave cooking brings out all the tomato's natural sweetness. If weight loss isn't a concern, you can stir a little sugar, white or brown, into the chopped vegetables. These lightened stewed tomatoes are beautiful, healthy and a fabulous accompaniment to simple grilled, roasted and broiled foods, or serve one as a light first course. A leftover will be delicious, cold at lunch, with a sandwich.

This is one of those odd recipes that does not work well in a low-wattage oven; the tomatoes do not cook evenly. *SERVES 4*

Per 1 tomato and ¼-cup (60-ml) sauce serving: 59 calories; 0 milligrams cholesterol; .5 gram fat; 35 milligrams sodium; 2.4 grams protein (5% RDA); 13 grams carbohydrate

RDA: calcium 3%; phosphorus 6%; iron 7%; 549 milligrams potassium; vitamin A 47%; thiamin 9%; riboflavin 6%; niacin 7%; vitamin C 70%

4 tomatoes (each 8 ounces; 227 g), cored, and skin pricked several times with a fork	1 teaspoon cornstarch
	¼ cup (60 ml) water
	¼ teaspoon celery seeds
6 ounces (170 g) onion, peeled and diced	Freshly ground black pepper, to taste
	2 teaspoons fresh lemon juice
2 ribs celery, peeled and diced	

1. Place tomatoes evenly spaced around a 2½-quart (2.5-l) soufflé dish. Scatter over onions and celery.

2. Stir together cornstarch and water in a small bowl, making sure there are no lumps. Add celery seeds and black pepper and pour mixture over tomatoes. Cover tightly with microwave plastic wrap. Cook at 100% for 12 minutes in a 650- to 700-watt oven. Prick plastic to release steam.

3. Remove from oven and uncover. Stir lemon juice into liquid and serve tomatoes with vegetables and liquid spooned over.

PROVENÇALE TOMATOES

Years ago, I learned one of my favorite recipes from a friend of mine who cooks almost nothing else. Those who are not on a diet can find the original recipe in *Food for Friends*. The premise of that recipe was to cook the tomatoes in olive oil very slowly—over an hour—which drives out all the water, leaving only the purest tomato taste. This made good tomatoes even out of winter's pale imitations. Now, thanks to the rapid evaporation of liquid from uncovered food cooked in a microwave oven, I can produce a very good version of this dish more rapidly with less calories.

I serve these tomatoes with roast leg of lamb (page 374); but it would be equally good with Braised Pork and Vegetables (page 367), especially when the vegetables are mashed.

There are two recipes for this dish, one using small tomatoes—in which the portion can be doubled—and one using larger tomatoes, where each half-tomato should be a portion. If you look at the nutrition for a half-tomato in each recipe, you will see that the larger-tomato portion contains roughly twice the amount of everything that's in the smaller. That's why you can double the portion.

Leftover tomatoes are good cold with lunch.

Provençale Tomatoes 1

SERVES 8 AS A SIDE DISH, 4 AS A FIRST COURSE

Per ½-tomato serving: 28 calories; .2 milligram cholesterol; .9 gram fat; 30 milligrams sodium; .8 gram protein (1.8% RDA); 4 grams carbohydrate

RDA: vitamin A 9%; vitamin C 11%

4 medium-size ripe tomatoes (each weighing about 3 ounces; 85 g)

6 tablespoons Seasoned Bread Crumbs (page 479)

1. Core tomatoes and prick all over with a fork. Cut in half horizontally and remove the seeds. Allow to drain a few minutes, skin side up, on paper towels.
2. Place skin side down around the inside edge of a 10-inch (25.5-cm) quiche dish. Cook, uncovered, at 100% for 4 minutes in a 650- to 700-watt oven. Preheat broiler.
3. Remove from microwave oven. Sprinkle bread crumbs over tomatoes evenly and brown under the broiler for a few minutes.
4. Remove from broiler and serve hot.

To serve 8. Prepare tomatoes as in Steps 1 and 2 and cook for 6 minutes, giving each piece a half-turn (180°) once. Finish recipe as in Steps 3 and 4.

Provençale Tomatoes 2

SERVES 4 AS A FIRST COURSE OR SIDE DISH

Per ½-tomato serving: 60 calories; .3 milligram cholesterol; 1.8 grams fat; 62 milligrams sodium; 1.8 grams protein (4% RDA); 10 grams carbohydrate

RDA: vitamin A 23%; thiamin 6%; vitamin C 30%

2 large tomatoes (each weighing about 8 ounces; 227 g)	6 tablespoons Seasoned Bread Crumbs (page 479)

1. Core tomatoes and prick all over with a fork. Cut in half horizontally and remove seeds. Allow to drain, skin side up, on paper towels. Preheat broiler.

2. Place in a 10-inch (25.5-cm) quiche dish. Cook, uncovered, at 100% for 2 minutes 30 seconds in a 650- to 700-watt oven.

3. Remove from microwave oven and sprinkle bread crumbs over. Brown under broiler for a few minutes.

4. Remove from broiler and serve hot.

To serve 4. Prepare tomatoes as in Steps 1 and 2 and cook for 4 minutes, giving each piece a half-turn (180°) once. Finish recipe as in Steps 3 and 4.

Ways to Prepare Tomatoes

Core tomatoes deeply with a small knife to remove all pale pith.

Cut into chunks.

Halve across and remove seeds with your finger.

Crosswise tomato slices, 1-inch (2.5-cm) cubes and wedges

CHINESE STEWED TOMATOES

*T*his was one of my favorite recipes in *Microwave Gourmet*. By the time I got to cooking it for this book, my taste had changed along with my point of view and I wanted less salt, less fat. It still tastes marvelous and can be used cold as a relish. If you like that idea, make the larger quantity. If you cut the tomatoes in small pieces before cooking, this will make a delicious, chunky sauce.   *SERVES 2*

Per ¾ cup (180-ml) serving: 53 calories; 0 milligrams cholesterol; 3 grams fat; 82 milligrams sodium; 1.3 grams protein (3% RDA); 7 grams carbohydrate

RDA: 244 milligrams potassium; vitamin A 28%; vitamin C 34%

1 clove garlic, smashed and peeled
½ scallion, green and white parts, cut
   into ½-inch (1-cm) pieces
2 tablespoons coriander leaves
1 teaspoon vegetable oil
2 small tomatoes (each about 4 ounces,
   113.5 g), cored and cut into 8
   wedges (about 1½ cups; 355 ml)

1 teaspoon Chinese salted black beans
1 teaspoon water
1 teaspoon rice wine vinegar
1½ teaspoons cornstarch

1. Place garlic, scallion and coriander leaves in a food processor. Process until coarsely chopped. Scrape into an $8 \times 8 \times 2$-inch ($20 \times 20 \times 5$-cm) dish. Stir in oil and cook, uncovered, at 100% for 2 minutes in a 650- to 700-watt oven.

2. Remove from oven. Stir in tomatoes and black beans. Cover tightly with microwave plastic wrap and cook for 2 minutes. Prick plastic to release steam.

3. Remove from oven and uncover. Stir together water, vinegar and cornstarch in a small bowl, making sure there are no lumps. Stir into tomato mixture and cook, uncovered, for 1 minute 30 seconds.

4. Remove from oven. Stir to combine and serve.

To serve 8. Use 6 cloves garlic, 2 scallions, ½ cup (120 ml) coriander leaves, 1 tablespoon vegetable oil, 8 medium tomatoes, 4 teaspoons black beans, 4 teaspoons water, 4 teaspoons rice wine vinegar and 2 tablespoons cornstarch. Cook as in Step 1 in a $14 \times 11 \times 2$-inch ($35.5 \times 28 \times 5$-cm) dish for 4 minutes. Cook as in Step 2 for 10 minutes. Finish as in Step 3, cooking for 3 minutes.

To serve 4. Use 2 cloves garlic, 1 scallion, ¼ cup (60 ml) coriander leaves, 2 teaspoons vegetable oil, 4 medium tomatoes, 2 teaspoons black beans, 2 teaspoons water, 2 teaspoons rice wine vinegar and 3 teaspoon cornstarch. Cook as in Step 1 in a $13 \times 10 \times 2$-inch ($33 \times 28 \times 5$-cm) dish for 4 minutes. Cook as in Step 2 for 4 minutes. Finish as in Step 3, cooking for 3 minutes.

To serve 2. Cook as in Step 1 for 3 minutes. Continue with Step 2, cooking for 3 minutes. Cook as in Step 3 for 2 minutes 30 seconds.

To serve 4. Cook as in Step 1 for 6 minutes. Cook as in Step 2 for 6 minutes. Finish as in Step 3, cooking for 5 minutes.

STEWED ARTICHOKE HEARTS

Good emergency rations—the artichoke hearts are in the freezer. Make it on a day when you want something saucy to go with a simple main course. There is enough good liquid to moisten your rice or noodles.   *SERVES 6*

Per ½-cup (120-ml) serving: 50 calories; 0 milligrams cholesterol; .6 gram fat; 50 milligrams sodium; 3 grams protein (6% RDA); 10 grams carbohydrate

RDA: phosphorus 5%; 234 milligrams potassium; riboflavin 7%; vitamin C 11%

2 9-ounce (255-g) boxes frozen
    artichoke hearts, defrosted in a sieve
    under warm running water
2 tablespoons cornstarch
1 cup (240 ml) Basic Chicken Broth
    (page 460), or unsalted or regular
    canned chicken broth

⅓ cup (80 ml) chopped fresh dill
2 tablespoons fresh lemon juice

1. Place artichoke hearts in a 2½-quart (2.5-l) soufflé dish or casserole with a tightly fitted lid. Stir together cornstarch and broth in a small bowl, making sure there are no lumps, and stir into artichokes. Cover tightly with microwave plastic wrap or with lid. Cook at 100% for 5 minutes in a 650- to 700-watt oven. If using plastic wrap, prick to release steam.
2. Remove from oven and uncover. Add dill and stir well. Re-cover and cook for 1 minute. If using plastic wrap, prick to release steam.
3. Remove from oven and uncover. Stir in lemon juice and serve.

To serve 6. Cook as in Step 1 for 8 minutes. Cook as in Step 2 for 2 minutes.

STEWED OKRA

You may think that you hate okra; but you won't once you've had it cooked in a microwave oven, where it remains green and stays slightly crisp without getting gooey. When trimming the stem end, try not to cut into the pod, revealing the little tubes inside. Stewed okra goes as well with complex but dry dishes, such as Jambalaya (page 323), as with simply cooked dishes. *SERVES 6*

Per generous ½-cup (120-ml) serving: 59 calories; 0 milligrams cholesterol; 2 grams fat; 132 milligrams sodium; 2 grams protein (4% RDA); 8 grams carbohydrate

RDA: calcium 6%; phosphorus 5%; iron 6%; vitamin A 23%; thiamin 8%; riboflavin 3%; niacin 4%; vitamin C 40%

¼ pound (113.5 g) onion, peeled and thinly sliced (about 1⅓ cups; 320 ml)

3 cloves garlic, smashed and peeled

1 tablespoon olive oil

1 pound (450 g) tomatoes, cut into wedges (about 3 cups; 705 ml)

½ pound (227 g) fresh okra, stem end trimmed, or 1 10-ounce (284-g) box frozen okra, defrosted in a sieve under warm running water

¼ cup (60 ml) fresh basil leaves, cut across into chiffonade

½ teaspoon kosher salt

1. Place onion, garlic and oil in a 2½-quart (2.5-l) soufflé dish or casserole with a tightly fitted lid. Cook, uncovered, at 100% for 3 minutes in a 650- to 700-watt oven.

2. Stir in tomatoes and okra. Cover tightly with microwave plastic wrap or casserole lid. Cook for 6 minutes (if using frozen okra, cook for 4 minutes). If using plastic, prick to release steam.

3. Leaving dish in oven, uncover carefully. Cook, uncovered, for 3 minutes.

4. Remove from oven. Stir in basil and salt and serve.

FOR 400- TO 500-WATT OVENS

To serve 6. Cook as in Step 1 for 5 minutes. In Step 2, cook for 12 minutes (if using frozen okra, cook for 6 minutes). Cook for 4 minutes (if using frozen okra, cook for 5 minutes) in Step 3. Finish as in Step 4.

BRAISED CELERY HEARTS

While this certainly makes a nice light side dish, you can also use it as a first course. Don't increase the portion, even though the calories are low, if you are watching your sodium. Celery has lots. *SERVES 4*

Per 1-celery-heart serving: 19 calories; 0 milligrams cholesterol; .2 gram fat; 192 milligrams sodium; 1 gram protein (2% RDA); 4 grams carbohydrate

RDA: vitamin C 12%

4 heads celery (each 1½ pounds; 680 g)　　　½ teaspoon fresh lemon juice
¼ cup (60 ml) Basic Chicken Broth
　　(page 460), or Vegetarian Broth II
　　(page 466), or unsalted or regular
　　canned chicken broth

1. Remove outer ribs of celery, leaving a celery heart with about 7 ribs (3 ounces; 85 g). Peel base of celery heart with a vegetable peeler and cut remaining heart into quarters lengthwise.

2. Arrange quarters spoke-fashion in a single layer with the root end toward the edge of the dish in a 10-inch (25.5-cm) pie plate or quiche dish. Pour over broth and lemon juice. Cover tightly with microwave plastic wrap. Cook at 100% for 10 minutes in a 650- to 700-watt oven. Prick plastic to release steam.

3. Remove from oven and uncover. Let stand 3 minutes before serving.

To serve 2. Use 2 heads celery, 2 tablespoons broth and ¼ teaspoon lemon juice. Prepare as in Step 1. Arrange as in Step 2 in an 8½ × 4½ × 2½-inch (21.5 × 11 × 6-cm) loaf pan. Cook for 7 minutes.

FOR 400- TO 500-WATT OVENS

To serve 4. Cook for 12 minutes.

To serve 2. Cook for 9 minutes.

Cut base from celery. Trim off stems to leave a 4-inch (10-cm) long heart.

Trim bottoms of hearts; peel outsides with a vegetable peeler.

Cut hearts lengthwise into quarters.

CURRIED CABBAGE

I think this is a spectacular and surprising dish to serve with chicken or fish. It's mildly spicy and quite smooth.   *SERVES 4*

Per ½-cup (120-ml) serving: 63 calories; <1 milligram cholesterol; 4 grams fat; 19 milligrams sodium; 2 grams protein (4% RDA); 7 grams carbohydrate

RDA: vitamin C 60%

1 tablespoon vegetable oil
1½ teaspoons curry powder
4 cups (1 l) shredded cabbage
4 ounces (113.5 g) onion, peeled and
   thinly sliced

1½ teaspoons fresh lemon or lime juice
2 tablespoons nonfat yogurt

1. Stir together oil and curry powder in a 13 × 10 × 2-inch (33 × 25.5 × 5-cm) oval dish. Cook, uncovered, at 100% for 2 minutes in a 650- to 700-watt oven.

2. Remove from oven and add cabbage and onion. Stir well to coat with the mixture. Cover tightly with microwave plastic wrap. Cook at 100% for 12 minutes, stirring once halfway through cooking. Prick plastic to release steam.

3. Remove from oven and uncover. Stir in remaining ingredients and serve.

FOR 400- TO 500-WATT OVENS

To serve 4. Cook as in Step 1 for 3 minutes. Cook as in Step 2 for 20 minutes, stirring once halfway through cooking.

ACORN SQUASH

I love simply cooked acorn squash. You can sprinkle it with balsamic vinegar, honey, maple syrup or lemon juice before cooking if you like; but I love it plain. Moreover, acorn squash is low in calories and a good source of carbohydrate; have a half instead of a baked potato.

PER 1 WHOLE ACORN SQUASH (8 OUNCES; 217 G) SERVING 2, WITH 3.44 OUNCES (97.5 G) OF FLESH EACH: 39 calories; 0 milligrams cholesterol; 0 grams fat; 3 milligrams sodium; .8 gram protein (2% RDA); 10 grams carbohydrate

YIELD: 1 pound (450 g) of acorn squash, cooked, yields ¾ cup (180 ml) purée.

RDA OF 2 SERVINGS: calcium 3%; phosphorus 4%; iron 4%; 338 milligrams potassium; vitamin A 7%; thiamin 9%; niacin 3%; vitamin C 18%

Cut squash in half. Remove seeds and fibers. Place in a dish just large enough to hold the halves and cover tightly with microwave plastic wrap.

8 ounces (227 g) squash
650- to 700-watt oven: 5 min.
400- to 500-watt oven: 7 min.

1 pound (450 g) squash
650- to 700-watt oven: 7 min.
400- to 500-watt oven: 10 min.

1½ pounds (680 g) squash
650- to 700-watt oven: 13 min.
400- to 500-watt oven: 19 min.

2 pounds (900 g) squash
650- to 700-watt oven: 15 min.
400- to 500-watt oven: Not recommended

RUTABAGA PURÉE

*B*ig, hard, yellow-fleshed winter turnips, which have a strong flavor, are not everybody's pleasure; but I think you will find they have a wonderful taste when diluted, as in this purée.   *SERVES 8*

Per ½-cup (120-ml) serving: 66 calories; 8 milligrams cholesterol; 2 grams fat; 240 milligrams sodium; 4 grams protein (10% RDA); 8 grams carbohydrate

RDA: calcium 13%; phosphorus 11%; iron 3%; vitamin A 3%; thiamin 4%; riboflavin 5%; niacin 3%; vitamin C 31%

1½ pounds (680 g) rutabaga, peeled
   and cut into 1-inch (2.5-cm) cubes
   (about 3 cups; 705 ml)
½ cup (120 ml) water
¾ cup (180 ml) part-skim ricotta
   cheese

¾ cup (180 ml) skim milk
1 teaspoon kosher salt
½ teaspoon ground cumin

1. Place rutabaga and water in an 8-cup (2-l) glass measure. Cover tightly with microwave plastic wrap. Cook at 100% for 15 minutes in a 650- to 700-watt oven. Prick plastic to release steam.

2. Remove from oven and uncover. Place in a food processor and process until smooth (mixture will be somewhat lumpy). Add remaining ingredients and process again until smooth.

FOR 400- TO 500-WATT OVENS

To serve 8. Cook for 27 minutes.

Vegetable Meals

You don't have to be a vegetarian to adore these vegetable meals, particularly in spring and summer when the vegetables are so good. They may be helpful when your other meal of the day has had more meat than usual, or even to follow a day of animal-protein self-indulgence.

SUMMER VEGETABLE STEW

Make this when the vegetables are at their peak. It's very pretty and good enough to be the base of a vegetarian meal. Serve it with some steamed new potatoes (page 220). Start with a soup. Add some bread and finish with a summery fruit dessert.   *SERVES 6 AS A SIDE DISH, 4 AS A MAIN COURSE*

Per scant 1-cup (240-ml) serving: 100 calories; 10 milligrams cholesterol; 4 grams fat; 143 milligrams sodium; 4 grams protein (9% RDA); 14 grams carbohydrate

RDA: phosphorus 10%; iron 10%; vitamin A 212%; thiamin 12%; vitamin C 52%

1½ pounds (680 g) zucchini (about 3 small zucchini), quartered lengthwise and cut across into ½-inch (1-cm) slices (about 6 cups; 1.5 l)

½ pound (227 g) carrots (3 medium carrots), peeled and thinly sliced (about 1½ cups; 355 ml)

3 cloves garlic, smashed, peeled and sliced

6 ounces (170 g) string beans, tipped, tailed and halved crosswise (about 1¾ cups; 410 ml)

1 cup (240 ml) fresh peas (shelled, about 6 ounces; 170 g), or same amount of frozen peas, defrosted in a sieve under warm running water

¼ cup (60 ml) chopped fresh parsley

¼ cup (60 ml) whole fresh tarragon leaves

2 tablespoons unsalted butter

½ teaspoon kosher salt, or to taste

1. Place zucchini, carrots and garlic in a 2½-quart (2.5-l) soufflé dish. Cover tightly with microwave plastic wrap. Cook at 100% for 6 minutes in a 650- to 700-watt oven. Prick plastic to release steam.

2. Remove from oven and uncover. Stir in remaining ingredients except tarragon, butter and salt. Cover tightly with microwave plastic wrap. Cook at 100% for 8 minutes. Prick plastic to release steam.

(continued)

3. Remove from oven. Uncover and stir in tarragon. Cook, uncovered, for 3 minutes more.

4. Remove from oven. Stir in butter and salt and serve hot.

To serve 3. Use ¾ pound (340 g) zucchini, ¼ pound (113.5 g) carrots, 2 small cloves garlic, 3 ounces (85 g) string beans, ½ cup (120 ml) peas, 2 tablespoons each parsley and tarragon, 1 tablespoon butter and ¼ teaspoon salt. Cook as in Step 1 for 4 minutes. Cook as in Step 2 for 6 minutes. Finish as in Steps 3 and 4, cooking for 2 minutes.

FOR 400- TO 500-WATT OVENS

To serve 6. Cook as in Step 1 for 10 minutes. Cook as in Step 2 for 15 minutes. Finish as in Steps 3 and 4, cooking for 5 minutes.

To serve 3. Cook as in Step 1 for 6 minutes. Cook as in Step 2 for 8 minutes. Finish as in Steps 3 and 4, cooking for 3 minutes.

RATATOUILLE

*T*his nonclassic ratatouille can be used in half-portions as a side dish; but it comes into its own as the centerpiece of a vegetarian meal. Put it, with all those happy vitamins, over cooked pasta or cooked barley (page 196), serve with a green salad, lots of bread, a glass of wine and a piece of cheese, and feel free to have dessert.   *SERVES 8*

Per 1-cup (240-ml) serving: 144 calories; 0 milligrams cholesterol; 8 grams fat; 292 milligrams sodium; 4 grams protein (10% RDA); 19 grams carbohydrate

RDA: phosphorus 10%; iron 15%; vitamin 37%; thiamin 13%; vitamin C 135%

1 large eggplant (1¼ pounds; 570 g), cut into 1-inch (2.5-cm) cubes (about 8⅔ cups; 2.2 l)

1 large onion (¾ pound; 340 g), peeled, halved and thinly sliced (about 3 cups; 705 ml)

12 cloves garlic, smashed and peeled

¼ cup (60 ml) well-flavored olive oil

3 small yellow squash (about 1¼ pounds; 570 g), halved lengthwise and cut into ½-inch (1-cm) slices (about 5 cups; 1.2 l)

2 pounds (900 g) tomatoes, cored and cut into ½-inch (1-cm) cubes (about 4½ cups; 1.1 l)

1½ teaspoons dried oregano

1½ teaspoons dried thyme

2 bell peppers (each 6 ounces; 170 g), stemmed, seeded, deribbed and cut into 1-inch (2.5-cm) squares (about 2 cups; 470 ml)

1 jalepeño pepper, seeded and thinly sliced

¼ cup (60 ml) chopped fresh parsley

¼ cup (60 ml) fresh basil chiffonade

1½ teaspoons kosher salt, or to taste

Freshly ground black pepper, to taste

1. Place eggplant, onion, garlic and oil in a 13 × 9 × 2-inch (33 × 23 × 5-cm) oval glass dish. Cook, uncovered, at 100% for 15 minutes in a 650- to 700-watt oven, stirring every 5 minutes.

2. Add squash, tomatoes, oregano and thyme. Cover tightly with microwave plastic wrap. Cook at 100% for 5 minutes. Prick plastic to release steam.

3. Remove from oven and uncover. Add bell peppers, hot peppers and parsley. Re-cover and cook at 100% for 5 minutes. Prick plastic to release steam.

4. Leaving dish in oven, uncover and cook for 12 minutes, stirring once. Remove from oven. Add basil, salt and pepper and serve hot or at room temperature.

To serve 4. Use ¾ pound (340 g) eggplant, 6 ounces (170 g) onion, 6 cloves garlic, 2 tablespoons oil, 1½ yellow squash (about 9 ounces; 255 g), 1 pound (450 g) tomatoes, ¾ teaspoon each oregano and thyme, 1 bell pepper (about 6 ounces; 170 g), ½ jalepeño pepper, 2 tablespoons each parsley and basil, ¾ teaspoon salt and pepper to taste. Cook as in Step 1 for 10 minutes, stirring 3 times. Continue as in Step 2, cooking for 3 minutes. Stir in peppers and parsley. Cook as in Step 3 for 3 minutes. Finish as in Step 4, cooking for 8 minutes.

FOR 400- TO 500-WATT OVENS

To serve 8. Cook as in Step 1 for 25 minutes, stirring 3 times. Cook as in Step 2 for 8 minutes. Continue cooking as in Step 3 for 8 minutes. Finish as in Step 4, cooking for 20 minutes and stirring twice.

To serve 4. Cook as in Step 1 for 15 minutes, stirring 3 times. Cook as in Step 2 for 5 minutes. Continue cooking as in Step 3 for 5 minutes. Finish as in Step 4, cooking for 12 minutes and stirring once.

VEGETABLE COUSCOUS

*T*he tiny Moroccan pasta, couscous, loves to sop up stew juices. It does just as well with a vegetable stew as with a meat one—perhaps better. When you look at the calories, remember that they include the couscous too. That's a lot of food, and you can still have a main course and dessert. It's a spectacular party dish. Put the couscous in a giant ring on a large round platter. Pour the vegetables into the center of the ring. Let everyone serve themselves.   *SERVES 6*

Per 1⅓ cups (320 ml) couscous with 1 cup (240 ml) vegetables serving: 295 calories; 0 milligrams cholesterol; 1 gram fat; 480 milligrams sodium; 11 grams protein (24% RDA); 66 grams carbohydrate

RDA: iron 19%; vitamin A 168%; thiamin 25%; niacin 20%; vitamin C 84%

3 cups (705 ml) tomato juice

6 garlic cloves, smashed, peeled and minced

FOR SPICE MIXTURE

½ teaspoon anise seeds

1 teaspoon ground cumin

1 teaspoon ground coriander

1 teaspoon ground ginger

⅛ teaspoon ground allspice

⅛ teaspoon ground nutmeg

½ teaspoon crushed red pepper flakes

½ teaspoon ground cardamom

¼ teaspoon ground cinnamon

6 ounces (170 g) carrots, peeled and cut into half-moons ½ inch (1 cm) thick (about 1 cup; 240 ml)

6 ounces (170 g) turnips, peeled and cut into ½-inch (1-cm) cubes (about 1⅓ cups; 320 ml)

8 ounces (227 g) eggplant, cut into 1-inch (2-cm) cubes (about 2 cups; 470 ml)

4 ounces (113.5 g) okra, defrosted in a sieve under warm running water, if frozen

4 ounces (113.5 g) frozen pearl onions, defrosted in a sieve under warm running water

4 ounces (113.5 g) drained, vacuum-packed canned corn niblets

1 pound (450 g) asparagus, woody stems snapped off, peeled and cut into 1-inch (2-cm) lengths (about 3½ cups; 825 ml)

2½ cups (590 ml) water

2½ cups (590 ml) uncooked instant couscous or regular couscous (page 181)

1 tablespoon chopped mint, optional

1.   Combine tomato juice, garlic and spice mixture in a small bowl. Pour 1 cup (240 ml) of this mixture into a 14 × 11 × 2-inch (35.5 × 28 × 5-cm) rectangular dish. Arrange carrots and turnips around the inside edge of the dish and place eggplant pieces in the center. Cover tightly with microwave plastic wrap. Cook at 100% for 9 minutes in a 650- to 700-watt oven. Prick plastic to release steam.

2. Remove from oven and uncover. With a spatula, move eggplant to the edge of the dish with the carrots and turnips. Arrange okra in a ring inside the other vegetables, with pearl onions in a ring inside the okra and the corn in the center. Scatter asparagus over all. Cover tightly and cook for 4 minutes. Prick plastic wrap.

3. Remove from oven and uncover. Keep warm while preparing the couscous.

4. Place remaining tomato juice mixture and water in a $13 \times 9 \times 2$-inch ($33 \times 23 \times 5$-cm) dish. Cover and cook for 4 minutes. Prick plastic wrap.

5. Remove from oven and uncover. Stir in instant couscous, re-cover and allow the mixture to stand 8 minutes, or until all liquid has been absorbed. See page 181 if using regular couscous.

6. Uncover and toss couscous with a fork to break up any lumps. To serve, mound couscous in a ring on a large serving platter. Place vegetables and their cooking liquid in the center. Sprinkle with chopped fresh mint, if desired.

FOR 400- TO 500-WATT OVENS

To serve 6. Arrange ingredients as in Step 1 in a $13 \times 9 \times 2$-inch ($33 \times 23 \times 5$-cm) oval dish. Cook for 15 minutes. Continue with Step 2, cooking for 15 minutes. Finish as in Step 3, and prepare couscous on top of the stove, according to manufacturer's instructions. Serve as in Step 6.

Vegetables arranged in concentric rings
with slowest-cooking vegetables
around the outside. Work toward
the center, placing quickest-cooking
vegetables in the center.

EGGPLANT SCALOPPINE

*T*his is one of those dishes that are meatless, but you won't feel any sense of loss or deprivation. You can have two slices as a main course with pasta, rice or any grain of your choice. One slice, a half-serving, is a good first course.

Sadly, the most that you can make in a low-wattage oven is four slices; the most in a 650- to 700-watt oven is six slices. However, these stay hot—cheese gets very hot in a microwave oven—and cook quickly, so it is feasible to have a second batch ready to slip into the oven as soon as the first batch comes out. That way you can serve this for from four to six people as a main course, depending on the wattage of your oven.   *SERVES 1 AS A MAIN COURSE, 2 AS A FIRST COURSE*

Per 2-slice serving: 255 calories; 42 milligrams cholesterol; 12 grams fat; 324 milligrams sodium; 20 grams protein (45% RDA); 19 grams carbohydrate

RDA: calcium 56%; phosphorus 41%; iron 16%; vitamin A 63%; riboflavin 19%; vitamin C 66%

3 ounces (85 g) eggplant, cut into 2
   slices, each ½ inch (1 cm) thick and
   4 inches (10 cm) across
2 tablespoons part-skim ricotta cheese
8 leaves fresh basil

½ cup (60 ml) Fresh Tomato Purée
   (page 468), or canned tomato purée
2 ounces (56 g) part-skim mozzarella
   cheese, grated (about ½ cup;
   120 ml)

*Eggplant cut in lengthwise and
crosswise (round) slices*

*Place eggplant on a flat surface.
Hold knife parallel to work surface
and cut across into slices.*

Cut slices lengthwise into strips.

Cut strips across into cubes.

1. Place eggplant in one layer in a 10-inch (25.5-cm) quiche dish or pie plate. Spread ricotta over eggplant and arrange basil leaves on ricotta.

2. Pour purée on top of basil and scatter mozzarella cheese over all. Cover tightly with microwave plastic wrap. Cook at 100% for 5 minutes in a 650- to 700-watt oven. Prick plastic to release steam.

3. Remove from oven and uncover. Serve hot.

To serve 2 as a main course, 4 as an appetizer. Use 4 slices eggplant, ¼ cup (60 ml) ricotta, 16 leaves basil, 1 cup (240 ml) purée and 4 ounces (113.5 g) mozzarella. Cook in a 9 × 13 × 2-inch (23 × 33 × 5-cm) oval dish as in Step 2 for 10 minutes.

To serve 3 as a main course, 6 as an appetizer. Use 6 slices eggplant, ⅓ cup (80 ml) ricotta, 24 basil leaves; 1½ cups (355 ml) purée and 6 ounces (170 g) mozzarella. Cook in a 11 × 14 × 2-inch (28 × 35.5.5-cm) dish as in Step 2 for 17 minutes.

FOR 400- TO 500-WATT OVENS

To serve 1 as a main course. Cook for 10 minutes.

To serve 2 as a main course. Cook for 15 minutes.

To serve 1 as a first course. Use 1½ ounces (42.5 g) eggplant, 1 tablespoon ricotta, 4 leaves basil, ¼ cup (60 ml) tomato purée and 1 ounce (28 g) mozzarella. Cook for 4 minutes.

STUFFED EGGPLANT

*I*f you can find small Japanese or Chinese eggplants, use four; halve them and proceed as below. You will still get an unspeakably nutritious and delicious main course. To lower the sodium content that comes from canned tomatoes, substitute Fresh Tomato Purée (page 468), using ¾ cup in Step 5 and ½ cup (120 ml) in Step 6.   *SERVES 4 AS A MAIN COURSE, 8 AS A FIRST COURSE*

Per half-eggplant serving: 195 calories; 0 milligrams cholesterol; 2 grams fat; 542 milligrams sodium; 6 grams protein (14% RDA); 42 grams carbohydrate

RDA: calcium 14%; phosphorus 19%; iron 18%; 902 milligrams potassium; vitamin A 16%; thiamin 23%; riboflavin 23%; niacin 16%; vitamin C 46%

2 medium eggplants (each about 1 pound; 450 g)
¾ cup (180 ml) water
½ cup (120 ml) bulgur
4 ounces (113.5 g) onion, peeled and coarsley chopped (about 1 cup; 240 ml)
3 cloves garlic, smashed, peeled and chopped
1 teaspoon vegetable oil

14 ounces (395 g) canned Italian plum tomatoes, drained, with the juice reserved
2 teaspoons chopped fresh mint
Freshly ground black pepper, to taste
2 teaspoons cornstarch
1 teaspoon kosher salt
Pinch cayenne pepper
3 tablespoons fresh lemon juice

1. Prick eggplants several times with a fork. Place on two layers of paper toweling directly on the carrousel of the oven. Cook, uncovered, at 100% for 12 minutes in a 650- to 700-watt oven. Remove from oven and let stand until cool.

2. When cool enough to handle, cut off stem ends and discard. Quarter each eggplant lengthwise and scoop out flesh with a spoon. Reserve flesh. Transfer eggplant-skin shells to a 14×11×2-inch (35.5×28×5-cm) dish and reserve.

3. Place water in a 2-cup (470-ml) glass measure. Cook, uncovered, for 3 minutes. Remove from oven and stir in bulgur. Cover loosely with paper toweling and let stand for 10 minutes while continuing with recipe.

4. Place onion, garlic and oil in a 2½-quart (2.5-l) soufflé dish. Cook, uncovered, for 3 minutes.

5. Remove from oven and scrape into the work bowl of a food processor. Add drained tomatoes and reserved eggplant. Process until coarsely chopped. Return mixture to soufflé dish and stir in bulgur, mint and black pepper. Mound about ½ cup (120 ml) stuffing into each reserved eggplant shell.

6. In a small bowl stir together cornstarch and tomato liquid, making sure there are no lumps. Add salt and cayenne. Pour mixture over stuffed eggplant shells. Cover tightly with microwave plastic wrap and cook for 9 minutes. Prick plastic to release steam.

7. Remove from oven and uncover. Pour over lemon juice and serve hot.

FOR 400- TO 500-WATT OVENS

To serve 4 as a first course. Use 1 eggplant, ⅓ cup (80 ml) water, ¼ cup (60 ml) bulgur, ½ onion (2 ounces; 60 g), 2 small cloves garlic, ½ teaspoon vegetable oil, 7 ounces (200 g) tomatoes, 1 teaspoon mint, pinch black pepper, 1 teaspoon cornstarch, ½ teaspoon salt, pinch cayenne and 1½ tablespoons lemon juice. Cook eggplants as in Step 1 for 10 minutes. Continue with Step 2. Heat water as in Step 3 for 4 minutes. Continue as in Step 4, cooking for 5 minutes. Cook as in Step 6 for 6 minutes.

*Arrange stuffed eggplant,
alternating wide ends with narrow
ends, in dish.*

BASICS, SAUCES AND SNACKS

―――――――――――――― ≈ ――――――――――――――

O *ne of the reasons restaurants can turn out so much food so rapidly and,*
seemingly, with less fuss than you or I is not just that they have so many
accomplished hands at work, but that they have their mise en place, basic prep-
arations, done ahead. It is a lesson well worth learning. They make their basics
just for the meal ahead. It makes more sense for the home cook to quickly make
enough for several meals in the microwave oven and to refrigerate these staples
to keep in the refrigerator or freezer—ready when needed.

There are few things that can make as much difference in the quality of your
food and the health of your diet as making some culinary basics from scratch.
Broths that used to take many hours can be made in twenty to forty minutes in
a microwave oven. They are better and cheaper than canned broths, bouillon
and stock cubes, and can be made without any salt. When tomatoes are in
season, ripe and inexpensive, is a good time to put up some Fresh Tomato Purée
for freezing. It will taste fresher and have less salt than anything you can buy.

The most important basics to start with are one or two stocks—perhaps
Basic Chicken Broth and Vegetarian Broth I—Egg White Mayonnaise, one or
two low-calorie salad dressings, Fresh Tomato Purée, Peanut Butter—if that's
one of your passions—a bread (pages 152–153) and some snack foods. If you
like spicy food, make Pickled Jalapeño Peppers. If you cannot find Fromage
Blanc in a nearby store, make it or Yogurt Cheese to eat with fruit and use in
your cooking or to provide a healthy snack.

Those basics should keep you happy and away from the temptation of salty,
caloric and cholesterol-ridden commercially prepared foods. Besides, your
homemade basics will taste better than commercial products. If you have the
homemade on hand, you will be able to make rapidly finished dishes full of
flavor and nutritious as well.

If you like ketchup, try making Early American Ketchup instead of ingesting
all the sodium and sweeteners in commercial varieties.

While most of these basics cook in the microwave oven in under a half hour,
some—such as many of the salad dressings—don't require any cooking. A
morning or afternoon will amply suffice to make the few basics that I have listed
above.

―――

Basic Broths

One of the real triumphs of the microwave oven is its ability to cook broths—the stocks basic to soups, stews and sauces—in twenty to forty minutes. I get real satisfaction from a beautifully made broth. I have been known to spend days on a double consommé for an elegant dinner and I probably will again; but some phases of that process have been shortened by the microwave oven. When it comes to broths for everyday use, I will never lug out the old, heavy stockpot again.

You can, if you prefer, add up to one cup of chopped vegetables and herbs to any basic broth recipe that makes four cups (1 l), and two cups of vegetables and herbs to one that makes eight cups (2 l), without changing anything else. Be careful; broths with vegetables or herbs will turn in hot weather unless refrigerated quickly.

My broths are unconventional in that they are made from nothing but bone or bone and meat—no seasonings, no vegetables. I find that this makes them most flexible in use and less likely to spoil, particularly on a hot day or in a hot kitchen. It is the vegetables that turn the soup. Also, I can always chop up any vegetables and herbs that I want in a food processor and infuse them into the premade broth for ten minutes in a microwave oven and get exactly the flavor I want. There is no longer any reason to make one dish taste very much like another just because the flavorings in the broth are the same and dominate.

Broths can be varied infinitely, but these are the basics. Freeze any you do not need right away in small amounts. Broths are not wildly nutritious unless they contain vegetables, so you will not find RDAs following a few of them. Also, the figures given are based on commercial products since it is not feasible to analyze homemade stocks. I always imagine homemade will be better. It certainly tastes better.

I also give numbers of servings; but it's slightly silly since these broths are usually used as ingredients in other dishes.

BASIC CHICKEN BROTH

*T*he message of many cultures makes me think that chicken broth is not just a cooking basic, but that it is the very basis of life itself. The chicken-soup remedy for colds is as widespread as are grandmothers, from China to Russia to America. There are even two medical studies, one from Mount Sinai Hospital in New York and another from England, that conclude that chicken soup may indeed have therapeutic value, mainly as a decongestant. What did Grandma tell you? If you want an old-fashioned chicken soup instead of broth, see page 120.

Basic Chicken Broth is basic in two other important ways: It is not in and of itself a soup, although the addition of a few seasonings, some vegetables or noodles will easily make it into one, and it is the base of many other dishes, a basic to keep in your kitchen and have on hand, refrigerated or in the freezer, so that it is always easy to make soups and stews in a hurry. *MAKES 4 CUPS (1 L), SERVES 4*

Per 1-cup (240-ml) serving: 30 calories; 0 milligrams cholesterol; 2 grams fat; 53 milligrams sodium; 2 grams protein (5% RDA); 2 grams carbohydrate

2 pounds (900 g) chicken bones and
  giblets or duck bones and giblets
  (except livers), without skin and fat
  if possible, cut into 2-inch (5-cm)
  pieces

4 cups (1 l) cold water

1. Combine bones and water in a 2½-quart (2.5-l) soufflé dish. Cover tightly with microwave plastic wrap. Cook at 100% for 20 minutes in a 650- to 700-watt oven; cook for 30 minutes for a strong broth and 40 minutes for a broth that will jell. Prick plastic to release steam.

2. Remove from oven. Uncover and strain broth through a fine sieve. Use or freeze in 1- or 2-cup portions. If you wish to skim the broth of fat, refrigerate until fat rises to the surface and skim with a large spoon.

To make 8 cups (2 l). Use 4 pounds (1.8 kg) bones and 8 cups (2 l) water. Cook as in Step 1 in a 5-quart (5-l) casserole covered with plastic wrap or a lid for 30 minutes; 45 minutes for a broth that will jell. Measure volume after cooking and add water if there has been any evaporation to have a full 8 cups (2 l).

FOR 400- TO 500-WATT OVENS

To make 4 cups (1 l). Cook for 45 minutes.

BASIC FISH BROTH

Basic fish broth can hardly be said to be as essential to most of the world's foods as chicken broth; but it is much more useful than many might think. In Provence and the Mediterranean in general, where fish is cheaper and more available than chicken, it is the base for a wide variety of dishes, including seafood stews.

When making Basic Fish Broth for general use, it is important to use only the heads and bones of white-fleshed fish; otherwise, it may be oily and have a darker color. The heads and bones of oily fish, including those of salmon, mackerel, sardines and sturgeon, are good if you are making a dish with those fish in it. Do not use the bones of flat fish such as sole or flounder, which tend to give a bitter taste to the broth.

A bitter-tasting broth can also occur if the gills and all blood have not been removed from the head and bones. The gills can be snipped out with a heavy-duty kitchen shears. The bones should be washed in running water to remove the blood.

You might like to try fish broth with pasta and some fennel or celery instead of a ubiquitous chicken soup with noodles. Garlic almost always goes well with fish broth, as do the Vietnamese and Thai seasonings, such as lemon grass and hot pepper.   *MAKES 4 CUPS (1 L), SERVES 4*

Per 1-cup (240-ml) serving: 46 calories; 22 milligrams cholesterol; <1 gram fat; 240 milligrams sodium; 6 grams protein (12% RDA); 5 grams carbohydrate

2 pounds (900 g) fish heads and bones, cleaned of any blood and cut into 2-inch (5-cm) pieces	4 cups (1 l) water, or 2 cups (470 ml) each of water and white wine

1. Combine bones and water in a 2½-quart (2.5-l) soufflé dish or casserole with a tightly fitted lid. Cover. Cook at 100% for 20 minutes in a 650- to 700-watt oven; cook for 30 minutes for a strong broth and 40 minutes for a broth that jells.

2. Remove from oven. Uncover and strain through a fine sieve lined with a dampened kitchen towel or cheesecloth.

To make 7 cups (1.7 l). Use 4 pounds (1.8 kg) bones and 8 cups (2 l) water or 4 cups (1 l) each of water and white wine in a 5-quart (5-l) casserole. Cover with lid and cook as in Step 1 for 60 minutes. Finish as in Step 2.

FOR 400- TO 500-WATT OVENS

To make 4 cups (1 l). Cook for 30 minutes, or 45 minutes for a jelling broth.

BASIC MEAT BROTH

While the recipe remains the same, the flavor varies wildly depending on the creature the bones come from. Lamb will quickly give the most strongly flavored broth, perfect for hot winter soups. Veal bones give a very gelatinous stock with a somewhat undefinable, but easily recognized on the second go-round, flavor that is ideal for giving texture to stews. Beef broth makes good soups and stews. Note that it is possible to use a combination of bones when making meat broth. A classic combination would be one part veal bones to two parts chicken or beef bones. The veal bones give a silky texture and a backbone, while the beef or chicken bones add the flavor top notes. *MAKES 4 CUPS (1 L), SERVES 4*

Per 1-cup (240-ml) serving: 18 calories; 0 milligrams cholesterol; .7 gram fat; 5 milligrams sodium; .5 gram protein (1% RDA); 3 grams carbohydrate

2 pounds (900 g) lamb, beef, chicken and/or veal bones, cut into 2-inch (5-cm) pieces

4 cups (1 l) water

1. Combine bones and water in a 2½-quart (2.5-l) soufflé dish. Cover tightly with microwave plastic wrap. Cook at 100% for 20 minutes in a 650- to 700-watt oven; cook for 30 minutes for a strong broth and 40 minutes for a broth that will jell. Prick plastic to release steam.
2. Remove from oven and uncover. Strain through a fine sieve and use immediately, refrigerate or freeze.

To make 8 cups (2 l). Use 4 pounds (1.8 kg) bones and 8 cups (2 l) water. Cook as in Step 1 in a 5-quart (5-l) casserole covered with plastic wrap or lid for 30 minutes. Measure volume after cooking and add water if there has been any evaporation so that you have 8 cups (2 l).

FOR 400- TO 500-WATT OVENS

To make 4 cups (1 l). Cook for 45 minutes.

RICH BEEF BROTH

This is a classic French meat broth or stock. When it is cooked, the meat can be used in a salad or a hash. The vegetables are best discarded.

MAKES 4 CUPS (1 L), SERVES 4

Per 1-cup (240-ml) serving: 27 calories; 5 milligrams cholesterol; 1 gram fat; 14 milligrams sodium; 2 grams protein (4% RDA); 3 grams carbohydrate

RDA: 95 milligrams potassium; vitamin A 20%

2 pounds (900 g) veal bones, cut into
    2-inch (5-cm) pieces
½ pound (227 g) lean beef stew meat
    (shin is good and cheap), cut into
    2-inch (5-cm) pieces
1 carrot (about 2½ ounces; 71 g),
    peeled and diced (about ½ cup;
    120 ml)

1 rib celery (2 ounces; 56 g), peeled
    and diced (about ¼ cup; 60 ml)
1 leek (4 ounces; 113.5 g), trimmed,
    cleaned and diced (about ¾ cup;
    180 ml)
4 cups (1 l) water

1. Combine all the ingredients for the broth in a 5-quart (5-l) soufflé or casserole with a tightly fitted lid. Cover tightly with microwave plastic wrap or casserole lid. Cook at 100% for 30 minutes in a 650- to 700-watt oven. If using plastic, prick to release steam and remove from oven.

2. Uncover and strain broth through a fine sieve. Measure volume after cooking and add water if there has been any evaporation so that you have 4 cups (1 l). Use or freeze in 1- or 2-cup portions. If you wish to skim the broth of fat, refrigerate until fat rises to the surface and skim with a large spoon.

FOR 400- TO 500-WATT OVENS

To make 4 cups (1 l). Cook as in Step 1 in a 2½-quart (2.5-l) soufflé dish or casserole with a lid for 45 minutes.

RICH VEAL BROTH

*T*his very concentrated broth has a beautiful color and a hint of sweetness. Use it in your most elegant veal dishes or sauces. A small oven evaporates the broth somewhat less, making four rather than three cups. It will be almost as strong. If you want a more intense broth from a small oven, continue to cook uncovered until it reduces slightly.   *MAKES 3 CUPS (705 ML), SERVES 3*

Per 1-cup (240-ml): 49 calories; 11 milligrams cholesterol; 4 grams fat; 43 milligrams sodium; <1 gram protein (<1% RDA); 3 grams carbohydrate

1 medium onion (4 ounces; 113.5 g),
   sliced thin
1 tablespoon butter

2½ pounds (1.15 kg) veal bones, cut
   into 2-inch (5-cm) pieces
4 cups (1 l) water

1. Combine onion and butter in a 5-quart (5-l) soufflé dish or casserole with a tightly fitted lid. Cover tightly with microwave plastic wrap or lid. Cook at 100% for 8 minutes in a 650- to 700-watt oven, or until onion is caramelized. If using plastic, prick to release steam.

2. Remove from oven and uncover. Add remaining ingredients, re-cover and cook for 40 minutes. If using plastic, prick to release steam.

3. Remove from oven and uncover. Strain broth through a fine sieve and use immediately, or refrigerate or freeze.

FOR 400- TO 500-WATT OVENS

To make 4 cups (1 l). Cook as in Step 1 for 12 minutes. Cook as in Step 2 for 60 minutes.

VEGETARIAN BROTH I

*T*his cloudy broth is greenish in color. It is best used in opaque soups and stews. If you want a clear green broth, omit the potato.   *MAKES 3 CUPS (705 ML), SERVES 3*

Per 1-cup (240-ml) serving: 28 calories; 0 milligrams cholesterol; <1 gram fat; 7 milligrams sodium; 1 gram protein (2% RDA); 6 grams carbohydrate

RDA: 199 grams potassium; vitamin C 14%

1 clove garlic, smashed, peeled and
   chopped
1 bay leaf
½ cup (120 ml) celery leaves
Stems from 1 bunch parsley
1 potato (10 ounces: 284 g), scrubbed
   and thinly sliced with its skin
½ medium onion (4 ounces; 113.5 g),
   peeled and coarsely chopped (about
   ½ cup; 120 ml)

½ ounce (14 g) dried mushrooms,
   broken into small pieces (about
   1 tablespoon)
1 cup (240 ml) spinach, washed and
   thinly sliced (about 8 ounces; 227 g)
4 cups (1 l) water

1. Stir together all ingredients in a 2½-quart (2.5-l) soufflé dish. Cover tightly with microwave plastic wrap. Cook at 100% for 16 minutes, or until potatoes are tender when pricked right through the plastic with the tip of a sharp knife, in a 650- to 700-watt oven. If the potatoes are not done, patch plastic and cook 2 minutes longer. Prick plastic to release steam.

2. Remove from oven. Uncover and strain through a fine sieve, being careful to press only lightly on the vegetables to extract broth.

FOR 400- TO 500-WATT OVENS

To make 3 cups (705 ml). Cook for 26 minutes.

STIRRING THROUGH PLASTIC WRAP

To stir food during cooking without removing plastic wrap, slit plastic with a knife.
Place a spoon through the slit and stir food. Patch plastic wrap.

VEGETARIAN BROTH II

Unlike the previous vegetarian broth, this one is clear. It has a paler color and somewhat more herbal flavor than the previous broth.
MAKES 3 CUPS (705 ML), SERVES 3

Per 1-cup serving: 25 calories; 0 milligrams cholesterol; 0 grams fat; 17 milligrams sodium; .8 gram protein (2% RDA); 6 grams carbohydrate

RDA: calcium 3%; iron 4%; 158 milligrams potassium; vitamin C 15%

4 cloves garlic, smashed and peeled
1 small onion (about 4 ounces;
   113.5 g), peeled and halved
Stems from 1 bunch parsley
1 medium carrot (about 4 ounces;
   113.5 g), trimmed, peeled and cut
   into 1-inch (2.5-cm) lengths

2 celery ribs, trimmed, peeled and cut
   into 1-inch (2.5-cm) lengths
4 cups (1 l) water
1 bay leaf
Pinch dried thyme
Pinch dried oregano

1. Place garlic, onion, parsley stems, carrot and celery in a food processor and process until coarsely chopped. Scrape into a 2½-quart (2.5-l) soufflé dish.

2. Add remaining ingredients. Cover tightly with microwave plastic wrap. Cook at 100% for 25 minutes in a 650- to 700-watt oven. Prick plastic to release steam.

3. Remove from oven and uncover. Strain through a fine sieve, pressing lightly on the vegetables. Use immediately, refrigerate or freeze.

FOR 400- TO 500-WATT OVENS

To make 3 cups (705 ml). Cook for 40 minutes.

BASIC GLAZE

Glazes are broths so reduced that, when cold, they form a heavy syrup. They freeze indefinitely and are a convenient way to add some extra flavor to stews.

To reduce 4 cups of broth to 1 cup, place in a 4-cup (1-l) glass measure. Cook, uncovered, at 100% in a 650- to 700-watt oven until liquid is reduced to 1 cup (240 ml). When cooking in a low-wattage oven, this may take more time than you want to spend.

Cooking Basics

There are many basic preparations that will make your cooking life quicker and easier if you prepare them ahead, not at the last minute when you need them. Many can be refrigerated or frozen to keep on hand. Freeze if you are likely to be tempted by a refrigerator full of delectable stuff. The time it takes to defrost something gives you time for a second thought. Making basics will also make your cooking less expensive if you do it when the basic products are in season or on special at your store.

Homemade basics are also lower in calories and sodium than those you buy. See Nutritional Comparison of Tomato Products below as an example. If you must substitute store-bought, learn to read labels carefully.

NUTRITIONAL COMPARISON OF TOMATO PRODUCTS

PRODUCT	CAL.	CARB. (g)	CALC. (mg)	IRON (mg)	SOD. (mg)
TOMATOES					
Tomatoes, raw (4.4 oz.; 123 g)	24	5	8	0.59	10
Tomatoes, canned in juice (½ cup; 120 ml)	34	8	34	0.61	285
Tomatoes, canned in thick purée (½ cup; 120 ml)	30	7	34	0.86	180
Tomato purée, canned (½ cup; 120 ml)	51	13	19	1.16	499
Tomato purée, canned, salt-free (½ cup; 120 ml)	51	13	19	1.16	25
Fresh Tomato Purée (page 468) (½ cup; 120 ml)	39	18	29	1.98	33
Tomato paste, canned (½ cup; 120 ml)	110	25	46	3.91	1,035
SAUCES					
Commercial spaghetti sauce, plain (½ cup; 120 ml)	136	20	35	0.81	618
Tomato Sauce Casalinga (page 167) (½ cup; 120 ml)	51	13	19	1.16	499
CONDIMENTS					
Tomato ketchup, commercial (1 tbsp.)	18	4	7	0.1	180
Early American Ketchup (page 469) (1 tbsp.)	9	2	4	1.3	3
Tomato Braised Onions (page 528) (¼ cup; 180 ml)	35	8	15	1	29
Red Tomato Salsa (page 522) (2 tbsp.)	7	2	4	<1	2

FRESH TOMATO PURÉE

*H*our for hour, making your own tomato purée is probably the best thing you can do for health, pocketbook and eating pleasure other than making basic broths. Make this in the summer, when tomatoes are good and cheap. If you use plum tomatoes, San Marzano or Roma, your purée will be thicker and sweeter than if you use American tomatoes. The American tomatoes will have a fresher taste. Make a batch of each. Freeze it in half-cup and cup quantities.

If you continue to cook the purée, uncovered, stirring from time to time, you will end up with homemade tomato paste.   *MAKES 4 CUPS OF PURÉE*

Per ¼-cup (60-ml) serving: 20 calories; 0 milligrams cholesterol; <1 gram fat; 8 milligrams sodium; 1 gram protein (2% RDA); 4 grams carbohydrate

RDA: vitamin A 23%; vitamin C 30%

4 pounds (1.8 kg) red, ripe tomatoes
   (about 12 medium tomatoes)

1. Core and cut an "X" through the skin of each tomato. Place in a 2½-quart (2.5-l) soufflé dish or casserole. Cook, uncovered, at 100% for 20 minutes in a 650- to 700-watt oven.
2. Remove from oven. Pass tomatoes through a food mill fitted with a medium disc. Return puréed tomatoes to soufflé dish. Cook, uncovered, at 100% for 45 minutes.
3. If not using immediately, freeze in 1-cup (240-ml) quantities.

To make 2 cups (470 ml). Use 2½ pounds (1.15 kg) tomatoes. Cook as in Step 1 for 12 minutes. Cook as in Step 2 for 20 minutes. Finish as in Step 3.

FOR 450- TO 500-WATT OVENS

To make 2 cups (470 ml). Cook as in Step 1 for 20 minutes. Cook as in Step 2 for 45 minutes.

EARLY AMERICAN TOMATO KETCHUP

You may have never thought of making ketchup; but our ancestors used to do it all the time from all sorts of ingredients, from oysters to mushrooms. Tomato ketchup came along very late; but when it did, oh my! If you look at the tomato nutrition comparisons above, you will notice that ketchup bought in a bottle is loaded with salt.

I got a version of this recipe from *Jennie June's American Cookery Book,* New York, 1878. Her recipe made gallons. This one makes much less, but has a wonderful thick texture and lots of flavor. It is also easy to make since, in the microwave oven, it doesn't require lots of stirring and risk scorching. It has no salt added and no sugar. I don't think that you will miss them. I like mine fairly spicy, so I use the larger amounts of red pepper and black pepper; but you can start with the smaller amounts and see how you feel. I like it without sugar. If you want a sweeter ketchup, stir in a sugar substitute to taste after the ketchup comes out of the oven. This recipe does not work in a low-wattage small oven.
MAKES 1⅔ CUPS, SERVES 25

Per 1-tablespoon serving: 9 calories; 0 milligrams cholesterol; < .1 gram fat; .3 gram protein (.8% RDA); 2 grams carbohydrate

RDA: vitamin A 9%; vitamin C 12%

2½ pounds (1.15 kg) plum tomatoes, cored and cut into quarters (about 6 cups; 1.5 l)
1 cup (240 ml) cider vinegar
½ teaspoon dry mustard

¼–½ teaspoon dried red pepper flakes
¼–½ teaspoon freshly ground black pepper
½ teaspoon ground mace

1. Coarsely chop tomatoes in a food processor. If your food processor is small, you may have to do this in two batches. You will have about 4½ cups (1.1 l) chopped tomatoes.

2. Stir together tomatoes and remaining ingredients in a 2½-quart (2.5-l) soufflé dish or casserole. Cook, uncovered, at 100% in a 650- to 700-watt oven for 40 minutes.

3. Remove from oven. Pass tomato mixture through a food mill fitted with the medium disc. Return mixture to soufflé dish. Cook, uncovered, for 17 minutes.

4. Remove from oven and transfer tomato mixture to a blender. Whir until smooth. Allow to cool, or can. Place in clean glass jars with tightly fitting lids and refrigerate.

GARLIC TO GO

Garlic is healthy; but many people dislike chopping it up; it goes bad quickly and it isn't equally good at all times of the year. In late winter and early spring it will begin to sprout a green shoot and turn bitter. When garlic is fresh and fat, make up a batch or two of Garlic to Go. It keeps better this way than peeled and stored in oil. It also tastes better and is less fattening.

It's easy to peel a large batch of garlic. Place the head of garlic on a large cutting board and cover it with a dish towel so that the cloves don't fly all over the room. Slam the flat bottom of a heavy pot onto the head of garlic. Lift the cloth. Separate the cloves and throw out any easily removed skins and roots. Pat the cloves into a single layer. Re-cover with cloth and whack a few more times. Remove cloth. The cloves will look smashed and you will be able to simply pick off the skins. No knife is needed.

If you want to smash and peel individual cloves, put them on your cutting board. With a heavy knife held flat and your hand and the knife handle away from the edge of the board, whack the clove. Once again, it will be smashed and peeled. That is how all garlic is handled in this book.

You can keep Garlic to Go in a jar in the refrigerator for up to two weeks, or freeze it in one-third-cup (80 ml) amounts. Defrost as needed for one and a half

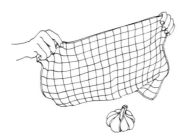

Cover head of garlic with a kitchen towel.

Smash garlic with a heavy pan.

Discard loose peels, separate cloves, cover and smash again if needed so that skin comes off easily.

Smash individual garlic clove with a large knife.

Remove remaining peels.

Remove green germ—if any— in the center of the garlic clove.

minutes at 100 percent in a full-wattage oven and two minutes in a low-wattage oven. Use one and a half teaspoons to replace a large clove of garlic. Add it after your food is cooked. On its own it makes a good pasta sauce with lots of black pepper. *MAKES 1 CUP (240 ML), SERVES 16*

Per 1-tablespoon serving: 41 calories; 0 milligrams cholesterol; 4 grams fat; 74 milligrams sodium; .4 gram protein (1% RDA); 2 grams carbohydrate

RDA: vitamin C 3%

30 cloves garlic, smashed and peeled
   (about 1½ heads; ⅔ cup; 160 ml)
¾ cup (180 ml) plus 2 tablespoons
   water

¼ cup (60 ml) olive oil
½ teaspoon kosher salt
Freshly ground black pepper, to taste

1. Place garlic and water in a 1½-quart (1.5-l) soufflé dish. Cover tightly with microwave plastic wrap. Cook at 100% for 8 minutes in a 650- to 700-watt oven. Prick plastic to release steam.

2. Remove from oven and uncover. Transfer mixture to a blender and add remaining ingredients. Blend until smooth. Store, tightly covered and refrigerated.

To make ⅓ cup (80 ml). Use 15 cloves garlic, ¼ cup (60 ml) water, 1 tablespoon oil, pinch salt and pepper to taste. Cook as in Step 1 for 5 minutes.

FOR 400- TO 500-WATT OVENS

To make 1 cup (240 ml). Cook for 12 minutes.

To make ⅓ cup (80 ml). Cook for 8 minutes.

SILKY PEPPER STRIPS

You can make these with any color of pepper; but red and yellow will be the prettiest. Homemade, they are much less expensive and have almost no sodium, unlike those bought canned. Cover leftover pepper strips with a good vinegar and store in the refrigerator virtually indefinitely, to use as needed.
MAKES 1 CUP (240 ML), SERVES 4

Per 3-pepper-strip serving (about ¼ cup; 60 ml): 23 calories; 0 milligrams cholesterol; 0 grams fat; 3 milligrams sodium; 1 gram protein (2% RDA); 5 grams carbohydrate

RDA: 181 milligrams potassium; vitamin A 106%; vitamin C 295%

1 pound (450 g) red, yellow or green
   bell peppers (3 small or 2 large
   peppers)

1. Peel peppers with a vegetable peeler. Cut small peppers lengthwise into quarters and larger peppers into sixths. (If necessary, finish peeling pepper strips at this point.) Remove core, stem and derib.
2. Arrange pepper strips skin side down in a 13×9×2-inch (33×23×5-cm) oval dish, with tapered ends toward the center. Cover tightly with microwave plastic wrap. Cook at 100% for 7 minutes, or until tender, in a 650- to 700-watt oven. Prick plastic to release steam.
3. Remove from oven. Let stand 1 minute and uncover. Remove and drain on paper towels.

To make 2 cups (470 ml). Use 2 pounds (900 g) bell peppers. Follow Step 1. In Step 2, arrange pepper strips in a 14×11×2-inch (35.5×28×5-cm) dish and cook for 12 minutes. Finish as in Step 3.

FOR 400- TO 500-WATT OVENS

To make 1 cup. Cook peppers for 12 minutes.

PICKLED JALAPEÑO PEPPERS

Where I live, fresh jalapeño peppers are not available year-round. I find the kind that come in cans slimy. They are also loaded with salt. It takes very little time to put them up yourself and, between the acidity of the peppers and that of the vinegar, they will keep indefinitely once refrigerated. Rinse them off before using. The spicy vinegar can be reused for more peppers, or it can add zip to a salad dressing.   *MAKES 1 POUND (450 G); 30 PEPPERS*

Per 1 pepper (½ ounce; 15 g): 7 calories; 0 milligrams cholesterol; <1 gram fat; 1 milligram sodium; <1 gram protein (1% RDA); 2 grams carbohydrate

RDA: vitamin C 61%

1 pound (450 g) jalapeño peppers
1 cup (240 ml) cider vinegar

1 cup (240 ml) water

1. Cook peppers at least one day before you plan to use them. Combine all ingredients in a 2½-quart (2.5-l) soufflé dish or casserole. Cover tightly with microwave plastic wrap. Cook at 100% for 12 minutes in a 650- to 700-watt oven. Prick plastic to release steam.

2. Remove from oven and uncover. Let cool to room temperature and pack into containers well covered with liquid. Refrigerate until needed. The peppers will absorb some of the liquid, so cover with more vinegar as needed.

FOR 400- TO 500-WATT OVENS

To make 1 pound (450 g). Cook for 18 minutes.

LETCHO

Letcho is an omnipresent dish in Hungary. It is served with eggs at breakfast, and with meat, fish or chicken at lunch and dinner. You can also top two strips of Basic Firm Polenta (page 216) with one serving, or one cup of cooked pasta, or top small rounds of toasted or grilled bread, as crostini, an Italian sort-of hors d'oeuvre, with a tablespoon of letcho to make a succulent snack with drinks. This dish works better in a 650- to 700-watt oven than in lower-wattage ovens. Using hot paprika or chili makes a relatively spicy dish. You can substitute ordinary paprika for a milder one.   *MAKES 4 CUPS (1 L), SERVES 16*

Per ¼-cup (60 ml) serving: 28 calories; 0 milligrams cholesterol; 1 gram fat; 18 milligrams sodium; 1 gram protein (2% RDA); 4 grams carbohydrate

RDA: 127 milligrams potassium; vitamin A 29%; vitamin C 81%

1 tablespoon vegetable oil
1 teaspoon hot paprika or chili powder without cumin
1½ pounds (680 g) yellow onions (3 large onions), peeled and thinly sliced (about 8 cups; 2 l)

1 pound (450 g) red bell peppers (2–3 large peppers), stemmed, seeded, deribbed and cut into strips (about 6 cups; 1.5 l)
2 tablespoons tomato paste

1. Combine oil and paprika in a 13×9×2-inch (33×23×5-cm) oval dish. Cook, uncovered, at 100% for 1 minute in a 650- to 700-watt oven. Stir in onions, coating them with the paprika and oil mixture. Cook, uncovered, for 6 minutes.

2. Remove from oven. Stir onions and mound peppers on top. Cover tightly with microwave plastic wrap. Cook for 8 minutes. Prick plastic to release steam.

3. Remove from oven and uncover. Stir well and cook, uncovered, for 6 minutes. Stir in tomato paste and cook, uncovered, for 18 minutes, stirring twice.

FOR 400- TO 500-WATT OVENS

To make 2 cups (470 ml). Use 1½ teaspoons oil, ½ teaspoon hot or mild paprika or chili powder, ¾ pound (340 g) onions (about 4 cups; 1 l), ½ pound (225 g) red bell peppers (about 3 cups; 705 ml) and 1 tablespoon tomato paste. Cook as in Step 1 for 2 minutes; add onions and cook for 5 minutes. Continue with Step 2, cooking for 8 minutes. Stir and cook, covered, 8 minutes more. In Step 3, you will cook the mixture covered for 4 minutes; uncover and stir; then cook uncovered for 8 minutes, stirring once.

SPICE MIX

I use this in Spicy Buttermilk Dressing (page 496); but its blend of seasonings can be sprinkled into Italian and Indian dishes to add oomph.   *MAKES ¼ CUP (60 ML)*

2 tablespoons coriander seeds
2 tablespoons mustard seeds
2 teaspoons cumin seeds
2 teaspoons fennel seeds

1 teaspoon celery seeds
½ teaspoon crushed red pepper
Large pinch ground cloves

1. Mix spices together and spread all ingredients in an even layer in a 10-inch (25.5-cm) quiche dish or pie plate. Cook, uncovered, at 100% for 6 minutes in a 650- to 700-watt oven.

2. Remove from oven and scrape spices into a spice grinder or clean coffee grinder. Grind to a fine powder. Store in an airtight container at room temperature.

To make 1½ tablespoons. Use 1 tablespoon each coriander and mustard seeds, 1 teaspoon each cumin and fennel seeds, ½ teaspoon celery seeds, ¼ teaspoon red pepper and a pinch ground cloves. Cook as in Step 1 for 6 minutes.

FOR 400- TO 500-WATT OVENS

To make ¼ cup (60 ml). Cook for 9 minutes.

To make 1½ tablespoons. Cook for 9 minutes.

Electric coffee grinder or spice grinder.
One not used for coffee is good for spices.

DIET PESTO SAUCE

I love pesto, not only on top of pasta but, in addition, to stir into soups and stews—a twenty-six-calorie tablespoonful may often be the right amount to add to a portion. Sadly, conventional pestos are very fattening, with their nuts and oil. This version takes advantage of the silky texture of garlic once it has been cooked in a microwave oven. It freezes well, so make it at the end of summer when basil is plentiful. You may want to reduce the salt slightly if you're watching your sodium.   *MAKES 2 CUPS (470 ML), SERVES 24*

Per 2-tablespoon serving: 52 calories; 0 milligrams cholesterol; <3 grams fat; 146 milligrams sodium; 1.6 grams protein (3% RDA); 6 grams carbohydrate

RDA: calcium 16%; phosphorus 4%; iron 16%; 259 milligrams potassium; vitamin A 13%; vitamin C 10%

3 heads garlic, cloves separated, smashed and peeled
1½ cups (355 ml) Basic Chicken Broth (page 460), or unsalted or regular canned chicken broth

6 cups (1.5 l) fresh basil leaves
3 tablespoons olive oil
1½ teaspoons kosher salt

1. Place garlic and broth in a 4-cup (1-l) glass measure. Cover tightly with microwave plastic wrap. Cook at 100% for 14 minutes in a 650- to 700-watt oven.
2. Prick plastic to release steam. Uncover and scrape into a food processor. Process until smooth. With the motor running, add the basil, then the oil and salt. Continue processing until smooth.

To make ⅔ cup (160 ml). Use 1 head garlic, ½ cup (120 ml) broth, 2 cups (470 ml) basil, 1 tablespoon oil and ½ teaspoon salt. Cook as in Step 1 for 8 minutes.

FOR 400- TO 500-WATT OVENS

To make ⅔ cup (160 ml). Cook for 15 minutes.

DIET DUXELLES

Duxelles is one of those nifty French inventions that are a real pain to make on top of the stove, since it has to be constantly stirred so that it doesn't scorch while it cooks over low heat until all the moisture evaporates. It's quicker in the microwave oven. More important, it doesn't require standing, hovering and stirring. Use it as a stuffing—farce—or a base for soups and sauces.

MAKES 2 CUPS (470 ML), SERVES 8

Per ¼-cup (60-ml) serving: 29 calories; 0 milligrams cholesterol; <1 gram fat; 206 milligrams sodium; 2 grams protein (4% RDA); 6 grams carbohydrate

RDA: 349 milligrams potassium; riboflavin 16%; niacin 12%; vitamin C 21%

1 pound (450 g) mushrooms, wiped clean and stems trimmed
½ pound (227 g) yellow onion, peeled and quartered
1 cup (240 ml) fresh parsley leaves

4 ribs celery, peeled and cut across into 2-inch (5-cm) pieces
2 teaspoons fresh lemon juice
2 teaspoons kosher salt
Freshly ground black pepper, to taste

1. Place mushrooms, onion, parsley and celery in a food processor and process until finely chopped.
2. Scrape vegetables into a 13 × 10 × 2-inch (33 × 25.5 × 5-cm) oval dish. Cover tightly with microwave plastic wrap. Cook at 100% for 15 minutes in a 650- to 700-watt oven. Prick plastic to release steam.
3. Leaving dish in oven, uncover. Cook, uncovered, for 15 minutes more. Remove from oven.
4. Stir in remaining ingredients.

To make 1 cup (240 ml). Use ½ pound (227 g) mushrooms, ¼ pound (113.5 g) onion, ½ cup parsley leaves, 2 ribs celery, 1 teaspoon each lemon juice and salt, and pepper to taste. Prepare as in Step 1. Cook as in Step 2 in a 10-inch (25.5-cm) quiche dish for 10 minutes. Cook as in Step 2 for 5 minutes.

FOR 400- TO 500-WATT OVENS

To make 2 cups (470 ml). Cook as in Step 2 for 20 minutes. Cook as in Step 3 for 20 minutes.

To make 1 cup (240 ml). Cook as in Step 2 for 15 minutes. Cook as in Step 3 for 10 minutes.

PEANUT BUTTER

No, this isn't a microwave recipe. Making your own peanut butter is so quick and so rewarding; no fat or sodium is added. If you can wait, this tastes better after a day in the refrigerator. *MAKES 1⅔ CUPS (400 ML), SERVES 25*

Per 1-tablespoon serving: 55 calories; 0 milligrams cholesterol; 5 grams fat; 0 milligrams sodium; 2 grams protein (5% RDA); 2 grams carbohydrate

RDA: niacin 6%

1¾ cups (410 ml) unsalted dry-roasted   1 cup (240 ml) water
   peanuts

1. Combine peanuts and water in a blender. Blend until smooth. Store, tightly covered and refrigerated. If mixture separates slightly, simply stir well before using.

DRIED BREAD CRUMBS

I'm sure that you find yourself with stale or leftover bread as often as I do. I cut the bread into pieces and crumble into coarse crumbs in a food processor. Then I dry the crumbs in the microwave oven and store them until needed. They keep practically forever.

The caloric and nutritional information on the bread crumbs will be the same as for the weight or amount of bread with which you started. All you are removing is the water. You will notice that your yield is less than that for fresh crumbs. *MAKES 1½ CUPS (355 ML)*

5 1-ounce (28-g) slices of bread

1. Tear bread into pieces. Place in a food processor and pulse until you have coarse crumbs.
2. Scrape crumbs into a layer in a 10-inch (25.5-cm) quiche dish or pie plate. Cook, uncovered, at 100% for 5 minutes in 650- to 700-watt oven, stirring once, or until completely dried.
3. Remove from oven. Scrape into a container with a tightly fitting lid. Allow to cool uncovered. Cover and store at room temperature.

To make 4 cups (1 l). Use a 1-pound (450-g) loaf of bread. Cook as in Step 2 for 9 minutes, stirring 3 times.

To make 3 tablespoons. Use ¾-ounce (21-g) bread. Cook as in Step 2 on a 7-inch (18-cm) round plate for 3 minutes without stirring.

FOR 400- TO 500-WATT OVENS

To make 1½ cups (355 ml). Cook as in Step 2 for 10 minutes, stirring once.

To make 4 cups (1 l). Cook as in Step 2 for 15 minutes, stirring 3 times.

To make 3 tablespoons. Cook as in Step 2 for 6 minutes.

SEASONED BREAD CRUMBS

*T*hese herbed and seasoned crumbs are a nice topping for cooked vegetable dishes like Cauliflower Gratin (page 426), Provençale Tomatoes (page 440) and simply cooked purées, and on Turkey Hash (page 334) if you can afford the calories. They add crunch, flavor and color, and let you brown the dish under a broiler. You can stir them into pastas dressed only with oil and garlic or Garlic to Go (page 470). These keep well at room temperature.   *MAKES 4 CUPS (1 L)*

Per 1-tablespoon serving: 27 calories; <1 gram cholesterol; 1 gram fat; 36 milligrams sodium; 1 gram protein (1% RDA); 4 grams carbohydrate

1 loaf white bread (1 pound, 450 g)	1 teaspoon dried sage
4 cloves garlic, smashed, peeled and minced	½ teaspoon dried thyme
	½ teaspoon dried savory
¼ cup (60 ml) olive oil	Freshly ground black pepper, to taste

1. Crumble bread into a food processor and process until finely chopped. Transfer to a 13 × 10 × 2-inch (33 × 25.5 × 5-cm) oval dish. Cook, uncovered, at 100% for 9 minutes in a 650- to 700-watt oven, stirring 3 times.
2. Remove from oven and reserve, stirring occasionally.
3. In a small bowl combine garlic, oil and dried herbs. Cook, uncovered, for 3 minutes.
4. Remove from oven. Pour this mixture over reserved bread crumbs and stir in black pepper. Cook, uncovered, for 3 minutes, stirring twice.
5. Remove from oven and let stand until cool, stirring frequently.

FOR 400- TO 500-WATT OVENS

To make 4 cups (1 l). Cook as in Step 1 for 9 minutes, stirring 3 times. Cook garlic and herb mixture as in Step 3 for 4 minutes. Cook as in Step 4 for 6 minutes.

CROUTONS

Some of us like to sprinkle croutons into our salads and soups. Commercial croutons are full of salt and oil. These are quickly made with neither. You can make large croutons for soup or little squares to have on your salad. The calories and other nutritional values will depend on the kind of bread that you use.

MAKES ¾ CUP (180 ML)

4 average slices bread, each about 1
   ounce (28 g), crusts removed and
   each slice quartered or cut into ½-
   inch (1-cm) dice

1. Place bread on two sheets of paper toweling in a single layer. Cook, uncovered, at 100% for 2 minutes 30 seconds in a 650- to 700-watt oven.
2. Remove from oven and allow to cool.

FOR 400- TO 500-WATT OVENS

To make ¾ cup (180 ml). Cook as in step 1 for 5 minutes.

Sauces

SALAD DRESSINGS

Any of you who have read the chapter before this one know how I feel about salads. It is not just a personal passion. Having salads every day, even twice a day, is good for your body, and if you're on a weight-loss diet, it helps with the diet as well. Why? Salads are rich in vitamins and fiber, the kind that we used to call roughage when I was a kid. They fill you up and deliver lots of flavor that can be varied by the ingredients in the salad and in the dressing.

The only hitch is that most salad dressings are fattening due to the amount of oil, and we use too much, making our salads limp and slimy, because we don't make the dressings flavorful enough. While there are many varieties of commercially bottled diet dressings on the market, they are to be avoided except in case of emergency or when dining out. Their calories may be low; but they tend to be high in sodium and to be made with saturated or polyunsaturated fats, which are not the best kinds of oils for our health. Additionally, they tend to be artificially thickened with vegetable gums and flavored with tired or artificial seasonings.

Instead of using those sad liquids, learn to make a few of the dressings below. You will soon find out which are your favorites. They take little time and will make your salad sing. Always feel free to add some herbs, minced garlic or another virtually calorie-less seasoning that pleases you. Except for the cooked dressings, quantities can easily be multiplied or divided.

Many of these salad dressings can be used as marinades—for vegetables and meats to be grilled or broiled—and sauces for simply cooked or raw foods. A few are good as dips.

Calorie counts are generally given by the tablespoon. Remember, that doesn't mean a heaping, but a level, tablespoon. Many of these dressings are so low in calories that you can feel free to use more than a tablespoon at a time.

With rare exceptions, salad dressings add little to your diet by way of vitamins and minerals. Therefore, I give the RDA listings only of those dressings that are interesting exceptions.

None of the recipes for the first group of dressings, except for the Rouille, requires any cooking. Those further on do, if only to develop the seasonings.

MAYONNAISE AND MAYONNAISE-BASED DRESSINGS

As far as taste goes, commercially prepared light or low-calorie mayonnaise or mayonnaise-type salad dressings are quite satisfactory, and they do have relatively few calories. However, a careful reading of their labels indicates that they also have cholesterol, polyunsaturated and saturated fats—rather than the healthier monounsaturated fats—and a more-than-healthy dose of sodium.

To solve the problem, I have come up with an Egg White Mayonnaise and some delicious variants of that basic. It is not the world's most thinning recipe; but the flavor is excellent and it has no cholesterol, little sodium and, if you use a monounsaturated oil, no cholesterol-provoking tendencies. While I like to use a good olive oil, I often cut it by mixing it half-and-half with a neutral tasting oil such as canola. By changing the oil, you can change the flavor. Use an olive-oil–based mayonnaise for Italian and other Mediterranean dishes. Use one made with canola oil for Tuna Salad (page 70) for sandwiches.

Refrigerated, mayonnaise keeps very well. Make a whole recipe and then use as much of it as you want to make one of the variations that follow, or one of your own imagining—say, mixed with cooked puréed spinach, herbs and capers. If that's too much temptation, you can make a half-batch of these recipes in a blender by pouring in the water alternately with the oil. All mayonnaise sauces will thicken as they get cold.

EGG WHITE MAYONNAISE

*T*his is a simple basic to keep on hand for a multitude of variations and uses. Just using it on sandwiches will improve your diet.   *MAKES 1½ CUPS (355 ML), SERVES 24*

Per 1-tablespoon serving: 82 calories; 0 milligrams cholesterol; 9 grams fat; 30 milligrams sodium; .13 gram protein (.3% RDA); .12 gram carbohydrate

1 egg white
¼ teaspoon kosher salt
Pinch freshly ground black pepper
1 tablespoon fresh lemon juice
2 teaspoons Dijon mustard

1 cup (240 ml) vegetable oil, preferably monounsaturated such as canola or olive, or a mixture of the two
¼ cup (60 ml) water

1. Place egg white, salt, pepper, lemon juice and mustard in the work bowl of a food processor. Process until smooth and creamy. Add oil in a thin stream through the feed tube.

2. When all of the oil has been incorporated, with the processor running, slowly pour in the water.

3. Use immediately, or remove to a clean glass jar and refrigerate, tightly covered.

AÏOLI

*T*his is called the butter of Provence, where its rich garlic-laden flavor is spread on bread, used in classic soups such as bourride—a white fish stew—and makes a festive of meal of its own when presented in bountiful bowls with an array of steamed or poached vegetables, meats, poultry and salt cod. I like it with micro-wave-cooked Sweet Potatoes (page 220)—an outstanding balance of sweet and pungent—or with an assortment of microwave-cooked vegetables. Sometimes I add a cooked chicken breast or fish fillet; but that's only for guests who might feel deprived without meat. I don't. Multiply as often as you want.

MAKES ½ CUP (120 ML), SERVES 8

Per 1-tablespoon serving: 83 calories; 0 milligrams cholesterol; 9 grams fat; 30 milligrams sodium; 0 grams protein; 0 grams carbohydrate

½ cup (120 ml) Egg White Mayonnaise   2 cloves garlic, smashed and peeled

1. In food processor or blender combine mayonnaise and garlic until garlic is invisible. Alternatively, add garlic to egg white, salt, pepper, lemon juice and mustard when making Egg White Mayonnaise.

2. Remove to a glass jar and refrigerate, tightly covered. It will grow stronger if left for a few hours.

ROUÏLLE

Watch out! This orangy traditional accompaniment to Riviera Fish Soup (page 138) is addictive. Make just what you need or you will start slathering it on everything. It is particularly good with cold meats on a sandwich. You can make more or less of this fiery red sauce by increasing or decreasing the amounts of aïoli, spices and vegetable oil proportionately. The spices will take the same amount of time to cook no matter what the quantity.
MAKES ¾ CUP (180 ML), SERVES 12

Per 1-tablespoon serving: 85 calories; 0 milligrams cholesterol; 9 grams fat; 30 milligrams sodium; .13 gram protein (.4% RDA); .15 gram carbohydrate

¼ teaspoon paprika
⅛ teaspoon cayenne

½ teaspoon vegetable oil
¾ cup (180 ml) Aïoli (page 483)

   1. Combine paprika, cayenne and oil in the center of a 1-quart (1-l) soufflé dish. Cook at 100%, uncovered, for 1 minute in a 650- to 700-watt oven.
   2. Combine paprika mixture with aïoli in a blender. Blend until thoroughly incorporated.
   3. Use immediately, or refrigerate in a clean glass jar, tightly covered.

FOR 400- TO 500-WATT OVENS

For ¾ cup (180 ml). Cook for 2 minutes 30 seconds.

TONNATO SAUCE

This is not a salad dressing. It is the classic Italian cold sauce to serve with thinly sliced, cool Poached Veal (page 381). It is equally good with fish, chicken, turkey scaloppine and pork tenderloin. It also makes a terrific dip for raw or lightly cooked vegetables at a cocktail party. If you are on a weight-loss diet, don't make this except for a party, or you will end up eating too much. Use up the extra half-can of tuna by feeding it to the cat, making Tuna Salad (page 70) or making a second batch of the sauce.   *MAKES 1½ CUPS (355 ML)*

Per 1-tablespoon serving: 78 calories; 1 milligram cholesterol; 8 grams fat; 37 milligrams sodium; 1 gram protein (2% RDA); <1 gram carbohydrate

1 recipe (1½ cups; 355 ml) Egg White Mayonnaise (page 482), or bottled diet mayonnaise

¼ cup (60 ml) drained chunk-light water-packed tuna, about half of a 3½-ounce (100-g) can

1 teaspoon capers, rinsed well and drained

1. Add tuna and capers to finished mayonnaise in a blender and blend until completely smooth.

2. Use immediately, or refrigerate in a clean glass jar, tightly sealed.

CURRY MAYONNAISE

A mild curry flavor can give a real lift to chicken, fish and vegetable salads. Think of that for using up leftovers. A strong Curry Mayonnaise is made with four teaspoons of curry powder and is used in dishes, such as Curried Chicken Salad (page 418), that have juicy ingredients that will dilute the flavor of the mayonnaise.   *MAKES 1 CUP (240 ML), SERVES 16*

Per 1-tablespoon serving: 63 calories; 0 milligrams cholesterol; 7 grams fat; 35 milligrams sodium; <1 gram protein (<1% RDA)

2–4 teaspoons curry powder
1 tablespoon vegetable oil

1 cup (240 ml) Egg White Mayonnaise (page 482), or bottled diet mayonnaise

1. Combine curry powder and vegetable oil in a 2-cup (470-ml) glass measure. Cook, uncovered, at 100% for 2 minutes in a 650- to 700-watt oven. Remove from oven and allow to cool. Stir in mayonnaise and store, tightly covered and refrigerated.

VINAIGRETTE DRESSINGS

These are the dressings that most of us think of when we think of salad dressing. They can be as various as the people who make them and as there are kinds of oils, vinegars, juices, herbs and spices. Let your imagination fly. Here are a few suggestions with carefully worked out nutrition to inspire and guide you.

Regardless of their actual acidity, milder, rounder-tasting vinegars can be used in a greater amount in proportion to the oil than sharp, one-note vinegars.

No matter how much dressing a recipe makes, the calorie count and nutritional figures are given by the tablespoon. A quarter-cup has four tablespoons. Keep that in mind when deciding how much dressing to use for a salad for a group. All dressings that are uncooked—most of these—can be increased or decreased proportionately. The nutrition remains the same. When dressings are made ahead, store them in the refrigerator in a clean glass jar with a lid. Shake them in their jar or whisk thoroughly before using. One tablespoon of dressing is usually sufficient for a side or small first-course salad.

If you dry your greens less than you have been taught—just shake them and then pat them with paper toweling—your dressing will go further.

You will notice that garlic is cooked in many of these recipes. It makes the flavor gentler and thickens your sauce.

BALSAMIC DRESSING

*B*alsamic vinegar is expensive; but it is well worth buying. It can be used alone, as a dressing or a dip, or turned into a salad dressing with very little oil. Use this on greens or as a marinade for fish. It's also good with artichokes.
MAKES ¼ CUP (60 ML), SERVES 4

Per 1-tablespoon serving: 31 calories; 0 milligrams cholesterol; 3 grams fat; 0 milligrams sodium; 0 grams protein; <1 gram carbohydrate

3 tablespoons balsamic vinegar   Freshly ground black pepper, to taste
1 tablespoon olive oil '

1. Place ingredients in a small bowl and whisk to combine.

ORANGE-CUMIN VINAIGRETTE

*T*his does well on main-course fruit salads. It is a good all-purpose dressing for the more pungent greens and for salads with a little cooked fish or chicken. Given the low calorie count of this dressing, I would be tempted to double the amount per person so that this would serve 8.   *MAKES 1 CUP (240 ML), SERVES 16*

Per 1-tablespoon serving: 28 calories; 0 milligrams cholesterol; 3 grams fat; 24 milligrams sodium; <1 gram protein (<1% RDA); 1 gram carbohydrate

RDA: iron 4%; vitamin C 7%

½ cup (120 ml) fresh orange juice
2 tablespoons plus 2 teaspoons cider vinegar
2 tablespoons plus 2 teaspoons ground cumin

2 tablespoons plus 2 teaspoons vegetable oil
2 teaspoons fresh lemon juice
¼ teaspoon kosher salt

1. Combine ingredients in a small bowl and whisk until thoroughly blended.

PERNOD DRESSING

*T*his unusual dressing is particularly good on fish and seafood salads.
MAKES ⅔ CUP (160 ML), SERVES 10

Per 1-tablespoon serving: 57 calories; 0 milligrams cholesterol; 5 grams fat; 148 milligrams sodium; <1 gram protein; 1 gram carbohydrate

¼ cup (60 ml) fresh orange juice
¼ cup (60 ml) olive oil
1 tablespoon fresh lemon juice

1 teaspoon kosher salt
1¼ tablespoons Pernod
Freshly ground black pepper, to taste.

1. Combine all ingredients in a bowl and whisk until thoroughly blended.

SESAME DRESSING

I love this dressing on all sorts of green salads and on cooked-vegetable salads. I'm not mad for it with tomatoes.   *MAKES ⅔ CUP (160 ML), SERVES 10*

Per 1-tablespoon serving: 69 calories; 0 milligrams cholesterol; 7 grams fat; 34 milligrams sodium; .16 gram protein (.36% RDA); 1 gram carbohydrate

5 cloves garlic, smashed and peeled
½ cup (120 ml) water
1½ teaspoons chopped fresh tarragon
  leaves, or ½ teaspoon dried tarragon
2 teaspoons rice vinegar

1 teaspoon tamari soy
¼ cup (60 ml) vegetable oil, preferably
  canola or avocado
1½ tablespoons Oriental sesame oil

1. Place garlic and water in a 1-cup (240-ml) glass measure. Cover with microwave plastic wrap. Cook at 100% for 4 minutes in a 650- to 700-watt oven. Prick plastic to release steam. Uncover and add dried tarragon, if using. Cook for 2 minutes more, uncovered.

2. Remove from oven and transfer to a food processor or blender. Add vinegar, soy and fresh tarragon, if using, and process until smooth.

3. With the motor running, add both oils in a thin stream.

FOR 400- TO 500-WATT OVENS

For ⅔ cup (160 ml). Cook garlic and water for 8 minutes. Add dried tarragon, if using, and cook for 4 minutes, uncovered. Finish as in Step 2 and 3.

GARLIC OREGANO DRESSING

This is a basic Italian salad dressing. *MAKES ¼ CUP (60 ML), SERVES 4*

Per 1-tablespoon serving: 63 calories; 0 milligrams cholesterol; 7 grams fat; 135 milligrams sodium; <1 gram protein (<1% RDA); 1 gram carbohydrate

RDA: vitamin C 6%

2 tablespoons water
½ teaspoon dried oregano
1 clove garlic, smashed, peeled and
   minced

2 tablespoons fresh lemon juice
¼ teaspoon salt
Pinch freshly ground black pepper
2 tablespoons olive oil

1. Combine water, oregano and garlic in a 1-quart (1-l) soufflé dish or casserole with a tightly fitted lid. Cover tightly with microwave plastic wrap or lid. Cook at 100% for 1 minute 30 seconds in a 650- to 700-watt oven. Prick plastic to release steam.

2. Remove from oven and let stand for 1 minute. Uncover and transfer to a blender. Add lemon juice, salt and pepper and blend until smooth. With blender motor running, add oil in a thin stream and blend until completely incorporated.

For 1¼ cups (300 ml). Use 5 tablespoons water, 1½ teaspoons oregano, 5 cloves garlic, ½ cup (120 ml) lemon juice, 1 teaspoon salt, a large pinch pepper and ¾ cup (180 ml) olive oil. Cook garlic mixture for 2 minutes. Finish as in Step 2.

FOR 400- TO 500-WATT OVENS

For ¼ cup (60 ml). Cook for 2 minutes 30 seconds.

For 1¼ cups (300 ml). Cook for 3 minutes.

CREAMY ITALIAN DRESSING

This is a fresher, low-sodium, less-caloric version of the popular salad-bar and bottled dressing. It is good on most green salads.   *MAKES ⅔ CUP (160 ML), SERVES 10*

Per 1-tablespoon serving: 31 calories; .5 milligram cholesterol; 3 grams fat; 67 milligrams sodium; .5 gram protein (1% RDA); 1 gram carbohydrate

SEASONINGS

½ teaspoon dried oregano
½ teaspoon dried thyme
¼ teaspoon rubbed sage
¼ teaspoon summer savory
Pinch rosemary *or*
1½ teaspoons Italian herbs

FOR THE DRESSING

½ cup (120 ml) buttermilk
3 cloves garlic, smashed, peeled and
   sliced
1 tablespoon white wine vinegar
2 tablespoons olive oil
¼ teaspoon kosher salt
Pinch fennel seeds
Freshly ground black pepper, to taste

1. Put seasonings or Italian herbs in 1-quart (1-l) soufflé dish with buttermilk and garlic. Cover tightly with microwave plastic wrap. Cook at 100% for 2 minutes in a 650- to 700-watt oven. Prick plastic wrap to release steam.
2. Remove from oven and let sit 1 minute. Do not worry if mixture looks curdled.
3. Scrape mixture into blender. Let blender run until there are no visible whole pieces. Add remaining ingredients except for pepper and blend for 1 minute.
4. Refrigerate with pepper stirred in.

FOR 400- TO 500-WATT OVENS

For ⅔ cup (160 ml). Cook for 3 minutes in Step 1. Proceed with other steps.

NOT VINAIGRETTES

There are many good dressings that are not vinaigrettes; some can be used as dipping sauces. They are not based on vinegar and oil. Some require cooking. Many are very low in calories. They are worth making. The rules for portions and how much to use are the same as for Vinaigrettes (page 486).

BUTTERMILK DRESSING

Low in calories, but with good coating qualities, this would be good on cabbage as an alternate to mayonnaise, or tossed with cooked vegetables of the cabbage family. Try making a hot or cold dish with cooked cauliflower.

MAKES 1 CUP (240 ML), SERVES 16

Per 1-tablespoon serving: 33 calories; <1 milligram cholesterol; 3 grams fat; 54 milligrams sodium; <1 gram protein (1% RDA); <1 gram carbohydrate

½ cup (120 ml) buttermilk
2 tablespoons cider vinegar
¼ cup (60 ml) olive oil
½ teaspoon kosher salt

Freshly ground black pepper, to taste
3 drops hot red pepper sauce
¼ teaspoon celery seeds
⅛ teaspoon Worcestershire sauce

1. Whisk together all ingredients. Store, tightly covered, in the refrigerator.

MUSTARD DRESSING

*T*his is one of the world's easiest dressings. It has a terrific flavor, and look—only 10 calories. Unfortunately, something had to give. The mustard has sodium; so does the dressing. If you like to use a lot of dressing, here is the solution. I like this on spinach, watercress, vegetable, meat and cheese salads. Keep it in a jar so that you can shake it up before using. You can also use this as a hot sauce. It would be great on kidneys (page 385).   *MAKES 1½ CUPS (355 ML), SERVES 24*

Per 1-tablespoon serving: 10 calories; <1 milligram cholesterol; <1 gram fat; 173 milligrams sodium; <1 gram protein (1% RDA); 1 gram carbohydrate

1 cup (240 ml) buttermilk   Freshly ground black pepper, to taste
½ cup (120 ml) Dijon mustard

1. Mix all ingredients together well in a bowl. Transfer to a jar and keep refrigerated. To make as a hot sauce, combine ingredients in a 4-cup (1-l) glass measure. Cover tightly with microwave plastic wrap and cook at 100% for 2 minutes 30 seconds in a 650- to 700-watt oven.

FOR 400- TO 500-WATT OVENS

To make 1½ cups (355 ml). Cook for 5 minutes.

Seven ounces (200 g) avocado, peeled and pitted: 325 calories; 0 milligrams cholesterol; 31 grams fat; 4 grams protein (9% RDA); 15 grams carbohydrate

AVOCADO DRESSING

Into anybody's life a little luck must fall from time to time. I was reading some pretty dry information about fats and oils when I stumbled over the fact that avocado fat—caloric though it may be—is entirely monounsaturated. I decided to make a salad dressing, but found that I had to add lots of liquid or it was too thick. Imagine my delighted surprise when the nutritional analysis came back and I found that there were only fourteen calories in a tablespoon of dressing. That's good, because you really need to use two tablespoons of this for a portion of salad.

If you reduce the water to three quarters of a cup, you have an only slightly more caloric dip for a party. If you like your dips spicy, add some Pickled Jalapeño Peppers (page 473) to the blender. Top the dip in its serving bowl with chopped fresh coriander—cilantro—or parsley.   MAKES 3 CUPS (705 ML), SERVES 32

Per 1½-tablespoon serving: 14 calories; <1 milligram cholesterol; 1 gram fat; 59 milligrams sodium; <1 gram protein (1% RDA); 1 gram carbohydrate

10 ounces (284 g) avocado (1 large
   avocado), peeled and pitted (about
   7 ounces; 200 g)
3 tablespoons fresh lemon juice
1 cup (240 ml) water

2 cloves garlic, smashed and peeled
1 teaspoon hot red pepper sauce
1 cup (240 ml) buttermilk
1 teaspoon kosher salt

1. Place all ingredients in a blender and blend until smooth. Store tightly covered and refrigerated.

ORANGE-YOGURT DRESSING

Make this at least one day before you wish to serve it so that the flavors have a chance to develop. You will be surprised at how much energy comes from only nine calories per tablespoon. This is a good, superlight all-purpose dressing; feel free to double the portion.   *MAKES 2¼ CUPS (530 ML), SERVES 36*

Per 1-tablespoon serving: 9 calories; 1 milligram cholesterol; <1 gram fat; 50 milligrams sodium; 1 gram protein (1% RDA); 1 gram carbohydrate

2 cups (470 ml) plain nonfat yogurt
¼ cup (60 ml) fresh orange juice
⅛ teaspoon ground cumin, heated in
  ½ teaspoon oil

¹⁄₁₆ teaspoon minced garlic
1 teaspoon kosher salt
Pinch freshly ground black pepper

1. Combine all ingredients in a food processor or blender. Process until mixed. Store, tightly covered, in the refrigerator. Make one day before serving.

MINT YOGURT DRESSING

This is the same dressing that is used to make raita, the shredded-cucumber cooling salad that so often accompanies curries. You can make your own inventions with other shredded vegetables, or simply use the dressing for a tomato, cucumber and lettuce salad. Substitute chives or dill for mint if you want to use this as a topping for baked potatoes or fish. You can use it lavishly, as it is so low in calories.   *MAKES ¾ CUP (180 ML), SERVES 12*

Per 1-tablespoon serving: 10 calories; 1 milligram cholesterol; <1 gram fat; 71 milligrams sodium; 1 gram protein (2% RDA); 1 gram carbohydrate

RDA: calcium 3%

2 cloves garlic, smashed, peeled and
  thinly sliced
2 tablespoons water
¾ cup (180 ml) low-fat yogurt

2 tablespoons chopped fresh mint
1½ teaspoons fresh lemon juice
½ teaspoon kosher salt
Freshly ground black pepper to taste

1. Place garlic and water in a 1-cup (240-ml) glass measure. Cover tightly with microwave plastic wrap. Cook at 100% for 2 minutes in a 650- to 700-watt oven. Prick plastic to release steam.

2. Remove from oven and uncover. Add remaining ingredients and mix well.

FOR 400- TO 500-WATT OVENS

To make ¾ cup (180 ml). Cook as in Step 1 for 3 minutes.

SPICY BUTTERMILK DRESSING

*T*his dressing is very similar to the one above and equally low in calories; again, feel free to double the portion. Make it another week as a slightly different all-purpose dressing.   *MAKES 2 CUPS (470 ML), SERVES 32*

Per 1-tablespoon serving: 10 calories; <1 milligram cholesterol; <1 gram fat; 8 milligrams sodium; <1 gram protein (1% RDA); 2 grams carbohydrate

RDA: vitamin C 5%

1½ tablespoons Spice Mix (page 475)
1 tablespoon cornstarch
1 cup (240 ml) orange juice

1 cup (240 ml) buttermilk
4 cloves garlic, smashed and peeled

1. Combine Spice Mix and cornstarch in a 4-cup (1-l) glass measure. Stir in liquid, making sure there are no lumps. Add garlic and cook at 100%, uncovered, for 5 minutes or until boiling in a 650- to 700-watt oven.

2. Remove from oven. Place in the refrigerator until chilled.

To make 4 cups (1 l). Use 3 tablespoons Spice Mix, 2 tablespoons cornstarch, 2 cups (470 ml) orange juice, 2 cups (470 ml) buttermilk and 8 cloves garlic. Combine spice mixture, cornstarch, 1 cup (240 ml) of orange juice and 1 cup (240 ml) of buttermilk in a 4-cup (1-l) measure as above. Add garlic and cook, uncovered, for 5 minutes. Stir in remaining juice and buttermilk and finish as above.

FOR 400- TO 500-WATT OVENS

To make 2 cups (470 ml). Combine Spice Mix, cornstarch, orange juice, buttermilk and garlic as in original recipe. Cook in a 4-cup (1-l) measure, uncovered, for 8 minutes or until boiling. Finish as above.

SKINNY TOMATO DRESSING

*T*he garden-fresh flavor of this dressing is one of my favorites for greens and cooked and cooled vegetables. If refrigerated for two days—up to three weeks—it will be stiff like a gelatin mold (I have been caught eating it by the guilty spoonful). Remove from the refrigerator for about fifteen minutes; shake. Replace any extra in the refrigerator. The sodium comes from the tomato juice and the Worcestershire sauce.   *MAKES 2 CUPS (470 ML), SERVES 32*

Per 1-tablespoon serving: 34 calories; 0 milligrams cholesterol; 3 grams fat; 93 milligrams sodium; <1 gram protein (<1% RDA); 1 gram carbohydrate

RDA: vitamin C 5%

1 teaspoon unflavored gelatin
1½ cups (355 ml) tomato juice
4 cloves garlic, smashed and peeled
½ cup (120 ml) olive oil
3 tablespoons fresh lemon juice
2 teaspoons Worcestershire sauce
1 teaspoon celery seeds

1 teaspoon kosher salt
1 teaspoon granulated sugar
¼ teaspoon freshly ground black
    pepper
½ teaspoon hot red pepper sauce,
    optional

1. Combine gelatin, 1 cup (240 ml) of the tomato juice and garlic in a 4-cup (1-l) glass measure. Cover tightly with microwave plastic wrap. Cook at 100% for 2 minutes in a 650- to 700-watt oven. Prick plastic to release steam.

2. Remove from oven. Uncover and stir well. Let cool for 10 minutes.

3. When cool, add remaining tomato juice to mixture and scrape into a food processor. Process for 1 minute. With the machine running, add oil in a thin stream. Add the remaining ingredients and pulse briefly to mix.

4. Refrigerate in a clean glass jar, tightly covered.

To make 4 cups. Use 2 teaspoons unflavored gelatin, 3 cups (705 ml) tomato juice, 8 cloves garlic, 1 cup (240 ml) olive oil, 6 tablespoons fresh lemon juice, 4 teaspoons Worcestershire sauce, 2 teaspoons celery seeds, 2 teaspoons kosher salt, 2 teaspoons granulated sugar, ½ teaspoon freshly ground black pepper and ½ teaspoon hot pepper sauce (optional). Combine gelatin, 1 cup of the tomato juice and garlic cloves. Cook in a 4-cup (1-l) measure for 2 minutes as in Step 1. Finish as in Steps 2, 3 and 4.

FOR 400- TO 500-WATT OVENS
To make 2 cups (470 ml) or 4 cups (1 l). Cook gelatin and 1 cup (240 ml) of the juice as in Step 1 for 3 minutes. Finish as in Steps 2, 3 and 4.

GREEN SALSA DRESSING

A thin version of a Mexican salsa, this can be used as a topping for beans and rice, or mixed with the beans to make a salad. Otherwise, use it to dress raw or cooked vegetables or over raw ripe tomatoes and/or cucumbers. If you can afford the calories, this is delicious with avocados alone or in a salad. If you omit the water, you increase the calories only slightly and have a good salsa for tortillas or as a dip.   *MAKES 1⅔ CUPS (400 ML), SERVES 25*

Per 1-tablespoon serving: 22 calories; 0 milligrams cholesterol; 2 grams fat; 57 milligrams sodium; <1 gram protein (<1% RDA); 1 gram carbohydrate

RDA: vitamin C 4%

½ pound (227 g) tomatillos, husks removed, cored and coarsely chopped

1 fresh jalapeño pepper or chili pepper, or 1 dried pepper

2 cloves garlic, smashed and peeled

2 scallions, green and white parts, cut into 1-inch (2.5-cm) lengths

⅓ cup (80 ml) water

2 tablespoons chopped fresh cilantro leaves

¼ cup (60 ml) vegetable oil, preferably canola (not olive)

1 teaspoon kosher salt

1 tablespoon fresh lime juice

1. Combine tomatillos, pepper, garlic, scallions and water in a 4-cup (1-l) glass measure. Cover tightly with microwave plastic wrap. Cook at 100% for 2 minutes in a 650- to 700-watt oven. Prick plastic to release steam.

2. Remove from oven and uncover carefully. Scrape into a blender. Add remaining ingredients and blend until smooth.

FOR 400- TO 500-WATT OVENS

To make 1⅔ cups (400 ml). Cook for 3 minutes 30 seconds.

PAPRIKA DRESSING

*B*efore America acquired all its newfound sophistication, French dressing used to be an odd, slightly sweet sauce made with paprika and shaken out of a bottle. I never liked it; but it did give me the idea for this bright orange dressing fragrant with freshly cooked paprika and sweetened with onion. Out of nostalgia or out of adventure, try this. The now-despised iceberg lettuce would do brilliantly.
MAKES ½ CUP (120 ML), SERVES 8

Per 1-tablespoon serving: 65 calories; 0 milligrams cholesterol; 7 grams fat; 45 milligrams sodium; <1 gram protein (1% RDA)

RDA: vitamin A 7%; vitamin C 3%

1 medium onion (4 ounces; 113.5 g), peeled and thinly sliced (2 cups; 470 ml)
¼ cup (60 ml) olive oil
1 teaspoon paprika

Small pinch cayenne
2 tablespoons white wine vinegar
¼ cup (60 ml) water
¼ teaspoon kosher salt

1. Combine onion, 1 tablespoon of the oil, paprika and cayenne in a 1½-quart (1.5-l) soufflé dish or casserole and toss until onion is well coated. Cook, uncovered, at 100% for 3 minutes in a 650- to 700-watt oven. Stir in vinegar and cook, uncovered, for 2 minutes.
2. Transfer onion mixture to a food processor. Add water and salt and process until smooth. With motor running, slowly add the remaining oil. Scraping down the sides as necessary, process until smooth.

FOR 400- TO 500-WATT OVENS

To make ½ cup (120 ml). Cook as in Step 1, uncovered, for 6 minutes. Stir in vinegar and cook, uncovered, for 3 minutes. Finish as in Step 2.

SATÉ DRESSING

*S*até are those barbecued skewers of Malaysian and Indonesian food. They are normally served with a dipping sauce that can be thick with finely ground peanuts or, as in Vietnamese cooking, thin with bits of fresh chopped peanuts and cucumber floating around. This inauthentic version makes a good salad dressing, a good dipping sauce and a good dip for fresh vegetables. It is a marvelous alternative to red sauces as an embellishment for cooked shrimp at a dinner party or a cocktail party.

You can multiply or divide this recipe as you wish. To keep the sodium and calories low, use your own Peanut Butter, or substitute commercially made peanut butter if these health concerns are none of yours.

MAKES 1¼ CUPS (300 ML), SERVES 20

Per 1-tablespoon serving: 37 calories; 0 milligrams cholesterol; 3 grams fat; 101 milligrams sodium; 1 gram protein (3% RDA); 1 gram carbohydrate

RDA: niacin 4%

⅔ cup (160 ml) Peanut Butter
  (page 478)
½ cup (120 ml) water
3 tablespoons rice wine vinegar
2 tablespoons tamari soy

1 teaspoon chili oil, or to taste
1 teaspoon Oriental sesame oil
1 ounce (28 g) peeled ginger, grated

1. Place all ingredients in the work bowl of a food processor. Process until smooth.

2. Transfer to a jar and store, tightly covered and refrigerated.

SAVORY SAUCES

Salads are not the only foods that welcome a sauce. It is good to have a repertoire to beautify and change the flavor of simply cooked fish, chicken and meats. Of course, they are also suitable with more elaborate dishes, such as the first-course timbales (pages 103–106) and spinach rolls (pages 106–109). Many are made by puréeing lightly cooked vegetables. This gives them body, intense color, a wide range of tastes and, unlike the salad dressings, vitamins and minerals.

RED PEPPER PURÉE

Nothing could be easier, simpler—only one ingredient—than this bright orange-red sauce. You can use lots of it instead of taking a vitamin pill; look at all that vitamin C and A. More important, the flavor is fabulous. If you look at the recipe for cold Red Pepper Soup (page 145), you will see that once you have made this sauce you are halfway to the finished product. Why don't you make the sauce. Use some for soup and have a dividend—hot or cold—for another meal or two. It keeps for a long time refrigerated; it's all that acidic vitamin C.   *MAKES 3 CUPS (705 ML) IF PURÉED IN FOOD PROCESSOR, 2½ CUPS (590 ML) IF IN FOOD MILL; SERVES 10–12*

Per ¼-cup (60-ml) serving: 19 calories; 0 milligrams cholesterol; <1 gram fat; 2 milligrams sodium; 1 gram protein (1% RDA); 4 grams carbohydrate

RDA: calcium <1%; phosphorus 2%; iron 5%; vitamin A 88%; thiamin 4%; riboflavin 2%; niacin 2%; vitamin C 246%

2½ pounds (1.15 kg) red bell peppers
    (about 5 large peppers), stemmed,
    seeded and deribbed

1. Place peppers in a microwave plastic bag and knot it loosely, or put them in a 2½-quart (2.5-l) soufflé dish and cover tightly with microwave plastic wrap. Cook at 100% for 15 minutes in a 650- to 700-watt oven. Prick plastic to release steam.
2. Remove from oven and uncover.
3. Purée peppers, using either a food mill fitted with a medium disc or a food processor or blender.

FOR 450- TO 500-WATT OVENS

To make 2½–3 cups (590–705 ml). Cook peppers for 25 minutes. Finish as in Steps 2 and 3.

FENNEL SAUCE

*F*ennel's gentle licorice scent and taste hint their way into this pale green sauce that can be made with chicken or vegetarian broth. It is a sauce that adds a minimum of calories and a nice little boost of nutrition. Its delicate flavor and color would set off scallops or salmon to perfection.

MAKES 2 CUPS (470 ML), SERVES 8

Per ¼-cup (60-ml) serving: 34 calories, 0 milligrams cholesterol; 2 grams fat; 87 milligrams sodium; 1 gram protein (3% RDA); 2 grams carbohydrate

RDA: calcium 4%; phosphorus 3%; iron 5%; vitamin A 2%; thiamin 2%; riboflavin 1%; niacin 3%; vitamin C 13%

1½ pounds (680 g) fennel bulbs, cored
   and cut into 1-inch (2.5-cm) chunks
   (about 4 cups; 1 l)
1½ cups (355 ml) Basic Chicken Broth
   (page 460), Vegetarian Broth II
   (page 466), or unsalted or regular
   canned chicken broth

1 tablespoon olive oil
Kosher salt, to taste
Freshly ground black pepper, to taste

1. Place fennel and broth in a 2½ quart (2.5-l) soufflé dish or casserole with a tightly fitted lid. Cover tightly with microwave plastic wrap or lid. Cook at 100% for 15 minutes or until fennel is tender, in a 650- to 700-watt oven. If using plastic, prick to release steam.

2. Remove from oven and uncover. Transfer to a blender and add oil. Blend until very smooth. Add salt and pepper to taste.

FOR 450- TO 500-WATT OVENS

To make 2 cups (470 ml). Cook for 24 minutes.

GREEN BEAN FRAPPÉ

Make this cold, frothy, green sauce in summer when the beans are tender and tasty—not woody. Enjoy it with cold first or main courses. You can make more or less sauce by multiplying or dividing the ingredients and using the basic green bean cooking times on page 421. While this is not the least fattening sauce, it is so rich in vitamins it is well worth trying.   *MAKES 1⅓ CUPS (320 ML), SERVES 4*

Per ⅓-cup (80-ml) serving: 103 calories; 0 milligrams cholesterol; 10 grams fat; 28 milligrams sodium; 2 grams protein (4% RDA); 8 grams carbohydrate

RDA: calcium 4%; phosphorus 4%; iron 6%; 218 milligrams potassium; vitamin A 13%; thiamin 5%; riboflavin 6%; niacin 4%; vitamin C 33%

1 pound (450 g) green beans, tipped and tailed	3 tablespoons fruity olive oil
¾ cup (180 ml) water	2 tablespoons fresh lemon juice
	Pinch kosher salt

1. Combine beans and ¼ cup (60 ml) of the water in a 9-inch (23-cm) glass or ceramic pie plate or quiche dish. Cover tightly with microwave plastic wrap. Cook at 100% for 9 minutes in a 650- to 700-watt oven. Prick plastic to release steam.

2. Remove from oven and uncover. Place green beans together with cooking liquid in a food processor. Purée until almost smooth. With machine running, add remaining ingredients in a thin stream, as for mayonnaise.

3. Use as is, or, for best quality, strain sauce through a fine sieve, pressing on solids to extract as much flavor as possible. Serve cold or at room temperature.

FOR 450- TO 500-WATT OVENS

To make 1⅓ cups (320 ml). Cook for 15 minutes.

RUBY BEET SAUCE

Cold or hot, this brilliant red sauce, sweet and sour, is unusual, maybe not for everyday; but try it with a fish or seafood terrine or a vegetable timbale for a smashing presentation. If you have a blender, it will make a smoother sauce. If the beet tops are young and tender, cook them briefly in the microwave oven for a garnish. *MAKES 2 CUPS (470 ML), SERVES 8*

Per ¼-cup (60-ml) serving: 32 calories; 0 milligrams cholesterol; 1 gram fat; 120 milligrams sodium; .21 gram protein (1.3% RDA); 7.6 grams carbohydrate

RDA: iron 3%; 164 milligrams potassium; vitamin C 29%

1 pound (450 g) beets, stems trimmed to 2 inches (5 cm)
1 cup (240 ml) unsweetened apple juice

2 tablespoons cider vinegar
½ teaspoon kosher salt

1. Wash beets. Place in a 3-inch (7.5-cm) deep ceramic or glass dish large enough to hold the beets in a single layer. Cover tightly with microwave plastic wrap. Cook at 100% for 12 minutes in a 650- to 700-watt oven. Prick plastic to release steam. Test beets for tenderness; if they are especially large, it may take up to 2 minutes longer until the tip of a knife easily pierces to the center of the beet.

2. Cool beets until you can handle them. Peel, then remove stems. In a blender or food processor, purée beets with remaining ingredients until sauce becomes a smooth liquid.

FOR 450- TO 500-WATT OVENS

To make 2 cups (470 ml). Cook for 18 minutes. Test beets as above and continue cooking if needed. Finish as in Step 2.

24 KARAT SAUCE

Vitamins can come from sauces just as much as from the main ingredient. The name of this carrot-based sauce is not just a pun. It is there to tell you about its brilliant color and two-day supply of vitamin A. The sauce quickly makes a party dish out of the most simply cooked fish or chicken, or it can go with vegetable first courses. It reheats well, so you can make it ahead; you can even freeze it.
MAKES 2 CUPS (470 ML), SERVES 8

Per ¼-cup (60-ml) serving: 63 calories; 10 milligrams cholesterol; 3 grams fat; 242 milligrams sodium; 4 grams protein (9% RDA); 6 grams carbohydrate

RDA: calcium 10%; phosphorus 8%; iron 4%; vitamin A 217%; thiamin 2%; riboflavin 4%; niacin 3%; vitamin C 6%

¾ pound (340 g) carrots, trimmed, peeled and cut into 1-inch (2.5-cm) thick rounds
¾ cup (180 ml) Basic Chicken Broth (page 460), or unsalted or regular canned chicken broth

1½ teaspoons ground cumin
1 cup (240 ml) part-skim ricotta cheese
1 teaspoon kosher salt

1. In a 9-inch (23-cm) glass pie plate or quiche dish, stir together carrots, broth and cumin. Cover tightly with microwave plastic wrap. Cook at 100% for 15 minutes in a 650- to 700-watt oven.

2. While carrots are cooking, purée ricotta in a blender until completely smooth, scraping down the sides from time to time.

3. When carrots are cooked, remove from oven and prick plastic with the tip of a small knife. Uncover carefully. Add carrots, broth and cumin to blender. Purée until smooth. Season to taste with salt.

FOR 400- TO 500-WATT OVENS

To make 2 cups. Cook carrots as in Step 1 for 20 minutes. Finish as in Steps 2 and 3.

WATERCRESS SAUCE

*T*his intensely green sauce is rich in taste, and meant to be served hot. The sauce that follows is cold. It's a question of taste.   *MAKES 1¾ CUPS (410 ML), SERVES 7*

Per ¼-cup (60-ml) serving: 20 calories; .4 milligram cholesterol; .4 gram fat; 31 milligrams sodium; 1 gram protein (2.5% RDA); 3 grams carbohydrate

RDA: calcium 3%; vitamin A 7%; vitamin C 5%

1½ cups (355 ml) watercress sprigs
  (about 1½ ounces; 42.5 g)
1¼ cups (300 ml) Basic Chicken Broth
  (page 460), or unsalted or regular
  canned chicken broth

2 tablespoons cornstarch
½ cup (120 ml) buttermilk
Kosher salt, to taste
Freshly ground black pepper, to taste

1. Place watercress and 1 cup (240 ml) of the broth in a blender. You can use a food processor; but the result will not be as fine. Purée for 1 minute. Pour into a 4-cup (1-l) glass measure.

2. Slowly, stir cornstarch into remaining broth to make a smooth slurry. Stir thoroughly into watercress mixture. Cover tightly with microwave plastic wrap. Cook at 100% for 4 minutes in a 650- to 700-watt oven. Prick plastic to release steam.

3. Remove from oven. Uncover and stir in buttermilk. Add salt and pepper to taste.

FOR 400- TO 500-WATT OVENS

To make 1¾ cups (410 ml). Cook as in Step 2 for 8 minutes. Finish as in Step 3.

RICH WATERCRESS SAUCE

*T*his cold sauce is a delight with fish and chicken. You can substitute skim milk for the heavy cream to make an even skinnier sauce, if you like.
MAKES 1¼ CUPS (300 ML), SERVES 5

Per ¼-cup (60-ml) serving: 15 calories; 4 milligrams cholesterol; 1 gram fat; 51 milligrams sodium; 1 gram protein (2% RDA); 1 gram carbohydrate

12 ounces (340 g) watercress, washed
   and stemmed (about 6 cups; 1.5 l)
½ cup (120 ml) part-skim ricotta
   cheese

2 tablespoons heavy cream
½ teaspoon kosher salt

1. Place watercress in a 2½-quart (2.5-l) soufflé dish. Cook, uncovered, at 100% for 4 minutes in a 650- to 700-watt oven.
2. Remove from oven. Transfer watercress to a blender or food processor. Add remaining ingredients and blend until completely smooth. Store, tightly covered and refrigerated.

FOR 400- TO 500-WATT OVENS
To make 1¼ cups (300 ml). Cook for 6 minutes.

GREEN SAUCE

*T*his is basically a mint sauce and is meant to be eaten as soon as it is prepared. The English would use it with cooked lamb and it's delicious that way. Cook the prepared sauce ingredients after your leg of lamb comes out of the oven and is resting. It is also good with vegetable timbales and simply cooked vegetables. It is a thin sauce, so you need less of it than you might of a thicker one.
MAKES A GENEROUS 1 CUP (240 ML), 8 SERVINGS

Per 2-tablespoon serving: 19 calories; 0 milligrams cholesterol; 4 grams sodium; <1 gram protein (1% RDA); 4 grams carbohydrate

RDA: iron 4%; vitamin A 26%; vitamin C 14%

1 cup (240 ml) whole mint leaves, from
    about 2 bunches (about 2 ounces; 56
    g), plus 1 tablespoon chopped leaves
1 cup (240 ml) Vegetarian Broth II
    (page 466)

1 tablespoon cornstarch
2 tablespoons chopped parsley
2 teaspoons cider vinegar
¼ teaspoon granulated sugar
¼ teaspoon kosher salt, or to taste

1. Place the whole mint leaves and ¼ cup (60 ml) of the broth in a 1-quart (1-l) soufflé dish. Cover tightly with microwave plastic wrap. Cook at 100% for 1 minute 30 seconds in a 650- to 700-watt oven. Prick plastic to release steam.

2. Remove from oven and uncover. Transfer leaves and liquid to a blender and purée until completely smooth. Pass through a very fine sieve back into the soufflé dish, pushing out all the liquid. Discard the pulp. Add enough of the remaining broth to make 1 cup (240 ml) liquid.

3. In a small bowl mix the cornstarch with 2 tablespoons of the broth mixture, making sure there are no lumps. Stir back into broth mixture. Cover and cook for 1 minute 30 seconds. Prick plastic to release steam.

4. Remove from oven and uncover. Stir in chopped mint and parsley. Re-cover and cook 1 minute 30 seconds. Prick plastic.

5. Remove from oven and uncover. Stir in remaining ingredients. Serve hot.

FOR 400- TO 500-WATT OVENS

To make 1 cup (240 ml). Cook as in Step 1 for 3 minutes. Continue with Steps 2 and 3, cooking for 3 minutes. Cook as in Step 4 for 1 minute 30 seconds. Finish as in Step 5.

DIET BÉCHAMEL

White Sauce

Béchamel, the classic white or cream sauce of French cooking, has fallen out of favor in recent years. I still like it, especially since I have discovered that I can quickly make a diet version. This group of sauces adds creaminess to all sorts of dishes that would be much too fattening and artery-hardening with real cream. The thickness of the sauce depends on the amount of cornstarch used. Béchamel is the standard thickness. Light Béchamel is used to give a creamy texture to other sauces . . . not to overwhelm the basic food. Thick Béchamel is used mainly to bind vegetable purées and hashes that need some body.

Although I give serving numbers, Béchamel is usually an ingredient, and quantities for a serving may vary. It is unseasoned; the seasoning comes in the finished dish.

BÉCHAMEL
DIET VERSION

MAKES 1 CUP (240 ML), SERVES 4

Per ¼-cup (60-ml) serving: 41 calories; 1.5 milligrams cholesterol; .1 gram fat; 40 milligrams sodium; .3 gram protein (6% RDA); 7 grams carbohydrate

RDA: calcium 9%; 127 milligrams potassium; riboflavin 4%

2 tablespoons cornstarch   1¼ cups (300 ml) skim milk

    1. Measure cornstarch into a 2½-quart (2.5-l) soufflé dish or casserole with a tightly fitted lid. Pour in a small amount of milk and stir until cornstarch is completely dissolved. Stir in remaining milk. Cover tightly with microwave plastic wrap or lid. Cook at 100% for 3 minutes in a 650- to 700-watt oven.
    2. Remove from oven and uncover. Scrape corners and bottom of dish well with a wooden spoon. Using a whisk, whisk well to dissolve all lumps. Cover tightly with plastic, return to oven and cook for 2 minutes. Prick plastic to release steam.
    3. Remove from oven and uncover. Serve hot.

To make 2 cups (470 ml). Use 4 tablespoons cornstarch and 2 cups (470 ml) skim milk. Follow Step 1 and cook for 3 minutes. Remove from oven, shake dish and cook for 3 minutes more. Finish as in Step 2.

To make ½ cup (120 ml). Use 1 tablespoon cornstarch and ½ cup (120 ml) skim milk. Combine cornstarch and milk as in Step 1 in a 4-cup (1-l) glass measure. Cook, tightly covered, for 1 minute. Follow Step 2 and cook for 1 minute.

FOR 400- TO 500-WATT OVENS

To make 1 cup (240 ml). Follow Step 1. Remove from oven, shake dish and cook for 3 minutes more. Finish as in Step 2.

To make 2 cups (470 ml). Follow Step 1 and cook for 4 minutes. Remove from oven, shake dish and cook for 4 minutes more. Finish as in Step 2.

To make ½ cup (120 ml). Combine cornstarch and milk as in Step 1 in a 4-cup (1-l) glass measure. Cook, tightly covered, for 3 minutes. Follow Step 2 and cook for 2 minutes.

THIN BÉCHAMEL

MAKES 1 CUP (240 ML), SERVES 4

Per ¼-cup (60-ml) serving: 38 calories; 1.5 milligrams cholesterol; .1 gram fat; 40 milligrams sodium; 3 grams protein (6% RDA); 6 grams carbohydrate

RDA: calcium 9%

1½ tablespoons cornstarch   1¼ cups (300 ml) skim milk

1. Measure cornstarch into a 2½-quart (2.5-l) soufflé dish or casserole with a tightly fitted lid. Pour in a small amount of milk and stir until cornstarch is completely dissolved. Stir in remaining milk. Cover tightly with microwave plastic wrap or lid. Cook at 100% for 3 minutes in a 650- to 700-watt oven.

2. Remove from oven and uncover. Scrape corners and bottom of dish well with a wooden spoon. Using a whisk, whisk well to dissolve all lumps. Cover tightly with plastic, return to oven and cook for 2 minutes.

To make 2 cups (470 ml). Use 3 tablespoons cornstarch and 2 cups (470 ml) skim milk. Follow Step 1 and cook for 3 minutes. Remove from oven, shake dish and cook for 3 minutes more. Finish as in Step 2.

To make ½ cup (120 ml). Use 2 teaspoons cornstarch and ½ cup (120 ml) skim milk. Combine cornstarch and milk as in Step 1 in a 4-cup (1-l) glass measure. Cook, tightly covered, for 1 minute. Follow Step 2 and cook for 1 minute.

FOR 400- TO 500-WATT OVENS

To make 1 cup (240 ml). Follow Step 1. Remove from oven, shake dish and cook for 3 minutes more. Finish as in Step 2.

To make 2 cups (470 ml). Follow Step 1 and cook for 4 minutes. Remove from oven, shake dish and cook for 4 minutes more. Finish as in Step 2.

To make ½ cup (120 ml). Combine cornstarch and milk as in Step 1 in a 4-cup (1-l) glass measure. Cook, tightly covered, for 3 minutes. Follow Step 2 and cook for 2 minutes.

THICK BÉCHAMEL

Per ¼-cup (60-ml) serving: 49 calories; 1.5 milligrams cholesterol; .1 gram fat; 40 milligrams sodium; 3 grams protein (6% RDA); 9 grams carbohydrate

RDA: calcium 9%

3 tablespoons cornstarch   1¼ cups (300 ml) skim milk

1. Measure cornstarch into a 2½-quart (2.5-l) soufflé dish or casserole with a tightly fitted lid. Pour in a small amount of milk and stir until cornstarch is completely dissolved. Stir in remaining milk. Cover tightly with microwave plastic wrap or lid. Cook at 100% for 3 minutes in a 650- to 700-watt oven.
2. Remove from oven and uncover. Scrape corners and bottom of dish well with a wooden spoon. Using a whisk, whisk well to dissolve all lumps. Cover tightly with plastic, return to oven and cook for 2 minutes.

To make 2 cups (470 ml). Use 6 tablespoons cornstarch and 2 cups (470 ml) skim milk. Follow Step 1 and cook for 3 minutes. Remove from oven, shake dish and cook for 3 minutes more. Finish as in Step 2.

To make ½ cup (120 ml). Use 1½ tablespoons cornstarch and ½ cup skim milk. Combine cornstarch and milk as in Step 1 in a 4-cup (1-l) glass measure. Cook, tightly covered, for 1 minute. Follow Step 2 and cook for 1 minute.

FOR 400- TO 500-WATT OVENS
To make 1 cup (240 ml). Follow Step 1. Remove from oven, shake dish and cook for 3 minutes more. Finish as in Step 2.

To make 2 cups (470 ml). Follow Step 1 and cook for 4 minutes. Remove from oven, shake dish and cook for 4 minutes more. Finish as in Step 2.

To make ½ cup (120 ml). Combine cornstarch and milk as in Step 1 in a 4-cup (1-l) glass measure. Cook, tightly covered, for 3 minutes. Follow Step 2 and cook for 2 minutes.

PAPRIKA-LEMON BÉCHAMEL

*T*his slightly jazzy version of béchamel is more of a finished sauce that can stand on its own than the other béchamels. It has a light orange color and is mildly spicy. The level of flavor and spiciness will depend on the kind of paprika you use. While most supermarket paprikas are very mild, if you find a specialty store or a good supermarket that has imported Hungarian paprika, you will notice that it comes in sweet, mild and hot. The hot is about as spicy as our own chili powder; but it has more sweet notes, a brighter color and, of course, no cumin added. I often use it instead of chili powder in non-Southwestern recipes.
MAKES 1 CUP (240 ML), SERVES 4

Per ¼-cup (60-ml) serving: 33 calories; 1 milligram cholesterol; .2 gram fat; 123 milligrams sodium; 2 grams protein (5% RDA); 6 grams carbohydrate

RDA: calcium 8%; phosphorus 7%; vitamin A 17%; riboflavin 6%; vitamin C 7%

1 tablespoon cornstarch
2 teaspoons paprika
¼ teaspoon kosher salt

1 cup (240 ml) skim milk
5 teaspoons fresh lemon juice
Freshly ground black pepper, to taste

1. Place cornstarch, paprika and salt in a 1½-quart (1.5-l) soufflé dish. Slowly whisk in the milk and continue to whisk until the cornstarch is completely dissolved.

2. Cover tightly with microwave plastic wrap. Cook at 100% for 2 minutes in a 650- to 700-watt oven. Prick plastic to release steam.

3. Remove from oven and uncover. Stir well, especially in the corners of the dish. Re-cover and cook for 1 minute. Prick plastic wrap.

4. Remove from oven, uncover and stir in the lemon juice and pepper to taste.

FOR 400- TO 500-WATT OVENS

To make 1 cup. Increase paprika to 2½ teaspoons. Cook as in Steps 2 and 3 for 6 minutes, stirring after 3 minutes. Finish as in Step 4.

ORIENTAL GLAZE

I glaze Oriental Shrimp (page 278) with this; but it would be equally good on pork or chicken for barbecuing. You don't need too much, as it's savory. Besides, one-quarter cup (60 ml), enough for four people, is sixty calories. It won't work out to much per portion. It keeps very well when refrigerated. Make it at the beginning of summer and keep it on hand.   *MAKES 1¼ CUPS (300 ML), SERVES 20*

Per 1-tablespoon serving: 15 calories; 0 milligrams cholesterol; 0 grams fat; 412 milligrams sodium; 1 gram protein (2% RDA); 3 grams carbohydrate

Grated zest of 2 lemons
2 tablespoons granulated sugar
1 tablespoon cornstarch
½ cup (120 ml) tamari soy
½ cup (120 ml) Basic Chicken Broth
    (page 460), or unsalted or regular
    canned chicken broth
¼ cup (60 ml) rice wine vinegar
1 tablespoon tomato paste

1 ounce (28 g) peeled and grated fresh
    ginger (about 1 tablespoon)
6 cloves garlic, smashed, peeled and
    minced
½ teaspoon ground cardamom
½ teaspoon ground coriander
¼ teaspoon hot red pepper sauce
1 teaspoon fresh lemon juice

1. Combine all ingredients except lemon juice in a 4-cup (1-l) glass measure. Cover tightly with microwave plastic wrap. Cook at 100% for 6 minutes in a 650- to 700-watt oven. Prick plastic to release steam.

2. Remove from oven and uncover. Stir in lemon juice and use immediately or store, tightly covered and refrigerated.

FOR 400- TO 500-WATT OVENS

To make 1¼ cups (300 ml). Cook for 10 minutes.

QUICK BARBECUE SAUCE

*T*his is an all-around sauce for American-style barbecue. A quarter cup (60 ml) may be enough for two people, in which case it's only twenty-one calories per serving. Keep it on hand.   *MAKES 4 CUPS (1 L), SERVES 16*

Per ¼-cup (60-ml) serving: 42 calories; 0 milligrams cholesterol; <.1 gram fat; 536 milligrams sodium; .6 gram protein (1.3% RDA); 10 grams carbohydrate

RDA: calcium 8%; iron 11%; 456 milligrams potassium; vitamin A 9%; vitamin C 20%

2 cups (470 ml) Fresh Tomato Purée (page 468), or canned tomato purée
½ cup (120 ml) dark molasses
3 tablespoons Dijon mustard
¾ cup (180 ml) cider vinegar
1½ ounces (42.5 g) Pickled Jalapeño Peppers (page 473), or canned jalapeño peppers, chopped (2 tablespoons)

8 cloves garlic, smashed, peeled and minced
1 tablespoon kosher salt
¼ teaspoon hot red pepper sauce, or to taste

1. Combine all ingredients except salt and pepper sauce in an 8-cup (2-l) glass measure. Cook, uncovered, at 100% for 10 minutes in a 650- to 700-watt oven.

2. Remove from oven. Stir in remaining ingredients and use immediately or store, tightly covered and refrigerated.

FOR 400- TO 500-WATT OVENS

To make 4 cups (1 l). Cook for 20 minutes.

Diet Spreads and Snacks

I've always felt sympathetic to A. A. Milne's king who only wanted "a bit of butter for his bread." Butter in moderation isn't the monster it's been made out to be; but when reducing calories, cholesterol and saturated and unsaturated fat, it's nice to have tasty alternatives. I also want quickly made alternatives to high-calorie, high-sodium dips for easy lunches and entertaining (cocktail parties)—to serve with raw vegetables or low-calorie crackers—and for easy additions to lunch and breakfast. Since almost none of these are cooked, they can be divided and multiplied at will.

Some of the best snacks are strips of cleaned vegetables prepared ahead and kept in cold water in the refrigerator. A piece of fruit (calories and nutrition on pages 532–533) is always good. Have an Oat Bran Wafer (page 161), or a store-bought low-calorie, low-sodium whole wheat crisp, or some of those vegetables with one of these dips. Popcorn that has no butter or salt—high in fiber, with only 23 calories per cup—is also a good and an easy snack. Watch out for the buttered and seasoned kinds.

Most of the dips are also excellent when you want something to serve before dinner. It's a good idea to give yourself a snack or a bowl of low-calorie soup before you go out to a cocktail party or a dinner that you think may be late. It's the old Scarlett O'Hara trick. You cut your appetite and are less liable to overindulge at the party.

YOGURT CHEESE

Nonfat yogurt cheese that you make at home is delicious and can be modified with a wide variety of ingredients, used to cook with or served alone as a cheese with salad. The only problem is that you have to plan ahead.
MAKES 1½ CUPS (355 ML), SERVES 12

Per 2-tablespoon serving: 33 calories; 1.5 milligrams cholesterol; 0 grams fat; 36 milligrams sodium; 4 grams protein (9% RDA); 4 grams carbohydrate

RDA: calcium 11%; phosphorus 19%; 134 milligrams potassium; riboflavin 7%

4 cups (1 l) nonfat yogurt

1. Line a fine sieve with a double thickness of damp cheesecloth. Set this over a bowl and pour yogurt into the sieve. Refrigerate for 24 hours.

SMOKED SALMON YOGURT CHEESE

I like this at brunch on half of a toasted bagel. A few chives are a pleasant addition if you have them.   *MAKES 1½ CUPS (355 ML), SERVES 12*

Per 2-tablespoon serving: 35 calories; 4 milligrams cholesterol; .5 gram fat; 112 milligrams sodium; 6 grams protein (13% RDA); 4 grams carbohydrate

RDA: calcium 11%; phosphorus 21%; 151 milligrams potassium; riboflavin 6%

1½ cups (355 ml) Yogurt Cheese
  (opposite page)

4 ounces (13.5 g) smoked salmon,
  finely chopped
Fresh lemon juice, to taste

1. Combine all ingredients in a small bowl. Let chill for several hours to allow the flavors to develop.

Making and draining yogurt cheese with dampened
cheesecloth and a sieve set over a bowl

CHIVE YOGURT CHEESE

*T*his is good at breakfast, or with a salad.   *MAKES 1½ CUPS (355 ML), SERVES 12*

Per 2-tablespoon serving: 33 calories; 1.5 milligrams cholesterol; <.1 gram fat; 38 milligrams sodium; 4 grams protein (9% RDA); 4 grams carbohydrate

RDA: calcium 11%; iron 19%; riboflavin 6%

1½ cups (355 ml) Yogurt Cheese
   (page 514)

2 tablespoons plus 2 teaspoons finely
   chopped fresh chives

    1. Combine cheese and chives in a small bowl. Cover and let chill for several hours to allow the flavors to develop.

LIPTAUER

*L*iptauer was served all over the Austro-Hungarian Empire, which included Czechoslovakia, either with drinks or as a late-night snack. I have lightened the recipe; but the idea and the flavors are still outstanding. Do try to find genuine Hungarian hot paprika for this. If you cannot, use three quarters of a teaspoon of sweet paprika and one quarter of a teaspoon of cayenne pepper.
MAKES 1½ CUPS (355 ML), 12 SERVINGS

Per 2-tablespoon serving: 35 calories; 1.5 milligrams cholesterol; <1 gram fat; 38 milligrams sodium; 4 grams protein (9% RDA); 4 grams carbohydrate

RDA: calcium 11%; phosphorus 20%; 146 milligrams potassium; vitamin A 4%; riboflavin 6%

1½ cups (355 ml) Yogurt Cheese
   (page 514)
2 teaspoons caraway seeds

½ teaspoon sweet paprika
1 teaspoon hot paprika
Freshly ground black pepper, to taste

    1. Combine all ingredients in a small bowl. Chill for several hours to allow the flavors to develop.

CURRIED RICOTTA SPREAD

*T*his makes a nice accompaniment to a salad or fruit at lunch.
MAKES 1 CUP (240 ML), SERVES 3

Per ⅓-cup (80-ml) serving: 23 calories; 5 milligrams cholesterol; 1 gram fat; 65 milligrams sodium; 2 grams protein (4% RDA); 1 gram carbohydrate

RDA: calcium 4%

1 tablespoon curry powder
1 cup (240 ml) part-skim ricotta cheese

½ teaspoon kosher salt
3 tablespoons fresh lemon juice

   1. Put curry powder in a small ramekin. Cook at 100%, uncovered, for 1 minute 30 seconds in a 650- to 700-watt oven.
   2. Place ricotta in a blender. Add curry powder and salt. Blend until smooth. Add lemon juice and let stand in the refrigerator overnight before serving.

CINNAMON COTTAGE CHEESE SPREAD

*T*his is a very quick low-calorie alternative to butter at breakfast.
MAKES ½ CUP (120 ML), SERVES 8

Per 1-tablespoon serving: 8 calories; 1 milligram cholesterol; <1 gram fat; 1 milligram sodium; 2 grams protein (3% RDA); <1 gram carbohydrate

½ cup (120 ml) low-fat cottage cheese
Pinch cinnamon

Sugar substitute, to taste

   1. Combine all ingredients. Serve over toast with a sprinkling of wheat germ, if desired.

COTTAGE CHEESE DIP

*T*his vegetable-cheese dip can be spread on bread at lunch or used in a double portion as the main part of lunch with bread and fruit.
MAKES 2 CUPS (470 ML), SERVES 8

Per ¼-cup (60-ml) serving: 49 calories; 4.5 milligrams cholesterol; .7 gram fat; 234 milligrams sodium; 7 grams protein (16% RDA); 3 grams carbohydrate

RDA: calcium 4%; phosphorus 8%; iron 3%; vitamin A 42%; riboflavin 6%; vitamin C 36%

1 small carrot (2 ounces; 56 g), peeled
   and cut into 1-inch (2.5-cm) pieces
4 ounces (113.5 g) green bell pepper,
   cut into 1-inch (2.5-cm) pieces
1 scallion, cut into 1-inch (2.5-cm)
   lengths

⅓ cup (80 ml) parsley leaves
16 ounces (450 g) low-fat cottage
   cheese
½ teaspoon freshly ground black
   pepper
Kosher salt, to taste

1. Place all vegetables and parsley in the work bowl of a food processor. Process until finely chopped but not puréed. Scrape into a bowl and stir in cottage cheese, pepper and salt. Store, tightly covered, in the refrigerator.

FROMAGE BLANC

*I*f you can find it, you can buy fromage blanc; but here is a way to make it using a starter available from New England Cheesemaking Supply Company, P.O. Box 85, Ashfield, MA, 01330 (413) 628-3808. They also have rennet tablets, which you can use to make Chocolate Junket (page 573). If you are a vegetarian or kosher, they also have a vegetarian starter with instructions.
MAKES 1 CUP, 8 PORTIONS

Per 2-tablespoon portion: 33 calories; 2.4 milligrams cholesterol; <1 gram fat; 42 milligrams sodium; 4 grams carbohydrate

RDA: calcium 10%; phosphorus 9%; vitamin A 5%; riboflavin 6%

4 cups (1 l) skim milk

1 package starter culture (1.75 g)

1. Place milk in a 2½-quart (2.5-l) soufflé dish. Cook uncovered for 12 minutes, or until milk reaches 198°F (92°C).

2. Remove from oven and cool over a bowl of iced water until it reaches 86°F (30°C). Stir in starter culture package. Cover and allow to stand in a warm place for 12 to 15 hours (or overnight).

3. Uncover and drain mixture through a sieve lined with damp cheesecloth. Allow to drain for 4 hours.

FOR 400- TO 500-WATT OVENS

To make 1 cup. Cook as in Step 1 for 20 minutes.

SUMMER GREEN DIP

*O*ne summer's day a group of friends called unexpectedly to say they were coming by for drinks. I really had nothing in the house. Fortunately, the garden was burgeoning. I picked a lot of greens and threw them in a food processor with some skim-milk ricotta. This is what came out. It was a great success.

MAKES 1½ CUPS (355 ML), SERVES 12

Per 2-tablespoon serving: 44 calories; 7 milligrams cholesterol; 2 grams fat; 176 milligrams sodium; 4 grams protein (8% RDA); 4 grams carbohydrate

RDA: calcium 12%; 232 milligrams potassium; vitamin A 34%; vitamin C 18%

12 ounces (340 g) spinach, washed and
  stemmed
3-ounce (85-g) bunch parsley, tops cut
  off and stems discarded (about 2
  ounces; 56 g)
2-ounce (56-g) bunch dill, tops cut off
  and stems discarded (about 1½
  ounces; 42 g)

1 cup (240 ml) part-skim ricotta cheese
½ cup (120 ml) nonfat yogurt
2 cloves garlic, smashed and peeled
1 teaspoon kosher salt
4 teaspoons fresh lemon juice

1. Place cleaned spinach leaves in a colander and squeeze out excess water. Transfer to a food processor.

2. Add parsley and dill tops to spinach along with the remaining ingredients. Process until finely chopped. Refrigerate, covered, for one hour before using.

BASIC CHEESE NUTRITIONAL DATA

All data below are based on a 1-ounce (28-g) portion, unless otherwise noted.

TYPE	CAL.	FAT (g)	CHOL. (mg)	CALC. (mg)	SOD. (mg)
American, pasteurized, processed	106	9	27	174	406
Blue	100	8	21	150	396
Brie	95	8	28	52	178
Cheddar	114	9	30	204	176
Cottage, 2% fat (½ cup; 120 ml), unpacked	102	2	10	78	459
Cream cheese	99	10	31	23	84
Feta	75	6	25	140	316
Fromage blanc (commercial)	20	<1	2.5	7.5	35
Fromage Blanc (homemade; page 518)	25	<.1	1.8	77	31
Gouda	101	8	32	198	232
Monterey Jack	106	9	N/A	212	152
Mozzarella, part skim	72	5	16	183	132
Parmesan, hard	111	7	19	336	454
Romano, solid	110	8	29	302	340
Roquefort	105	9	26	188	513
Swiss	107	8	26	272	74
Yogurt Cheese, skim milk (homemade; page 514)	32	<1	2.4	108	42

SARDINE DIP

You may be startled to see that the bones are included in this dip, which also makes a nice sandwich spread. By the time they have been puréed in a blender, the bones disappear. If you only have a food processor, remove the bones as it won't pulverize them; but you will also be removing calcium.
MAKES ⅔ CUP (160 ML), SERVES 5

Per 2-tablespoon serving: 27 calories; 9 milligrams cholesterol; 1 gram fat; 45 milligrams sodium; 3 grams protein (6% RDA); 2 grams carbohydrate

RDA: calcium 7%; phosphorus 6%

1 ounce (28 g) drained canned sardines (about 4 small sardines), with their skin and bones
½ cup (120 ml) nonfat yogurt

2 teaspoons fresh lemon juice
3 scallions, green parts only, cut into 3-inch (7.5-cm) lengths
Freshly ground black pepper, to taste

1. Combine sardines, yogurt, lemon juice and scallions in a blender. Purée until smooth. Add pepper to taste.

SHRIMP DIP

I make this if I have leftover shrimp after a party. You can always make the shrimp on purpose and multiply and divide amounts following the shrimp cooking times.   MAKES 1½ CUPS (355 ML), SERVES 12

Per 2-tablespoon serving: 24 calories; 37 milligrams cholesterol; <1 gram fat; 50 milligrams sodium; 5 grams protein (10% RDA); 1 gram carbohydrate

½ pound (227 g) cooked shelled shrimp (page 267)
½ cup (120 ml) nonfat yogurt
1 scallion, white and green parts, cut into 1-inch (2.5-cm) pieces

1 teaspoon fresh lemon juice
1 tablespoon fresh dill sprigs
Dash hot red pepper sauce
Kosher salt, to taste
Freshly ground black pepper, to taste

1. Place all ingredients in a food processor and purée until almost smooth.
2. Transfer to a small bowl and refrigerate until ready to use.

RED TOMATO SALSA

*T*his is one of the great inventions of the American Southwest. It needs no cooking, but should be served shortly after being made or it becomes too watery. To avoid last-minute work, prepare all your ingredients ahead. Chop the onions, coriander and garlic. Leave in food processor. A half hour before serving, add tomatoes and jalapeño to food processor and chop. Stir in other ingredients.

Depending on your taste, you may want to add more or less jalapeño. The seeds and interior ribs of jalapeños are the hottest parts. Remove or not as you see fit. If you are unused to working with hot peppers, wear rubber gloves and do not touch any part of your face with them.

Salsa can be served as a dip or as a spicy sauce with Skinny Chili (page 357) or any bean or rice dish. As this is uncooked, you can multiply and divide the recipe as you wish. I find it goes very well at an outdoor grilling party or on a buffet. Since this is low in calories, fat and sodium while it is rich in vitamins, you can eat much more.

If you have leftovers, purée in a food processor or blender until quite finely chopped—the consistency of a thick soup. Stir in a quarter-teaspoon of olive oil for each cup of soup, adding about ten calories per portion. Chill thoroughly and you have gazpacho. The entire amount of salsa will make three generous cups of soup.   *MAKES 3½ CUPS (825 ML); 28 SERVINGS OF SAUCE*

Per 2-tablespoon serving: 7 calories; 0 milligrams cholesterol; <.1 gram fat; 2 milligrams sodium; .3 gram protein (.6% RDA); 2 grams carbohydrate

RDA: vitamin A 6%; vitamin C 11%

6 ounces (170 g) red onion, peeled and
   cut into 1-inch (2.5-cm) chunks
   (about 2 cups; 470 ml)
1 cup (240 ml) fresh coriander leaves
1 large clove garlic, smashed and
   peeled, optional
4 medium tomatoes, each about 6
   ounces (170 g), cored and cut into
   1-inch (2.5-cm) pieces (about 3¾
   cups; 885 ml)

1 Pickled Jalapeño Pepper (page 473),
   stemmed and seeded (about 1
   ounce), or fresh or canned
¼ cup (60 ml) fresh lime juice

1. Place onion, coriander and garlic clove, if using, in the work bowl of a food processor. Process until coarsely chopped. Add the tomatoes and jalapeño and process until almost finely chopped.

2. Transfer mixture to a glass or ceramic bowl and stir in the lime juice. Cover and refrigerate 30 minutes. Serve.

RED PEPPER SPREAD

*T*his is another low-sodium and low-fat version of an old standby from *Food for Friends*. If you can afford the calories, a little olive oil could not go amiss. You can double the recipe by using the larger version of Silky Pepper Strips and doubling the other ingredients. This is a perfect way to start an evening. Have as much as you want; it's good for you—look at all those vitamins.

Serve some more-fattening Diet Spicy Glazed Walnuts (page 525), the slim Summer Green Dip (page 519) and an assortment of vegetables. You can even add two or three Kalamata olives per person. Now you have a party.

MAKES 1 CUP (240 ML)

Per ¼-cup (60-ml) serving: 28 calories; 0 milligrams cholesterol; <1 gram fat; 40 milligrams sodium; <1 gram protein; 6 grams carbohydrate

RDA: iron 7%; vitamin A 106%; vitamin C 301%

1 cup (240 ml) Silky Pepper Strips (page 472)
2 teaspoons capers, drained and rinsed
1 tablespoon plus 2 teaspoons fresh lemon juice
3 cloves garlic, smashed and peeled
Freshly ground black pepper, to taste

1. Combine pepper, capers, lemon juice and garlic in a food processor. Process until smooth. Add freshly ground pepper to taste.

PEAR CHUTNEY

Most chutneys are loaded with salt and sugar. I like this somewhat pale-colored chutney—after all, they are pears—very well indeed. It can be used with curry; but it is just as good with grilled fish, poultry and meat.

I make a tea sandwich with very thin slices of white bread, trimmed of their crusts and cut in half. Two half-slices make a tea sandwich. I purée one and a half teaspoons of chutney per tea sandwich in a food processor or blender—obviously, feel free to multiply. I spread the puréed chutney on one half-slice of bread and top with a very thin half-slice of tomato. On goes the other half-slice of bread. It's worthy of Oscar Wilde.   *MAKES 3 CUPS (705 ML), 12 SERVINGS*

Per ¼-cup (60-ml) serving: 53 calories; 0 milligrams cholesterol; <1 gram fat; 125 milligrams sodium; .4 gram protein (1% RDA); 13 grams carbohydrate

RDA: vitamin C 14%

1½ pounds (680 g) firm pears (about 3 medium-size), peeled, cored and cut into ½-inch (1-cm) cubes (about 4 cups; 1 l)
½ cup (120 ml) cider vinegar
¼ cup (60 ml) frozen apple juice concentrate, defrosted
8 cloves garlic, smashed and peeled
1 tablespoon plus 1 teaspoon peeled and grated fresh ginger

1 teaspoon black mustard seeds
1 teaspoon cumin seeds
¼ teaspoon turmeric
¼ teaspoon ground nutmeg
5 cardamom pods, hulled and crushed
¼ teaspoon hot red pepper flakes
¼ cup (60 ml) water
2 tablespoons cornstarch
1 teaspoon fresh lemon juice
1 teaspoon kosher salt

1. In a 2½-quart (2.5-l) soufflé dish or casserole with a tightly fitted lid, toss together the pears with the vinegar. Add the apple juice concentrate, garlic, ginger and spices. Mix well to coat. Cover tightly with microwave plastic wrap or lid. Cook at 100% for 9 minutes in a 650- to 700-watt oven, stirring once during cooking. If using plastic, prick to release steam.

2. Remove from oven and uncover. In a small bowl mix together the water and cornstarch, making sure there are no lumps. Add mixture to the chutney with the lemon juice and salt and stir well.

3. Allow to cool and store refrigerated.

FOR 400- TO 500-WATT OVENS

To make 3 cups (705 ml). Cook for 15 minutes.

DIET SPICY GLAZED WALNUTS

If you cannot manage to eat just a few nuts, don't make these if you are on a weight-loss diet. Although their spiciness may help to keep your consumption in check. Other than calories, they are perfectly healthful.   *MAKES 5⅓ CUPS*

Per 2-tablespoon serving: 91 calories; 0 milligrams cholesterol; 9 grams fat; 54 milligrams sodium; 2 grams protein (4% RDA); 3 grams carbohydrate

1¼ pounds (564 g) shelled unsalted
 walnuts (about 5⅓ cups; 1.3 l)
4 cups (1 l) cold water
2 teaspoons vegetable oil

1½ teaspoons kosher salt
2 tablespoons granulated sugar
1½ teaspoons cayenne pepper

1. Place walnuts and water in a 14×11×2-inch (35.5×28×5-cm) dish. Cook, uncovered, at 100% for 10 minutes in a 650- to 700-watt oven.
2. Remove from oven. Drain, rinse and dry nuts. Rinse and dry dish and return walnuts to it.
3. Combine remaining ingredients in a small bowl. Add to walnuts and stir to coat. Cook, uncovered, for 8 minutes, stirring several times.
4. Remove from oven. Spread on wax paper to dry.

To make 2½ cups (590 ml). Use 10 ounces (284 g) nuts (about 2½ cups; 590 ml), 2 cups (470 ml) cold water, 1 teaspoon vegetable oil, ¾ teaspoon kosher salt, 1 tablespoon sugar and ¾ teaspoon cayenne pepper. Cook as in Step 1 in a 13×10×2-inch (33×25.5×5-cm) oval dish for 7 minutes. Continue with Step 2. Cook as in Step 3 for 5 minutes. Finish as in Step 4.

FOR 400- TO 500-WATT OVENS

To make 2½ cups (590 ml). Cook as in Step 1 for 15 minutes. Continue with Step 2. In Step 3 cook for 8 minutes. Finish as in Step 4.

RADISH PICKLES

A crisp and mildly spicy pickle to have with a drink, or before a party to stave off hunger. *MAKES 12 HALF-PINT JARS, SERVES ABOUT 48*

Per ¼-jar (¼-cup; 60 ml) serving: 11 calories; 0 milligrams cholesterol; .3 gram fat; 192 milligrams sodium; .5 gram protein (1% RDA); 3 grams carbohydrate

RDA: vitamin C 13%

4½–5 pounds daikon radish (or white or black radishes if daikon is not available)
1 tablespoon celery seeds
2 tablespoons coriander seeds
2 tablespoons yellow mustard seeds

2¼ cups tarragon vinegar
2¼ cups water
2 tablespoons kosher salt
1 teaspoon dried tarragon
6 shallots, peeled and halved

1. Sterilize 12 half-pint canning jars with their lids according to manufacturer's instructions.

2. Peel and trim radish. Cut into 2½ × ½ × ½-inch (6 × .5 × .5-cm) sticks or, if using young white radishes, leave whole. Reserve radish.

3. Place the celery, coriander and mustard seeds in a mound on one side of a kitchen towel. Fold the towel over the seeds. Pound with a heavy saucepan until spices are crushed. Pour into an 8-cup (2-l) glass measure. Stir in vinegar, water, salt and tarragon. Cover tightly with microwave plastic wrap. Cook at 100% in a 650- to 700-watt oven for 7 minutes, or until boiling.

4. Prick plastic to release steam. Remove from oven and uncover. Divide reserved radish evenly among jars, fitting the pieces snugly, upright, in the jars. Place half a shallot in the center of each jar. Pour vinegar mixture over radishes to cover them completely, leaving ½ inch (.5 cm) headroom in each jar.

5. Arrange filled jars around the outside edge of the carrousel. Cook at 100% for 12 minutes, or until radish is just tender.

6. Remove from oven and cover with lids. Let cool slightly. Refrigerate at least overnight and up to several months. Serve chilled.

FOR 400- TO 500-WATT OVENS

To make 4 half-pint jars of pickles. Use 1½ pounds radish, 1 teaspoon celery seeds, 2 teaspoons each coriander and mustard seeds, ¾ cup each vinegar and water, ¼ teaspoon tarragon, 2 teaspoons salt and 2 shallots. Sterilize jars and lids as above. Prepare radish. Crush seeds and mix with vinegars, salt and tarragon in a 4-cup (1-l) glass measure. Cover and cook for 6 minutes, or until boiling. Prepare jars as above and arrange around the edge of a wind-up carrousel. Cook for 10 minutes, or until just tender. Cover and chill as above.

CRUNCHY CAULIFLOWER PICKLE

*T*his inexpensive pickle is delicious, crisp and low in calories. I make it for a diabetic friend who is glad to note that it has no sugar. It has, like most pickles, some salt; watch it if you are on a low-sodium diet.   *MAKES 4 PINTS (2 L), SERVES 24*

Per ¼-cup (60-ml) serving: 9 calories; 0 milligrams cholesterol; 0 grams fat; 211 milligrams sodium; 1 gram protein (1% RDA); 2 grams carbohydrate

RDA: vitamin C 26%

1 head cauliflower (2–2½ pounds; 900 g–1.15 kg), trimmed and cut into small florets (about 5½ cups; 1.3 l)
1 cup (240 ml) loosely packed fresh dill sprigs
2 teaspoons dill seeds
1 teaspoon hot red pepper flakes

1½ tablespoons kosher salt
4 cloves garlic, smashed, peeled and chopped
1 teaspoon coriander seeds
2 cardamom pods, hulled and crushed
2 cups (470 ml) cider vinegar
2 cups (470 ml) water

1. Sterilize 4 pint jars and lids according to the manufacturer's directions. Divide cauliflower and dill sprigs among jars; reserve.
2. Combine remaining ingredients in an 8-cup (2-l) glass measure. Cover tightly with microwave plastic wrap. Cook at 100% for 5 minutes in a 650- to 700-watt oven. Prick plastic to release steam.
3. Remove from oven and uncover. Pour mixture over reserved cauliflower and dill, dividing liquid, garlic and spices evenly among the jars. Arrange jars in a circle on an oven carrousel. Cook, uncovered, for 10 minutes.
4. Remove from oven and cover jars tightly with sterilized lids.
5. Refrigerate for crispness.

FOR 400- TO 500-WATT OVENS

To make 4 pints (2 l). Prepare as in Step 1. Cook as in Step 2 for 10 minutes. Cook as in Step 3 for 15 minutes.

TOMATO BRAISED ONIONS

I serve this as a pleasant and low-sodium alternative to ketchup—not on a sandwich, but as a relish with broiled meats.   *MAKES 4½ CUPS (1.1 L), SERVES 6*

Per ¼-cup (60-ml) serving: 35 calories; 0 milligrams cholesterol; <1 gram fat; 29 milligrams sodium; 1 gram protein (2% RDA); 8 grams carbohydrate

RDA: vitamin A 12%; vitamin C 21%

½ pound (227 g) small white onions (about 8 onions), peeled and cut in half crosswise

⅔ cup (300 g) Fresh Tomato Purée (page 468), or canned tomato purée

1 tablespoon balsamic vinegar
2 tablespoons dark raisins
1 tablespoon tomato paste
½ teaspoon granulated sugar

1. Combine all ingredients in a 9-inch (23-cm) quiche dish or pie plate. Cover tightly with microwave plastic wrap. Cook at 100% for 7 minutes in a 650- to 700-watt oven. Prick plastic to release steam.
2. Remove from oven and uncover. Stir well.

To serve 12. Use 1 pound (450 g) small white onions, 1⅓ cups tomato purée, 2 tablespoons balsamic vinegar, ¼ cup (60 ml) dark raisins, 2 tablespoons tomato paste and 1 teaspoon sugar. Follow Step 1 and cook for 15 minutes, stirring 3 times.

FOR 400- TO 500-WATT OVENS

To serve 6. Cook for 14 minutes.

Other Foods for Snacking

I always seem to get hungry between three and four in the afternoon, whether I have had lunch or not. I like snacks. I also like them late in the evening if dinner has been unusually early. Where we fit in our snacks will depend on our pattern of eating and hunger. No matter when they are eaten, they should be as healthy as the rest of our food. If we are losing weight, they shouldn't sabotage the diet.

There are many snack recipes and suggestions besides the ones above in other chapters of this book. Sadly, the portion size for a snack isn't always as ample as that for mealtime usage. On the opposite page is a list of some snacks that I like, along with a suggested portion size, the amount of calories that portion involves and a page number so that you can find it in the book.

RECIPE	PORTION SIZE	CALORIES	PAGE
Strawberry Shake	½ cup (120 ml)	60	58
Carrot Shake	¾ cup (180 ml)	64	58
Spicy Chicken Broth	1 cup (240 ml)	52	59
Banana Shake	½ cup (120 ml)	64	60
Pineapple-Protein Shake	Generous ⅓ cup (80 ml)	68	61
Curried Yogurt Drink	1 cup (240 ml)	69	62
Hot Cocoa	½ cup (120 ml)	61	63
Pita Pizza	½ pita	75	72
Eggplant Purée with Tomato and Green Pepper, with vegetables or crackers	½ cup (120 ml)	48	88
Small artichoke, or half of a large artichoke	6 ounces (170 g)	75	99
Garlic Escarole Soup	1 cup (240 ml)	39	118
Fennel Soup	¾ cup (180 ml)	34	119
Quick Tomato Soup	1 cup (240 ml)	48	126
Majic Whole-Grain Bread	2 slices	88	152
Oat Bran Wafers	2 wafers	48	161
Baked potato, ½	3 ounces (85 g)	66	219
Fruit portion		80–100	532
Summer Fruit Salad	½ cup (120 ml)	28	537
Winter Fruit Salad	½ cup (120 ml)	34	538
Exotic Fruit Salad	½ cup (120 ml)	22	539
Peppered Strawberries	¾ cup (180 ml)	50	535
Minted Melon	⅔ cup (160 ml)	38	536
Apple Sauce	¼ cup (60 ml)	48	548
Oat Bran Crisps	1 crisp	56	574
Cornmeal Cookies	1 cookie	18	532
Meringue Clouds	2 meringues	16	585
Apricot Leather	1 × 11-inch (2.5 × 28-cm) strip	34	594
Prune Leather	1 × 11-inch (2.5 × 28-cm) strip	57	595
Cranberry Leather	1 × 11-inch (2.5 × 28-cm) strip	45	596
Diet Duxelles on toast	2 tablespoons	14	477
Peanut Butter	1 tablespoon	54	478
Diet Spreads and Snacks			514

DESSERTS

Sweet Endings

I really cannot masquerade as Barbara the Spartan. I have wolfed down sundaes, particularly in the late-lamented days of Schrafft's. My downfall is hot fudge—extra, please—over vanilla or coffee ice cream—no nuts, no cherry, but maybe some whipped cream if it's real, not out of an air-head can. I am saved only because so few people make really good hot fudge anymore. Homemade doesn't work; it's a soda fountain dream. Good hot fudge used to sit at the end of the counter in a pot that kept it hot and needed occasional stirring. Its smell filled the air like the sirens' song. Hot butterscotch wasn't bad either.

I still stumble into a place and a mood that involves me in a hot fudge sundae, and I fall. What I do now is to skip dinner after such a spree. At most, I have a large salad. Not the best way to eat; but better than compounding the error.

Nevertheless, I feel slightly like a fake. Unlike my friends who still work their way through a meal in high anticipation of dessert, who when they ask you what you had for dinner at a restaurant or a party mean: "What did you have for dessert?" I rarely eat dessert, and that certainly helps to keep my weight down. Conversely, one of my thinnest friends, a man, is a dessert fiend. He exercises a great deal, which may help to explain the dual phenomenon; but sugar isn't really that fattening. The killers—not just for your diet—are the heavy cream, the egg yolks and the shortenings. They are loaded with cholesterol or saturated fats, or both.

In some of these desserts, I do indeed use sugar. Almost none call for artificial sweeteners. When artificial sweeteners are used, they are generally added after the cooking time. If such a sweetener is used in a recipe that calls for heating it, the specific type is mentioned since others may do less well in that procedure. Read labels.

It is possible to indulge from time to time. If you have been eating from the recipes in this book, your cholesterol and weight should be way down. Even on the way down, there are desserts that you can eat and enjoy without feeling deprived. Since the world seems to be full of enticing books that give recipes for the richest, butteriest desserts, I will keep my recipes in the healthful category. I do use small amounts of egg yolk, butter and cream from time to time for those who crave it.

I have only a few suggestions to make about those incredibly fattening, guilt-inducing desserts. Don't make large cakes: too many tempting leftovers. Buy the best ingredients and store-bought desserts. If you are going to do it, do it right;

but limit the purchase. Buy just the amount of the best sweet butter you need. After all, it comes in quarter-pound amounts. Try to find bakeries—often French—that have smallish individual portions. Buy just as many as you need.

Finally, another confession: Many of those succulent baked desserts are not at their best made in a microwave oven. Now is the time to heat up your conventional oven and your kitchen. Save the microwave oven for melting the chocolate and the butter or making glazes. It's all in Microwave Gourmet.

These desserts start with the simplest of raw fruits, and go on to poached fruits and some fancy cooked-fruit desserts. There are nonfruit desserts, cookies, sauces and nonmicrowave desserts. Finally, for the persistent sweet tooth, there are some jams, preserves and sweet snacks.

Sometimes you will notice that no RDA percentages are given for a specific recipe. That means it has only its pretty face and delicious taste to recommend it.

Fruit As Dessert

I really like fruit, which is the great ally in the lose-weight and keep-weight-off battles. Fruit also provides ample amounts of carbohydrate, vitamins and minerals as well as fiber, both soluble and insoluble. If you stick to fruits that are in season, they will be cheaper and taste better. Stick to the organically grown if at all possible. If using canned or frozen fruits, look for those in unsweetened juice or light syrup.

Fruits can quickly be made into very good desserts in a microwave oven. Since you need to add no or little liquid, the flavor isn't diminished and you need to add no or little sugar. The natural sweetness of the fruit will come out.

Of course, fruits need not be cooked at all. Eat them alone as desserts or snacks. Mix them into salads. Have them with Fromage Blanc (page 518) or Yogurt Cheese (page 514) or a low-fat, low-sodium store-bought cheese. Top them with Whipped Ricotta Topping (page 581) or serve them with a little light sorbet (pages 552–556).

First you need to know how much of a given fruit makes a portion and how much you are getting nutritionally.

THE FRUIT PORTIONS

A fruit portion contains between eighty and one hundred calories. All calorie counts are for fresh unsweetened fruit. One portion of fruit is the specified amount in the menus in Microslim Gourmet Diets and Menus (pages 46–73) and elsewhere in the book. The quantity of each kind of fruit varies according to its calorie count. You may double the serving if you are large-framed or active. Unless a portion is one whole fruit, the portion size—either the number of pieces of fruit or volume—is given in parentheses after the name of the fruit.

FRUIT NUTRITION

TYPE	CAL.	CARB. (g)	CALC. (% RDA)	IRON (% RDA)	SOD. (mg)	POT. (mg)	VIT. C (% RDA)	VIT. A (% RDA)
Apple	81	19	1	1	1	159	13	1
Applesauce, unsweetened (¾ cup; 180 ml)	79	21	0.6	1.2	3	136	65	1
Apricot (4)	67	16	2	4	1	416	23	73
Banana	105	27	0.7	1.9	1	451	17	2
Blackberries (1 cup; 240 ml)	74	18	4.6	4.6	0	282	50	5
Blueberries (1 cup; 240 ml)	82	20	0.99	1.3	9	129	31	3
Cherries, sour, pitted (1 cup; 240 ml)	77	19	2.4	0.50	5	268	26	40
Cherries, sweet, pitted (1 cup; 240 ml)	104	24	2.1	3.1	1	325	17	6
Figs (2 large)	94	24	4.4	2.6	2	396	4	2
Fruit salad, canned: lt. syrup (½ cup; 120 ml)	73	19	0.8	2.1	7	104	5	11
water-packed (1 cup; 240 ml)	37	10	0.8	2	4	95	8	22
Grapefruit (½ large or 1 small whole)	38	10	1.4	0.6	0	167	69	3
Grapes (1 cup; 240 ml); American type	58	16	1.3	1.5	2	176	6	2
European type	114	28	1.7	2.3	3	296	29	2
Kiwi fruit (2 medium)	92	22	4	3.4	8	504	190	5
Mango (½)	67	18	1.1	0.7	2	161	48	81
Melon Cantaloupe (½)	94	22	2.8	3.2	23	825	188	172
Casaba (2 cups; 470 ml) in large cubes (about 1 lb. [450 g] or ⅙ of a melon, peeled and seeded)	90	22	1.8	7.6	40	714	91	2
Honeydew (1.5 cup; 355 ml) in large cubes (about 6 oz. [170 g] or ⅛ of a melon, peeled and seeded)	90	24	1.5	1	26	692	105	2
Watermelon (2 cups; 470 ml) in large cubes (about 1¼ lbs. [570 g], peeled and seeded)	100	22	2.6	3.1	6	372	51	23

TYPE	CAL.	CARB. (g)	CALC. (% RDA)	IRON (% RDA)	SOD. (mg)	POT. (mg)	VIT. C (% RDA)	VIT. A (% RDA)
Nectarine (1½)	101	24	0.9	1.7	0	438	18	30
Orange (large)	62	15	5.2	0.7	0	237	98	5
Papaya	117	30	7.2	1.7	8	780	313	122
Peach (2)	73	19	0.9	0.19	1	334	19	19
Pear	98	25	1.9	2.3	1	208	11	1
Pineapple, diced								
(1 cup; 240 ml)	77	19	1.1	3.2	1	175	40	1
Plum (2)	72	18	0.4	0.8	0	226	21	9
Raspberies								
(1½ cups; 355 ml)	91	21	4.1	5.8	0	281	77	5
Strawberries								
(2 cups; 470 ml)	90	20	4.2	6.3	4	494	282	2
Tangerine (2)	74	18	2.4	1	2	264	86	31
DRIED FRUITS								
Apricots (10 halves)	83	22	1.6	9.2	3	482	1.4	51
Currants (¼ cup; 60 ml)	102	27	3.1	6.5	3	321	2.8	tr
Prune (5 halves)	100	27	2.2	5.8	2	313	2.3	17
Raisins (2 tbsp., packed)	62	16	1	2.7	2	155	1	0

Some of these are raw, some are cooked and some are just barely prepared. All are quick and taste good. Serve berries with Fromage Blanc (pages 518) and some nonfat yogurt on the side. Sprinkle with sugar or a sugar substitute if you wish. I don't.

Almost all the raw fruit desserts can be multiplied or divided by increasing or decreasing the ingredients for the desired number of portions.

While these are certainly desserts, on purpose or by chance of leftovers, most make filling lunches with some bread and a light cheese.

GINGERED ORANGES

Nothing could be simpler or fresher. This would be ideal after a curry main course or any somewhat heavy winter meal. It can be multiplied by the number of guests, so it's good for a party; it can also be made up to a day ahead. Add some cookies for those who are less weight-conscious, or Meringue Clouds (page 585) for even those who are thinning. Serve the chilled orange slices in overlapping rounds. You can top each round with a sprig of mint if you like.

As you might expect, this is rich in vitamin C; you can forget the breakfast juice. I was surprised by the healthy amount of thiamin. *SERVES 2*

Per 6-slice serving: 79 calories; 0 milligrams cholesterol; 0 grams fat; 0 milligrams sodium; 1 gram protein (3% RDA); 20 grams carbohydrate

RDA: calcium 7%; thiamin 11%; vitamin C 126%

2 juice oranges (each 8 ounces; 227 g)   Pinch ground cumin, optional
1 tablespoon peeled and grated fresh
   ginger, from about a 1-ounce (28-g)
   piece

1. Peel oranges, being careful to remove all the white pith, over a bowl to catch any juices. Cut across into ½-inch (1-cm) slices and seed. Add ginger and stir to combine. Refrigerate until well chilled. Sprinkle with cumin before serving, if desired.

PEPPERED STRAWBERRIES

*T*his odd-sounding dish is delicious. It was my Russian father who taught me how brilliantly black pepper brought out the sweetness of fruit. He used to put it on melon. He never heard of balsamic vinegar. You can use red wine. After sitting for a few minutes, the sugar in the strawberries and the vinegar or the wine combine to make a syrup. Leftovers can be puréed to make a delicious sauce.

I had a little problem here with measurements. I call for a pint of strawberries because that is how they are sold. The box is always more than full and, depending on the size of the strawberries, you will actually get more or less strawberry weight for your pint. Fortunately, strawberries are so low in calories, it won't make much difference. Large strawberries should be cut up; small local strawberries can be left whole. All strawberries should be hulled. Don't just cut off the leafy part. Take the tip of a paring knife and make a conical incision into the top of the strawberry to remove all the pithy white parts.

You can let this sit for a couple of hours, during which time it will evolve into a surprisingly unctuous sauce with the strawberries and vinegar mysteriously combining into a syrup. Use a quarter-cup per person for only seventeen calories. If you have the whole portion fresh as dessert, you get lots of vitamin C for your calories. *SERVES 2*

Per ¾-cup (180-ml) serving: 50 calories; 0 milligrams cholesterol; <1 gram fat; 2 milligrams sodium; 1 gram protein (2% RDA); 12 grams carbohydrate

RDA: 276 milligrams potassium; vitamin C 151%

1 pint (470 ml) fresh strawberries, washed, hulled and quartered	Pinch freshly ground black pepper, or to taste
2 tablespoons balsamic vinegar	

1. Combine all ingredients in a small serving bowl. Let stand for 5 minutes. Serve at room temperature.

Deeply hull strawberries with a small knife to remove all white pith.

MINTED MELON

When melons are good, no dessert is easier. Don't try to make this too far ahead or the melon will shrink, giving its juices to the sauce. If using a melon baller seems like wasted work, just cut the peeled and seeded melon into about three-quarter-inch (2-cm) dice.   *MAKES 5 CUPS (1.2 L), SERVES 4*

Per 1¼-cup (300-ml) serving: 77 calories; 0 milligrams cholesterol; <1 gram fat; 21 milligrams sodium; 1 gram protein (2% RDA); 20 grams carbohydrate

RDA: 579 milligrams potassium; thiamin 11%; vitamin C 93%

1 honeydew melon (about 4 pounds; 1.8 kg), halved, seeded and scooped out with a 1-inch (2.5-cm) melon baller (about 5 cups; 1.2 l)

3 tablespoons chopped fresh mint
3 tablespoons fresh lime juice

1. Combine all ingredients in a large serving bowl. Serve chilled.

Fruit salads can be varied according to what is in season. Substitute fruits that have roughly the same nutritional value from the list on pages 532–533. Recipes can be multiplied or divided at will. If you like, toss each three cups (705 ml) with one tablespoon kirsch or other white fruit brandy for an added forty-one calories. I have allotted a cup and a half of each fruit salad so that you will really feel full; but you may not want that much. The quantity makes a good lunch with some bread and nonfat yogurt, nonfat cottage cheese, Yogurt Cheese (page 514) or Fromage Blanc (page 518).

SUMMER FRUIT SALAD

*S*ummer offers a virtually endless possibility of good fruit salads that can end a party buffet as well as a daily dinner. Leftovers can be eaten at breakfast; but don't make too much, as these fruit salads will stay fresh for only a day or so in the refrigerator. Because of the varied fruits, this gives you a substantial amount of vitamin A along with your vitamin C.   *MAKES 12 CUPS (3 L), SERVES 12*

Per 1½-cup (355-ml) serving: 84 calories; 0 milligrams cholesterol; 1 gram fat; 3 milligrams sodium; 2 grams protein (3% RDA); 20 grams carbohydrate

RDA: potassium 375 milligrams; vitamin A 32%; vitamin C 75%

4 apricots, pitted and cut into wedges
    (about 2 cups; 470 ml)
1 cup (240 ml) diced cantaloupe melon
1½ nectarines, pitted and cut into
    wedges (about 1½ cups; 355 ml)
2 peaches, pitted and cut into wedges
    (about 2 cups; 470 ml)

2 plums, pitted and cut into wedges
    (about 1½ cups; 355 ml)
1 cup (240 ml) blueberries
1½ cups (355 ml) raspberries
2 cups (470 ml) strawberries, hulled
    and halved if large

1. Combine all ingredients in a large serving bowl, adding the berries just before serving.

WINTER FRUIT SALAD

Winter offers fewer fruits for our salads; but their rarity may make them that much more desirable. If you find good out-of-season fruit, such as melons, enjoy the variation. Winter may have less of a fruit selection; what there is will still provide you with vitamin C and potassium.   *MAKES 9 CUPS (2.24 L), SERVES 8*

Per 1½-cup (355-ml) serving: 102 calories; 0 milligrams cholesterol; 1 gram fat; 2 milligrams sodium; 1 gram protein (3% RDA); 26 grams carbohydrate

RDA: 344 milligrams potassium; vitamin C 93%

1 large grapefruit, peeled and sectioned over a bowl to retain juices (2½ cups; 590 ml)

1 cup (240 ml) seedless grapes

2 kiwi fruit, peeled and thinly sliced across

2 navel or juice oranges, peeled and sectioned over a bowl to retain juices (1½ cups; 355 ml)

1 cup (240 ml) peeled, cored and cubed pineapple

1 pear (8 ounces; 227 g), peeled, cored, cut into cubes and tossed with fresh lemon juice—to taste—to prevent discoloration (about 1⅔ cups; 400 ml)

1 Granny Smith or other tart apple (8 ounces; 227 g), cored and cut into chunks (about 1⅔ cups; 400 ml)

1 banana, peeled, sliced and tossed with fresh lemon juice—to taste—to prevent discoloration

1. Except for the banana, combine all ingredients, including their juices, in a large serving bowl. Refrigerate. Add banana just before serving.

PREPARING CITRUS FRUITS AND ZESTS

Peel citrus fruit with a small knife, making sure to remove all white pith.

To section, cut on both sides of the membranes to release sections.

To obtain citrus zests, cut off thinly with a vegetable peeler, making sure not to cut into the white pith.

EXOTIC FRUIT SALAD

*T*here are times when what northerners think of as normal fruits are in sparse supply. It is then that the hot-climate fruits we think of as exotic come into their own and can provide a splendidly colorful and naturally sweet dessert. Fresh lychees are available only for a short time in the spring. If you use canned, be sure to drain and rinse them well—they come in heavy syrup (lots of calories). You will still be increasing the calories per serving; but since this has such a modest calorie count to begin with, it's not a disaster.

If the papaya seeds are not bitter—they often are—rinse them in water and sprinkle some of these black pearls on top of the salad. If you have access to fresh mint or lemon balm, it goes well with this salad.

Exotic doesn't mean fattening—quite the opposite—or lacking in vitamins. You still get plentiful vitamins C and A.   *SERVES 8*

Per 1½-cup (355-ml) serving: 66 calories; 0 milligrams cholesterol; <1 gram fat; 2 milligrams sodium; 1 gram protein (2% RDA); 17 grams carbohydrate

RDA: 22 milligrams potassium; vitamin A 36%; vitamin C 89%

2 cups (470 ml) peeled, cored and cubed fresh pineapple

1 papaya, peeled, seeded and cut into ½-inch (1-cm) cubes (about 4½ cups; 1.1 l)

1 mango, peeled, sliced, pit removed and cut into 1-inch (2-cm) cubes (about 4½ cups; 1.1 l)

15 fresh lychees, peeled and seeded (about 1 cup; 240 ml), or 11-ounce (310-g) can, thoroughly drained and rinsed with cold water

1. Stir together all ingredients in a large serving bowl. Sprinkle papaya seeds over, if desired.

SUMMER FRUIT COMPOTE

Good as raw fruit is, we may tire of it in the halcyon days of summer. Also, it spoils quickly when dead ripe. Cooked in a compote it keeps and offers welcome variation. This dessert, beautiful in its darkly colored sauce, may have somewhat fewer vitamins than some of the other fruit desserts, but 22 percent of your vitamin A and 31 percent of your vitamin C is still plentiful.   *SERVES 8*

Per generous ¾-cup (180-ml) serving: 145 calories; 0 milligrams cholesterol; 1 gram fat; <1 milligram sodium; 2 grams protein (3% RDA); 36 grams carbohydrate

RDA: vitamin A 22%; vitamin C 31%

3 Anjou pears (each 9 ounces; 255 g), peeled, cored and cut into 1-inch (2.5-cm) cubes (about 4 cups; 1 l)

1 tablespoon fresh lemon juice, sprinkled over pear to prevent discoloring

2 peaches (each 7 ounces; 200 g), halved, pitted and cut into 1-inch (2.5-cm) chunks (about 2 cups; 470 ml)

2 cups (470 ml) blackberries

3 apricots (each 3 ounces; 85 g), halved, pitted and cut into 1-inch (2.5-cm) chunks (about 1½ cups; 355 ml)

8 ounces (227 g) sweet cherries, stems removed

¼ cup (60 ml) granulated sugar

Zest from ½ lemon (2 teaspoons)

½ cup (120 ml) water

1 vanilla bean, split lengthwise

1. Arrange pears around the inside edge of a 13 × 11 × 2-inch (33 × 28 × 5-cm) dish. Place peaches inside pears. Place blackberries in the center of the dish and set apricot halves on top of them. Tuck cherries into spaces between fruit. Add remaining ingredients. Cover tightly with microwave plastic wrap. Cook at 100% for 16 minutes in a 650- to 700-watt oven. Prick plastic to release steam.

2. Remove from oven and uncover carefully. Serve each portion warm or refrigerated with some of the cooking liquid.

FOR 400- TO 500-WATT OVENS

To serve 8. Cook as in Step 1 for 25 minutes.

SUMMER FRUIT COMPOTE II

If I prefer one of the summer fruit compotes, it's this one. You may notice that the raspberry measurements don't seem to make sense. That's because containers of raspberries are usually filled beyond their brim. The cup and milliliter measurements should help straighten things out. The reason I include frozen cherries as an option is that all the other fruits may be available fresh for a longer season than sweet dessert cherries such as Bing. *SERVES 8*

Per generous ¾-cup (180-ml) serving: 135 calories; 0 milligrams cholesterol; 1 gram fat; <1 milligram sodium; 1 gram protein (3% RDA); 33 grams carbohydrate

RDA: 290 milligrams potassium; vitamin C 33%

3 Anjou pears (each 9 ounces; 255 g), peeled, cored and cut into 1-inch (2.5-cm) cubes (about 4 cups; 1 l)

1 tablespoon fresh lemon juice, sprinkled over pears to prevent discoloring

2 nectarines (each 7 ounces; 200 g), halved, pitted and cut into 1-inch (2.5-cm) cubes (2 cups; 470 ml)

2 plums (each 4 ounces; 113.5 g), halved, pitted and quartered (1½ cups; 355 ml)

8 ounces (227 g) fresh—pitted and stemmed—sweet cherries, or frozen sweet cherries (no sugar added), defrosted in a sieve under warm running water (1 cup; 240 ml)

1 pint fresh raspberries (2½ cups; 590 ml)

¼ cup (60 ml) granulated sugar

Zest from ½ lemon (2 teaspoons)

½ cup (120 ml) water

1 vanilla bean, split lengthwise

1. Arrange pears around the inside edge of a 13 × 11 × 2-inch (33 × 28 × 5-cm) oval dish. Place nectarines and plums inside pears, and place cherries and raspberries in the center of the dish.

2. Stir together remaining ingredients and pour over the fruit. Cover tightly with microwave plastic wrap. Cook at 100% for 16 minutes in a 650- to 700-watt oven. Prick plastic to release steam.

3. Remove from oven and uncover. Serve at room temperature or chilled.

FOR 400- TO 500-WATT OVENS

To serve 8. Cook as in Step 2 for 25 minutes.

WINTER FRUIT COMPOTE

I like this as much for a cold winter's day breakfast with a slice of toast and something hot to drink as I do for dessert. In addition to everything else, this is loaded with fiber and, considering the absence of fresh fruit, has good vitamin A and C; the potassium is spectacular.   *MAKES 3¾ CUPS (885 ML), SERVES 5*

Per ¾-cup (180-ml) serving: 163 calories; 0 milligrams cholesterol; 1 gram fat; 3 milligrams sodium; 1 gram protein (3% RDA); 42 grams carbohydrate

RDA: 417 milligrams potassium; vitamin A 20%; vitamin C 29%

1½ ounces (42.5 g) small dried apricot halves (about 12 halves; ¼ cup; 60 ml)

¼ cup (60 ml) kirsch or other unsweetened white fruit brandy

½ cup (120 ml) water

3 juniper berries, crushed with your fingers

2 whole cloves

¼ teaspoon mace

Pinch cinnamon

7 ounces (200 g) peeled, cored and cut across into ½-inch (1-cm) chunks fresh pineapple (about 1½ cups; 355 ml)

7½ ounces (214 g) tart apple, peeled, quartered and cut across into ½-inch (1-cm) slices (about 1⅔ cups; 400 ml), mixed with:

1 tablespoon fresh lemon juice

½ vanilla bean, split lengthwise

8 ounces (227 g) pears, peeled, quartered and cut across into 1-inch (2.5-cm) slices (about 1⅔ cups; 400 ml)

3 ounces (85 g) pitted whole prunes (about 8 prunes; ½ cup; 120 ml)

⅓ cup (80 ml) orange juice

4 teaspoons granulated sugar

1 tablespoon slivered almonds, optional

1. Place apricot halves in a circle inside the rim of a 2½-quart (2.5-l) soufflé dish or casserole with a tightly fitted lid. In a small bowl, stir together kirsch, water, juniper berries, cloves, mace and cinnamon and pour over apricots. Cover tightly with microwave plastic wrap or casserole lid. Cook at 100% for 3 minutes in a 650- to 700-watt oven. If using plastic, prick to release steam.

2. Remove from oven and uncover. Place pineapple in a ring on top of the apricots. Put apples in center of ring and top with pieces of vanilla and then pears. Place prunes in a ring on top of pineapple. Pour orange juice over all and sprinkle with sugar. Re-cover and cook for 8 minutes. Prick plastic wrap.

3. Remove from oven and uncover. Stir in almonds, if desired, and refrigerate until chilled.

FOR 400- TO 500-WATT OVENS

To serve 5. Cook as in Step 1 for 6 minutes. Cook as in Step 2 for 12 minutes. Finish as in Step 3.

RUMMY BAKED PINEAPPLE

*H*ot pineapple—you may shudder; but it's very good. The lucky souls who don't have to watch their weight or cholesterol will enjoy some cold vanilla ice cream with this. Pineapple Sorbet (page 556), while not quite as succulent, could reward the health-conscious who don't need to lose weight.   *SERVES 6*

Per ⅙-pineapple serving: 115 calories; 0 milligrams cholesterol; .6 gram fat; 2 milligrams sodium; .6 gram protein (1% RDA); 29 grams carbohydrate

RDA: iron 3%; 170 milligrams potassium; thiamin 9%; riboflavin 3%; niacin 3%; vitamin C 38%

1 whole pineapple (3¾ pounds; 1.6
   kg), top and bottom trimmed off
½ cup (120 ml) dark rum

⅓ cup (80 ml) granulated sugar
3¼-inch (.5-cm) slices fresh ginger

1. Cut pineapple lengthwise into 6 wedges. Trim off core. Slide a knife between the skin and the flesh, freeing it but not removing it. Cut flesh across into ½-inch (1-cm) chunks; leave flesh on top of skin. Place pineapple wedges spoke-fashion in a 14×11×2-inch (35.5×28×5-cm) dish. Reserve.

2. Combine remaining ingredients in a 4-cup (1-l) glass measure. Stir well to dissolve sugar. Cover tightly with microwave plastic wrap. Cook at 100% for 2 minutes in a 650- to 700-watt oven. Prick plastic to release steam.

3. Remove from oven and uncover. Strain syrup through a fine sieve. Pour syrup over reserved pineapple wedges. Cover tightly with microwave plastic wrap. Cook for 10 minutes. Prick plastic to release steam.

4. Remove from oven and uncover. Serve each wedge with some of the syrup spooned over.

FOR 400- TO 500-WATT OVENS

To serve 6. Prepare pineapple as in Step 1. Cook syrup as in Step 2 for 4 minutes. Cook 3 wedges at a time in a 10-inch (25.5-cm) quiche dish as in Step 3 for 8 minutes each.

LIGHT POACHED PEARS

*I*t isn't true that every recipe I cooked prior to this book was destined to bard the hips and thicken the waist. This almost-unchanged recipe from *Microwave Gourmet* was as light and delicious then as it is now. You will be surprised at how sweet the pears are cooked without any sugar. They also cook beautifully and evenly. They are not mushy on the outside and undercooked on the inside, but perfect throughout. Serve with Tart Apricot Sauce (page 579) and a sprig of mint if you want, or, more unusual but good, with Chocolate Sauce (page 580).
SERVES 6

Per 1-pear serving: 101 calories; 0 milligrams cholesterol; 1 gram fat; <1 milligram sodium; 1 gram protein (1% RDA); 26 grams carbohydrate

RDA: 218 milligrams potassium; vitamin C 19%

6 Bosc pears, peeled and thoroughly cored through the bottom
2 tablespoons fresh lemon juice

6 pieces lemon zest, each 2 × ¼ inches (5 × .5 cm)
6 pieces orange zest, each 2 × ¼ inches (5 × .5 cm)

1. Rub pears inside and out with lemon juice to prevent discoloration. Place 1 piece lemon zest and 1 piece orange zest inside each core cavity.
2. Arrange pears in a circle around the inside rim of a 2½-quart (2.5-l) soufflé dish. Cover tightly with microwave plastic wrap. Cook at 100% for 8 minutes in a 650- to 700-watt oven. Prick plastic to release steam.
3. Remove from oven. Uncover. Serve either hot or cold.

To serve 4. Use 4 pears, 1½ tablespoons lemon juice and 4 pieces each lemon zest and orange zest. Cook as in Step 2 for 7 minutes.

To serve 2. Use 2 pears, 1 tablespoon lemon juice and 2 pieces each lemon zest and orange zest. Cook as in Step 2 for 4 minutes 30 seconds.

FOR 400- TO 500-WATT OVENS

To serve 6. Cook for 12 minutes.

To serve 4. Cook for 11 minutes.

To serve 2. Cook for 8 minutes.

RASPBERRY POACHED PEARS

*I*t's true that this recipe only provides half a pear per person; but in exchange it offers a pale raspberry sauce that can be made in winter. When I finish cooking the pears, I turn them over before serving so that they are evenly rosy.   *SERVES 4*

Per serving: 76 calories; 0 milligrams cholesterol; <1 gram fat; <1 milligram sodium; 1 gram protein (1% RDA); 19 grams carbohydrate

RDA: 143 milligrams potassium; vitamin C 12%

2 Bosc pears (each 7–8 ounces;
 200–227 g), peeled, halved and
 cored
1 teaspoon fresh lemon juice
¼ cup (60 ml) raspberry purée, from
 2½ ounces (70 g) raspberries frozen
 in light syrup, defrosted, puréed and
 sieved

¼ cup (60 ml) water
1 whole clove
1-inch (2.5-cm) long strip lemon zest

1. Rub pears inside and out with fresh lemon juice to prevent discoloration. Arrange pears halves, core side up, spoke-fashion, with fat ends against the inside edge of a 10-inch (25.5-cm) quiche dish.

2. Stir together the rest of the ingredients. Pour over pears. Cover tightly with microwave plastic wrap. Cook at 100% for 6 minutes in a 650- to 700-watt oven. Prick plastic to release steam.

3. Remove from oven and uncover. Turn pears over. Re-cover and cook for 6 minutes more. Prick plastic to release steam.

4. Remove from oven and uncover. Serve pears core side up with the sauce spooned over.

To serve 8. Use 4 pears, 2 teaspoons lemon juice, ½ cup (120 ml) raspberry purée, ½ cup (120 ml) water, 2 cloves, and 2 strips lemon zest. Cook as in Step 2 for 8 minutes. Continue cooking as in Step 3 for 8 minutes.

FOR 400- TO 500-WATT OVENS

To serve 4. Cook as in Step 2 for 9 minutes. Cook as in Step 3 for 9 minutes.

To serve 8. Cook as in Step 2 for 12 minutes. Cook as in Step 3 for 12 minutes.

PEARS POACHED IN RED WINE

*T*his is a classic French dessert, made lighter and quicker but left delicious in your microwave oven. The pears will be lightly tinted by the red wine. If you want a darker color, leave the pears in their syrup for a few hours, turning them from time to time. An easy way to core the pears is with a melon baller. Make sure you take out the stringy part of the core that goes toward the stem. If your pears are fully ripe or soft, cooking times will be shorter.   *SERVES 8*

Per half-pear serving with 3 tablespoons syrup: 88 calories; 0 milligrams cholesterol; <1 gram fat; 1.6 milligrams sodium; .5 gram protein (1% RDA); 23 grams carbohydrate

RDA: vitamin C 7%

¼ cup (60 ml) granulated sugar
2 cups (470 ml) red wine
1 piece cinnamon stick, 1½ inches
  (4 cm) long
4 whole allspice berries

Pinch freshly grated nutmeg
2 whole cloves
4 firm Bosc pears (each 8 ounces;
  227 g), peeled, cored and halved

1. Combine all ingredients except pears in an 8-cup (2-l) glass measure. Cook, uncovered, at 100% for 3 minutes in a 650- to 700-watt oven.
2. Remove from oven and stir well. Cover tightly with microwave plastic wrap. Cook at 100% for 5 minutes. Prick plastic to release steam.
3. Remove from oven and uncover. Arrange pear halves in a 13 × 11 × 2-inch (33 × 25.5 × 5-cm) oval dish, core side up, alternating wide and narrow ends. Pour liquid over pears. Cover tightly with microwave plastic wrap. Cook at 100% for 5 minutes. Prick plastic to release steam.
4. Remove from oven and uncover. Turn pears over. Re-cover and cook for 5 minutes more. Prick plastic to release steam.
5. Remove from oven and uncover. Let pears cool in syrup and serve each half with about 3 tablespoons of the syrup poured on top.

To serve 4. Cook, in a 4-cup (1-l) glass measure, 2 tablespoons sugar, 1 cup (240 ml) red wine, 1 piece cinnamon stick 1-inch (2.5-cm) long, 2 allspice berries, a small pinch of nutmeg and 1 clove as in Step 1 for 1 minute 30 seconds. Cook as in Step 2 for 3 minutes. In Step 3, arrange halves of 2 pears in a 9-inch pie plate and cook with syrup for 4 minutes. Cook as in Step 4 for 4 minutes.

To serve 8. Cook as in Step 1 for 6 minutes, as in Step 2 for 10 minutes, as in Step 3 for 7 minutes and as in Step 4 for 7 minutes.

To serve 4. Cook as in Step 1 for 3 minutes, as in Step 2 for 5 minutes, as in Step 3 for 5 minutes and as in Step 4 for 5 minutes.

PEACHES WITH CHERRY SAUCE

Make this only in summer, when you can get beautiful peaches or nectarines and cherries—terrific. *SERVES 6*

Per serving: 100 calories; 0 milligrams cholesterol; 0 grams fat; 0 milligrams sodium; 1 gram protein (3% RDA); 25 grams carbohydrate

RDA: vitamin A 15%; vitamin C 18%

6 medium peaches or nectarines (about   1 recipe Cherry Sauce (page 577)
   3 pounds; 1.4 kg), peeled if desired

1. Cut a thin slice off the bottom of each peach or nectarine so that it will stand up straight. Place peaches or nectarines in a ring around the inside rim of a 2½-quart (2.5-l) soufflé dish. Cover tightly with microwave plastic wrap. Cook at 100% for 8 minutes in a 650- to 700-watt oven. Prick plastic to release steam.
2. Remove from oven and uncover. Drain any cooking liquid into a 4-cup (1-l) glass measure to use in cherry sauce. Place peaches on a serving platter or on individual serving plates and serve with cherry sauce spooned over or on the side.

To serve 6. Cook for 12 minutes.

APPLESAUCE

*U*nsweetened applesauce is a marvelous basic. You may want to make the largest amount and freeze it in small quantities. Defrosting times are the same as those for thick pasta sauce (page 166).

Mix a little horseradish into the applesauce and use it as a sauce with pork. Flavor it with cinnamon, nutmeg and lemon juice for a dessert. Mix with some of the Peppered Strawberries (page 535) that have turned to sauce for a brilliantly colored dessert. Since the apples are cooked with their skins, the color of the applesauce itself will vary with the kind of apples used.

You will notice that this recipe doesn't add any water and may make an applesauce that is denser than the commercial kinds that you are used to, especially since some apple varieties are particularly dense to begin with. You can always add some water to thin this sauce to the texture that you like. Since this sauce is dense with apples, it has more calories than commercially made sauces. If you add a quarter-cup (60 ml) of water to each half-cup (120 ml) of sauce, the calories and texture will come out about even with the commercial kind.
MAKES 1 CUP (240 ML), SERVES 4

Per ¼-cup (60-ml) serving: 48 calories; 0 milligrams cholesterol; <1 gram fat; 0 milligrams sodium; <1 gram protein; 13 grams carbohydrate

RDA: vitamin C 7%

2 Granny Smith or McIntosh apples (each about 6–8 ounces; 170–227 g), cut into 8 wedges and cored

1 teaspoon fresh lemon juice

1. Mix together apple wedges and lemon juice in a 2½-quart (2.5-l) soufflé dish. Cover tightly with microwave plastic wrap. Cook at 100% for 7 minutes in a 650- to 700-watt oven, stirring once. Prick plastic to release steam.

2. Remove from oven and uncover. Pass mixture through a food mill. Scrape into bowl and store, tightly covered, in the refrigerator or freezer.

To make ½ cup (120 ml). Use 1 apple and ½ teaspoon lemon juice. Cook for 5 minutes as in Step 1.

To make 1½ cups (355 ml). Use 3 apples and 1½ teaspoons lemon juice. Cook for 9 minutes as in Step 1.

To make 2 cups (470 ml). Use 4 apples and 2 teaspoons lemon juice. Cook for 11 minutes as in Step 1.

To make 3 cups (720 ml). Use 6 apples and 1 tablespoon lemon juice. Cook in a 5-quart (5-l) casserole as in Step 1 for 13 minutes.

FOR 400- TO 500-WATT OVENS

To make 1 cup (240 ml). Cook for 10 minutes.

To make ½ cup (120 ml). Cook for 7 minutes.

To make 1½ cups (355 ml). Cook for 14 minutes.

To make 2 cups (470 ml). Cook for 16 minutes.

APPLE SNOW

When I first learned this recipe from a Belgian cook named Berthe, it seemed like a miracle. The pectin of the apples turns to a foamy mousse when beaten vigorously for a long time. I never make this without a large electric mixer with a whisk attachment, but it can be done with a lot of goodwill, muscle and a balloon whisk. It is very glamorous served icy cold in glass dishes; those coupe Champagne glasses that I no longer use for the bubbly are ideal.   *SERVES 2*

Per ¾-cup (180-ml) serving: 80 calories; 0 milligrams cholesterol; 0 grams fat; 25 milligrams sodium; 2 grams protein (4% RDA); 18 grams carbohydrate

RDA: vitamin C 6%

1 McIntosh or other tart apple (about
 ⅓ pound; 150 g), cut into 8 wedges
 and cored
2-inch (5-cm) piece cinnamon stick
2-inch (5-cm) piece vanilla bean, split
 lengthwise

Pinch ground allspice
1 egg white
1 tablespoon granulated sugar
½ teaspoon finely grated lemon zest
2 drops fresh lemon juice

1. Combine apple, cinnamon, vanilla and allspice in a 4-cup (1-l) glass measure. Cover tightly with microwave plastic wrap. Cook at 100% for 5 minutes in a 650- to 700-watt oven. Prick plastic to release steam.
2. Remove from oven and uncover. Pass mixture through a food mill fitted with a medium disc. Allow to cool to room temperature or refrigerate.
3. Scrape into a mixing bowl. Add egg white and beat (a whisk attachment is ideal) about 10 minutes until the mixture forms soft peaks. Add sugar and beat until shiny. Fold in lemon zest and juice.
3. Chill for 2–6 hours.

(continued)

To serve 4. Cook 2 apples, a 3-inch piece of cinnamon, a 3-inch piece of vanilla bean and a large pinch of allspice in a 2½-quart (2.5-l) soufflé dish as in Step 1 for 7 minutes. Put through a food mill as in Step 2. Beat as in Step 3 using 2 egg whites until soft peaks form; add 2 tablespoons sugar and beat until shiny. Fold in 1 teaspoon of lemon zest and ⅛ teaspoon lemon juice. Chill.

To serve 8. Cook 4 apples, a whole stick of cinnamon, a whole vanilla bean (split), and ⅛ teaspoon allspice in a 2½-quart (2.5-l) soufflé dish as in Step 1 for 11 minutes. Put through a food mill as in Step 2. Beat as in Step 3 using 4 egg whites until soft peaks form; add ¼ cup (60 ml) sugar and beat until shiny. Fold in 2 teaspoons of lemon zest and ¼ teaspoon lemon juice. Chill.

FOR 400- TO 500-WATT OVENS

To serve 2. Cook for 7 minutes.

To serve 4. Cook for 10 minutes.

To serve 8. Cook for 16 minutes.

HONEY BAKED APPLES

*B*aked apples make one of the most comforting of winter desserts. Serve them hot, or make extras and have them cold instead of juice at breakfast or as part of your lunch after a salad and a small pita bread, or something as simple as nonfat cottage cheese and some sliced tomatoes. The apples provide the carbohydrate. They are so good I give instructions for cooking several amounts. If you like it, maple syrup can be substituted for the honey. If you are not trying to lose weight, the walnuts add a nice crunch and forty-seven calories per person.

Six apples will not fit in or cook evenly in a low-wattage oven.   *SERVES 2*

Per 1-apple serving (without walnuts): 117 calories; 0 milligrams cholesterol; 1 gram fat; 0 milligrams sodium; .5 gram protein (1% RDA); 30 grams carbohydrate

RDA: vitamin C 20%

2 small McIntosh or Granny Smith
   apples (each 6 ounces; 170 g), cored
   and 1 inch (2.5 cm) peeled off
   around the top of each apple
1 teaspoon fresh lemon juice

2 teaspoons fresh orange juice
2 teaspoons honey
2 tablespoons chopped walnuts,
   optional

1. Rub lemon juice on exposed areas of apples and prick the skin of each in several places. Place opposite each other in a 1½-quart (1.5-l) soufflé dish. Pour remaining lemon juice and orange juice around apples. Spoon honey into the core of each. Cover tightly with microwave plastic wrap. Cook at 100% for 3 minutes, or until tender, in a 650- to 700-watt oven. Prick plastic to release steam.

2. Remove from oven and uncover carefully. Remove apples to a serving plate and spoon liquid over. Sprinkle walnuts on top, if desired, and serve.

To serve 1. Use 1 apple, ½ teaspoon lemon juice, 1 tablespoon walnuts, if desired, 1 teaspoon honey, and 1 teaspoon orange juice. Put in center of a 1-quart (1-l) soufflé dish and cook for 2 minutes.

To serve 4. Use 4 apples, 2 teaspoons lemon juice, ¼ cup (60 ml) walnuts, if desired, 1 tablespoon plus 1 teaspoon orange juice, and 1 tablespoon plus 1 teaspoon honey. Arrange in a circle in a 2½-quart (2.5-l) soufflé dish and cook for 5 minutes.

To serve 6. Use 6 apples, 1 tablespoon lemon juice, ⅓ cup (80 ml) walnuts, if desired, 2 tablespoons honey, and 2 tablespoons orange juice. Arrange in a circle in a 5-quart (5-l) casserole and cook for 7 minutes.

FOR 400- TO 500-WATT OVENS

To serve 2. Cook for 4 minutes to 4 minutes 30 seconds.

To serve 1. Cook for 3 minutes.

To serve 4. Cook for 7 minutes.

SORBETS

Sorbets do take some work and some forethought; but they are well worth it. At a party, instead of making dessert all of one sorbet, you may want to give a small amount of several different flavors. Small ice cream scoops—the French have attractive oval ones—can make the portions look deliberate instead of meager. If using scoops, know how much they scoop up. Sorbets should not be served so cold that you cannot taste them. If you freeze them ahead, take them out of the freezer about ten minutes before you want to serve them, or place, uncovered, in the microwave oven for one minute at 100 percent.

At parties, a dish of sorbet can look more festive with a plump strawberry, a fanned strawberry, a half-slice of orange, a sprinkling of smaller berries and/or a sprig of mint.

Those who are not on weight-loss diets can increase their portions. Trying to use a sugar substitute will not work well. It is the cooked sugar syrup that keeps the sorbet from getting grainy.

Recipes can be increased or decreased by using the same proportions of fruit or flavoring to simple syrup.

For those who do not have ice cream machines, the sorbet can be put either in an ice cube tray without dividers and stirred from time to time as it chills in the freezer, or in an ice cube tray with dividers and, just before it freezes hard, whirred in a food processor, then replaced in the freezer.

Since Simple Syrup (opposite page) isn't tempting on its own, I make it ahead and keep it in the refrigerator so that I can make just the amount of tempting sorbet that I need. The usual proportion is one cup of simple syrup to each two cups of puréed fruit. I almost always add some lemon juice to help preserve the color of the fruit. It also perks up the flavor.

I find that the two-to-one simple syrup (two parts water by liquid measure to one of sugar) is sufficiently sweet for me and keeps the calories down. Those of you who have a sweet tooth and are unworried about your weight can use the one-to-one simple syrup, which is the conventional proportion.

The odd-size serving is given for the nutrition to avoid scaring you to death. It is also the amount of syrup that usually shows up in a single serving of sorbet. If you change from two-to-one syrup to the more caloric one-to-one syrup, you can see what you are adding by way of calories to a single serving—about forty-four.

SIMPLE SYRUP

Combine sugar and water in container indicated. Cook, uncovered, at 100% for first time indicated. Stir well. Cover tightly with microwave plastic wrap and cook for second time indicated. Prick plastic to release steam and uncover. Store, tightly covered and refrigerated, for up to two weeks.

TWO-TO-ONE SYRUP

PER 2½–TABLESPOON SERVING: 48 calories; 0 milligrams cholesterol; 0 grams fat; < 1 milligram sodium; 0 grams protein; 12 grams carbohydrate

SUGAR	WATER	CONTAINER	650- TO 700- WATT OVEN	400- TO 500- WATT OVEN	YIELD
1 cup	2 cups	2½-quart	3 minutes	5 minutes	2½ cups
(240 ml)	(470 ml)	(2.5-1)	5 minutes	9 minutes	(2.5-1)
½ cup	1 cup	4-cup measure	2 minutes	4 minutes	1⅓ cups
(120 ml)	(240 ml)	(1-1)	3 minutes	6 minutes	(320 ml)
¼ cup	½ cup	4-cup measure	1 minute	2 minutes	⅔ cup
(60 ml)	(120 ml)	(1-1)	2 minutes	3 minutes	(160 ml)

ONE-TO-ONE SYRUP

PER 2½–TABLESPOON SERVING: 92 calories; 0 milligrams cholesterol; 0 grams fat; < 1 milligram sodium; 0 grams protein; 24 grams carbohydrate

SUGAR	WATER	CONTAINER	650- TO 700- WATT OVEN	400- TO 500- WATT OVEN	YIELD
2 cups	2 cups	2½-quart	3 minutes	5 minutes	2¾ cups
(470 ml)	(470 ml)	(2.5-1)	6 minutes	11 minutes	(650 ml)
1 cup	1 cup	2½-quart	3 minutes	4 minutes	1⅓ cups
(240 ml)	(240 ml)	(2.5-1)	6 minutes	9 minutes	(320 ml)
½ cup	½ cup	4-cup measure	2 minutes	4 minutes	¾ cup
(120 ml)	(120 ml)	(1 1)	4 minutes	8 minutes	(180 ml)

PEAR SORBET

*I*t's easy to see from this recipe that adding some fruit to the simple syrup changes it from a nutritional and tasteless wasteland to a delicious and reasonably healthy dessert.   *SERVES 8*

Per ½-cup (120-ml) serving: 87 calories; 0 milligrams cholesterol; <1 gram fat; <1 milligram sodium; 1 gram protein (1% RDA); 22 grams carbohydrate

RDA: 177 milligrams potassium; vitamin C 14%

6 Light Poached Pears (page 544)
1⅓ cups (320 ml) Two-to-One Simple
   Syrup (page 553)

2 tablespoons fresh lemon juice
⅛ teaspoon ground cardamom

   1. Cut pears into quarters and place in the work bowl of a food processor. Purée until smooth.
   2. Add simple syrup, lemon juice and cardamom to purée and process to combine. Refrigerate until cold.
   3. Transfer to ice cream maker and freeze according to manufacturer's instructions.

PEACH SORBET

A very light sorbet that is delicious only when peaches are ripe in season. Then the peaches are so sweet, you don't need any more sugar than this.   *SERVES 8*

Per ½-cup (120-ml) serving: 87 calories; 0 milligrams cholesterol; 0 grams fat; 0 milligrams sodium; 1 gram protein (1% RDA); 22 grams carbohydrate

RDA: vitamin A 9%; vitamin C 14%

2 pounds (900 g) peaches (about 4
   medium)
½ cup (120 ml) granulated sugar

1½ cups (355 ml) water (approx.)
3 tablespoons fresh lemon juice

   1. Peal and pit peaches over a 4-cup (1-l) glass measure to catch any juices. Reserve peaches. Place pits and skins in measure. Add sugar and enough water to

measure 1½ cups (355 g). Cover tightly with microwave plastic wrap. Cook at 100% for 6 minutes 30 seconds in a 650- to 700-watt oven. Prick plastic to release steam. Remove from oven.

2. Mix reserved peaches with lemon juice in a food processor or blender and purée until smooth. Scrape into a 4-cup (1-l) glass measure. Cover tightly with plastic wrap and cook for 5 minutes. Prick plastic to release steam.

3. Uncover syrup. Strain through a fine sieve and reserve.

4. Remove peaches from oven and uncover. Pour syrup into peach purée and stir to combine. Cover tightly and refrigerate overnight. Freeze in an ice cream machine according to manufacturer's instructions.

FOR 400- TO 500-WATT OVENS

To serve 8. Cook as in Step 1 for 8 minutes. Continue with Step 2, cooking for 10 minutes. Finish as in Steps 3 and 4.

STRAWBERRY SORBET

*S*ince air is beaten into this as the ice cream machine paddles whirl, it turns out to be a deep pink rather than bright red. It is beautiful and the taste is brightly refreshing. *SERVES 8*

Per ½-cup (120-ml) serving: 85 calories; 0 milligrams cholesterol; <1 gram fat; 1 milligram sodium; 1 gram protein (1% RDA); 21 grams carbohydrate

RDA: 163 milligrams potassium; vitamin C 93%

2 pint boxes strawberries, hulled, washed and halved (about 4 cups; 1 l)

1⅓ cups (320 ml) cold Two-to-One Simple Syrup (page 553)
¼ cup (60 ml) fresh lemon juice

1. Place strawberries in a food processor or blender and purée until almost smooth (making about 2⅔ cups [630 ml] purée). Stir in simple syrup along with lemon juice and process to combine.

2. Transfer to ice cream maker and proceed according to manufacturer's instructions.

PINEAPPLE SORBET

*T*his sorbet gets delightfully light and fluffy when made in an ice cream machine. It may take a little longer than other sorbets to get firm—not hard. Since it is virtually white, I often sprinkle on a few berries for color.   *SERVES 10*

Per ½-cup (120-ml) serving: 103 calories; 0 milligrams cholesterol; <1 gram fat; 1 milligram sodium; <1 gram protein (1% RDA); 26 grams carbohydrate

RDA: 130 milligrams potassium; vitamin C 31%

1 whole ripe pineapple (about 2½ pounds; 1.15 kg), peeled, cored and cut into chunks (about 5 cups; 1.2 l)
1⅓ cups cold Two-to-One Simple Syrup (page 553)

2 tablespoons fresh lemon juice, or to taste

1. Place pineapple in a food processor or blender and purée until smooth (making about 3 cups [705 ml] purée). Mix in syrup and lemon juice, to taste.
2. Freeze in an ice cream machine according to manufacturer's instructions.

CHOCOLATE SORBET

*T*his is absolutely divine and worth the extra calories—more than fruit sorbets—that you will get. Besides, the richness is deeply satisfying.   *SERVES 5*

Per generous ½-cup (120-ml) serving: 134 calories; 0 milligrams cholesterol; 6 grams fat; 1 milligram sodium; 1 gram protein (3% RDA); 23 grams carbohydrate

2 ounces (56 g) unsweetened chocolate
2 cups (470 ml) water

½ cup (120 ml) granulated sugar

1. Combine chocolate and ⅓ cup (80 ml) of the water in an 8-cup (2-l) glass measure. Cook, uncovered, at 100% for 1 minute 30 seconds in a 650- to 700-watt oven.
2. Remove from oven. Stir until smooth. Combine remaining water and sugar in a small bowl and stir to dissolve sugar. Add to chocolate mixture, stirring well to make sure mixture is smooth. Cover tightly with microwave plastic wrap. Cook for 3 minutes. Prick plastic to release steam.

3. Remove from oven and uncover. Let mixture stand until cool and then refrigerate until chilled. Freeze in an ice cream machine according to manufacturer's instructions.

FOR 400- TO 500-WATT OVENS

To serve 5. Cook as in Step 1 for 3 minutes. Continue with Step 2, cooking for 6 minutes. Finish as in Step 3.

COFFEE GRANITÉ

*T*his Italian favorite is like the best essence of coffee melting in your mouth. Have it as it is, or top with Whipped Ricotta Topping (page 581) if you are being very virtuous, or with a little whipped cream. Make only what you need by reducing or increasing according to the simple syrup quantities (page 553); otherwise it will disappear as if into the air. *SERVES 4*

Per ½-cup (120-ml) serving: 73 calories; 0 milligrams cholesterol; 0 grams fat; 1 milligram sodium; <1 gram protein (<1% RDA); 19 grams carbohydrate

1 cup (240 ml) very strong coffee
1⅓ cups (320 ml) Two-to-One Simple
   Syrup (page 553)

1. Combine ingredients in a mixing bowl. Refrigerate until chilled. Spread in a 10½ × 7 × 2-inch (26.5 × 18 × 5-cm) dish and freeze at least 4 hours or overnight. The mixture will not freeze hard.

2. Remove from freezer just before serving. Break up with a fork or coarsely chop in a food processor.

LIGHT WHITE ICE CREAM

Yes, if you tell people what's in this they will be very surprised. It is rich and smooth, unlike ice milk. You have to pay for the voluptuousness with some extra calories and some cholesterol; but it's much leaner than normal ice cream.
SERVES 6

Per generous ½-cup (120-ml) serving: 163 calories; 27 milligrams cholesterol; 7 grams fat; 146 milligrams sodium; 13 grams protein (28% RDA); 11 grams carbohydrate

RDA: calcium 27%; phosphorus 19%; riboflavin 12%

¼ cup (60 ml) water
2¼ teaspoons unflavored gelatin
  (1 envelope; 7 grams)
2 cups (240 ml) part-skim ricotta
  cheese

1 cup (120 ml) buttermilk
2 tablespoons granulated sugar
¼ teaspoon vanilla extract
2 tablespoons unsweetened fruit brandy
2 tablespoons fresh lemon juice

1. Place water in a small glass bowl and sprinkle gelatin over. Allow to stand for 1 minute. Cook, uncovered, at 100% for 45 seconds in a 650- to 700-watt oven. Remove from oven and reserve.
2. Place ricotta in a blender and process until smooth, scraping down sides occasionally with a rubber spatula. Add reserved gelatin and remaining ingredients. Process to combine. Scrape mixture into an ice cream maker and freeze according to manufacturer's directions.

FOR 400- TO 500-WATT OVENS

To serve 6. Cook gelatin and water as in Step 1 for 1 minute. Finish recipe as in Step 2.

These seemingly rich desserts are gala enough for any entertainment and can be made a day ahead. Some of them use the microwave oven only to melt the gelatin; but the real points are how good they taste and how well their reduced calorie counts are disguised. Don't tell.

Many of them rely on unflavored gelatin to hold their shapes. Lest we forget— it was a surprise to me—a single packet (2¼ teaspoons; 7 g) has twenty-five calories and enough jelling power to set two cups of liquid.

The easiest way to use gelatin is to sprinkle the amount you will need for the total recipe over a small amount of the liquid. In a minute or so, the water will combine with the gelatin layer to turn it transparent. Briefly heat the gelatin-water combination, uncovered, in a microwave oven, or place the container holding the gelatin in a water bath and heat on top of stove until it dissolves.

Allow gelatin mixture to cool slightly before adding to cold liquids, or slowly stir some of the cold liquids into the dissolved gelatin before adding to the cold liquids. This is to prevent the cold liquid from setting the gelatin in streaks or bits before it gets thoroughly incorporated.

If the dessert needs to be beaten after almost entirely jelling, it will need to be cooled. It can be jelled either by setting in the refrigerator or by placing the stainless steel bowl that it will be whisked in in an ice-water bath and stirring the dessert mixture with a spatula from time to time, making sure to scrape carefully the sides and the bottom of the bowl. If your mixture gets away from you and sets up firm before you get a chance to beat it, put it at room temperature for a few minutes or until you have the proper texture.

I usually chill the mixture in the metal bowl of a mixer so that it can quickly be placed in the mixer.

Those who don't want to use gelatin, which is an animal product, can look at pages 587–588 to substitute agar agar.

Most of the molded gelatin desserts in this chapter come out of their molds very easily. Place your serving plate upside down over the mold. Holding the plate tightly on the mold with one hand and the mold in the other, quickly turn plate and mold over. Set plate down on a table and lift off mold.

To unmold chilled gelatin desserts that don't seem to want to come out of their mold: Run the tip of a sharp knife between the top edge of the dessert and the mold. Next to your serving plate, place a large bowl half full of very hot water. Briefly dip the mold in the water. Remove and unmold as above.

STRAWBERRY BAVARIAN

I have always had a weakness for strawberry Bavarian. I think this low-calorie version is a rich, pink triumph. If you use a ring mold, you can fill the center of the unmolded dessert with strawberries.   *SERVES 6*

Per generous ½-cup (120-ml) serving: 111 calories; 13 milligrams cholesterol; 3 grams fat; 53 milligrams sodium; 8 grams protein (17% RDA); 14 grams carbohydrate

RDA: calcium 12%; 183 milligrams potassium; vitamin C 75%

¼ cup (60 ml) water
3½ teaspoons unflavored gelatin (1½ envelopes; 11 g)
1 pound (450 g) strawberries, washed, hulled and cut in half

3 tablespoons granulated sugar
¼ cup (60 ml) fresh lemon juice
1 cup (240 ml) part-skim ricotta cheese

1. Place water in a small glass bowl and sprinkle gelatin over. Allow to stand for 1 minute. Cook, uncovered, at 100% in a 650- to 700-watt oven for 1 minute. Remove from oven and reserve.

2. Place strawberries, sugar and lemon juice in a blender and purée until smooth. Scrape into a metal bowl and reserve.

3. Place ricotta in the blender and purée until smooth, scraping the sides down with a spatula. With the motor running, add the dissolved gelatin and process to combine.

4. Stir ricotta mixture into reserved strawberry purée. Place bowl inside a larger bowl filled with ice. Allow to stand for about 20 minutes, or until almost set, stirring occasionally with a spatula.

5. Fill a 4-cup (1-l) metal mold or bowl with ice water and set aside while finishing the recipe.

6. When the mixture is almost set, remove bowl from ice and whisk strawberry mixture until light and foamy. Pour ice water out of the mold. Scrape Bavarian into mold. Refrigerate until set, about 20 minutes.

7. When ready to serve, remove from refrigerator and unmold onto a serving platter.

FOR 400- TO 500-WATT OVENS

To serve 6. Cook water and gelatin as in Step 1 for 1 minute 30 seconds.

LEMON BAVARIAN

*T*his rich, tart dessert is the perfect end for a small or medium-size dinner party. If you grate the lemon zest before you juice the lemons, you should come out about even.   *SERVES 4*

Per ½-cup (120-ml) serving: 123 calories; 19 milligrams cholesterol; 5 grams fat; 79 milligrams sodium; 10 grams protein (23% RDA); 11 grams carbohydrate

RDA: calcium 17%; vitamin C 18%

½ cup (120 ml) water
2¼ teaspoons unflavored gelatin
   (1 envelope; 7 grams)
1 cup (240 ml) part-skim ricotta cheese

2 tablespoons granulated sugar
¼ cup (60 ml) fresh lemon juice
2 tablespoons grated lemon zest

1. Place water in a small glass bowl and sprinkle gelatin over. Allow to stand for 1 minute. Cook, uncovered, at 100% in a 650- to 700-watt oven for 45 seconds. Remove from oven and reserve.

2. Place ricotta in a blender and purée until smooth. Add reserved gelatin and remaining ingredients. Process to combine.

3. Scrape mixture into a small metal bowl and place inside a larger bowl filled with ice. Allow to stand for about 20 minutes, or until almost set, stirring occasionally.

4. Fill a 4-cup (1-l) metal mold or bowl with ice water and set aside while finishing the recipe.

5. When lemon mixture is almost set, remove bowl from ice and whisk mixture until light and foamy. Pour ice water out of and pour the Bavarian into the mold. Refrigerate, covered, until set, about 20 minutes.

6. When ready to serve, remove from refrigerator and unmold onto a serving platter.

To serve 8. Dissolve 4½ teaspoons gelatin in ½ cup (120 ml) water as in Step 1 for 1 minute 30 seconds. In Step 2, add ½ cup cold water and use 2 cups (480 ml) part-skim ricotta, ¼ cup (60 ml) sugar, ½ cup (120 ml) lemon juice and ¼ cup (60 ml) lemon zest. In Step 4 use an 8-cup (2-l) mold or bowl. Finish as above.

FOR 400- TO 500-WATT OVENS

To serve 4. Cook water and gelatin as in Step 1 for 1 minute.

To serve 8. Cook water and gelatin as in Step 1 for 2 minutes.

PLUM TIMBALES

When red plums are ripe and in season, they are usually eaten out of hand; but think of them for this vivid party dessert. You can add a dollop of Whipped Ricotta Topping (page 581), a wedge of raw plum, even a sprig of mint, to each plate. *SERVES 8*

Per ½-cup (120-ml) timbale serving: 74 calories; 0 milligrams cholesterol; <1 gram fat; 2 milligrams sodium; 2 grams protein (5% RDA); 17 grams carbohydrate

RDA: vitamin C 14%

1½ pounds (680 g) red plums, pitted
    and cut into wedges (about 5 cups;
    1.2 l)
1 tablespoon fresh lemon juice

¼ cup (60 ml) granulated sugar
4½ teaspoons unflavored gelatin
    (2 envelopes; 14 g)
1½ cups (355 ml) water

    1. Combine plums, lemon juice and sugar in an 8-cup (2-l) glass measure.

    2. In a small bowl, sprinkle gelatin over water and let stand until it is translucent. Stir gelatin mixture into plums. Cover tightly with microwave plastic wrap. Cook at 100% for 8 minutes in a 650- to 700-watt oven. Prick plastic to release steam.

    3. Remove from oven. Uncover and pass through the finest blade of a food mill. Divide mixture among 8 ½-cup (120-ml) timbale molds or ramekins. Refrigerate overnight.

    4. Unmold each timbale (as on page 559) onto individual dessert plates.

To serve 4. Use ¾ pound (340 g) red plums, 1½ teaspoons lemon juice, 2 tablespoons sugar, 1 envelope gelatin and ¾ cup (180 ml) water. Combine in an 8-cup (2-l) measure. Cook as in Step 2 for 6 minutes, or until plums are tender. Finish as above, using 6 ½-cup (120-ml) ramekins.

FOR 400- TO 500-WATT OVENS

To serve 4. Cook for 8–9 minutes, or until plums are tender.

TANGERINE PUDDING

We all need glamorous end-of-party desserts. This pale tangerine cream that sets like a Bavarian is perfect, especially after group-feeds of Salmon in Red Wine (page 259), Fish Tagine (page 260), Fish Couscous (page 262), Green Shrimp Curry (page 282) or Tomato-Beef Curry (page 356). It can be made ahead.
SERVES 8

Per ⅔-cup (160-ml) serving: 147 calories; 1 milligram cholesterol; <1 gram fat; 33 milligrams sodium; 1 gram protein (3% RDA); 36 grams carbohydrate

RDA: vitamin C 31%

4 tangerines (each about 5 ounces; 142 g), skins left on and quartered
3 cups (705 ml) water
¾ cup (180 ml) granulated sugar

3 tablespoons fresh lemon juice
⅔ cup (160 ml) cornstarch
1 cup (240 ml) buttermilk

1. Remove all visible seeds from the tangerines. Place in a 2½-quart (2.5-l) soufflé dish or casserole with a tightly fitted lid. Stir together water and sugar and pour over tangerines. Cover soufflé dish with lid. Cook at 100% for 15 minutes, or until tangerines are cooked through, in a 650- to 700-watt oven.

2. Remove from oven and uncover. Place a food mill fitted with a medium disc over a large bowl. Remove tangerines from syrup with a slotted spoon and purée in food mill.

3. Strain cooking liquid through a fine sieve into tangerine purée along with lemon juice. Stir well.

4. Rinse out and dry casserole. In it, slowly combine ½ cup (120 ml) of the tangerine mixture with the cornstarch, stirring well to make sure there are no lumps. Thoroughly stir in remaining tangerine mixture. Cover with lid and cook for 8 minutes, stirring once halfway through cooking.

5. Remove from oven and uncover. Let stand until cool. When cool, stir in buttermilk. Divide among 8 ½-cup (120-ml) ramekins (each 3½ × 1½ inches; 9 × 4 cm), or pour into a large serving bowl. Refrigerate, covered, until set, about 3 hours.

FOR 400- TO 500-WATT OVENS

To serve 8. Cook as in Step 1 for 25 minutes. Continue with Steps 2 and 3. Cook as in Step 4 for 12 minutes, stirring once halfway through cooking.

MANGO MOUSSE

*T*his is another glamorous after-the-party solution with a beautiful color. It may be glamorous, but peeling and cutting the mangoes isn't. It's messy. Wear old clothes. Peel the mango with a sharp paring knife. Cut slices from the edge toward the pit and separate with your knife. I have a friend who does this naked in a bathtub. Garnish the mousse with a slice of fresh peeled mango (ten calories) if you like.   *SERVES 14*

Per ½-cup (120-ml) serving: 66 calories; 0 milligrams cholesterol; 0 grams fat; 20 milligrams sodium; 2 grams protein (5% RDA); 15 grams carbohydrate

RDA: vitamin A 35%; vitamin C 21%

3 ripe mangoes (each 12–16 ounces; 340–453 g), peeled, pitted and cut into chunks (about 4½ cups; 1.1 l)
1½ cups (355 ml) water
⅓ cup (80 ml) granulated sugar
⅛ teaspoon cinnamon
⅛ teaspoon nutmeg
⅛ teaspoon allspice
1½ tablespoons cornstarch
3½ teaspoons unflavored gelatin (1½ envelopes; 11 g)
1½ cups (355 ml) nonfat yogurt

1. Purée mango in a blender or food processor until smooth. Reserve in the refrigerator.

2. Reserve 3 tablespoons of the water. In an 8-cup (2-l) glass measure, stir together thoroughly the remaining water, sugar, cinnamon, nutmeg and allspice. Cook, uncovered, at 100% for 4 minutes in a 650- to 700-watt oven.

3. Remove from oven. Stir together reserved 3 tablespoons water and cornstarch, making sure there are no lumps. Stir into hot syrup. Sprinkle gelatin over syrup. Cover tightly with microwave plastic wrap. Cook for 2 minutes. Prick plastic to release steam.

4. Remove from oven and uncover. Pour into a metal bowl and cool in the freezer for 20 minutes or place in the refrigerator until cool.

5. When the mixture is cool, whip with an electric mixer until pale and frothy. Return to freezer for 5 minutes more.

6. Fold reserved mango purée into whipped mixture. Fold in yogurt and carefully transfer to a decorative metal mold that has been rinsed out with ice water. Chill for at least 4 hours.

7. Unmold as on page 559.

To serve 7. Use 1½ mangoes, ¾ cup (180 ml) water, 3 tablespoons sugar, pinch each cinnamon, nutmeg and allspice, ¾ tablespoon cornstarch, ¾ envelope gelatin, ¾ cup (180 ml) yogurt. Cook as in Step 2 in a 4-cup (1-l) measure for 2 minutes. Continue as in Step 3, cooking for 2 minutes. Finish as in Steps 4–6.

FOR 400- TO 500-WATT OVENS
To serve 7. Cook as in Step 2 for 4 minutes. Cook as in Step 3 for 4 minutes.

CRANBERRY KISSEL

Kissel is a traditional Russian dessert, with the favorite Russian taste blend of sweet and sour. I love it made with American cranberries. Although it is simple to make, its ruby-red glow makes it festive enough for a party. Serve some whipped cream on the side. Have a spoonful yourself, keeping your cholesterol down; let the others indulge.   *SERVES 8*

Per ½-cup (120-ml) serving: 81 calories; 0 milligrams cholesterol; <1 gram fat; 1 milligram sodium; <1 gram protein; 21 grams carbohydrate

RDA: vitamin C 12%

12 ounces (340 g) cranberries (fresh or unsweetened frozen berries)
½ cup (120 ml) granulated sugar
1 cup (240 ml) water

3 tablespoons cornstarch
2 tablespoons fresh lemon juice
¼ cup (60 ml) heavy cream, optional

1. Combine cranberries and sugar in an 8-cup (2-l) glass measure. Cover tightly with microwave plastic wrap. Cook at 100% for 10 minutes in a 650- to 700-watt oven. Prick plastic to release steam.

2. Remove from oven and uncover. Transfer to a food processor and purée until smooth. Pass mixture through a fine sieve and transfer back into the measure.

3. Stir together water and cornstarch in a small bowl. Stir into purée. Cover tightly with microwave plastic wrap. Cook for 4 minutes. Prick plastic to release steam.

4. Remove from oven and uncover. Stir in lemon juice. Divide mixture among 8 ½-cup (120-ml) ramekins (3½ × 1½ inches; 9 × 4 cm), or put in a large serving bowl. Refrigerate until set. Just before serving, whip cream and serve each portion with 1 tablespoon of cream, if desired.

FOR 400- TO 500-WATT OVENS
To serve 8. Cook as in Step 1 for 14 minutes. Continue as in Step 2. Cook as in Step 3 for 6 minutes. Finish as in Step 4.

Some Fruitless Desserts

"Aha!" you may be thinking by now. "Sure, she can make them skinny. They're all fruit." True so far, except for the Chocolate Sorbet above, but now we go on to extremely pleasant fruitlessness.

RICE PUDDING

*R*ice pudding is one of childhood's soothers. As a grown-up, I still turn to it with pleasure and find that my guests do as well. Serve it warm or refrigerated. It is higher in calories than many of the desserts and maybe you should save it for a time when you are not on a weight-loss diet. The rest of the time, rejoice in the high carbohydrate and calcium.

This is one of those recipes in which the timings look funny in the low-wattage oven version. That's because the low-wattage oven cooks at 100 percent power at just about the same level of energy as the high-wattage oven at 50 percent power. Another odd thing happens in this recipe. The high-wattage version requires one-quarter cup more milk than the low-wattage version. That makes a slight difference in the nutrition. It adds sixty-three calories per serving. *SERVES 7*

Per generous ½-cup (120-ml) serving: 166 calories; 3 milligrams cholesterol; .3 gram fat; 70 milligrams sodium; 6 grams protein (14% RDA); 33 grams carbohydrate

RDA: calcium 17%; phosphorus 16%; iron 5%; 262 milligrams potassium; thiamin 11%; riboflavin 11%; niacin 5%

1 cup (240 ml) Carolina rice	2 tablespoons granulated sugar
3¾ cups (885 ml) skim milk	1 1-inch (2.5-cm) piece vanilla bean
¼ teaspoon cinnamon	2 tablespoons raisins

1. Combine rice and 1 cup (240 ml) of the milk in a 2½-quart (2.5-l) soufflé dish or casserole with a tightly fitted lid. Cover with lid and cook at 100% for 6 minutes in a 650- to 700-watt oven.

2. Remove from oven. Uncover and stir in 1 cup (240 ml) milk, cinnamon, sugar and vanilla bean. Cover and cook at 50% for 8 minutes. Stir in 1 cup (240 ml) milk and raisins. Re-cover and cook at 50% for 8 minutes.

3. Stir in ½ cup (120 ml) milk. Re-cover and cook at 50% for 4 minutes.

4. Remove from oven. Let stand, covered, until rice is cooked through and most of the milk is absorbed, about 30 minutes. Stir in remaining ¼ cup (60 ml) milk.

To serve 7. Use 1 cup (240 ml) rice, 3½ cups (825 ml) skim milk, ¼ teaspoon cinnamon, 2 tablespoons sugar, 1-inch (2.5-cm) piece vanilla bean and 2 tablespoons raisins. Cook as in Step 1 for 10 minutes. Cook as in Step 2 for times given above. Omit Step 3. You will have ½ cup milk (120 ml) left. Finish as in Step 4, adding remaining milk at end of waiting time.

TAPIOCA PUDDING

When I was a child, schools used to serve a dessert we called "fish eyes and glue." It was tapioca. Tapioca pudding made with instant tapioca in a microwave oven is a whole other animal, creamy and delicate. If you haven't given tapioca a try since childhood, take my word and chance it now, warm or refrigerated.
SERVES 4

Per ¾-cup (180-ml) serving: 98 calories; 2 milligrams cholesterol; <1 gram fat; 89 milligrams sodium; 6 grams protein (13% RDA); 17 grams carbohydrate

RDA: calcium 15%; phosphorus 13%; 227 milligrams potassium; riboflavin 12%

2 cups (470 ml) skim milk	2 egg whites
3 tablespoons tapioca (instant type)	1 teaspoon vanilla extract
1½ tablespoons granulated sugar	

1. Stir together the milk, tapioca and sugar in an 8-cup (2-l) glass measure. Cover tightly with microwave plastic wrap. Cook at 100% for 5 minutes in a 650- to 700-watt oven. Prick plastic to release steam.

2. Remove from oven and uncover. Stir well and cook, uncovered, for 4 minutes.

3. Remove from oven and stir well. In a medium bowl, beat together the egg whites and vanilla extract. Stirring constantly, pour ½ cup (120 ml) of the tapioca mixture into the egg whites to warm them. Stir mixture back into the tapioca. Cook, uncovered, for 1 minute.

4. Remove from oven and stir well. Cover the surface with a piece of microwave plastic wrap to prevent a skin from forming. Serve warm or chilled.

To serve 4. Cook as in Step 1 for 8 minutes. Cook as in Step 2 for 6 minutes. Continue as in Step 3, cooking for 1 minute 30 seconds.

CHOCOLATE TAPIOCA PUDDING

Want a chocolate fix? Here is tapioca with a smooth chocolate flavor for a few extra calories.   *SERVES 4*

Per ¾-cup (180-ml) serving: 111 calories; 2 milligrams cholesterol; 1 gram fat; 89 milligrams sodium; 6 grams protein (14% RDA); 20 grams carbohydrate

RDA: calcium 16%; phosphorus 14%; riboflavin 13%

2 tablespoons unsweetened cocoa powder (preferably Dutch process)	2 tablespoons granulated sugar
2 cups (470 ml) skim milk	2 egg whites
3 tablespoons tapioca (instant type)	1 teaspoon vanilla extract

1. Stir together cocoa and ¼ cup (60 ml) of the milk in a small bowl, crushing any lumps and making a smooth paste. Combine this mixture with remaining milk, tapioca and sugar in an 8-cup (2-l) glass measure. Cover tightly with microwave plastic wrap. Cook at 100% for 5 minutes in a 650- to 700-watt oven. Prick plastic to release steam.

2. Remove from oven and uncover. Stir well and cook, uncovered, for 4 minutes.

3. Remove from oven and stir well. In a small bowl, beat together egg whites and vanilla extract. Stirring constantly, pour ½ cup (120 ml) of the tapioca mixture into the egg whites to warm them. Stir mixture back into the tapioca. Cook, uncovered, for 1 minute.

4. Remove from oven and stir well. Cover the surface with a piece of microwave plastic wrap to prevent a skin from forming. Serve warm or chilled.

FOR 400- TO 500-WATT OVENS

To serve 4. Cook as in Step 1 for 8 minutes. Cook as in Step 2 for 6 minutes. Continue as in Step 3, cooking for 1 minute 30 seconds.

PURPLE PUDDING

*T*his surprisingly purple dessert is a spectacular for a large party. It can be made equally well with grits and white cornmeal. The grits version will be slightly less creamy; but I think I really like the slightly grainy texture. Now that it is possible to buy blueberries frozen without any sugar, this can be made as well in winter as in summer. This is so low in calories that you can add a fruit sauce such as apricot (page 579); but I don't think you will need it. I might strew each portion with a few extra blueberries to let people know where the purple is coming from. You can unmold it before your dinner; but replace it in the refrigerator, otherwise it may leak some water. If it does, simply blot up with paper towels.
MAKES 5 CUPS (1.2 ML), SERVES 16

Per 1-inch (2.5-cm) slice: 58 calories; 0 milligrams cholesterol; <1 gram fat; <1 milligram sodium; 1 gram protein (2% RDA); 13 grams carbohydrate

1 cup (240 ml) blueberries, fresh or
    unsweetened frozen (if frozen,
    defrost in a sieve under warm
    running water)
2 teaspoons fresh lemon juice
4 cups (1 l) water

¾ cup (180 ml) grits or white cornmeal
½ cup (120 ml) granulated sugar
Grated zest of 1 lemon
1 teaspoon vanilla extract
Nonstick cooking spray for the mold

1. Place blueberries and lemon juice in a 1½-quart (1.5-l) soufflé dish. Cook, uncovered, at 100% for 4 minutes in a 650- to 700-watt oven.

2. Remove from oven, stir well and reserve.

3. Stir together water, grits or cornmeal, sugar and lemon zest in an 8-cup (2-l) glass measure. Cook, uncovered, for 12 minutes, stirring twice.

4. Remove from oven and let stand for 10 minutes, stirring twice. Add vanilla. Spray a 6-cup (1.5-l) mold or pudding bowl—something taller than it is wide, but tapering, not a cylinder—with the cooking spray.

5. Fold reserved blueberry mixture into the pudding, stirring just until marbled. Pour into sprayed mold. Chill for 4 hours or until firm.

6. To serve, unmold onto a serving dish.

FOR 400- TO 500-WATT OVENS

To serve 16. Cook blueberries as in Step 1 for 6 minutes. Cook grits or cornmeal as in Step 3 for 24 minutes, stirring twice. Finish as above.

CREAMY CUSTARD
(VANILLA, ORANGE, ALMOND OR COFFEE)

*T*hese custards do have some cholesterol. They are your reward for being so good with the rest of your food. They are lower in cholesterol and fat than standard custard recipes and taste just as good.

Custard is one of the dishes on which I have had a change of mind. I find that they cook better at 50 percent power—"medium"—in 650- to 700-watt ovens. Low-wattage ovens are at an equivalent power when cooking at 100 percent power.

If you want to make more than four servings of these custards, make two batches. They really need to be on a carrousel to cook evenly, and that's all the carrousel will hold.   *SERVES 4*

Per ½-cup (120-ml) serving: 126 calories; 139 milligrams cholesterol; 3 grams fat; 100 milligrams sodium; 7 grams protein (16% RDA); 17 grams carbohydrate

RDA: calcium 11%; phosphorus 12%; 183 milligrams potassium; riboflavin 12%

1¼ cups (300 ml) skim milk
2 whole eggs, graded large
2 egg whites
¼ cup (60 ml) granulated sugar
1 teaspoon vanilla extract

OPTIONAL FLAVORINGS

2 1-inch (2.5-cm) strips orange zest, minced
or
1 teaspoon almond extract
or
½ teaspoon powdered instant coffee

1. Place milk in a 4-cup (1-l) glass measure. Heat, uncovered, at 100% for 2 minutes in a 650- to 700-watt oven.

2. Whisk together eggs, whites and sugar. Pour in hot milk, stirring constantly but not vigorously. Add vanilla and one additional flavoring, if desired.

3. Pour into 4 ½-cup (120-ml) ramekins (½ × 1½ inches; 9 × 4 cm), and skim any foam from the top of each. Place cups, evenly spaced, around the carrousel. Cook, uncovered, at 50% for 6–7 minutes, or until firm.

4. Remove from oven and serve at room temperature or lightly chilled.

To serve 2. Use ⅔ cup (160 ml) milk, 1 egg, 1 white, 2 tablespoons sugar and ½ teaspoon vanilla. Cook as in Step 1 in a 2-cup (470-ml) glass measure for 1 minute. Continue with Step 2. Cook as in Step 3 in 2 ½-cup (120-ml) ramekins at 50% for 4 minutes.

To serve 4. Heat milk in a 4-cup (1-l) measure as in Step 1 for 4 minutes. Finish recipe as above, cooking custards as in Step 3 at 100% for 6 minutes.

To serve 2. Heat milk in a 2-cup (470-ml) measure as in Step 1 for 2 minutes. Finish recipe as above, cooking custards as in Step 3 at 100% for 4 minutes.

PUMPKIN PUDDING

*T*his book could not have been written without Joy Horstmann. Neither the planning of her own wedding nor my own fussiness has dissuaded her from organized intelligence, creative testing and, in this case, recipe development. It's a lovely dessert for Thanksgiving, when the richer pies may make you rue the festivities for days. It is so good I don't think you will feel deprived; it tastes rich. Thanksgiving is a time when there are liable to be a lot of people around, so Joy has thoughtfully given versions for up to twelve servings. After that, do it twice or do something else.   *SERVES 4*

Per ½-cup (120-ml) serving: 126 calories; 70 milligrams cholesterol; 2 grams fat; 54 milligrams sodium; 4 grams protein (9% RDA); 24 grams carbohydrate

RDA: calcium 11%; phosphorus 10%; 313 milligrams potassium; vitamin A 14%; vitamin C 21%

1 cup (240 ml) skim milk
5 tablespoons fresh orange juice
2 tablespoons cornstarch
1 egg, grade A large
¼ cup (60 ml) packed light brown
   sugar
¾ cup (180 ml) pumpkin purée,
   unsweetened canned, or use an
   equivalent amount of acorn squash
   (page 447)

½ teaspoon ground cinnamon
¼ teaspoon dried ground ginger
⅛ teaspoon freshly grated nutmeg
⅛ teaspoon ground cardamom

1. Heat milk, uncovered, in an 8-cup (2-l) glass measure at 100% for 3 minutes in a 650- to 700-watt oven.
2. Remove from oven. Whisk in remaining ingredients. Cover tightly with microwave plastic wrap. Cook for 4 minutes. Prick plastic to release steam.
3. Remove from oven and uncover. Divide among 4 ½-cup (120-ml) ramekins or place in a serving bowl. Cover each with plastic wrap and refrigerate until chilled.

(continued)

To serve 8. Use 2 cups (470 ml) milk, ⅔ cup (160 ml) orange juice, ¼ cup (60 ml) cornstarch, 2 eggs, ½ cup (120 ml) sugar, 1½ cups (355 ml) purée, 1 teaspoon cinnamon, ½ teaspoon ginger and ¼ teaspoon each nutmeg and cardamom. Cook milk as in Step 1 for 6 minutes. Continue with Step 2, cooking for 8 minutes. Finish as in Step 3.

To serve 12. Use 3 cups (705 ml) milk, 1 cup (240 ml) orange juice, 6 tablespoons cornstarch, 3 eggs, ¾ cup (180 ml) sugar, 2¼ cups (530 ml) purée, 1½ teaspoons cinnamon, ¾ teaspoon ginger and ½ teaspoon each nutmeg and cardamom. Cook milk as in Step 1 in a 5-quart (5-l) casserole for 9 minutes. Continue with Step 2, cooking for 15 minutes. Finish as in Step 3.

FOR 400- TO 500-WATT OVENS

To serve 4. Cook as in Step 1 for 5 minutes. Cook as in Step 2 for 6 minutes. Finish as in Step 3.

To serve 8. Cook as in Step 1 for 9 minutes. Cook as in Step 2 for 12 minutes. Finish as in Step 3.

TRICKY CHOCOLATE PUDDING

I consider this recipe one of the triumphs of this book. I love chocolate pudding and this makes me very happy. The calories and the cholesterol are so low, I sometimes allow myself a teaspoon or two of heavy cream floated on top. Chocolate pudding addicts are divided into the no-skin-on-top and the skin-on-top crowds. I, myself, like the skin. For no skin, cover the serving dish tightly with plastic wrap before refrigerating. For a skin, leave uncovered. Do not substitute a 2½-quart (2.5-l) soufflé dish for the measuring cup. If you don't have the measuring cup, use a glass or ceramic bowl of about the same capacity. Here, the shape of the container changes the cooking.   *SERVES 4*

Per ⅓-cup (80-ml) serving: 75 calories; 2 milligrams cholesterol; 1 gram fat; 48 milligrams sodium; 3 grams protein (8% RDA); 15 grams carbohydrate

RDA: calcium 12%; riboflavin 7%

4 teaspoons unsweetened cocoa powder (preferably Dutch-process)	2 tablespoons granulated sugar
2 tablespoons cornstarch	1½ cups (355 ml) skim milk

1. Combine all ingredients in a blender or food processor and blend well, making sure there are no lumps.

2. Pour into an 8-cup (2-l) glass measure. Cover tightly with microwave plastic wrap. Cook at 100% in a 650- to 700-watt oven for 4 minutes to 4 minutes 30 seconds, or until mixture boils. Prick plastic to release steam.

3. Remove from oven and uncover carefully. Whisk pudding thoroughly and strain through a fine sieve. Divide among 4 3½ × 1½-inch (9 × 4-cm) ramekins or pour into a serving bowl. Cover tightly with plastic wrap and refrigerate until cold.

To serve 8. Use 3 tablespoons cocoa, ¼ cup (60 ml) cornstarch, ¼ cup (60 ml) sugar and 3 cups (705 ml) milk. Prepare as in Step 1. Cook as in Step 2 for 7 minutes. Finish as in Step 3.

FOR 400- TO 500-WATT OVENS

To serve 4. Cook for 9–10 minutes, or until boiling and thickened.

CHOCOLATE JUNKET

*T*his is a good dessert when you want something low in calories and high in satisfaction that can be ready about an hour after you walk in the door. By the time you have had your first course, it will be time to put the junket in the refrigerator. By the time you've had your main course, it will be ready to eat. It is not a dessert that holds; it starts to bleed whey if it sits too long.

Note: Rennet is an animal product that is used to set milk into curds for cheese or dessert. It can be bought from those who sell supplies for making cheese. For additional information, see Fromage Blanc (page 518). *SERVES 4*

Per ½-cup (120-ml) serving: 59 calories; 2 milligrams cholesterol; .5 gram fat; 78 milligrams sodium; 4 grams protein (10% RDA); 10 grams carbohydrate

RDA: calcium 15%; phosphorus 13%; 224 milligrams potassium; riboflavin 10%

2 cups (470 ml) skim milk	½ rennet tablet (.22 g) (see note)
1 tablespoon cocoa powder	1 tablespoon water
1 tablespoon granulated sugar	

1. Place milk, cocoa and sugar in a 1½-quart (1.5-l) soufflé dish. Cover tightly with microwave plastic wrap. Cook at 100% for 2 minutes in a 650- to 700-watt oven. Prick plastic to release steam.

2. Remove from oven and uncover. Reserve. Crush the half rennet tablet in a small bowl and mix with the water. Add to the cocoa mixture and stir to com-

(continued)

Chocolate Junket (cont.)

bine. Cover loosely and allow to stand for 20 minutes. Transfer to the refrigerator and chill for 15 minutes.

FOR 400- TO 500-WATT OVENS

To serve 4. Cook as in Step 1 for 4 minutes.

WITH A GLASS OF MILK

Of course, by now you know that it's skim milk with which you want a cookie. You can also look at those cooked in a conventional oven—Ginger Crisps (page 586) and Meringue Clouds (page 585). If you are not trying to lose weight, serve a few of these along with fruit salads, compotes and sorbets.

OAT BRAN CRISPS

As cookies go, these beige spice cookies are good for you. Don't eat too many; have one with your sorbet or fruit salad.   *MAKES 18 COOKIES*

Per 1-cookie serving: 56 calories; 10 milligrams cholesterol; 4 grams fat; 6 milligrams sodium; 1 gram protein (2% RDA); 4 grams carbohydrate

½ cup (120 ml) oat bran
¼ cup (60 ml) granulated sugar
½ teaspoon cinnamon
Pinch freshly grated nutmeg

Pinch mace
6 tablespoons unsalted butter, cut into small pieces
2 egg whites

1. Combine oat bran, sugar, cinnamon, nutmeg and mace in a food processor. Process just to combine. Add butter, pulsing on and off. Add egg whites and process until mixture is smooth.

2. Line a 9-inch (23-cm) pie plate or quiche dish with parchment paper cut to fit. Drop teaspoonfuls of batter onto the paper, leaving 1 inch (2.5 cm) between each cookie (you will get about 6 cookies in a batch). Cook, uncovered, at 100% for 3 minutes in a 650- to 700-watt oven. Repeat with remaining batter until it is used up.

3. Remove from oven. Let cookies stand on the plate for several minutes to cool and harden slightly. With a wide metal spatula, remove to a cooling rack and let stand until completely cool. Store, tightly covered, for up to one week.

FOR 400- TO 500-WATT OVENS

To make 18 cookies. Cook each batch for 5 minutes.

PEANUT BUTTER BLONDIES

These are like slim, pale brownies; but with less cholesterol. If you use commercially prepared peanut butter, the sodium and the cholesterol will both rise.
SERVES 16

Per brownie: 85 calories; 6 milligrams cholesterol; 5 grams fat; 18 milligrams sodium; 2 grams protein (3% RDA); 10 grams carbohydrate

3 tablespoons unsalted butter
½ cup (120 ml) Peanut Butter (page 478), or commercial peanut butter
½ cup (120 ml) packed light brown sugar
1 egg white

1 teaspoon vanilla extract
½ cup (120 ml) sifted cake flour, not self-rising
¼ teaspoon baking powder
Pinch kosher salt

1. Place butter in a 1½-quart (1.5-l) soufflé dish. Cook, uncovered, at 100% in a 650- to 700-watt oven for 2 minutes.
2. Remove from oven. Stir in peanut butter, sugar, egg white and vanilla extract. Sift together flour, baking powder and salt. Stir into mixture. Allow to sit for 5 minutes.
3. Scrape batter into a 8×8×2-inch (20×20×5-cm) dish. Cook, uncovered, for 4 minutes, or until set.
4. Remove from oven. Cut into 16 squares. Remove from dish and allow to cool on a wire rack.

FOR 400- TO 500-WATT OVENS

To make 16 blondies. Cook as in Step 1 for 3 minutes. In Step 3, cook for 6 minutes.

CORNMEAL COOKIES

*T*hese are a little different from any cookie around. They are like modestly firm miniature pancakes and can be eaten hot or cool. They never get crisp. The cornmeal is cooked in the microwave oven. See Basic Firm Polenta (page 216) for other quantities to increase or decrease the recipe. The cookies themselves are baked in a conventional oven. If you prefer to eat these warm, make the batter ahead, spread on the prepared baking sheets, preheat the oven and bake at the last minute.   *MAKES ABOUT 20 COOKIES*

Per 1-cookie serving: 18 calories; 1 milligram cholesterol; <1 gram fat; 15 milligrams sodium; <1 gram protein (1% RDA); 3 grams carbohydrate

1½ cups (355 ml) water
¼ cup (60 ml) yellow cornmeal
1 tablespoon granulated sugar
2 teaspoons unsalted butter
¼ cup (60 ml) all-purpose flour

½ teaspoon baking powder
Large pinch nutmeg
Large pinch cinnamon
Pinch kosher salt

1. Place rack in center of conventional oven. Preheat to 425°F (218°C).
2. Stir together water, cornmeal and sugar in a 1½-quart (1.5-l) soufflé dish. Cook, uncovered, in a 650- to 700-watt microwave oven at 100% for 3 minutes 30 seconds, stirring once.
3. Remove from oven and beat in remaining ingredients.
4. Cover a metal cookie sheet with parchment paper. For each cookie, use a level tablespoon of the mixture. With the back of a spoon, spread onto the paper each tablespoon of mixture into a flat 2½-inch (6-cm) round, leaving a space of about ½ inch (1 cm) between each round. You will have about 5 rows of 4 cookies each.
5. Place in the conventional oven and bake for 15 minutes.
6. Remove from oven. With a metal spatula, carefully turn the cookies over. Return to oven and cook 3 minutes longer.
7. Remove from oven. Transfer cookies to a cooling rack. Serve warm or cool.

FOR 400- TO 500-WATT OVENS

To make 20 cookies. Cook as in Step 2 for 5 minutes, stirring once.

Sweet Sauces

Sometimes a simple sauce will make all the difference to a portion of poached fruit, or even to a more elaborate dessert. Look carefully at the calories in each serving to see how much you can feel free to add. Many are fruit sauces, and they go well with almost any dessert. All the fruit sauces can be frozen to avoid the temptation of eating more than you should.

CHERRY SAUCE

*T*his sauce has a beautiful, rich color. The alcohol cooks out, but it can be omitted for the wary. The calorie count will come down.
MAKES 1¼ CUPS (300 ML), 10 SERVINGS

Per 2-tablespoon serving: 22 calories; 0 milligrams cholesterol; <1 gram fat; <1 milligram sodium; <1 gram protein (<1% RDA); 5 grams carbohydrate

½ pound (227 g) sweet cherries (about 30 cherries), stemmed and pitted, or frozen unsweetened cherries, defrosted in a bowl to catch juice
2 tablespoons granulated sugar

1 tablespoon kirsch
2 tablespoons water, or juice from fruit that is being poached (see Peaches with Cherry Sauce, page 547)

1. Combine cherries, sugar and kirsch in a 4-cup (1-l) glass measure. Cover tightly with microwave plastic wrap. Cook at 100% for 3 minutes in a 650- to 700-watt oven. Prick plastic to release steam.
2. Remove from oven and uncover. Transfer to a food processor and purée until smooth. Stir in water, if desired, or any liquid from frozen cherries.

FOR 400- TO 500-WATT OVENS

To make 1¼ cups (300 ml). Cook for 6 minutes.

STRAWBERRY SAUCE

*T*his brilliant red sauce is one of the few recipes in which I use an artificial sweetener. The strawberry taste will be so strong and pronounced that you won't notice any off taste from the sweetener.   *MAKES 3 CUPS (705 ML), 24 SERVINGS*

Per 2-tablespoon serving: 14 calories; 0 milligrams cholesterol; <1 gram fat; <1 milligram sodium; <1 gram protein (<1% RDA); 4 grams carbohydrate

RDA: vitamin C 42%

3 pints fresh strawberries, hulled (about 2½ pounds; 1.15 kg); if strawberries are very large, halve them

½ teaspoon fresh lemon juice, or more to taste

4 packages artificial sweetener, or to taste

1. Place one third of the strawberries in the food processor and purée until smooth. Pass through a fine sieve. You should have 1 cup (240 ml) of purée.

2. Place the purée in a 10-inch (25.5-cm) quiche dish and cover tightly with microwave plastic wrap. Cook, uncovered, at 100% for 2 minutes in a 650- to 700-watt oven.

3. Stir in remaining whole or halved strawberries. Cook, uncovered, for 6 minutes more.

4. Remove from oven and let cool slightly. Add lemon juice and sweetener to taste. Store tightly covered and refrigerated.

FOR 400- TO 500-WATT OVENS

To make 3 cups (705 ml). Prepare as in Step 1. Cook purée as in Step 2 for 4 minutes. Cook as in Step 3 for 9 minutes. Finish as in Step 4.

TART APRICOT SAUCE

*T*his makes a brightly colored, fairly thick sauce loaded with fiber. If you want a thinner sauce, you can add back some of the cooking liquid to taste after you make the purée. You will proportionately decrease the calories and the nutritional value.   *MAKES 1½ CUPS (355 ML), 6 PORTIONS*

Per ¼-cup (60-ml) portion: 27 calories; 0 milligrams cholesterol; <1 gram fat; 1 milligram sodium; <1 gram protein (<1% RDA); 7 grams carbohydrate

RDA: 132 milligrams potassium; vitamin A 14%

8 ounces dried apricots (about 1½ cups; 355 ml)
1½ cups (355 ml) water

2-inch (5-cm) piece of vanilla bean
2 tablespoons granulated sugar
2 tablespoons fresh lemon juice

1. Combine apricots, water, vanilla bean, and sugar in a 4-cup (1-l) glass measure. Cover tightly with microwave plastic wrap. Cook at 100% for 7 minutes in a 650- to 700-watt oven. Prick plastic to release steam.

2. Remove from oven and uncover carefully.

3. Drain apricots, reserving juice, and discard vanilla bean. Scrape apricots into a food processor or blender. Add lemon juice and purée until smooth. Add as much of the reserved cooking liquid as you wish to get a texture that you like.

FOR 400- TO 500-WATT OVENS

To make 1½ cups (355 ml). Cook as in Step 1 for 11 minutes.

CHOCOLATE SAUCE

No, it's not hot fudge. On the other hand, it won't overwhelm you with calories and cholesterol. If you want a hot sauce, use it just after it comes out of the oven. Do not reheat or the sweeteners will change on you. It's fine as a cold sauce, particularly with fruit and cold puddings.   *MAKES ¾ CUP (180 ML), 6 SERVINGS*

Per 2-tablespoon serving: 47 calories; 8 milligrams cholesterol; 4 grams fat; 11 milligrams sodium; 2 grams protein (4% RDA); 3 grams carbohydrate

½ cup (120 ml) skim milk
¼ cup (60 ml) unsweetened cocoa
    powder (preferably Dutch process)

1½ tablespoons unsalted butter, cut
    into small pieces
2 teaspoons artificial sweetener

1. In a 2-cup (470-ml) glass measure, slowly stir the milk into the cocoa powder to avoid lumps. Cover tightly with microwave plastic wrap. Cook at 100% for 2 minutes in a 650- to 700-watt oven. Prick plastic to release steam.

2. Remove from oven and uncover. Whisk in butter until completely melted and sauce is smooth. Stir in sweetener and serve warm or refrigerate.

FOR 400- TO 500-WATT OVENS

To make ¾ cup (180 ml). Cook as in Step 1 for 4 minutes.

WHIPPED RICOTTA TOPPING

*I*f you have been reading through this chapter, this recipe may look familiar. It is the base for Light White Ice Cream (page 558). I make it most often to use as a topping to replace the more-caloric and cholesterol-laden whipped cream. For the sake of comparison, a tablespoon of heavy cream (two tablespoons whipped cream) has fifty-two calories, twenty-one milligrams of cholesterol and six grams of fat. This will keep for a week in the refrigerator. To substitute agar agar, see pages 587–588.   *MAKES 1½ CUPS (355 ML), ABOUT 16 SERVINGS*

Per 1 heaped-tablespoon serving: 19 calories; 3 milligrams cholesterol; 1 gram fat; 20 milligrams sodium; 6 grams protein (4% RDA); 1 gram carbohydrate

2 tablespoons water
¾ teaspoon unflavored gelatin (¼ envelope; 4 g)
½ cup (120 ml) part-skim ricotta cheese

⅓ cup (80 ml) buttermilk
1½ teaspoons granulated sugar
2 drops vanilla extract

1. Place water in a small glass bowl and sprinkle gelatin over. Allow to stand for 1 minute. Cook, uncovered, at 100% for 20 seconds in a 650- to 700-watt oven. Remove from oven and reserve.

2. Place the ricotta in a blender and purée until smooth, scraping down the sides occasionally with a rubber spatula. Add remaining ingredients and the dissolved gelatin and process to combine.

3. Scrape mixture into a metal bowl and set over a larger bowl of ice. Allow to stand for about 15 minutes, until almost set, stirring occasionally with a rubber spatula. Whisk until light and foamy.

4. Scrape into a container and store, covered, in the refrigerator.

FOR 400- TO 500-WATT OVENS

To make 1½ cups (355 ml). Cook gelatin and water as in Step 1 for 30 seconds. Finish recipe as above.

Conventional Baking

Wheat flour is one of those things the microwave oven handles erratically at best. Since the goodies into which it is usually baked for dessert are often high in calories and cholesterol, I haven't felt guilty about mainly avoiding such recipes in this book for the microwave oven. Below, I give some recipes for conventionally baked desserts that will neither damage attempts at weight-loss or health.

If you've gotten out of the conventional-oven habit, remember that you will be dealing with a hot kitchen, hot oven sides and racks and very hot metal baking tins. Be careful.

ANGEL FOOD CAKE

I have always loved a good angel food cake and am happy to report that even a good-sized slice is not laden with calories. It also is remarkable among cakes for its absence of cholesterol. It makes a gala party dessert served with a fruit sauce (pages 577–579), fresh berries or sorbet.

Such cakes are a little tricky. The pans must be scrupulously clean or the cake will not rise properly. After washing the pan with soap and water, rinse it with vinegar or lemon juice and then rinse well with clear cold water. It is possible to make this by whisking by hand; but it is very tiring. Small hand-held mixers will not give you optimum volume when you beat the egg whites. I suggest a strong stationary mixer.

Angel food cakes should not be cut with knives; they crush. In my childhood, some people had angel-food forks, which looked like huge metal combs with very long teeth and a handle. Since most of us don't have these, use two forks—one in each hand—pulling your hands in opposite directions to separate what are called slices. If you must use a knife, make sure it is a heavily serrated one and cut gently, sawing back and forth.

Per ¹⁄₁₂-cake serving: 156 calories; 0 milligrams cholesterol; <1 gram fat; 103 milligrams sodium; 3 grams protein (7% RDA); 36 grams carbohydrate

⅔ cup (160 ml) plus ¾ cup (180 ml) superfine sugar
½ cup (120 ml) confectioners' sugar
⅔ cup (160 ml) cake flour (not self-rising)
3 tablespoons cornstarch

10 large egg whites at room temperature (about 1 cup; 240 ml)
¾ teaspoon cream of tartar
½ teaspoon kosher salt
¾ teaspoon vanilla extract

1. Carefully clean a 10-inch (25.5-cm) tube pan. Dry thoroughly.

2. Sift ⅔ cup (160 ml) of the sugar three times and reserve. In a medium bowl, sift together the remaining ¾ cup (180 ml) sugar, confectioners' sugar, flour and cornstarch three times. Reserve.

3. In a large bowl with an electric mixer, beat egg whites on medium speed until frothy, about 3 minutes. Add salt and cream of tartar. Beat to very soft peaks.

4. Continue beating and add the reserved sifted sugar 2 tablespoons at a time. End by adding vanilla. Beat for 1½ minutes longer; the mixture will be very shiny and rather sticky, like marshmallow cream. Do not overbeat.

5. Remove bowl from mixer. Sift one third of the reserved flour mixture over the beaten whites. With a rubber spatula, fold it in until about half incorporated. Sift another third of the flour mixture over the whites and fold it in with 3 or 4 strokes. Sift over remaining flour and fold in completely.

6. Pour batter into prepared pan. Bake on the center rack of a preheated 350°F (177°C) oven for 50–60 minutes, or until cake is firm when pressed with a finger.

7. Remove cake from oven. Let cool, inverted on a bottle, for one hour. Run a sharp knife between the cake and the pan to loosen and carefully turn it out onto a rack. Allow to cool.

ARMAGNAC-PRUNE SOUFFLÉ

*T*his may sound odder to you than apricot soufflé, but it is very good and reminiscent of Southwestern France, where Armagnac is king.   *SERVES 4*

Per serving: 129 calories; 0 milligrams cholesterol; <1 gram fat; 53 milligrams sodium; 4 grams protein (10% RDA); 30 grams carbohydrate

RDA: vitamin A 17%; riboflavin 9%

4 egg whites   Nonstick cooking spray
¾ cup (180 ml) Armagnac-Prune Purée
   (page 589)

1. Preheat oven to 375°F (190°C). Spray a 1½-quart (1.5-l) ceramic soufflé mold with nonstick cooking spray.

2. Beat egg whites until they hold peaks, but are not stiff or dry. Fold into purée.

3. Pour soufflé mixture into the mold and bake in preheated conventional oven for 20 minutes. Serve immediately.

APRICOT SOUFFLÉ

Like all soufflés, this will not wait for your guests. Unlike most of them, it has no cholesterol and is low in calories. If you're not on a weight-loss diet, add some Tart Apricot Sauce (page 579) to the bowl after serving.   *SERVES 4*

Per serving: 85 calories; 0 milligrams cholesterol; <1 gram fat; 55 milligrams sodium; 4 grams protein (9% RDA); 18 grams carbohydrate

RDA: 350 milligrams potassium; vitamin A 31%; riboflavin 7%

4 egg whites   Nonstick cooking spray
¾ cup (180 ml) Apricot Purée (page
  588)

1. Preheat the oven to 375°F (190°C). Spray a 1½-quart (1.5-l) soufflé dish with nonstick cooking spray.
2. Beat egg whites until they hold peaks but are not stiff and dry.
3. Fold half the egg whites into the purée until evenly combined. Add purée mixture to the remaining whites and fold until well mixed, taking care not to collapse the whites.
4. Place mixture in sprayed soufflé dish. Smooth the top of the mixture with a spatula and cook for 20 minutes. Serve immediately.

MERINGUE CLOUDS

*T*hese are conventionally made meringues in a cookie size. Meringues usually need lots of sugar or they are sticky. These are made with very little sugar, yet they are crisp and delicate. Artificial sweetener can be used in this recipe because the baking temperature is so low. Have one of these as a reward after a virtuous lunch, or serve along with a sorbet. Two or three make a good snack when you feel like you need a sweet fix and your spirits are dragging. Don't make more at a time unless you are giving a party—too tempting.   *MAKES 10–12 MERINGUES*

Per 1-meringue serving: 8 calories; 0 milligrams cholesterol; 0 grams fat; 10 milligrams sodium; 1 gram protein (1% RDA); 1 gram carbohydrate

2 egg whites
1 tablespoon granulated sugar

Scant 1 teaspoon artificial sweetener
(aspartame)

1. Preheat conventional oven to 200°F (93°C). Line a baking sheet with parchment paper.
2. Place egg whites in the large bowl of an electric mixer. Beat until stiff. Gradually add granulated sugar and sweetener.
3. Drop meringues with a teaspoon onto lined baking sheet.
4. Place in oven and turn oven off. Leave in oven until meringues are cool and dry. This may take hours. Leaving them overnight is just fine.

GINGER CRISPS

*T*hese delicious cookies may not be an everyday event for weight-loss dieters; but eat one at a party with a fruit compote, salad or sorbet, and let the guests have what they will.   *MAKES 30 COOKIES*

Per 1-cookie serving: 69 calories; 8 milligrams cholesterol; 3 grams fat; 11 milligrams sodium; 1 gram protein (2% RDA); 10 grams carbohydrate

½ cup (120 ml) granulated sugar
½ teaspoon ground ginger
4 ounces (113.5 g) unsalted butter, cut
   into 1-inch (2.5-cm) pieces
3 egg whites
1 cup (240 ml) sifted all-purpose flour

Pinch kosher salt
1 teaspoon fresh lemon juice
1 teaspoon grated fresh ginger
30 ¼-inch (.5-cm) pieces crystallized
   ginger

1. Place sugar and ground ginger in a food processor and process just to combine. Add butter and process until smooth.

2. With machine running, add egg whites, flour, salt, lemon juice and grated ginger. Process until smooth. Let batter stand for 15 minutes.

3. Preheat oven to 400°F (204°C). Butter and flour two cookie sheets. Drop the batter by rounded teaspoonful onto cookie sheets, at least 2 inches (5 cm) apart. Press a piece of crystallized ginger into each cookie. Cook for 8 minutes, or until edges are golden brown.

4. Remove cookies to a cooling rack with a wide metal spatula. Store airtight for up to 3 days.

Jams and Preserves

These are not so much sweet endings as beginnings. While there are some quite good, calorically reduced fruit preserves on the market, some of us like to make our own. They don't take very long in a microwave oven, and are nice not only for eating but also as gifts.

Since most preserves need to thicken, which is usually accomplished with a mixture of pectin—inherent in the fruit or added—and sugar (caloric en masse), for some of these preserves I use an ingredient that may be new to many of us: agar agar.

Agar agar is a vegetarian gelatin. Besides being vegetarian, it has the advantage of not needing to be cold to retain its firming qualities. It used to be much more popular than it is today. You will probably have to get it in a health-food store. It may come in either long strips, sheets or powdered form. If it is not already powdered, break up the pieces and grind in a blender or coffee mill until pulverized.

Agar agar is a little tricky in that it needs to be cooked long enough to dissolve but not so long that it overcooks and no longer thickens. Three tablespoons of agar agar flakes (7 g) will jell about four cups (1 l) of a clear liquid. Thicker mixtures such as the preserves may need more, as indicated in the recipes. One and a half tablespoons of flakes make, when pulverized, the same quantity contained in an envelope of gelatin and will set two cups (470 ml) liquid just as the gelatin does.

You can always re-liquefy agar agar in the microwave oven by heating for about one minute. Even though agar agar will set at room temperature—good for jams—it is not a wonderful idea to leave things made with it out of the refrigerator for a long time. In laboratories it is used as a culture medium.

AGAR AGAR YIELDS

FLAKES	POWDER
1½ tablespoons	2¼ teaspoons
2 tablespoons	3½ teaspoons
3 tablespoons	1 tablespoon plus 1½ teaspoons

You can substitute agar agar in recipes above using gelatin. If the gelatin in the recipe is simply dissolved in a small amount of water before being used, do the same with agar agar. Since the agar agar jells quickly at room temperature, particularly in small quantities, as soon as the agar agar is taken out of the microwave oven, always stir some of the mixture to which it is being added into it and then add it back to the mixture, stirring thoroughly.

AGAR AGAR	WATER	650- TO 700- WATT OVENS	400- TO 500- WATT OVENS
1½ teaspoons	¼ cup (60 ml)	3 minutes	5 minutes
2¼ teaspoons	½ cup (120 ml)	4 minutes	6 minutes
3½ teaspoons	1⅓ cups (320 ml)	5 minutes	9 minutes
1 tablespoon plus 1½ teaspoons	1½ cups (355 ml)	6 minutes	10 minutes

Not all of these recipes require all this fussing. Some are made from dried fruits. The drying process removes the water that would have had to be jelled, and so when the fruits are cooked and puréed, they are already thickened. Those who do not need to lose weight will find these purées valuable adjuncts to baking.

All preserves should be packed in sterile jars with sterile lids. See manufacturer's instructions, and, if worried, refrigerate preserves. I recommend using small jars so that only a few days' worth of servings get opened at one time—less temptation and less boredom.

APRICOT PURÉE

I like this on breakfast toast, where a whole tablespoon will only cost me twenty-three calories. The serving size given below can be entirely consumed with more toast by those who do not need to watch their weight—lavish. It is also the approximate quantity per person when it is used as the base of Apricot Soufflé (page 584).

MAKES ¾ CUP (180 ML), 4 NON–WEIGHT-LOSS SERVINGS, 12 WEIGHT-LOSS SERVINGS

Per 3-tablespoon serving: 69 calories; 0 milligrams cholesterol; <1 gram fat; 5 milligrams sodium; 1 gram protein (2% RDA); 17 grams carbohydrate

RDA: 305 milligrams potassium; vitamin A 31%

3 ounces (85 g) dried apricots
¾ cup (180 ml) water
1 tablespoon granulated sugar

2-inch (5-cm) piece of vanilla bean,
    split lengthwise
3 tablespoons lemon juice

1. Combine all ingredients in a 1½-quart (1.5-1) soufflé dish. Cover tightly with microwave plastic wrap. Cook at 100% for 8 minutes in a 650- to 700-watt oven. Prick plastic to release steam.

2. Remove from oven. Uncover and discard vanilla bean.

3. Pour into a blender and purée until smooth.

4. Pack in sterilized jars, or freeze for long storage.

FOR 400- TO 500-WATT OVENS

To make ¾ cup (180 ml). Cook for 12 minutes.

ARMAGNAC-PRUNE PURÉE

Armagnac-Prune Purée will cost you thirty-eight calories for an on-the-bread one-tablespoon serving. Warmed and thinned with a little water, it makes a delicious ice cream sauce (whoops!) or accompaniment to Rice Pudding (page 566) or poached fruit.

MAKES ¾ CUP (180 ML), 4 NON–WEIGHT-LOSS SERVINGS, 12 WEIGHT-LOSS SERVINGS

Per 3-tablespoon serving: 113 calories; 0 milligrams cholesterol; <1 gram fat; 2 milligrams sodium; 1 gram protein (2% RDA); 29 grams carbohydrate

RDA: 322 milligrams potassium; vitamin A 17%

6 ounces (170 g) pitted prunes (about
  17 prunes; 1 cup; 240 ml)
½ vanilla bean (4 inches; 10 cm)

½ cup (120 ml) water
1 tablespoon fresh lemon juice
2 tablespoons Armagnac or brandy

1. Combine prunes, vanilla bean and water in a 1½-quart (1.5-1) soufflé dish. Cover tightly with microwave plastic wrap. Cook at 100% for 5 minutes in a 650- to 700-watt oven. Prick plastic to release steam.

2. Remove from oven and uncover. Transfer prunes to a food processor along with 2 tablespoons of the cooking liquid, lemon juice and brandy. Purée until smooth. Discard remaining cooking liquid.

3. Pack in sterilized jars, or freeze for long storage.

STRAWBERRY JAM

*T*his is indeed one of those preserves that obliges the use of agar agar (page 587); but since it provides wonderful flavor for only thirteen calories per tablespoon—which certainly permits what would seem to be wildly self-indulgent quantities for breakfast (up to four tablespoons for those not losing weight)—the effort is worthwhile.

MAKES 4 CUPS, 16 NON–WEIGHT-LOSS SERVINGS, 64 WEIGHT-LOSS SERVINGS

Per 1-tablespoon serving: 13 calories; 0 milligrams cholesterol; <1 gram fat; <1 milligram sodium; <1 gram protein (<1% RDA); 3 grams carbohydrate

RDA: vitamin C 18%

2 quarts (2 l) fresh strawberries, hulled
½–1 cup (120 to 240 ml) water
   (amount depends on strawberries)
½ cup (120 ml) granulated sugar

3 tablespoons powdered agar agar
2 teaspoons fresh lemon juice, or to
   taste

1. Place one quart of the strawberries in a food processor or blender. Purée until smooth. Pass purée through a fine sieve into a 4-cup (1-l) measure. Add enough water to measure 2½ cups (590 ml). Stir in sugar and agar agar. Cover tightly with microwave plastic wrap. Cook at 100% for 10 minutes in a 650- to 700-watt oven. Prick plastic to release steam.

2. Remove from oven. Uncover and stir in remaining strawberries. Cook, uncovered, for 7 minutes.

3. Remove from oven. Stir in lemon juice. Divide among sterilized jars and store, tightly covered and refrigerated.

FOR 400- TO 500-WATT OVENS

To make 2 cups (470 ml). Use 1 quart strawberries, ¼–½ cup (60–120 ml) water, ¼ cup (60 ml) granulated sugar, 1½ tablespoons powdered agar agar and 1 teaspoon fresh lemon juice, or to taste. Prepare, using 2 cups (470 ml) berries as in Step 1, adding enough water to make 1¼ cups (300 ml) purée and cooking in an 11 × 8½ × 2-inch (28 × 21.5 × 5-cm) oval dish for 10 minutes. Continue with Step 2, cooking for 10 minutes, or until it jells. Finish as in Step 3.

PEACH CONSERVE

I make this when peaches are inexpensive and I can buy them by the half-bushel. Those kind may be small and require your digging out various imperfections; but they are fragrantly ripe and sweet. At only eleven calories per tablespoon, there is very little limit to what the non–weight-loss dieter can eat.

MAKES 3 CUPS (705 ML), 24 NON–WEIGHT-LOSS SERVINGS, 48 WEIGHT-LOSS SERVINGS

Per 1-tablespoon serving: 11 calories; 0 milligrams cholesterol; <1 gram fat; <1 milligram sodium; <1 gram protein (<1% RDA); 3 grams carbohydrate

3 pounds (1.4 kg) peaches; 1½ pounds (680 g) peeled and pitted, and 1½ pounds (680 g) cut into 1-inch (2.5-cm) chunks and reserved

¼ cup (60 ml) granulated sugar
3 tablespoons powdered agar agar
1 teaspoon fresh lemon juice

1. Place peeled peaches in the work bowl of a food processor. Process until smooth. Scrape into a 14 × 11 × 2-inch (35.5 × 28 × 5-cm) dish. Stir in sugar and agar agar. Cover tightly with microwave plastic wrap. Cook at 100% for 10 minutes in a 650- to 700-watt oven. Prick plastic to release steam.

2. Remove from oven. Uncover carefully and stir in remaining peaches. Cook, uncovered, for 7 minutes.

3. Remove from oven. Stir in lemon juice and divide among sterilized jars. Process according to manufacturer's instructions.

FOR 400- TO 500-WATT OVENS

To make 3 cups (705 ml). Cook as in Step 1 for 10 minutes. Continue with Step 2, cooking for 10 minutes.

LEMON MARMALADE

*T*his is not a low-low-calorie preserve; but it is so fresh to wake up to, so full of vitamins, that I thought we could all indulge from time to time. Those whose weight is already down there can indulge at will, rejoicing in the strong boost of vitamin C; but not in vast quantities. This recipe would take forever in a low-wattage oven. *MAKES 4 CUPS (1 L), 64 SERVINGS*

Per 1-tablespoon serving: 52 calories; 0 milligrams cholesterol; <1 gram fat; 1 milligram sodium; <1 gram protein (<1% RDA); 15 grams carbohydrate

RDA: vitamin C 26%

12 lemons   4 cups (1 l) granulated sugar

1. Working over a bowl, slice off both ends of the lemons and discard. Peel them, removing both the peel and the pith. Reserve lemons in bowl with collected juice.

2. Place the peel in the work bowl of a food processor. Process until coarsely chopped. Scrape into an 8-cup (2-l) glass measure. Add cold water to cover. Cover tightly with microwave plastic wrap. Cook at 100% for 12 minutes in a 650- to 700-watt oven. Prick plastic to release steam.

3. Remove from oven and uncover. Strain peel in a colander or sieve and rinse with cold water. Return to measure, cover with cold water and cook, covered, for 12 minutes more. Prick plastic.

4. Remove from oven and uncover. Strain through a colander and rinse with cold water. Place in a 13×9×2-inch (33×23×5-cm) oval glass or ceramic dish and reserve.

5. Cut the lemons in half and remove as many seeds as possible. Remove ¼ cup (60 ml) of the juice collected in the bottom of the bowl and reserve. Place lemons and any remaining juice in the work bowl of a food processor. Process until coarsely chopped. Add to the reserved peel and stir in sugar. Cook, uncovered, for 40 minutes, or until jelled, stirring every 10 minutes. Add reserved lemon juice and cook for 3 minutes more.

6. Pack marmalade into sterilized jars and process according to manufacturer's instructions.

TOMATO JAM

*T*omato jam may not be everybody's idea of a morning treat; but I love its spicy sweetness and relish the scantiness of the calories. After all, tomatoes are fruits, and beautifully colored ones as well. If you don't welcome the thought at breakfast, consider it as a teatime snack with toast.   *MAKES 4 CUPS (1 L), 32 SERVINGS*

Per 2-tablespoon serving: 27 calories; 0 milligrams cholesterol; <1 gram fat; 98 milligrams sodium; 1 gram protein (1% RDA); 7 grams carbohydrate

RDA: 147 milligrams potassium; vitamin A 13%; vitamin C 27%

4 pounds (1.8 kg) tomatoes (about 8 large tomatoes)
1 lemon, quartered, seeded and cut into 1-inch (2.5-cm) chunks
1 juice orange (8 ounces; 227 g), quartered, seeded and cut into 1-inch (2.5-cm) chunks

3 cloves garlic, smashed and peeled
5 quarter-size slices fresh ginger, peeled
½ cup (120 ml) dark brown sugar
½ teaspoon ground mace
½ teaspoon freshly grated nutmeg
2 teaspoons kosher salt
1 tablespoon fresh lemon juice

1.   Core tomatoes and cut an "X" in the bottom of each. Place in a 2½-quart (2.5-l) soufflé dish or casserole. Cook, uncovered, at 100% for 20 minutes in a 650- to 700-watt oven, stirring halfway through cooking.

2.   Remove from oven. Pass tomatoes through the medium disc of a food mill. Return to dish and cook, uncovered, for 45 minutes longer, or until you have a thick tomato purée.

3.   Place lemon, orange, garlic and ginger in food processor. Process until coarsely chopped.

4.   Remove tomatoes from oven. Stir in chopped mixture, sugar, mace, nutmeg and salt. Cook, uncovered, for 5 minutes.

5.   Remove from oven and stir in lemon juice. Divide among sterilized jars and process according to manufacturer's instructions.

FOR 400- TO 500-WATT OVENS

To make 2 cups (470 ml). Use 2 pounds (900 g) tomatoes, ½ lemon, ½ orange, 2 small cloves garlic, 2 quarter-size slices ginger, ¼ cup (60 ml) sugar, ¼ teaspoon each mace and nutmeg, 1 teaspoon salt and 1½ teaspoons lemon juice. Cook as in Step 1 for 20 minutes, stirring halfway through cooking. Continue as in Step 2, cooking for 45 minutes. Continue as in Step 3. Cook as in Step 4 for 7 minutes. Finish as in Step 5.

Fruit Leathers

If you tend to get the sweet-munchies, these reduced and barely sweetened strips of dried-fruit purees are very satisfying and take a while to chew. Take one or two strips to the office and nibble when temptation comes along in the shape of a canteen cart or a friend with a candy bar.

APRICOT LEATHER

Moroccans, and other Near Eastern dwellers in hot climates with good fruit, discovered that fruit cooked down so far that it contains almost no water can be preserved in brightly colored semipliable sheets—like the fruit rolls full of sugar that you can buy in the store.   *SERVES 8*

Per 1 × 11-inch (2.5 × 28-cm) strip serving: 34 calories; 0 milligrams cholesterol; <1 gram fat; 2 milligrams sodium; <1 gram protein (<1% RDA); 9 grams carbohydrate

RDA: vitamin A 15%

¾ cup (180 ml) Apricot Purée (page
   588)

1. Line a 14 × 11 × 2-inch (35.5 × 28 × 5-cm) dish with parchment paper. Spread the purée over the parchment. Cook, uncovered, at 100% for 11 minutes in a 650- to 700-watt oven. Reduce oven power to 50% and cook for 11 minutes more.
2. Remove from oven. Let stand, uncovered, until completely cool and dry. Peel from paper and cut into strips.

FOR 400- TO 500-WATT OVENS

To serve 4. Use generous ⅓ cup (80 ml) purée. Spread in a 13 × 9 × 2-inch (33 × 23 × 5-cm) oval dish as in Step 1. Cook for 8 minutes. Finish as in Step 2.

PRUNE LEATHER

You may think yuck; but wait until you start muching on this delicious, dark brown fruit leather; you will change your mind.   *SERVES 8*

Per 1 × 11-inch (2.5 × 28-cm) strip serving: 57 calories; 0 milligrams cholesterol; <1 gram fat; 1 milligram sodium; 1 gram protein (1% RDA); 14 grams carbohydrate

RDA: 161 milligrams potassium; vitamin A 8%

¾ cup (180 ml) Armagnac-Prune Purée
  (page 589)

1. Line a 14 × 11 × 2-inch (35.5 × 28 × 5-cm) dish with parchment paper. Spread the purée over the parchment. Cook, uncovered, at 100% for 11 minutes in a 650- to 700-watt oven. Reduce oven power to 50% and cook for 11 minutes more.

2. Remove from oven. Let stand, uncovered, until completely cool and dry. Peel from paper and cut into strips.

FOR 400- TO 500-WATT OVENS

To serve 4. Use generous ⅓ cup (80 ml) purée. Spread in a 13 × 9 × 2-inch (33 × 23 × 5-cm) oval dish as in Step 1. Cook for 8 minutes. Finish as in Step 2.

CRANBERRY LEATHER

A little piece of Burgundy-red leather. It's just big enough to carry to the office and pull pieces off of during the day for snacks. Over the course of a day, you can eat the whole thing.　*SERVES 4*

Per 2 × 13-inch (5 × 33-cm) slice: 45 calories; 0 milligrams cholesterol; <1 gram fat; <1 milligram sodium; <1 gram protein (<1% RDA); 12 grams carbohydrate

RDA: vitamin C 10%

6 ounces (170 g) cranberries, fresh or frozen	3 tablespoons water
	2 tablespoons granulated sugar

1. Combine all ingredients in an 8-cup (2-l) glass measure. Cover tightly with microwave plastic wrap. Cook at 100% for 8 minutes in a 650- to 700-watt oven. Prick plastic to release steam.
2. Remove from oven and uncover. Transfer mixture to a food mill and purée using a fine blade.
3. Line a 13 × 9 × 2-inch (33 × 23 × 5-cm) oval dish with parchment paper. Spread cranberry purée over paper. Cook, uncovered, at 100% for 3 minutes. Decrease oven power to 50% and cook for 3 minutes more.
4. Remove from oven. Let stand, uncovered, until completely cool and dry. Peel from paper and cut into strips.

LEARNING MICROWAVE

Why learn microwave? Because it is not just a way of reheating or defrosting. It does those things, but at its best it is a splendid way to cook in a hurry and cook well—not everything; but many, many things—preserving more of the nutrients that are in the food, along with the flavor and the color. Fish, poultry, vegetables and most carbohydrates do brilliantly. You are not cheating when you use a microwave oven. It is cooking. Don't feel guilty just because your work gets done in a fraction of the time.

Evidently, the microwave oven doesn't clean and cut up your vegetables, or walk the dog. That time remains the same. To minimize it, use the electrical appliances where feasible.

A few microwave cooking times may not appear to be much briefer than the conventional cooking times. There are several reasons for the microwave alternative. It may provide better quality. It will certainly be cooler. It may actually be shorter because the omnipresent conventional cooking instruction "Bring to a boil" doesn't exist in microwave cooking. The time for boiling the liquid is in the recipe. It may also be shorter because it liberates the cook from standing and stirring to do other chores or preparation, such as setting the table. Risotto is a good instance.

I wrote another book, Microwave Gourmet, which explains how to cook using a microwave oven. I would like to believe that all of you already have and use that book or are going to run right out and buy it; but, of course, it isn't true. So here it goes. I hope that with time I have become clearer and more succinct. While I will give you all the basic information that you need, I cannot cover it in as much detail as I did in Microwave Gourmet. Also, you will find that much of the cooking information you need is provided in each chapter. If you have questions about how to cook a certain food, how to arrange it in your cooking dish, indeed what cooking dish to use, look in the Index and it will guide you to a specific solution.

How Do Microwaves Cook?

I am tempted to say, by exaggeration. The other flip answers are, quickly and well. Of course, food cooks in microwave ovens just as it does in any other mode of cooking. The food gets hot. A microwave oven is another tool for heating—cooking—food. Your barbecue may use wood or charcoal or even butane gas. Your stove and conventional oven use electricity or gas. In the south of Italy, home cooks still sometimes make their jams by setting the wide bowls of fruit out in the hot sun to cook. The microwave oven uses microwaves. Don't be confused by all the slang and industry jargon. Microwaves have no more relationship to X rays or atomic radiation than your light bulb does.

Each way of cooking has its own rules and problems; but the basic flavors of food and the joys of cooking remain the same.

However flippant it is, my first answer has much truth to it. The microwave oven is, as we shall see, much like a little kid who cannot help exaggerating everything. It cooks faster, evaporates more, tends to have more-pronounced hot spots, and the microwaves themselves run out of energy more quickly—like that same kid at the end of a day. Also like that child, they are short and they don't do arithmetic normally.

What does all that mean in practical terms to your fish, your chicken, your vegetables? Microwaves pass through the surface of the food and produce heat among the molecules in the interior of it. The energy penetrates from all sides, but only reaches one and a half inches into the food. This means that the ideal piece of food for microwave cooking is of an even thickness and shape. Small evenly sized pieces of chicken breast, for example, cook well. A whole large fish also cooks well. Remember to keep the pieces of food separated by a small space; the microwave oven will read touching pieces as if they were one piece.

Microwave energy acts on food in liquid—a stew, for instance—as if it were one mass. To get around this problem, cook with as little liquid as possible, only enough to cover the bottom of the container or just to cover the food. The microwave oven produces wet heat, so you do not need to worry about the food drying out. It will cook more quickly with little or no liquid added. For example, if you are making a soup, cook the vegetables in just enough liquid to cover and then add the rest of the liquid just to heat.

Microwave energy cooks food from the outside of the cooking dish toward the center. This is the opposite from the way food cooks on top of the stove. When you put something in the frying pan, the food in the center of the pan gets cooked first. In the microwave oven, the food around the outside of the dish gets cooked first. This is both good and bad. On the positive side, it means that you can put evenly sized pieces of chicken or vegetables around the inside edge of a dish and they will all be cooked in the same amount of time. However, it presents a problem for cooking custards, which tend to set around the outside before the center is cooked. To get around that particular problem, you have to stir from the outside of the dish toward the center, moving the undercooked portion from the center to the outside. You can also arrange foods in the dish according to how quickly they cook.

To find out how to arrange other kinds of foods for even cooking, see the illustrations in the appropriate chapters.

While the entire dish of food cooks from the outside toward the center, an individual piece of food itself cooks from the inside out. This means that it usually does not brown. It cooks with humidity, which can come from the water content of the food itself. Uncovered, this moisture evaporates more quickly than in other forms of cooking—exaggeration again. This makes it important to cover most foods cooked in the microwave oven.

If you are cooking a very small piece of food and overcook it, the result may not be apparent on the surface; but inside, where the microwaves overlap, the food will be overcooked or oven-burned.

As the size of the pieces is important, so is the size of the dish. Changing the size of a cooking container is like changing the size of a layer-cake pan. Try to approximate as closely as possible the cooking dish size given in the recipes.

What the food is made of will also influence the way it cooks. Microwave heating and consequent cooking of food has often been described as the water molecules in the food becoming agitated and their friction causing heat. Whether that is accurate or not, fat draws microwaves like a magnet, as does sugar. In this book, that will not be very relevant. It's more relevant that protein also cooks quickly in a microwave oven, which makes it imperative that high-protein foods such as meats not be overcooked or they will toughen.

The Oven

THE POWER

Microwave ovens come in several different sizes and wattages. A full-power oven has 650–700 watts of power, a medium-power oven has 500–600 watts of power and a low-power oven has 400–500 watts of power. It is important to know the power of your oven since the power affects the speed with which your food will cook and the evenness of the cooking. If you already have an oven and don't know how much power it has, look in the instruction book or call the manufacturer with your model number to find out.

To a certain extent, the wattage of your oven can be compared with the horsepower of a car. If I ask you to my house for dinner and tell you that it will take you an hour to get there, I am working on the assumption that your car will go at the speed limit of fifty-five miles an hour. If your car can go only twenty-five miles an hour, you will be over an hour late. You will be late and dinner will be ruined.

It will take you approximately one and a half times as long to cook something in a low-power oven as it takes to cook it in a full-power oven. But as I said earlier, this is not a hard-and-fast arithmetic formula. Since the oven is less powerful as well as less rapid, it will often not microwave large amounts of food well. If you are buying a new oven, I strongly recommend that you get a 650- to 700-watt oven.

Most ovens, except for the smallest ones, also come with several power settings, which is what is meant when an oven is called "variable power." Unless you select a specific power setting on the oven, it will start cooking at its default setting. When you turn the microwave oven on, it will automatically start cooking at 100 percent power, which is the highest setting on your oven. Almost all microwave cooking in this book is done at 100 percent power, both for rapidity and efficiency.

Clearly, if you have an oven that has about half the power of a full-power one—that is, it has 400 instead of 700 watts of power—that 100 percent will be working half as hard. Therefore, recipes in this book give different timings so that you can choose the proper version for your oven.

Sometimes there are also different techniques for the same recipe, depending on the wattage of the oven. When a low-wattage oven is on at 100 percent power, it is the equivalent of a full-wattage oven at 50 percent power. When an occasional recipe is cooked at 50 percent power in a full-wattage oven, it will be cooked at 100 percent power in a low-wattage oven. Many low-wattage ovens have only a single setting, of 100 percent. Examples of such differences in versions of a recipe would be those for timbales (pages 103–106).

To defrost, you should learn how to set a full-power oven to 30 percent power—defrost or low or 3. The 50 percent power—medium or 5—setting is used primarily for custards.

It should be noted that there are convection-microwave ovens. I do not find them advantageous unless you are short of conventional oven space and wish to use the convection power for an additional oven. I should point out that while microwave ovens use very little electric power, convection-microwaves, when used in combination, use quite a good deal. While it is better to have a separate electric line for even power for your microwave oven, it is not essential. It is imperative for a convection-microwave; otherwise, you may well blow fuses. To use a convection-microwave, you will have to learn how a convection oven works.

Unfortunately, most ovens do not use the convection and microwave powers simultaneously. They cycle between the two, which makes it almost impossible to give instructions for their use. It should be noted that while microwaves cook quickly by barely penetrating the food, convection ovens cook by the conventional means of conduction, passing heat from one part to the next relatively slowly. Trying to use both at the same time exaggerates the difference between the two modes of cooking. To brown food, which the microwave oven does poorly, it is more expedient either to brown it under a conventional broiler after microwave cooking or to brown it on top of the stove before microwave cooking.

Additionally, ovens made for convection-microwave cooking have exposed-metal walls rather than coated-metal walls. This makes them sweat—give off moisture in drops—which loosens the seal of plastic wrap. It also reflects heat, which may scorch small amounts of hot fat such as butter or chocolate unless cooking times are reduced.

OVEN SIZE

Ovens come in many sizes with a variety of interior configurations. A large-size oven, with 1.5 cubic feet (425 cubic cm) of interior space, will permit you to cook not only for yourself but also for company. It is also better to have an oven with a relatively square cavity. Ovens that are rectangular may not have a very high cavity, which makes it hard to stir things.

CONTROLS

Since ovens vary so wildly in the form of their controls, you will have to read the instruction book that comes with the oven in order to learn how to turn it on, set the clock and set the cooking time and the power. I prefer ovens with digital controls—easier to read. They are set like a digital clock, with minutes set as numerals: One and a half minutes is set and given in this book as one minute and thirty seconds.

The cooking time turns the oven off and on, as does opening the door. There can be no emission of microwaves when the door is open. Normally, after the time is set there is also a start button to turn the oven on. This means that you can put the food in the oven and set the time without pushing the start button. Push the start button at a time figured so that the food will come out when you are ready. If you interrupt the cooking by opening the door in order to stir the food, be sure to close the door and push the start button again to complete the set cooking time. Alternatively, you can set the time to remind you to stir, and then reset it for the remaining cooking time.

Many ovens will have many other controls, such as computer controls. They are not only unnecessary but virtually useless as well.

OTHER OVEN FEATURES

Some ovens come with carrousels, which rotate the food and cooking dishes through the cavity. I prefer these. The tight covering that I recommend obviates much of the unevenness in temperature and evaporation of most other recipes. Stirring the food will also help; but the carrousel is an aid when cooking an uncovered dish or a number of separate foods, such as baking potatoes, artichokes or pears. If your oven does not have a carrousel, you can buy a simple wind-up one that will fit in the smallest ovens.

Some ovens come with racks so that more than one dish can be cooked in it at the same time. If yours does not have one, buy an inexpensive plastic rack with folding legs.

CLEANING THE OVEN

Most ovens come with a glass tray at the bottom that is removable. This glass tray or a carrousel permits the food to cook from the bottom. If something should spill or boil over, remove this tray—using pot holders—and wash it as you would a plate. Anything on the walls of the oven can normally be wiped off with a wet sponge with or without a little mild detergent. If you use detergent, be sure to wipe well with another sponge or paper towel moistened with clean water. You don't want a detergent smell in your food.

The microwave oven rarely gets really dirty; but it may accumulate cooking odors. Think of these as odors that aren't getting into your house. To remove odors from your machine, put a few large slices of cucumber on a plate and cook at 100 percent power for 4–5 minutes. The odor will be gone and you can put the cucumber into a soup or throw it out.

Cooking Containers

See page 27 for the sizes you will be using most often. They are worth finding and buying if you don't have them. When choosing cooking dishes for microwave cooking, I prefer those with rounded corners when possible. The microwaves tend to get caught in sharp corners and cause local overcooking.

Try to use containers that are as close as possible in size to those in the recipes. Changing the size and shape is like changing the size and shape of a baking pan in conventional cooking.

Use glass, ceramic, porcelain and earthenware dishes. Any that are not entirely coated with a metallic glaze and do not have gold or platinum trim are usable. A small amount of a coppery-red or cobalt-blue glaze in decoration will not matter.

Beware of cooking pots that are enameled. They may look like ceramic, but will have a heart of metal.

I generally avoid plastic cooking dishes, since the covers that come with them cannot be used in the microwave oven and microwave plastic wrap doesn't make a tight seal on many of them. They also tend to discolor. I do use plastic containers for freezing food and then defrosting it. Be sure to use plastic containers that are meant for microwave-oven use. Others will get unpleasantly soft and are dangerous—the risk of spilling hot liquids is one danger.

Remove the lids from the freezing containers. Cover them as best as you can with microwave plastic wrap.

Plastic is transparent to microwaves. If you substitute a plastic cooking dish for the kind suggested, you may have to reduce the cooking time slightly. This transparency has been taken into account in the timings for defrosting of frozen foods.

Always use pot holders or kitchen towels—not paper—when removing a dish or container from the microwave oven. While the dish itself is not heated by the microwaves, the food in the dish can get very hot and in turn heat the dish, and if you pick up the dish bare-handed, you will get a nasty and dangerous surprise.

Coverings

For most recipes in this book, your containers and dishes will be covered. Microwave cooking exaggerates unevenness in cooking and evaporation. Covering the dish makes something like the balanced system of a terrarium, evening out the moisture and heat. Covering will also change cooking times, because steam is retained in the cooking dish. Additionally, retaining the steam means that the surface of the food does not cool because of all the evaporation that would take place if the food were not tightly covered. Tight covering then means more safety because of even cooking and hotter food. Dishes that are meant to have evaporation occur as part of the cooking technique—risotto, for example—will normally need to be stirred during the cooking.

When—in this book—dishes are covered for cooking, they are covered with either microwave plastic wrap or the tightly fitted lid that comes with the dish, depending on the recipe. Sometimes they can be used interchangeably. From time to time, the dish may be loosely covered with paper toweling.

Many casseroles come with covers, and some soufflé dishes intended for micro-wave cooking now come with lids, or you may find that one of your non-metallic oven-proof lids will fit your soufflé dishes or use a glass pie plate. Lids are nor-mally used or given as alternatives for foods such as stews, where the recipe is for a large quantity and contains a substantial amount of liquid.

Microwave plastic wrap comes in two basic kinds—stretchy and more rigid—depending on a given manufacturer's formula. Whatever the kind, you need to use a piece large enough so that it covers the entire open space of the dish and extends down the sides, or around the handle of a measuring cup, to make a tight seal. This is what is meant by tight-sealing. It occurs because the wrap clings to the container, particularly as the container gets hot. The seal will be less effective

When covering a measuring cup with plastic wrap, place square of wrap on the diagonal. Make sure to wrap around handle to get a tight seal.

Cover dishes with microwave plastic wrap, easing if wrap is stiff. Let wrap extend down sides of dish.

Plastic wrap may swell and form a bubble; prick to release steam.

Remove plastic wrap by pulling it away and then up from cooking dish.

with plastic containers. If need be, overlap two sheets of wrap to get a large enough piece. The wrap will stick to itself.

When using the stretchy kind, you can draw the wrap as tightly as you wish. When using the rigid kind, it is better to leave a few pleats or gussets in the top—basically a little loose wrap—so that the steam has room to expand. In the spec-ified dishes, there is generally enough headroom for the steam in any case.

Always pierce the plastic wrap immediately after cooking. This permits the steam to escape before you remove the wrap, and keeps the plastic from being

If one piece of wrap will not completely cover dish, overlap two pieces, patting them so that they stick together. Do not completely double the wrap.

sucked back down on top of the food as the steam cools. Today's information is that it is better if the wrap does not touch the food.

To remove the wrap, pull a piece that is hanging over the side of the cooking dish away from the dish and then up, keeping your hands away from the dish. You can use cooking tongs. In this way you will avoid any steam that may remain in the dish.

When using paper toweling to cover a dish loosely so that the food will not spatter, or under a food like a potato to absorb moisture, use those that are clearly marked for microwave use or microwavable. Normally there will be no designs, nor will they be reinforced with plastic. Do not be virtuous and use recycled paper. It may contain metallic traces that will ignite in the oven.

Similarly, if you are using microwave plastic bags, avoid the ties that come with them because they often have wire hidden inside. Instead, loosely knot the plastic bag.

You will notice that metal isn't popular in microwave circles. It blocks the microwaves and, improperly used, can cause sparks, called arcing. Aluminum foil can be used within a cooking dish to shield—wrap—part of a piece of food and keep it from overcooking. Metal foil should not touch exposed-metal oven walls or racks.

What the Microwave Does Badly

The microwave cannot roast, grill, broil, sauté or stir-fry. See pages 346–349 for alternative instructions. It browns food seldom and badly. See page 350 if you want a browned surface on your food. You cannot cook a main course for thirty; the oven isn't big enough. It's inefficient to cook two completely different dishes at the same time. It is not useful for cooking any significant quantity of pasta. It is less than splendid with wheat flour and gluten. See conventional baking recipes for bread (pages 151–153) and desserts (pages 582–585).

For other bakery or pastry shop–type desserts—probably not on your diet— see *Microwave Gourmet* or good all-purpose conventional-baking books.

A microwave oven is only one of the tools in your kitchen. It does many things superbly. Use it for those and use the rest of your kitchen for the other things. Boil the water for the pasta on top of the stove while the microwave oven cooks the sauce. Just remember to start that water early enough. Cooking in the micro-wave oven is very rapid.

For nutritional data about basic ingredients, see page numbers set in **boldface** type. *Italic* page numbers refer to illustrations.

Brown rice, about, 31, **183**
  cooking, 181
  reheating, 182
  yields, 182
  basic cooking times, 199
Buckwheat, about, 29
Bulgur wheat. *See* Tabbouleh
Burger, skinny, 302
Butter, about, 43
Buttermilk
  about, 44
  dill sauce, gravlax with, 90
  dressing, 491
    mustard, 492
    spicy, 495

Cabbage, **391**
  coleslaw, 394
  curried, 446
  Napa, shredded salad, 408
  red
    pork with braised, 372
    salad, grated, 396
    soup, curried, 133
Cajun shrimp boil, 281
Cake, angel food, 582
Cake flour, about, 32
Calories and nutritional information section of
    recipes, 19
Cannellini beans with garlic, 208
Canola oil, about, 35
Cantaloupe, nutritional information, 532
Capelli d'angelo, about, 30
Capellini, about, 30
Caprese salad, 80
Caraway seeds, about, 36
Carbohydrates, 16, 20, 148–49. *See also* Grains
    and other starches
  menu planning and, 47
  for soup, **117**
Cardamom, about, 37
Carrot(s), **391, 436**
  about, 40
  cooking times for, 436
  and mushrooms with cumin, 82
  Oriental, 437
  paupiettes with carrot sauce stuffed with, 253
  purée, 438
  salad
    cooked, with raisins and walnuts, 399
    grated, 395
  shake, 58
  soup, 24 karat, 144
  timbale, 105
  24 karat sauce, 504
    gilded chicken with, 308
Carrousel for microwave oven, 27, 27
Casaba melon, **532**
Casseroles, 27

Cauliflower, **391, 425**
  cooking times for, 425
  to cut into small florets, 425
  gratin, 426
  pickle, crunchy, 527
  purée, 427
  timbale, 106
Cayenne pepper, about, 37
Celery, **391**
  about, 40
  chicken with, 314
  hearts, braised, 445
  to peel (string), *131*
  salad of spinach, mushroom, and, 401
  soup, 122
  trimming and cutting of to make hearts, *445*
  in Waldorf salad, 406
Celery root rémoulade, 77
Celery seed, about, 37
Chamomile, about, 36
Cheese, **520**
  about, 44
  cottage, **520**
    and cinnamon spread, 517
    dip, 518
    filling, spinach roulade with, 109
  fromage blanc, 518, **520**
    about, 44
    filling, spinach roulade with, 109
  grated, 166
  low-fat, low-salt, about, 44
  mozzarella, **520**
    about, 44
    in Caprese salad, 80
    in chopped salad, 417
  Parmesan, **520**
    about, 166
    turkey, 331
  ricotta
    about, 44
    light white ice cream made with, 558
    spread, curried, 517
    summer green dip, 519
    topping, whipped, 581
  yogurt, 514, *515*, **520**
    chive, 516
    liptauer, 516
    smoked salmon, 515
Cheese graters, *166*
Cherry(-ies), **532**
  sauce, 577
    peaches with, 547
Chicken, 289–329, **294**, *341*
  to arrange in cooking dish, *291, 296, 309*
  barbecued, 297
  broth
    about, 33
    basic, 460
    calorie and sodium content in bouillon,